SEEING OURSELVES

READINGS ON

DATE DUE

Alfred A. Knopf New York

SEEING OURSELVES

second edition

READINGS ON SOCIOLOGY AND SOCIETY

Edited by

PETER I. ROSE

Smith College

THIS IS A BORZOI BOOK PUBLISHED BY ALFRED A. KNOPF, INC.

Library of Congress Cataloging in Publication Data

Rose, Peter Isaac, 1933–   comp.
   Seeing ourselves.

   Includes bibliographical references.
   1. Sociology—Addresses, essays, lectures.
I. Title.
HM51.R824   1975   301'.08   75–20251
ISBN O–394–30128–5

Manufactured in the United States of America

Second Edition

987654321

Picture Editor, R. Lynn Goldberg

PHOTO CREDITS

Page 9: Alison Ozer; **38:** Lonnie Wilson/Photo Trends; **65:** Joanne
Leonard/Woodfin Camp & Associates; **92:** Mark Haven; **108:** Joel
Gordon/Photo Trends; **121:** Alison Ozer; **175:** Mark Haven; **204:** Martin
Weaver/Woodfin Camp & Associates; **242:** George W. Gardner; **264:**
Philip Teuscher; **282:** Arthur Tress; **332:** Leonard Freed/Magnum; **372:**
Courtesy, A. T. & T. Co.; **424, 448, 475:** Mark Haven.

PREFACE

The famous Scottish poet, Robert Burns, once wrote

> O wad some Power the giftie gie us
> To see oursels as ithers see us!*

   This book offers an opportunity to see ourselves and various aspects of our society as professional observers see us. It is a series of brief, incisive, and intimate commentaries on the subject matter of sociological inquiry.
   The efforts of former Alfred A. Knopf editors David Bartlett, Lynne Farber, and Walter Kossmann on behalf of this project and their many kindnesses to me are gratefully acknowledged. Thanks are also extended to Fred Burns for his assistance in the completion of this second edition.

Northampton, Massachusetts   Peter I. Rose

---

* From Robert Burns, "To A Louse: On Seeing One on a Lady's Bonnet at Church," 1786.

CONTENTS

NOW—AND IN THE FUTURE

REPRISE

INTRODUCTION

TO SEE OURSELVES

This book is about the stuff of sociology. It is about people. And it is about the patterns of social behavior—personal and professional and political—in which people, in this case American people, engage.

The writers are professional observers. Most are sociologists though some are social critics, journalists, and fiction writers. Together they provide a literate approach to some of the principal areas of sociological and social concern.

As you examine each article you will note that these are not light-hearted, frivolous pieces, though some are tinged with a bittersweet humor. They are very much down to earth. Each is a commentary on some aspect of life that should be familiar to, if not clearly compre-hended by, those who read them. Some should evoke that "light bulb" flash as one recognizes the message being conveyed about social bonds, prejudices, or class differences. Other essays should stimulate the reader to ponder what it would be like to be transported into another social context: to have lived in Haight Ashbury several years ago instead of in Scarsdale, to have been born white instead of black or female instead of male. And still other selections should help in under-standing movements like "Women's Lib" or "resurging ethnicity" that make little sense perhaps because we are reluctant to find out about them.

The readings included in this augmented edition of *Seeing Ourselves* are grouped in eight parts as in the original version. Each section has new material added along with the articles published in the first edition. The first part, "Sociologists and Society," introduces the subject of sociology and offers several views of what it is and what it is apt to become. The layman's problem of defining sociologists is discussed, as is the sociologist's problem of using the techniques appropriate to the task. There is further consideration of sociology as a discipline both in its own right and in relation to other fields.

Next comes "Body and Soul." Here there is a mixed bag of essays on the bathroom and the bedroom, on lifestyles of people in different social settings, on love and beauty, and on growing old. It is followed by "Roles and Relationships," portrayals of social ties and social strains in the family, school, military, and neighborhood.

"In Communities," the fourth part, offers intimate views and analyses of some very different types of American communities, as well as a glimpse at people who have no sense of place. Included are reports on "Main Street," Levittown, Haight Ashbury, and the West Side of Manhattan. Significantly, the first three places, though different, have the characteristics usually associated with community; the last is but an area of residence. And one further essay extends the notion of homelessness to an extreme—Richard Nixon and the people with whom he surrounded himself.

There are two sections on social stratification. The first includes a theoretical essay on symbols of class status, descriptions of poverty and working-class aspirations, an examination of forgotten middle-class Americans, and a commentary on the bigotry of some upper-class liberals. The next section deals with "minorities"—blacks, women, students, and white ethnics. It looks at their grievances and their attempts to redress them.

"Action and Apathy," the seventh part, is about involvement in the political process, including a variation of community pressure tactics Tom Wolfe calls "Mau-Mauing the Flak Catchers." The volume concludes with a discussion of the constructive uses of anarchy, the corruption of values, a critique of Charles Reich's The Greening of America, and three commentaries on the future. A very pointed reprise, offering a chance to ponder what has gone before, comes last.

These readings were chosen for students to see sociology and society from the inside. Careful reading with guidance from skilled instructors should indicate how important the key concepts of sociology—society and culture, institutions and roles, community and group, class and status and power and all the others—are for putting labels on social behavior. But most important is the manifest intent to be able to see ourselves—warts and all.

SOCIOL-
OGISTS
AND
SOCIETY

robert a. nisbet

Sociology is a life science in the sense that human interaction is its core subject. Like other scientists, sociologists depend on observations to explain the phenomena in which they are interested. But there is something else. Sociologists are also a part of what they study, and their experiences—both planned and random—contribute to the "data bank" on which they depend. This can lead to all sorts of difficulties of maintaining the proper distance from the subjects of their inquiry.

Few sociologists have stated these thoughts more succinctly than Robert A. Nisbet, author of many books and articles on the history of sociology, on sociology and contemporary life, and on *The Social Bond*. The following excerpt is from that recent text.

In the pages to follow, Nisbet introduces the student to the nature of the sociological enterprise and shows why he feels it is essential to distinguish between the problems of sociology and social problems.

The Objectives of Sociology

The fundamental objectives of sociology are the same as those of science generally—discovery and explanation. To *discover* the essential data of social behavior and the connections among the data is the first objective of sociology. To *explain* the data and the connections is the second and larger objective. Science makes its advances in terms of both of these objectives. Sometimes it is the discovery of a new element or set of elements that marks a major breakthrough in the history of a scientific discipline. Closely related to such discovery is the discovery of relationships of data that had never been noted before. All of this is, as we know, of immense importance in science. But the drama of discovery, in this sense, can sometimes lead us to overlook the greater importance of explanation of what is revealed by the data. Sometimes decades, even centuries, pass before known connections and relationships are actually explained. Discovery and explanation are the two great interpenetrating, interacting realms of science.

The order of reality that interests the scientist is the *empirical* order, that is, the order of data and phenomena revealed to us through observation or experience. To be precise or explicit about what is, and is not, revealed by observation is not always easy, to be sure. And often it is necessary for our natural powers of observation to be supplemented by the most intricate of mechanical aids for a given object to become "empirical" in the sense just used. That the electron is not as immediately visible as is the mountain range does not mean, obviously, that it is any less empirical. That social behavior does not lend itself to as quick and accurate description as, say, chemical behavior of gases and compounds does not mean that social roles, statuses, and attitudes are any less empirical than molecules and tissues. What is empirical and observable today may have been nonexistent in scientific consciousness a decade ago. Moreover, the empirical is often data *inferred* from direct observation. All of this is clear enough, and we should make no pretense that there are not often shadow areas between the empirical and the nonempirical. Nevertheless, the first point to make about any science, physical or social, is that its world of data is the empirical world. A very large amount of scientific energy goes merely into the work of expanding the frontiers, through discovery, of the known, observable, empirical world.

From observation or discovery we move to *explanation.* The explanation sought by the scientist is, of course, not at all like the explanation sought by the theologian or metaphysician. The scientist is not interested—not, that is, in his role of scientist—in ultimate, transcendental, or divine causes of what he sets himself to explain. He is interested in explanations that are as empirical as the data themselves. If it is the high incidence of crime in a certain part of a large city that requires explanation, the scientist is obliged to offer his explanation in terms of factors which are as empirically real as the phenomenon of crime itself. He does not explain the problem, for example, in terms of references to the will of God, demons, or original sin. A satisfactory explanation is one that is not only empirical, however, but one that can be stated in the terms of a *causal proposition.* Description is an indispensable point of beginning, but description is not explanation. It is well to stress this point, for there are all too many scientists, or would-be scientists, who are primarily concerned with data gathering, data counting, and data describing, and who seem to forget that such operations, however useful, are but the first step. Until we have accounted for the problem at hand, explained it causally by referring the data to some principle or generalization already established, or to some new principle or generalization, we have not explained anything.

An example of the foregoing, and one highly relevant to sociology, is provided by the study of suicide. What, it is asked, causes certain persons to take their own lives? No doubt every person has his own explanation, one based upon what he believes to have been operative perhaps in some friend or acquaintance who killed himself. A "common sense" approach might be to shrug when the question is asked and say that there is no accounting, that insight into the motive dies with the individual himself, or that the suicide was the will of God, which is beyond human detection.

But scientific *discovery* has made it very clear that the incidence of suicide varies in the human race from people to people, nation to nation, and, within a given people or nation, from one ethnic, professional, or residential group to another. We find, for instance, that suicide is much higher in incidence in the United States than in certain other countries (Mexico, for instance) and that within the United States it is virtually absent among some ethnic or occupational groups and extremely high in incidence among others. All of this, be it noted, is not explanation. It is discovery. But discovery is the beginning of science, and with respect to the study of suicide it is quite plain that until the variable incidence of suicide was discovered among human beings, any possibly sound explanation would have been impossible. Plainly, explanations that do not rest on all the data, or at least all relevant data, are of only the most limited value. So, discovery of data is by no means to be depreciated. Some, though not all, of the greatest episodes in the history of science have been inaugurated by discovery of data—of processes, events, connections, substances, and so forth—which had not previously been known. Going back to suicide, no mean step was taken when someone in the nineteenth century first became aware, through studies of official registers, of the highly variable incidence of suicide in populations.

Still, the next step is the more notable, the step we call explanation. How do we explain the fact that year after year, decade after decade, middle-class, white, professional men are more likely to commit suicide than individuals in other sectors of the population, and that this likelihood becomes even greater if they are unmarried or, if married, childless and cut off from the ties of religion or a similar community of ethical purpose? Bear in mind that we are not saying that each and every individual answering to the description just given will commit suicide or that he probably will. To think sociologically is to be able to think in terms of aggregates of people, of rates of incidence or frequency among these aggregates. Our sociological question is, How do we explain the manifest rate of suicide among certain individuals in the population? What are the causal relations? What are the operating processes that link suicide with human behavior generally and with the norms and structures which form the cultural environment of human beings who commit suicide? We can dispense with explanations drawn from biology, for there is no evidence—not yet at least—that suicides are differently constituted than nonsuicides. Psychological explanations, while potentially more helpful or relevant, are rendered suspect by the patterns we have discovered of the incidence of suicide: the patterns are social and economic, not biological or psychological.

Emile Durkheim, one of the greatest of modern sociologists, working in the 1890s on precisely this problem—the variable incidence of suicide in the population—offered an explanation that in its larger outlines can be taken as a very model of what a scientific explanation should be in sociology.[1] The rates of suicide, Durkheim declared, vary inversely with the degree of social and moral cohesion of the groups of which individuals are parts. In those parts of the population where social ties and moral values tend to be close and authoritative in the life of the individual, suicide is rare or nonexistent. But in those sectors of society, such as in contemporary middle-class, industrial or professional sectors, where opposite conditions prevail, the incidence of suicide is much higher. And this holds true irrespective of race, nationality, or geography.

In short, through the variable factors of social cohesion and normative rigor Durkheim explained those patterns of connection among the data of suicide incidence that others had long been aware of but had failed to explain crucially. But his explanation did not stop simply with a demonstration of the unvarying correlation between high incidence of suicide and social and moral disorganization. For, although this *is* explanation, in that it throws light upon the original problem (that is, the incidence of suicide in its variable manifestations in a society), it is what we would have to call a low order of explanation. After all, the subject of sociology is man himself and, more particularly, man's social behavior. Until we have been able to relate what we find in the data to man himself—his personality, social needs, drives, and psychosocial processes generally—we have failed in attaining the order of explanation that any scientist desires.

It was not enough, then, for Durkheim simply to note the high correlation between greater or lesser intensities of the social bond and greater or smaller numbers of suicides. What he attempted to do was relate this association to that wider area of scientific knowledge concerned with the nature of social behavior generally. We thus find in Durkheim's great study an effort to explain, through still higher or more general levels of knowledge about man and his behavior, what his studies had revealed with respect to suicide and social cohesion. Unhappily this aspect of Durkheim's work is not as successful as the former. By the standards of contemporary principles in the study of social behavior, Durkheim's theory of social order and personality is not wholly adequate in its effort to explain.

This, however, is of no importance to our point. What is important is the type of data, the type of question asked, the discovery of crucial variables, and, finally, the efforts, in ascending degrees of generality, to *explain* the data and the connections of the data which earlier discovery had made manifest. And all of this is made as vivid in Durkheim's study of suicide as it could be through any example chosen from chemistry or physics.

The Framework of Science

We must now turn to the method, or as I prefer to put it, the *framework* within which the objectives of discovery and explanation are characteristically to be found in any science. After all, discovery and explanation by themselves are inalienable attributes of all intellectual behavior, whether at the ordinary behavioral level, or in scholarship, philosophy, art, and religion. And indeed we should remind ourselves that there is a lasting affinity between science and other types of intellectual activity, especially art. The sources of the creativity that finds expression in the discoveries and explanations of science are, in strictly psychological terms, much the same for the scientist and the artist. Nothing in the way of mere technique or procedure can ever take the place of imagination, insight, sustained vision, and sheer intellectual comprehension. These are intellectual qualities as vital to the artist and scholar as they are to the scientist.

Nevertheless, science is different from these other activities, at least in its mode of expression, which I have called its framework. And it is to the difference that I now turn.

First and foremost in the scientific framework is the *question* that is asked by the scientist. At bottom, leaving out all niceties and rhetorical flourishes, this question is a simple one: *How does it operate?* Whatever the sphere of empirical reality at hand, the stellar universe, the chromosomal composition of the human body, the family, or a criminal conspiracy, what the scientist wants to know is, first of all, what the crucial component elements are, what the key processes of action or behavior are, and what the fundamental relationships, internal and external, are. In short, he wants to know how it operates. The whole of science, physical, biological, or social, may be regarded as a vast collection of questions of this sort, made specific and relevant to the data at hand, of the means involved in seeking the answers to the questions, and, ultimately, of the answers themselves. Naturally, our standards of what constitutes an acceptable answer, that is, a valid explanation, become ever more exacting and precise. But the fundamental question itself of how things work, operate, or behave in time and space remains the lasting point of departure of the scientist's work.

But for the scientist this question calls for a certain type of answer. Scientific answers or explanations must be capable of empirical verification by others, proceeding in the same way toward the same end. The answers cannot derive from some special *mystique* or from the peculiar and unique character of the scientist's own set of faculties and dispositions, or from his religion, his patriotism, his commitment to a given social-action cause, or from any factor that he alone possesses. Science is by its nature universal, and the unity of science comes from the fact that the same question directed to the same body of data can produce the same answer to all, assuming they follow the procedures dictated by the character of the problem. This is what we mean by the objectivity and universality of science. In science an answer or conclusion is valid irrespective of one's personal, political, or religious likes and dislikes.

In this respect science differs from certain other forms of what many would call "knowledge." No one would argue that the "truth" of the artist's or religious mystic's work depends upon others being able to reach precisely the same result with the same expenditure of effort, system, and materials. How often have we looked at some painting or listened to a piece of music or read a poem that illuminated experience in a way that it had never been illuminated before? Who, looking at Picasso's Spanish Civil War paintings, could say that some special form of understanding was not transmitted? Or perhaps listening to a Beethoven or Ravel quartet, reading a poem by Blake or Randall Jarrell, or walking through the Sistine Chapel or a Frank Lloyd Wright building? From all of these experiences we derive, in one degree or another, some form of illumination, some deepening of understanding that we are prone to say "adds to my knowledge." And so it does, taking the word "knowledge" in its largest sense. But no one would ever suppose that any amount of sheer preparation, sheer perfecting of method and technique, or sheer hard work would enable him to duplicate what is distinctive in a great painting, poem, or musical composition. Nor would anyone, however advantaged he might feel in the way of knowledge from one or another of these artistic experiences, suppose that it either could be or should be "verified."

But verification, or possibility of verification, is the very essence of science. Science, in short, is concerned with answers, conclusions, and principles which are, as we commonly say, testable. If I were to declare suicide a consequence of mankind's imperishable urge to destroy itself,

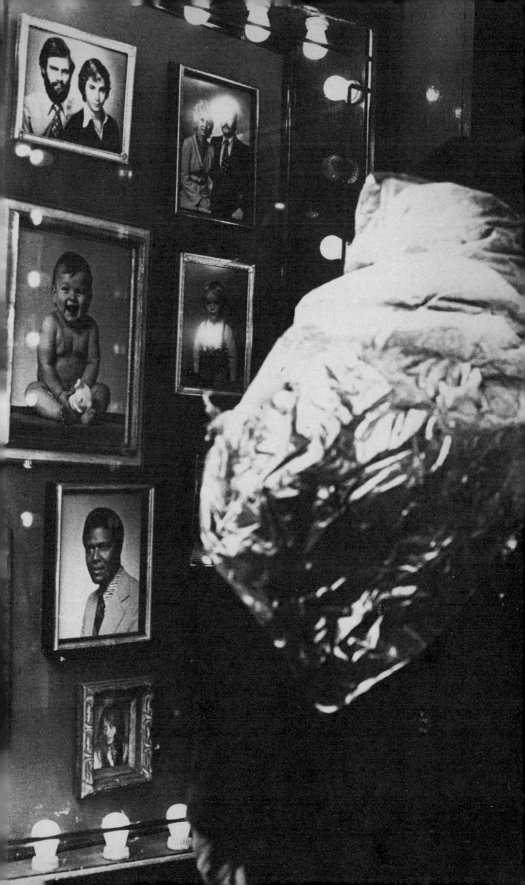

this might be true in some ultimate religious or metaphysical sense. But the conclusion would not be verifiable or testable. If, on the other hand, I declare that frequency of suicides in the population is determined by the weather, this answer is verifiable; which is to say that it can be determined to be right or wrong. So also with respect to war, crime, violence, poverty. We may choose to declare each a manifestation of God's will, and in the ultimate reach of imagination this may well be true. But there is, obviously, no way of testing or verifying it. Thus a scientific answer to the question of the causes of war, poverty, violence, ethnic discrimination, or of any other part of the social order must limit itself to those conditions and factors which, in the form of some hypothesis that is itself a *tentative* answer, can be verified.

What I am saying here does not, of course, rule out the strong possibility that our hypotheses, our postulates, even our ways of seeing the data before us, may be conditioned and shaped by nonscientific, nonrational factors. No one is completely a scientist or a rationalist. No one is immune to the operation of influences that may be governed by self-interest, ideology, or political or religious faith. And there is the further fact that however rational and logical a given scientific formulation may be in the presentation, its actual psychological roots may lie anywhere—in fantasy, in reverie, in sheer unstructured imagination. But irrespective of source or conditioning influence, what gives identity to the scientific statement in the long run is its verifiability by others.

This conclusion leads us to a frequently misunderstood aspect of science: *prediction.* The test of a science, it is commonly said, is its power to predict. There is a sense in which this is true, but the sense has nothing whatsoever to do with the revelation of "things to come," with ability to read the future in the fashion of the fortuneteller. Scientific prediction is not in any way concerned with the forecasting of unprecedented or unique events in history. Prediction in any scientific sense is no more than a statement of the high probability of the occurrence, or recurrence, of some form of behavior, physical or social, *that is inseparable from a previously discovered regularity in nature.* When the astronomer "predicts" an eclipse of the sun for some hour and day in the future, he is not really extracting from the future, as we commonly think of the future. He is merely noting that among the great regularities of relation of earth, moon, and sun is that which periodically manifests itself by obscuration of the light of the sun by the intervention of the moon for a very brief period between the sun and a point of the earth. That it is possible for the astronomer to give this a precise date in the future—the "future," that is, within our own arbitrary, man-made, system of reckoning time—is but incidental to the vital point, which is that the eclipse is simply a point on a great, endlessly recurrent cycle of motions in the relation of earth, moon, and sun. Predicting an eclipse is not one bit different from predicting that the sun will rise tomorrow morning.

So with all scientific prediction. When the epidemiologist predicts that an influenza epidemic of a certain type is highly probable he is doing nothing more than drawing from what is known of a previously discovered causal relationship. Repeated experiences have made clear that the outbreak of influenza epidemics is closely related to the presence of certain crucial, functionally related conditions having to do with increased incidence of virus strains, foreseeable congestion of people in, say, the Christmas holiday period of the year, normal incidence of mild respiratory ailments, and so on. Predicting an influenza epidemic is not very different from predicting that the individual who allows himself to be exposed to certain types of disease will in all probability fall victim to the disease.

Do we predict in the social sciences? Of course we do. Not, to be sure, with the same degree of success or accuracy that is to be found in astronomy with respect to eclipses, for the materials that the social scientist works with do not fall within regularities as fixed as those which confront the astronomer. Making allowance for the possibility of an accuracy in the social sciences in the future that we have not yet achieved, the unbanishable element of *choice* in human behavior will doubtless forever make fixed laws and also accurate prediction unlikely. Social science predicts, nonetheless, and, all things considered, with quite a high degree of success. But such success is contingent upon the social scientist's ability to rigorously avoid temptations to match wits with the card-reader or haruspex and his determination to stay within the framework of science.

We may go back once again to the study of suicide in society. On the basis of careful studies of the conditions or causes of high incidence of suicide, it is possible to predict that rates of suicide will go up in a given population as the result of certain changes of social structure already apparent. Or that rates will go down as the result of opposite types of change. Such prediction, to the degree that it is successful, is no more than a reaping of the rewards of sound studies of social causation in suicide. It is emphatically not a foretelling of the future as we popularly understand this. Repeated studies of urban violence have shown clearly that the prelude to massive outbreaks of violence is a certain set of conditions: poverty coupled with strong feelings of resentment, the presence of potential leaders of such violence, ineffective police protection, climatic conditions favoring large assemblies, and so on. It is, then, possible to predict violence on the basis of the known existence of these conditions.

Where prediction is successful in science we can be sure that prior studies have revealed certain fixed, or largely fixed, regularities of relationship. We can be certain, in sum, that we have managed to find out "how things work," which, as I have said, is the fundamental question of all science. What is important really is not prediction but the causal or functional relationships we have managed to discover and to explain.

Insofar as our discoveries have been relevant and our explanations sound, prediction—in the scientific sense—will also be sound. But again warning must be voiced: in the social sciences such causal relationships and such predictions will always be more uncertain and precarious than in the physical sciences. The subject of the social sciences is man himself, and a rather highly developed cerebrum allows him, if not what used to be called free will, at least a range and diversity of possible responses unknown to atoms and viruses. Still, man's plasticity' of response notwithstanding, his behavior in society does fall within institutionalized regularities that permit scientific statements analogous to those of the physical sciences.

Something must be said at this point about scientific statements, or propositions, as we more commonly call them. There are many references in the literature of and about science to "hypotheses," "laws," and "principles." All of these, let it be stressed, are *statements about natural or social behavior*. Each, in varying degree of probability or certainty, is an explanatory statement about the patterns of behavior which the scientist has studied. Some statements have so high a degree of validity and reliability that we call them "laws." The law of gravitation in physics is the classic example. Others, dealing with more complex and uncertain phenomena, or proceeding from still-imperfect understanding, are less likely to be referred to as laws. But they are nonetheless scientific statements in as full a sense as the other. A "hypothesis" is also a statement about observed phenomena, but of so tentative and unverified a character that we refrain from calling it a law or principle. It is a statement whose validity remains hypothetical or speculative until an investigator can test it, verify it, or otherwise reinforce the statement through its exposure to the crucial data.

The important point here, however, is that neither laws nor principles in the world of science are enacted or decreed as are the laws that govern us in civilized society. Social laws do not lie out in nature waiting to be discovered, as so much popular conception of science would have it. Alexander Pope's famous couplets on Newton and the physical world exemplify an attitude nearly as rife today as then: "Nature and nature's laws lay hid in night; God said, Let Newton be, and all was light." But laws lie nowhere save in the scientist's consciousness. They may be of absolute and unvarying validity, but they are still propositions or statements that serve to explain phenomena and connections among phenomena.

There is today, in certain quarters of the social sciences, a rather deep conviction that before one can study society scientifically he must know "methodology." What this commonly turns out to be is statistics, supplemented perhaps by analysis of case study or survey techniques. Today, the gathering of statistics is highly important, even indispensable, for the social scientist. It is indeed a mode of literacy, for how else than through knowledge of the real significance of averages, means, medians, and the like, can one hope to read and understand contemporary population, crime, divorce, marriage, education, and other reports on populations? We have no way of discovering the all-important connections among data and classes of data, when these are vast or complex, except through statistical techniques that arrange our data for proper explanation. Survey techniques, case-study techniques, and other modes of disciplining or refining observation are also important. No science can do without its techniques, and techniques vary from discipline to discipline.

But this said, we must nevertheless constantly bear in mind that the *method* of science is none of these. It is not statistics, not case study, not survey, not mathematics, not experiment. All of these are techniques that serve, in their different ways, the scientist's efforts to discover and to explain. In certain areas of sociology mathematics is fundamental to any approach whatsoever to the subject matter; in other areas experiment has the same role of importance. But both mathematics and experiment remain techniques nonetheless. They are not, in themselves, the method of sociology. The method of sociology is inseparable from the disciplined imagination of the scientist when he is making discoveries or seeking explanations. He does so with respect to the question of how things operate and casts his results in the form of statements that are understandable and, potentially at least, verifiable.

It is well to make use here of an old and very sound distinction between the *logic of discovery* and the *logic of demonstration*. The latter can be stated simply enough. It is no more than the propositions themselves but set forth in a sequential and ordered fashion, with hypothesis, arrangements of data, techniques, and ultimate conclusions all articulated in such a way as to be understood easily by others. The logic of discovery, however, is frequently as random and disordered as the human imagination itself. When we talk about the logic of discovery we are talking about the ways by which the scientist has in fact reached his conclusion; we are often in the presence of modes of intuition and insight which are anything but ordered and sequential. The conclusion may come in a single, sudden flash of inspiration after months of seemingly hopeless effort. It is this aspect of the matter that has led so many of the really great scientists to deny that anything resembling the orderly processes of a "method" was involved in their work.

In fact, there *is* a method, and I would not wish to seem to imply the contrary. But this method—I am referring to the method or logic of *discovery*—is bound up with the kind of question that is asked and the kind of conclusion that is reached in science in contrast to art, metaphysics, or religion. The method is emphatically *not* something that can be reduced to simple and sequential steps derived from a manual. Least of all is method in the social sciences identical with any one or another of the numerous techniques by which observation, discovery, and explanation are aided.

There is, finally, one other important element in what I have called the framework of sociology. This is the set of concepts that gives distinctiveness and identity to the discipline. Every science is known by the signal ideas or concepts through which reality is approached in the terms of that discipline. It would be impossible either to describe or to work within physics, for example, except in the terms of the fundamental concepts of energy, mass, quantum, and the like. The same is true of each of the other sciences. I am not suggesting that such concepts are hard and fast within any science. The opposite is true. Nothing is more evident in the present period of scientific efflorescence than the breakdown of what were once thought to be fixed and eternal boundaries among the sciences. Today, more or less despairingly, we are prone to say that chemistry is what chemists do and physics is what goes on in the physics buildings on the campus. Also, the concepts of one science extend dramatically into the work of another. Within the last generation biology has been revolutionized by what it has drawn from, first, chemistry, then physics, in its studies of the elements of life. Nowhere has the phenomenon of extension of concept been more vivid than among the social sciences. One need only compare introductory textbooks in each of the social sciences written a half-century ago with those of the present day to be made aware of the breaking of boundaries, the borrowing and lending of concepts here as in the physical sciences.

So much is true. But equally true is the fact that at any given moment each science is a complex of concepts that give it identity—no matter how rapidly some of the concepts may seem to come and go or be otherwise changed. And in the largest sense the "method" of any science is the application of these concepts to the world of things and processes that does not itself know any disciplinary boundaries but, as experience has shown, can best be approached from the large number of specialized viewpoints to be found in the different sciences.

The method of sociology is in *general* the method of each of the other sciences. But the distinctive and *specific* method of sociology derives directly from the fundamental concepts of sociology and their use in offering explanation of the myriad ways of human behavior. Concepts such as *social role, status, norm, group,* and *function* are not merely descriptive counters to be arranged and rearranged for reassurance of what we already know. They are windows to the outside world; they are the operating means of shedding light upon the same residual subject matter that all of the social sciences take for their province. I repeat, there is no such thing as strictly sociological subject matter in the living world of reality; no more is there a strictly economic or political or anthropological subject matter. The common concern of all the social sciences is the behavior of human beings in culture and society. But it has been made clear beyond further doubt that in the interpretation of social behavior—in both discovery and explanation, in both prediction and control of social behavior—the concepts I have mentioned, along with others, provide indispensable means. The distinctive method of sociology is, in sum, inseparable from the fundamental concepts that give it content.

. . . Before leaving the subject I would like to utter a word of warning against obsessive concern with concepts. We cannot too often remind ourselves that the subject matter of sociology is not, ultimately, concepts or social systems, social wholes, or abstract forms of rhetoric misconceived as social theory. *The subject matter of sociology is social behavior*—the behavior of individual human beings as we find them. This, in the present context, may seem a mere platitude. But no one can read very far in the modern literature of sociology without becoming aware of how preoccupation with concepts sometimes actually replaces concern with the empirical stuff of social behavior. We find some sociologists declaring in effect that until we have refined and polished our concepts, made them epistemologically pure and logically faultless, we cannot proceed with our real mission, which is the study of social behavior.

To this misconception I can reply only with the gist of what the great scientist Wolfgang Köhler had to say on the subject. Had Galileo and Newton and the other pioneering figures in modern physics been too much preoccupied with the epistemological purity of their concepts of gravitation and energy instead of going ahead in a pragmatically naïve and happily undisturbed way, physics would never have become a science. To which may be added the statement that zoology, botany, and geology did not start out as sciences with correct and adequate definitions of plants and animals. The real work in the science of sociology has only just begun; there is immense need at the present time for new data to be discovered and for new explanations which are more in accord with the data we have.

The Problems of Sociology

A science is also known by its problems. Someone has said that the great men of science are not those who solved the problems but those who discovered them. Herbert Butterfield, distinguished historian of science, has told us that some of the most revolutionary changes in modern science have taken place *not* as the results of new observations or additional evidence but by transpositions taking place in the minds of the scientists themselves. Fundamentally these transpositions had to do with ways in which problems were envisaged. Too often a "problem" in a discipline can hang on and on through inertia even when its very statement is predicated in circularities or known misconceptions.

Of all forms of intellectual activity one of the most difficult is that of confronting or handling the same data as before but, as Professor Butterfield notes, *placing them in a new system of relations with one another by giving them a different framework*. Or, in other words, by stating the question or problem differently. Michael Polanyi, distinguished physical scientist and notable philosopher, writes:

> It is a commonplace that all research must start from a problem. Research can be successful only if the problem is good; it can be original only if the problem is original. But how can one see a problem, any problem, let alone a good and original problem? For to see a problem is to see something that is hidden. It is to have an intimation of the coherence of hitherto not comprehended particulars.[2]

Polanyi tells us that this applies to even the most radically novel discoveries. In sheer brilliance and lasting importance nothing exceeds the quantum theory in physics set forth by the remarkable Max Planck in 1900. But Polanyi notes that all the material on which Planck founded his theory was open to inspection by other physicists. Polanyi writes, "He alone saw inscribed in it a new order transforming the outlook of man." What Max Planck did, most fundamentally, was find a completely new way of posing the problem. This example demonstrates the absolute importance, whatever may be the necessary restraints of method and technique in science, of preserving at all costs unobstructed perceptions and uncluttered imagination.

What are the fundamental problems of sociology? . . . It will suffice to say at this point that the problems of sociology are those of *the nature of the social bond*: the patterns of social interaction, the social aggregates, the systems of authority, the social roles, statuses, and norms which form the social bond. The problems are also, of course, the processes by which these patterns and elements are changed. Earlier, I described this book as one concerned with the essential concepts of sociology. But there is always a close and mutually determining relation between the concepts and the problems of any science. Science, which has been well described as a never ending quest, draws its concepts from its attacks upon problems and its problems from its consideration of existing concepts.

Here a very important distinction is in order between the *problems of sociology* and what we commonly call *social problems*. Few things have led to more misconception of the nature of sociology as a science than the failure to make this distinction. When we refer to social problems we have in mind such matters as crime, racial tensions, juvenile delinquency, mental disorders, family breakdown, and international war. Plainly, all of these reflect disruptions of the social bond. Equally plainly, all of them deserve our best efforts to correct them. They are and should be subjects of social policy at all levels of government and society.

But not one of them is *as such* a constitutive problem of sociology. That sociology can and does throw much light upon these and other social problems is not to be denied. But so does each of the other social sciences. The essential point here is that social problems are common property of *all* the social sciences. Consider crime alone. It is indeed a problem to which sociology, with its primary interests in social behavior, can contribute significant insight. But crime is also an economic matter; it cannot be divorced from the economic system—from matters of property and wealth. In addition, crime is a phenomenon with psychological aspects: there are students of the subject who have made personality deficiencies or abnormalities the point of departure for understanding criminal behavior. Crime is also a subject for the political scientist, for we have discovered repeatedly that methods of framing, administering, and interpreting laws have much to do with the incidence and types of criminal behavior in a society. What is true of crime is true as well of each of the other great social problems in our time. Without exception they are subjects for all the social sciences.

There is another aspect of the matter that should be stressed. When we think of social problems we are dealing with matters which are inseparable from *policy*, that is, public policy, the policy that is ultimately decided by citizens, elected officials, and the administrators of a society. Science is an invaluable aid to the formation of public policy; but it cannot be, by itself, the formulator of policy for a people. Moral, legal, and other considerations, including those of personal freedom, are bound to influence judgment when policy is being formed. Consider the use of tobacco, for example. Ample research has by now made it clear that tobacco, especially in the form of cigarettes, is harmful to human health. Few persons, however, would wish to judge the matter of public policy on tobacco—that is, political legislation designed to prevent or lessen smoking—solely in the terms presented by scientists. Most of us would consider extreme legislation along this line, however beneficently intended, as a violation of our freedom. Policy on tobacco is obviously subject to more than scientific considerations. The same is true with respect to other matters that enter public consciousness as problems: urban violence, crime, drugs, sexual deviance, mental illness, and so on. Each embodies behavior that is or should be within the province of the scientist in his search for causes, conditions, and effects. Wise public policy on any of these matters deserves and needs the advice of scientists qualified to provide it. Such advice should be influential and often followed meticulously. But it should never be controlling as such, for public policy in a free society must also draw from considerations that are outside the province of science.

In sum, the problems of the science of sociology, like the problems of any science, are specialized, limited to the sphere formed by the kind of data and concepts sociology works with, and addressed to the universal question of all science: *How does it operate?* Inherently, there is no more reason to assume that social problems such as crime and family disorganization are the problems of the discipline of sociology than to assume that public health problems such as tuberculosis and venereal diseases are the problems of physiology. Obviously physiology as a basic science can contribute to what eventually becomes control of these diseases. But control will be established only after the results of physiology have been fused with those of other disciplines and transferred from the realm of basic science to that of applied science.

Sociology is one of the basic sciences, and as such its progress involves ever greater specialization, just as is so manifestly the case in physics, biology, and the other sciences. It is in the applied disciplines —medicine for the biological sciences, public administration and social work among the social sciences—that the specialized and necessarily limited results of the several basic sciences are brought together and then focused on specific practical or social problems.

The true problems of sociology, then, are but specialized refinements of the underlying question of how social behavior operates. They are simply the problems of the nature of social behavior and its changes in time.

NOTES

1. Emile Durkheim, *Suicide: A Study in Sociology.* Published in 1897, Durkheim's book is justly regarded as a classic in the social sciences. Whatever its deficiencies—inevitable in any truly original or pioneering work—the larger conclusions are as valid today as they were in Durkheim's time.
2. Michael Polanyi, *The Tacit Dimension* (New York: Doubleday, 1966), p. 21.

bennett m. berger

It may seem a strange thing to begin explaining who one is by telling you what one is not. But such is often the case with sociologists. As Bennett Berger points out, as a category they are more frequently badly caricatured than adequately characterized, especially by those who know little of the field. One common portrait has them as ineffective "bumblers," purveyors of the obvious, wordsmiths whose neologisms smack of Orwellian "newspeak," or just plain hacks "who," as one commentator once wrote, "spend thousands of dollars to find a house of prostitution."

Others say sociologists are Machiavellian manipulators, in it for the power they may be able to wield over the lives of others, exploiters of the poor and the oppressed, complete "diabolists."

In truth, few sociologists fall under either rubric. They are scientists of social behavior whose laboratories are to be found everywhere men gather. Most are able social scientists whose lives are spent trying to study, understand, and explain everyday life. Some, Bennett Berger among them, seem to have a special sense or ability that places them in the very camp of the "intellectuals" alongside those who are often sociology's loudest critics.

Reprinted from *The Antioch Review*, vol. 17, no. 3, by permission of the editors. This article was originally entitled "Sociology and the Intellectuals: An Analysis of a Stereotype."

I

The stereotype of the sociologist has two dimensions, founded in contradictory beliefs which, in turn, have their source in the structure of the intellectual professions. The image of the sociologist as a pathetically ignorant and pompous bumbler (jargon-ridden, pretentious, and without insight) is based on the conviction that sociology has no special subject matter, and is therefore no science; its technical apparatus and methodological strictures are hence not only presumptuous but futile, and result only in pretentiousness and banality. The image of the sociologist as a Machiavellian manipulator, however, clearly rests on a recognition of the efficacy of scientific, especially statistical, techniques in dealing with a human subject matter. But both of these—the perceived failure as well as the perceived success of sociology—have elicited from the intellectuals a hostile response.

The Problem of Subject Matter: The Sociologist as Bumbler The tendency to specialization in the intellectual professions submits them to pressure to define specifically a subject matter uniquely their own, in order to justify their existence in a procession- and specialty-conscious culture, to establish and preserve their identities with foundations and university administrations, and to demonstrate their utility and their consequent right to public support. As new specializations develop, and claim professional status, entirely reasonable questions of justification can be raised. What can you do that others not trained in your profession cannot do? What competence has your training conferred on you that is denied to others because of their lack of such training? I take it that the flourishing health of the image of the sociologist as bumbler can in part be attributed to the failure of sociologists to answer these questions satisfactorily. Any discipline which claims as its special subject matter the domain of "social relations" or "social systems" or "society" or any of the other textbook-preface definitions claims not a special subject matter but the whole gamut of human experience, a claim which thousands of scholars and intellectuals are with good reason likely to dispute. Louis Wirth's definition of sociology as the study of that which is true of men by virtue of the fact that they have everywhere and at all times lived a group life, strikes the eye as somewhat better, but runs into the difficulty of generally assuming that pretty nearly everything that is true of men is true by virtue of this fact.

It is in part due to this failure to meet the responsibility of defining one's professional competence simply and clearly to interested laymen that sociological "jargon," for example, is met with such resistance and resentment. Laymen react with no such rancor to the technical vocabularies of mathematics, the physical and natural sciences, and engineering because by an act of faith (based, to be sure, on a common-sense understanding of what those disciplines do) they decide that behind the jargon, which they do not understand (because it is a descriptive shorthand, familiarity with which requires special training), lies a *special subject matter amenable to technical treatment* which they *could* understand *if* they took the trouble. Thus the intelligent layman feels no shame or outrage at not being able to understand a technical article in a chemistry journal—or, for that matter, in not understanding the job specifications in a newspaper want ad for engineers. No such toleration is likely toward the technical vocabulary of sociology until it is accepted as a legitimate scientific profession.

That this acceptance is not forthcoming is due partly to the belief of many intellectuals that the technical vocabulary is not a natural concomitant of scientific enterprise, but rather an attempt to disguise the banality of the results of sociological studies: sociologists "belabor the obvious"; they lack insight, and substitute in its place a barrage of carefully "proven" platitudes. Doubtless, some sociologists do, but every intellectual discipline has its share of brilliant people, as well as hacks, and there is no reason to suppose that sociology has more than a normal complement of either. That the hacks are identified as *representative* of sociology is probably due more to judgments regarding the quality of sociological prose rather than to any analysis of the significance of its contents. Certainly, the prose of sociologists may seem clumsy when compared to the efforts of those whose business it is to write well. But whereas the results of scientific endeavor can legitimately be expected to be true and important, one cannot legitimately expect either that science be beautiful or that scientists be literary stylists.

In short, then, the hue and cry about the jargon and turgidity of sociological prose, about the pretentiousness of its methodology and the banality of its preoccupations, is meaningful as criticism only if one assumes that sociology has no special subject matter amenable to technical treatment; if it has not, then it must be judged by the same criteria as general essays on social and cultural topics. But as long as sociologists commit themselves to the traditions of science, and address their work not to a general literate audience, but to a community of their colleagues, these criticisms cannot seem other than beside the point. For the continuing application of aesthetic criteria of judgment to a nonaesthetic pursuit reveals only a refusal to grant to sociology the status of a science.

The Threat of Technique: The Sociologist as Diabolist Stereotypes generally contain contradictory elements, and the stereotype of the sociologist is no exception. For along with his alleged gifts for the labored cliché and the clumsy, inept sentence, the sociologist is also credited with the diabolical potential of making puppets out of men, of destroying their individuality with IBM machines, of robbing them of their "individual human dignity," and presiding, finally, over their total mechanization. This image of the sociologist as diabolist rests not on a conviction regarding the failure to define a specific subject matter, but on a fear regarding the success of sociological techniques, particularly statistics, which is seen by some intellectuals as *threatening* in two ways. First, the possibility of a science of society apparently implies the possibility of human behavior being controlled or manipulated by those who know its "causes" or by those with access to this knowledge. This vision, fostered by stimulus-response psychology, nourished by the "sociological perspective," which finds the source of individual behavior in group influences (and thus runs head on into the myth of the autonomous individual), and made fearful by reports of brain washing and by novels like *1984* and *Brave New World*, is perhaps responsible for the peculiar ambivalence felt by some intellectuals toward the very *desirability* of a science of society. Sociology is thus seen as a potential threat to democratic society. Second, and more relevant in the present context, is the fact that the application of the techniques of science to human behavior is perceived as a threat to the viability of the most basic function of intellectuals in the Western tradition: to comment on and to interpret the meaning of contemporary experience.

II

The noun "intellectual" is one of those words which, in spite of lack of consensus regarding their meaning, continue to flourish in common usage. Attempts to define the term, to ask who the intellectuals are or what the intellectuals do, while useful, have seemed to me inconclusive. Certainly some intellectuals are "detached" or "free-floating"; surely a great number are "alienated"; doubtless "neurosis" is widespread among them; "irresponsibility," although currently out of fashion, is nevertheless affirmed by some of them. There is great magic in some of their bows; but, like Philoctetes, they often carry a corresponding wound whose stench forces them to live somewhat marginally. Finally, it is true that they create and transmit cultural values—sometimes. There are, however, two difficulties with these and similar attempts at definition. First, the relation between the key criteria of the definitions and the perspectives of the definers is generally only too transparent. Second, and for my purposes more interesting, is that although the word is part of common usage, the attempts to define it have generally ignored this fact. I propose here first to ask not who the intellectuals are or what they do, but rather who they are *thought* to be—whom do people have in mind when they use the term?—and only then to go on to the other questions.

In this connection, I was present a few years ago at a forum on "The Role of the Intellectual in Modern Society" held at the Museum of Modern Art in New York. The panel members were Granville Hicks, Clement Greenberg, W. H. Auden, and Robert Gorham Davis. Auden spoke last, and at one point in his remarks he looked around at his colleagues on the platform as if to take note of the experts chosen to talk on this topic. Hicks, he said, was a novelist and literary critic; Davis was a literary critic and English professor; Greenberg was an art critic and an editor of *Commentary*; and Auden identified himself as a poet and critic. Had this forum been held in the Middle Ages, he pointed out, we panel members would have been mostly members of the clergy; in the sixteenth and seventeenth centuries, we would have been mostly natural scientists; in the twentieth century, we are mostly literary men. Auden did not attempt to answer the question that he had left implicit, but the question is a very leading one because the contemporary image of the intellectual *is*, I believe, essentially a literary one—and in two senses: he is conceived *as* a literary man, and this conception has been reinforced by the fact that it is literary men who have been most interested in, and who have written most on, the problem of the intellectual.

But it would be a mistake to assume that, because the intellectual is conceived in the image of the literary man, his essential property is that he is an artist or a student of literature. His identification as an intellectual rests not on the aesthetic value of his novels, plays, poems, essays, or literary criticism, but on his assumption, through them, of the role of *commentator on contemporary culture and interpreter of contemporary experience*. But if the intellectuals are those who assume this role, Auden's implicit question still remains: Why, in our time, has it been typically literary men who have assumed the role of the intellectual? It is in attempting to answer this question that the relation between "the intellectuals" and the stereotyping of sociologists will become clear.

In our time literary men have pre-empted the intellectual's role because of (A) their maximal freedom from the parochial demands of technical specialization, (B) their freedom (within their status as literary men) to make large and uncompromising judgments about values, and (C) their maximal freedom from institutional restraints.

Specialization Intellectuals, I have said, are commentators on contemporary culture and interpreters of contemporary experience; they are critics, liberal or conservative, radical or reactionary, of contemporary life. The range of their competence is not circumscribed; it includes nothing less than the entire cultural life of a people. If they are academic men, they may be specialists in various subjects; but their professional specialties do not generally interfere with their being intellectuals. In the humanities, and particularly in literature, a specialty usually consists of *expertise* regarding a given historical period and the figures important to one's discipline who are associated with it: Dr. Johnson and the English literature of the eighteenth century; the significance of Gide in the French literature of the twentieth century; Prince Metternich and the history of Europe after 1815; Kant, Hegel, and German Idealism 1750–1820. Specialties like these do not militate against one's assuming the role of the intellectual, because the traditions of humanistic study encourage the apprehension of cultural wholes; they encourage commentary and interpretation regarding the "backgrounds"—social, cultural, intellectual, spiritual—of the subject matter one is expert about. The humanities—and particularly literature—offer to intellectuals a professional status which impedes little if at all the fulfillment of their function as intellectuals. On the other hand, the commitment of empirical sociology to "scientific method" frequently renders it incompetent to deal with the "big problems," and often instills in sociologists a trained incapacity to say anything they cannot prove.

Values In commenting on contemporary culture and in interpreting contemporary experience, intellectuals are under no seriously sanctioned injunction to be "detached" or "objective." Unlike the sociologist, who functions under the rule of strict separation between facts and values, the intellectual is expected to judge and evaluate, to praise and blame, to win adherents to his point of view and to defend his position against his intellectual enemies. In the context of free debate among intellectuals, the exercise of this function takes the form of polemics; in an academic context, it develops into the phenomenon of "schools of thought." The point is that, whereas in sociology the existence of schools of thought is an embarrassment to everyone (since it is a constant reminder that not enough is *known*—in science, opinion is tolerated only where facts are not available), in the humanities the existence of schools of thought is accepted as normal and proper, because the humanities actively encourage evaluation, the development of point of view, and heterogeneity of interpretation.

Freedom from Institutional Restraints Literary men have been able, more than members of other intellectual professions, to resist the tendencies toward the bureaucratization of intellectual life. This has been possible because of the large market for fiction in the United States, and because of the opportunities of selling critical and interpretive articles to the high- and middle-brow magazines, which, in spite of repeated protestations to the contrary, continue to flourish in this country. The ability of free lance writers to support themselves without depending upon a salary from a university or other large organization maximizes their freedom to be critics of contemporary life. Such opportunities are not typically available to sociologists. In addition, major sociological research is increasingly "team" research, while literary and humanistic research in universities is still largely a matter of individual scholarship. Obviously, collective responsibility for a work restrains the commentaries and interpretations of its authors; the individual humanistic scholar, usually responsible only to himself, is free from the restraints imposed by the conditions of collective research.

The purpose of this discussion of the intellectuals has been to highlight the fact that although sociology has arrogated to itself the right to *expertise* regarding society and culture, its commitment to the traditions of science (narrow specialization, objectivity, and team research) militates against sociologists assuming the role of the intellectual. The business of intellectuals has always been the critical discussion and evaluation of the affairs of contemporary men, or, if I may repeat it once more, to comment on contemporary culture and interpret contemporary experience. When the sociologist arrogates *expertise* regarding the affairs of contemporary men, he is perceived as saying, in effect, that he *knows* more about the affairs of contemporary men than the intellectual does; and once this implication is received into the community of intellectuals, the issue is joined. The fact of this implication becomes one more fact of contemporary experience to which the intellectuals can devote their critical faculties—and with considerable relish, because the implication seems to threaten the basis of their right to the position which, as intellectuals, they hold.

Even those intellectuals with sympathies for the goals of sociology often exhibit a fundamental underestimation of the consequences of its commitment to science. The characteristic plea of these people is an exhortation to "grapple with the *big* problems." Although this advice is without doubt well intentioned, it characteristically underestimates the degree to which the mores of science and the responsibility of foundations and university research institutes can command the type of work sociologists do. I mean by this simply that the sociologist is responsible to the community of social scientists for the *scientific* value of his work, and that university research institutes are sensitive to charges of financing "biased" or "controversial" research (a possibility that is maximized when one deals with the "big problems"). And when the "big problems" *are* grappled with, for example, in books like *The American Soldier* and *The Authoritarian Personality*, or in other types of work like *The Lonely Crowd*, *White Collar*, and *The Power Elite*, controversy and polemic follow. For the sympathetic intellectual's exhortation to the sociologist to "grapple with the big problems" says, in effect, "don't be a scientist, be a humanist; be an intellectual." This implication is supported by the respectful (if not totally favorable) reception given by intellectuals to the works of Riesman and Mills (least encumbered with the trappings of science), and their utter hostility to works like *The American Soldier*, which fairly bristles with the method of science.

There is one more source of the intellectual's hostility to sociology that I would like to examine, a source that was anticipated by Weber in his lecture on science as a vocation. For if it is true that intellectualization and rationalization, to which science commits itself and of which it is a part, means "that principally there are no mysterious incalculable forces that come into play, but rather that one can, in principle, master all things by calculation," then it is not only true, as Weber said, that "the world is disenchanted," but also true that the social scientist is perceived as challenging that tradition of humanism and art which has subsisted on the view that the world *is* enchanted, and that man is the mystery of mysteries. To the carriers of this tradition, every work of art and every poetic insight constitutes further proof that the world is enchanted, and that the source of man's gift to make art and to have poetic insight is a mystery made more mysterious by each illumination. The power of this tradition should not be underestimated; it is well rooted in the thinking of modern literature, with its antiscientific temper and its faith in the recalcitrance of men to yield up their deepest secrets to the generalizations of science. From Wordsworth's "to dissect is to kill," to Mallarmé's "whatever is sacred, whatever is to remain sacred, must be clothed in mystery," to Cummings' "mysteries alone are significant," the tradition has remained strong. And surely, it must have reached its apotheosis when, before a Harvard audience, Cummings made the following pronouncement:

I am someone who proudly and humbly affirms that love is the mystery of mysteries, and that nothing measurable matters "a very good God damn": that "an artist, a man, a failure," is no mere whenfully accreting mechanism, but a givingly eternal complexity—neither some soulless and heartless ultra-predatory infra-animal nor any un-understandingly knowing and believing and thinking automation, but a naturally and miraculously whole human being—a feelingly illimitable individual; whose only happiness is to transcend himself, whose every agony is to grow. (E. E. Cummings, *six nonlectures*, Cambridge: Harvard University Press, 1955, pp. 110–111.)

Intellectuals in this tradition seem to believe that the fulfillment of the goals of social science necessarily means that the creative powers of man will be "explained away," that his freedom will be denied, his "naturalness" mechanized, and his "miraculousness" made formula; that Cummings' "feelingly illimitable individual" will be shown up as a quite limited and determined "social product," whose every mystery and transcendence can be formulated, if not on a pin, then within the framework of some sociological theory. It is no wonder, then, that a vision as fearsome as this can provoke the simultaneous convictions that a science of society is both impossible and evil.

III

It is no great step from the stereotypes consequent to ethnic and racial diversity to the stereotypes consequent to the diversity of occupational specialization. In those occupations which claim technical, professional status, occupations in which advanced, specialized training is necessary, it is likely that occupational stereotypes should find fertile ground because those on the "outside" have only secondary, derivative "knowledge" of the occupation. It is likely to be even more true of those professions which, like sociology, are so new that the nature of their subject matter is still being discussed by their members, and *still* more true if the new profession, by arrogating to itself a field of study formerly "belonging" to someone else (or to everyone else), raises, either intentionally or unintentionally by implication, invidious questions of relative competence.

Noteworthy in this regard is the fact that the social sciences which have been most active in the "interdisciplinary" tendencies of recent years are sociology, cultural anthropology, and psychology—precisely those disciplines with the most broadly defined subject matter. Each of these claims nothing less, in effect, than the totality of man's non-physiological behavior as the field of its special competence; and it is no wonder that economics and political science, whose claims are considerably more modest (i.e., whose subject matter is relatively clearly and narrowly defined), have not found it strikingly to their interests to participate much in this convergence. For it is no doubt partly a matter of common professional interest as well as a matter of theoretical clarification that is behind this pooling of their intellectual resources by sociologists, anthropologists, and psychologists. The satire (which invokes the extant stereotype) to which social scientists are submitted is of common concern to them, for the public image of the social sciences, largely created by the commentaries of intellectuals on them, is related to the amount of public support that the social sciences receive.

The stereotype of sociology and sociologists is part of a larger configuration which stereotypes social science in general; sociology, however, is the most successfully maligned of the social sciences. This special vulnerability is due largely to its relative lack of the sources of prestige available to the other social sciences. Economics commands a respect consequent to its age, to the generally accepted legitimacy of its subject matter, to its demonstrated usefulness, and to the wide variety of jobs available to people trained in it. Cultural anthropology borrows scientific prestige from physical anthropology and archeology, and gets some of its own as a result of its concern with the esoteric subject matter of primitive peoples. Political science has the prestigious correlates of law, diplomacy, and international relations. Clinical psychology has the towering figure of Freud, an affinity to medicine, and the presence of the almost mythic dimensions of The Psychiatrist. Unlike economics, sociology has no hoary past, and no long line of employers clamoring for access to its skills. Unlike clinical psychology, it has no founding figure generally recognized as seminal in the history of western science; and the tenuousness of the concept of a "sick society" denies to sociology the status of a clinical discipline, and hence the prestige that accrues to The Healer. Unlike political science, it has neither an empirical nor an historical relation to the high concerns of nations, governments, or law; and unlike cultural anthropology, it has neither empirical roots nor an esoteric subject matter. Not only is sociology's subject matter not esoteric, but its traditional concern with such peripheral problems of social life as crime, delinquency, and divorce, and others conventionally classified under the rubric "social disorganization," quite likely tends, as Merton has suggested, to diminish its prestige.

Sociology, then, is *vulnerable* to stereotyping; its position in the contemporary structure of the intellectual professions exposes it to criticism from all sides. In numbers the weakest of the social sciences, it is the bastard son of the humanities, from which it gets its subject matter, and the sciences, from which it gets its methods. Fully acknowledged by neither parent, it finds itself in the role of *upstart*, now utilizing the existing methods of science, now improvising new scientific methods, in an attempt to make the enchanted data of the humanities yield up their mysteries.

Like ethnic stereotypes, which are fostered by segregation and reinforced by the consequent cultural isolation, intellectual stereotypes are fostered by professional specialization and reinforced by the diverse (and sometimes conflicting) perspectives developed in each. The lack of an intellectual perspective that transcends the provincialism generated by the limitations of a specialized perspective makes one susceptible to clichés and stereotypic thinking about related fields of study. In race and interethnic relations, the marginal man has, with his proverbial "one foot in each culture," provided this transcendent perspective. Humanist intellectuals can fulfill this function in intellectual life by addressing their criticisms of sociology *to sociologists*, rather than to their own colleagues; for it is the ironic fact that in writing to his own colleagues about sociology, the humanist intellectual himself tends to use obvious clichés to which his immersion in his own perspective blinds him. The kind of cross-fertilization that might be achieved by having humanist intellectual perspectives critically directed at an *audience of sociologists*, perhaps *in* a sociological journal, might go a long way toward providing this transcendent perspective.

ruth harriet jacobs

Journalists are out to write a "story," sociologists to do a piece of "research." Ruth Jacobs, a journalist turned sociologist, illustrates this in remembering the admonition of her first city editor to "never let the facts get in the way of a good story."

"Journalism seeks today's headlines: yesterday's story is wrapping for today's garbage. . . . Social science, on the other hand, accumulates knowledge carefully and painfully." This is only one of the differences noted by Ms. Jacobs. Others include approach to subject matter, the public's understanding of each, and judgments by professional peers.

Feeling that the gulf between the two fields is wider than generally perceived, the author of the following article thinks that sociologists who use journalistic techniques "should specify their changed status and hang out their journalist's shingle."

Not all sociologists would agree with Jacobs' interpretation and, as shall be seen in some of the essays that follow, there are even those who argue that few sociologists can match the perceptive insights of such writers as Lewis Lapham, Peter Schrag, Michael Lerner, and Tom Wolfe.

Reprinted from *The American Sociologist* 1970, Vol. 5 (November): 348–350, by permission of the author and the American Sociological Association. This article was originally entitled "The Journalistic and Sociological Enterprises as Ideal Types."

Sociological jargon and depth analysis characterize the "new reportage" of journalism. Some activist sociologists, in attempting to communicate their concerns, utilize certain techniques and audiences of journalists. At a time of considerable public interest in sociology and pressure on and within the profession, laymen are sometimes confused about the differences between sociological and journalistic observations and analyses, and even sociologists may feel some confusion. Consequently, there may be value in discussing several aspects of the journalistic and sociological enterprises that are diverse despite their surface commonalities. In a sense, journalism and sociology are ideal types of research. Ideal type analysis by its nature hopefully clarifies the essence of the phenomenon studied. Perhaps this is a time when sociologists should scrutinize the essentials of their profession because of the temptation to abandon or short-cut them.

Though a new Ph.D. sociologist, I immodestly attempt such an analysis because I was formerly a journalist and reported in a quite different manner and for very different purposes the phenomena I now study as a sociologist. From 1943 through 1949, I "covered" for the *Boston Traveler* and *Boston Herald* deviance, politics, education, disasters, so-called human-interest news, and collective behavior in many forms. From 1949 to 1961, while home raising a. family, I was a freelance journalist. After receiving a B.S. from Boston University in 1964, I entered Brandeis University and there obtained my advanced degrees. In the process of initiation to sociology, I had much to unlearn, and I painfully acquired a sense of the divergence between sociology and journalism.

Both disciplines gather information, but with diverse methods. My initial graduate school field-work problems did not include the doorbell-ringing anxieties of the neophyte field worker. To probe various people, communities, and organizations had been part of my newspaper-reporting experience. This background was not pure advantage, however, because I had to discard inappropriate journalistic objectives, methods, and ethics. In my first field-work course, I was able to obtain information more rapidly and completely than my younger, non-journalistically trained classmates, but I caught myself in various slips. One was where I typed "the reporter" instead of "the student" or "the field worker" in an early report; another came when I said I was going out on a "story" instead of out on a field-work assignment.

My task was to salvage that which could be properly transferred to sociology and to reject unusable newspaper-reporting techniques. My first city editor had repeatedly insisted, "never assume anything; find out the facts." In sociology, this helped me to avoid biased observation or expedient closures of theoretical constructs. But I had to abandon the editor's second law, "never let the facts get in the way of a good story."

As reporters, we operated within this paradox by finding, on every assignment, the facts that would protect our paper (and ourselves) from libel or public outcry of misrepresentation and inaccuracy. From these facts we would produce readable, exciting copy. Our criteria for this involved timeliness, public interest, and the values of the publisher and readers. We went after a story with an idea of what would be newsworthy. The experienced reporter knows he must produce a snappy lead paragraph and he seeks out colorful incidents and good quotations. Such goals are not ideal for sociological inquiry, though they may be utilized where there is pressure to publish in a timely area.

In my first field work, I looked automatically for what could be my gestalt. I set out with a list of things needed for a smooth overview. In talking with a dozen people, I sought to extract colorful illustrations from them to back up my "lead" or notion of the community. In only a few hours I was able to obtain nineteen pages of information. I did not pursue or write what would not be good copy, and in this, apparently, I succeeded: the comment on my paper was, "This is a first rate report, well worked out and quite rich in information. It reveals you to be quite alert and sensitive in the field situation." But, the reader added, "I would have to see your field notes for a more detailed critique."

This latter was a shrewd observation. My field notes would have revealed why my report was so "well worked out." My notes were fragmentary and included just what I had sought for the report and used in it. I had operated as in the newspaper business, that is, I had concentrated on getting a colorful story fast.

It was hard to stop doing this and to learn that significant data come from long immersion and do not always come as expected. I had extreme difficulty in making myself take notes. In the daily rush of news stories, writing had usually immediately followed the event—many reporters manage with very few notes. Sometimes it was impossible or unwise to record, and I had trained myself in selective remembering, which I came to trust and depend upon for unconscious synthesizing. Journalism seeks today's headlines: yesterday's story is wrapping for today's garbage, and details are not worth space in a reporter's notebook.

Social science, on the other hand, accumulates knowledge carefully and painfully. Though my instructors emphasized the importance of recording, I found it hard to make extensive notes. In fact, the requirement to do so annoyed me. I trusted myself to remember what was important, and I rationalized that note-taking impeded unobtrusiveness, informant-rapport, spontaneity, and kinesthetic clues. There was, of course, some truth to this. Eventually I worked out a satisfactory compromise for note-taking. I felt that my recall immediately after an interview would be dependable, so I continued minimal recording when talking with many shy informants or in certain observational situations, and then I went immediately to my car, drove long enough to leave the neighborhood, and wrote a full account.

At first, I was just going through the motions of doing busy work for my professors. A month later, when I re-read my notes, I was shocked to find things I had forgotten. I started to record more enthusiastically. I also began to find that what seemed unimportant at the recording might later prove to be valuable. For example, in a study of a family, I realized what Everett Hughes meant when he told our class to record everything in order to check on ourselves. After completing my last interview with a Mrs. C. (Jacobs, 1969), I found the notes of my early observations extremely useful in evaluating impressions after transference and counter-transference had developed. My early notes, in which I had recorded Mrs. C's behavior at a rally, also balanced later interviews in her home. The details of her community performance would have been forgotten if I had not been recording everything, because I observed many people at that event and had no realization then that Mrs. C. would become a major informant.

In the area of personal interaction, the approaches of the sociologist and the journalist are markedly different. While the personality of either worker may color the "truth" of the responses he gets, what is an ethical and veracious dilemma for the journalist is a scientific and methodological problem for the sociologist, who has to exhaust every possible means of weighing his impact on the data. For the newspaperman, an unpromising casual acquaintance will sometimes prove a valuable source, and just as scientific breakthroughs come "accidentally," prime feature stories often develop out of unplanned encounters and casual conversations. This, of course, is not the way sociological problems are pursued.

The news writer and editor have more clearly defined public and subjective legitimation of what they make public than does the participant-observer sociologist. This is because when a journalist identifies himself to an informant, he serves notice that what is told to him is possible public information. If the contact wishes to protect himself, he may say that the information is "off the record" or he may request secrecy regarding its source. The matter, of course, is more complex than this, as Westin (1967) and others have pointed out: there are libel-constraints in the background, and there are always decisions to make about freedom and responsibility of the press in reporting what public figures do not want reported; certain officials cannot expect privacy in acts that have public impact. So, too, sociology deals with publicly accountable behavior, as Rainwater and Pittman state (1967:364):

There are some situations for which the offer of confidentiality may be both unnecessary and technically a bad choice. In some situations, the applicability of research findings to applied goals will be rendered almost impossible if true confidentiality is maintained. And in some other situations it may be impossible to communicate the findings once the informants have been told that what we see and hear will be kept confidential.

A journalist has the self-protection of knowing that people understand what reporters do: they print the news. I soon discovered that informants lack a knowledge of what sociologists do. Though told they are being studied, many informants reveal more than they realize, and they confide facts that they do not expect to go beyond the listener. For example, on election day I rode about with an off-duty law enforcement official who was driving voters to the polls. Although I told him my interest in writing about the entire town, he saw me only in terms of the day's election. Consequently, he guarded political disclosures but gossiped freely about such matters as preferential treatment for favored law-breakers. He wished to impress me, and I was Simmel's "stranger" to whom he could safely ventilate his feelings. The information he gave me could have been used to his detriment, and he is unlikely to have given such information to a newspaper reporter.

Sociologists' informants often confuse them with social workers, clinical psychologists, and psychiatrists, seeing all as therapists. They consequently reach for help, and the sociologist's problem is not so much establishing rapport but being ethically responsible for controlling it. Many anxious, lonely people will seek help from anyone who seems to offer understanding. A sociologist often seems such a person, and he must beware of seeming to promise help that he cannot deliver.

The sociologist must also protect himself from suffering because of involvement beyond his capacity. Newspapermen are perhaps less vulnerable to such involvement because of their more transitory and surface approaches. An unkept promise to put a name or picture in the paper (or perhaps keep something out) may be less traumatic for the journalist than a poorly managed encounter is for the sociologist. While a journalist may become closely involved with his informants, he is less likely than the sociologist to be regarded as omnipotent and a dispenser of aid. Subjects may seek to utilize the newsman's influence or knowledge, but they do not see him in a scientist's halo. The medical motto to do no harm is not far from the code of most responsible sociologists and journalists.

Sociological probing, more subtle and less public than journalism, must protect its subjects. Erikson (1967:368) has pointed to disguised observations by social scientists as "an ugly invasion of privacy" plus painful misleading in a human transaction. Such issues are acute in the profession and sociologists have, to some extent, codified their concerns (Newsletter of Society for the Study of Social Problems, 1969; The American Sociologist, 1968).

In publishing, both the sociologist and the journalist are aware of the power to influence. The sociologist has a deeper responsibility because his biases are more subtle than are those of the journalist. Journalists sometimes attempt to borrow the authority of sociologists by writing, "as sociologists say." Sociologists may be put into double jeopardy where news headlines boldly state as actuality things carefully qualified by social scientists.

This points to another dichotomy between the two kinds of reporting. The work of the scientist will be reviewed, criticized, and questioned by his peers, and the sociologist will offer conclusions with caution. The journalist does not write for his peers and he may be more effective when he disregards them. His ignorance of the fact that a story has been told before allows him to recapitulate it for an audience that never tires of particular themes. For example, my output as an eighteen-year-old reporter was considerable because my curiosity and youth made everything seem exciting. I found news everywhere. As I matured, it became increasingly tedious for me to find feature stories because things no longer seemed novel. Had I continued, I might have ended in the haven of trained incapacity, the copy desk. Curiosity, as Berger (1963) points out, is also the earmark of sociologists, but they must heed the curiosity of others about the same matter. Good journalism can be repetitive; good sociology must be cumulative.

Unlike journalism, sociology is not confined to reporting and interpretation. Public interest and novelty justify journalism, but sound theory justifies sociology. The journalist may create his reputation by uncovering facts and reporting them accurately and colorfully. The sociologist who only reports facts or writes well will rank low among his peers—a situation, of course, that has encouraged some rather shaky theory-building and some skimpy testing. An essential difference between journalism and sociology is that journalists write from the top down, in triangle fashion, and sociologists do the opposite. The most important and sensational items of a journalist are put in the lead, with less newsworthy items at the end. The sociologist puts his data first and his conclusions at the end. A reader of science must read the full article for complete information, but a reader of news may get the "cream" in the first paragraph or two. Only the publication's reputation is the newsman's validation. Lay readers who find scientific writing cumbersome and inconclusive prefer the rewrites of the journalists. Presenting college students with journalistically adapted reports, as is sometimes done, may be doing them and their disciplines an ultimate disservice. While journalism and sociology may seem akin, they are essentially two very different enterprises. Sociologists resent journalists' borrowing their sociological language and mantle, and they resent superficial or distorted reports of their findings. But sociologists must eliminate attributes more appropriately left to journalism. If, as concerned citizens, they choose to use journalistic techniques in this time of crisis, they should specify their changed status and hang out their journalist's shingle.

However, as sociologists know, ideal types exist only as constructs. It is likely that the sociological and journalistic enterprises will continue to have characteristics somewhere between the poles described above.

REFERENCES

The American Sociologist. 1968. "Toward a code of ethics for sociologists." Vol. 3 (November):316–318.

Berger, Peter. 1963. Invitation to Sociology. New York: Anchor Books.

Erikson, K. T. 1967. "A comment on disguised observation in sociology." Social Problems 14 (Spring):366–373.

Jacobs, R. 1969. "Mobility pains: a family in transition." Family Coordinator 18 (April):129–134.

Newsletter of Society for the Study of Social Problems. 1969. "Revised statement regarding rights of human subjects in social research." (May):8–10.

Rainwater, L., and D. J. Pittman. 1967. "Ethical problems in studying a politically sensitive and deviant community." Social Problems 14 (Spring):357–366.

Westin, Alan F. 1967. Privacy and Freedom. New York: Atheneum.

william b. cameron

Here is an insider's critique of certain trends in sociology, particularly what might be called "the strain toward quantophrenia," the tendency to believe that only what you can count counts.

With tongue in cheek, William B. Cameron pointedly exposes the naivety of many social scientists who think they know what the "mean" really means, who substitute correlation for causation, who confuse that which is mathematically possible with that which is empirically true, who confuse "significance" for importance.

Cameron is not opposed to the use of statistics but feels one must approach percentages and samples and partial correlations with a healthy skepticism. If not, he argues, one might fall into the trap of believing that all women are crazy on the basis of having taken a 100 percent sample—the total universe—of the adult females at home and then interviewing one's wife!

Scientific writers assure us that mathematics is rapidly becoming the language of all the sciences. In my own field, sociology, a casual survey of the journals shows that it already competes strongly with sociologese, which is an argot singularly difficult to displace. In any field which strives for impartiality and objectivity in its descriptions of nature, the cool and dispassionate language of numbers has its appeals, but statistics, that promising younger daughter of mathematics, is constantly threatened with seductions into easy virtue hardly matched since the *Perils of Pauline*.

The basic value and potential fault of numbers is that they are remote from reality, abstract, and aloof from the loose, qualitative differences which immediately impinge upon our senses. Numerous selections, generalizations, and discriminations take place before any aspect of sense experience can be reduced to a number, and most of the time we are hardly aware of these abstractions even as we make them. The simplest and most basic statistical operation is counting, which means that we can identify something clearly enough so that we can recognize it when we meet it again and keep track of the number of such events which occur. This sounds simple enough until we actually try to count objects, such as, let us say, students in various colleges in the university. It is easy enough to simply count everyone who enrolls, but deans, board members, and newspaper reporters want to know how many there are in various divisions. Suppose a student is finishing his undergraduate work and taking a few graduate courses as well. Is he one undergraduate, one graduate, or one of each? If someone takes a single course in evening college, is he then one evening student, or only one-fifth of a student? (Remember, we are trying to keep our private passions out of this description!) How many times he should be counted obviously depends on what it is we are trying to count, and for administrative purposes it may be best to count his *appearance* in each of these divisions; but unfortunately, any public listing of 5000 appearances is very likely to be interpreted as 5000 skinsful of student body, whereas we might find only 3000 epidermal units, or if you prefer clichés, 3000 noses. Equally obvious, 100 evening college students taking one two-hour course each are in no meaningful way equivalent to 100 day students, each with a sixteen-hour load. The moral is: Not everything that can be counted counts.

If we have counted things to our satisfaction, we can express the numerical value of one class of objects in terms of the number of some other, as a fraction or rate or ratio (*e.g.*, one teacher to each twenty-five students). The meaning of this, of course, depends first of all on how we counted teachers and students. To avoid argument with academics, we might better redefine our units as people who meet classes, and enrollees. Also we must remind ourselves that the real persons do not necessarily, if indeed ever, confront each other in the frequencies the ratio suggests. The ratio is merely a casual guess as to the most likely arrangement to expect by chance, and contrary to the opinion of some people, academic affairs rarely proceed entirely by chance.

One of the most useful modifications of the ratio is a statement of relationships in percentage or a ratio standardized to a base of one hundred. A minimum of four mathematical operations have been performed to obtain a percentage: two classes of events have been counted, the frequency of one has been divided into the frequency of the other, and

the result multiplied by one hundred. Considered in this way, it is obvious that there is plenty of room for simple errors, but the simplest of all is the bland acceptance of the end figure as a kind of real object having a life of its own. In other words, people tend to treat percentages like match sticks, or houses, or dollar bills, rather than high-powered abstractions.

A parable: A teacher took a job as instructor at X college, and the second year he received a raise of ten per cent. The third year enrollment fell off, and the college was forced to cut everyone's salary ten per cent. "Oh well," he said philosophically, "easy come, easy go. I'm right back where I started." Not if he was a math teacher, he didn't! If this example trapped you, figure it out on paper with a starting salary for the instructor of, say $30,000, which is just as realistic as thinking that ten per cent equals ten per cent, if you have not first made certain that the two percentages are computed from the same, and reasonable, base. Even comparing figures as percentages of the same base is misleading if the base figure is not understandably related. As an example, compare your salary to that of the head coach at a university as percentages of (a) your son's weekly allowance, and (b) the national debt, and see which one, if either, makes you feel better. The sober, unhappy point is that both of these two kinds of errors are offered constantly in newspapers, journals, speeches, and elsewhere, and often the author blandly omits any definition of the base whatsoever, *viz*: "Things are looking better. Business volume is up ten per cent!"

Moral: 400 per cent is better in baseball than in taxes.

Our society has so often eulogized man's best friend that only the most obtuse statistician would conclude that a typical man-and-his-dog average three legs, but every day good, average people make errors just as gratuitous on the average in using averages. To speak of the average height of a group of men and women or the average age of the audience at a grade school play may yield results which, while less shocking, are fully as bizarre. Here again, as with most common statistical devices, few people really understand mathematically what the formulas mean, and yet they develop a kind of mystical feel for their use. "Average man" calls up an image of the man who lives across the alley. "Average day" means one distinguished from the rest neither by drama nor by excessive monotony. In fact, most people's approach to the whole business of averages is so intuitive that when the statistician writes "mean" they automatically translate it to "feel," because the mean is meaningless.

To be sure, the sophisticated have learned that average includes medians and modes, and many even know that for some reason salaries are better discussed in terms of the median (that coach is somehow involved in this again), but very few people have learned that there are times when you should not "take an average" at all. Most of us go ahead and take them on general principles, just like Grandpa took physic. Of course, when Grandpa had appendicitis, the physic killed him. You can't go against nature (or God) that way. But nature (or God) is less prompt in punishing statistical errors, with the result that many folks develop a real talent for sin.

Moral: How mean can you get?

Correlation is one of the handiest devices yet devised, and correspondingly, one of the least understood. Unless you have had a course in statistics, you probably do not know the formulas for this one, which may be just as well, considering how many people take means and how popular a catchword correlation has become. Most people think it is a high-powered word for cause. Actually it is not. In fact, "it" is not anything, because "it" is a "they." While correlation customarily refers to Pearsonian r (because this is an easy formula for people with easy consciences), there are numerous ways of computing correlations, each with subtly different meanings but all with one thing in common: correlations are simply mathematical statements about the degree to which some varying things tend (or don't tend) to vary together. A long time ago, John Stuart Mill painstakingly explained that even when causes were somehow involved, you could not safely infer that one of the variables in the correlation was causing the other; but Mill is out of fashion these days, and correlations are popular. Perhaps a good example of spurious causal reasoning might be the very high positive correlation between the number of arms and the number of legs in most human populations, which clearly proves what I have claimed all along, that arms cause legs.

There is no point in the math-fearing layman's even trying to grasp when and how to use the various correlation formulas. You simply must study some mathematics to gain even a hint of the restrictions, because the restrictions grow in part out of the kind of data with which you deal and in part out of the mathematical assumptions you make in trying to get the job done. If the mathematical assumptions are not met reasonably well by the data (and they almost never are!), the resulting statement about relationships among the data is, in greater or lesser part, grounds for libel. But data, like nature and God, are slow to respond to statistical calumny; so let us only seek to protect the reader.

Two other forms of correlation are beginning to appear in public, with their own characteristic misinterpretations: these are multiple and partial correlation. If correlation means the mathematical relation between two sets of variables, then multiple correlation means relationships between three sets or more. Fair enough? This is especially handy when trying to describe a complex set of interactions, such as rush hour traffic, or the stock market, or many human behaviors in which opposing and cooperating forces are working, pushing, and shoving, not working in any clearcut simple direction, but nonetheless producing some kind of result. The "feel" most people have for correlation carries over into multiple correlation, with probably not much greater inaccuracy. Instead of feeling one thing affecting another, they can go on feeling several things affecting another.

The real fun comes with partials. Multiples are confusing "because of" (or correlated strongly with) the fact that they describe complex situations. Partials are confusing because with them we symbolically do what we can't do in actual practice (but would love to!): we simplify the situation by making everything hold still except the one thing we wish to examlne.

"Now," says the layman, "you're getting somewhere. I *knew* there was a simple answer to all this if you would just produce it. What was that partial correlation for income and juvenile delinquency again?" Alas, we are worse off than before, because with multiple correlation we convinced him the problem was complicated (although not for exactly the reasons he supposed); but now we have inadvertently proven to him that it is all very simple, and that all effects may be understood in terms of simple, discrete causes. If I become inarticulate here, it is because in my town a layman (nice, average sort of man) published a statement in which he said income had virtually no relation to juvenile delinquency, and cheerfully cited a partial correlation to prove it.

What he did not know and I failed to explain to him was that partials rule out the joint effects of several variables *mathematically*, although these effects may be present and important *empirically*. For example (and here my analogies really strain their mathematical bonds!), in samples of water, the multiple correlation between hydrogen and oxygen and the phenomenon called wetness is high. The partial correlation for hydrogen and wetness, holding oxygen constant, is near zero. The same goes for the partial between oxygen and wetness, with hydrogen held constant. At this point I hope the readers bellow in a chorus, "You idiot, it takes both hydrogen and oxygen *together* to produce water!" Amen, and it probably takes low income, broken homes, blighted residential property, and a host of other things, all intricately intertwined, to produce juvenile delinquency. To say that the partial correlation with low income, all other factors held mathematically constant, is near zero, does not mean we can forget it in real life. It more probably means that this one factor is the constant companion of all the rest.

Clearer illustration of multiple and partial correlation may be seen in the *State Fair* mince pie, to which each member of the family surreptitiously added brandy. Each did just a little, but the whole effect on the judge was a lulu. To attribute some portion of the binge to any single person's brandy contribution would have only symbolic meaning, and hardly would be identifiable empirically, but it could not be ruled out. Moral: Camels may ultimately collapse under straws.

Most teachers have been exposed to the Normal Curve, usually in the form of an edict from the administration concerning the proper distribution of grades to hand out. In fact, in one institution some misguided administrator computed the percentage distribution of grades for my class of six students and compared it to the proposed institutional curve. The curve is what you might expect to find if the frequencies of events ranged around some mid-point purely by chance, like the impact points of artillery shells fired as exactly as possible at a given target. The mathematical specifications of the curve are complicated, but the basic point to remember is that this is a curve of chance occurrences; in fact, some people call it the curve of error. If any factor, however small, consistently biases the possibilities of events, they will not group themselves in this sort of curve, and it is sheer tyranny for us to insist that they should do so. It is true that over a large number of cases (say ten thousand) of students taking a given test with a similar general background of ability and interest, the grades will *approximate* this sort of curve. But the principle on which the curve is predicted says explicitly in fine print that any given small portion (sample) of those ten thousand (universe) might pile up at either end, or in the middle, or might scatter all over it from here to Hoboken. This small sample is your class and mine, and it may not be just your imagination: it is perfectly possible, statistically, that they really are all F's this year! Another year they may be all A's.

Moral: The normal curve will never replace the *Esquire* calendar.

The theory of sampling is a beautiful and fearful thing to behold and none but the statistical priesthood should be trusted to gaze upon it. But the laiety should at least become pious and agree to some key points in the creed. First of all, size of sample is much (underline *much*) less important than almost everything else about the sample. A carefully designed sample of two hundred cases can tell more than a sloppily collected sample of two thousand. The basic problem in sampling is to get a sample which faithfully represents the whole population or universe from which it was drawn. All the elaborate machinery of sampling is set up to serve this purpose, and if the rules are not followed, the sample might as well not be drawn at all. Good sampling is neither cheap nor easy, while bad sampling is sometimes both. The casual layman who wants to know how to make a sample should be given the same advice as the man who asked a doctor at a dance what he would suggest in a hypothetical case of illness. You will recall that the M.D. said, "I would advise that man to see a doctor." The best advice before trying to draw a sample is to see your local statistician. Otherwise, don't do it yourself unless you are sure you know how.

Moral: A free sample may be good for a disease you don't have.

The question which must be answered about most information derived from sample surveys is: "Is this statistically significant?" What this means is: "Could the kind of frequencies of events we have discovered have occurred purely by chance?" On this kind of answer rests our confidence in the Salk vaccine, radar, strategy in sales campaigns, and many other kinds of events where the improvement or change we seek is not total but is nevertheless desirable. In some cases, as small a change as two or three per cent may be significant—that is to say, is not likely to have occurred merely by chance; while in others, a twenty or thirty per cent change may not be significant. The techniques of determining significance are a serious study in themselves, but the common sense cautions in using them may be summed up in two statements: a difference that does not make a difference is not a difference; and, there is a vast difference between statistical significance and importance.

john o'neill

The following selection consists of excerpts from an article by a British sociologist who takes issue with the more traditional views outlined by Robert A. Nisbet in the first essay in this volume. John O'Neill is opposed to the highly professional orientation of most sociologists. He wants them to relate more to their subjects, their students, the world, to recognize, as he would put it that, at bottom, sociology is a "skin trade."

Unlike Nisbet, O'Neill does not draw a distinction between the problems of sociology and social problems. They are one and the same. Indeed, the relationship between sociologist and subject must be symbiotic.

The controversy over the extent of involvement and the degree of detachment is as old as the discipline of sociology. It is still being debated.

Students, . . . sullen-looking and apparently self-obsessed, come to sociology because they believe it is concerned with people and that it contributes to the understanding and practical improvement of human relations. They expect with the aid of some sociological training to find themselves in a position to "work with people."

From "Sociology as a Skin Trade" by John O'Neill, excerpted from *Sociological Inquiry* (Winter 1970), by permission of the author and publisher.

Now nothing is more likely to throw the sociological profession into turmoil than the persistence of this popular belief that sociology involves working with people. Students who will still believe this are called radicals and activists. They are regarded as throwbacks from the days when the academic establishment did not distinguish sex, socialism, and sociology. Sociology's status as a science was won very painfully and depends very much upon the segregation of those whose sympathies are with social work, or political and community action.

Now there are signs that this conception of the professional role belongs more to the generation which worked its way up with sociology than to the contemporary generation of students who do not have the same status qualms about science or affluence. For it is not the professionally alienated or poorer sociology students who retain the activist and populist conception of sociology. The truth which the older generation of social science professionals must confront is the return of bad times and the inescapable involvement of sociology with the ills of society. Curiously enough, whereas the older professionals saw the priest as the specter of bad times, nowadays the young sociologist regards the older technicians and professionals as the high-priests of the bureaucratization of spirit and imagination to which they attribute much of our social malaise.

Working with people creates a bewildering variety of practices which I shall call skin trades. People need haircuts, massage, dentistry, wigs and glasses, sociology and surgery, as well as love and advice. A vast number of people are involved in trades which fit out, adorn, repair, amuse, cajole, confine and incarcerate other people. A special aura attaches to working with people. The work of the priest, judge, doctor, and missionary is regarded as holy. The work of the prostitute, the pickpocket, and undertaker is considered profane. In reality, these trades are all involved in dirty work with people. Alternatively, with the exception of the pickpocket, all of these trades may be regarded as holy occupations because of the sublimity of their purpose, to restore and make whole the person.

Working with people is a precarious undertaking and thus the skin trades are especially marked with the ambivalent aura of sacredness and profanity which surrounds the human body. For this reason, every society defines rituals of approach and avoidance to govern contacts between people, between the sexes, and between trades. The vast symbiosis of social life is naturally represented as a body in which the spiritual functions are relieved for prayer and thought through the excremental services of the lower-orders.

In this scheme of things, the skin trades have been traditionally low-caste, their services being required in order to keep the higher castes free from bodily impurities and thus holy. The lower castes cut hair, wash clothes, clean latrines, and dress corpses. In the dutiful performance of these tasks, the lower castes exchange the possibility of mobility in this life for the certainty of it in the next life. This social division of labor is again expressed in the concentration of the skin trades in a locality of the city, for example, around ports, railway stations, and markets. With their teeming produce and swarming crowds, these areas are also the scenes of bar-fights, prostitution, hustling, miscegeny, and missionary work. Ports, markets, and railway centers are the body orifices of society. As such they arouse the anxiety of the forces of law and order housed in the symbolic center of the social organism. Once sociology enters the house of government it too becomes anxious about margins, disorder and deviations.

Sociology is best thought of as a skin trade. This does not mean that sociology is not a profession and a science. It merely implies that sociology is obliged to claim the status of a science and a profession because that is the dilemma of the skin trades in the modern world. It suggests, too, that some of the scientific equipment of the sociologist, like that of the dentist, cosmetician, and pharmacist, may be more related to status management than the real nature of his task.

Consider the dentist's dilemma. As a mouth-miner he is employed in a dark hole filling cavities, stopping odors, uprooting and removing debris. To save face as a professional it is essential for him to spend more time on the surface than in mouth-mining. Thus the office decor, receptionist, nurse, and para-surgical front of the dentist's suite furnishes the necessary choreography of his professional activity. It enables him to reconstruct his mouth-work in the frame of the professional-client relationship.

Much of the sociological apparatus functions, I suggest, to support a ritual of decontamination between the scientist and his subject. It is essential that the sociologist view his subject only with professional eyes and that he resist the look in the eyes of the sick, the poor, and the aimless who turn his questions back upon him. In this way the erotic symbiosis of talk is reduced to the interview schedule or attitude survey in which the client comes clean before the professional *voyeur*. As the sociological apparatus increases in size and complexity it has to be housed in offices and institutes and its services can only be afforded by wealthy clients. This has the disadvantage of shutting sociology out of crowd scenes, disasters and riots. It also demands standards of decorum from the sociologist which make it difficult for him to pass in the underworld of crime, sex, race and poverty. The professional sociologist is curiously caught in his own caste.

In my view sociology is a symbiotic science. Its promise is to give back to the people what it takes from them. This is true of all culture but sociology more than any other discipline promises to make this a practical truth. This is not to say that sociology does not need the other sciences. On the contrary, it presupposes other physical and social sciences. But it has its own task in the need to articulate the connections between individual experience and the transvaluation of human sensibilities worked by the institutional settings of technology, science, and politics.

But, in its aspiration to become a science and to bestow professional status upon its members, sociology has uncritically assumed all the trappings of science. It has lodged itself in the bureaucratic organizations which are the institutional expression of the process of rationalization that has made the fortune of modern science and technology. The same processes of rationalization control the selection and organization of data collected for the sake of client projects parasitic upon the public life and concerns of the people.

The apprentice sociologist is as much exploited by these projects as the people they are intended to benefit. He learns the collection and manipulation of data chosen as much for their machine-culinary properties as for any relevance to practical social or theoretical concerns. However, in exchange for domesticating his imagination with trivial generalizations or with the more frequent correlations which litter the sociological journals, the apprentice sociologist is assured of his acceptance to the sociological profession. He is all the more converted when he contemplates the power of professional method and organization which can produce an instant sociology of the Berkeley Free Speech Movement or of Watts, or of crime and violence in the streets, of poverty, or of affluence.

The most profound shock which the apprentice sociologist experiences occurs when he is confronted with the professional neutering of his sense of relevance and concern. This is achieved in a number of ways. Every freshman learns the distinction between facts and values. The effect of this distinction is to convince him that the classroom is a laboratory which can only be contaminated by his everyday knowledge of class, race, war, poverty, sex and the body.

To put it another way, many students come to sociology because its questions are raised for them in their everyday contact with one another, with the ghetto, the police, the military, and the administration. They have met "the system" in their high schools, in their fights with university administrators, the city-fathers, and the sublime indifference of most people. They are not content with the abstract problem of how organizations handle uncertainty. They would like to know which in particular are the most powerful corporations. What is life like in these institutions? What is the ethnic composition of their labor force? What percentage of their production is destined for military purposes? What do their activities in colonial countries mean for the lives of those people? In short, they would like to know which organizations determine the distribution of comfort and security for some and poverty and danger for others. They know they cannot get answers to these questions from a sociology which relies on statistical data never intended to probe the consequences of organizational rationality.

These questions are often dismissed as the concerns of activists. This is short-sighted. Such questions really call upon sociology to reexamine its own sense of the relevance of things. They remind the professional sociologist that his own "isms"—careerism, scientism, and opportunism —are showing through. They challenge the optimistic assumption of middle-range theory that somehow the data will pile itself up into the big answer to the big question with which no one meanwhile need concern himself.

There is no single road to sociological disenchantment. The fact-value distinction is only one of the devices for altering the student's sense of relevance. Another favorite is the method of "sociological vertigo." The strategy in this case is to confound the ethnocentrism of young students with a bewildering tour of the most exotic sociological and anthropological scenes. The purpose here seems to be to convince the sociology student that everything might be some other way—a terror usually reserved for students in introductory philosophy courses.

Nowadays such "trips" are losing their power to convert students who live their lives experimentally and at short notice. In any case, once they discover that the sociologist's "high" is on functionalism or social determinism and that he never understood what *they* meant by individualism and community, they turn off on the paid-piper. For the striking thing is that so many young students have thought through for themselves what it means to encounter other people as they are and to know them without needing the way in to be marked esoterically or the way out to be anything else than the time-in-between-people.

Each time one meets a class of sociology students one knows that sociology cannot escape into itself. This is possible only if we allow our jargon to turn meaning away from language and the world toward which it carries us. Yet sociology must speak in its own voice and according to its own experience.

Much of what I have said may seem highly critical of professional sociology. If it were nothing more, then it would not serve young sociologists. What I mean to do is to awaken the sense of some of the root metaphors which apply to sociology as a "trade," a "craft," or a "field." These metaphors remind us of the care and sweat in doing sociology. At the same time, they remind us that sociology is only a way of earning a living and cannot presume to contribute more than others to the public good. It means that when we teach we take others into our care and in turn we must lend ourselves to what they need in order to grow and to become themselves.

Young people are looking for work. We must show them the fields and how we care for them so that they will want to share the work. There is no way of legislating what sociologists should do even though we may be clear about what is urgent and important in their task. The practicing sociologist must answer for himself and to his colleagues and to the rest of men.

In calling sociology a skin trade I want to restore its symbiotic connections with the body-politic and to situate it in relation to the exchange of organic needs and the utopian celebration of libidinal community which surpasses all understanding. This means that the rhetoric of scientism in sociology as well as its humanism must be tested against the commonsense relevances of everyday life. It is a reminder that society is richer than sociology and that for all our science the world is still the mystery and passion of being with our fellow men.

6/BODY RITUAL AMONG THE NACIREMA

horace miner

American anthropologists have long been intrigued by the seemingly exotic behavior of peoples whose manners and mores markedly differ from their own. They have probed and described the cultural patterns and collective psyches of Trobriand Islanders and Bushmen, of Eskimos and Australian Aborigines, of Indian villagers and Thai peasants. And, typically, their reports have included detailed interpretations of the most intimate aspects of everyday life, seeing all sorts of connections between what goes on in one institutional sphere and another, often, as William B. Cameron might have put it, substituting alleged correlation with causation.

Few have ever come to study the mysterious Nacirema or tried to interpret their ways of life. In this delightful and pointed piece of social-science fiction, anthropologist Horace Miner does precisely that. Taking but a tiny portion of the daily routine of his subjects and relating it to what he knows about the culture, Miner attempts to explain "Body Ritual Among the Nacirema."

The anthropologist has become so familiar with the diversity of ways in which different peoples behave in similar situations that he is not apt to be surprised by even the most exotic customs.

Reproduced by permission of the American Anthropological Association from *American Anthropologist*, vol. 58, no. 3, 1956, and by permission of the author.

In fact, if all of the logically possible combinations of behavior have not been found somewhere in the world, he is apt to suspect that they must be present in some yet undescribed tribe. This point has, in fact, been expressed with respect to clan organization by Murdock.[1] In this light, the magical beliefs and practices of the Nacirema present such unusual aspects that it seems desirable to describe them as an example of the extremes to which human behavior can go.

Professor Linton first brought the ritual of the Nacirema to the attention of anthropologists twenty years ago,[2] but the culture of this people is still very poorly understood. They are a North American group living in the territory between the Canadian Cree, the Yaqui and Tarahumare of Mexico, and the Carib and Arawak of the Antilles. Little is known of their origin, although tradition states that they came from the east. According to Nacirema mythology, their nation was originated by a culture hero, Notgnihsaw, who is otherwise known for two great feats of strength— the throwing of a piece of wampum across the river Pa-To-Mac and the chopping down of a cherry tree in which the Spirit of Truth resided.

Nacirema culture is characterized by a highly developed market economy which has evolved in a rich natural habitat. While much of the people's time is devoted to economic pursuits, a large part of the fruits of these labors and a considerable portion of the day are spent in ritual activity. The focus of this activity is the human body, the appearance and health of which loom as a dominant concern in the ethos of the people. While such a concern is certainly not unusual, its ceremonial aspects and associated philosophy are unique.

The fundamental belief underlying the whole system appears to be that the human body is ugly and that its natural tendency is to debility and disease. Incarcerated in such a body, man's only hope is to avert these characteristics through the use of the powerful influences of ritual and ceremony. Every household has one or more shrines devoted to this purpose. The more powerful individuals in the society have several shrines in their houses and, in fact, the opulence of a house is often referred to in terms of the number of such ritual centers it possesses. Most houses are of wattle and daub [wood and plaster] construction, but the shrine rooms of the more wealthy are walled with stone. Poorer families imitate the rich by applying pottery plaques to their shrine walls.

While each family has at least one such shrine, the rituals associated with it are not family ceremonies but are private and secret. The rites are normally only discussed with children, and then only during the period when they are being initiated into these mysteries. I was able, however, to establish sufficient rapport with the natives to examine these shrines and to have the rituals described to me.

The focal point of the shrine is a box or chest which is built into the wall. In this chest are kept the many charms and magical potions without which no native believes he could live. These preparations are secured for a variety of specialized practitioners. The most powerful of these are the medicine men, whose assistance must be rewarded with substantial gifts. However, the medicine men do not provide the curative potions for their clients, but decide what the ingredients should be and then write them down in an ancient and secret language. This writing is understood only by the medicine men and by the herbalists who, for another gift, provide the required charm.

The charm is not disposed of after it has served its purpose, but is placed in the charm box of the household shrine. As these magical materials are specific for certain ills, and the real or imagined maladies of the people are many, the charm-box is usually full to overflowing. The magical packets are so numerous that people forget what their purposes were and fear to use them again. While the natives are very vague on this point, we can only assume that the idea in retaining all the old magical materials is that their presence in the charm-box, before which the body rituals are conducted, will in some way protect the worshipper.

Beneath the charm-box is a small font. Each day every member of the family, in succession, enters the shrine room, bows his head before the charm-box, mingles different sorts of holy water in the font, and proceeds with a brief rite of ablution. The holy waters are secured from the Water Temple of the community, where the priests conduct elaborate ceremonies to make the liquid ritually pure.

In the hierarchy of magical practitioners, and below the medicine men in prestige, are specialists whose designation is best translated "holy-mouth-men." The Nacirema have an almost pathological horror of and fascination with the mouth, the condition of which is believed to have a supernatural influence on all social relationships. Were it not for the rituals of the mouth, they believe that their teeth would fall out, their gums bleed, their jaws shrink, their friends desert them, and their lovers reject them. They also believe that a strong relationship exists between oral and moral characteristics. For example, there is a ritual ablution of the mouth for children which is supposed to improve their moral fiber.

The daily body ritual performed by everyone includes a mouth-rite. Despite the fact that these people are so punctilious about care of the mouth, this rite involves a practice which strikes the uninitiated stranger as revolting. It was reported to me that the ritual consists of inserting a small bundle of hog hairs into the mouth, along with certain magical powders, and then moving the bundle in a highly formalized series of gestures.

In addition to the private mouth-rite, the people seek out a holy-mouth-man once or twice a year. These practitioners have an impressive set of paraphernalia, consisting of a variety of augers, awls, probes, and prods. The use of these objects in the exorcism of the evils of the mouth involves almost unbelievable ritual torture of the client. The holy-mouth-man opens the client's mouth and, using the above mentioned tools, enlarges any holes which decay may have created in the teeth. Magical materials are put into these holes. If there are no naturally occurring holes in the teeth, large sections of one or more teeth are gouged out so that the supernatural substance can be applied. In the client's view, the purpose of these ministrations is to arrest decay and to draw friends. The extremely sacred and traditional character of the rite is evident in the fact that the natives return to the holy-mouth-man year after year, despite the fact that their teeth continue to decay.

It is to be hoped that, when a thorough study of the Nacirema is made, there will be careful inquiry into the personality structure of these people. One has but to watch the gleam in the eye of a holy-mouth-man, as he jabs an awl into an exposed nerve, to suspect that a certain amount of sadism is involved. If this can be established, a very interesting pattern emerges, for most of the population shows definite masochistic tendencies. It was to these that Professor Linton referred in discussing a distinctive part of the daily body ritual which is performed only by men. This part of the rite involves scraping and lacerating the surface of the face with a sharp instrument. Special women's rites are performed only four times during each lunar month, but what they lack in frequency is made up in barbarity. As part of this ceremony, women bake their heads in small ovens for about an hour. The theoretically interesting point is that what seems to be a preponderantly masochistic people have developed sadistic specialists.

The medicine men have an imposing temple, or *latipso*, in every community of any size. The more elaborate ceremonies required to treat very sick patients can only be performed at this temple. These ceremonies involve not only the thaumaturge [Miracle worker] but a permanent group of vestal maidens who move sedately about the temple chambers in distinctive costume and headdress.

The *latipso* ceremonies are so harsh that it is phenomenal that a fair proportion of the really sick natives who enter the temple ever recover. Small children whose indoctrination is still incomplete have been known to resist attempts to take them to the temple because "that is where you go to die." Despite this fact, sick adults are not only willing but eager to undergo the protracted ritual purification, if they can afford to do so. No matter how ill the supplicant or how grave the emergency, the guardians of many temples will not admit a client if he cannot give a rich gift to the custodian. Even after one has gained admission and survived the ceremonies, the guardians will not permit the neophyte to leave until he makes still another gift.

The supplicant entering the temple is first stripped of all his or her clothes. In every-day life the Nacirema avoids exposure of his body and its natural functions. Bathing and excretory acts are performed only in the secrecy of the household shrine, where they are ritualized as part of the body-rites. Psychological shock results from the fact that body secrecy is suddenly lost upon entry into the *latipso*. A man, whose own wife has never seen him in an excretory act, suddenly finds himself naked and assisted by a vestal maiden while he performs his natural functions into a sacred vessel. This sort of ceremonial treatment is necessitated by the fact that the excreta are used by a diviner to ascertain the course and nature of the client's sickness. Female clients, on the other hand, find their naked bodies are subjected to the scrutiny, manipulation and prodding of the medicine men.

Few supplicants in the temple are well enough to do anything but lie on their hard beds. The daily ceremonies, like the rites of the holy-mouth-men, involve discomfort and torture. With ritual precision, the vestals awaken their miserable charges each dawn and roll them about on their beds of pain while performing ablutions, in the formal movements of which the maidens are highly trained. At other times they insert magic wands in the supplicant's mouth or force him to eat substances which are supposed to be healing. From time to time the medicine men come to their clients and jab magically treated needles into their flesh. The fact that these temple ceremonies may not cure, and may even kill the neophyte, in no way decreases the people's faith in the medicine men.

There remains one other kind of practitioner, known as a "listener." This witch-doctor has the power to exorcise the devils that lodge in the heads of people who have been bewitched. The Nacirema believe that parents bewitch their own children. Mothers are particularly suspected of putting a curse on children while teaching them the secret body rituals. The counter-magic of the witch-doctor is unusual in its lack of ritual. The patient simply tells the "listener" all his troubles and fears, beginning with the earliest difficulties he can remember. The memory displayed by the Nacirema in these exorcism sessions is truly remarkable. It is not uncommon for the patient to bemoan the rejection he felt upon being weaned as a babe, and a few individuals even see their troubles going back to the traumatic effects of their own birth.

In conclusion, mention must be made of certain practices which have their base in native esthetics but which depend upon the pervasive aversion to the natural body and its functions. There are ritual fasts to make fat people thin and ceremonial feasts to make thin people fat. Still other rites are used to make women's breasts larger if they are small, and smaller if they are large. General dissatisfaction with breast shape is symbolized in the fact that the ideal form is virtually outside the range of human variation. A few women afflicted with almost inhuman hypermammary development are so idolized that they make a handsome living by simply going from village to village and permitting the natives to stare at them for a fee.

Reference has already been made to the fact that excretory functions are ritualized, routinized, and relegated to secrecy. Natural reproductive functions are similarly distorted. Intercourse is taboo as a topic and scheduled as an act. Efforts are made to avoid pregnancy by the use of magical materials or by limiting intercourse to certain phases of the moon. Conception is actually very infrequent. When pregnant, women dress so as to hide their condition. Parturition takes place in secret, without friends or relatives to assist, and the majority of women do not nurse their infants.

Our review of the ritual life of the Nacirema has certainly shown them to be a magic-ridden people. It is hard to understand how they have managed to exist so long under the burdens which they have imposed upon themselves. But even such exotic customs as these take on real meaning when they are viewed with the insight provided by Malinowski when he wrote:[3]

> Looking from far and above, from our high places of safety in the developed civilization, it is easy to see all the crudity and irrelevance of magic. But without its power and guidance early man could not have mastered his practical difficulties as he has done, nor could man have advanced to the higher stages of civilization.

NOTES

1. George P. Murdock, *Social Structure* (New York: The Macmillan Co., 1949).
2. Ralph Linton, *The Study of Man* (New York: D. Appleton-Century Co., 1936).
3. Bronislaw Malinowski, *Magic, Science, and Religion* (Glencoe: The Free Press, 1948).

william simon

We now live in what William Simon describes as a relatively lush erotic landscape, in a society in which sex has taken on new meaning —at least in terms of public consciousness. Sexual styles and behavior are no longer the secret purview of lovers alone but the stuff of everyday discussion. There is a new openness about such once forbidden subjects as autoerotic behavior, homosexuality, and cosmetic sexuality. But sexual relations are not the only thing that have appeared to change. Indeed, sexual behavior is dominated by sociocultural factors.

One learns what is appropriate sexual activity (and what the limits are) from others in his or her social milieu. In a period of rapid change, all areas of society are in a state of flux. So, too, with the attitudes toward sex. As Simon points out "many of the facets of sexuality . . . are related to major shifts in the life styles and public values of the American middle class."

In less than half a century sex in American life has rocketed from the unmentionable to a topic of almost obsessive public concern. The management of sexual activity, either as a social or personal phenomenon, has become a high-priority preoccupation for vast segments of our society. The major theme of preoccupation that emerges from this talk, study and activity is: What has changed in American sexual styles and behavior?

In earlier periods the silence kept everyone at a distance from the question itself. Because of pluralistic ignorance—no one had any idea what anybody else was doing or feeling—it was possible to hang onto a vague sense of some natural order of things in sex. And despite all that we have learned about sexual matters—and it is not nearly enough—this notion of the natural order of things persists; it is a major theme whenever the sexual dimension of man is considered. We should also note that our increase in knowledge about sex has won acceptance largely because the researchers worked under the rubric of the natural sciences—the zoological commitment of Kinsey, the medical context of Masters and Johnson. Thus, we began to talk aloud about sex, and a many-sided public dialogue continues. Some see this increased sexual knowledge as a rare opportunity for personal growth and maturity. Others see it as a portent of a crumbling society. The only agreement seems to be that we are in the process of change, and that the change is possibly profound.

This agreement that there are profound changes, even though the changes are often vaguely defined, has led to the clamor about the so-called sex revolution. The very ability to embrace a concept of sex revolution may in itself be truly revolutionary. Yet, to talk about sexual revolution in purely sexual terms makes as little sense as talking about political revolutions in exclusively political terms. There is one promising facet of the preoccupation with sex: it may help us consider the sexual dimension in the context of on-going social and psychological life. This would certainly be an improvement over most of our past in which the specter of sexuality was an isolated figure in a denuded social and psychological landscape or, at best, was accompanied by the gray figure of orthodox morality. The point is that for the first time we have an opportunity to pursue this subject in breadth.

There is, however, a dual aspect of sexuality that generates complexity in both sexual activity and social regulation of it. The sexual dimension links man to his evolution and gives him a sense of participation in species life and species survival. The sexual component also remains a powerful reminder of the mediating and limit-setting functions of the body. But perhaps most important, man's sexuality can be an equally powerful reminder of how unnatural and unprogrammed the human experience is. We need only look across cultures or through the histories of single cultures to see the impressive variety of adaptations and meanings that are possible. For in acting upon his sexuality, man simultaneously celebrates one of his most universal aspects as well as his utter dependence upon the sociocultural moment. What, after all, is more unnatural to most of our contemporaries than the nude human body in a sexual posture?

Changes in the definition or representation of the sexual dimension in American cultural life since World War II have proceeded at a gallop. In looking at them, it is important to differentiate between the public and private faces of sex. The changes in the public face of sexuality are easy to discern. The hard part is to find the implications of these public changes for the private face of sexuality.

With nationwide media systems, we are surrounded by sexual imagery more explicitly erotic than any we have had before in our society. This erotic environment may be seen in two distinct dimensions. The first involves the limits of permissible public or quasi-public representation of the sexual. This boundary has shifted markedly, particularly in the last decade. Some part of this growing permissiveness is a direct result of the federal judiciary's handling of a number of major cases involving erotic materials. The courts may be somewhat ahead of the social consensus in this permissiveness, but there are substantial continuities involved in both the production and consumption of culture in our society. Both the popular and the more traditional arts are living in closer collaboration with what had previously been their underground. In fact, the underground itself becomes increasingly a special part of our public culture. To indicate how far and how quickly we have come, it might be noted that in 1948 the *New York Times* refused to carry the conservative, medical-textbook publisher's advertising for the first Kinsey report. By the mid-1960s the *Times* was carrying, without apparent reluctance, rather lurid ads for books that were previously almost unavailable except in the locked library cases of Kinsey's Institute for Sex Research.

What is publicly permissible, however, only suggests what is available to the society. Contrary to the would-be censors' predictions, permissiveness did not attract massive portions of the population to the new erotic frontiers. Relatively few people in our society are gourmets of the extremely and/or exclusively erotic.

In fact, the second dimension of the new erotic environment may be even more important; it is the extent to which the sexual is included in conventional public discourse, without new images or language. Here we can see a profound increase in concern for the sexual. Consumer advertising, the popular arts, the middle-range sources of information such as women's magazines and TV documentaries—all provide occasion and language for both thinking and talking about sex in social situations. Educators appear almost but not quite ready to admit that there may be more to sex education than studies in reproductive biology and social etiquette. The new liberal theologies—particularly those infected with the new morality—find in the sexual an imagery that achieves a kind of instant salience. All at once we find sex at center stage instead of on the fringes of self-awareness.

The result is that we now live in a relatively lush erotic landscape, and it is increasingly difficult to separate that which is expressive of disturbed fantasies and aroused anxieties from that which is descriptive of the present and/or prototypical of the future. There is almost a shift from the question of the legitimacy of what one is doing and wants to do to the question of what more should one do or should want to do.

The sexual images we are now offered are confused and frequently contradictory. In the wake of Masters and Johnson's powerful study, the ladies' magazines appear to have established the legitimacy, if not the necessity, of female orgasm almost before they have established the necessity of sexual intercourse. Thus we can talk about orgasm more easily than we can talk about intercourse. Wife-swapping, for example, is talked about in ways that define it rather curiously as a social problem. One is all at once unsure of what is an appropriate response. One senses, however, that there is more talk about wife-swapping than there is actual swapping, and that participation is extremely marginal. Much the same is true of what the young are reputed to be doing sexually.

A point to remember is that often significant social change does not come about merely because behavior patterns change. The point of change may be simply the point at which given forms of behavior appear plausible. An example of this phenomenon is the current status of homosexuality as a public topic. There is no evidence of recent growth in the proportion of our population that has homosexual preferences. Of course, the number of such persons has increased along with the total population. But, aside from relatively localized situations, little has changed in the life situation of the homosexual. He must still face both the risks of arrest, conviction and imprisonment and the frequently more feared risk of rejection by family, friends and employers.

Nevertheless, in recent years homosexuality has become part of the standard fare on the frontiers of cultural consumption. The subject is the pivotal theme in an increasing number of novels, plays and motion pictures. It is covered by television, newspapers and magazines. This implies that ultimately society will respond more rationally to the homosexual. Even more important is the implication for the future status of heterosexuality. Our thinking about homosexuality conditions our thinking about heterosexuality and sexuality in general.

All these changes in the public representation of the sexual—be it of the homosexual, the alleged youthful vanguard of the sexual revolution, the female doubly liberated by the pill and the language of the multiple orgasm, etc.—could represent a watershed where both the status and content of sexuality are transformed. Unless one sees the sexual as a nearly immutable evolutionary inheritance, one must assess the complex process in which the idea of the sexual is formed and transformed, the process within which—one might say—it is invented.

The author sees sexual behavior as dominated by sociocultural factors. This view is supported by cross-cultural research and by study of data restricted to the United States. The individual can learn sexual behavior as he learns other behavior—through the interaction of complex social and psychological factors and not as the result of some masked primordial drive. This means that sexual behavior can often express and serve nonsexual motives. For most people, including most of the young, a heightened awareness of the sexual dimension need not be followed by an ability to incorporate this awareness into their own sexual commitments.

It is not uncommon for those who view the sexual component as a high-order biological constant to see it as pressing against the layers of experiences and adopted roles that describe the individual. These layers of experience, in this view, may provide an authentic expression of the sexual while other layers cause distortion and repression. The contrary perspective describes these layers of experience and role incumbency as essentially creating the sexual or at least forming the frameworks within which our respective sexual scripts are formed and evolve. It is not surprising that the notion of the high-order biological constant has achieved such great currency. Because for all but a very few individuals in our society a sense of the sexual self is typically experienced as something discontinuous with other—more public— senses of self. Despite the seeming remoteness of the sexual, the very capacity to be sexual appears to be linked to larger senses of self and linked in very fundamental ways. To understand possible changes in the sexual dimension, then, we must first understand something of these other aspects of identity.

The sex act is obviously more than the joining of sex organs. A crucial sense of gender not only shapes the performance, but also may be a necessary precondition for something sexual to happen in the first place. Consistent with this is the finding reported by Kagen and Moss that the most powerful predictor of adult sexual commitment may be the quality of the nonsexual sex-role learning during the later years of childhood— ages six to 10. The importance of the gender role for sexual activity has two dimensions. One, what kinds of acts are consistent with what kinds of commitments to concepts of masculinity and femininity? And, two, what kinds of sex-role characteristics make it possible for one to see another person as potentially erotic? As these crucial gender roles undergo change we may begin to expect changes in sexual patterns far more dramatic than those presumed to be prompted by the pill or sexy movies. Major shifts in just these social definitions of gender roles may be now in process. There is far less data on this topic than its significance requires.

Impressionistically there appears to be a growing tendency toward greater and greater tolerance for deviation from narrow, stereotypic definitions of appropriate male and female behavior. There always was more such tolerance at the higher socioeconomic levels, and this apparent shift may reflect only a widespread affluence. The people in higher socioeconomic levels have an out-size role in creating public images of private life, in determining the modalities of self-image. The middle-class urban young who are mixing gender symbols freely with hair and dress may be expressing just this kind of shift of gender-role learning. And our current crop of young appear to have an earlier and possibly greater capacity for heterosociality, which is likely to have an effect on their capacity for heterosexuality. Their sexual style will probably continue to be expressive of the assimilation of these changing gender roles. But one's sexual style need not be a test of one's gender commitment, as it is for so very many adults today.

There is, to be sure, a great deal of continuity as well as change. For many, including many of the young, sex continues to be a fearful test that must confirm what it can confirm only provisionally. For males the fear of sociosexual inadequacy and incompetence and for females the double fear of being too little sexual and too much sexual will keep the sexual game precisely that: a game in which the costs of losing often outweigh the rewards of victory. But the trends we have noted earlier do represent a new countervailance and the prospect for a cooler attitude.

The trends need not have immediate implications for what people do or the frequency with which they do it. The important changes may be in the attitude with which they approach sex. Instead of acting out of need (the need for social-psychological validation rather than a response to inarticulate strivings of the body) people may develop a heightened ability to act out of desire. This in turn suggests that casualness might affect both style and frequency. But such a change does not necessarily mean stepped-up sexuality. On the contrary, it might produce a marked lessening among those to whom sexual commitment was an imperative, a test or ordeal.

For the time being, however, new patterns will strain for accommodation with older patterns. Adolescent boys will continue to make strong commitments to their own sexuality by masturbating and by spinning complex fantasies. For most of them masturbation, as commitment and rehearsal, will continue to be organized around fantasy themes that feed directly from their own sense of emerging masculinity. This sense of masculinity will tend to be aggressive and direct in ways that will almost never find expression in heterosocial communication. But there will also be strong pulls toward engagement in sociosexual activity as success on this level wins social support and social reward.

For girls, on the other hand, there is little reason to expect an immediate or marked shift to increased sexual activity, either masturbatory or sociosexual, during the early or even the middle years of adolescence. They will continue learning how to appear sexual and will receive social support and rewards for success at it. But there still will be no rewards for sexual activity as such.

This cosmetic sexuality will form in a rhetorical atmosphere of social competence and competence in the managing of emotional relations, abilities that make sociosexual activity legitimate. Until now the legitimating conditions for sexual activity for most females have been tied to family formation or courtship in very fundamental ways.

Many of the facets of sexuality that we have considered are related

to major shifts in the life styles and public values of the American middle class. In a situation where decisions that commit the total society —such as the tragedy of Vietnam or even factors that affect the immediate quality of community life—appear remote to most people, the sexual takes on a significance and power beyond that which is intrinsic to it. Nowadays one strives for competence and self-actualization which, as goals, are far more flexible than the traditional achievement that one sought before. In fact, the so-called new morality involves a shift from the morality of significant acts to the morality of personal competence. Sexuality gives the individual at least the sense of making moral decisions. Not only may his sense of personal effectiveness thus be enhanced but his focus is shifted from the act to the quality of his motives. This takes the form of personal competence. Management of sexuality, as a consequence, becomes significant in self-identity. The negative aspect is that sexuality increasingly must demonstrate achievement and competence. Whether a relatively limited sexual capacity can sustain such additional burdens is questionable; we still cannot put that very private capacity into the competition for social reward and validation.

The constant affluence experienced by the American middle class since World War II also creates certain pressures on sexuality. The young, who have only the most abstract notions about nonaffluence, increasingly demand that the landscape on the other side of traditional achievement be described in terms that make sense as experience. Affluence generates a kind of anomie all its own. The ease and abundance with which certain goals are achieved trivialize the goals. One response to the anomie of affluence, as seen long ago by Durkheim, is a quest for new, more intense experience. Something of this phenomenon can be seen in the pursuit of drug experience by many middle-class young people. Sexuality obviously is a key way station in the pursuit of intense experience.

In the long run both of these trends—for personal competence and for intense experiences—should encourage all of society—young and not-so-young—to become even more concerned with sex, more sexually active and possibly more sexually experimental. This suggests not only a narrowing of gender distinctions but quite possibly a narrowing of generational distinctions. Parents and children might increasingly share sexual style and commitment as the young become sexual earlier and the old remain sexual longer. Generational difference could erode considerably, and in fact, may already have begun to do so.

Although exotic and marginal sex is at center stage, most sexual activity still is aimed at family formation and maintenance. But as the imagery of sex changes, there are changes in the character of the family and in its relation to the larger society. Students of family life have for some time commented upon the narrowing of family control and the shift of socializing functions among the young to places outside the home. Along with these changes, new weight has been given to inter-personal attachments—as against external constraints—in the main-tenance of a viable family life. Again, sexuality is taking new relevance; it may have to serve as both content and visible proof of enduring attachment. This is seen in the emphasis now placed upon sexual competence in marriage, one that borders on sexual athleticism.

This poses a difficulty. One still finds it hard to get social recognition and support for his sexual competence in marriage. For many, making competent conversation about sex becomes a bid for this social recog-nition. This is reflected in the growing demand for technical and pseudo-technical information. The results are mixed. Some find reassurance in their verbal performance. Yet, the more one talks sex, the more detail one has against which to compare his direct sexual experience. This does not always enhance one's sense of competence or even one's identity.

In general, the sexual dimension in our society comprises a limited biological capacity that is harnessed and amplified by varied social uses. Within that context we have sketched both possible uses and modes of amplification. We have emphasized that the expression of the sexual component is the celebration of a social and psychological drama rather than a natural response. We have suggested that there may be sub-stantial change in this social drama. In the past the drama has been a silent charade. Now we appear to be giving the drama a sound track and inviting the audience to participate. Competence increasingly replaces guilt as the major source for amplifying complexity. Guilt had the power of endowing limited behavior with enduring emotions. Competence may require an enlargement of the scope of the behavior. Keynes may have to replace Adam Smith as the metaphorical cartographer for our sexual style. Whether the principle of "the more you spend the more you have" can apply to the body any more effectively than it applies to the economy is questionable. For while physiology may not be our destinies, it can still be a major source of their frustration.

susan sontag

Growing old is rough. And according to Susan Sontag, growing old and being a woman is doubly rough. As a woman in our culture ages she suffers a variety of social penalties. She is perceived as less attractive and loses sexual desirability. Men do not have such problems. Indeed, older men are often considered more attractive than younger ones and their preference for younger women is seen as perfectly understandable.

Women spend much time, effort, and money attempting to stave off the inevitable scourge of aging. They use various pastes and powders trying to maintain a facade of youthfulness. But it seldom works. Reviewing the situation, Ms. Sontag suggests that "Women should allow their faces to show the lives they have lived. Women should tell the truth." But using her own arguments, we might add that men —and women themselves—must be willing to accept that truth. And this involves some major changes in the ways all of us see our bodies.

"How old are you?" The person asking the question is anybody. The respondent is a woman, a woman "of a certain age," as the French say discreetly. That age might be anywhere from her early twenties to her late fifties. If the question is impersonal—routine information requested when she applies for a driver's license, a credit card, a passport—she will probably force herself to answer truthfully. Filling out a marriage license application, if her future husband is even slightly her junior, she may long to subtract a few years; probably she won't. Competing for a job, her chances often partly depend on being the "right age," and if hers isn't right, she will lie if she thinks she can get away with it. Making her first visit to a new doctor, perhaps feeling particularly vulnerable at the moment she's asked, she will probably hurry through the correct answer. But if the question is only what people call personal—if she's asked by a new friend, a casual acquaintance, a neighbor's child, a co-worker in an office, store, factory—her response is harder to predict. She may side-step the question with a joke or refuse it with playful indignation. "Don't kou know you're not supposed to ask a woman her age?" Or, hesitating a moment, embarrassed but defiant, she may tell the truth. Or she may lie. But neither truth, evasion, nor lie relieves the unpleasantness of that question. For a woman to be obliged to state her age, after "a certain age," is always a miniature ordeal.

If the question comes from a woman, she will feel less threatened than if it comes from a man. Other women are, after all, comrades in sharing the same potential for humiliation. She will be less arch, less coy. But she probably still dislikes answering and may not tell the truth. Bureaucratic formalities excepted, whoever asks a woman this question—after "a certain age"—is ignoring a taboo and possibly being impolite or downright hostile. Almost everyone acknowledges that once she passes an age that is, actually, quite young, a woman's exact age ceases to be a legitimate target of curiosity. After childhood the year of a woman's birth becomes her secret, her private property. It is something of a dirty secret. To answer truthfully is always indiscreet.

The discomfort a woman feels each time she tells her age is quite independent of the anxious awareness of human mortality that everyone has, from time to time. There is a normal sense in which nobody, men and women alike, relishes growing older. After thirty-five any mention of one's age carries with it the reminder that one is probably closer to the end of one's life than to the beginning. There is nothing unreasonable in that anxiety. Nor is there any abnormality in the anguish and anger that people who are really old, in their seventies and eighties, feel about the implacable waning of their powers, physical and mental. Advanced age is undeniably a trial, however stoically it may be endured. It is a shipwreck, no matter with what courage elderly people insist on continuing the voyage. But the objective, sacred pain of old age is of another order than the subjective, profane pain of aging. Old age is a genuine ordeal, one that men and women undergo in a similar way. Growing older is mainly an ordeal of the imagination—a moral disease, a social pathology—intrinsic to which is the fact that it afflicts women much more than men. It is particularly women who experience growing older (everything that comes *before* one is actually old) with such distaste and even shame.

The emotional privileges this society confers upon youth stir up some anxiety about getting older in everybody. All modern urbanized societies —unlike tribal, rural societies—condescend to the values of maturity and heap honors on the joys of youth. This revaluation of the life cycle in favor of the young brilliantly serves a secular society whose idols are ever-increasing industrial productivity and the unlimited cannibalization of nature. Such a society must create a new sense of the rhythms of life in order to incite people to buy more, to consume and throw away faster. People let the direct awareness they have of their needs, of what really gives them pleasure, be overruled by commercialized *images* of happiness and personal well-being; and, in this imagery designed to stimulate ever more avid levels of consumption, the most popular metaphor for happiness is "youth." (I would insist that it is a metaphor, not a literal description. Youth is a metaphor for energy, restless mobility, appetite: for the state of "wanting.") This equating of well-being with youth makes everyone naggingly aware of exact age—one's own and that of other people. In primitive and pre-modern societies people attach much less importance to dates. When lives are divided into long periods with stable responsibilities and steady ideals (and hypocrisies), the exact number of years someone has lived becomes a trivial fact; there is hardly any reason to mention, even to know, the year in which one was born. Most people in noindustrial societies are not sure exactly how old they are. People in industrial societies are haunted by numbers. They take an almost obsessional interest in keeping the score card of aging, convinced that anything above a low total is some kind of bad news. In an era in which people actually live longer and longer, what now amounts to the latter *two-thirds* of everyone's life is shadowed by a poignant apprehension of unremitting loss.

The prestige of youth afflicts everyone in this society to some degree. Men, too, are prone to periodic bouts of depression about aging—for instance, when feeling insecure or unfulfilled or insufficiently rewarded in their jobs. But men rarely panic about aging in the way women often do. Getting older is less profoundly wounding for a man, for in addition to the propaganda for youth that puts both men and women on the defensive as they age, there is a double standard about aging that denounces women with special severity. Society is much more permissive about aging in men, as it is more tolerant of the sexual infidelities of husbands. Men are "allowed" to age, without penalty, in several ways that women are not.

This society offers even fewer rewards for aging to women than it does to men. Being physically attractive counts much more in a woman's life than in a man's, but beauty, identified, as it is for women, with youthfulness, does not stand up well to age. Exceptional mental powers can increase with age, but women are rarely encouraged to develop their minds above dilettante standards. Because the wisdom considered the special province of women is "eternal," an age-old, intuitive knowledge about the emotions to which a repertoire of facts, worldly experience, and the methods of rational analysis have nothing to contribute, living a long time does not promise women an increase in wisdom either. The private skills expected of women are exercised early and, with the exception of a talent for making love, are not the kind that enlarge with experience. "Masculinity" is identified with competence, autonomy, self-control—qualities which the disappearance of youth does not threaten. Competence in most of the activities expected from men, physical sports excepted, increases with age. "Femininity" is identified with incompetence, helplessness, passivity, noncompetitiveness, being nice. Age does not improve these qualities.

Middle-class men feel diminished by aging, even while still young, if they have not yet shown distinction in their careers or made a lot of money. (And any tendencies they have toward hypochondria will get worse in middle age, focusing with particular nervousness on the specter of heart attacks and the loss of virility.) Their aging crisis is linked to that terrible pressure on men to be "successful" that precisely defines their membership in the middle class. Women rarely feel anxious about their age because they haven't succeeded at something. The work that women do outside the home rarely counts as a form of achievement, only as a way of earning money; most employment available to women mainly exploits the training they have been receiving since early childhood to be servile, to be both supportive and parasitical, to be unadventurous. They can have menial, low-skilled jobs in light industries, which offer as feeble a criterion of success as housekeeping. They can be secretaries, clerks, sales personnel, maids, research assistants, waitresses, social workers, prostitutes, nurses, teachers, telephone operators—public transcriptions of the servicing and nurturing roles that women have in family life. Women fill very few executive posts, are rarely found suitable for large corporate or political responsibilities, and form only a tiny contingent in the liberal professions (apart from teaching). They are virtually barred from jobs that involve an expert, intimate relation with machines or an aggressive use of the body, or that carry any physical risk or sense of adventure. The jobs this society deems appropriate to women are auxiliary, "calm" activities that do not compete with, but aid, what men do. Besides being less well paid, most work women do has a lower ceiling of advancement and gives meager outlet to normal wishes to be powerful. All outstanding work by women in this society is voluntary; most women are too inhibited by the social disapproval attached to their being ambitious and aggressive. Inevitably, women are exempted from the dreary panic of middle-aged men whose "achievements" seem paltry, who feel stuck on the job ladder or fear being pushed off it by someone younger. But they are also denied most of the real satisfactions that men derive from work—satisfactions that often do increase with age.

The double standard about aging shows up most brutally in the conventions of sexual feeling, which presuppose a disparity between men and women that operates permanently to women's disadvantage. In the accepted course of events a woman anywhere from her late teens through her middle twenties can expect to attract a man more or less her own age. (Ideally, he should be at least slightly older.) They marry and raise a family. But if her husband starts an affair after some years of marriage, he customarily does so with a woman much younger than his wife. Suppose, when both husband and wife are already in their late forties or early fifties, they divorce. The husband has an excellent chance of getting married again, probably to a younger woman. His ex-wife finds it difficult to remarry. Attracting a second husband younger than herself is improbable; even to find someone her own age she has to be lucky, and she will probably have to settle for a man considerably older than herself, in his sixties or seventies. Women become sexually ineligible much earlier than men do. A man, even an ugly man, can remain eligible well into old age. He is an acceptable mate for a young, attractive woman. Women, even good-looking women, become ineligible (except as partners of very old men) at a much younger age.

Thus, for most women, aging means a humiliating process of gradual sexual disqualification. Since women are considered maximally eligible in early youth, after which their sexual value drops steadily, even young women feel themselves in a desperate race against the calendar. They are old as soon as they are no longer very young. In late adolescence some girls are already worrying about getting married. Boys and young men have little reason to anticipate trouble because of aging. What makes men desirable to women is by no means tied to youth. On the contrary, getting older tends (for several decades) to operate in men's favor, since their value as lovers and husbands is set more by what they do than how they look. Many men have more success romantically at forty than they did at twenty or twenty-five; fame, money, and, above all, power are sexually enhancing. (A woman who has won power in a competitive profession or business career is considered less, rather than more, desirable. Most men confess themselves intimidated or turned off sexually by such a woman, obviously because she is harder to treat as just a sexual "object.") As they age, men may start feeling anxious about actual sexual performance, worrying about a loss of sexual vigor or even impotence, but their sexual eligibility is not abridged simply by getting older. Men stay sexually possible as long as they can make love. Women are at a disadvantage because their sexual candidacy depends on meeting certain much stricter "conditions" related to looks and age.

Since women are imagined to have much more limited sexual lives than men do, a woman who has never married is pitied. She was not found acceptable, and it is assumed that her life continues to confirm her unacceptability. Her presumed lack of sexual opportunity is embarrassing. A man who remains a bachelor is judged much less crudely. It is assumed that he, at any age, still has a sexual life—or the chance of one. For men there is no destiny equivalent to the humiliating condition of being an old maid, a spinster. "Mr.," a cover from infancy to senility, precisely exempts men from the stigma that attaches to any woman, no longer young, who is still "Miss." (That women are divided into "Miss" and "Mrs.," which calls unrelenting attention to the situation of each woman with respect to marriage, reflects the belief that being single or married is much more decisive for a woman than it is for a man.)

For a woman who is no longer very young, there is certainly some relief when she has finally been able to marry. Marriage soothes the sharpest pain she feels about the passing years. But her anxiety never subsides completely, for she knows that should she re-enter the sexual market at a later date—because of divorce, or the death of her husband, or the need for erotic adventure—she must do so under a handicap far greater than any man of her age (*whatever* her age may be) and regardless of how good-looking she is. Her achievements, if she has a career, are no asset. The calendar is the final arbiter.

To be sure, the calendar is subject to some variations from country to country. In Spain, Portugal, and the Latin American countries, the age at which most women are ruled physically undesirable comes earlier than in the United States. In France it is somewhat later. French conventions of sexual feeling make a quasi-official place for the woman between thirty-five and forty-five. Her role is to initiate an inexperienced or timid young man, after which she is, of course, replaced by a young girl. (Colette's novella *Chéri* is the best-known account in fiction of such a love affair; biographies of Balzac relate a well-documented example from real life.) This sexual myth does make turning forty somewhat easier for French women. But there is no difference in any of these countries in the basic attitudes that disqualify women sexually much earlier than men.

Aging also varies according to social class. Poor people look old much earlier in their lives than do rich people. But anxiety about aging is certainly more common, and more acute, among middle-class and rich women than among working-class women. Economically disadvantaged women in this society are more fatalistic about aging; they can't afford to fight the cosmetic battle as long or as tenaciously. Indeed, nothing so clearly indicates the fictional nature of this crisis than the fact that women who keep their youthful appearance the longest—women who lead unstrenuous, physically sheltered lives, who eat balanced meals, who can afford good medical care, who have few or no children—are those who feel the defeat of age most keenly. Aging is much more a social judgment than a biological eventuality. Far more extensive than the hard sense of loss suffered during menopause (which, with increased longevity, tends to arrive later and later) is the depression about aging, which may not be set off by any real event in a woman's life, but is a recurrent state of "possession" of her imagination, ordained by society—that is, ordained by the way this society limits how women feel free to imagine themselves.

There is a model account of the aging crisis in Richard Strauss's sentimental-ironic opera *Der Rosenkavalier*, whose heroine is a wealthy and glamorous married woman who decides to renounce romance. After a night with her adoring young lover, the Marschallin has a sudden, unexpected confrontation with herself. It is toward the end of Act I; Octavian has just left. Alone in her bedroom she sits at her dressing table, as she does every morning. It is the daily ritual of self-appraisal practiced by every woman. She looks at herself and, appalled, begins to weep. Her youth is over. Note that the Marschallin does not discover, looking in the mirror, that she is ugly. She is as beautiful as ever. The Marschallin's discovery is moral—that is, it is a discovery of her imagination; it is nothing she actually *sees*. Nevertheless, her discovery is no less devastating. Bravely, she makes her painful, gallant decision. She will arrange for her beloved Octavian to fall in love with a girl his own age. She must be realistic. She is no longer eligible. She is now "the old Marschallin."

Strauss wrote the opera in 1910. Contemporary operagoers are rather shocked when they discover that the libretto indicates that the Marschallin is all of thirty-four years old; today the role is generally sung by a soprano well into her forties or in her fifties. Acted by an attractive singer of thirty-four, the Marschallin's sorrow would seem merely neurotic, or even ridiculous. Few women today think of themselves as old, wholly disqualified from romance, at thirty-four. The age of retirement has moved up, in line with the sharp rise in life expectancy for everybody in the last few generations. The *form* in which women experience their lives remains unchanged. A moment approaches inexorably when they must resign themselves to being "too old." And that moment is invariably—objectively—premature.

In earlier generations the renunciation came even sooner. Fifty years ago a woman of forty was not just aging but old, finished. No struggle was even possible. Today, the surrender to aging no longer has a fixed date. The aging crisis (I am speaking only of women in affluent countries) starts earlier but lasts longer; it is diffused over most of a woman's life. A woman hardly has to be anything like what would reasonably be considered old to worry about her age, to start lying (or being tempted to lie). The crises can come at any time. Their schedule depends on a blend of personal ("neurotic") vulnerability and the swing of social mores. Some women don't have their first crisis until thirty. No one escapes a sickening shock upon turning forty. Each birthday, but especially those ushering in a new decade—for round numbers have a special authority—sounds a new defeat. There is almost as much pain in the anticipation as in the reality. Twenty-nine has become a queasy age ever since the official end of youth crept forward, about a generation ago, to thirty. Being thirty-nine is also hard; a whole year in which to meditate in glum astonishment that one stands on the threshold of middle age. The frontiers are arbitrary, but not any less vivid for that. Although a woman on her fortieth birthday is hardly different from what she was when she was still thirty-nine, the day seems like a turning point. But long before actually becoming a woman of forty, she has been steeling herself against the depression she will feel. One of the greatest tragedies of each woman's life is simply getting older; it is certainly the *longest* tragedy.

Aging is a movable doom. It is a crisis that never exhausts itself, because the anxiety is never really used up. Being a crisis of the imagination rather than of "real life," it has the habit of repeating itself again and again. The territory of aging (as opposed to actual old age) has no fixed boundaries. Up to a point it can be defined as one wants. Entering each decade—after the initial shock is absorbed—an endearing, desperate impulse of survival helps many women to stretch the boundaries to the decade following. In late adolescence thirty seems the end of life. At thirty, one pushes the sentence forward to forty. At forty, one still gives oneself ten more years.

I remember my closest friend in college sobbing on the day she turned twenty-one. "The best part of my life is over. I'm not young any more." She was a senior, nearing graduation. I was a precocious freshman, just sixteen. Mystified, I tried lamely to comfort her, saying that I didn't think twenty-one was *so* old. Actually, I didn't understand at all what could be demoralizing about turning twenty-one. To me, it meant only something good: being in charge of oneself, being free. At sixteen, I was too young to have noticed, and become confused by, the peculiarly loose, ambivalent way in which this society demands that one stop thinking of oneself as a girl and start thinking of oneself as a woman. (In America that demand can now be put off to the age of thirty, even beyond.) But even if I thought her distress was absurd, I must have been aware that it would not simply be absurd but quite unthinkable in a *boy* turning twenty-one. Only women worry about age with that degree of inanity and pathos. And, of course, as with all crises that are inauthentic and therefore repeat themselves compulsively (because the danger is largely fictive, a poison in the imagination), this friend of mine went on having the same crisis over and over, each time as if for the first time.

I also came to her thirtieth birthday party. A veteran of many love affairs, she had spent most of her twenties living abroad and had just returned to the United States. She had been good-looking when I first knew her; now she was beautiful. I teased her about the tears she had shed over being twenty-one. She laughed and claimed not to remember. But thirty, she said ruefully, that really is the end. Soon after, she married. My friend is now forty-four. While no longer what people call beautiful, she is striking-looking, charming, and vital. She teaches elementary school; her husband, who is twenty years older than she, is a part-time merchant seaman. They have one child, now nine years old. Sometimes, when her husband is away, she takes a lover. She told me recently that forty was the most upsetting birthday of all (I wasn't at that one), and although she has only a few years left, she means to enjoy them while they last. She has become one of those women who seize every excuse offered in any conversation for mentioning how old they really are, in a spirit of bravado compounded with self-pity that is not too different from the mood of women who regularly lie about their age. But she is actually fretting much less about aging than she was two decades ago. Having a child, and having one rather late, past the age of thirty, has certainly helped to reconcile her to her age. At fifty, I suspect, she will be ever more valiantly postponing the age of resignation.

My friend is one of the more fortunate, sturdier casualties of the aging crisis. Most women are not as spirited, nor as innocently comic in their suffering. But almost all women endure some version of this suffering: A recurrent seizure of the imagination that usually begins quite young, in which they project themselves into a calculation of loss. The rules of this society are cruel to women. Brought up to be never fully adult, women are deemed obsolete earlier than men. In fact, most women don't become relatively free and expressive sexually until their thirties. (Women mature sexually this late, certainly much later than men, not for innate biological reasons but because this culture retards women. Denied most outlets for sexual energy permitted to men, it takes many women *that* long to wear out some of their inhibitions.) The time at which they start being disqualified as sexually attractive persons is just when they have grown up sexually. The double standard about aging cheats women of those years, between thirty-five and fifty, likely to be the best of their sexual life.

That women expect to be flattered often by men, and the extent to which their self-confidence depends on this flattery, reflects how deeply women are psychologically weakened by this double standard. Added on to the pressure felt by everybody in this society to look young as

long as possible are the values of "femininity," which specifically identify sexual attractiveness in women with youth. The desire to be the
"right age" has a special urgency for a woman it never has for a man.
A much greater part of her self-esteem and pleasure in life is threatened
when she ceases to be young. Most men experience getting older with
regret, apprehension. But most women experience it even more painfully:
with shame. Aging is a man's destiny, something that must happen because he is a human being. For a woman, aging is not only her destiny.
Because she is that more *narrowly* defined kind of human being, a
woman, it is also her vulnerability.

To be a woman is to be an actress. Being feminine is a kind of
theater, with its appropriate costumes, *décor*, lighting, and stylized
gestures. From early childhood on, girls are trained to care in a
pathologically exaggerated way about their appearance and are profoundly mutilated (to the extent of being unfitted for first-class adulthood) by the extent of the stress put on presenting themselves as
physically attractive objects. Women look in the mirror more frequently
than men do. It is, virtually, their duty to look at themselves—to look
often. Indeed, a woman who is not narcissistic is considered unfeminine.
And a woman who spends literally *most* of her time caring for, and
making purchases to flatter, her physical appearance is not regarded in
this society as what she is: a kind of moral idiot. She is thought to be
quite normal and is envied by other women whose time is mostly used
up at jobs or caring for large families. The display of narcissism goes
on all the time. It is expected that women will disappear several times
in an evening—at a restaurant, at a party, during a theater intermission,
in the course of a social visit—simply to check their appearance, to see
that nothing has gone wrong with their make-up and hairstyling, to make
sure that their clothes are not spotted or too wrinkled or not hanging
properly. It is even acceptable to perform this activity in public. At the
table in a restaurant, over coffee, a woman opens a compact mirror and
touches up her make-up and hair without embarrassment in front of her
husband or her friends.

All this behavior, which is written off as normal "vanity" in women,
would seem ludicrous in a man. Women are more vain than men
because of the relentless pressure on women to maintain their appearance at a certain high standard. What makes the pressure even more
burdensome is that there are actually several standards. Men present
themselves as face-and-body, a physical whole. Women are split, as
men are not, into a body and a face—each judged by somewhat different
standards. What is important for a face is that it be beautiful. What is
important for a body is two things, which may even be (depending on
fashion and taste) somewhat incompatible: first, that it be desirable
and, second, that it be beautiful. Men usually feel sexually attracted to
women much more because of their bodies than their faces. The

traits that arouse desire—such as fleshiness—don't always match those that fashion decrees as beautiful. (For instance, the ideal woman's body promoted in advertising in recent years is extremely thin: the kind of body that looks more desirable clothed than naked.) But women's concern with their appearance is not simply geared to arousing desire in men. It also aims at fabricating a certain image by which, as a more indirect way of arousing desire, women state their value. A woman's value lies in the way she *represents* herself, which is much more by her face than her body. In defiance of the laws of simple sexual attraction, women do not devote most of their attention to their bodies. The well-known "normal" narcissism that women display—the amount of time they spend before the mirror—is used primarily in caring for the face and hair.

Women do not simply have faces, as men do; they are identified with their faces. Men have a naturalistic relation to their faces. Certainly they care whether they are good-looking or not. They suffer over acne, protruding ears, tiny eyes; they hate getting bald. But there is a much wider latitude in what is esthetically acceptable in a man's face than what is in a woman's. A man's face is defined as something he basically doesn't need to tamper with; all he has to do is keep it clean. He can avail himself of the options for ornament supplied by nature: a beard, a mustache, longer or shorter hair. But he is not supposed to disguise himself. What he is "really" like is supposed to show. A man lives through his face; it records the progressive stages of his life. And since he doesn't tamper with his face, it is not separate from but is completed by his body—which is judged attractive by the impression it gives of virility and energy. By contrast, a woman's face is potentially separate from her body. She does not treat it naturalistically. A woman's face is the canvas upon which she paints a revised, corrected portrait of herself. One of the rules of this creation is that the face *not* show what she doesn't want it to show. Her face is an emblem, an icon, a flag. How she arranges her hair, the type of make-up she uses, the quality of her complexion—all these are signs, not of what she is "really" like, but of how she asks to be treated by others, especially men. They establish her status as an "object."

For the normal changes that age inscribes on every human face, women are much more heavily penalized than men. Even in early adolescence, girls are cautioned to protect their faces against wear and tear. Mothers tell their daughters (but never their sons): You look ugly when you cry. Stop worrying. Don't read too much. Crying, frowning, squinting, even laughing—all these human activities make "lines." The same usage of the face in men is judged quite positively. In a man's face lines are taken to be signs of "character." They indicate emotional strength, maturity—qualities far more esteemed in men than in women. (They show he has "lived.") Even scars are often not felt to be unattractive; they too can add "character" to a man's face. But lines of aging, any scar, even a small birthmark on a woman's face, are always regarded as unfortunate blemishes. In effect, people take character in men to be different from what constitutes character in women. A woman's character is thought to be innate, static—not the product of her experience, her years, her actions. A woman's face is prized so far as it remains unchanged by (or conceals the traces of) her emotions, her physical risk-taking. Ideally, it is supposed to be a mask—immutable, unmarked. The model woman's face is Garbo's. Because women are identified with their faces much more than men are, and the ideal woman's face is one that is "perfect," it seems a calamity when a woman has a disfiguring accident. A broken nose or a scar or a burn mark, no more than regrettable for a man, is a terrible psychological wound to a woman; objectively, it diminishes her value. (As is well known, most clients for plastic surgery are women.)

Both sexes aspire to a physical ideal, but what is expected of boys and what is expected of girls involves a very different moral relation to the self. Boys are encouraged to *develop* their bodies, to regard the body as an instrument to be improved. They invent their masculine selves largely through exercise and sport, which harden the body and strengthen competitive feelings; clothes are of only secondary help in making their bodies attractive. Girls are not particularly encouraged to develop their bodies through any activity, strenuous or not; and physical strength and endurance are hardly valued at all. The invention of the feminine self proceeds mainly through clothes and other signs that testify to the very effort of girls to look attractive, to their commitment to please. When boys become men, they may go on (especially if they have sedentary jobs) practicing a sport or doing exercises for a while. Mostly they leave their appearance alone, having been trained to accept more or less what nature has handed out to them. (Men may start doing exercises again in their forties to lose weight, but for reasons of health—there is an epidemic fear of heart attacks among the middle-aged in rich countries—not for cosmetic reasons.) As one of the norms of "femininity" in this society is being preoccupied with one's physical appearance, so "masculinity" means *not* caring very much about one's looks.

This society allows men to have a much more affirmative relation to their bodies than women have. Men are more "at home" in their bodies, whether they treat them casually or use them aggressively. A man's body is defined as a strong body. It contains no contradiction between what is felt to be attractive and what is practical. A woman's body, so far as it is considered attractive, is defined as a fragile, light body. (Thus, women worry more than men do about being overweight.) When they do exercises, women avoid the ones that develop the muscles, particularly those in the upper arms. Being "feminine" means looking physically weak, frail. Thus, the ideal woman's body is one that is not of much practical use in the hard work of this world, and one that must continually be "defended." Women do not develop their bodies, as men do. After a woman's body has reached its sexually acceptable form by late adolescence, most further development is viewed as negative. And it is thought irresponsible for women to do what is normal for men: simply leave their appearance alone. During early youth they are likely to come as close as they ever will to the ideal image—slim figure, smooth firm skin, light musculature, graceful movements. Their task is to try to maintain that image, unchanged, as long as possible. Improvement as such is not the task. Women care for their bodies—against toughening, coarsening, getting fat. They *conserve* them. (Perhaps the fact that women in modern societies tend to have a more conservative political outlook than men originates in their profoundly conservative relation to their bodies.)

In the life of women in this society the period of pride, of natural honesty, of unself-conscious flourishing is brief. Once past youth women are condemned to inventing (and maintaining) themselves against the inroads of age. Most of the physical qualities regarded as attractive in women deteriorate much earlier in life than those defined as "male." Indeed, they perish fairly soon in the normal sequence of body transformation. The "feminine" is smooth, rounded, hairless, unlined, soft, unmuscled—the look of the very young; characteristics of the weak, of the vulnerable; eunuch traits, as Germaine Greer has pointed out. Actually, there are only a few years—late adolescence, early twenties—in which this look is physiologically natural, in which it can be had without touching-up and covering-up. After that, women enlist in a quixotic enterprise, trying to close the gap between the imagery put forth by society (concerning what is attractive in a woman) and the evolving facts of nature.

Women have a more intimate relation to aging than men do, simply because one of the accepted "women's" occupations is taking pains to keep one's face and body from showing the signs of growing older. Women's sexual validity depends, up to a certain point, on how well they stand off these natural changes. After late adolescence women become the caretakers of their bodies and faces, pursuing an essentially defensive strategy, a holding operation. A vast array of products in jars and tubes, a branch of surgery, and armies of hairdressers, masseuses, diet counselors, and other professionals exist to stave off, or mask, developments that are entirely normal biologically. Large amounts of women's energies are diverted into this passionate, corrupting effort to defeat nature: to maintain an ideal, static appearance against the progress of age. The collapse of the project is only a matter of time. Inevitably, a woman's physical appearance develops beyond its youthful form. No matter how exotic the creams or how strict the diets, one cannot indefinitely keep the face unlined, the waist slim. Bearing children takes its toll: the torso becomes thicker; the skin is stretched. There is no way to keep certain lines from appearing, in one's mid-twenties, around the eyes and mouth. From about thirty on, the skin gradually loses its tonus. In women this perfectly natural process is regarded as a humiliating defeat, while nobody finds anything remarkably unattractive in the equivalent physical changes in men. Men are "allowed" to look older without sexual penalty.

Thus, the reason that women experience aging with more pain than men is not simply that they care more than men about how they look. Men also care about their looks and want to be attractive, but since the business of men is mainly being and doing, rather than appearing, the standards for appearance are much less exacting. The standards for what is attractive in a man are permissive; they conform to what is possible or "natural" to most men throughout most of their lives. The standards for women's appearance go against nature, and to come anywhere near approximating them takes considerable effort and time. Women must try to be beautiful. At the least, they are under heavy social pressure not to be ugly. A woman's fortunes depend, far more than a man's, on being at least "acceptable" looking. Men are not subject to this pressure. Good looks in a man is a bonus, not a psychological necessity for maintaining normal self-esteem.

Behind the fact that women are more severely penalized than men are for aging is the fact that people, in this culture at least, are simply less tolerant of ugliness in women than in men. An ugly woman is never merely repulsive. Ugliness in a woman is felt by everyone, men as well as women, to be faintly embarrassing. And many features or blemishes that count as ugly in a woman's face would be quite tolerable on the face of a man. This is not, I would insist, just because the esthetic standards for men and women are different. It is rather because the esthetic standards for women are much higher, and narrower, than those proposed for men.

Beauty, women's business in this society, is the theater of their enslavement. Only one standard of female beauty is sanctioned: the *girl*. The great advantage men have is that our culture allows two standards of male beauty: the *boy* and the *man*. The beauty of a boy resembles the beauty of a girl. In both sexes it is a fragile kind of beauty and flourishes naturally only in the early part of the life-cycle. Happily, men are able to accept themselves under another standard of good looks—heavier, rougher, more thickly built. A man does not grieve when he loses the smooth, unlined, hairless skin of a boy. For he has only exchanged one form of attractiveness for another: the darker skin of a man's face, roughened by daily shaving, showing the marks of emotion and the normal lines of age. There is no equivalent of this second standard for women. The single standard of beauty for women dictates that they must go on having clear skin. Every wrinkle, every line, every grey hair, is a defeat. No wonder that no boy minds becoming a man, while even the passage from girlhood to early womanhood is experienced by many women as their downfall, for all women are trained to want to continue looking like girls.

This is not to say there are no beautiful older women. But the standard of beauty in a woman of any age is how far she retains, or how she manages to simulate, the appearance of youth. The exceptional woman in her sixties who is beautiful certainly owes a large debt to her genes. Delayed aging, like good looks, tends to run in families. But nature rarely offers enough to meet this culture's standards. Most of the women who successfully delay the appearance of age are rich, with unlimited leisure to devote to nurturing along nature's gifts. Often they are actresses. (That is, highly paid professionals at doing what all women are taught to practice as amateurs.) Such women as Mae West, Dietrich, Stella Adler, Dolores Del Rio, do not challenge the rule about the relation between beauty and age in women. They are admired precisely because they *are* exceptions, because they have managed (at least so it seems in photographs) to outwit nature. Such miracles, exceptions made by nature (with the help of art and social privilege), only confirm the rule, because what makes these women seem beautiful to us is precisely that they do not look their real age. Society allows no place in our imagination for a beautiful old woman who does look like an old woman—a woman who might be like Picasso at the age of ninety, being photographed outdoors on his estate in the south of France, wearing only shorts and sandals. No one imagines such a woman exists. Even the special exceptions—Mae West & Co.—are always photographed indoors, cleverly lit, from the most flattering angle and fully, artfully clothed. The implication is they would not stand a closer scrutiny. The idea of an old woman in a bathing suit being attractive, or even just acceptable looking, is inconceivable. An older woman is, by definition, sexually repulsive—unless, in fact, she doesn't look old at all. The body of an old woman, unlike that of an old man, is always understood as a body that can no longer be shown, offered, unveiled. At best, it may appear in costume. People still feel uneasy, thinking about what they might see if her mask dropped, if she took off her clothes.

Thus, the point for women of dressing up, applying make-up, dyeing their hair, going on crash diets, and getting face-lifts is not just to be attractive. They are ways of defending themselves against a profound level of disapproval directed toward women, a disapproval that can take the form of aversion. The double standard about aging converts the life of women into an inexorable march toward a condition in which they are not just unattractive, but disgusting. The profoundest terror of a woman's life is the moment represented in a statue by Rodin called *Old Age*: a naked old woman, seated, pathetically contemplates her flat, pendulous, ruined body. Aging in women is a process of becoming obscene sexually, for the flabby bosom, wrinkled neck, spotted hands, thinning white hair, waistless torso, and veined legs of an old woman are felt to be obscene. In our direst moments of the imagination, this transformation can take place with dismaying speed—as in the end of *Lost Horizon*, when the beautiful young girl is carried by her lover out of Shangri-La and, within minutes, turns into a withered, repulsive crone. There is no equivalent nightmare about men. This is why, however much a man may care about his appearance, that caring can never acquire the same desperateness it often does for women. When men dress according to fashion or now even use cosmetics, they do not expect from clothes and make-up what women do. A face-lotion or perfume or deodorant or hairspray, used by a man, is not part of a disguise. Men, as men, do not feel the need to disguise themselves to fend off morally disapproved signs of aging, to outwit premature sexual obsolescence, to cover up aging as obscenity. Men are not subject to the barely concealed revulsion expressed in this culture against the female body—except in its smooth, youthful, firm, odorless, blemish-free form.

One of the attitudes that punish women most severely is the visceral horror felt at aging female flesh. It reveals a radical fear of women installed deep in this culture, a demonology of women that has crystallized in such mythic caricatures as the vixen, the virago, the vamp, and the witch. Several centuries of witch-phobia, during which one of the cruelest extermination programs in Western history was carried out, suggest something of the extremity of this fear. That old women are repulsive is one of the most profound esthetic and erotic feelings in our culture. Women share it as much as men do. (Oppressors, as a rule, deny oppressed people their own "native" standards of beauty. And the oppressed end up being convinced that they *are* ugly.) How women are psychologically damaged by this misogynistic idea of what is beautiful parallels the way in which blacks have been deformed in a society that has up to now defined beautiful as white. Psychological tests made on young black children in the United States some years ago showed how early and how thoroughly they incorporate the white standard of good looks. Virtually all the children expressed fantasies that indicated they considered black people to be ugly, funny looking, dirty, brutish. A similar kind of self-hatred infects most women. Like men, they find old age in women "uglier" than old age in men.

This esthetic taboo functions, in sexual attitudes, as a racial taboo. In this society most people feel an involuntary recoil of the flesh when imagining a middle-aged woman making love with a young man—exactly as many whites flinch viscerally at the thought of a white woman in bed with a black man. The banal drama of a man of fifty who leaves a wife of forty-five for a girlfriend of twenty-eight contains no strictly sexual outrage, whatever sympathy people may have for the abandoned wife. On the contrary. Everyone "understands." Everyone knows that men like girls, that young women often want middle-aged men. But no one "understands" the reverse situation. A woman of forty-five who leaves a husband of fifty for a lover of twenty-eight is the makings of a social and sexual scandal at a deep level of feeling. No one takes exception to a romantic couple in which the man is twenty years or more the woman's senior. The movies pair Joanne Dru and John Wayne, Marilyn Monroe and Joseph Cotten, Audrey Hepburn and Cary Grant, Jane Fonda and Yves Montand, Catherine Deneuve and Marcello Mastroianni; as in actual life, these are perfectly plausible, appealing couples. When the age difference runs the other way, people are puzzled and embarrassed and simply shocked. (Remember Joan Crawford and Cliff Robertson in *Autumn Leaves*? But so troubling is this kind of love story that it rarely figures in the movies, and then only as the melancholy history of a failure.) The usual view of why a woman of forty and a boy of twenty, or a woman of fifty and a man of thirty, marry is that the man is seeking a mother, not a wife; no one believes the marriage will last. For a woman to respond erotically and romantically to a man who, in terms of his age, could be her father is considered normal. A man who falls in love with a woman who, however attractive she may be, is old enough to be his mother is thought to be extremely neurotic (victim of an "Oedipal fixation" is the fashionable tag), if not mildly contemptible.

The wider the gap in age between partners in a couple, the more obvious is the prejudice against women. When old men, such as Justice Douglas, Picasso, Strom Thurmond, Onassis, Chaplin, and Pablo Casals, take brides thirty, forty, fifty years younger than themselves, it strikes people as remarkable, perhaps an exaggeration—but still plausible. To explain such a match, people enviously attribute some special virility and charm to the man. Though he can't be handsome, he is famous; and his fame is understood as having boosted his attractiveness to women. People imagine that his young wife, respectful of her elderly husband's attainments, is happy to become his helper. For the man a late marriage is always good public relations. It adds to the impression that, despite his advanced age, he is still to be reckoned with; it is the sign of a continuing vitality presumed to be available as well to his art, business activity, or political career. But an elderly woman who married a young man would be greeted quite differently. She would have broken a fierce taboo, and she would get no credit for her courage. Far from being admired for her vitality, she would probably be condemned as predatory, willful, selfish, exhibitionistic. At the same time she would be pitied, since such a marriage would be taken as evidence that she was in her dotage. If she had a conventional career or were in business or held public office, she would quickly suffer from the current of disapproval. Her very credibility as a professional would decline, since people would suspect that her young husband might have an undue influence on her. Her "respectability" would certainly be compromised. Indeed, the well-known old women I can think of who dared such unions, if only at the end of their lives—George Eliot, Colette, Edith Piaf—have all belonged to that category of people, creative artists and entertainers, who have special license from society to behave scandalously. It is thought to be a scandal for a woman to ignore that she is old and therefore too ugly for a young man. Her looks and a certain physical condition determine a woman's desirability, not her talents or her needs. Women are not supposed to be "potent." A marriage between an old woman and a young man subverts the very ground rule of relations between the two sexes, that is: whatever the variety of appearances, men remain dominant. Their claims come first. Women are supposed to be the associates and companions of men, not their full equals—and never their superiors. Women are to remain in the state of a permanent "minority."

The convention that wives should be younger than their husbands powerfully enforces the "minority" status of women, since being senior in age always carries with it, in any relationship, a certain amount of power and authority. There are no laws on the matter, of course. The convention is obeyed because to do otherwise makes one feel as if one is doing something ugly or in bad taste. Everyone feels intuitively the esthetic rightness of a marriage in which the man is older than the woman, which means that any marriage in which the woman is older creates a dubious or less gratifying mental picture. Everyone is addicted to the visual pleasure that women give by meeting certain esthetic requirements from which men are exempted, which keeps women working at staying youthful-looking while men are left free to age. On a deeper level everyone finds the signs of old age in women esthetically offensive, which conditions one to feel automatically repelled by the prospect of an elderly woman marrying a much younger man. The situation in which women are kept minors for life is largely organized by such conformist, unreflective preferences. But taste is not free, and its judgments are never merely "natural." Rules of taste enforce structures of power. The revulsion against aging in women is the cutting edge of a whole set of oppressive structures (often masked as gallantries) that keep women in their place.

The ideal state proposed for women is docility, which means not being fully grown up. Most of what is cherished as typically "feminine" is simply behavior that is childish, immature, weak. To offer so low and demeaning a standard of fulfillment in itself constitutes oppression in an acute form—a sort of moral neo-colonialism. But women are not simply condescended to by the values that secure the dominance of men. They are repudiated. Perhaps because of having been their oppressors for so long, few men really *like* women (though they love individual women), and few men ever feel really comfortable or at ease in women's company. This malaise arises because relations between the two sexes are rife with hypocrisy, as men manage to love those they dominate and therefore don't respect. Oppressors always try to justify their privileges and brutalities by imagining that those they oppress belong to a lower order of civilization or are less than fully "human." Deprived of part of their ordinary human dignity, the oppressed take on certain "demonic" traits. The oppressions of large groups have to be anchored deep in the psyche, continually renewed by partly unconscious fears and taboos, by a sense of the obscene. Thus, women arouse not only desire and affection in men but aversion as well. Women are thoroughly domesticated familiars. But, at certain times and in certain situations, they become alien, untouchable. The aversion men feel, so much of which is covered over, is felt most frankly, with least inhibition, toward the type of woman who is most taboo "esthetically," a woman who has become—with the natural changes brought about by aging—obscene.

Nothing more clearly demonstrates the vulnerability of women than the special pain, confusion, and bad faith with which they experience getting older. And in the struggle that some women are waging on behalf of all women to be treated (and treat themselves) as full human beings—not "only" as women—one of the earliest results to be hoped for is that women become aware, indignantly aware, of the double standard about aging from which they suffer so harshly.

It is understandable that women often succumb to the temptation to lie about their age. Given society's double standard, to question a woman about her age is indeed often an aggressive act, a trap. Lying is an elementary means of self-defense, a way of scrambling out of the trap, at least temporarily. To expect a woman, after "a certain age," to tell exactly how old she is—when she has a chance, either through the generosity of nature or the cleverness of art, to pass for being somewhat younger than she actually is—is like expecting a landowner to admit that the estate he has put up for sale is actually worth less than the buyer is prepared to pay. The double standard about aging sets women up as property, as objects whose value depreciates rapidly with the march of the calendar.

The prejudices that mount against women as they grow older are an important arm of male privilege. It is the present unequal distribution of adult roles between the two sexes that gives men a freedom to age denied to women. Men actively administer the double standard about aging because the "masculine" role awards them the initiative in courtship. Men choose; women are chosen. So men choose younger women. But although this system of inequality is operated by men, it could not work if women themselves did not acquiesce in it. Women reinforce it powerfully with their complacency, with their anguish, with their lies.

Not only do women lie more than men do about their age but men forgive them for it, thereby confirming their own superiority. A man who lies about his age is thought to be weak, "unmanly." A woman who lies about her age is behaving in a quite acceptable, "feminine" way. Petty lying is viewed by men with indulgence, one of a number of patronizing allowances made for women. It has the same moral unimportance as the fact that women are often late for appointments. Women are not expected to be truthful, or punctual, or expert in handling and repairing machines, or frugal, or physically brave. They are expected to be second-class adults, whose natural state is that of a grateful dependence on men. And so they often are, since that is what they are brought up to be. So far as women heed the stereotypes of "feminine" behavior, they *cannot* behave as fully responsible, independent adults.

Most women share the contempt for women expressed in the double standard about aging—to such a degree that they take their lack of self-respect for granted. Women have been accustomed so long to the protection of their masks, their smiles, their endearing lies. Without this protection, they know, they would be more vulnerable. But in protecting themselves as women, they betray themselves as adults. The model corruption in a woman's life is denying her age. She symbolically accedes to all those myths that furnish women with their imprisoning securities and privileges, that create their genuine oppression, that inspire their real discontent. Each time a woman lies about her age she becomes an accomplice in her own underdevelopment as a human being.

Women have another option. They can aspire to be wise, not merely nice; to be competent, not merely helpful; to be strong, not merely graceful; to be ambitious for themselves, not merely for themselves in relation to men and children. They can let themselves age naturally and without embarrassment, actively protesting and disobeying the conventions that stem from this society's double standard about aging. Instead of being girls, girls as long as possible, who then age humiliatingly into middle-aged women and then obscenely into old women, they can become women much earlier—and remain active adults, enjoying the long, erotic career of which women are capable, far longer. Women should allow their faces to show the lives they have lived. Women should tell the truth.

stanford m. lyman, marvin b. scott

In this article, Stanford M. Lyman and Marvin B. Scott look at some often neglected but central aspects of social behavior, the ways in which people respond in various stressful social situations. They describe different contexts in our society (among the Nacerima) where one is implicitly and, sometimes, explicitly called on to "play it cool." Situations ranging from the embarrassing to the dangerous are considered.

Lyman and Scott show how cultural training provides guidelines for "coolness" that, if effective, are readily acknowledged by the one who properly uses space, props, clothing, body, and voice and by those with whom he interacts. Many examples are given to illustrate how, in an age of "otherdirectedness," one must learn to deal with what Erving Goffman calls "role distance." Today, the authors suggest, everyone must learn about the preservation of poise under pressure.

"Don't lose your cool!"

A common enough phrase and one easily recognized in contemporary urban America. But, sociologically speaking, what does this new moral imperative mean? What does one lose when he loses his cool? Our task is to answer these questions by analyzing the social observable features in everyday life.[1]

From Stanford M. Lyman, and Marvin B. Scott, "Coolness in Everyday Life" from Marcello Truzzi (ed.), *Sociology and Everyday Life*, © 1968. Reprinted by permission of Prentice Hall, Inc., Englewood Cliffs, New Jersey.

Coolness is exhibited (and defined) as poise under pressure. By pressure we mean simply situations of considerable emotion or risk, or both. *Coolness, then, refers to the capacity to execute physical acts, including conversation, in a concerted, smooth, self-controlled fashion in risky situations, or to maintain affective detachment during the course of encounters involving considerable emotion.*[2]

We may distinguish three types of risk under which an individual might display coolness. First there is *physical risk* to the person in the form of danger to life and limb. The moral worth of many of the heroes of the Western world is displayed in their willingness and ability to undergo trials of pain and potential death with stylized equanimity and expert control of relevant motor skills. Modern fictional heroes, such as James Bond and Matt Dillon, for example, face death constantly in the form of armed and desperate killers; yet they seem never to lose their nerve or skill. It is not merely their altruistic service in the cause of law and country that makes them attractive, but also, and perhaps more importantly, their smooth skill—verbal and physical—that never deserts them in times of risk.

Secondly, there is *financial* risk. Financial risk entails not only the possible loss of income and status, but also the loss of character associated with the venture. Captains of industry, professional gamblers, and those who play the stock market are supposed to withstand the losses sometimes occasioned in the process with calmness, detachment, even cavalier abandon.

Finally, the most crucial for our concerns, there is *social* risk. Social risks may arise whenever there is an encounter. In every social encounter a person brings a "face" or "mask"—which constitutes the value he claims for himself.[3] Given that an individual stakes this value in every encounter, it follows that encounters are morally serious occasions fraught with great risks where one puts on the line a public face. This is the most serious of risks, for in risking it—he risks his very self-hood. When the interactants are *aware* that each is putting on a public face, they will look for cues to glean some "real self" presumably lurking beneath the mask.[4] The capacity to maintain face in such situations constitutes a display of coolness.

As suggested, encounters are hazardous because of the ever present possibility that identity and status will be disconfirmed or damaged by behavior. Whenever an individual or a group has to stage an encounter before a particular audience in order to establish a distinctive identity and meaning, the management of the staging becomes crucial to the endeavour. The effort can fail not simply because of the inadequacies or the conflict of the presented material, but also, and perhaps more importantly, because of the failure to maintain expressive identity and control. Thus individuals and teams—for a successful performance—must not only manage what they have planned, but also carry off the presentation smoothly in the face of interruptions, intrusions, and prop failures.

Smoothness of performance can be seriously interrupted by "prop" failure. Some engagements involve the maintenance in good order of a particular setting. Included here at the minimum is the apparel of the actor. A professor lecturing before his class might be completely discomfited if he discovers his fly is unzipped; and he is indeed hard pressed to re-establish his seriousness of purpose if he is unable to repair the situation with discretion. Professional stage actors must immediately and smoothly construct dialogue to suit a situation in which the stage sets unexpectedly collapse.

Smooth performance can also be challenged by interruption or intrusion. In certain societies—England, for example—public political speeches are traditionally interrupted by hecklers, and on some occasions, objects are flung at the speaker. English politicians try to develop a style that prepares them for responding to such interruptions by having in readiness a repertoire of clever remarks. Interruption can also be occasioned by a sudden and unexpected event that would normally upset the average man. During the Second World War many actors and concert performers earned reputations for coolness under extreme situations when they continued to play out their performances after an air raid had begun.

Interruptions, intrusions and prop failures are of two sorts with respect to coolness. The first type requires deft and casual repair of self or self-possessions in order for coolness to be displayed. The professor who, aware that the class perceives his unzipped fly, casually zips it up without interrupting the flow or tone of his lecture is likely to be recognized as cool. Similarly, the Walter Mitty-like flyer who sets the broken bone of his arm while maneuvering his plane to a safe landing under hazardous conditions will be known for his coolness.

The second type of intrusion, interruption or prop failure involves those situations that require immediate action because the entire situation has been altered by their presence. Fires in theaters, air raids, tornadoes, assassinations of presidents and other major calamities are illustrations. Those who maintain presence of mind in the face of the disastrous event, and especially those who by their own example prevent others from riotous or panicky behavior, place a stamp of moral worth upon themselves.

The exhibition of coolness under situations of potential panic can be a source of leadership. Formal leaders may be thrust from their posts because they panic, and unknown persons raised to political heights because of their publicly displayed ability to remain calm. Much popular folk-lore perceives calamitous situations as those providing just the right opportunity for a person otherwise unqualified to assume a dominant position. Indeed, if his acts are sufficiently skillful and smooth, the displayer of coolness may be rewarded with future rights of charismatic authority. A doctor who performs delicate surgery in the midst of an earthquake may by that act establish rights to administer the hospital in

which he works. And a teacher who manfully but non-violently prevents
a gang of hoodlums from taking over a school may by his performance
take over the school himself.

Embarrassment is one of the chief nemeses of coolness. Any encounter is likely to be suddenly punctuated by a potentially embarrassing
event—a gaffe, a boner, or uncontrollable motor response—that casts
new and unfavorable light upon the actor's performance. In some instances, the audience will save the actor from needless embarrassment
by studiously overlooking the event; however, this tactful inattention
may itself cause embarrassment as each person in the engagement manfully seeks to overlook the obvious. In other instances, the actor himself
will be on his mettle to attend or disattend to the disturbance in such a
manner that it does not detract from his performance. A skillful self-
rescue from a potentially embarrassing situation can win the actor more
than he intended, since he may gain not only his directly intended objective but also a boost in his moral worth as well.

Thus, coolness is both a quality to be lost and a prize to be gained in
any engagement. That is, coolness may be lost or gained by qualities
exhibited in the behavior. A failure to maintain expressive control, a
giving way to emotionalism, flooding out, paleness, sweatiness, weeping,
or violent expressions of anger or fear are definite signs of loss of cool.[5]
On the other hand, displays of *savoir-faire,* aplomb, *sang-froid,* and
especially displays of stylized affective neutrality in hazardous situations
are likely to gain one the plaudits associated with coolness.

Coolness does not, therefore, refer to routine performance in a role.
However, an affectively manifest departure from a role can disconfirm
the presence of an actor's coolness just as a remarkable exhibition of
sang-froid can gain for one the reputation of having it. To be cool, then,
is to exhibit a definite form of expressive control during the performance
of a role. Thus, we can distinguish three kinds of role performance: cool
role behavior, routinized role behavior, and role behavior that indicates
loss of cool.

Card playing is one type of social gathering in which all three kinds of
role behavior might be exhibited. The "cool player" may push the deed to
his family home into the pile of money in the center of the table with
the stylized casualness of a Mississippi gambler, neither his smooth,
softly smiling face nor his calm, unshaking hands indicating that he is
holding only a pair of deuces. The "routine player" may take his bet with
a grimace indicating seriousness of purpose and awareness of risk, but
not entirely losing composure or calling undue attention to himself. The
"uncool player" may become ashen, burst into tears, shriek obscenities,
or suddenly accuse his opponents of cheating when his prized and final
bet is raised beyond his ability to respond. The card game, like the
battlefield, is a moral testing ground.

While the display of coolness is a potential in all encounters, there
are certain typical situations where such a display is a social expecta-

tion. These involve situations in which the risks are patently obvious—e.g., bullfighting, automobile racing, and war. Literature dealing with these subjects typically portrays characterological coolness and invests it with honor and virtue. Indeed, if one wishes to find examples and evidence of coolness one need but look in the literature about activities considered risky.

Two other types of situations calling for the display of coolness are the *innovative* and the *anomic*. Innovative situations include activities associated with the rites of passage—all those "first times" in the life cycle in which one has to be poised in the face of the as yet unexperienced event. Examples include the wedding night for virgins, first days in school, and the first witnessing of death. Anomic situations are those in which at least one of the actors does not know the rules of conduct and must carry off an engagement in the face of those who do. Typically immigrants, newcomers, and parvenus find themselves in such situations—situations in which poise is at a premium.[6]

A display of coolness is often a prerequisite to entrance into or maintenance of membership in certain social circles. Since in nearly all societies coolness is taken to be part of the character syndrome of elites, we may expect to find a universal condition and a variety of forms of character testing of the elite. European nobility were expected to acquire adeptness at coquetry and repartee; the stylized insult and the witty return were highly prized and regularly tested.[7] Among would-be samurai in Japan, the martial skills were highly prized but even more highly prized was presence of mind. A samurai in training was constantly subjected to contrived sudden dangers, but if he exercised little cathectic control over his skill and strength he would be severely reproved by his zen master.[8] Another coolness test for membership—one involving sexual self-control—is a commonplace of college fraternity initiations. A "stag" film will be shown, and immediately upon its completion, the lights will be flashed on and the initiates ordered to stand up. Those who have "lost their cool" are then observable.

Tests of coolness among peers usually take the form of some contest relation. Teenage Italian-American slumdwellers engage in "a series of competitive encounters intended to assert the superiority and skillfulness of one individual over the other, which take the form of card games, short physical scuffles, and endless verbal duels."[9] And American ghetto-dwelling Negroes have developed a highly stylized dialogue of insult which reaches its quintessential manifestation in "sounding" or the game known as " the dozens."[10]

To successfully pass coolness tests one must mobilize and control a sizable and complex retinue of material and moral forces. First one must master all those elements of self and situation whose unmastered presence constitutes the condition of embarrassment. These include spaces, props, equipment, clothing, and body.[11] Maladroit usage of these often constitutes a definite sign of loss of coolness, while deft and skillfull management of any intrusive action by these can signify the presence of coolness.

Coolness tests also require one to control all those elements of self which, if evidenced, constitute the sign of emotional incapacity. In addition to the body—and here we refer to its carriage, litheness, deftness and grace—there is the special case of the face, perhaps the most vulnerable agent of, as well as the most valuable instrument for, poise under pressure.[12] The eyes, nostrils, and lips are all communicators of one's mental ease and personal control. Failures here—such as a look of fear in the eyes, a flare of the nostrils, or quivering lips—communicate characterological faults that deny coolness. Finally, the color of the face must be kept neutral if coolness is to be confirmed. Those who blush or pale quickly are hard put to overcome the outward physical sign that they are not poised.

Among the most significant instruments for coolness is the voice. Both form and content are relevant here, and each must be coordinated in the service of savoir-faire if that character trait is to be confirmed. In institutionalized verbal contests—such as the Negro game of the "dozens"—vocal controls are the principal element of style. For these games as for other verbal artistic endeavours "style is nothing if it is not an overtly conscious striving for design on the part of the artist."[13] To engage expertly in "the dozens," and other Negro word games, one has to employ "noncasual utterances"—i.e., use of language for restricted purposes—in subculturally prescribed but seemingly effortless syntactic constructions and specified elements of diction. Of course voice control as an element of the establishment and maintenance of poise under pressure has its place in circles beyond that of the ghetto Negro. In parlor repartee, covert exchanges of hostility among colleagues, joking relations, and teasing, not only the content but also the tone and timbre count for much.

Courtship and dating are perhaps the most widespread institutions in which poise is expected and thus they require mobilization of those material, anatomical, physiological, and moral forces which together, under coordinated control, constitute the armamentarium by which the coolness game may be won.[14] Activities which require for their execution a mobilization of passions—e.g., sexual intercourse—are sometimes regarded as peculiarly valuable for testing poise through affective detachment. Italian-American men admire a person "who is able to attract a good-looking woman and to conquer her without becoming involved."[15] Chinese clan rules warn husbands about the dangers created by emotional expression in sexual relations with their wives.[16] And youthful male prostitutes count it as a proof of their strong character that they do not become emotionally excited during professional acts of sexual intercourse.[17]

Where coolness is considered a positive trait, attempts will be made to demonstrate it. However, there are those statuses and situations that typically are thought to be devoid of risk and whose incumbents must therefore search out or create situations in which coolness can be demonstrated if that trait is desired. For some, then, coolness must be staged. Since, as we have said, coolness is imputed to individuals only insofar as the person's actions are seen to occur in risk-taking situations, those who strive after a reputation for coolness will seek out risky situations wherein it can be manifested. Thus, children often attempt to show emotional poise by "risky" riding on merry-go-round horses.[18] Adolescents escalate both the nature of the risk and the poise required in games of "chicken." Not surprisingly we find that slumdwelling adolescents—who highly prize the character attribute of coolness—distinguish time in terms of its potential for action (and by inference, for displays of character). "Dead" time is time devoid of such potential.[19]

Conclusions

Although the term "coolness" is of recent vintage, the phenomenon or trait to which it refers is universal, appearing under a variety of rubrics: nonchalance, sophistication, *savoir-faire*, "blase character," and so on. For Simmel, coolness—or blase character, as he called it—was a trait of urbanized man.[20] Although Simmel attributes this blase character to the preponderance of a money economy, the rapidity of change, and the interdependence of roles in cities, it would seem that these are but major sources of risk that generate the conditions for displaying the character trait of coolness. These sources of risk may be matched by other types of risk and thus other forms of coolness and character development appropriate to them may be found in non-urban settings.[21]

Coolness is often associated with nobility and wealth; indeed, it is from among the ranks of the risk-taking rich that *savoir-faire* and finesse are usually noted and often expected, but it is not exclusively so. Bandits and burglars exhibit many of the traits associated with coolness and sometimes explicitly link these up to aspirations toward or identification with the nobility. Thus Robin Hood is portrayed as a wronged lord who, although forced to flee into the forest and adopt the outlaw life, remains noble, courageous, temperate, and capable of considerable finesse.[22]

Note, too, that coolness is not only associated with those of high rank but also among those who are so low in the social order that the most prized possession they have is personal character—a personal status that can be acknowledged or disconfirmed in everyday encounters and demonstrated particularly in the skill and finesse with which word games are played. Such people, Negroes in America are an outstanding example, develop considerable verbal ability—a pervasive pride in their own individuality, and—because of the permanent danger of character as well as physical assassination—skill in social and personal defense. And it is among quite ordinary American Negroes and persons similarly situated that we find the creative imagination developed toward posturing and prevarication and characterological coolness.[23]

On the contemporary American scene, however, the trait of coolness is not limited to any one segment of the social order. David Riesman and others have suggested that the era of moral absolutism, accompanied by the trait of inner-directedness, has declined, and among the concomitant changes is a shift in the concept of strong character.[24] In the era of inner-directedness moral character was summed up in the admonition to do one's duty. Today, such a seemingly simplistic moral model has been exchanged for the chameleon-like, radar-attuned actor who keeps pace with the rapid changes in form, content, and style. Although poise under pressure was an issue in the era of rugged individualism and unfettered capitalism, the nature of the risks involved was both different in content and differentially distributed. Modern society has changed the issue in risk and democratized it.[25] Keeping cool is now a problem for everyone.

In the place of the earlier isolated individuality accompanied by morally clear doctrines of guilt and shame, there has arisen the coordinated group accompanied by loneliness and affected by a ubiquitous sense of anxiety. The fictional heroes of the eras reflect these changes. The Lone Ranger—perhaps the last fully developed prototype of morally correct inner direction—was a silent, skillful devotee of law and order. He traveled the uncharted trails of the frontier West accompanied only by an Indian, both in but not of their society. He spoke seldom and then in short, clipped, direct statements. He seemed to have no needs; neither women, wealth, nor power attracted or wounded him. The problems he solved were simple in form; they were *only* dangerous to life and limb: a gang of evil-doers threatened the town. Only their removal from the scene would restore the unquestionably desirable *status quo ante*.

By contrast Maverick is the prototype hero of the modern age. He is a gambler and, like Riesman's other-directed man, a cosmopolitan. For Maverick, the problems are not simple. His interest is to get through life with the maximum of pleasure, the minimum of pain. He recognizes no moral absolutes except physical and characterological survival. For him the only weapon is his wits; the only skill, verbal repartee. Only if he loses his cool will he lose to his more powerful and often ill-defined and impersonal opponents. The moral lesson implied in Maverick is quite clear. The modern age is one of permanent complex problems. They neither lend themselves to direct solution nor do they gradually disappear.[26] It is rather that the hazardous nature of life becomes ordinary, the impermanence of things and relationships becomes fixed, and to survive man must adopt the character associated with the routinization of anxiety. Its most salient feature is what we call coolness. Its manifestations are the recognition of danger in the *presentation* of self in everyday life, the risk in *attachment* to things or people, and the positive value of what Goffman calls "role distance."[27]

Despite the ubiquity of coolness in the modern world, its study may be enhanced if we look at the form and content of life for those who are relatively permanent outsiders in society. Career deviants must manifest a considerable display of *savoir-faire* if they are to survive and especially—if like abortionists[28]—they deal with a clientele who are only situationally deviant. Minorities whose status is both anomalous and precarious have evidenced a remarkable ability to build a subculture resting in large part on the artful development of coolness forms. Here, then, are the strategic research sites.

The study of coolness—its meaning, manifestations, and metamorphosis—is surely a topic deserving further investigation, for all men in society are subject to the problems of personal risk and the preservation of poise under pressure.

NOTES

1. This paper explores a theoretical avenue opened up by Erving Goffman. Our orientation and some of its conceptual categories used here are derived from the various writings of this seminal thinker.
2. This definition closely follows the one suggested by Goffman in "Where the Action Is," unpublished manuscript, University of California, Berkeley, p. 29.
3. Goffman, "On Face Work," *Psychiatry*, 18 (August, 1955), pp. 213–231.
4. The hazards of social encounters are not universally recognized with the same degree of seriousness. Thus, in Japanese culture the face engagements of individuals are always regarded as character tests. Individuals are expected to be aware at all times of the proprieties. Loss of face can occur at any time. On the other hand, in American culture it would appear that social risks are not recognized as an ingredient of every encounter, but only of those that have a retro- or pro-active effect on the participants. For an analysis of the Japanese as veritable models of poise under pressure, see Nyozekan Hasegawa, *The Japanese Character*, Tokyo: Kodansha International, 1966, esp. pp. 29–34 and 90–94. See also George De Vos, "A Comparison of the Personality Differences in Two Generations of Japanese Americans By Means of the Rorschach Test," *Nagoya Journal of Medical Science* (August, 1954), pp. 164–165, 252–261; and William Caudill, "Japanese American Personality and Acculturation," *Genetic Psychology Monographs*, 45 (1952), pp. 3–102.
5. The loss of cool is not everywhere a stigma. Among Shtetl Jews, for example, displays of overt emotionalism are culturally approved. See Mark Zborowski and Elizabeth Herzog, *Life is With People: The Culture of the Shtetl*, N.Y.: Schocken Books, 1962, p. 335.
6. In some instances the fears and apprehensions among newcomers are so great that not even ordinary calmness can prevail until special restorative

measures are employed. For a most dramatic illustration of the point see *Equiano's Travels: The Interesting Narrative of the Life of Olaudah Equiano or Gustavus Vassa the African,* edited by Paul Edwards, N.Y.: Praeger, 1967 originally published in 1789), pp. 30–31.

7. Repartee and other word games apparently came into full bloom in courtly circles after women and intellectuals were admitted to participate. See Florian Znaniecki, *Social Relations and Social Roles,* San Francisco: Chandler, 1965, pp. 175–176.
8. Hasegawa, *op. cit.,* p. 88.
9. Herbert J. Gans, *The Urban Villagers,* N.Y.: The Free Press of Glencoe, 1962, p. 81.
10. See John Dollard, "The Dozens: Dialectic of Insult," *The American Imago,* Vol. I (November, 1939), pp. 3–25; Ralph E. Berdie, "Playing the Dozens," *Journal of Abnormal and Social Psychology,* V. 42 (January, 1947), pp. 120–121; Corneleus L. Golightly and Israel Scheffler, "Playing the Dozens: A Research Note," *Journal of Abnormal and Social Psychology,* V. 43 (January, 1948), pp. 104–105; Roger D. Abrahams, *Deep Down in the Jungle,* Hatboro, Penn.: Folklore Associates, 1964, pp. 41–65, 89–98, 259–262. Abrahams (p. 50) describes sounding as follows: "Sounding occurs only in crowds of boys. One insults a member of another's family; others in the group make disapproving sounds to spur on the coming exchange. The one who has been insulted feels at this point that he must reply with a slur on the protagonist's family which is clever enough to defend his honor (and therefore that of his family). This, of course, leads the other (once again, due more to pressure from the crowd than actual insult) to make further jabs. This can proceed until everyone is bored with the whole affair, until one hits the other (fairly rare), or until some other subject comes up that interrupts the proceedings (the usual state of affairs)."
11. Edward Gross and Gregory P. Stone, "Embarrassment and the Analysis of Role Requirements," *American Journal of Sociology,* 70 (July, 1964), pp. 6–10. See also Erving Goffman, "Embarrassment and Social Organization," *American Journal of Sociology,* 62 (November, 1956), pp. 264–271.
12. See Georg Simmel, "The Aesthetic Significance of the Face," in Kurt Wolff, editor, *Georg Simmel, 1858–1918,* Columbus: Ohio State University Press, 1959, pp. 276–281. Also Goffman, "On Face Work," *op. cit.*
13. Charles T. Scott, *A Linguistic Study of Persian and Arabic Riddles: A Language-Centered Approach to Genre Definition,* unpublished Ph.D. dissertation, University of Texas, 1963, p. 12.
14. For a piquant instance in which these forces were unexpectedly tested by a Kikuyu youth studying in America see R. Mugo Gatheru, *Child of Two Worlds: A Kikuyu's Story,* Garden City: Doubleday-Anchor, 1965, pp. 153–154.
15. Gans, *op. cit.,* p. 190.
16. Hui-chen Wang Liu, *The Traditional Chinese Clan Rules,* Locust Valley, N.Y.: J. J. Augustin, 1959, pp. 60–93.
17. Albert J. Reiss, "The Social Integration of Queers and Peers," in Howard S. Becker, ed., *The Other Side,* N.Y.: The Free Press of Glencoe, 1964, pp. 181–210.
18. For a discussion of the behavioristic elements in riding a merry-go-round and other games of equipoise see Erving Goffman, "Role Distance," in *Encounters,* Indianapolis: Bobbs-Merrill, 1961, pp. 105–110.
19. Gans, *op. cit.,* pp. 27–32; Jules Henry, "White People's Time, Colored People's Time," *Trans-Action* (March-April, 1965), pp. 31–34; John Horton,

"Time and Cool People," *Trans-Action* (April, 1967), pp. 5–12.

20. Georg Simmel, "The Metropolis and Mental Life," in *Sociology of Georg Simmel*, N.Y.: The Free Press of Glencoe, 1950, pp. 413–414.

21. One such setting is the chivalric ideal of the fifteenth century. See Diaz de Gamez, "The Chivalric Ideal," in James B. Ross and Mary M. McLaughlin, eds., *The Portable Medieval Reader*, N.Y.: Viking Press, 1949, esp. pp. 91–92.

22. See Maurice Keen, *The Outlaws of Medieval Legend*, London: Routledge and Kegan Paul, 1961. For further evidence of the generalized character of bandits and outlaws see Eric J. Hobsbawn, *Social Bandits and Primitive Rebels*, N.Y.: Free Press of Glencoe, 1959, pp. 1–29. For a characterological analysis of the modern day fictional Robin Hood, namely, Raffles, see George Orwell, "Raffles and Miss Blandish," in *Dickens, Dali and Others*, N.Y.: Reynal and Co., 1946, pp. 202–221. These legendary bandits—Robin Hood, Raffles, etc.—are characterized by taking extra risks in the name of sportsmanship, or aesthetic reasons, and in so doing amply display strong character.

23. See Richard Wright, "The Psychological Reactions of Oppressed People," in *White Man, Listen!*, Garden City: Doubleday-Anchor, 1957, pp. 17–18.

24. David Riesman, Nathan Glazer, Reuel Denny, *The Lonely Crowd*, Garden City: Doubleday-Anchor, 1950, 1953.

25. See Talcott Parsons and Winston White, "The Link Between Character and Society," in S. M. Lipset and L. Lowenthal, editors, *Culture and Social Character*, N.Y.: The Free Press of Glencoe, 1961, pp. 89–135.

26. For an analysis of the modern world in these terms see Robert Nisbet, *Community and Power*, N.Y.: Oxford Galaxy, 1962.

27. Goffman, "Role Distance," *Encounters, op. cit.*

28. See Donald Ball, "An Abortion Clinic Ethnography," *Social Problems*, V. 14 (Winter, 1967), pp. 293–301.

john horton

Time means different things to different people. To many middle-class Americans it is a commodity. It is used, borrowed, saved, wasted. But this is not true of all Americans nor of many others beyond our borders. Even so, as John Horton points out, some sociologists have failed to understand or, perhaps, accept the fact that not all perceive of time in rational, impersonal ways. While warning that one must not simply reverse the majority stereotype, saying, for example, "the lower class has no sense of future time," he shows how important time is to all men.

Horton focuses attention on those thought to be the most irrational in their sense of time, unemployed street-corner men who live in the ghettoes of America. Answering a series of rhetorical questions, he describes the phenomenon of the "rhythm of street time" as he observed it in 1965 and 1966 while intensively interviewing a number of "dudes" in the black section of Venice, California. He discusses the difference between "live" and "dead" time, indicates the irrelevance of the regular clock to those on the street, and describes the uncertain predictability of personal time "on the set."

Horton's essay is not only an excellent description of street time but also an inside view of the problems of "playing it cool," problems described by Lyman and Scott in the previous article.

Time in industrial society is clock time. It seems to be an external, objective regulator of human activities. But for the sociologist, time is not an object existing independent of man, dividing his day into precise units. Time is diverse; it is always social and subjective. A man's sense of time derives from his place in the social structure and his lived experience.

The diversity of time perspectives can be understood intellectually— but it is rarely tolerated socially. A dominant group reifies and objectifies its time; it views all other conceptions of time as subversive—as indeed they are.

Thus, today in the dominant middle-class stereotype, standard American time is directed to the future; it is rational and impersonal. In contrast, time for the lower class is directed to the present, irrational and personal. Peasants, Mexican-Americans, Negroes, workers are "lazy"; they do not possess the American virtues of ambition and striving for success. Viewed solely from the dominant class norm of rationality, their presumed orientation to present time is seen only as an irrational deviation, something to be controlled and changed. It is at best an epiphenomenon produced in reaction to the "real, objective" phenomenon of middle-class time.

Sociologists have not been completely exempt from this kind of reified thinking. When they universalize the middle-class value of rational action and future time and turn it into a "neutral" social fact, they reinforce a negative stereotype: Lower classes are undependable in organized work situations (they seek immediate rewards and cannot defer gratification); in their political action, they are prone to accept immediate, violent, and extreme solutions to personal problems; their sense of time is dysfunctional to the stability of the economic and political orders. For example, Seymour Martin Lipset writes, in a paper significantly entitled "Working Class Authoritarianism":

> This emphasis on the immediately perceivable and concern with the personal and concrete is part and parcel of the short time perspective and the inability to perceive the complex possibilities and consequences of action which often results in a general readiness to support extremist political and religious movements, and generally lower level of liberalism on noneconomic questions.

To examine time in relation to the maintenance or destruction of the dominant social order is an interesting political problem, but it is not a sociology of time; it is a middle-class sociology of order or change in its time aspect. Surely, a meaningful sociology of time should take into account the social situation in which time operates and the actor's as well as the observer's perspective. The sociologist must at least entertain the idea that lower-class time may be a phenomenon in and of itself, and quite functional to the life problems of that class.

Of course, there are dangers in seeking the viewpoint of a minority: The majority stereotypes might be reversed. For example, we might find out that no stereotype is more incorrect than that which depicts the lower classes as having no sense of future time. As Max Weber has observed, it is the powerful and not the powerless who are present-oriented. Dominant groups live by maintaining and expanding their present. Minority groups survive in this present, but their survival is nourished by a dream of the future. In "Ethnic Segregation and Caste" Weber says:

> The sense of dignity that characterizes positively privileged status groups is natural to their "being" which does not transcend itself, that is, to their beauty and excellence. Their kingdom is of this world. They live for the present by exploiting the great past. The sense of dignity of the negatively privileged strata naturally refers to a future lying beyond the present whether it is of this life or another. In other words it must be nurtured by a belief in a providential "mission" and by a belief in a specific honor before God.

It is time to reexamine the meaning of time, the reality of the middle-class stereotype of itself, as well as the middle-class stereotype of the lower class. In this article I explore the latter: the meaning of time among a group most often stereotyped as having an irrational, present sense of time—the sporadically unemployed young Negro street corner population. I choose the unemployed because they live outside of the constraints of industrial work time; Negroes because they speak some of the liveliest street language, including that of time; young males because the street culture of the unemployed and the hustler is young and masculine.

To understand the meaning of street time was to discover "what's happening" in the day-to-day and week-to-week activities of my respondents. Using the middle-class stereotype of lower-class time as a point of departure, I asked myself the following questions:

> In what sense is street time personal (not run by the clock) and present-oriented?

> What kind of future orientation, if any, exists?

> Are street activities really irrational in the sense that individuals do not use time efficiently in the business of living? I have attempted to answer the questions in the language and from the experience of my respondents.

Street culture exists in every low income ghetto. It is shared by the hustling elements of the poor, whatever their nationality or color. In Los Angeles, members of such street groups sometimes call themselves "street people," "cool people," or simply "regulars." Whatever the label, they are known the world over by outsiders as hoods or hoodlums, persons who live on and off the street. They are recognizable by their own fashions in dress, hair, gestures, and speech. The particular fashion varies with time, place, and nationality. For example, in 1963 a really sharp Los Angeles street Negro would be "conked to the bone" (have processed hair) and "togged-out" in "continentals." Today "natural" hair and variations of mod clothes are coming in style.

Street people are known also by their activities—"duking" (fighting or at least looking tough), "hustling" (any way of making money outside the "legitimate" world of work), "gigging" (partying)—and by their apparent nonactivity, "hanging" on the corner. Their individual roles are defined concretely by their success or failure in these activities. One either knows "what's happening" on the street, or he is a "lame," "out of it," "not ready" (lacks his diploma in street knowledge), a "square."

There are, of course, many variations. Negroes, in particular, have contributed much to the street tongue which has diffused into both the more hip areas of the middle class and the broader society. Such expressions as "a lame," "taking care of righteous business," "getting down to the nitty-gritty," and "soul" can be retraced to Negro street life.

The more or less organized center of street life is the "set"—meaning both the peer group and the places where it hangs out. It is the stage and central market place for activity, where to find out what's happening. My set of Negro street types contained a revolving and sometimes disappearing (when the "heat," or police pressure, was on) population of about 45 members ranging in age from 18 to 25. These were the local "dudes," their term meaning not the fancy city slickers but simply "the boys," "fellas," the "cool people." They represented the hard core of street culture, the role models for younger teenagers. The dudes could be found when they were "laying dead"—hanging on the corner, or shooting pool and "jiving" ("goofing" or kidding around) in a local community project. Isolated from "the man" (in this context the man in power—the police, and by extension, the white man), they lived in a small section of Venice outside the central Los Angeles ghetto and were surrounded by a predominantly Mexican and Anglo population. They called their black "turf" "Ghost-town"—home of the "Ghostmen," their former gang. Whatever the origin of the word, Ghost-town was certainly the home of socially "invisible" men.

In 1965 and 1966 I had intensive interviews with 25 set members. My methods emerged in day to day observations. Identified as white, a lame, and square, I had to build up an image of being at least "legit" (not working for police). Without actually living in the area, this would have been impossible without the aid of a key fieldworker, in this case an outsider who could be accepted inside. This field worker, Cowboy, was a white dude of 25. He had run with "Paddy" (white), "Chicano" (Mexican), and "Blood" (Negro) sets since the age of 12 and was highly respected for having been president of a tough gang. He knew the street, how to duke, move with style, and speak the tongue. He made my entry possible. I was the underprivileged child who had to be taught slowly and sympathetically the common-sense features of street life.

Cowboy had the respect and I the toleration of several set leaders. After that, we simply waited for the opportunity to "rap." Although sometimes used synonymously with street conversation, "rap" is really a special way of talking—repartee. Street repartee at its best is a lively way of "running it down," or of "jiving" (attempting to put someone on), of trying "to blow another person's mind," forcing him "to lose his cool," to give in or give up something. For example, one needs to throw a lively rap when he is "putting the make on a broad."

Sometimes we taped individuals, sometimes "soul sessions." We asked for life histories, especially their stories about school, job, and family. We watched and asked about the details of daily surviving and attempted to construct street time schedules. We probed beyond the past and present into the future in two directions—individual plans for tomorrow and a lifetime, and individual dreams of a more decent world for whites and Negroes.

The set can be described by the social and attitudinal characteristics of its members. To the observer, these are expressed in certain realities of day to day living: not enough skill for good jobs, and the inevitable trouble brought by the problem of surviving. Of the 25 interviewed, only four had graduated from high school. Except for a younger set member who was still in school, all were dropouts, or perhaps more accurately kicked-outs. None was really able to use or write formal language. However, many were highly verbal, both facile and effective in their use of the street tongue. Perhaps the art of conversation is most highly developed here where there is much time to talk, perhaps too much—an advantage of the *lumpen*-leisure class.

Their incomes were difficult to estimate, as "bread" or "coins" (money) came in on a very irregular basis. Of the 17 for whom I have figures, half reported that they made less than $1,400 in the last year, and the rest claimed income from $2,000-4,000 annually. Two-thirds were living with and partially dependent on their parents, often a mother. The financial strain was intensified by the fact that although 15 of 17 were single, eight had one or more children living in the area. (Having children, legitimate or not, was not a stigma but proof of masculinity.)

At the time of the interview, two-thirds of them had some full- or part-time employment—unskilled and low-paid jobs. The overall pattern was one of sporadic and—from their viewpoint—often unsatisfactory work, followed by a period of unemployment compensation, and petty hustling whenever possible and whenever necessary.

When I asked the question, "When a dude needs bread, how does he get it?" the universal response was "the hustle." Hustling is, of course, illegitimate from society's viewpoint. Street people know it is illegal, but they view it in no way as immoral or wrong. It is justified by the necessity of surviving. As might be expected, the unemployed admitted that they hustled and went so far as to say that a dude could make it better on the street than on the job: "There is a lot of money on the street, and there are many ways of getting it," or simply, "This has always been my way of life." On the other hand, the unemployed, the part-time hustlers, usually said, "A dude could make it better on the job than on the street." Their reasons for disapproving of hustling were not moral. Hustling meant trouble. "I don't hustle because there's no security. You eventually get busted." Others said there was not enough money on the street or that it was too difficult to "run a game" on people.

Nevertheless, hustling is the central street activity. It is the economic foundation for everyday life. Hustling and the fruit of hustling set the rhythm of social activities.

What are the major forms of hustling in Ghost-town? The best hustles were conning, stealing, gambling, and selling dope. By gambling, these street people meant dice; by dope, peddling "pills" and "pot." Pills are "reds" and "whites"—barbiturates and benzedrine or dexedrine. Pot is, of course, marijuana—"grass" or "weed." To "con" means to put "the bump" on a "cat," to "run a game" on somebody, to work on his mind for goods and services.

The "woman game" was common. As one dude put it, "If I have a good lady and she's on County, there's always some money to get." In fact, there is a local expression for getting county money. When the checks come in for child support, it's "mother's day." So the hustler "burns" people for money, but he also "rips off" goods for money; he thieves, and petty thieving is always a familiar hustle. Pimping is often the hustler's dream of the good life, but it was almost unknown here among the small-time hustlers. That was the game of the real professional and required a higher level of organization and wealth.

Hustling means bread and security but also trouble, and trouble is a major theme in street life. The dudes had a "world of trouble" (a popular song about a hustler is "I'm in a World of Trouble")—with school, jobs, women, and the police. The intensity of street life could be gauged in part by the intensity of the "heat" (police trouble). The hotter the street, the fewer the people visible on the street. On some days the set was empty. One would soon learn that there had been a "bust" (an arrest). Freddy had run amok and thrown rocks at a police car. There had been a leadership struggle; "Big Moe" had been cut up, and the "fuzz" had descended. Life was a succession of being picked up on suspicion of assault, theft, possession, "suspicion of suspicion" (an expression used by a respondent in describing his life). This was an ordinary experience for the street dude and often did lead to serious trouble. Over half of those interviewed claimed they had felony convictions.

Keeping cool and out of trouble, hustling bread, and looking for something interesting and exciting to do created the structure of time on the street. The rhythm of time is expressed in the high and low points in the

day and week of an unemployed dude. I stress the pattern of the unemployed and full-time hustler because he is on the street all day and
night and is the prototype in my interviews. The sometimes employed
will also know the pattern, and he will be able to hit the street whenever
released from the bondage of jail, work, and the clock. Here I describe
a typical time schedule gleaned through interviews and field observation.

Characteristically the street person gets up late, hits the street in
the late morning or early afternoon, and works his way to the set. This
is a place for relaxed social activity. Hanging on the set with the boys
is the major way of passing time and waiting until some necessary or
desirable action occurs. Nevertheless, things do happen on the set.
The dudes "rap" and "jive" (talk), gamble, and drink their "pluck"
(usually a cheap, sweet wine). They find out what happened yesterday,
what is happening today, and what will hopefully happen on the weekend
—the perpetual search for the "gig," the party. Here peer socialization
and reinforcement also take place. The younger dude feels a sense of
pride when he can be on the set and throw a rap to an older dude. He
is learning how to handle himself, show respect, take care of business,
and establish his own "rep."

On the set, yesterday merges into today, and tomorrow is an emptiness to be filled in through the pursuit of bread and excitement. Bread
makes possible the excitement—the high (getting loaded with wine,
pills, or pot), the sharp clothes, the "broad," the fight, and all those good
things which show that one knows what's happening and has "something
going" for himself. The rhythm of time—of the day and of the week—is
patterned by the flow of money and people.

Time is "dead" when money is tight, when people are occupied elsewhere—working or in school. Time is dead when one is in jail. One is
"doing dead time" when nothing is happening, and he's got nothing
going for himself.

Time is alive when and where there is action. It picks up in the evening when everyone moves on the street. During the regular school year
it may pick up for an hour in the afternoon when the "broads" leave
school and meet with the set at a corner taco joint. Time may pick up
when a familiar car cruises by and a few dudes drive down to Johnny's
for a "process" (hair straightening and styling). Time is low on Monday
(as described in the popular song, "Stormy Monday"), Tuesday,
Wednesday, when money is tight. Time is high on Friday nights when
the "eagle flies" and the "gig" begins. On the street, time has a personal
meaning only when something is happening, and something is most
likely to happen at night—especially on Friday and Saturday nights.
Then people are together, and there may be bread—bread to take and
bread to use.

Human behavior is rational if it helps the individual to get what he
wants whether it is success in school or happiness in the street. Street

people sometimes get what they want. They act rationally in those situations where they are able to plan and choose because they have control, knowledge, and concern, irrationally where there are barriers to their wants and desires.

When the street dude lacks knowledge and power to manipulate time, he is indeed irrational. For the most part, he lacks the skills and power to plan a move up and out of the ghetto. He is "a lame" in the middle class world of school and work; he is not ready to operate effectively in unfamiliar organizations where his street strengths are his visible weaknesses. Though irrational in moving up and out of the street, he can be rational in day to day survival in the street. No one survives there unless he knows what's happening (that is, unless he knows what is available, where to get what he can without being burned or busted). More euphemistically, this is "taking advantage of opportunities," exactly what the rational member of the middle class does in his own setting.

To know what's happening is to know the goods and the bads, the securities, the opportunities, and the dangers of the street. Survival requires that a hustling dude know who is cool and uncool (who can be trusted); who is in power (the people who control narcotics, fences, etc.); who is the "duker" or the fighter (someone to be avoided or someone who can provide protection). When one knows what's happening he can operate in many scenes, providing that he can "hold his mud," keep cool, and out of trouble.

With his diploma in street knowledge, a dude can use time efficiently and with cunning in the pursuit of goods and services—in hustling to eat and yet have enough bread left over for the pleasures of pot, the chicks, and the gig. As one respondent put it, "The good hustler has the knowledge, the ambition to better himself. He conditions his mind and must never put his guard too far down, to relax, or he'll be taken." This is street rationality. The problem is not a deficient sense of time but deficient knowledge and control to make a fantasy future and a really better life possible.

The petty hustler more fully realizes the middle class ideal of individualistic rationality than does the middle class itself. When rationality operates in hustling, it is often on an individual basis. In a world of complex organization, the hustler defines himself as an entrepreneur; and indeed, he is the last of the competitive entrepreneurs.

The degree of organization in hustling depends frequently on the kind of hustling. Regular pimping and pushing require many trusted contacts and organization. Regular stealing requires regular fences for hot goods. But in Ghost-town when the hustler moved, he usually moved alone and on a small scale. His success was on him. He could not depend on the support of some benevolent organization. Alone, without a sure way of running the same game twice, he must continually recal-

culate conditions and people and find new ways of taking or be taken himself. The phrase "free enterprise for the poor and socialism for the rich" applies only too well in the street. The political conservative should applaud all that individual initiative.

Negro street time is built around the irrelevance of clock time, white man's time, and the relevance of street values and activities. Like anyone else, a street dude is on time by the standard clock whenever he wants to be, not on time when he does not want to be and does not have to be.

When the women in school hit the street at the lunch hour and he wants to throw them a rap, he will be there then and not one hour after they have left. But he may be kicked out of high school for truancy or lose his job for being late and unreliable. He learned at an early age that school and job were neither interesting nor salient to his way of life. A regular on the set will readily admit being crippled by a lack of formal education. Yet school was a "bum kick." It was not his school. The teachers put him down for his dress, hair, and manners. As a human being he has feelings of pride and autonomy, the very things most threatened in those institutional situations where he was or is the under-developed, unrespected, illiterate, and undeserving outsider. Thus what-ever "respectable" society says will help him, he knows oppresses him, and he retreats to the streets for security and a larger degree of personal freedom. Here his control reaches a maximum, and he has the kind of autonomy which many middle class males might envy.

In the street, watches have a special and specific meaning. Watches are for pawning and not for telling time. When they are worn, they are decoration and ornaments of status. The street clock is informal, per-sonal, and relaxed. It is not standardized nor easily synchronized to other clocks. In fact, a street dude may have almost infinite toleration for individual time schedules. To be on time is often meaningless, to be late an unconsciously accepted way of life. "I'll catch you later," or simply "later," are the street phrases that mean business will be taken care of, but not necessarily now.

Large areas of street life run on late time. For example, parties are not cut off by some built-in alarm clock of appointments and schedules. At least for the unemployed, standard time neither precedes nor follows the gig. Consequently, the action can take its course. It can last as long as interest is sustained and die by exhaustion or by the intrusion of some more interesting event. A gig may endure all night and well into another day. One of the reasons for the party assuming such time dimensions is purely economic. There are not enough cars and enough money for individual dates, so everyone converges in one place and takes care of as much business as possible there, that is, doing what-ever is important at the time—sex, presentation of self, hustling.

Events starting late and lasting indefinitely are clearly street and class phenomena, not some special trait of Afro-Americans. Middle class

Negroes who must deal with the organization and coordination of activities in church and elsewhere will jokingly and critically refer to a lack of standard time sense when they say that Mr. Jones arrived "CPT" (colored people's time). They have a word for it, because being late is a problem for people caught between two worlds and confronted with the task of meshing standard and street time. In contrast, the street dudes had no self-consciousness about being late; with few exceptions they had not heard the expression CPT. (When I questioned members of a middle class Negro fraternity, a sample matched by age to the street set, only three of the 25 interviewed could not define CPT. Some argued vehemently that CPT was the problem to be overcome.)

Personal time as expressed in parties and other street activities is not simply deficient knowledge and use of standard time. It is a positive adaption to generations of living whenever and wherever possible outside of the sound and control of the white man's clock. The personal clock is an adaption to the chance and accidental character of events on the street and to the very positive value placed on emotion and feeling. (For a discussion of CPT which is close to some of the ideas presented here, see Jules Henry, "White People's Time, Colored People's Time," *Trans-action*, March/April 1965).

Chance reinforces personal time. A dude must be ready on short notice to move "where the action is." His internal clock may not be running at all when he is hanging on the corner and waiting for something to do. It may suddenly speed up by chance: Someone cruises by in a car and brings a nice "stash" of "weed," a gig is organized and he looks forward to being well togged-out and throwing a rap to some "boss chick," or a lame appears and opens himself to a quick "con." Chance as a determinant of personal time can be called more accurately *uncertain predictability*. Street life is an aggregate of relatively independent events. A dude may not know exactly what or when something will happen, but from past experience he can predict a range of possibilities, and he will be ready, in position, and waiting.

In white middle class stereotypes and fears—and in reality—street action is highly expressive. A forthright yet stylized expression of emotion is positively evaluated and most useful. Street control and communication are based on personal power and the direct impingement of one individual on another. Where there is little property, status in the set is determined by personal qualities of mind and brawn.

The importance of emotion and expression appears again and again in street tongue and ideology. When asked, "How does a dude make a rep on the set?" over half of the sample mentioned "style," and all could discuss the concept. Style is difficult to define as it has so many referents. It means to carry one's self well, dress well, to show class. In the ideology of the street, it may be a way of behaving. One has style if he is able to dig people as they are. He doesn't put them down for what they do. He shows toleration. But a person with style must also show respect. That means respect for a person as he is, and since there is power in the street, respect for another's superior power. Yet one must show respect in such a way that he is able to look tough and inviolate, fearless, secure, "cool."

Style may also refer to the use of gestures in conversation or in dance. It may be expressed in the loose walk, the jivey or dancing walk, the slow cool walk, the way one "chops" or "makes it" down the street. It may be the loose, relaxed hand rap or hand slap, the swinger's greeting which is used also in the hip middle class teen sets. There are many refined variations of the hand rap. As a greeting, one may simply extend his hand, palm up. Another slaps it loosely with his finger. Or, one person may be standing with his hand behind and palm up. Another taps the hand in passing, and also pays his respect verbally with the conventional greeting "What's happening, Brother." Or, in conversation, the hand may be slapped when an individual has "scored," has been "digging," has made a point, has got through to the person.

Style is a comparatively neutral value compared to "soul." Soul can be many things—a type of food (good food is "soul food," a "bowl of soul"), music, a quality of mind, a total way of acting (in eating, drinking, dancing, walking, talking, relating to others, etc.). The person who acts with soul acts directly and honestly from his heart. He feels it and tells it "like it is." One respondent identified soul with ambition and drive. He said the person with soul, once he makes up his mind, goes directly to the goal, doesn't change his mind, doesn't wait and worry about messing up a little. Another said soul was getting down to the nitty-gritty, that is, moving directly to what is basic without guise and disguise. Thus soul is the opposite of hypocrisy, deceit, and phoniness, the opposite of "affective neutrality," and "instrumentality." Soul is simply whatever is considered beautiful, honest, and virtuous in men.

Most definitions tied soul directly to Negro experience. As one hustler puts it, "It is the ability to survive. We've made it with so much less. Soul is the Negro who has the spirit to sing in slavery to overcome the monotony." With very few exceptions, the men interviewed argued that soul was what Negroes had and whites did not. Negroes were "soul brothers," warm and emotional—whites cold as ice. Like other oppressed minorities these street Negroes believed they had nothing except their soul and their humanity, and that this made them better than their oppressors.

Soul is anchored in a past and present of exploitation and deprivation, but are there any street values and activities which relate to the future? The regular in the street set has no providential mission; he lives personally and instrumentally in the present, yet he dreams about the day when he will get himself together and move ahead to the rewards of a good job, money, and a family. Moreover, the personal dream coexists with a nascent political nationalism, the belief that Negroes can and will make it as Negroes. His present-future time is a combination of contradictions and developing possibilities. Here I will be content to document without weighing two aspects of his orientation: *fantasy personal future* and *fantasy collective future.* I use the word fantasy because street people have not yet the knowledge and means and perhaps the will to fulfill their dreams. It is hard enough to survive by the day.

When the members of the set were asked, "What do you really want out of life?" their responses were conventional, concrete, seemingly realistic, and—given their skills—rather hopeless. Two-thirds of the sample mentioned material aspirations—the finer things in life, a home, security, a family. For example, one said, in honest street language, "I want to get things for my kids and to make sure they have a father." Another said, jokingly, "a good future, a home, two or three girls living with me." Only one person didn't know, and the others deviated a little from the material response. They said such things as "for everyone to be on friendly terms—a better world . . . then I could get all I wish," "to be free," "to help people."

But if most of the set wanted money and security, they wanted it on their own terms. As one put it, "I don't want to be in a middle class bag, but I would like a nice car, home, and food in the icebox." He wanted the things and the comforts of middle class life, but not the hypocrisy, the venality, the coldness, the being forced to do what one does not want to do. All that was in the middle class bag. Thus the home and the money may be ends in themselves, but also fronts, security for carrying on the usual street values. Street people believed that they already had something that was valuable and looked down upon the person who made it and moved away into the middle class world. For the observer, the myths are difficult to separate from the truths—here where the truths are so bitter. One can only say safely that street people dream of a high status, and they really do not know how to get it.

The Negro dudes are political outsiders by the usual poll questions. They do not vote. They do not seek out civil rights demonstrations. They have very rudimentary knowledge of political organization. However, about the age of 18, when fighting and being tough are less important than before, street people begin to discuss their position in society. Verbally they care very much about the politics of race and the future of the Negro. The topic is always a ready catalyst for a soul session.

The political consciousness of the street can be summarized by noting those interview questions which attracted at least a 75 percent rate of agreement. The typical respondent was angry. He approves of the Watts incident, although from his isolated corner of the city he did not actively participate. He knows something about the history of discrimination and believes that if something isn't done soon America can expect violence: "What this country needs is a revolutionary change." He is more likely to praise the leadership of Malcolm X than Lyndon Johnson, and he is definitely opposed to the Vietnam war. The reason for his opposition is clear: Why fight for a country which is not mine, when the fight is here?

Thus his racial consciousness looks to the future and a world where he will not have to stand in the shadow of the white man. But his consciousness has neither clear plan nor political commitment. He has listened to the Muslims, and he is not a black nationalist. True, the Negro generally has more soul than the white. He thinks differently, his women may be different, yet integration is preferable to separatism. Or, more accurately, he doesn't quite understand what all these terms mean. His nationalism is real as a folk nationalism based on experience with other Negroes and isolation from whites.

The significance of a racial future in the day to day consciousness of street people cannot be assessed. It is a developing possibility dependent on unforeseen conditions beyond the scope of their skill and imagination. But bring up the topic of race and tomorrow, and the dreams come rushing in—dreams of superiority, dreams of destruction, dreams of human equality. These dreams of the future are salient. They are not the imagination of authoritarian personalities, except from the viewpoint of those who see spite lurking behind every demand for social change. They are certainly not the fantasies of the hipster living philosophically in the present without hope and ambition. One brother summarized the Negro street concept of ambition and future time when he said:

The Negro has more ambition than the whites. He's got farther to go. "The man" is already there. But we're on your trail, daddy. You still have smoke in our eyes, but we're catching up.

ROLES AND RELATION- SHIPS

maya angelou

Few contemporary writers have captured the quality of human relationships more successfully or poignantly than Maya Angelou. In *I Know Why the Caged Bird Sings*, she provides an intimate portrait of life and socialization for blacks in the southern United States. Particularly important is the description of the special social bonds between certain relatives.

One of the central figures in the story is her grandmother, "Momma," in whose candy store Maya spent much of her young life watching, playing, and learning the hardships of being black. In many ways her whole story is telescoped into a few brief pages in which she relates an encounter between a white dentist and Momma. The reader should pay careful attention to the fantasies described near the end of the piece to fully understand the "inside" meaning of what sociologists call "primary relationships."

The Angel of the candy counter had found me out at last, and was exacting excruciating penance for all the stolen Milky Ways, Mounds, Mr. Goodbars and Hersheys with Almonds. I had two cavities that were rotten to the gums. The pain was beyond the bailiwick of crushed aspirins or oil of cloves. Only one thing could help me, so I prayed earnestly that I'd be allowed to sit under the house and have the building collapse on my left jaw.

Since there was no Negro dentist in Stamps, nor doctor either, for that matter, Momma had dealt with previous toothaches by pulling them out (a string tied to the tooth with the other end looped over her fist), pain killers and prayer. In this particular instance the medicine had proved ineffective; there wasn't enough enamel left to hook a string on, and the prayers were being ignored because the Balancing Angel was blocking their passage.

I lived a few days and nights in blinding pain, not so much toying with as seriously considering the idea of jumping in the well, and Momma decided I had to be taken to a dentist. The nearest Negro dentist was in Texarkana, twenty-five miles away, and I was certain that I'd be dead long before we reached half the distance. Momma said we'd go to Dr. Lincoln, right in Stamps, and he'd take care of me. She said he owed her a favor.

I knew there were a number of whitefolks in town that owed her favors. Bailey and I had seen the books which showed how she had lent money to Blacks and whites alike during the Depression, and most still owed her. But I couldn't aptly remember seeing Dr. Lincoln's name, nor had I ever heard of a Negro's going to him as a patient. However, Momma said we were going, and put water on the stove for our baths. I had never been to a doctor, so she told me that after the bath (which would make my mouth feel better) I had to put on freshly starched and ironed underclothes from inside out. The ache failed to respond to the bath, and I knew then that the pain was more serious than that which anyone had ever suffered.

Before we left the Store, she ordered me to brush my teeth and then wash my mouth with Listerine. The idea of even opening my clamped jaws increased the pain, but upon her explanation that when you go to a doctor you have to clean yourself all over, but most especially the part that's to be examined, I screwed up my courage and unlocked my teeth. The cool air in my mouth and the jarring of my molars dislodged what little remained of my reason. I had frozen to the pain, my family nearly had to tie me down to take the toothbrush away. It was no small effort to get me started on the road to the dentist. Momma spoke to all the passers-by, but didn't stop to chat. She explained over her shoulder that we were going to the doctor and she'd "pass the time of day" on our way home.

Until we reached the pond the pain was my world, an aura that haloed me for three feet around. Crossing the bridge into whitefolks' country, pieces of sanity pushed themselves forward. I had to stop moaning and start walking straight. The white towel, which was drawn under my chin and tied over my head, had to be arranged. If one was dying, it had to be done in style if the dying took place in whitefolks' part of town.

On the other side of the bridge the ache seemed to lessen as if a whitebreeze blew off the whitefolks and cushioned everything in their neighborhood—including my jaw. The gravel road was smoother, the stones smaller and the tree branches hung down around the path and nearly covered us. If the pain didn't diminish then, the familiar yet strange sights hypnotized me into believing that it had.

But my head continued to throb with the measured insistence of a bass drum, and how could a toothache pass the calaboose, hear the songs of the prisoners, their blues and laughter, and not be changed? How could one or two or even a mouthful of angry tooth roots meet a wagonload of powhitetrash children, endure their idiotic snobbery and not feel less important?

Behind the building which housed the dentist's office ran a small path used by servants and those tradespeople who catered to the butcher and Stamps' one restaurant. Momma and I followed that lane to the back-stairs of Dentist Lincoln's office. The sun was bright and gave the day a hard reality as we climbed up the steps to the second floor.

Momma knocked on the back door and a young white girl opened it to show surprise at seeing us there. Momma said she wanted to see Dentist Lincoln and to tell him Annie was there. The girl closed the door firmly. Now the humiliation of hearing Momma describe herself as if she had no last name to the young white girl was equal to the physical pain. It seemed terribly unfair to have a toothache and a headache and have to bear at the same time the heavy burden of Blackness.

It was always possible that the teeth would quiet down and maybe drop out of their own accord. Momma said we would wait. We leaned in the harsh sunlight on the shaky railings of the dentist's back porch for over an hour.

He opened the door and looked at Momma. "Well, Annie, what can I do for you?"

He didn't see the towel around my jaw or notice my swollen face.

Momma said, "Dentist Lincoln. It's my grandbaby here. She got two rotten teeth that's giving her a fit."

She waited for him to acknowledge the truth of her statement. He made no comment, orally or facially.

"She had this toothache purt' near four days now, and today I said, 'Young lady, you going to the Dentist.' "

"Annie?"

"Yes, sir, Dentist Lincoln."

He was choosing words the way people hunt for shells. "Annie, you know I don't treat nigra, colored people."

"I know, Dentist Lincoln. But this here is just my little grandbaby, and she ain't gone be no trouble to you . . ."

"Annie, everybody has a policy. In this world you have to have a policy. Now, my policy is I don't treat colored people."

The sun had baked the oil out of Momma's skin and melted the Vaseline in her hair. She shone greasily as she leaned out of the dentist's shadow.

"Seem like to me, Dentist Lincoln, you might look after her, she ain't nothing but a little mite. And seems like maybe you owe me a favor or two."

He reddened slightly. "Favor or no favor. The money has all been repaid to you and that's the end of it. Sorry, Annie." He had his hand on the doorknob. "Sorry." His voice was a bit kinder on the second "Sorry," as if he really was.

Momma said, "I wouldn't press on you like this for myself but I can't take No. Not for my grandbaby. When you come to borrow my money you didn't have to beg. You asked me, and I lent it. Now, it wasn't my policy. I ain't no moneylender, but you stood to lose this building and I tried to help you out."

"It's been paid, and raising your voice won't make me change my mind. My policy . . . " He let go of the door and stepped nearer Momma. The three of us were crowded on the small landing. "Annie, my policy is I'd rather stick my hand in a dog's mouth than in a nigger's."

He had never once looked at me. He turned his back and went through the door into the cool beyond. Momma backed up inside herself for a few minutes. I forgot everything except her face which was almost a new one to me. She leaned over and took the doorknob, and in her everyday soft voice she said, "Sister, go on downstairs. Wait for me. I'll be there directly."

Under the most common of circumstances I knew it did no good to argue with Momma. So I walked down the steep stairs, afraid to look back and afraid not to do so. I turned as the door slammed, and she was gone.

Momma walked in that room as if she owned it. She shoved that silly nurse aside with one hand and strode into the dentist's office. He was sitting in his chair, sharpening his mean instruments and putting extra sting into his medicines. Her eyes were blazing like live coals and her arms had doubled themselves in length. He looked up at her just before she caught him by the collar of his white jacket.

"Stand up when you see a lady, you contemptuous scoundrel." Her tongue had thinned and the words rolled off well enunciated. Enunciated and sharp like little claps of thunder.

The dentist had no choice but to stand at R.O.T.C attention. His head dropped after a minute and his voice was humble. "Yes, ma'am, Mrs. Henderson."

"You knave, do you think you acted like a gentleman, speaking to me like that in front of my granddaughter?" She didn't shake him, although she had the power. She simply held him upright.

"No, ma'am, Mrs. Henderson."

"No, ma'am, Mrs. Henderson, what?" Then she did give him the tiniest of shakes, but because of her strength the action set his head and arms

to shaking loose on the ends of his body. He stuttered much worse than Uncle Willie. "No, ma'am, Mrs. Henderson, I'm sorry."

With just an edge of her disgust showing, Momma slung him back in his dentist's chair. "Sorry is as sorry does, and you're about the sorriest dentist I ever laid my eyes on." (She could afford to slip into the vernacular because she had such eloquent command of English.)

"I didn't ask you to apologize in front of Marguerite, because I don't want her to know of my power, but I order you, now and herewith. Leave Stamps by sundown."

"Mrs. Henderson, I can't get my equipment . . ." He was shaking terribly now.

"Now, that brings me to my second order. You will never again practice dentistry. Never! When you get settled in your next place, you will be a vegetarian caring for dogs with the mange, cats with the cholera and cows with the epizootic. Is that clear?"

The saliva ran down his chin and his eyes filled with tears. "Yes, ma'am. Thank you for not killing me. Thank you, Mrs. Henderson."

Momma pulled herself back from being ten feet tall with eight-foot arms and said, "You're welcome for nothing, you varlet, I wouldn't waste a killing on the likes of you."

On her way out she waved her handkerchief at the nurse and turned her into a crocus sack of chicken feed.

Momma looked tired when she came down the stairs, but who wouldn't be tired if they had gone through what she had. She came close to me and adjusted the towel under my jaw (I had forgotten the toothache; I only knew that she made her hands gentle in order not to awaken the pain). She took my hand. Her voice never changed. "Come on, Sister."

I reckoned we were going home where she would concoct a brew to eliminate the pain and maybe give me new teeth too. New teeth that would grow overnight out of my gums. She led me toward the drugstore, which was in the opposite direction from the Store. "I'm taking you to Dentist Baker in Texarkana."

I was glad after all that that I had bathed and put on Mum and Cashmere Bouquet talcum powder. It was a wonderful surprise. My toothache had quieted to solemn pain, Momma had obliterated the evil white man, and we were going on a trip to Texarkana, just the two of us.

On the Greyhound she took an inside seat in the back, and I sat beside her. I was so proud of being her granddaughter and sure that some of her magic must have come down to me. She asked if I was scared. I only shook my head and leaned over on her cool brown upper arm. There was no chance that a dentist, especially a Negro dentist, would dare hurt me then. Not with Momma there. The trip was uneventful, except that she put her arm around me, which was very unusual for Momma to do.

The dentist showed me the medicine and the needle before he deadened my gums, but if he hadn't I wouldn't have worried. Momma stood right behind him. Her arms were folded and she checked on everything he did. The teeth were extracted and she bought me an ice cream cone from the side window of a drug counter. The trip back to Stamps was quiet, except that I had to spit into a very small empty snuff can which she had gotten for me and it was difficult with the bus humping and jerking on our country roads.

At home, I was given a warm salt solution, and when I washed out my mouth I showed Bailey the empty holes, where the clotted blood sat like filling in a pie crust. He said I was quite brave, and that was my cue to reveal our confrontation with the peckerwood dentist and Momma's incredible powers.

I had to admit that I didn't hear the conversation, but what else could she have said than what I said she said? What else done? He agreed with my analysis in a lukewarm way, and I happily (after all, I'd been sick) flounced into the Store. Momma was preparing our evening meal and Uncle Willie leaned on the door still. She gave her version.

"Dentist Lincoln got right uppity. Said he'd rather put his hand in a dog's mouth. And when I reminded him of the favor, he brushed it off like a piece of lint. Well, I sent Sister downstairs and went inside. I hadn't never been in his office before, but I found the door to where he takes out teeth, and him and the nurse was in there thick as thieves. I just stood there till he caught sight of me." Crash bang the pots on the stove. "He jumped just like he was sitting on a pin. He said, 'Annie, I done tole you, I ain't gonna mess around in no niggah's mouth.' I said, 'Somebody's got to do it then,' and he said, 'Take her to Texarkana to the colored dentist' and that's when I said 'If you paid me my money I could afford to take her.' He said, 'It's all been paid.' I tole him everything but the interest been paid. He said ' 'Twasn't no interest.' I said ' 'Tis now. I'll take ten dollars as payment in full.' You know, Willie, it wasn't no right thing to do, 'cause I lent that money without thinking about it.

"He tole that little snippity nurse of his'n to give me ten dollars and make me sign a 'paid in full' receipt. She gave it to me and I signed the papers. Even though by rights he was paid up before, I figger, he gonna be that kind of nasty, he gonna have to pay for it."

Momma and her son laughed and laughed over the white man's evilness and her retributive sin.

I preferred, much preferred, my version.

nancy frazier, myra sadker

While overt racial segregation may no longer be tolerated in the elementary classroom, Nancy Frazier and Myra Sadker contend that this is far from the case concerning sex. Boys and girls have been and continue to be segregated as a part of a hidden curriculum.

This hidden curriculum is sometimes called incidental learning, but what happens to the pupils as they are tracked toward their socially prescribed male or female roles appears to be far from incidental. Schooling turns out to be a sexist activity.

Schooling as a Sexist Activity

There is no course in the official curriculum called "Male Role Development," or "Learning How to be a Girl," but such learning takes place incidentally, and a variety of signals—some obvious, some hidden—insure that sex typing will be reinforced.

One obvious way sex typing occurs is by dress code regulations that many schools still maintain. Regulations that insist that girls wear skirts or dresses rather than slacks have a much deeper impact than on mere appearance. When a girl complies with such regulations she relinquishes freedom—freedom to run as fast as she is able, freedom to sit in complete comfort, and freedom to turn a somersault at recess on the play yard. Because of the clothes she is forced to wear, her physical mobility is hampered and restrained. It is a symbolic confinement.

Recently dress codes have been widely challenged as is illustrated by the following memo sent out by a Massachusetts principal to his faculty:

> I am being beseiged by 6th grade girls who want to wear slacks to school. May I have your opinions?
>
> Do you think we ought to permit slacks? In cold weather only?—In any weather?—any slacks (dungarees, chinos, etc?)
>
> Any other comments about dress?
>
> This will be one topic of discussion for Friday.

This memo is not only indicative of a few cracks beginning to appear in the sartorial armor; it is also indicative of how basically solid the armor still is.

Another distinction children learn, and we are still dealing with the obvious examples, is that boys are supposed to be stronger than girls. When school maintenance chores are assigned, boys draw those tasks requiring heavier manual labor whereas girls are asked to help in quieter, more sedentary ways. This separation of tasks is often inappropriate and forced since some girls mature faster than boys, and in the early grades, are frequently as big and as strong. However, if stacks of heavy texts are to be moved from one room to another, a small boy may be found struggling under their weight, while a girl—perhaps larger and stronger—sits and watches.

School against boys   There are many learnings about sex role behavior that are less obvious. To begin with, we will concentrate on the incidental learnings that are reserved for the elementary school boy. One of his early unhappy learnings may be that he and school don't get along very well. Let's look at an active 6-year old's first encounter with school.

It is Tommy's first day in the first grade. With a sense of bewilderment, he surveys the unknown faces, the shelves of books, the collage of bulletin board pictures, the rows of desks that comprise the classroom. Despite his confusion, he does receive certain definite impressions.

First of all, he finds that the person in charge of his new life is a woman. She seems annoyed whenever he leaves his desk, or talks to the boy in front of him, or spills his crayons on the floor.

He particularly hates following directions and being neat about it. In the arithmetic lesson, the teacher instructs the class to divide their papers into three boxes and to draw one lollipop in the first, two flags in the second, and three ice cream cones in the third. Tommy begins drawing the objects before the instructions are completed. Consequently, he mixes up the number of lollipops and ice cream cones, and since he has forgotten to bring an eraser, he desparately tries to rub the error out with spit. When the teacher stops by his desk to check his work, she reprimands him for the messy hole that has emerged in the middle of his lollipops.

Obviously not a very pleasant or rewarding encounter for Tommy. It is a beginning attempt to check the independence and mastery training that he has profited from in his home environment—one that, along with numerous variations, will occur again and again throughout the early grades.

Many educators feel that the cards are stacked against the elementary school boy. At age 6 when he enters the first grade, he may be twelve months behind his female classmate in developmental age, and by nine this discrepancy has increased to eighteen months.[1] Thus he is working side by side with a female who may be not only bigger than he, but who seems able, as we shall see, to handle school more competently and more comfortably. Added to this handicap is the fact that the elementary school boy must function in an environment that is antithetical to the independent life style he has been encouraged to develop up until then. He is in a situation where neatness, good manners, and docility appear to be keys to success. Writers and cartoonists often depict him as a male misfit in a female world, a young bull whose every move seems to disrupt the delicate balance of the china shop.

Patricia Sexton is one educator who has frequently expressed concern for the development of the young boy in the "feminine" elementary school. In a *Saturday Review* article titled "Are Schools Emasculating Our Boys?" she has stated:

> Boys and the schools seem locked in a deadly and ancient conflict that may eventually inflict mortal wounds on both. . . . The problem is not just that teachers are too often women. It is that the school is too much a woman's world, governed by women's rules and standards. The school code is that of propriety, obedience, decorum, cleanliness, physical and, too often, mental passivity.[2]

She is not alone in her analysis. A review of the recent educational literature discloses a number of articles with titles that reflect similar concern: "Males: A Minority Group in the Classroom" (*Journal of Learning Disabilities*),[3] "Are Girls Really Smarter?" (*Elementary School Journal*),[4] "For Johnny's Reading Sake," (*Reading Teacher*),[5] "Elementary Education—A Man's World," (*Instructor*).[6] Numerous other articles with titles less explicit deal with problems young boys experience in their encounter with the elementary school. No corresponding concern anywhere near such magnitude can be found for the elementary school girl.

The conflict between boy and school has also provided a fertile source of material for humorists. One of the major themes of school cartoons has been that of the mischievous boy doing battle with the weary and rattled female teacher—chuckling with anticipation as he places a thumbtack on her chair, subdued as he trudges home with her retaliation in hand, a report card of Ds and Fs. Cartoonists also draw these rebellious young boys conspiring together with advice such as, "Play it dumb for the first few weeks, then start producing. The teacher will think she's doing wonders with you." They are also pictured as continually trying to explain the bad grades they get to their parents: "You can see she's against me—she has me even dumber than I was last month, and you know that's impossible," or, "I'm saving my brains for real life."[7]

What does the young boy learn from this feminine environment that stresses passivity, neatness, and docility? For one thing, he may learn how to be more quiet, neat, and docile—although for many this is not likely. He may instead learn—that school is a girl's world, one that has little appeal, meaning, or pertinence for him. In fact, one study has shown that elementary school children, both boys and girls, labeled school objects such as blackboard, book, page of arithmetic, and school desk as feminine rather than neuter or masculine.[8]

In a sense the femininity of the school is paralleled by the femininity of the home. The home, like the classroom, is usually organized by a woman, and we can safely guess that, if a similar study were done and children were asked to label home objects such as sink and table, they would label them feminine also. However, in each situation the young boy is treated quite differently. The woman in the home is more likely to foster her son's independence so that he will develop the appropriate "manly" qualities. The woman who runs the classroom, with thirty children on her hands, may fear that unless independence and activity are checked, her room will explode and she will lose control.

Thus, the young boy must spend approximately a thousand hours a year at an institution that restrains and checks him. This lack of comfortable fit between the more active behavior allowed at home and the passivity demanded in school may force young boys into open rebellion. We can see how this happens as we take another look at boys in the elementary school.

The scene is a restless and unruly afternoon in Miss Hodgkins' fifth-grade class. She has issued warning after warning trying to get the class to quiet down, but she has little success. Finally she explodes, "I've had just all I'm going to take! As usual, the boys are causing all the trouble, so, as usual, all the boys will stay after school. If only you boys could be nice and quiet like the girls, what a pleasure teaching would be."

How likely is it that this scene (or some reasonable facsimile) will occur in an elementary school? Educational research suggests that it is quite likely indeed. Those who study what goes on in classrooms have focused much attention on classroom interaction patterns, who talks with whom, how much of a lesson is teacher talk, who is criticized, who is praised and how often. One finding of these studies is that a different pattern of interaction emerges for boys than for girls.

Researchers studied how teachers dispensed reward and disapproval in three sixth-grade classrooms. Children in these classes were asked to nominate those classmates who received the teacher's approval and those who received her disapproval. Both classroom observers and the children themselves noted that the teachers expressed greater approval of girls and greater disapproval of boys.[9] In another study it was found that boys receive eight to ten times as many prohibitory control messages (warnings like: "That's enough talking, Bill. Put that comic book away, Joe.") as their female classmates. Moreover, this same researcher has also found that when teachers criticize boys, they are more likely to use harsh or angry tones than when talking with girls about an equivalent misdemeanor.[10]

However, it has been found that teachers not only disapprove of boys more, but also interact with them more in general. In a large study involving twenty-one fourth- and sixth-grade classes (thirteen taught by male teachers and eight by female teachers) it was found that teachers interacted more with boys in four major categories of teaching behavior: approval, instruction, listening to the child, and disapproval.[11] So it seems that teachers not only reprimand boys more, but also talk with them about subject matter more frequently and listen to what they have to say more often. In short, boys are receiving more than their share of the teacher's active attention.

Although it is difficult to assess the impact of all this attention, including negative attention, on boys, one researcher suggests the following result: "One consequence might be a cumulative increase in independent, autonomous behavior by boys as they are disapproved, praised, listened to, and taught more actively by the teacher."[12]

We have been discussing school as a feminine environment in which boys rebel against the network of restrictions imposed upon them. It also appears that boys view this feminine environment as an inappropriate arena for combat and achievement. They are consistent losers when school laurels in the form of grades are given out.

The teacher has just handed back a major unit test to her third grade class. She states that she has stars to put on the papers of those who received A's and B's, and she requests that children with the appropiate grade come up to her desk to claim their reward. The line that circles her desk is overwhelmingly female.

Elementary school boys appear to be quite unsuccessful when it comes to winning good grades. Among boys and girls of comparable IQ, girls are more likely to receive higher grades than boys. Also, boys who do equally as well as girls on achievement tests get lower grades in school. In fact, throughout elementary school two-thirds of all grade repeaters are boys.[13] Within this general pattern of low achievement, one subject is singled out for particularly poor performance.

It is ten o'clock. A glance at the daily lesson plan shows that reading is scheduled, and if one steps inside the classroom, (s)he will find the teacher calling upon Johnny to read a selection in the basal reader. Johnny stumbles his way through the passage—his reversals and omissions turning the printed word into a tortured garble. The teacher sighs with impatience and then calls on Loretta who reads the section fluently.

Reading is a subject that seems to be a good deal more difficult for boys than for girls. In a study of one thousand first graders in Maryland, it was found that for every girl with a reading problem, there were about two boys.[14] Other researchers have found that three times more boys than girls have trouble with reading.[15]

There is evidence that shows that this difficulty is not something inherently male, but rather one of the more pernicious examples of incidental learning. John McNeil studied seventy-two kindergarten boys and sixty kindergarten girls who were enrolled in a reading program that consisted of programmed instruction. In this program, the children sat in individual cubicles; they were presented identical segments of reading material at a common pace, and they received the same number of taped comments of encouragement. The boys and girls were given equal opportunity to respond, and the same number of responses were demanded daily from all learners. On a word recognition test administered after the program had been in operation for four months, boys made significantly higher scores than girls did. After completing this program, the children were placed in a regular classroom situation where they received their reading instruction from female teachers. After four months of classroom reading, a similar test was administered. This time the boys did not do as well as the girls.

In an attempt to figure out reasons for the shift in test scores, McNeil asked the children to nominate those in their reading group who received negative comments from the teacher such as "Sit Up!" "Pay attention." The nominations indicated that boys not only received more negative admonitions, but also were given less opportunity to read.[16] Thus it appears that boys may be taught reading in a more punitive manner, and these negative contacts may be associated with difficulties boys have in beginning reading.

A cross-cultural study also makes the point that the young boy's trouble with reading is a socially learned disability. Reading achievement levels of over a thousand students in Germany and over a thousand students in the United States were analyzed. In the United States, mean scores for girls were higher than mean scores for boys. In Germany, however, the opposite was true; boys had the higher scores. It was noted in the study that teachers in Germany are primarily male, and this may have contributed to the boys' superior reading scores.[17] It appears that reading disability in either sex can be attributed to cultural factors. However, one cannot assume that male teachers will necessarily result in higher reading performance by male students. Other studies report no difference in reading gains made by students with teachers of either sex.[18]

In many ways the experience of schooling reinforces the already partially formed sex role stereotypes that boys bring to it. Often the nuclear family environment is a feminine one from which the father departs early in the morning and does not return until evening, possibly even after the youngster has gone to bed. Mother and child spend long unbroken hours in one another's company. Typically, the elementary school classroom is also a "feminine" environment organized and administered by a woman. A difference emerges in the way the young boy is treated in these two environments. At home an independent life style is fostered. In the classroom, where approximately thirty individuals are packed into close quarters, activity and independence are frowned upon. There, docility is the message of the hidden curriculum. Often boys rebel. This rebellion brings increased teacher disapproval, but also increased teacher attention in general. As they refuse to buy this message of docility, as they interact more directly and actively with teachers, their approach to learning becomes increasingly independent and autonomous.

That is a positive result of the boy's conflict with school. There are negative effects, too. School may become so distasteful that he drops out. He may do this literally, but he can also drop out in a less concrete fashion. Although he may remain a firmly entrenched figure in the second seat, fourth row, his thoughts and energy are everywhere but in the classroom. This kind of dropping out can be seen in high male failure rates, in bad grades, and in the expressed hatred of school.

School against girls Educators have not spent as much time worrying about what happens to girls in elementary school. A review of the educational literature does not disclose numerous articles pleading, "Let's Give the Girls a Break" or asking, "Is School Destroying our Daughters?" Until very recently, that is. The women's liberation movement has caused increased awareness and indignation at unequal treatment of females in all institutions of society, and as one of these institutions, attention is focused on the school. Most frequently, discrimination is being examined at the university level. However, girls learn harmful lessons at all rungs of the educational ladder, and the groundwork for future discrimination is established early.

If the young girl has experienced sex typing at home, it is likely she will enter school already somewhat compliant and passive. These characteristics are well in line with the norms of the elementary school; it seems that the young female student should feel very much at home there. In order to see if the sex typing is reinforced, let's visit the classroom again. Let's join Mary-Alice as she experiences her first day at school and the arithmetic lesson that went so unhappily for Tommy.

Amid the noise and confusion of thirty five- and six-year-olds settling into their desks, Mary-Alice was led to her seat. The busy turmoil of the classroom confused her and a hundred different vignettes competed for her attention: mothers waving goodbye, colorful pictures on the bulletin board, a cage with a hamster, bookcases lined with picture books, children whispering together in the corridor. She was puzzled and anxious about her new surroundings, and she waited cautiously at her seat to see what would happen.

After introducing herself to the class, the teacher gave instructions for a lesson in arithmetic. Mary-Alice listened very carefully, and then working slowly and methodically, she took her ruler and divided her paper into three equal compartments. In the first box she drew one lollipop, in the second, two flags, and in the third, three ice cream cones. When the teacher stopped by her desk to check her work she was delighted: "This is the most attractive paper in the class. I'm going to put it on the bulletin board so that everyone can see it." Mary-Alice smiled and silently vowed that tomorrow she would try to make her paper even neater and prettier.

Mary-Alice does indeed feel at home in elementary school—and therein lies the problem. Jerome Bruner summarizes the result of this too comfortable fit:

Observant anthropologists have suggested that the basic values of the early grades are a stylized version of the feminine role in society, cautious rather than daring, governed by a lady-like politeness. . . . Girls in the early grades who learn to control their fidgeting earlier are rewarded for excelling in their feminine values. The reward can be almost too successful in that in later years it is difficult to move girls beyond the orderly virtues they learned in their first school encounters. The boys, more fidgety in the first grades get no such reward, and as a consequence may be freer in their approach to learning in the later grades.[19]

Girls are reinforced for silence, for neatness, for conformity—and in this dispensation of rewards, the process of learning is thwarted. One study, concerned with fifth-grade children, points up the unhappy effects that reward-seeking can have on intellectual curiosity. It shows that when students are anxious to receive good grades and teacher praise, they hide their academic weaknesses from the teacher and avoid situations of intellectual challenge.[20] Thus the young girl, programmed into dependency on rewards, will be more likely to avoid the academically challenging problem wherein lies the possibility of failure and loss of teacher approval but also the potential for greater academic growth and stimulation.

In fact it has been shown that grade school girls are more likely to avoid possible failure than are boys of a corresponding age. One very interesting study was concerned with nursery and elementary school children. Each child was given two seven-piece wooden puzzles and was told that (s)he had one and a half minutes to complete each. The experimenter, however, only pretended to time the children's performances, and in actuality manipulated success and failure. The children were allowed to complete only one of the puzzles. The other was removed after five pieces had been connected, even if the time limit had not been reached. After the children had attempted to complete both puzzles, the experimenter announced that there was a little extra time to work on one of them again. The children were asked to choose the puzzle they wished to work on a second time. For the nursery school group, no significant difference was found between the repetition choices of boys and girls. For the grade school group, however, a telling pattern emerged. Boys more often chose to return to the puzzle they had failed to complete. In contrast, *girls more often repeated the puzzle that they had put together successfully.* They avoided the failure situation.[21]

Owing to the teachers' bestowal and withdrawal of rewards and an environment that stresses docility, the elementary school directly reinforces the passivity that the young female student may bring with her from home. The result is a bizarre distortion of the learning process. Neatness, conformity, docility, these qualities for which the young girl receives good grades and teacher's praise have little to do with active intellectual curiosity, analytical problem solving, and the ability to cope with challenging material. For good grades and teachers' praise, the grade school girl relinquishes the courage that it takes to grapple with difficult material. This naive young bargainer of seven or eight has made an exchange that will cost her dearly.

This passive approach to learning, this avoidance of the challenging situation, this fear of failure are obviously unfortunate, detrimental attitudes. What is even more disturbing is the fact that they can literally be translated into a decline of ability. It has been found that during the formative childhood years some children's IQs increase, some remain constant, and some decline. Eleanor Maccoby depicts the children at age six whose IQs will be likely to increase by the time they reach age ten. They are "competitive, self-assertive, independent, and dominant in interaction with other children. The children who show declining IQs during the next four years are children who are passive, shy, and dependent."[22] These are attitudes that tend to differentiate boys and girls. In effect, a devastating paradoxical theft has been committed. By effectively reinforcing a passive approach to learning, the school runs the risk of decreasing the female student's ability. Ironically, while attempting to increase student potential, the school, in reality, may be likely to limit it.

As was mentioned earlier, boys look around the elementary school and find that the school is staffed by female teachers; the result may be a conflict between their active life style and the school environment. Girls, however, experience their own difficulties with the staffing patterns of the elementary school.

Joanne is in the sixth grade at Barnes Elementary School. She has gone there all her life, and all her teachers have been women. Joanne has seen that sometimes students get fresh and hard to handle, and then the teacher sends these students to the principal's office. She has also noted that whenever the teacher doesn't know the answer to a question about school rules and regulations, the teacher says that she will find out the answer from the principal. All her teachers have taken their orders from the principal and have gone to him when they need help. And the principal is a man. Joanne wonders if, in every profession, women always get directions and orders from men.

It may be that elementary school is a woman's world, but a male captain heads the ship. Furthermore, the trend is toward replacing more and more of these principalships with men. According to a 1928 National Education Association report, 55 percent of elementary school principals were women.[23] In 1966, men out-numbered women in these principalships by a ratio of three to two.[24] In 1971, although women comprised 88 percent of elementary school teachers, they were only 22 percent of elementary school principals.[25]

The woman principal is a vanishing breed, and apparently her extinction is not coming about because men are better at the job. In a 1955 study, which has since been replicated, it was found that female principals were more democratic and were more concerned with the objectives of teaching, with pupil participation, and with the evaluation of learning.[26] This indication of the superiority of the female principal is not necessarily a sign that women are more capable administrators. Rather it points up the far richer female talent pool that is available to begin with. Not only do more women than men go into elementary education, but there is also evidence that women who choose education for a profession are brighter than men who choose this field. In 1968, 268 male and 811 female merit scholarship finalists and semifinalists chose secondary education for a career, and for elementary education, the figures were two men and 146 women.[27] Evidently, when administrative talent is selected, the brightest is not the best.

As one climbs higher on the administrative ladder, there are fewer and fewer women to be found. In 1971, there were only two women among the thirteen thousand district superintendents in the United States.[28] Moreover, as of 1960 more than one-half of all school boards, key centers of decision making, had no women members.[29]

Thus, women swell the base of the educational pyramid, feminizing the elementary school, and men perch along the structure's top, issuing their directives and decisions. The pattern is familiar. It can be seen in the business office where a pool of secretaries, armed with memo pad and typewriter, put into operation the orders of their male commander; it happens on the hospital ward where female nurses, equipped with bedpan and thermometer, carry out the instructions of the male doctor. In education as in other fields, women have their place—and it is not on top.

How does this imbalance in the school staffing pattern affect the elementary school girl? She may be quite unaware of many of the male bosses. School board members and superintendents may be little more than shadowy, undefined figures who shuffle papers and talk incessantly in some unimportant corner of her school world. However, the male boss in the form of the principal does emerge as an important figure. Whenever an issue is too big or troublesome for the teacher (usually female) to handle, the principal (usually male) is called upon to offer the final decision, to administer the ultimate punishment or reward. And children, so alert to body cues, so sensitive to messages transmitted through the silent language, must detect the teacher's change in demeanor, the slight shift in posture that transforms confidence into deference and respect. It would be hard to misinterpret the relationship. The teacher is the boss of the class; the principal is boss of the teacher. And the principal is a man. In the child's mind associations form. When a woman functions professionally, she takes orders from a man, and the image of female inferiority and subservience begins to come across.

Children seldom see a female superintendent, and the woman principal is becoming harder and harder to find. There is another staffing rarity, and this is the opportunity for children to work with a teacher who is noticeably pregnant, for many schools have written policies that require discontinuance of teaching at a specific time during pregnancy, sometimes as early as the third month. Women teachers who have been harmed by such regulations are taking their grievances to court, contending that such policies violate their equal protection rights under the fourteenth amendment.

A Virginia school teacher, Susan Cohen, is the first woman to successfully challenge the constitutionality of regulations concerning mandatory maternity leave. In her federal court suit, the judge noted, "Decision of when a pregnant teacher should discontinue working are matters best left up to the woman and her doctor."[30]

But even as Mrs. Cohen was winning her suit in Virginia, two women teachers in Cleveland lost their case against compulsory maternity leave. The following are comments taken from actual court records. They represent the puritanical views that some board members and educators hold about pregnant women.

> Teachers suffered many indignities as a result of pregnancy, which consisted of children pointing, giggling, laughing, and making snide remarks.

> Although no child was born in the classroom, a few times it was very close.

> Where the possibility of violence and accident exists, pregnancy greatly magnifies the probability of serious injury.

> The kids might think she has a watermelon in her belly.[31]

As increasing numbers of women challenge these attitudes and the regulations in which they are embodied, they are receiving assistance from the National Education Association through the Du Shane Emergency Fund. Lawsuits have now been instituted in situations involving forced maternity leave, loss of salary and retirement benefits, endangered tenure and seniority rights, and inequitable policies relative to reemployment after childbirth.

The dismissal of pregnant teachers also harms children, for pregnancy and birth can be presented and discussed in schools in a highly positive manner. A second-grade teacher brought his wife, who was eight months pregnant, into class to talk to the children. They were fascinated as she told them how the baby was growing inside her and a few, who felt the baby kick when they placed their hands on her stomach, were delighted and amazed. Almost daily after her visit they asked about the progress of mother and baby and with the teacher's help built a chart for the bulletin board on the development of a fetus. Later the teacher brought his wife to class again, this time with their four-month-old daughter, and a whole new learning area was opened— how to take care of a newborn infant.

Compulsory maternity leaves and related policies obviously do a disservice to women teachers. They deprive children as well, teaching them by omission that a pregnant woman is someone to giggle at or be embarrassed about and also denying them involvement in the fascinating process of birth.

Curricular materials as they now exist also harm elementary school children—particularly girls. What do girls learn about themselves from the image of women in school texts?

Sara's fourth-grade class has spent the past month studying the early history of America. The children's history text tells of the colonists' refusal to accept "taxation without representation," the war with England, and the struggle to conceptualize a new form of government. The text is replete with pictures and biographical sketches of George Washington, Ben Franklin, Paul Revere, Sam Adams. Although Sara has examined the text carefully, the only woman she can find mentioned is Betsey Ross. She wonders if there simply weren't any women in the colonies or if women never did anything worth writing about. It seems to her to have been a rather lopsided birth of the nation —having only founding fathers.

. . .

NOTES

1. Frances Bentzen, "Sex Ratios in Learning and Behavior Disorders," *National Elementary Principal*, 46, no. 2 (November 1966), 13–17.
2. Patricia Sexton, "Are Schools Emasculating Our Boys?," *Saturday Review*, 48 (19 June 1965), p. 57.
3. William J. Goldman and Anne May, "Males: A Minority Group in the Classroom," *Journal of Learning Disabilities*, 3, no. 3 (May 1970), 276–278.
4. William McFarland, "Are Girls Really Smarter?," *Elementary School Journal*, 70, no. 10 (1968), 14–19.
5. Michael Palardy, "For Johnny's Reading Sake," *Reading Teacher*, 22, no. 8 (May 1969), 720–724.
6. Le Trippot, "Elementary Education—A Man's World," *Instructor*, 78, no. 3 (November 1968), 50–52.
7. Timothy Weaver, "Humor and Education," *Phi Delta Kappan*, 52, no. 3 (November 1970), 1966–1968.
8. Jerome Kagan, "The Child's Sex Role Classification of School Objects," *Child Development*, 35, no. 4 (December 1964), 1051–1056.
9. William Meyer and George Thompson, "Teacher Interactions with Boys, as Contrasted with Girls," in Raymond Kuhlens and George Thompson, eds., *Psychological Studies of Human Development*, New York, Appleton-Century-Crofts, 1963, pp. 510–518.
10. Phil Jackson and Henriette Lahaderne, "Inequalities of Teacher-Pupil Contacts," in Melvin Silberman, ed., *The Experience of Schooling*, New York, Holt, Rinehart and Winston, 1971, pp. 123–134.
11. Robert Spaulding, "Achievement, Creativity, and Self-Concept Correlates of Teacher-Pupil Transactions in Elementary School," Cooperative Research Project No. 1352, 1963, U.S. Dept of Health, Education and Welfare, Office of Education, Washington, D.C.
12. Pauline Sears and David Feldman, "Teacher Interactions with Boys and Girls," *National Elementary Principal*, 46, no. 2 (November 1966), 30–35.

13. Gary Peltier, "Sex Differences in the School: Problem and Proposed Solution," *Phi Delta Kappan*, *50*, no. 3 (November 1968), 182–185.
14. Bentzen, "Sex Ratios in Learning and Behavior Disorders," *op. cit.*
15. Richard Waite *et al.*, "First-Grade Reading Textbooks," *Elementary School Journal*, *67*, no. 7 (April 1967), 366–374.
16. John McNeil, "Programmed Instruction Versus Visual Classroom Procedures in Teaching Boys to Read," *American Educational Research Journal*, *1*, no. 2 (March 1964), 113–120.
17. Ralph Preston, "Reading Achievement of German and American Children," *School and Society*, *90*, no. 2214 (October 1962), 350–354.
18. Steven Asher and John Gottman, "Sex of Teacher and Student Reading Achievement," paper presented at the American Educational Research Association, April 1972.
19. Jerome Bruner, *Toward a Theory of Instruction*, Cambridge, Mass., Belknap Press of Harvard University, 1966, pp. 123–124.
20. Melvin Silberman, "Classroom Rewards and Intellectual Courage," in Silberman, ed., *The Experience of Schooling, op. cit.*
21. Vaughn Crandall and Alice Rabson, "Children's Repetition Choices in an Intellectual Achievement Situation Following Success and Failure," *Journal of Genetic Psychology*, *97*, (September 1960), 161–168.
22. Eleanor Maccoby, "Woman's Intellect," in Seymour Farber and Roger Wilson, eds., *The Potential of Woman*, New York, McGraw-Hill, 1963, p. 33.
23. Norma Hare, "The Vanishing Woman Principal," *National Elementary Principal*, *45*, no. 5 (April 1966), 12–13.
24. Patricia Sexton, *The Feminized Male*, New York, Random House (Vintage), 1969, pp. 141–143.
25. Material presented by Bernice Sandler for the record to the Committee on the Judiciary, House of Representatives, 92nd cong., Hearings on Equal Rights of Men and Women, 1971.
26. Hare, *op. cit.*
27. Sexton, *The Feminized Male, op. cit.*
28. Sandler, *op. cit.*
29. Sexton, *The Feminized Male, op. cit.*
30. NEA Du Shane Emergency Fund Division, "Discriminating Against the Pregnant Teacher," *Today's Education*, *60*, no. 9 (1971), 33–35.
31. *Ibid.*, p. 33.

edgar z. friedenberg

In the American high school one learns many things: history and English, science and math, and also, according to sociologist Edgar Z. Friedenberg, how to play particular subservient social roles.

Friedenberg is highly critical of the high school whose principal population, the students, are on the verge of entering adulthood and yet are often treated as little children who must be protected and constantly disciplined. While some learn restraint as they play out their prescribed roles and follow regulations more often geared to the teachers' fears than the real needs of adolescents, others chafe at the bit.

Friedenberg's essay on socialization in the modern high school was written a decade ago. What is striking is that, despite changes in dress codes and smoking regulations, very little has actually changed. Indeed, the inclination to turn to peers rather than teachers for guidance and leadership has become more intense in an age when more and more high-school students seek to emulate their older brothers and sisters in challenging established authority. And the authorities in most high schools are far less willing to give in to demands than are those in the universities.

Not far from Los Angeles, though rather nearer to Boston, may be located the town of Milgrim, in which Milgrim High School is clearly the most costly and impressive structure. Milgrim is not a suburb. Although it is only fifty miles from a large and dishonorable city and a part of its conurbation, comparatively few Milgrimites commute to the city for work. Milgrim is an agricultural village which has outgrown its nervous system; its accustomed modes of social integration have not yet even begun to relate its present, recently acquired inhabitants to one another. So, though it is not a suburb, Milgrim is not a community either.

Milgrim's recent, fulminating growth is largely attributable to the rapid development of light industry in the outer suburbs, with a resulting demand for skilled labor. But within the past few years, further economic development has created a steady demand for labor that is not skilled. In an area that is by no means known for its racial tolerance or political liberalism, Milgrim has acquired, through no wish of its own, a sizable Negro and Puerto Rican minority. On the shabby outskirts of town, a number of groceries label themselves Spanish-American. The advanced class in Spanish at Milgrim High School makes a joyful noise—about the only one to be heard.

Estimates of the proportion of the student body at Milgrim who are, in the ethnocentric language of demography, non-white, vary enormously. Some students who are clearly middle-class and of pinkish-gray color sometimes speak as if they themselves were a besieged minority. More responsible staff members produce estimates of from 12 to 30 per cent. Observations in the corridors and lunchrooms favor the lower figure. They also establish clearly that the non-whites are orderly and well behaved, though somewhat more forceful in their movements and manner of speech than their light-skinned colleagues.

What is Milgrim High like? It is a big, expensive building, on spacious but barren grounds. Every door is at the end of a corridor; there is no reception area, no public space in which one can adjust to the transition from the outside world. Between class periods the corridors are tumultuously crowded; during them they are empty. But at both times they are guarded by teachers and students on patrol duty. Patrol duty does not consist primarily in the policing of congested throngs of moving students, or the guarding of property from damage. Its principal function is the checking of corridor passes. Between classes, no student may walk down the corridor without a form, signed by a teacher, telling where he is coming from, where he is going, and the time, to the minute, during which the pass is valid. A student caught in the corridor without such a pass is sent or taken to the office; there a detention slip is made out against him, and he is required to remain after school for two or three hours. He may do his homework during this time, but he may not leave his seat or talk.

There is no physical freedom whatever at Milgrim. Except during class breaks, the lavatories are kept locked, so that a student must not only obtain a pass but find the custodian and induce him to open the facility. Indeed Milgrim High's most memorable arrangements are its corridor passes and its johns; they dominate social interaction. "Good morning, Mr. Smith," an attractive girl will say pleasantly to one of her teachers in the corridor. "Linda, do you have a pass to be in your locker after the bell rings?" is his greeting in reply. There are more classifications of washrooms than there must have been in the Confederate Navy. The common sort, marked just "Boys" and "Girls," are generally locked. Then there are some marked, "Teachers, Men" and "Teachers, Women," unlocked. Near the auditorium are two others marked simply, "Men" and "Women," which are intended primarily for the public when the auditorium is being used for some function. During the school day cardboard signs saying "Adults Only" are placed on these doors. Girding up my maturity, I used this men's room during my stay at Milgrim. Usually it was empty; but once, as soon as the door clicked behind me, a teacher who had been concealed in the cubicle began jumping up and down to peer over his partition and verify my adulthood.

He was not a voyeur; he was checking on smoking. At most public high schools, students are forbidden to smoke, and this is probably the most common source of friction with authorities. It focuses, naturally, on the washrooms which are the only place students can go where teachers are not supposed to be. Milgrim, for a time, was more liberal than most; last year its administration designated an area behind the school where seniors might smoke during their lunch period. But, as a number of students explained to me during interviews, some of these seniors had "abused the privilege" by lighting up before they got into the area, and the privilege had been withdrawn. No student, however, questioned that smoking was a privilege rather than a right.

The concept of privilege is important at Milgrim. Teachers go to the head of the chow line at lunch; whenever I would attempt quietly to stand in line the teacher on hall duty would remonstrate with me. He was right, probably; I was fouling up an entire informal social system by my ostentation. Students on hall patrol also were allowed to come to the head of the line; so were seniors. Much of the behavior that Milgrim depends on to keep it going is motivated by the reward of getting a government-surplus peanut butter or tuna fish sandwich without standing in line.

The lunchroom itself is a major learning experience, which must make quite an impression over four years time. There are two large cafeterias which are used as study halls during the periods before and after the middle of the day. The food, by and large, is good, and more tempting than the menu. The atmosphere is not quite that of a prison, because the students are permitted to talk quietly, under the frowning scrutiny of teachers standing around on duty, during their meal—they are not supposed to talk while standing in line, though this rule is only sporadically enforced. Standing in line takes about a third of their lunch period, and leaves plenty of time for them to eat what is provided them. They may not, in any case, leave the room when they have finished, any more than they could leave a class. Toward the end of the period a steel gate is swung down across the corridor, dividing the wing holding the cafeterias, guidance offices, administrative offices, and auditorium from the rest of the building. Then the first buzzer sounds, and the students sweep out of the cafeteria and press silently forward to the gate. A few minutes later a second buzzer sounds, the gate is opened, and the students file out to their classrooms.

During the meal itself the atmosphere varies in response to chance events and the personality of the teachers assigned supervisory duty; this is especially true in the corridor where the next sitting is waiting in line. The norm is a not unpleasant chatter; but about one teacher in four is an embittered martinet, snarling, whining, continually ordering the students to stand closer to the wall and threatening them with detention or suspension for real or fancied insolence. On other occasions, verbal altercations break out between students in the cafeteria or in line and the *student* hall patrolmen. In one of these that I witnessed, the accused student, a handsome, aggressive-looking young man, defended himself in the informal but explicit language of working-class hostility. This roused the teacher on duty from his former passivity. He walked over toward the boy, and silently but with a glare of contempt, beckoned him from the room with a crooked finger and led him along the corridor to the administrative office: the tall boy rigid in silent protest, the teacher, balding and stoop-shouldered in a wrinkled suit, shambling ahead of him. The youth, I later learned, was suspended for a day. At some lunch periods all this is drowned out by Mantovani-type pop records played over the public address system.

What adults generally, I think, fail to grasp even though they may actually know it, is that there is no refuge or respite from this: no coffee-break, no taking ten for a smoke, no room like the teachers' room, however poor, where the youngsters can get away from adults. High schools don't have club rooms; they have organized gym and recreation. A student cannot go to the library when he wants a book; on certain days his schedule provides a forty-five-minute library period. "Don't let anybody leave early," a guidance counselor urged during a group-testing session at Hartsburgh, an apparently more permissive school that I also visited. "There really isn't any place for them to go." Most of us are as nervous by the age of five as we will ever be, and adolescence adds to the strain; but one thing a high-school student learns is that he can expect no provision for his need to give in to his feelings, or swing out in his own style, or creep off and pull himself together.

The little things shock most. High-school students—and not just, or even particularly, at Milgrim—have a prisoner's sense of time. They don't know what time it is outside. The research which occasioned my presence at Milgrim, Hartsburgh, and the other schools in my study required me to interview each of twenty-five to thirty students at each school three times. My first appointment with each student was set up by his guidance counselor; I would make the next appointment directly with the student and issue him the passes he needed to keep it. The student has no *open* time at his own disposal; he has to select the period he can miss with least loss to himself. Students well-adapted to the school usually pick study halls; poorer or more troublesome students pick the times of their most disagreeable classes; both avoid cutting classes in which the teacher is likely to respond vindictively to their absence. Most students, when asked when they would like to come for their next interview, replied, "I can come any time." When I pointed out to them that there must, after all, be some times that would be more convenient for them than others, they would say, "Well tomorrow, fourth period" or whatever. But hardly any of them knew when this would be in clock time. High-school classes emphasize the importance of punctuality by beginning at regular but uneven times like 10:43 and 11:27, which are, indeed, hard to remember; and the students did not know when this was.

How typical is all this? The elements of the composition—the passes, the tight scheduling, the reliance on threats of detention or suspension as modes of social control are nearly universal. The usurpation of any possible *area* of student initiative, physical or mental, is about as universal. Milgrim forbids boys to wear trousers that end more than six inches above the floor, and has personnel fully capable of measuring them. But most high schools have some kind of dress regulation; I know of none that accepts and relies on the tastes of students.

There are differences, to be sure, in tone; and these matter. They greatly affect the impact of the place on students. Take, for comparison and contrast, Hartsburgh High. Not fifteen miles from Milgrim, Hartsburgh is an utterly different community. It is larger, more compact, and more suburban; more of a place. Hartsburgh High is much more dominantly middle class and there are few Negroes in the high school there.

First impressions of Hartsburgh High are almost bound to be favorable. The building, like Milgrim, is new; unlike Milgrim's, it is handsome. External walls are mostly glass, which gives a feeling of light, air, and space. At Hartsburgh there is none of the snarling, overt hostility that taints the atmosphere at Milgrim. There are no raucous buzzers; no bells of any kind. Instead, there are little blinker lights arranged like the Mexican flag. The green light blinks and the period is over; the white light signals a warning; when the red light blinks it is time to be in your classroom. Dress regulations exist but are less rigorous than at Milgrim. Every Wednesday, however, is dress-up day; boys are expected to wear ties and jackets or jacket-sweaters, the girls wear dresses rather than skirts and sweaters. The reason is that on Wednesday the school day ends with an extra hour of required assembly and, as the students explain, there are often outside visitors for whom they are expected to look their best.

Students at Hartsburgh seem much more relaxed than at Milgrim. In the grounds outside the main entrance, during lunch period, there is occasional horseplay. For ten minutes during one noon hour I watched three boys enacting a mutual fantasy. One was the audience who only sat and laughed, one the aggressor, and the third—a pleasant, inarticulate varsity basketball player named Paul—was the self-appointed victim. The two protagonists were portraying in pantomime old, silent-movie type fights in slow motion. The boy I did not know would slowly swing at Paul, who would sink twisting to the ground with grimaces of anguish; then the whole sequence would be repeated with variations, though the two boys never switched roles. In my interviews with Paul I had never solved the problem arising from the fact that he was eloquent only with his arms and torso movements, which were lost on the tape recorder, and it was a real pleasure to watch him in his own medium. This was a pleasure Milgrim would never have afforded me. Similarly, in the corridors at Hartsburgh I would occasionally come upon couples holding hands or occasionally rather more, though it distressed me that they always broke guiltily apart as soon as they saw me or any adult. One of my subjects, who was waiting for his interview, was dancing a little jig by himself in the corridor when I got to him. This was all rather reassuring.

It was also contrary to policy. There is a regulation against couples holding hands and they are punished if caught by the kind of teacher who hates sexuality in the young. The air and space also, subtly, turn out to be illusions if you try to use them. Hartsburgh High is built around a large, landscaped courtyard with little walks and benches. I made the mistake of trying to conduct an interview on one of these benches. When it was over we could not get back into the building except by disturbing a class, for the doors onto this inviting oasis can only be opened from inside, and nobody ever goes there. Since the courtyard is completely enclosed by the high-school building, this arrangement affords no additional protection from intruders; it merely shuts off a possible place for relaxation. The beautiful glass windows do not open enough to permit a body to squirm through and, consequently, do not open enough to ventilate the rooms, in which there are no individual controls for the fiercely effective radiators. Room temperature at Hartsburgh is a matter of high policy.

Teachers do not hide in the washrooms at Hartsburgh; but the principal recently issued a letter warning that any student caught in the vicinity of the school with "tobacco products" would be subject to suspension; students were directed to have their parents sign the letter as written acknowledgment that they were aware of the regulation and return it to the school. Staff, of course, are permitted to smoke. At Hartsburgh a former teacher, promoted to assistant principal serves as a full-time disciplinarian, but students are not dragged to his office by infuriated teachers, as sometimes happens at Milgrim. Instead, during the first period, two students from the school Citizenship Corps go quietly from classroom to classroom with a list, handing out summonses.

Along with having a less rancorous and choleric atmosphere than Milgrim, Hartsburgh seems to have more teachers who like teaching and like kids. But the fundamental pattern is still one of control, distrust, and punishment. The observable differences—and they are striking—are the results almost entirely, I believe, of *structural* and demographic factors and occur despite very similar administrative purposes. Neither principal respects adolescents at all or his staff very much. Both are preoccupied with good public relations as they understand them. Both are inflexible, highly authoritarian men. But their situations are different.

At Milgrim there is a strong district superintendent; imaginative if not particularly humane, he is oriented toward the national educational scene. He likes to have projects, particularly in research guidance. Guidance officers report through their chairman directly to him, not to the building principal; and the guidance staff is competent, tough, and completely professional. When wrangles occur over the welfare of a student they are likely to be open, with the principal and the guidance director as antagonists; both avoid such encounters if possible, and neither can count on the support of the district office; but when an outside force—like an outraged parent—precipitates a conflict, it is fought out. At Hartsburgh, the district superintendent is primarily interested in running a tight ship with no problems. To this end, he backs the authority of the principal whenever this might be challenged. The guidance office is vestigal and concerned primarily with college placement and public relations in the sense of inducing students to behave in socially acceptable ways with a minimum of fuss.

In these quite different contexts, demographic differences in the student bodies have crucial consequences. At Milgrim, the working-class students are not dominant—they have not quite enough self-confidence or nearly enough social savvy to be—but they are close enough to it to be a real threat to the nice, college-bound youngsters who set the tone in their elementary and junior high school and who expect to go on dominating the high school. These view the rapid influx of lower-status students as a rising wave that can engulf them, while the newcomers, many of whom are recent migrants or high-school transfers from the city, can remember schools in which they felt more at home.

The result is both to split and to polarize student feeling about the school, its administration, and other students. Nobody likes Milgrim High. But the middle-class students feel that what has ruined it is the lower-class students, and that the punitive constraint with which the school is run is necessary to keep them in line. In some cases these students approach paranoia: one girl—commenting on a mythical high school described in one of our semi-projective research instruments—said, "Well, it says here that the majority of the students are Negro—about a third" (the actual statement is "about a fifth").

The working-class students are hard-pressed; but being hard-pressed they are often fairly realistic about their position. If the Citizenship Corps that functions so smoothly and smugly at Hartsburgh were to be installed at Milgrim, those who actually turned people in and got them in trouble would pretty certainly receive some after-school instruction in the way social classes differ in values and in the propensity for non-verbal self-expression. At Milgrim, the working-class kids know where they stand and stand there. They are exceptionally easy to interview because the interviewer need not be compulsively non-directive. Once they sense that they are respected, they respond enthusiastically and with great courtesy. But they do not alter their position to give the interviewer what they think he wants, or become notably anxious at disagreeing with him. They are very concrete in handling experience and are not given to generalization. Most of them seem to have liked their elementary school, and they share the general American respect for education down to the last cliché—but then one will add, as an afterthought, not bothering even to be contemptuous, "Of course, you can't respect *this* school." They deal with their situation there in correspondingly concrete terms. Both schools had student courts last year, for example, and Hartsburgh still does, though few students not in the Citizenship Corps pay much attention to it. Student traffic corpsmen give much attention to it. Student traffic corpsmen give out tickets for corridor offenses, and these culprits are brought before an elected student judge with an administrative official of the school present as adviser. But Milgrim had a student court last year that quickly became notorious. The "hoody element" got control of it, and since most of the defendants were their buddies, they were either acquitted or discharged on pleas of insanity. The court was disbanded.

The struggle at Milgrim is therefore pretty open, though none of the protagonists see it as a struggle for freedom or could define its issues in terms of principles. The upper-status students merely assent to the way the school is run, much as middle-class white Southerners assent to what the sheriff's office does, while the lower-status students move, or get pushed, from one embroilment to the next without ever quite realizing that what is happening to them is part of a general social pattern. At Hartsburgh the few lower-status students can easily be ignored rather than feared by their middle-class compeers who set the tone. They are not sufficiently numerous or aggressive to threaten the middle-class youngsters or their folkways; but, for the same reason, they do not force the middle-class youngsters to make common cause with the administration. The administration, like forces of law and order generally in the United States, is accepted without deference as a part of the way things are and work. Americans rarely expect authority to be either intelligent or forthright; it looks out for its own interests as best it can. Reformers and troublemakers only make it nervous and therefore worse; the best thing is to take advantage of it when it can help you and at other times to go on living your own life and let it try to stop you.

This is what the Hartsburgh students usually do, and, on the whole, the results are pleasant. The youngsters, being to some degree ivy, do not constantly remind the teachers, as the Milgrim students do, that their jobs have no connection with academic scholarship. Many of the teachers, for their part, act and sound like college instructors, do as competent a job, and enjoy some of the same satisfactions. The whole operation moves smoothly. Both Milgrim and Hartsburgh are valid examples— though of very different aspects—of American democracy in action. And in neither could a student learn as much about civil liberty as a Missouri mule knows at birth.

What is learned in high school, or for that matter anywhere at all, depends far less on what is taught than on what one actually experiences in the place. The quality of instruction in high school varies from sheer rot to imaginative and highly skilled teaching. But classroom content is often handled at a creditable level and is not in itself the source of the major difficulty. Both at Milgrim and Hartsburgh, for example, the students felt that they were receiving competent instruction and that this was an undertaking the school tried seriously to handle. I doubt, however, that this makes up for much of the damage to which high-school students are systematically subjected. What is formally taught is just not that important, compared to the constraint and petty humiliation to which the youngsters with few exceptions must submit in order to survive.

The fact that some of the instruction is excellent and a lot of it pretty good *is* important for another reason; it makes the whole process of compulsory schooling less insulting than it otherwise would be by lending it a superficial validity. Society tells the adolescent that he is sent to school in order to learn what he is taught in the classroom. No anthropologist and very few high-school students would accept this as more than a rationalization; but rationalizations, to be at all effective, must be fairly plausible. Just as the draft would be intolerable if the cold war were wholly a piece of power politics or merely an effort to sustain the economy, so compulsory school attendance would be intolerable if what went on in the classrooms were totally inadequate to students' needs and irrelevant to their real intellectual concerns. Much of it is, but enough is not, to provide middle-class students, at least, with an answer when their heart cries out "For Christ's sake, what am I doing here?"

But far more of what is deeply and thoroughly learned in the school is designed to keep the heart from raising awkward, heartfelt issues—if design governs in a thing so subtle. It is learned so thoroughly by attendance at schools like Milgrim or even Hartsburgh that most Americans by the time they are adult cannot really imagine that life could be organized in any other way.

First of all, they learn to assume that the state has the right to compel adolescents to spend six or seven hours a day, five days a week, thirty-six or so weeks a year, in a specific place, in charge of a particular group of persons in whose selection they have no voice, performing tasks about which they have no choice, without remuneration and subject to specialized regulations and sanctions that are applicable to no one else in the community nor to them except in this place. Whether this law is a service or a burden to the young—and, indeed, it is both, in varying degrees—is another issue altogether. As I have noted elsewhere,* compulsory school attendance functions as a bill of attainder against a particular age group. The student's position is that of a conscript, who is protected by certain regulations but in no case permitted to use their breach as a cause for terminating his obligation. So the first thing the young learn in school is that there are certain sanctions and restrictions that apply only to them; that they do not participate fully in the freedoms guaranteed by the state, and that *therefore, these freedoms do not really partake of the character of inalienable rights.*

Of course not. The school, as schools continually stress, acts *in loco parentis;* and children may not leave home because their parents are unsatisfactory. What I have pointed out is no more than a special consequence of the fact that students are minors, and minors do not, indeed, share all the rights and privileges—and responsibilities—of citizenship. Very well. However one puts it, we are still discussing the same issue. The high school, then, is where you really learn what it means to be a minor.

For a high school is not a parent. Parents may love their children, hate them, or like most parents, do both in a complex mixture. But they must nevertheless permit a certain intimacy and respond to their children as persons. Homes are not run by regulations, though the parents may think they are, but by a process of continuous and almost entirely unconscious emotional homeostasis, in which each member affects and accommodates to the needs, feelings, fantasy life, and character structure of the others. This may be, and often is, a terribly destructive process; I intend no defense of the family as a social institution. But children grow up in homes or the remnants of homes; are in physical fact dependent on parents, and too intimately related to them to permit their area of freedom to be precisely defined. This is not because they have no rights or are entitled to less respect than adults, but because intimacy conditions freedom and growth in ways too subtle and continuous to be defined as overt acts.

Free societies depend on their members to learn early and thoroughly

* See "An Ideology of School Withdrawal," *Commentary,* June 1963.

that public authority is not like that of the family; that it cannot be expected—or trusted—to respond with sensitivity and intimate perception to the needs of individuals but must rely basically, though as humanely as possible, on the impartial application of general formulae. This means that it must be kept functional, specialized, and limited to matters of public policy; the meshes of the law are too coarse to be worn to the skin. Especially in an open society, where people of very different backgrounds and value systems must function together, it would seem obvious that each must understand that he may not push others further than their common undertaking demands, or impose upon them a manner of life that they feel to be alien.

After the family, the school is the first social institution an individual must deal with—the first place in which he learns to handle himself with strangers. The school establishes the pattern of his subsequent assumptions as to what relations between the individual and society are appropriate and which constitute invasions of privacy and constraints on his spirit—what the British, with exquisite precision, call "taking a liberty." But the American public school evolved as a melting pot, under the assumption that it had not merely the right but the duty to impose a common standard of genteel decency on a polyglot body of immigrants' children and thus insure their assimilation into the better life of the American dream. It accepted, also, the tacit assumption that genteel decency was as far as it could go. If America has generally been governed by the practical man's impatience with other individuals' rights, it has also accepted the practical man's determination to preserve his property by discouraging public extravagance. With its neglect of personal privacy and individual autonomy the school incorporates a considerable measure of Galbraith's "public squalor." The plant may be expensive—for this is capital goods; but little is provided graciously, liberally, simply as an amenity, either to teachers or students, though administrative offices have begun to assume an executive look.

The first thing the student learns, then, is that as a minor, he is subject to peculiar restraints; the second is that these restraints are general, not limited either by custom or by the schools' presumed commitment to the curriculum. High-school administrators are not professional educators in the sense that a physician, an attorney, or a tax accountant are professionals. They do not, that is, think of themselves as practitioners of a specialized instructional craft, who derive their authority from its requirements. They are specialists in keeping an essentially political enterprise from being strangled by conflicting community attitudes and pressures. They are problem-oriented, and the feelings and needs for growth of their captive and unenfranchised clientele are the least of their problems; for the status of the "teen-ager" in the community is so low that even if he rebels, the school is not blamed for the conditions against which he is rebelling. He is simply a truant or a juvenile delinquent; at worst the school has "failed to reach him." What high-school personnel become specialists in, ultimately, is the *control* of large groups of students even at catastrophic expense to their opportunity to learn. These controls are not exercised primarily to facilitate instruction, and particularly, they are in no way limited to matters bearing on instruction. At several schools in our sample boys had been ordered—sometimes on the complaint of teachers—to shave off beards. One of these boys had played football for the school; he was told that, although the school had no legal authority to require him to shave, he would be barred from the banquet honoring the team unless he complied. Dress regulations are another case in point.

Of course these are petty restrictions, enforced by petty penalties. American high schools are not concentration camps. But I am not complaining about their severity; what disturbs me is what they teach their students concerning the proper relationship of the individual to society, and in this respect the fact that the restrictions and penalties are unimportant in themselves makes matters worse. Gross invasions are more easily recognized for what they are; petty restrictions are only resisted by "troublemakers." What matters in the end is that the school does not take its own business of education seriously enough to mind it.

The effects on the students are manifold. The concepts of dignity and privacy, notably deficient in American adult folkways, are not permitted to develop here. The school's assumption of custodial control of students implies that power and authority are indistinguishable. If the school's authority is not limited to matters pertaining to education, it cannot be derived from its educational responsibilities. It is a naked, empirical fact, to be accepted or controverted according to the possibilities of the moment. In such a world, power counts more than legitimacy; if you don't have power, it is naïve to think you have rights that must be respected . . . wise up. High-school students experience regulation only as control, not as protection; they know, for example, that the principal will generally uphold the teacher in any conflict with a student, regardless of the merits of the case. Translated into the high-school idiom, *suaviter in modo, fortiter in re* becomes "If you get caught, it's just your ass."

Students do not often resent this; that is the tragedy. All weakness tends to corrupt, and impotence corrupts absolutely. Identifying, as the weak must, with the more powerful and frustrating of the forces that impinge upon them, they accept the school as the way life is and close their minds against the anxiety of perceiving alternatives. Many students like high school; others loathe and fear it. But even the latter do not object to it on principle; the school effectively obstructs their learning of the principles on which objection might be based; though these are among the principles that, we boast, distinguish us from totalitarian societies.

Yet, finally, the consequence of continuing through adolescence to submit to diffuse authority that is not derived from the task at hand—as a doctor's orders or the training regulations of an athletic coach, for example, usually are—is more serious than political incompetence or weakness of character. There is a general arrest of development. An essential part of growing up is learning that, though differences of power among men lead to brutal consequences, all men are peers; none is omnipotent, none derives his potency from magic, but only from his specific competence and function. The policeman represents the majesty of the state, but this does not mean that he can put you in jail; it means, precisely, that he cannot—at least not for long. Any person or agency responsible for handling throngs of young people—especially if he does not like them or is afraid of them—is tempted to claim diffuse authority and snare the youngster in the trailing remnants of childhood emotion which always remain to trip him. Schools succumb to this temptation, and control pupils by reinvoking the sensations of childhood punishment, which remain effective because they were originally selected, with great unconscious guile, to dramatize the child's weakness in the face of authority. "If you act like a bunch of spoiled brats, we'll treat you like a bunch of spoiled brats," is a favorite dictum of sergeants, and school personnel, when their charges begin to show an awkward capacity for independence.

Thus the high school is permitted to infantilize adolescence; in fact, it is encouraged to by the widespread hostility to "teen-agers" and the anxiety about their conduct found throughout our society. It does not allow much maturation to occur during the years when most maturation would naturally occur. Maturity, to be sure, is not conspicuously characteristic of American adult life, and would almost certainly be a threat to the economy. So perhaps in this, as in much else, the high school is simply the faithful servant of the community.

There are two important ways in which it can render such service. The first of these is through its impact on individuals: on their values, their conception of their personal worth, their patterns of anxiety, and on their mastery and ease in the world—which determine so much of what they think of as their fate. The second function of the school is Darwinian; its biases, though their impact is always on individual youngsters, operate systematically to mold entire social groups. These biases endorse and support the values and patterns of behavior of certain segments of the population, providing their members with the credentials and shibboleths needed for the next stages of their journey, while they instill in others a sense of inferiority and warn the rest of society against them as troublesome and untrustworthy. In this way the school contributes simultaneously to social mobility and to social stratification. It helps see to it that the kind of people who get ahead are the kind who will support the social system it represents, while those who might, through intent or merely by their being, subvert it, are left behind as a salutary moral lesson.

lewis h. lapham

Socialization takes place in many settings: the home, the neighborhood, the school, the church—and, for some, in the army. Through directives of parents and peers, teachers and preachers, one learns the roles appropriate to certain social circumstances and, to a marked degree, internalizes them. In a real sense, one defines oneself in terms of others' expectations.

Nowhere is socialization more thorough than in the religious cloister or the officer corps of a military organization. In both cases one lives in a separate social world in which special relationships are encouraged and an intense loyalty is demanded.

Here journalist Lewis H. Lapham describes the senior reaches of army life as he observed it. His interviews offer an interesting portrait of the officer corps—"a man who has been an officer for some years can go anywhere in the world and find the same routine, the same attitudes. . . ." He also shows how far removed the generals are from the country they serve, even as they are the most loyal of all patriots.

The following observations on the United States Army should be read in the spirit of a travel essay, as if, for the past several months, I had been wandering in a distant country. A country with certain likenesses to my own, and yet in many ways foreign.

Setting forth to write about the ethos of the officer class, I arrived at the main gates of Army posts with doubtful credentials. My own country is urban and secular, the eclectic milieu of a man who has lived for ten years in New York City and who has attended, however unwillingly, to the noisy dramatics of new fashion. (I think of a vast and cheerless stage, loud with the cries of clever people shifting the political and cultural scenery.) I was the wrong age for the nation's recent wars, and as a journalist I am sometimes a maker of heresies.

All of which inclined most officers to grave and not unfounded suspicion. The Army is a rural society pervaded by a feeling of small-town neighborliness and governed by the regulations of small-town morality. The residential quarters of the larger posts invariably reminded me of a town painted by Norman Rockwell: the great, good American place protected by a white picket fence from the barbarian hordes gathered on the frontiers. I remember shade trees and station wagons, Little League football games and afternoon tea.

The Army also resembles the medieval church, preserving what every good officer believes to be "the true American virtues" in the midst of a decadent temporal society riven by disillusion and despair. Once having accepted the tenets of the military theology, a man inherits a knowledge of good and evil. He knows precisely where he stands in the annual order of merit, and he can be reasonably sure that his worthiness will be rewarded by promotions or medals and that his transgressions will be punished by loss of command or exile to a supply depot on Guam.

For the most part I found myself in the company of men whom I liked. Although often I couldn't agree with their prejudices or enthusiasms (most notably, in the customary phrase, for "knocking off Cong"), I admired them as men of their word, and I envied them the unquestioning fervor of their belief. The education of an Army officer does not admit of doubt, and theirs is not an existential habit of mind. They are expected to ask and answer questions 1 through 7; questions 8 through 10 they ignore. (The kind of man who insists on the later questions retires as a major.) Their innocence reminded me of the simplicities of my youth, and sometimes I found myself wishing I were back on the team, assuring the coach that I could play the last fifteen minutes with a broken hand.

I also felt that their lives had been more various and dramatic than the lives of the people I knew in New York (during the course of twenty years an officer might serve as a soldier, a bureaucrat, a politician, and a teacher); they seemed less preoccupied with themselves, and as I listened to them talk of past wars and present policy, the affairs of my literary acquaintances seemed to recede toward the backwaters of idle gossip. Gradually I understood that most writers are practical men posing as romantics, and that most Army officers are romantics posing as what they are pleased to call "realists." "Hard-nosed" and "realistic" are two much-admired adjectives in the Army, but often the men whom they supposedly describe are dreamers accustomed to gazing upon secret maps and believing that the nations of the world can be played with like so many children's blocks.

I made no attempt to talk to enlisted men, and I didn't travel to the desolate places of the Army. More often than not I was looking at a fine view of a parade ground or the Potomac River, drinking sherry with a general and remarking pleasantly on the collapse of the American moral structure. The distance was always long enough for me to briefly imagine that the soldiers enjoyed their marching, and that everything worked the way it said in the book.

Two Generals

The two generals who will figure most prominently in these notes are both headmasters of important Army schools; both are ambitious men, and either of them conceivably could become, within a matter of a few years, Chief of Staff. I came to know each of them quite well, and although possessed of very different qualities, they seemed to contain between them most of the attitudes that I encountered among their colleagues elsewhere in the Army.

Brigadier General Ira Augustus Hunt, forty-six years old, West Point 1945, presently the assistant commandant of the Engineer School at Fort Belvoir, Virginia.

Hunt appealed to me as a man of extraordinary charm. He could give way to elusive and paradoxical enthusiasms, and his sudden moods were reflected in his haunted face, like clouds moving across quiet water. His mind didn't work by the numbers, and the transitions in his thought could be very abrupt. Within the space of a sentence he could shift from fond recollections of a Vermeer painting or an Italian landscape to equally fond recollection of "pounding the shit out of the little VC bastards" in Vietnam. Also he had a habit of delivering conspiratorial asides, as if he were an actor confiding to the audience at a play.

Once, while talking about his years building roads in Korea, he remembered how he'd been walking across the headquarters compound on a clear, blue day, congratulating himself on his good fortune; suddenly he was hit in the face by an overthrown softball that broke his nose. Having recalled the incident, he paused and stared out the window. In an abstracted voice, he said, "I always like those little things that get your attention."

He divided his life into periods in exactly the way a painter might mark the evolution of a style. He graduated from West Point too late to take part in World War II; the next five years with occupation troops in Germany and Italy he described as "a time for soldiers." During the

1950s he spent most of his time at school, either teaching mechanics (at West Point and Annapolis) or studying for advanced degrees (at MIT and the French engineering school at Grenoble). He traveled widely during his years in Europe, and he could remember eating wild boar at a country inn in Provence, or a sunset beyond the Pont-du-Gard at Nîmes, or the texture of the winter light along the canals at Delft.

The 1960s Hunt defined as "administrative." He worked for Defense Secretary Robert McNamara and for the Chief of Army Engineers in Washington, drawing up the earliest plans for travel to the moon. In 1968 he was given the opportunity of commanding an infantry brigade in Vietnam. Combat command is a rare thing among engineering officers, and Hunt welcomed it with his habitual zeal.

"I'd missed two goddamn wars," he said, "and this one I was going to get into for all it was worth."

He commanded the brigade for three months and acquired a reputation for fierce heroics. The division newspaper likened his performance to that of a lineman who knew he would never again get hold of a live football. Hunt liked to talk about the war, and he always did so with great animation, waving his arms and banging his hand on a table. He applied the formulas of systems analysis to the business of killing, and each of the companies under his command had a daily quota of dead Cong.

Often he would bring out maps and souvenirs. Some of the maps had been captured from the VC and showed the movements of a battle in which Hunt had directed the attack from the other side. Pointing to the lines drawn with blue and red crayon on cheap rice paper, he said, "We had a hell of a good body count that day."

On another afternoon he let me read a report that he'd written about the same engagement. The fighting continued into the small hours of morning, and Hunt had been moved by the dramatic effects.

"Although the guns were spewing destruction," he wrote, "the patterns of the varied tracers reminded me of colored lacework."

Brigadier General James V. Galloway, fifty-one years old, ROTC at Ohio University in 1940, the assistant commandant of the Armor School at Fort Knox, Kentucky.*

Whereas Hunt could succumb to the emotional response of an aesthete, Galloway had the cautious instincts of a country politician. He is a large and conventionally handsome man, with an easy sense of humor and a memory for people's names. The friendly slowness of his speech concealed a shrewd intelligence, and I could imagine him also as a successful banker, content to meet with the other regular guys in town and think of ways to merchandize ths American Dream.

---

* Since this article was written, Galloway has been promoted to Major General and now commands the First Armored Division in southern Germany.

Although he had served as a junior aide to General George S. Patton in the North African and Sicilian campaigns, Galloway seldom discussed the war, and I suspected that he had disapproved of Patton. He is not a man who is fond of fighting; neither is he a man who has much patience for flamboyant violations of the rules. He takes pleasure in the formalities of the Army, and I suspect that he would prefer to settle all disputes in a back room with a bottle of bourbon and a cigar.

Throughout most of World War II, Galloway was associated with a headquarters of some kind or other, rising in rank from lieutenant to major and learning to accommodate himself to the whims of senior officers. Each of his superiors he remembered as "a fine old gentleman." He once showed me the letters he'd received on his promotion to general, and it was characteristic of him that he'd arranged the letters in order of rank, Westmoreland's on top, and so forth through the hierarchy.

Whenever I talked with men who had known Galloway, they never failed to mention his wife Eve. She is a vivacious and pretty woman, the daughter of an Army officer and an heir to the genteel traditions of the old Army between the world wars; like her husband she is politically astute, and I recognized her as a woman who would always know the appropriate thing to say.

On two occasions Galloway and I played golf together, and on several evenings we sat up drinking and talking in the large neo-Georgian house allotted to him as a prerogative of rank. It resembles a house in a pleasant suburb, comfortably furnished with the possessions acquired over twenty years of traveling between Army posts in Germany, the United States, and Southeast Asia. Similar but slightly smaller houses (those assigned to colonels) stand on either side of it, all of them protected by shade trees and with lawns cluttered by children's bicycles.

Galloway obviously dotes on his own four children, and most of the time as he sat in a favorite chair with his pipe I could think of him as the kindly paterfamilias. And yet he could be suddenly and unconsciously demonic. Talking one night about Vietnam he said that the remarkable thing about the war was that the Army hadn't taken matters into its own hands; instead the Pentagon had "swallowed its pride" and meekly accepted the bungling weakness of civilian indecision. He had long since advocated the bombing of the dams above Hanoi and Haiphong, a solution he still thought satisfactory. The ensuing flood, he said, would "erase" both cities. When I asked him how many people would drown, he irritably waved his hand.

"A million . . . a million and a half."

Autumn Evening at Fort Knox

There were twelve of us for dinner at the Galloways', and I had the feeling of being introduced into a safe and orderly community in which all things could be conveniently explained. The men were senior officers who shared not only an identical image of the world but also an almost identical experience of it (they had served together at other times and places, and they could remember the same view of the Rhine or the same line of trees on a Korean hillside); their wives had long since fitted themselves into the forms of Army life, and I was struck by the graciousness of their manners. "Iron butterflies," Eva Galloway once called them, to whom promotions translated into larger houses, additional servants, and more interesting invitations.

Before dinner, a colonel named Kimball took me aside to make sure that my opinions were sound. He knew that I'd come to Fort Knox to write about General Galloway, and he didn't want the general to expose himself to unnecessary risks. (Like most officers, the colonel preferred to think of the Eastern press establishment as a conspiracy of assassins.) We stood near the fireplace, decorously holding our drinks with paper cocktail napkins and talking about the death that week of coach Vince Lombardi.

"Without discipline," the colonel said, "nobody can do anything."

He is a handsome man with a weathered face and fine blue eyes. He spoke in a soft voice that became more intense as he extended his thought about Lombardi to encompass the protests against the war in Vietnam. He wanted to know what was the matter with the country; what was the matter with the kids and with Senator Fulbright and all the other self-appointed critics.

"You don't question the quarterback or argue about the play in the huddle," he said. "You carry out your assignment and hit that guy with everything you've got."

Accepting me as a traveler from the East and therefore familiar with anathema, he asked for explanations. Certain weird phenomena had appeared in the country, and he didn't know what to make of them.

"It's nonsense," he said. "All that stuff about the individual. How can anything be accomplished if everybody is encouraged to do their own thing?"

He wasn't angry, but rather profoundly troubled and confused. For himself he had found a meaningful way of life, and he didn't understand why other people couldn't see that. He had learned to devote himself to something larger than himself, and he believed that only in that direction could a man find purpose or happiness. It was as if he stood at a crossroads, pointing out the way to the Delectable Mountains and yet obliged to watch so many pilgrims stumble into the Slough of Despond.

"They're selfish, you see . . . They have no sense of obligation . . . no sense of community . . ."

But at that moment we were interrupted by a woman asking about the new clothes in New York and whether everybody really was buying the midi length, and were they wearing boots? The colonel withdrew apologetically, as if fearful that he'd said too much.

At dinner I understood one of the reasons for his confusion. I happened to sit between the colonel's wife and Mrs. Galloway, and at first the conversation drifted across the polite, suburban subjects: real estate values and the stock market, children and school and Scouts, football and missed five-iron shots. It was a warm night and candles flickered on the white wooden tables in the garden. I remember music playing, a moon sliding behind low clouds, and far off, on the artillery ranges, the sound of mortar fire. It was a sound I had become used to on Army posts, always in the distance like the cries of children in a school playground.

Mrs. Galloway talked about the 1930s at old Fort McKinley in the Philippines. Her first language had been Spanish, and her mother, although afflicted with recurrent malaria and therefore forbidden to take liquor, nevertheless gave such wonderful lawn parties. There was an elegance then, an elegance and a sense of time passing slowly on wide verandas. It was always pleasant to beat the cavalry at polo, because polo, of course, was the cavalry's game.

With the coffee and liqueurs at the end of dinner, Colonel Kimball's wife talked about her son who had been a literary agent in New York. He married a girl who was studying astrology, which seemed to Mrs. Kimball pointless, but then he divorced her and dropped out to write two pornographic novels. The novels didn't sell, and so he went off to Lawrence, Kansas, to run for sheriff. I gathered that he was into pot and Richard Brautigan and Consciousness III. Mrs. Kimball spoke of him with delight and surprise, pleased about his quixotic adventures but slightly puzzled about the windmills with which he'd chosen to joust. For a moment she looked into the distance, and then she said something that seemed to clarify everything else I had learned about the Army in the many months of traveling.

"We're innocents," she said. "We really don't know what is going on outside."

The Movable Small Town

Usually when I first met a general, he would take the trouble to explain that the Army was just like anywhere else, that it really wasn't so different from business, or law, or the electronics industry. At the end of a few months I came to understand that few generals believed that. Most of them take pride in the distinction between the Army and civilian society, the latter commonly referred to as "the outside" and thought to be inferior. An officer obliged to live away from an Army post is said to be "living on the economy"; the customary inflection of the phrase implies foraging in hostile country. The distinction rests upon the premise that civilian society is dominated by "the commercial values" (i.e., money and greed) whereas the Army is seen as being governed by the ideals of honor, duty, and country. The expression of the prejudice takes various forms. I remember Galloway talking about the Army's system of promotion, a subject to which he'd given considerable thought.

"A man's got to be aggressive and ambitious," he said. "He wouldn't be worth a damn if he wasn't. But the competition isn't vicious or cut-throat like it is in business."

Or it was Hunt, in a more rhetorical style, making wide sweeping gestures and declaiming about the sense of mission in the Army.

"I could run a drive-in, but so what? What is that? Where is the satisfaction in coming home to announce that you've served 5,000 hamburgers that day?"

Or it was another general addressing a class of young lieutenants at Fort Benning and telling them that unless they measured up to the beau ideal of the infantry officer, they might as well go back to farming or selling toilet paper.

Most explicitly it was the sentiment that Galloway had framed under glass and placed on the wall of his office at Fort Knox: "War is an ugly thing, but not the ugliest of things. The decayed and degraded state of moral and patriotic feeling which thinks nothing worth a war is worse . . . A man who has nothing which he cares about more than his personal safety is a miserable creature who has no chance of being free, unless made and kept so by the existence of better men than himself."

The prejudice is further confirmed by the citizens of the towns immediately adjacent to Army posts within the United States. The merchants sell high-priced but shoddy stuff to the enlisted men, the pawnbrokers prosper, and the eminent people in the community (bankers, landowners, breeders of horses, etc.) seldom condescend to treat with the officers. The orderliness of an Army post contrasts markedly with the neon clutter of pizza stands and used-car lots sprawled along the roads just beyond the main gates.

The society within is both conservative and socialist, imbued with the fading courtliness of the Old South. (At the moment there are about 500 generals in the U.S. Army, and I would guess that maybe 400 of them were born in small Southern towns.) Nobody wants to meddle with the status quo; everybody would concede, although sometimes reluctantly, that the well-being of the Army as a whole takes precedence over the well-being of any individual. The regulations define the expected behavior, and the bureaucracy provides all those things supposedly provided by a socialist state: structure, meaning, rewards, punishments, free schools and medical attention, housing, a controlled press, and cut rates at the commissary. Those men who are deemed valuable to the system receive the additional advantages of servants, cars, aides, and white-pillared houses. Also they discover a great many people who laugh at their jokes, and seldom do they hear anybody disagree with them. The women share the rank with their husbands, and the wife of a commanding general rules by divine right.

(The prerogatives diminish in Washington, and all but the most senior officers consider duty at the Pentagon "a rough cut." Not only must they live in a suburb, but also they forfeit the expansive feeling of command.

"Around here," a brigadier general said, "the lieutenant colonels do the work, and the lieutenant generals make the decisions. The rest of us make snuffling noises."

He told me of a friend who took his brigadier's flag home to Arlington at night and posed with it in front of a mirror so that he would recognize himself as a general.)

All Army posts, whether in the United States or abroad, are more or less the same place. A man who has been an officer for some years can go anywhere in the world and find the same routine, the same food, and the same attitudes with which he has been familiar since he was a recruit. He will continue to run across the same friends in different combinations, and he will begin to remember different posts as the places where his children were born; his wife will share with other wives the same chronicles of godforsaken housing and furniture lost in transit.

The coincidences can be very dramatic. Eve Galloway, for instance, remembered an accident at sea when she was an infant: the transport ship bound for Manila hit a reef outside Panama, and the sudden list of the deck threatened to slide her overboard in her blue bassinet. She was saved by a boy of nine, also the child of an Army officer. Many years later, during her husband's tour at the War College in Carlisle, Pennsylvania, she was telling the story to a number of friends at dinner. The man seated next to her, now a colonel, had been the boy who had rescued her.

Whenever I talked to officers about the rewards of Army life, they inevitably mentioned "a sense of belonging." Their offices were always crowded with memorabilia—signed photographs, plaques, models of tanks, ceremonial swords, and ornamental spurs. Those things are talismans; like the ribbons on a man's uniform they provide a substitute for the continuity of place, and establish tenuous connections in a society of nomads.

But if that society offers the comforts of a small town, it also insists upon the moral rectitude (or at least the appearance of moral rectitude) proper to a small town. The code is puritanical, and if a man is discovered in his wickedness he can expect the traditional punishment. No aspect of his conduct escapes judgment, and he is exposed at all times to the scrutiny of his peers and the gossip of their wives. "It isn't like working for Macy's," Hunt once said. "You're in the Army twenty-four hours a day."

At least once a year every officer receives an efficiency report, a form that resembles a grammar school report card. He is graded not only on the performance of his duty, but also according to a roster of character traits that include "appearance," "enthusiasm," and "sociability." The form is filled out by a man's immediate superior officer, and the grades range from 1 (excellent) through 5 (reason for dismissal). Generals rate colonels, colonels rate majors, and so forth through the entire sequence of command. Together with all other relevant documents (letters of recommendation or censure, medical statements, decorations, etc.), the efficiency reports accumulate in a file at the Pentagon. It is on the basis of his file that a man is promoted.

The moral code forbids philandering and disapproves of a second divorce. Conceivably an officer could survive a promiscuous wife (on the grounds that the lady is psychotic and yet her husband remains loyal), but if he himself indulges in lewdness, his career comes to an end. One divorce can be excused because it assumes that the lady didn't enjoy the Army life, but to make the mistake twice suggests poor judgment.

A man's children and appearance also become testaments to his character. If his sons behave badly, then obviously he can't keep order in his own house; a man who cannot command a household cannot command a division. If he is fit and athletic, then he probably possesses solid opinions. A fat man begins as a doubtful prospect who must prove himself otherwise.

The Tickets

The structure of the movable small town depends upon rank, and the man who would make a successful upward passage must "punch the tickets" in the proper sequence. Like most things in the Army, the promotional system appears on paper as a perfect geometrical shape (in this instance a pyramid); also, like most things in the Army, it doesn't quite work that way.

We will begin with the official model displayed by the briefing officers within the Officer Personnel Directorate (OPD). The directorate manages the careers of all officers below the rank of general, shunting them onto their required tracks like so many freight cars in a marshalling yard. The most prestigious branches of the Army are the combat arms (armor, infantry, artillery), and for the sake of example the OPD presents the rise of the ideal infantry officer. Over the course of twenty years he should collect the following tickets: command of a platoon as a lieutenant, of a company as a captain, of a battalion as a lieutenant colonel, and of a brigade as a full colonel; field staff as a major and high-level staff in the Pentagon at both grades of colonel; attendance at the principal Army schools (among them the Command and General Staff College at Fort Leavenworth and either the National or Army War College); appropriate decorations at all ranks; letters of praise from senior officers who themselves rise to high places; no blunders or trouble with the newspapers.

Each ticket must be punched within a specific period of time (a lieutenant colonel, for instance, has about five years in rank), and the punching of ticket C makes it that much easier to punch ticket D. One statistic will suffice to give an idea of the competition: there are roughly 15,000 lieutenant colonels in the Army and only 240 battalions for them to command. Certain rules apply throughout:

At all ranks, command in combat is preferable to command in garrison. The promotion boards search the records for what is called "the sound of the guns," and a man who has not heard that sound has the same kind of difficulty that a rich man has with the eye of a needle.

A staff assignment with the Joint Chiefs of Staff is preferable to a similar assignment in an outlying headquarters.

If translated into a graph, a man's record should reduce to a smooth, upward curve, without sudden or erratic waverings. The graph corresponds to a man's spiritual worth in the same way a rich business corresponded to a man's salvation in John Calvin's Geneva.

The entire system moves more rapidly during a war, and it is better to have taken part in a present or recent war than in an old war. In 1968 the OPD was rotating 25,000 officers a year through Saigon, a procedure comparable to sending the sophomores into the big game so that they could win their letter.

The assignments and promotions through the lower ranks work entirely off the documents in a man's file. The gathering of satisfactory efficiency reports requires an ability to assess the temperament of the officer who writes it, and a man who would succeed must acquire the tact of a courtier. By the time he reaches his middle thirties (in the rank of major or lieutenant colonel), his file has begun to reveal a pattern. Those men whose files suggest clear promise are known as "hard-chargers," "studs," or "burners," and it is at this point in their careers that politics becomes important. Although everybody insists that only the records determine promotion, nobody will deny that it doesn't hurt to know people. OPD sets up an elaborate system of directions, and then the ambitious men proceed to work out the alternate routes. Again, as with the official model, certain principles remain constant:

Never, even as a young major, go someplace where you don't know anybody.

Always do the best you can because you never know whom you might impress and why that may become important later.

Take the harder assignment in the more remote place. It is better to succeed as a company commander in Korea than as a military attaché in Paris.

Never get bogged down in a specialty. The man who learns too much about ballistics or Southeast Asia will retire as a knowledgeable colonel.

The relatively small size of the bureaucracy, particularly as a man ascends in rank and becomes one of the happy few, allows for special pleadings. If OPD sends you to an undesirable place, perhaps you know somebody in the OPD office who can arrange something else. Or maybe you know a general in Germany who can ask for your transfer to his division. (The wishes of the commanders outside the United States supersede the dictates of OPD; not only can they request their friends, but they can also refuse to accept strangers.) Or possibly you can get over to Vietnam as a staff officer and wait around until an operations officer is killed, wounded, or relieved for incompetence.

The combinations are infinite, and through Galloway I acquired at least a dim understanding of the mathematics. Listening to him talk, I could imagine the connections between people as if they were strands in an immensely convoluted tapestry, the complete design of which could be seen only by the older men. At breakfast one morning in the officers' club we discussed his promotion to brigadier in 1966. We were to play golf that afternoon, and Galloway was in an amiable mood; arranging the foursome, the day before, he had said to his aide: "Get me two colonels."

In 1966, he said, he figured it was his year to become a general. His file contained, among other pieces of paper, a recent decoration and a letter of recommendation from General Earle Wheeler (then Chief of Staff). Also he counted four friends on the promotion board, and he'd been assigned as the Army's representative in 1967 to the School of International Relations at Harvard University. But the brigadier's list was published in the summer, and Galloway's name was absent. He smiled, and with sardonic understatement he said, "I'll admit I was disappointed. I didn't come into the Army to die a colonel."

He went to Washington to ask the general then running OPD what had happened; the general, an old friend of Galloway's, assured him that he would make the list the next time around. The trouble, he said, was that Galloway had not had an unaccompanied tour of duty in Korea or Vietnam. (Some officers prefer the simplicities of the battlefield and do not object to the separation from their families; to a man like Galloway, who cherishes his family and enjoys the complexities of the Pentagon, the separation seems pointless.)

Having talked to OPD he decided to call upon Creighton Abrams, a friend from the 1950s in Germany who was then in Desk Operations and close to the wellsprings of power. Walking through the corridor to Abrams' office, Galloway realized that he couldn't complain openly (a mark of bad form), and so he resolved to volunteer for Vietnam. Abrams laughed at him.

"The old man," Galloway said, "knew exactly what was in my mind."

Abrams advised him to take the appointment to Harvard, in itself a very good ticket, and to put in a volunteer statement so that at least a belligerent intention would show up in the record. The following year Galloway studied under Henry Kissinger, and in April 1967 he received orders to Saigon. The brigadier's list came out two days after his arrival, and this time his name was on it. "So you see," he said, "I didn't have to go at all."

It is characteristic of his luck that when eventually he was sent to the Americal Division, he arrived the day before the My Lai incident and thus was not, as he remarked of the other officers implicated, "mentioned in dispatches."

shirley jackson

**Fiction often reflects—even amplifies—life, particularly when written
by as sensitive a writer as the late Shirley Jackson.**

**In "After You, My Dear Alphonse," a very short story, the author of
The Lottery provides an intimate glimpse at the effects of socialization
on the racial attitudes and relationships of the "respectable middle
class."**

**One is introduced to the white Mrs. Wilson who, in trying to help
Boyd, her son's black friend, reveals all the confusing results of racism
tempered or masked by liberal paternalism. It is a story to think about
—and to discuss—for many who read it will feel an uncomfortable
sense of having been one of the characters themselves: Mrs. Wilson,
or Johnny, or, perhaps, Boyd.**

Mrs. Wilson was just taking the gingerbread out of the oven
when she heard Johnny outside talking to someone.

"Johnny," she called, "you're late. Come in and get your
lunch."

"Just a minute, Mother," Johnny said. "After you, my dear
Alphonse."

"After *you*, my dear Alphonse," another voice said.

"No, after *you,* my dear Alphonse," Johnny said.

Mrs. Wilson opened the door. "Johnny," she said, "you come in this minute and get your lunch. You can play after you've eaten."

Johnny came in after her, slowly. "Mother," he said, "I brought Boyd home for lunch with me."

"Boyd?" Mrs. Wilson thought for a moment. "I don't believe I've met Boyd. Bring him in, dear, since you've invited him. Lunch is ready."

"Boyd!" Johnny yelled. "Hey, Boyd, come on in!"

"I'm coming. Just got to unload this stuff."

"Well, hurry, or my mother'll be sore."

"Johnny, that's not very polite to either your friend or your mother," Mrs. Wilson said. "Come sit down, Boyd."

As she turned to show Boyd where to sit, she saw he was a Negro boy, smaller than Johnny but about the same age. His arms were loaded with split kindling wood. "Where'll I put this stuff, Johnny?" he asked.

Mrs. Wilson turned to Johnny. "Johnny," she said, "what did you make Boyd do? What is that wood?"

"Dead Japanese," Johnny said mildly. "We stand them in the ground and run over them with tanks."

"How do you do, Mrs. Wilson?" Boyd said.

"How do you do, Boyd? You shouldn't let Johnny make you carry all that wood. Sit down now and eat lunch, both of you."

"Why shouldn't he carry the wood, Mother? It's his wood. We got it at his place."

"Johnny," Mrs. Wilson said, "go on and eat your lunch."

"Sure," Johnny said. He held out the dish of scrambled eggs to Boyd. "After you, my dear Alphonse."

"After *you*, my dear Alphonse," Boyd said.

"After *you*, my dear Alphonse," Johnny said. They began to giggle.

"Are you hungry, Boyd?" Mrs. Wilson asked.

"Yes, Mrs. Wilson."

"Well, don't you let Johnny stop you. He always fusses about eating, so you just see that you get a good lunch. There's plenty of food here for you to have all you want."

"Thank you, Mrs. Wilson."

"Come on, Alphonse," Johnny said. He pushed half the scrambled eggs onto Boyd's plate. Boyd watched while Mrs. Wilson put a dish of stewed tomatoes beside his plate.

"Boyd don't eat tomatoes, do you, Boyd?" Johnny said.

"*Doesn't* eat tomatoes, Johnny. And just because you don't like them, don't say that about Boyd. Boyd will eat *any*thing."

"Bet he won't," Johnny said, attacking his scrambled eggs.

"Boyd wants to grow up and be a big strong man so he can work hard," Mrs. Wilson said. "I'll bet Boyd's father eats stewed tomatoes."

"My father eats anything he wants to," Boyd said.

"So does mine," Johnny said. "Sometimes he doesn't eat hardly anything. He's a little guy, though. Wouldn't hurt a flea."

"Mine's a little guy too," Boyd said.

"I'll bet he's strong, though," Mrs. Wilson said. She hesitated. "Does he . . . work?"

"Sure," Johnny said. "Boyd's father works in a factory."

"There, you see?" Mrs. Wilson said. "And he certainly has to be strong to do that—all that lifting and carrying at a factory."

"Boyd's father doesn't have to," Johnny said. "He's a foreman."

Mrs. Wilson felt defeated. "What does your mother do, Boyd?"

"My mother?" Boyd was surprised. "She takes care of us kids."

"Oh. She doesn't work, then?"

"Why should she?" Johnny said through a mouthful of eggs. "You don't work."

"You really don't want any stewed tomatoes, Boyd?"

"No, thank you, Mrs. Wilson," Boyd said.

"No, thank you, Mrs. Wilson, no, thank you, Mrs. Wilson, no, thank you, Mrs. Wilson," Johnny said. "Boyd's sister's going to work, though. She's going to be a teacher."

"That's a very fine attitude for her to have, Boyd." Mrs. Wilson restrained an impulse to pat Boyd on the head. "I imagine you're all very proud of her?"

"I guess so," Boyd said.

"What about all your other brothers and sisters? I guess all of you want to make just as much of yourselves as you can."

"There's only me and Jean," Boyd said. "I don't know yet what I want to be when I grow up."

"We're going to be tank drivers, Boyd and me," Johnny said. "Zoom." Mrs. Wilson caught Boyd's glass of milk as Johnny's napkin ring, suddenly transformed into a tank, plowed heavily across the table.

"Look, Johnny," Boyd said. "Here's a foxhole. I'm shooting at you."

Mrs. Wilson, with the speed born of long experience, took the gingerbread off the shelf and placed it carefully between the tank and the foxhole.

"Now eat as much as you want to, Boyd," she said. "I want to see you get filled up."

"Boyd eats a lot, but not as much as I do," Johnny said. "I'm bigger than he is."

"You're not much bigger," Boyd said. "I can beat you running."

Mrs. Wilson took a deep breath. "Boyd," she said. Both boys turned to her. "Boyd, Johnny has some suits that are a little too small for him, and a winter coat. It's not new, of course, but there's lots of wear in it still. And I have a few dresses that your mother or sister could probably use. Your mother can make them over into lots of things for all of you, and I'd be very happy to give them to you. Suppose before you leave I make up a big bundle and then you and Johnny can take it over to your mother right away . . ." Her voice trailed off as she saw Boyd's puzzled expression.

"But I have plenty of clothes, thank you," he said. "And I don't think my mother knows how to sew very well, and anyway I guess we buy about everything we need. Thank you very much, though."

"We don't have time to carry that old stuff around, Mother," Johnny said. "We got to play tanks with the kids today."

Mrs. Wilson lifted the plate of gingerbread off the table as Boyd was about to take another piece. "There are many little boys like you, Boyd, who would be very grateful for the clothes someone was kind enough to give them."

"I didn't mean to make you mad, Mrs. Wilson," Boyd said.

"Boyd will take them if you want him to, Mother," Johnny said.

"Don't think I'm angry, Boyd. I'm just disappointed in you, that's all. Now let's not say anything more about it."

She began clearing the plates off the table, and Johnny took Boyd's hand and pulled him to the door. " 'Bye, Mother," Johnny said. Boyd stood for a minute, staring at Mrs. Wilson's back.

"After you, my dear Alphonse," Johnny said, holding the door open.

"Is your mother still mad?" Mrs. Wilson heard Boyd ask in a low voice.

"I don't know," Johnny said. "She's screwy sometimes."

"So's mine," Boyd said. He hesitated. "After *you*, my dear Alphonse."

IN COMMU- NITIES

peter schrag

Sinclair Lewis' novel, *Main Street*, was first published in 1920. It was then considered the quintessential portrait of smalltown America. Now, after half a century, Peter Schrag asks, "Is Main Street still there?"

It is—and it isn't.

Schrag visited Mason City, Iowa, and similar communities in 1970 and found that the outside world and the national culture have been intruding on "Main Street" at an ever increasing rate. There are new styles, new politics and politicians, "new" organizations like the NAACP and the League of Women Voters, new models for the young to imitate. Still, he found, much of the old remained.

There is still something special or different about the Mason Cities of America. Maybe what makes them unique (they used to be typical!) is that, despite the traditional prejudices and fears of change, or perhaps because of them, what remains is a sense of community, a faith in being able to cope.

One wonders for how long this will be the case.

Mason City, Iowa. Pop. 32,642. Meat packing, Portland cement, brick and tile, beet sugar, dairy products, commercial feeds, soybean oil and meal, thermopane windows and mobile homes. At

From *Out of Place in America*, by Peter Schrag. Copyright © 1970 by Peter Schrag. Reprinted by permission of Random House, Inc.

the intersection of Highways 18 and 65, 135 miles south of Minneapolis, 125 miles north of Des Moines. Three major railroads. Ozark Airlines. Daily newspapers, one local television station. Library, art museum.

Among the most difficult things in any small American town is to stay for more than a few days and remain an outsider. There seems to be a common feeling that anyone—even a writer from New York—is, somewhere in his heart, a small-town boy come home. The light but unceasing stream of traffic that moves through Main Street—Federal Avenue in Mason City—north to Minneapolis and beyond, south to Des Moines, reinforces the belief that this flat, open place is part of a great American continuity extending through other Main Streets, across the fields of corn and beets, past tractor depots and filling stations, past grain elevators and loading pens to the very limits of the national imagination. It must make it difficult to conceive of anyone as a total stranger, for being here —local pride notwithstanding—cannot seem very different from being anywhere else.

They take you in, absorb you, soak you up; they know whom you've seen, where you've been, what you've done. In Mississippi hamlets, the sheriff follows you around; here it is The Word. *Small towns co-opt* (you tell yourself), *and nice small towns co-opt absolutely.* But it is not just them, it's you. The things that you bring with you—your sense of yourself as a friendly sort, the wish to believe that the claims of small-town virtue are valid, your particular kind of chauvinism—all these make you a willing collaborator. So maybe they're right. *Maybe we're all just small-town boys come home.* Yes, you're willing to come to dinner, to visit the Club, to suspend the suspicion that all this is some sort of do-it-yourself Chamber of Commerce trick. Later perhaps (says the Inner Voice of Reason) you will be able to sort things out, to distinguish Main Street from the fantasies that you and a lot of other people from New York have invented for it. Later.

You have come here to see what is happening to the heart of this country, to ask how the great flat democracy responds to Vietnam and Black Power, to marijuana and Mark Rudd, to see how it is taking technology and the Bomb—all the things that overwhelm the visible spectrum of public concern. Is there something here that can survive in New York and Chicago? Is there an Americanism that will endure, or will it perish with the farm and the small town? What, you ask, is happening to Main Street? Later. For the moment you are simply in it, listening to them worry about a proposed civic center, about the construction of a mall, about taxes and industrial development, and about something called "the traffic problem," which, by even the more placid standards of New York, seems more imagined than real.

There are ghosts in this country—local ghosts, and ghosts that you bring with you, that refuse to stay behind: shades of brawling railroad workers and dispossessed farmers; frontiersmen and Babbitts; the old remembered tales of reaction and America First, of capital "R" Republicanism and the Ku Klux Klan; the romance of Jefferson and Frederick Jackson Turner, the yeoman farmer and the self-made man. As a place of literary irony, Middle America is celebrating its golden anniversary. "Main Street," wrote Sinclair Lewis in 1920, "is the climax of civilization. That this Ford car might stand in front of the Bon Ton Store, Hannibal invaded Rome and Erasmus wrote in Oxford cloisters. What Ole Jensen the grocer says to Ezra Stowbody the banker is the new law for London, Prague, and the unprofitable isles of the sea; whatsoever Ezra does not know and sanction, that thing is heresy, worthless for knowing and wicked to consider." But that irony, too, may be a ghost—now as much myth, perhaps, as the self-flattering cultural propositions invented to answer it. ("Right here in Mason City," someone tells you, "we sell 300 tickets each year for the Metropolitan Opera tour performances in Minneapolis.") The life of Babbittry, you tell yourself, follows the life (and art) of others. But the models are no longer clear. Main Street once insisted on rising from Perfection (rural) to Progress (urban): Sauk Centre and Zenith were trying to do Chicago's "thing," but what does Chicago have to offer now? The Main Street boosters are still there, hanging signs across the road proclaiming "A Community on the March," but their days are numbered. How would Lewis have portrayed the three hundred marchers of the Vietnam Moratorium in Mason City? How would he deal with the growing number of long-haired, pot-smoking kids? Here, too, Mason City follows New York and Chicago. (The Mafia, you are told, controls the floating dice games that occasionally rumble through the back rooms of a local saloon.) The certainty of Lewis's kind of irony was directed to the provincial insularity that war, technology, and television are rendering obsolete. Main Street lives modern not in its dishwashers and combines—not even in Huntley-Brinkley and Walter Cronkite—but in its growing ambivalence about the America that creates them, the America that crosses the seas of beets and corn, and therefore about itself.

It is not a simple place, and perhaps never was. You see what you expect, and then begin to see (or imagine) what you did not. Standard America, yes: the Civil War monument in the square; the First National Bank; Osco's Self-Service Drugs; the shoe store and movie theaters; Damon's and Younkers' ("Satisfaction Always"); Maizes' and Penney's; Sears and Monkey Ward. Middle America the way it was supposed to be: the farmers coming to shop on Saturday afternoon; the hunting and fishing; the high school football team Friday night; the swimming and sailing at Clear Lake, a small resort nine miles to the west. You cannot pass through town without being told that Mason City is a good place to raise a family, without hearing praise for the schools, and without incessant reminders that Meredith Wilson's musical play *The Music Man* was *about* Mason City, that Willson was born here, and that the town was almost renamed River City because of it. (There *is* a river, the Winnebago, which makes itself known only at times of flood.) Mr. Toot, the figure of a trombone-blowing bandsman (says a man at the Chamber of Commerce), is now the town symbol. "We hope," says the man, "that we can make our band festival into a major event." Someday, you imagine, this could be the band capital of the nation, the world, and maybe the whole wicked universe.

Mason City, they tell you, is a stable community: steady population, little unemployment, no race problem (there are, at most, 300 Negroes in town), clean water, and—with some huffy qualifications (dust from one of the cement plants, odor from the packing house)—clean air. A cliché. In the *Globe Gazette,* the editor, Bob Spiegel, suggests that the problems and resources of the large cities be dispersed to all the Mason Cities in America. A Jeffersonian, Mr. Spiegel, and a nice guy: "The smaller communities need the plants and the people that are polluting the urban centers—not in large doses, but steadily, surely. . . . The small communities are geared up. They have comprehensive plans. They know they can't stand still or they will be passed by." Stable, perhaps, but what is stable in a relativistic universe? The very thing that Spiegel proposes seems to be happening in reverse. The community is becoming less pluralistic: it has fewer Negroes, fewer Jews, and fewer members of other minorities than it had twenty years ago. "After the war," said Nate Levinson, an attorney, who is president of the synagogue, "we had eighty Jewish families. Now we have forty. We can't afford a rabbi anymore." On the few occasions that Mason City has tried to attract Negro professionals, they refused to come or to stay. There is nobody to keep them company, and the subtle forms of discrimination—in housing and employment—are pervasive enough to discourage pioneers. ("My maid says if she hears any more about Black Power she'll scream. . . . I wouldn't mind one living next door, if he mowed the grass and kept the place neat.") The brighter kids—black and white—move away, off to college, off to the cities, and beneath that migration one can sense the fear that the city's declining agricultural base will not be replaced by enough industrial jobs to maintain even the stability that now exists.

Mason City is not a depressed town, although in its stagnating downtown shopping area it often looks like one. (Shopping centers are thriving on the periphery; the farmers come in to shop, but not all the way.) The city shares many of the attributes of other small Middle Western communities, competing with them for industry, counting, each week, another farm family that is selling out or giving up, counting the abandoned houses around the county, counting the number of acres (now exceeding 200) required for an efficient agricultural operation. An acre of land costs $500, a four-row combine $24,000. If you stop in such places as Plymouth, a town of 400, nine miles from Mason City, you hear the cadences of compromise and decline: men who have become part-time

farmers and make ends meet, at $2.25 an hour, by working in the sugar mill in Mason City. Independence becomes, ever more, a hopeful illusion belied by abandoned shops and boarded windows, and by tales of success set in other places—an engineer in California, a chemist in Detroit, a teacher in Oregon.

Iowa, you realize, not just from statistics, but from faces, is a state of old people: "What do the kids here want to do? What do the kids in Mason City want to do? What do the kids in Iowa want to do? They want to get out. I'd get out, go to California if I could." There is a double migration, from farms into towns, from towns into cities, and out of the state. More than 10 per cent of Mason City's work force is employed at the Decker packing plant on the north side of town. (The plant is a division of Armour and Company.) At the moment the plant is prosperous; it pays good wages. (A hamboner—who does piece work—can make $6 to $7 an hour). But what would happen, said one of the city's corporate managers, if the place should succumb to the increasing efficiency of newer plants? "What'll we do the day—and don't quote me—when the place has to shut down?"

It is the fashion to worry slow, worry with a drawl. Urgency and crisis are not the style. Through most of its history, Mason City was dominated by a few families, and to some extent it still is—not because they are so powerful, but because Federal Avenue once thought they were. Small towns create their own patriarchs, tall men who look even taller against the flatness of history, producing—inevitably—a belief that civic motion and inertia are the subtle work of Big Men: bankers, real estate operators, and corporate managers. Mason City still talks about the General, Hanford MacNider (banking, cement, real estate), who was an Assistant Secretary of War under Coolidge, ambassador to Canada, an aspirant for the 1940 Republican nomination for President, and, for a time, a supporter of America First. (In Mason City, MacNider was *Secretary* of War and barely missed becoming President.) The MacNiders gave the city land for parks, for the public library, and for a museum. (The General was also a founder of the Euchre and Cycle Club, a lunch-and-dinner club—all the best people—which still has no Jewish members, and he is remembered, among other things, as the man who did not lower his flag for thirty days after John F. Kennedy was killed.) "My father," said Jack MacNider, now president of the Northwestern States Portland Cement Company, "was quite a guy. Some people thought he was tough. To some he was a patron saint. You should have known him."

The General's shadow has survived him, and there are still people who are persuaded that nothing of major consequence can be accomplished in Mason City against the opposition of the family. Is that true, you ask Jack, sitting in his second-story office overlooking Federal Avenue. (There is a picture of the General, in full uniform, behind Jack's desk.) "I'm flattered," he answers, not defensively, but with some amuse-

ment, saying more between the lines than on the record, telling you—
you imagine—that the MacNiders take the rap for a lot of small-town
inertia they can't control, and that they suffer (or enjoy) a visibility for
which they haven't asked. At this very moment, a young lawyer named
Tom Jolas, a second generation Greek, is challenging the Establishment
(such as it is) in his campaign for mayor; you both know that Jolas is
likely to win (on November 4 he did win, handily) and that the city's
style and mood are now determined as much by younger businessmen
and professionals—and by hundreds of packing house workers and
cement workers—as they are by the old families. "This must be a fish
bowl for the MacNiders," you say, and Jack offers no argument. And
when you speak about prejudice in Mason City, Jack agrees—yes, there
is—but you can't be sure whether he means against Catholics, Jews, and
Negroes (or Greeks, and Chicanos), or also against the MacNiders. The
shadow is still there, but the General is dead.

Mason City's traditional style of politics and political behavior was
nicely represented by sixty-five-year-old George Mendon, who was mayor
for sixteen years until Jolas beat him. Small towns always create the illusion of responsiveness—you can call any public official, any corporate
manager, with little interference from secretaries who ask your business,
your name, and your pedigree—and you thus can walk into Mendon's
office unannounced and receive an audience. But you are never sure that,
once in, you have really arrived anywhere. The action must be someplace
else. The room is almost bare, the desk virtually clean, the man without
visible passion. Yes, jobs and industrial development are a problem, and
Mason City has done pretty well, but there are 20,000 other towns trying
to attract industry, and, you know, these things take time. Yes, they
would like to hire some Negroes for the police force, but none have been
qualified. Yes, the MacNiders had been good to the city—all that land
they'd given (and all those tax deductions?) but. . . . When Mendon was
challenged during the campaign about operating an underpaid and under-
trained police force, he answered that the city had the most modern
equipment, including riot guns, Mace, and bulletproof vests. What are
they for, you ask, and Mendon, rattling the change in his pocket, identifies himself. "Our colored population is peaceful," he said. "They
wouldn't riot. But you never know when people from the outside might
come in and try to start something." Mason City is prepared for Watts
and Newark, and somewhere in its open heart there lurks an edge of
apprehension that the fire next time might burn even here. But when
Mendon spoke about his riot guns at an open meeting, the general response was tempered by considerable facetious amusement, and the
people who were amused went out to vote against him, and beat him.

There is no single current running against the old style of politics, or
against the Mendons and the Establishment they are supposed to represent. In 1968, Mason City voted for Nixon, for the conservative Congress-

man, H. R. Gross, and for Harold Hughes, a liberal Democrat. ("We helped elect Gross the first time he ran," said a union official, "and we've been sorry ever since.") Sociology and political calculations don't help much. "The issue here," said Bud Stewart, who runs a music store and worked for Jolas, "is generational," implying that whatever was young and progressive supported the challenger against the older Establishment. Jolas campaigned under the slogan "Time for a Change," including, among other things, concern for public housing (which the city does not have, but desperately needs), more attention to the problems of youth, and the creation of a modern police force that could meet what he called the rising rate of crime. (And which meant, I was told, getting rid of the reactionary police chief who had bought all the riot junk.) But what Jolas said was clearly not as important as what he is: young, energetic, and, beneath it all, ambiguously liberal, and unambiguously decent. "I had my hair long and wore sideburns," he tells you (two years ago, he managed a teen-age rock band), "but my friends said I couldn't win with it; so I cut it short. But maybe after the election I might get a notion and let it grow again."

Jolas's great political achievement before he ran for mayor was to force the state to reroute a projected interstate highway so that it would pass within a few miles of Mason City, but it was undoubtedly personality rather than politics that elected him. ("You know what they're saying about me?" he mused one day toward the end of the campaign. "They're saying that, if I'm elected, the Greeks and the niggers are going to take over Mason City. I even had someone charge that I belong to the Mafia—the Greek Mafia.") More than anything else, Jolas seems to have a sense of concern about youth—not a program—but an awakening awareness of how kids are shortchanged by schools, by politicians, by adults. ("He knows," I wrote in my notes, "that the world screws kids.")

What Jolas can achieve is doubtful. He will not have a sympathetic city council nor perhaps even a sympathetic community, and his commitment to a downtown civic center and mall as a means of restoring the vitality of the central business area may be more the token of modernism than the substance of progress; yet it is clear that Jolas received the support, and represented the aspirations, of whatever liberalism (black, labor, professional) the city could muster. If you sit in his storefront headquarters long enough, you learn how far Main Street has come from Babbittry. You meet Marie Dresser, the recently widowed wife of a physician, who, as president of the Iowa League of Women Voters, carried a reapportionment fight through the legislature and who speaks of how, when their son decided to grow a mustache, she and her husband decided to back him against the school authorities and how, eventually, they won; Jean Beatty, the wife of a psychologist, answering phone calls and stuffing Jolas envelopes, and shuttling between meetings of the league and the local branch of the NAACP, knowing that the organization should be run by black people, but knowing also that its precariously weak membership cannot sustain it without help; or Jim Shannon, the county Democratic chairman, who has worked for the Milwaukee Railroad all his life, and who has gone back to the local community college (working nights, studying economics during the day), speaking in his soft, laconic, infinitely American cadences about the campaign for Bobby Kennedy in 1968, about a decade of legislative fights, reminding you, without meaning to, or even mentioning it, that liberalism wasn't invented in New York, that the Phil Harts, the Frank Churches, the Fred Harrises, and the George McGoverns weren't elected by professors.

If that were all—if one could merely say that Mason City and Middle America are going modern—it would all be easy, but it is not. (What, after all, is modern—uniquely modern—after you've dispensed with the technology?) The national culture is there—mass cult, high, middle, and low, mod and trad: Bud Stewart in the Edwardian double-breasted suits that he orders from advertisements through the local stores; the elite trooping off to Minneapolis to hear the Met when it comes on tour, or to Ames to catch the New York Philharmonic (mostly, say the cynics, to be conspicuous, not for love of music); the rock on the radio and in the jukes (the Fifth Dimension, Blood, Sweat and Tears, new Dylan and old Baez, plus some leavening from the likes of Johnny Cash); the long hair and the short skirts, the drugs and the booze. (At the same time, beer, rather than pot, seems still to be the preponderant, though not the exclusive, form of adolescent sin.) But somehow what Mason City receives through the box and the tube—and from trips to Minneapolis and Des Moines, where some of the ladies do almost weekly shopping—it seems to shape and reshape into its own forms. There is a tendency to mute the decibels of public controversy and social friction, perhaps because people are more tolerant and relaxed, perhaps because they are simply less crowded. There is talk about crime and violence, but the most common local examples seem usually to involve the theft of bicycles and the destruction of Halloween pumpkins. (Another way of staking a claim on the modern?) If you ask long enough, you can get some of the blue-collar workers to speak about their resentment against welfare, taxes, and student demonstrators (not at Harvard, mind you, but at the State University of Iowa), but it is commonly only television and the newspapers that produce the talk. And so it tends to be dispassionate, distant, and somewhat abstract. Bumper stickers and decals are scarce; you rarely see American flags on the rear windows of automobiles because, one might assume, there aren't many people at whom to wave them, not many devils to exorcise. The silent majority here is an abstraction, a collage of minorities, except when it comes to the normalcy of the ladies' study clubs and bridge clubs, the football, the hunting and fishing, and the trip to the lake. And every two years they go back, most of them, and vote for H. R. Gross.

And yet, here are the kids, high school students and students at the Community College, organizing a moratorium march, running a little

newspaper, semi-underground within the high school, and with the bless-
ing of the school authorities; here are the clergymen, not all, but a few,
giving their support for the march from the pulpit (when she heard her
minister that Sunday, one prominent parishioner promptly resigned from
the church); and here are ordinary people responding to the critics of
dissent with their own protest. In a letter to the *Globe Gazette*:

> We supported the Moratorium Day demonstration. We have a son in Vietnam.
> We love our country. We fly the American flag.
>
> But we do not believe in blindly following our leader as the Germans did
> when their leader decided to exterminate the Jews or as some Americans
> would do if our leader should decide to exterminate the Indians.
>
> We feel our country was wrong to send 40,000 of our boys to their death,
> not defending their own shores.
>
> Supporting the Moratorium was our way of saying we love our country
> right or wrong, and this time it was wrong.

Given the reputation of the average small town in America, the greatest surprise is the school system which, under Rod Bickert, the superintendent, and John Pattswald, the high school principal, has managed to
move well beyond the expected, even in the conventional modern suburb.
Mason City has abandoned dress codes in its high school, has instituted
flexible-modular scheduling (meaning that students have only a limited
number of formal lecture classes, and can do their own thing—in "skill"
and study centers, in the library or the cafeteria—as they will) and has
begun to experiment, in the high school, with an "open mike" where any
student can talk to the entire school on anything he pleases. There are
no bells, no monitors. As you walk through the halls (modern, sprawling,
corporate style), Pattswald, a Minnesotan, explains that he first came to
the school as a disciplinarian. "It was a conservative school and I ran a
tight ship." When he became principal he turned things around. "We're
something of an island, and when some of the parents first heard about
it they thought it was chaos. We had an open meeting—parents and students—to explain the flex-mod schedule, but most of the parents wanted
to know about dress. (You know, we have everything here, including girls
in miniskirts and pants suits.) The students helped us carry it. They know
that some sort of uproar could blow this thing right out of the water, but
I think they can do the job."

Every day Pattswald spends a couple of hours visiting classes, asking
students irreverent questions that are, at least tangentially, directed to
the teachers. "I ask them why they're doing what they're doing; what's
the significance of this, why study at all? Sure, we have some weak
teachers, but now when I hire people I role-play with them a little, I want
to see how they take pressure. In the classroom it's too easy for the
teachers always to be the last resort and to put the screws down. That's
no way to improve the climate of learning." The conversation is frequently interrupted while Pattswald stops to talk with students (he
knows many by name), and later to tell you about them. "Kids are my

life," he says, rounding a corner after a brief encounter with two boys. "The whole point is to get them to appreciate the worth of an individual. We have to reach the ones who are overlooked, like one boy they were taunting and who talked about himself as 'a ball that they always kick around.' Those are the ones we have to reach. But I think we're coming."

The militant students seek you out. Mason City is still a confining place, and they find the visitor from New York, the outsider, walking through the hall alone: the organizers of the moratorium, the editors of the mimeographed paper, the *Bitter End* (not quite underground, not quite official), the activists, sons and daughters of the affluent lawyers and doctors, all local people, not carpetbaggers from the East. The school, they say, is divided between "pointy heads like us" and "the animals." (A group passes through the hall after school and the pointy heads, through a glass door, follow the herd with "Moo-moo," "Oink-oink.") The radicals still see the school as a fraud. "There is no way to get a decent education in a public school. Everybody's too uptight." Like what? "Like being allowed to leave school during your unstructured time to make a movie. You can get a release to dish hamburgers at McDonald's, so why not to make movies?" One of them gets threatening letters for his part in the peace movement, another loses his allowance because he won't cut his hair. Their lives are no different, nor are their parents', from those of similar people in Scarsdale or Shaker Heights or Winnetka. (Some of them, said Pattswald, "have told their parents to go to hell.") What is surprising is that, although they are a lonely minority, they are in Mason City (bands, football, cheerleaders, Toot)—that they are in this community at all.

For the majority of the young, the concerns are universal: cars, dances, sports. You hear them in Vic's ("Real Dago Pizza"): "It's a '65 Chevvy. I traded it for that car that was sitting in the grass by the Hub . . . paid three hundred and fifty dollars and put a new engine in it and it runs great." They want to go to college, to get jobs—more than half the high school students work—so they can maintain those automobiles, get married. The modest dream is to become an airline stewardess; "if I'm not too clumsy," to enlist in the Army; to learn a trade. On Friday nights they cruise up and down Federal, shuttling from a root-beer stand at the south end to a drive-in at the other. There is some talk about establishing a teen center, a place Where Kids Can Go, but the proposal draws little enthusiasm from adults and less from the kids. And yet, even among the majority—the animals, the apathetic—something may be happening. The war perhaps, or television, or the music. There was a time, said a school administrator, "when the war seemed very distant." Mason City's enlistment rate was always high, the college students were exempt anyway, and the draft wasn't much of an issue. But in the past year eight recent graduates of Mason City High were killed in Vietnam, making death and change more personal. Nearly a hundred turned out to hear discussions about the war inside the school, and while the patriotic speakers still come to address the assembly, other messages are being heard as well. The hair gets longer, the music a little harder, and the news is on everybody's set.

The young are slowly becoming mediators of the culture, they receive the signals from the outside and interpret the messages for adults. And that's new for all America, not just for Mason City. "The kids are having an effect on their parents," said a mental-health worker, one of the few clinicians in town, apparently, that the adolescents are willing to trust. "People here are friendly and uptight at the same time. Many of them take the attitude that the children should have their fun, that eventually they'll come around to their parents' view. But people have been jarred —by TV and by their own children, and they know, some of them at least, that they've got to listen. They're trying to become looser."

But becoming looser is still a struggle and, given the conditions of life, an imperative that can be deferred. ("I'm *not* going to send my son to Harvard," says a Harvard graduate. "An eighteen-year-old is not mature enough to handle SDS and all that other garbage.") The space, the land, the weather, the incessant reminders of physical normalcy make it possible to defer almost anything. Church on Sunday, football on Friday and the cycle of parties, dinners, and cookouts remain more visible (not to say comprehensible) than the subtleties of cultural change or social injustice. If the churches and their ministers are losing some of their influence among the young (and if the call for psychiatrists is increasing), they are still holding their members, and if the Catholic Monsignor, Arthur Breen, has to schedule a folk mass at Holy Family every Sunday (in addition to four other masses) he nonetheless continues to pack them in.

What you see most of all (see is not a good word; feel, maybe) is a faith in the capacity of people and institutions to be responsive, the belief that, finally, things are pretty much what they seem, that Things Work. "This is just a big farm town," said a Mason City businessman. "You don't check people's credit here. You just assume they'll pay their bills. In Waterloo, which is really an industrial city, even though it isn't very big, you check everybody out." The answer to an economic problem is to work harder, to take a second job, or to send your wife to work, usually as a clerk or a waitress. (Wages for women are extremely low.) On the radio, *Junior Achievement* makes its peace with modernism by setting its jingle to "Get With It" to a rock beat, but the message of adolescent enterprise (Babbittry?) is the same, and around the lunch tables at the Green Mill Restaurant or the bar at Tom MacNider's Chart House it is difficult to convince anyone that sometimes even people with the normal quota of ambition can't make it.

The advantages of that faith are obvious, but the price is high. "This is a nice town as long as you don't rock the boat," said Willis Haddix, a meat packer, who is president of the struggling Mason City chapter of

NAACP. "What's wrong here is in the secret places": in subtle discrimination in housing and jobs; in the out-of-sight, dilapidated frame houses at the north and south ends of town, buildings surrounded with little piles of old lumber, rusting metal chairs, decaying junk cars once slated for repair; in the lingering aroma of personal defeat; and in the cross between arrogance and apathy that declares "there are no poor people in this area." On Sundays, while most people are packing their campers for the trip home, or making the transition between church and television football, the old, who have little to do, wander into the Park Inn for lunch —hot roast beef sandwiches for $1.25—and to talk about Medicare. And against theirs you hear other voices: Murray Lawson, for example, a civilized, compassionate man, who represents Mason City in the legislature, saying, "We've been generous with education, but not so generous with the old. We've had a rough time with nursing homes"; Jim Shannon, who supports his wife and seven children on the salary of a railroad clerk and janitor, describing the effects of a regressive sales tax that victimizes the small man but makes little impact on the rich; the official of the local O E O poverty agency talking about the county's third welfare generation and reflecting that "an admission of poverty is an admission of failure, and people here don't do that"; Tom Jolas describing Mason City's enthusiasm for the New York Mets when they won the World Series after a ninth place finish in 1968, because "people believe in coming off the bottom."

And then you learn something else—about yourself, and about the phenomenon you choose to call Main Street. You hear them complain about Eastern, urban provincialism, about those people who cannot believe that Mason City has television ("You must get it from the West Coast"), let alone an art museum, a decent library, or a couple of go-go joints (or that you can buy Philip Roth, Malcolm X, and Henry Miller in the bookstore), and you begin to understand, almost by suggestion, what the barriers of comprehension are all about. Is it really surprising that Main Street cannot fully comprehend talk about police brutality, police rigidity, or social disillusionment? If the system works here, why doesn't it work everywhere else? Main Street's uniquely provincial vice lies in its excessive, unquestioning belief (in the Protestant ethic, hard work, honesty, and conventional politics); New York's in the conviction that most of the time nothing may make much difference, that institutions and public life are by their very nature unresponsive. And if New York has come to doubt the values and the beliefs of tradition, it still hasn't invented anything to replace them. The anger of the blue-collar worker—at welfare, students, Negroes—is rooted in the frustrated ethic of Main Street, frustrated in not only its encounters with urban problems and technology, but in the growing doubt of the Best people—Wallace's pointy heads, Agnew's effete impudent snobs—that it still has merit. Among the characteristic excesses of rural populism (whether expressed by William Jennings Bryan, Joe McCarthy, or Spiro Agnew) was a paranoia about Them: the bankers, the railroads, the Eastern Establishment, the Communists in government. But paranoia is surely also one of the characteristic defenses of almost every other inhabitant of New York. (If you try to explain the vicissitudes of dealing with Con Edison or the New York Telephone Company, most people in Mason City stare at you in disbelief; if you speak about rents and housing, they're certain you've gone mad.) Every rural or small-town vote against some proposal for the alleviation of a problem in New York or Chicago or Cleveland is not merely an act of self-interest (keeping taxes low, protecting the farmers) but also a gesture of disbelief that Main Street's ethic and tactics—if they were really applied—would be ineffective in the Big City.

At the end, sitting in the waiting room at the Municipal Airport (all flights from Chicago are late, naturally), you detach yourself. You hear, still, one of the Federal Avenue lawyers saying, "This town is solid. It's solid as a commercial center, and as a medical and cultural center for a large region." You see his nearly bare office, the brown wood furniture, the linoleum floors, and the fluorescent lights, see his partner in a sleeveless, gray pullover walking through the outer office (Clarence Darrow?), and hear the trucks stopping for the red light at the intersection below. You hear Jack MacNider speaking about the gradual movement of the "iron triangle"—the Midwestern industrial region—into north central Iowa, speaking about the ultimate industrialization of the area around the city. You see the high school homecoming queen, fragile and uncomfortable in the back of an open convertible in the wind-chilled stadium; see the wide residential streets with their maples and time-threatened elms, the section of magnificent houses by Prairie School architects (one of them by Frank Lloyd Wright) and the crumbling streets at the south end, near the Brick and Tile; and you hear, in that same neighborhood, two NAACP ladies, one white, one Negro, discussing the phrasing of a letter to the school board politely protesting the use of *Little Black Sambo* in the elementary grades. And then, finally, you hear again all those people speaking about how good Mason City is for raising a family, and you wonder what kind of society it is that must separate growing up and rearing of children from the places where most of its business is transacted, its ideas discussed, and its policies determined. And then you wonder, too, what would happen if something ever came seriously to disturb Main Street's normalcy, if direct demands were ever made, if the letters ceased being polite, if the dark places—the discrimination and disregard—were probed and, for the first time, tested. Small towns do co-opt, you think, not by what they do, not by their hospitality, but by what we wish they were—because all of us, big city boys and small, *want* to believe. And yet, when Ozark 974 rises from the runway, off to Dubuque, over the corn and beets, over the Mississippi, off to Chicago, you know that you can't go home again, that the world is elsewhere, and that every moment the distances grow not smaller but greater. Main Street is far away.

herbert j. gans

"Main Street" used to be the typical American town. As Peter Schrag pointed out in the last article, we are now in another age. Suburbia is where most people live—or aspire to live. And as Mason City, home of "The Music Man," becomes more and more a living legacy of an older, more staid America, so Levittown, whether in New York or New Jersey or Pennsylvania or California, has become the exemplar of the new. In fact, Levittowners are often the children of Main Streeters. Middle America has a new, if highly mobile, home.

For several years urbanologist Herbert J. Gans lived in and observed the new community of Levittown, New Jersey. Here is part of his report.

Of particular interest are Gans' discussions of how people met and began to establish relationships, how cliques formed and stratification developed, and how instant "traditions" were created. The author also offers a useful typology to summarize the patterns of voluntary associations he witnessed among the Levittowners.

The Beginnings of Group Life

The first Levittowners occupied their homes in the second week of October 1958. Awaiting them was a township government which in the past had only to maintain the roads, and a school system which in the previous year taught 85 pupils in grades 1 through 9. The township also boasted a Methodist church with attached social organizations, a YMCA with its own (but ramshackle) building, a PTA for the local school, and a Levittown Civic Association, founded the year before to prepare for the newcomers and to integrate them into the existing community. Township and county residents, most of whom were Protestants, were eyeing the new community with some trepidation, because rumors had it that many of the newcomers were Catholics leaving Philadelphia slums to escape Negroes, and some were Italians who carried knives. Elected officials were equally fearful, for the township and the county had always been Republican, and most Levittowners were expected to be Democrats. Even so, everyone was waiting to welcome, and if possible to coopt, the 25 families who moved in that October week and the 3000 others who followed them during the course of this study.

Among the Levittowners themselves, the first signs of group life began to appear even before they moved in. As they inspected the model homes, many were also inspecting the other people who were looking at the homes with them. Those who decided to buy were called back to Levittown a few weeks later to select their lots, and at that time some met the people who would live near them. Most did not, but even so, they were ready to assume that they would be agreeable neighbors and perhaps even good friends. Later, only 9 percent recalled being "very much concerned about not knowing [their] neighbors beforehand." Reassured by the people they had seen around the model homes area and by the builder's credit check, they felt, as one man put it, "the people who could afford this type of house would be good people." Besides, everyone was looking forward to occupying his new home, and this engendered a spirit of optimism and the trust that other purchasers shared this spirit. After all, Levittown would be a new community, and newness is often identified with perfection in American culture.

Before moving in, only a few people were looking forward to getting together with their neighbors, at least according to the mail questionnaire results. However, once they had occupied the house and had gotten it and themselves settled, they began to look for playmates for their young children and then to find companions for themselves among their new neighbors. For the first two weeks they worked mainly at getting the house in shape, limiting themselves to exchanging cheerful hellos across the street or backyard. Once the initial nest-making period was over, however, people were ready to meet and, in this process, they got some help from an unexpected source—salesmen.

On moving day the first people to greet the new homeowners had not been their neighbors but an unending parade of milkmen, bread salesmen, and other merchants hoping to sign them up for home delivery until the shopping center was completed. At first, the constant callers were a bother, but when the moving-in chores were over, the salesmen became social intermediaries, telling people about their neighbors, and pointing out the ones with similar backgrounds or interests. Children, too, were a catalyst. They were let out of the house at once to allow mothers to get the house settled, and immediately began to find age mates on the block. This brought parents of roughly similar age together. Where such playmates were not available, or if the children were too young, mothers would take them in hand and knock on a few doors to find out if children of similar age were nearby. The women then had an excuse to meet their neighbors.

The speed with which people met depended in part on the season. Winter arrivals could not get out of the house much and in some cases had to wait until spring, being lonely in the meantime. But the initial section was occupied when the weather was still warm, and the very first Levittowners came together quite quickly. Bad weather does not prevent socializing; it is, rather, that most people need an excuse to meet each other. The intrepid and extrovert few can go up and introduce themselves, but for most people such a frontal assault, with its tacit admission of loneliness and the possibility of being rejected, is impossible. In good weather, however, opportunities and excuses were at hand. One could take the children outside, and spend some time with them until a neighbor appeared, or one could work on the lawn for the same covert purpose. If these methods did not work, people could—and did—walk up and down the street with baby carriages or tricycling children as a way of extending the exchange of hellos to a meeting. Since everyone was dying of curiosity, such excuses were acceptable forms of breaking the isolation.

The feeling of optimism that neighbors would be friendly was not enough; there had to be some sign that there would be no rejection. Women asked, "Are you settled yet?" If the answer was positive, then invitations could be exchanged to look at each others' houses. Being settled meant that the house was in sufficient shape to express the image that the women wanted to create among their neighbors. The men, knowing that they would be less dependent on their neighbors for social activities, could be more casual, although they did help their wives, working on the front lawn to make sure that the image outside was as good as that inside.

Once the image was ready, and an initial meeting produced no rejection, people were prepared to exchange information and to look for common backgrounds or interests that would bind them together. They described where they had come from, and their—or their husbands'—

occupations, and went on to cover child-rearing methods and plans for fixing the house (women), the lawn, cars, and work (men). Every topic served either to bring people closer together or to pull them apart, by indicating where differences existed and what topics were taboo. For example, one of my neighbors was an Army pilot, and on our initial meeting—produced by a washout on our front lawns—we exchanged occupations. After I mentioned being a professor, he made a crack about another neighbor, a blue collar worker, to indicate that, although he referred to himself as "a glorified truck driver," he was, nevertheless, a white collar worker like me. He went on by talking about a relative who was studying for his Ph.D., but, aware that most professors were liberal and agnostic, he also let me know that he shared Southern race attitudes and was a fundamentalist Baptist. Disagreements would surely come up about race and religion, and if we were to be good neighbors, these subjects should not be discussed.

After the first bits of personal and family information had been exchanged, adjacent neighbors traded invitations to come in for coffee. If a social entrepreneur had moved onto the block, there might even be a block party, but as a rule, large gatherings needed another rationale so as to leave enough social distance between potentially incompatible people. One such device was a card party; another was a party at which a national manufacturer of plasticware or small appliances exhibited and sold his products to a group of invited women. Although the hostess of such a party might appear to trade on her social contacts in order to obtain material benefit—she received free products for holding the gathering—it was never interpreted in this fashion. "It gives me a chance to meet people I've wanted to meet," one such hostess explained. "It's just not right to go up to someone to say I want to meet you; that you only do with next-door neighbors. I'm not out to make money; it's just an excuse for partying." On the blocks that settled later, people got together after attending community-wide meetings or were introduced to each other through the charity fund drives. These were usually run by women experienced in community activity or by those who could knock on doors without trepidation, but even for the less courageous, collecting for the heart or cancer fund was an entree and, of course, a chance to meet the neighbors. Finally, such holidays as the Fourth of July, Hallowe'en, and Christmas allowed neighbors moving in just before then to throw a party without seeming too bold socially.

All of these occasions were structured to make overtures as successful as possible. Initial rejection was, of course, rare, for no one could be curt to a neighbor who would be living on the same block for several years. Too much social aggressiveness was out of the question, however, for most Levittowners were uncomfortable with "forward" people.

First encounters took anywhere from two weeks to a month or two;

they were followed by a period of considerable informal visiting and entertaining, lasting perhaps two to six months. These visits provided companionship and mutual support in the early period of living in a new community, for a new house in a still almost rural area created not only loneliness but also a variety of problems which were solved by getting together and "sharing ideas."

Each contact between neighbors could advance people closer to friendship, or it could bring out differences that would indicate that friendship was not possible. Both alternatives developed quickly. On one block a group of women had established a bridge club a month after arrival; on another, four women had a daily coffee-klatsch after about two months. On my block all of this happened so precipitously that by mid-December one neighbor could say, "I feel I have been in Levittown for years, the place is so settled."

The culture of the block jelled quite rapidly too. Standards of lawn care were agreed upon as soon as it was time to do something about the lawn, and by unspoken agreement, the front lawn would be cared for conscientiously, but the backyard was of less importance. Those who deviated from this norm—either neglecting their lawn or working on it too industriously—were brought into line through wisecracks. When I, in a burst of compulsive concern, worked very hard on my lawn at the start, one of my neighbors laughed and said he would have to move out if I was going to have "that fancy a lawn." Since I was not interested in a "fancy lawn," I found it easy to take the hint, but those who wanted a perfect lawn stayed away from the talkfests that usually developed evenings and on Saturday mornings when the men were ostensibly working on the lawns, so as not to be joked about and chastised as ratebusters.

Perhaps the best illustration of the rapid definition of block norms came at a party around Christmas time. A former New York suburbanite invited everyone to a stand-up cocktail party, but within an hour it had turned into an informal gathering, climaxed by a slightly drunken group sing. The almost immediate transformation from an upper middle class party to a lower middle class get-together took place for several reasons. Most of the guests were unfamiliar with cocktail parties and were not willing to stand up in the prescribed fashion. The hostess was dressed up in bright Capri pants, but one of the neighbors, of working class background, had never seen such pants, and thinking they were pajamas, concluded the party had been called off. Only when guests started arriving did she realize her error and later everyone, she included, laughed about it. The hostess' husband had objected to what he called a "Westchester County party" from the start, and the hostess went along with the dramatic metamorphosis too. She had not been putting on airs, but had thought her neighbors were like those in New York. From then on, social life on the block followed the norms of lower middle class entertaining.

Informal Clubs As people decided how they felt about their nearby neighbors, a sorting and departure process developed. Those who had become friends set up block cliques, others moved into multi-block ones, and yet others looked for friends elsewhere, particularly for evening visiting. The earliest departures took place among social and cultural *minority groups,* especially working and upper middle class people, older ones, and Jews—and all others who felt themselves out of place among their neighbors and needed or wanted to find their social life elsewhere. With this departure, the community stratification process began in earnest.[1]

Many of the Jewish women had come from predominantly Jewish areas in the cities and for a significant number, Levittown was the first real contact with non-Jewish neighbors. Some made friends, but many were not comfortable enough and began quite early to search for other Jewish women. The salesmen helped, but the process was immeasurably hastened by an unpredictable factor. One of the ministers who was forming a church had long admired the Jews. As he made the rounds looking for people for his church, he ran into a Jewish couple who mentioned the need for a synagogue in Levittown, and thereafter he passed on the names of all Jews he encountered. As a result, only five weeks after the first Levittowners had arrived, the twenty-six Jewish families among them met to discuss the formation of a synagogue. The meeting acquainted Jews with each other, and the first Levittown organization was set up a few days later—a mahjong club for Jewish women. It was not really a formal club, but by this time the county daily newspaper had added a society column, and the society editor was so short of news that she pounced on any grouping and promptly dubbed it a club.

Another sorting process occurred among a group of women on a block adjacent to mine. Although people chose their lots individually, the high proportion of Catholics brought it about that four women of that religion, all of them from working class backgrounds, lived close to each other. Since they differed from the evolving block culture, they began to meet every day for lengthy coffee-klatsches, partly in common defense against the middle class ethos. In fact coffee-klatsch cliques sprang up all over Levittown, although not half as many as the suburban myth claimed or as I had expected. Women not of a minority culture took occasional coffee with their neighbors, but they did not huddle together as closely.

Some of the coffee-klatsch groups expanded into block clubs, involving a dozen neighbors on adjacent blocks, which met fortnightly or monthly for conversation and/or cards, with individual members getting together in between. Some were formed by enterprising women who had belonged to similar clubs in other suburbs, but most developed among people with minority backgrounds or interests. They usually evolved after the summer, as block sociability waned and women wanted to make sure that they would see each other in winter, when people who do not visit each other regularly have little opportunity to meet. On one block, it was a group of older women; on another, a group of wives with traveling husbands—salesmen, pilots, or merchant seamen. Elsewhere, it was a group of Catholic women whose men had become involved in the organization of the Catholic parish and had told their wives, "You'd better get busy if you want companionship." Indeed, the clubs were often formed by women whose husbands were away from the house a lot. Most clubs were strictly female, although sometimes the men later formed card-playing clubs. One informal group, called the Happy Hours club, consisted of previously urban and primarily Italian couples who liked to stay up late and complained that their neighbors went to bed at 10 P.M. every night.

Most of the groups remained together for at least the three years that I was in touch with them. Some had become regular clubs when the group lost its initial enthusiasm and structure was needed as an adhesive. Sometimes, the organization was involuntary, as when the society reporter from the county daily wanted to write about them and asked them to take a name and become a club. Usually, the women did not want publicity, partly because neighbors who had not been invited to join would feel excluded.

Other minority group members had a more difficult time in finding friends close by and had to enter the larger community. Among these were professional and upper middle class people and, especially, college-educated women. They felt isolated on the blocks, and of course their dissatisfaction separated them further from the neighbors. Their feeling of estrangement in the pervasive lower middle class culture encouraged them to establish community-wide voluntary associations which could attract other Levittowners with similar social and cultural interests.

The Evolution of Social Life   The development of social relationships reached an equilibrium rapidly, for 75 percent of the interview respondents reported having settled down both in the house and in the community within six months, and fully half indicated it took even less time than that. After two years in Levittown, 47 percent reported that they were doing about as much individual visiting with neighbors as they had after six months; 30 percent said they were doing more. Nighttime visiting with other couples increased, 43 percent reporting more, 34 percent about the same, and the rest, less. About a third indicated the couples they spent most of their time with were neighbors, while 24 percent mentioned people they met in community organizations, and 13 percent, those met at church. Only 20 percent indicated that none of their friends were neighbors. The people who did more visiting with other couples than after arrival also said they visited with neighbors more, and vice versa. About a quarter of the respondents reported less visiting with couples and neighbors than before, however, and these respondents were primarily low-status people with less than a high school education, and with blue collar jobs.

Over time, the block system had stabilized as well, ranging from close friendship among some to open hostility among a few, but mostly calling for friendly coexistence and occasional visiting among those who were not friends. Holiday parties increased cohesion temporarily, and if an accident or illness befell a neighbor everyone pitched in to help as much as he could, regardless of how people felt about the family.

The prevailing equilibrium was most often interrupted by two phenomena: the turnover of residents and fights among neighbors. The latter were not frequent, but when they happened, they could produce lasting feuds. Most squabbles generated over the children. If children quarrel—and they often do—parents naturally take sides. If one set of parents feels that the other child is in the wrong and has not been sufficiently punished or that his wrongdoing is a result of what it considers poor parental supervision, the children's conflict is likely to become one between parents. This may continue long after the children have forgotten the fight. Parental conflicts, of course, expressed deeper disagreements between neighbors; friends do not fight over their children's battles. Sometimes there was an eventual reconciliation, but often people just stopped talking to each other.

Turnover was then slight and stemmed largely from transfers by employers, but if the relationship with neighbors had been intense, the family who took over the house was not invited to join the group. If ties were less close and the newcomer amicable and of similar age and background, she was usually welcomed. As one pointed out, "I had to push a little at first to get people to talk to me, but now there's no problem. There isn't much coffee-klatsching here, we are all too busy cleaning. But I'm pregnant, and the gal next door just had a baby too, so that made for a common interest."

The arrival of a baby was always an event in Levittown—where it was an everyday occurrence—and there was likely to be a baby shower and renewed interest in the mother among the neighbors. A first pregnancy also incorporated old-time residents into the block society. One of my neighbors had worked prior to her pregnancy, and had not been around for the weekday exchange of coffee visits. When the baby came, she was at once visited by another neighbor, also pregnant, and then became part of the block, even though it had been two years since they had all arrived.

The Founding of Voluntary Associations

In a new community, organizations can be started by outsiders or by residents, that is, by *external* or *internal initiative*. The residents can act *intentionally* to achieve community aspirations held before arrival, or *unintentionally*, responding to community conditions of the moment. This suggests three types of origin: *External, Internal-Intended,* and *Internal-Unintended*.[2] For simplicity's sake, I will call the first *External*, the second *Internal*, and the third *Unintended*.

In Levittown, almost a third of all organizations set up in the first two years were External. These were usually branches of nationwide associations, especially service clubs, veterans' groups, and women's social clubs. Since Levittown's opening had been widely heralded for some time, and a community of 12,000 or more families were expected, the associations saw a golden opportunity to expand their roster of branches and members. Some used professional organizers who go from community to community, but most asked or encouraged branches in nearby towns to organize their new neighbor. Many associations give annual awards to the local branches which set up the most new groups and enroll the most new members, and the winners obtain increased political strength within the national association. Indeed, a man who wants to be a national or state officer in a service or veterans' club is materially aided in his rise up the hierarchy by getting a reputation as a "starter." This incentive extends to professional organizers as well. Almost two years before Levittown opened, national Boy Scouts headquarters had requested the county office to start tooling up for forming troops in Levittown. A young executive was added to the county staff; he had taken a pay cut to come, knowing full well that he would be able to organize many troops, thereby enhancing his chances for rapid career advancement in the future.

Most organizations waited until the community was settled, but then went into action quickly in the hope of bringing the potential leaders and active participants among the Levittowners into their group before others had a chance to attract them. As a result, the Veterans of Foreign Wars (VFW) arrived on the scene after only three months, when Levittown had barely two hundred families, and the Lions, Kiwanis, and the Junior Chamber of Commerce followed shortly afterwards. Later, O.R.T. (a Jewish women's service organization), 4-H, a B'nai B'rith Lodge for men, a county hospital auxiliary, a civil defense group, the Optimists (a men's service club), B'rith Sholom (a Jewish fraternity), and the American Legion were founded in a similar manner.

The Internal method of organization was used principally by women's groups, with a Levittowner who had been active in the group in the past and had intended to start a new branch doing so as soon as enough potential members seemed to be available. The founders' motives varied. Some were looking for advancement in the national organizational hierarchy; others wanted to be the first president of the new group; but for most, the organization had become integral to their lives. A founder of a Jewish women's group explained her initiative by saying, "I could not conceive of living without Hadassah." Among other groups founded in this fashion were Deborah, a women's organization supporting a national tuberculosis hospital, a B'nai B'rith Lodge for women, the Federated Women's Club, the League of Women Voters, and Beta Sigma Phi, a sorority for women without college degrees.

Externally and Internally founded organizations were usually national branches, but sometimes people who had been active in local groups in their former communities came with the intention of starting one in Levittown. A Texan imported the Lords and Ladies Club, which held monthly dances at county supper clubs for middle class managerial families who wanted but could not afford a country club. The Emergency Ambulance Squad was initiated by a man who had been an officer of one in his previous community.

Most local groups were Unintended, founded in response to some felt community or individual need. Usually people with similar interests came together, sometimes accidentally, sometimes because they were a minority which needed to be together, and sometimes because they could gain from formal organization. Several ham radio operators met by sheer accident, having heard each other over the air. A Ham Club was started when it became possible to obtain civil defense funds to convert their hobby into a community service.

On the other hand, a number of Unintended groups arose because members individually could not do without them, particularly women who were lonely and could not find compatible neighbors. One woman turned to the national office of Pan-Hellenic, a sorority for college graduates to which she had once belonged. Her decision to form a branch was primarily a function of class difference; she found herself uninterested in block-club card games and gossip. On the other hand, the Levittown Women's Club, a branch of the Federated Women's Clubs of America, was founded without premeditation by a lonely resident who had been active in a branch elsewhere and had simply enjoyed her membership. In many cases, wives whose husbands were frequently out of town became Unintended founders. The organizer of the Women's Club and the two neighbors with whom she worked were married to salesmen or pilots. Subsequently, women whose traveling husbands worked in the same firm or line also started groups. For instance, the local newspaper reported of the "RCA Wives" that "from the first meeting it is evident that a lot of the wives whose husbands are away a great deal are more than eager to constructively fill their time."[3]

Similar clubs were organized by the wives of merchant seamen and Air Force pilots.

In other cases, the impetus was culturally based. An All-Nations club of foreign wives, and before that a British Wives club, were organized, as were a dramatic society, a ceramics club, a folk dance group, an art club, and branches of two national groups, the Great Books Club and the Buxom Belles (devoted to group weight reduction). In two neighborhoods the scarcity of baby-sitters encouraged the formation of cooperatives in which women exchanged baby-sitting services for each other. They were popular with Jewish women who wanted to get out for club meetings but whose husbands worked evenings in stores in the Philadelphia area.

Community needs and issues generated a number of spontaneous civic and political groups. Dissatisfaction with Board of Education policies brought about the Citizens' Association for Public Schools; the Levittown Youth Sports Association was founded by the police chief in the hope of keeping adolescents busy to prevent juvenile delinquency; and doctors organized a professional group to protect themselves against the osteopaths who outnumbered them in the area.

As the community matured, a number of Unintended groups arose in opposition to already established ones. A Jewish fraternity sprang up because men wanting social activities were dissatisfied with the existing Jewish men's club, primarily dedicated to fund raising for the synagogue, and civic associations developed in the later neighborhoods to defend their interests before elected officials who came largely from the initially settled areas. The service and veterans' groups stimulated women's auxiliaries, generally Externally, but sometimes on an Unintended basis because the wives wanted to help their husbands, and share a common organizational affiliation. Unintended groups also sprang up in later neighborhoods because the residents were unwilling to join groups formed by residents from the initial neighborhoods, feeling they would not be welcomed by the older residents, or because they thought they had more in common with people who had moved in at the same time. Besides, an ambitious founder could organize a new group more easily than enter an established group and work his way up.

The Organizational Process   Anyone can start an organization, but it can only survive by attracting members, and for this reason the organizational process was often the same. The first step was, of course, to get in touch with potential members. National organizations used mailing lists to find members who had just moved to Levittown or had the school send invitations home via the students. There were newspaper ads and stories and announcements at meetings of other organizations. But perhaps most successful was the practice of enrolling friends and neighbors. People who wanted to start an organization often called on their neighbors for help, exploiting the cohesion developed on the block; people curious enough to come to a first meeting brought a neighbor for company and security. Later interviews showed that of the people who had not intended to join groups, fully 36 percent had been drawn in by neighbors.[4] This banding together affected the organizational process in two ways. Founders who called on friends to help them quickly developed leadership cliques. This often speeded up the organizing process, but in some cases it led to protests that the group was run by a clique, and then to rival cliques. It also made many groups into virtual neighborhood clubs, and discouraged joiners from other neighborhoods. Thus, new clubs with the same manifest aim, such as service clubs, appeared when new neighborhoods were settled because the previously organized clubs were in effect exclusive.

These consequences were quite unintended, for all groups were open to any person wanting to join. Even those which had membership requirements—for example, service clubs which in other towns took only men in retail business—opened their rolls to anyone who was interested. The opportunity to be a charter member—or an officer—was publicized to get people into the organization and to establish it as quickly as possible on a firm basis. The next step was the election of officers and development of program. Both stages also proceeded with great haste in order to secure the existence of the organization as quickly as possible. Once the group was chartered, the program could be used to attract further members, making available more people and funds to recruit others, expand the organization, and thus guarantee its survival. Officers were usually elected at either the first or second meeting, often before people had a chance to get acquainted. Ambitious leaders could generally get themselves elected and put their friends into office as well, although occasionally attendance was so small that everyone present became an officer willy-nilly. Most of the time, the wish to get the group organized and chartered immediately preempted the selection of the right people for the position. For example, one founder had persuaded the newspaper to run a picture of the elected officers, and the election had to be hurried so that a slate of officers could pose for the photographer when he came. Another meeting was thrown into an uproar by one Levittowner who argued that the norms of democracy demanded the postponement of elections until people knew the candidates and each other, but those in attendance wanted the organization, a neighborhood PTA, established that night, and voted to elect a slate nominated by the founder and her friends.

The Definitional Struggle The rapidity of the organizing process created a considerable amount of conflict in many organizations. These conflicts were usually ascribed to "personalities," reflecting the inability of people to get along. Some were generated by the newness of the community, for, as one leader put it, "When you don't know each other, it is hard to separate the workers from the talkers."[5] More often, the fights between personalities were actually *definitional struggles* about the purpose, composition, and program of the group, especially in organizations without nationally prescribed activities. Probably the most important source of differences was class. For example, the VFW, the first male organization in Levittown, initially attracted both working class and a smaller number of middle class people. From the start, working class members wanted a primarily social organization; the middle class, a community service group. The confrontation was relatively brief, however; after a few weeks, the middle class leaders left to organize the Catholic Church. Where such alternative outlets were not available, factions and bitter struggles developed over the election of the second year's set of officers.

In one women's club, the definitional struggle was over the amount of innovation permissible in club tradition. This involved differences of age and of class. The traditionalists, who were somewhat older and more restrictively lower middle class, wanted a closed group with a statusful program of "culture"; the innovators, more expansive, called for open admission and a program of "community service." The crucial but never stated issue was over the admission of working class women; this came out when the leader of the traditional faction described her opponent as wanting to run the club as if it were a firehouse—a historical preserve for the working class.[6] The adherents of open admission won, and the leader of the traditionalists retired to set up an art club, while the victorious advocate of community service later went into politics.

There was also constant debate over the speed of organization, with "go-slow" factions who wanted the group to establish itself firmly before it indulged in too many activities, and "go-fast" ones which argued—usually successfully—that a rapid pace was needed to advertise the organization in order to enroll new members. A similar conflict was noticeable in leadership struggles. Founders were often dynamic and even charismatic people who attracted publicity and thus members, but then tended to order the more active ones around and alienated them. Whether praised as "starters" or discredited as "pushers," they would eventually be replaced by more diplomatic officers, administrators who were able to get people to work together. Of twelve officers who had succeeded founders, eleven indicated that the one thing they were doing differently was "stabilizing the organization" or "delegating authority to a much greater extent."[7] In some working class groups, the founder sometimes lacked administrative skills and later gave way to a better-educated, lower middle class member who was more able to run meetings and manage relations with other groups.

Most definitional struggles ended with the acquiescence of the losing faction and the gradual departure of its members. Eventually, many organizations achieved a measure of stability, both in number of members and in programs, with occasional innovation in activities, particularly of the community service variety that would publicize the group anew. If membership lagged, there were likely to be periods of organizational revival, sparked by the appearance of a new leader whose dynamism and willingness to work enabled him to move rapidly into the organization's ruling circle. The new arrivals were usually people who had previously belonged to the organization elsewhere.

Not all groups underwent definitional struggles, however. In many national organizations, the leaders had been active in other suburbs and other new branches and thus had a ready answer to the inevitable first question: How should we get started? Indeed, almost all groups tried to find members with past experience in new (or old) groups, hoping that their "ideas" would work in Levittown. Often then, the young organizations relied on traditional solutions, although when definitional struggles developed, the voices of experience were not respected.

The haste with which organizations sought to get started is shown by the chronological pattern of founding. During the first nine months of Levittown's existence, when the population was small and most people were still settling into house and block, 14 groups sprang up (not counting churches and church-related ones), and from September 1959 to June 1960, when the population enlarged and more people were ready to look beyond the block, 36 were founded. The peak had already been reached, however; only 14 additional groups appeared during the 1960–1961 season and just 13 more in the next four years—for a grand total of 77.[8] Only a handful of these failed to survive, although some have carried on with just a few members. When interviewed after two years, about 70 percent of the respondents reported belonging to at least one of these organizations.

Externally founded groups and branches of national ones were of course able to mobilize more quickly, and regardless of how they were founded, those appealing to ethnic or class minorities were set up earlier than those appealing to the dominant lower middle class population. Among the churches, for example, the Jews and the fundamentalist Baptists were the first, and organizations appealing to lower-status groups preceded those of higher status. Among the men's groups, the order was exactly in terms of status; the VFW arriving first, followed shortly thereafter by the Lions, Kiwanis, and Junior Chamber of Commerce, with the Optimists and Rotarians waiting until the community was two years old. Higher-status organizations can afford to wait because they know that people will join whenever they appear, and such groups even bide their time to see who the highest-status leaders are. Low-status groups benefit from early establishment, for this gives them an opportunity to attract higher-status people who want to become active immediately. Among the women's groups, lower-status groups also preceded higher ones, although those enrolling a large proportion of

Jews came before all others. Groups with similar programs and appealing to the same types of people organized almost *seriatim* so as not to be left behind in the competition for members.

Organizational Origin and Residents' Aspirations. If the aspirations Levittowners volunteered before arrival had guided the founding process, most organizations would have been started Internally by people to whom they were important. Civic groups would have outnumbered social clubs and both would have been surpassed by home-and-family-centered groups such as PTAs, Scouts, and garden clubs.

As it turned out, however, only 24 percent of the organizations emerging in the first two years were Internal, 31 percent were External, and the remaining 45 percent were Unintended. More were social than were civic—28 percent were purely social and cultural; 28 percent, mixed social and service; and 16 percent, civic. Only 14 percent were family-centered, although that proportion would triple if churches were considered in this category. (The rest included "occupational" groups, such as the Medical Club, an investment club, and, of course, a garden club.)

It is worthwhile asking, therefore, why the groups that sprang up were not those that people wanted before they came, why almost a third could be organized by outsiders who knew nothing about the new community, and whether the large number of Unintended groups, which sprang up on the spur of the moment, represented the impact of community conditions on the origin process.

One answer suffices for all three questions. How organizations were founded was ultimately less relevant than what happened to them once they were founded. No organization, however it started, could exist beyond the initial meeting without responding to some needs among the members it attracted, and these needs were not only more important than founders' or members' preoccupancy aspirations, but they developed largely after people had lived in Levittown for a while. External, Internal, and Unintended groups alike responded to these needs, which turned out to be more social than civic or familial; or to put it another way, civic and familial needs were satisfied by public agencies and political groups, leaving the voluntary associations to fill the social needs.

Aside from the few civic groups, which tried to intervene in municipal affairs, and the men's service clubs, which provided "community-minded" activities for the lawyers, salesmen, realtors, and politicians who needed to advertise themselves in the community, the organizations were primarily *sorting* groups which divided and segregated people by their interests and ultimately, of course, by socioeconomic, educational, and religious differences. On the block, people who shared a common space could not really express their diversity; the community sorting groups came into being for this purpose.

Men could divide and segregate themselves on the job, but the women had to do it in the community, and partly for this reason most organizations were sexually separated, with only some of those appealing to upper middle class people providing "coeducational" activities. The total array of women's groups offered the opportunity for extremely fine sorting. Well-educated women would be likely to find compatible people and activities in the American Association for University Women, the League of Women Voters, Great Books, or the Better Schools Committee, and, if they were more socially inclined, the Pan-Hellenic Society; those with less than a college degree could choose from among a dozen groups. Working class women clung to the church—the Altar and Rosary Society was the town's largest club a year after it was started—or joined the auxiliaries of their husbands' groups. Religious sorting was also available, for every church had men's and women's groups, and some secular organizations became predominantly Catholic, others Protestant or Jewish. The Jews had their own secular clubs which sorted by age and class. Occupational specialties were honored; ex-nurses worked in hospital auxiliaries and ex-teachers became active in the PTA. One Levittowner even talked about a Texas club; she too wanted to be "with her own."

Organizational programs reflected these diversities. The organizations of the college-educated stressed cultural activities and local or national political issues; those of the high school graduates scheduled fashion shows and lectures on beauty, home management, and child care. The highly educated shunned "gossip," their own version of it being buried in the discussion of social issues. Games, always major organizational sidelines, were also stratified, ranging from poker, pinochle, and hearts up to canasta, scrabble, and bridge. Municipal services and formal governmental institutions still being in a primitive stage, most groups combined social sorting with a variety of community service activities. The upper middle class groups put on candidates' night and community forums; the working class groups concentrated on sports for the children, fire-fighting, and Fourth of July ceremonies; the lower middle class groups' activities ranged from rolling bandages, running Miss Levittown contests, and collecting books for the library to helping the Superintendent of Schools.

Needless to say, the kinds of sorting groups that Levittown would require could not be determined until after people had lived there for a while and could see how many friends they could find on the block and what charitable and civic activities needed to be supplied. As a result, they could not have anticipated before arrival what kinds of organizations they would actually join.[9] Likewise, the organizations could not anticipate their members' demands and needs in advance, but once they knew them, they adapted to them. This was particularly true of national and Externally founded groups, which developed new functions in Levittown having little to do with the reasons they came or with the aims in their national charters.[10] These groups succeeded only because they were able to bend to local needs when necessary.[11] For example, two Jewish national women's groups became essentially neighborhood clubs for young, managerial upper middle class women and older, lower middle class women, respectively. Most of their members knew little about the national organization but simply wanted Jewish companionship. A 4-H group was rescued after a poorly attended organizational meeting because the county agent chanced on a clique of teenage girls who needed a club to keep the group together, although they were not particularly interested in the 4-H program. The national groups were rarely aware of how their branches changed in Levittown—but then they did not care particularly, so long as they could add to their membership rolls.

The Unintentionally founded clubs were not much different from the others. Although they did not have to alter themselves to succeed, they too functioned primarily as sorting groups. Some were, of course, generated by community conditions, for example, the Sitters clubs, which responded to the shortage of baby-sitters, and a Juvenile Discussion group which met to do something about juvenile delinquency. Sometimes community conditions hastened the arrival of groups that would eventually have developed anyway. The Jewish community organized almost immediately because Jewish women found themselves ill at ease with their neighbors, and an institution was needed to celebrate Chanukah so the children could be discouraged from demanding Christmas trees.

Yet none of the sorting needs and community conditions were so distinctive as to require unique organizations. The ability of national groups to bend to local priorities helped, but even the local associations, 40 percent of the total, were modeled on similar organizations elsewhere and none was entirely original to Levittown. They were, rather, typical of those found in most other suburbs and communities of young families of similar class. In fact, although they considered themselves community-wide organizations, almost half of thirty-six for which membership addresses were available drew most of their people from one or two neighborhoods. Clearly, people cared less about the nominal purpose and scope of the group than to be with fellow residents who had come to Levittown at about the same time and were compatible in other ways.

NOTES

1. For descriptions of similar processes in other new developments, see R. H. Danhof, "The Accommodation and Integration of Conflicting Cultures in a Newly Established Community," *American Journal of Sociology*, 9, July 1943, 14–23; William H. Form, "Status Stratification in a Planned Community," *American Sociological Review*, 10, October 1945, 605–13, reprinted in William M. Dobriner, ed., *The Suburban Community* (New York: G. P. Putnam's Sons, 1958), pp. 209–24; and particularly William H. Form, "Stratification in Low

and Middle Income Housing Areas," *Journal of Social Issues*, 7 (1951), Nos. 1 and 2, 109–31; Robert Gutman, "Population Mobility in the American Middle Class," in Leonard J. Duhl, ed., *The Urban Condition* (New York: Basic Books, 1963), pp. 172–83; Henrik F. Infield, "A Veterans' Cooperative Land Settlement and Its Sociometric Structure," *Sociometry*, 10, February 1947, 50–70; Eva Rosenfeld, "Social Stratification in a Classless Society," *American Sociological Review*, 16, December 1951, pp. 766–74; and William H. Whyte, Jr., *The Organization Man* (New York: Simon & Schuster, 1956), chaps. 25 and 26.

2. An Unintended organization could, of course, be Externally founded, with outsiders starting a group in the new community in order to protect their own interests. This explains the formation of the Levittown Civic Association, but no other.

3. *Levittown Life*, July 6, 1961.

4. A national study of volunteers for the March of Dimes found that the largest proportion, 52 percent, joined after being asked by friends. David Sills, *The Volunteers* (New York: Free Press of Glencoe, 1957), pp. 102–103.

5. Conversely, a woman who participated in a telephone survey to find mothers for the PTA mentioned that she could tell from the person's voice and the topic of conversation whether that individual was "officer material."

6. When Levittown was racially integrated, this club was one of the few which debated the exclusion of Negroes, but eventually decided not to do so.

7. William M. Michelson, *Adult Voluntary Association in Levittown* (Princeton University, Department of Sociology: Unpublished senior thesis, April 1961), p. 91.

8. If the neighborhood PTAs and the men's, women's, youth, and couples' clubs organized by the churches were included, the total would easily reach 100.

9. Later, all belonging to social and civic groups and 73 percent belonging to the men's service clubs said they had not intended to join these groups before coming to Levittown, as compared to only 31 percent of those in the PTA, the Scouts, and other child-centered organizations.

10. Although 61 percent of memberships in national organizations were intended before arrival, as compared to none in local groups, this reflected mainly the willingness of Mobiles and Transients to rejoin groups in which they had been active before.

11. Men's needs seemed more predictable; 73 percent of their groups were intended, as compared to only 48 percent of the women's, the latters' founding responding more directly to the sorting needs that developed in the community. Also, middle class founders were more responsive to their fellow residents than working class ones; 56 percent of organizations with predominantly working class memberships depending on External founders, and only 6 percent on Internal ones. Among middle class groups, only 9 percent were founded Externally and 48 percent Internally.

fred davis

San Francisco's Haight Ashbury is no longer the mecca of the Hip Generation. Yet, it still symbolizes a new type of community that is more than miles away from Levittown—and Mason City. To many, "Hashbury's" brief period of glory and sudden decline is but a sampling of what we can expect in the future.

Fred Davis studied the Hippies of the Haight, their lifestyles and values. His report begins with a comment on why middle-class attitudes are being rejected by the children of affluence. He then attempts to deal with the meaning of the subculture they and their counterparts in Berkeley, Cambridge, New York, Amsterdam, Copenhagen, and elsewhere are creating and the characteristics of a community that transcends political boundaries.

Davis offers personal observations and comments on three areas of special concern to—and rejection by—the members of the community: "compulsive consumption," "passive spectatorship," and "the time scale of experience."

And thus in love we have declared the purpose of our hearts plainly, without flatterie, expecting love, and the same sincerity from you, without grumbling, or quarreling, being Creatures of your own image and mould, intending no other matter herein, but to observe the Law of righteous action, endeavoring to shut out of the Creation, the cursed thing, called Particular Propriety, which is the cause of all wars, bloodshed, theft, and enslaving Laws, that hold the people under miserie.

Signed for and in behalf of all the poor oppressed people of England, and the whole world.

Gerrard Winstanley and others   June 1, 1649

From Fred Davis, "Why All of Us May Be Hippies Someday," copyright © December 1967 by *Transaction*, Inc., New Brunswick, New Jersey.

This quotation is from the leader of the Diggers, a millenarian sect of communistic persuasion that arose in England at the time of Oliver Cromwell. Today in San Francisco's hippie community, the Haight-Ashbury district, a group of hippies naming themselves after this sect distributes free food to fellow hippies (and all other takers, for that matter) who congregate at about four o'clock every afternoon in the district's Panhandle, an eight-block strip of urban green, shaded by towering eucalyptus trees, that leads into Golden Gate Park to the west. On the corner of a nearby street, the "Hashbury" Diggers operate their Free Store where all—be they hip, straight, hostile, curious, or merely in need—can avail themselves (free of charge, no questions asked) of such used clothing, household articles, books, and second-hand furniture as find their way into the place on any particular day. The Diggers also maintained a large flat in the district where newly arrived or freshly dispossessed hippies could stay without charge for a night, a week, or however long they wished—until some months ago, when the flat was condemned by the San Francisco Health Department. Currently, the Diggers are rehabilitating a condemned skid-row hotel for the same purpose.

Not all of Haight-Ashbury's 7500 hippies are Diggers, although no formal qualifications bar them; nor, in one sense, are the several dozen Diggers hippies. What distinguishes the Diggers—an amorphous, shifting, and sometimes contentious amalgam of ex-political radicals, psychedelic mystics, Ghandians, and Brechtian avant-garde thespians—from the area's "ordinary" hippies is their ideological brio, articulateness, good works, and flair for the dramatic event. (Some are even rumored to be over 30.) In the eyes of many Hashbury hippies, therefore, the Diggers symbolize what is best, what is most persuasive and purposive, about the surrounding, more variegated hippie subculture—just as, for certain radical social critics of the American scene, the hippies are expressing, albeit elliptically, what is best about a seemingly ever-broader segment of American youth: its openness to new experience, puncturing of cant, rejection of bureaucratic regimentation, aversion to violence, and identification with the exploited and disadvantaged. That this is not the whole story barely needs saying. Along with the poetry and flowers, the melancholy smile at passing and ecstatic clasp at greeting, there is also the panicky incoherence of the bad LSD trip, the malnutrition, a startling rise in V.D. and hepatitis, a seemingly phobic reaction to elementary practices of hygiene and sanitation, and—perhaps most disturbing in the long run—a casualness about the comings and goings of human relationships that must verge on the grossly irresponsible.

But, then, social movements—particularly of this expressive-religious variety—are rarely of a piece, and it would be unfortunate if social scientists, rather than inquiring into the genesis, meaning, and future of the hippie movement, too soon joined ranks (as many are likely to, in any case) with solid burghers in an orgy of research into the "pathology" of it all: the ubiquitous drug use (mainly marihuana and LSD, often amphetamines, rarely heroin or other opiates), the easy attitudes toward sex ("If two people are attracted to each other, what better way of showing it than to make love?"), and the mocking hostility toward the middle-class values of pleasure-deferral, material success, and—ultimately—the whole mass-media-glamorized round of chic, deodorized, appliance-glutted suburban existence.

The Hip Scene Is the Message

Clearly, despite whatever real or imagined "pathology" middle-class spokesmen are ready to assign to the hippies, it is the middle-class scheme of life that young hippies are reacting against, even though in their ranks are to be found some youth of working-class origin who have never enjoyed the affluence that their peers now so heartily decry. To adulterate somewhat the slogan of Marshall McLuhan, one of the few non-orientalized intellectuals whom hippies bother to read at all, *the hip scene is the message,* not the elements whence it derives or the meanings that can be assigned to it verbally. (Interestingly, this fusion of disparate classes does not appear to include any significant number of the Negro youths who reside with their families in the integrated Haight-Ashbury district or in the adjoining Negro ghetto, the Fillmore district. By and large, Negroes view with bewilderment and ridicule the white hippies who flaunt, to the extent of begging on the streets, their rejection of what the Negroes have had scant opportunity to attain. What more revealing symbol of the Negro riots in our nation's cities than the carting off of looted TV sets, refrigerators, and washing machines? After all, aren't these things what America is all about?)

But granting that the hippie scene is a reaction to middle-class values, can the understanding of any social movement—particularly one that just in the process of its formation is so fecund of new art forms, new styles of dress and demeanor, and (most of all) new ethical bases for human relationships—ever be wholly reduced to its reactive aspect? As Ralph Ellison has eloquently observed in his critique of the standard sociological explanation of the American Negro's situation, a people's distinctive way of life is never solely a reaction to the dominant social forces that have oppressed, excluded, or alienated them from the larger society. The cumulative process of reaction and counterreaction, in its historical unfolding, ceates its own ground for the emergence of new symbols, meanings, purposes, and social discoveries, none of which are ever wholly contained in embryo, as it were, in the conditions that elicited the reaction. It is, therefore, less with an eye toward explaining "how it came to be" than toward explaining what it may betoken of life in the future society that I now want to examine certain facets of the Hashbury hippie subculture. (Of course, very similar youth movements, subcultures, and settlements are found nowadays in many parts of the affluent Western world—Berkeley's Telegraph Avenue teeny-boppers; Los Angeles' Sunset Strippers; New York's East Village hippies; London's mods; Amsterdam's Provos; and the summer *Wandervögel* from all over Europe who chalk the pavement of Copenhagen's main shopping street, the Strøget, and sun themselves on the steps of Stockholm's Philharmonic Hall. What is culturally significant about the Haight-Ashbury hippies is, I would hazard, in general significant about these others as well, with—to be sure—certain qualifications. Indeed, a certain marvelous irony attaches itself to the fact that perhaps the only genuine cross-national culture found in the world today builds on the rag-tag of beards, bare feet, bedrolls, and beads, not on the cultural-exchange programs of governments and universities, or tourism, or—least of all—ladies' clubs' invocations for sympathetic understanding of one's foreign neighbors.)

What I wish to suggest here is that there is, as Max Weber would have put it, an *elective affinity* between prominent styles and themes in the hippie subculture and certain incipient problems of identity, work, and leisure that loom ominously as Western industrial society moves into an epoch of accelerated cybernation, staggering material abundance, and historically-unprecedented mass opportunities for creative leisure and enrichment of the human personality. This is not to say that the latter are the *hidden causes* or tangible *motivating forces* of the former. Rather, the point is that the hippies, in their collective, yet radical, break with the constraints of our present society, are—whether they know it or not (some clearly do intuit a connection)—already rehearsing *in vivo* a number of possible cultural solutions to central life problems posed by the emerging society of the future. While other students of contemporary youth culture could no doubt cite many additional emerging problems to which the hippie subculture is, willy-nilly, addressing itself (marriage and family organization, the character of friendship and personal loyalties, the forms of political participation), space and the kind of observations I have been able to make require that I confine myself to three: the problems of *compulsive consumption*, of *passive spectatorship*, and of the *time-scale of experience*.

Compulsive Consumption

What working attitude is man to adopt toward the potential glut of consumer goods that the new technology will make available to virtually all members of the future society? Until now, modern capitalist society's traditional response to short-term conditions of overproduction has been to generate—through government manipulation of fiscal devices—greater purchasing power for discretionary consumption. At the same time, the aim has been to cultivate the acquisitive impulse—largely through mass advertising, annual styling changes, and planned obsolescence—so that, in the economist's terminology, a high level of aggregate demand could be sustained. Fortunately, given the great backlog of old material wants and the technologically-based creation of new wants, these means have, for the most part, worked comparatively well—both for advancing (albeit unequally) the mass standard of living and ensuring a reasonably high rate of return to capital.

But, as Walter Weisskopf, Robert Heilbroner, and other economists have wondered, will these means prove adequate for an automated future society in which the mere production of goods and services might easily outstrip man's desire for them, or his capacity to consume them in satisfying ways? Massive problems of air pollution, traffic congestion, and waste disposal aside, is there no psychological limit to the number of automobiles, TV sets, freezers, and dishwashers that even a zealous consumer can aspire to, much less make psychic room for in his life space? The specter that haunts post-industrial man is that of a near worker-less economy in which most men are constrained, through a variety of economic and political sanctions, to frantically purchase and assiduously use up the cornucopia of consumer goods that a robot-staffed factory system (but one still harnessed to capitalism's rationale of pecuniary profit) regurgitates upon the populace. As far back as the late 1940s sociologists like David Riesman were already pointing to the many moral paradoxes of work, leisure, and interpersonal relations posed by a then only nascent society of capitalist mass abundance. How much more perplexing the paradoxes if, using current technological trends, we extrapolate to the year 2000?

Hippies, originating mainly in the middle classes, have been nurtured at the boards of consumer abundance. Spared their parents' vivid memories of economic depression and material want, however, they now, with what to their elders seems like insulting abandon, declare unshamefacedly that the very quest for "the good things of life" and all that this entails—the latest model, the third car, the monthly credit payments, the right house in the right neighborhood—are a "bad bag." In phrases redolent of nearly all utopian thought of the past, they proclaim that happiness and a meaningful life are not to be found in things, but in the cultivation of the self and by an intensive exploration of inner sensibilities with like-minded others.

Extreme as this antimaterialistic stance may seem, and despite its probable tempering should hippie communities develop as a stable feature on the American landscape, it nonetheless points a way to a solution of the problem of material glut; to wit, the simple demonstration of the ability to live on less, thereby calming the acquisitive frenzy that would have to be sustained, and even accelerated, if the present scheme of capitalist production and distribution were to remain unchanged. Besides such establishments as the Diggers' Free Store, gleanings of this attitude are even evident in the street panhandling that so many hippies engage in. Unlike the street beggars of old, there is little that is obsequious or deferential about their manner. On the contrary, their approach is one of easy, sometimes condescending casualness, as if to say, "You've got more than enough to spare, I need it, so let's not make a degrading charity scene out of my asking you." The story is told in the Haight-Ashbury of the patronizing tourist who, upon being approached for a dime by a hippie girl in her late teens, took the occasion to deliver a small speech on how delighted he would be to give it to her—provided she first told him what she needed it for. Without blinking an eye she replied, "It's my menstrual period and that's how much a sanitary napkin costs."

Passive Spectatorship

As social historians are forever reminding us, modern man has—since the beginnings of the industrial revolution—become increasingly a spectator and less a participant. Less and less does he, for example, create or play music, engage in sports, dance or sing; instead he watches professionally-trained others, vastly more accomplished than himself, perform their acts while he, perhaps, indulges in Mitty-like fantasies of hidden graces and talents. Although this bald statement of the spectator thesis has been challenged in recent years by certain social researchers— statistics are cited of the growing numbers taking guitar lessons, buying fishing equipment, and painting on Sunday—there can be little doubt that "doing" kinds of expressive pursuits, particularly of the collective type, no longer bear the same *integral* relationship to daily life that they once did, or still do in primitive societies. The mere change in how they come to be perceived, from what one does in the ordinary course of life to one's "hobbies," is in itself of profound historical significance. Along with this, the virtuoso standards that once were the exclusive property of small aristocratic elites, rather than being undermined by the oft-cited revolutions in mass communications and mass education, have so diffused through the class structure as to even cause the gifted amateur *at play* to apologize for his efforts with some such remark as, "I only play at it." In short, the cult of professionalism, in the arts as elsewhere, has been institutionalized so intensively in Western society that the ordinary man's sense of expressive adequacy and competence has progressively atrophied. This is especially true of the college-educated, urban middle classes, which—newly exposed to the lofty aesthetic standards of high culture—stand in reverent, if passive, awe of them.

Again, the problem of excessive spectatorship has not proved particularly acute until now, inasmuch as most men have had other time-consuming demands to fill their lives with, chiefly work and family life, leavened by occasional vacations and mass-produced amusements. But what of the future when, according to such social prognosticators as Robert Theobald and Donald Michael, all (except a relatively small cadre of professionals and managers) will be faced with a surfeit of leisure time? Will the mere extension of passive spectatorship and the professional's monopoly of expressive pursuits be a satisfactory solution?

Here, too, hippies are opening up new avenues of collective response to life issues posed by a changing socio-technological environment. They are doing so by rejecting those virtuoso standards that stifle participation in high culture; by substituting an extravagantly eclectic (and, according to traditional aestheticians, reckless) admixture of materials, styles, and motifs from a great diversity of past and present human cultures; and, most of all, by insisting that every man can find immediate expressive fulfillment provided he lets the socially-suppressed spirit within him ascend into vibrant consciousness. The manifesto is: All men are artists, and who cares that some are better at it than others; we can all have fun! Hence, the deceptively crude antisophistication of hippie art forms, which are, perhaps, only an apparent reversion to primitivism. One has only to encounter the lurid *art nouveau* contortions of the hippie posters and their Beardsleyan exoticism, or the mad mélange of hippie street costume—Greek-sandled feet peeking beneath harem pantaloons encased in a fringed American Indian suede jacket, topped by pastel floral decorations about the face—or the sitar-whining cacophony of the folk-rock band, to know immediately that one is in the presence of *expressiveness* for its own sake.

In more mundane ways, too, the same readiness to let go, to participate, to create and perform without script or forethought is everywhere evident in the Hashbury. Two youths seat themselves on the sidewalk or in a store entranceway; bent beer can in hand, one begins scratching a bongo-like rhythm on the pavement while the other tattoos a bell-like accompaniment by striking a stick on an empty bottle. Soon they are joined, one by one, by a tambourinist, a harmonica player, a penny-whistler or recorder player, and, of course, the ubiquitous guitarist. A small crowd collects and, at the fringes, some blanket-bedecked boys and girls begin twirling about in movements vaguely resembling a Hindu dance. The wailing, rhythmic beating and dancing, alternately rising to peaks of intensity and subsiding, may last for as little as five minutes or as long as an hour, players and dancers joining in and dropping out as whim moves them. At some point—almost any—a mood takes hold that "the happening is over"; participants and onlookers disperse as casually as they had collected.

Analogous scenes of "participation unbound" are to be observed almost every night of the week (twice on Sunday) at the hippies' Parnassus, the Fillmore Auditorium, where a succession of name folk-rock bands, each more deafening than the one before, follow one another in hour-long sessions. Here, amidst the electric guitars, the electric organs, and the constantly metamorphizing show of lights, one can see the gainly and the graceless, the sylph bodies and rude stompers, the crooked and straight—all, of whatever condition or talent, *dance* as the flickering of a strobe light reduces their figures in silhouette to egalitarian spastic bursts. The recognition dawns that this, at last, is dancing of utterly free form, devoid of fixed sequence or step, open to all and calling for no Friday after-school classes at Miss Martha's or expensive lessons from Arthur Murray. The sole requisite is to tune in, take heart, and let go. What follows must be "beautiful" (a favorite hippie word) because it is *you* who are doing and feeling, not another to whom you have surrendered the muse.

As with folk-rock dancing, so (theoretically, at least) with music, poetry, painting, pottery, and the other arts and crafts: expression over performance, impulse over product. Whether the "straight world" will in time heed this message of the hippies is, to be sure, problematical. Also, given the lavish financial rewards and prestige heaped upon more talented hippie artists by a youth-dominated entertainment market, it is conceivable that high standards of professional performance will develop here as well (listen to the more recent Beatles' recordings), thus engendering perhaps as great a participative gulf between artist and audience as already exists in the established arts. Despite the vagaries of forecasting, however, the hippies—as of now, at least—are responding to the incipient plenitude of leisure in ways far removed from the baleful visions of a Huxley or an Orwell.

The Time-Scale of Experience

In every society, certain activities are required to complete various tasks and to achieve various goals. These activities form a sequence— they may be of short duration and simple linkage (boiling an egg); long duration and complex linkage (preparing for a profession); or a variety of intermediate combinations (planting and harvesting a crop). And the activity sequences needed to complete valued tasks and to achieve valued goals in a society largely determine how the people in that society will subjectively experience *time*.

The distinctive temporal bent of industrial society has been toward the second of these arrangements, long duration and complex linkage. As regards the subjective experience of time, this has meant what the anthropologist Florence Kluckhohn has termed a strong "future orientation" on the part of Western man, a quality of sensibility that radically

distinguishes him from his peasant and tribal forebears. The major
activities that fill the better part of his life acquire their meaning less
from the pleasure they may or may not give at the moment than from
their perceived relevance to some imagined future state of being or
affairs, be it salvation, career achievement, material success, or the
realization of a more perfect social order. Deprived of the pursuit of
these temporal distant, complexly modulated goals, we would feel that
life, as the man in the street puts it, is without meaning.

This subjective conception of time and experience is, of course, admi-
rably suited to the needs of post-18th century industrial society, needs
that include a stable labor force; work discipline; slow and regular accumulation of capital with which to plan and launch new investments and
to expand; and long, arduous years of training to provide certain people
with the high levels of skill necessary in so many professions and technical fields. If Western man had proved unable to defer present gratifications for future rewards (that is, if he had not been a future-oriented
being), nothing resembling our present civilization, as Freud noted, could
have come to pass.

Yet, paradoxically, it is the advanced technology of computers and
servo-mechanisms, not to overlook nuclear warfare, that industrial civilization has carried us to that is raising grave doubts concerning this
temporal ordering of affairs, this optimistic, pleasure-deferring, and magically rationalistic faith in converting present effort to future payoff. Why
prepare, if there will be so few satisfying jobs to prepare for? Why defer,
if there will be a superabundance of inexpensively-produced goods to
choose from? Why plan, if all plans can disintegrate into nuclear dust?

Premature or exaggerated as these questions may seem, they are
being asked, especially by young people. And merely to ask them is to
prompt a radical shift in time-perspective—from what *will be* to what *is*,
from future promise to present fulfillment, from the mundane discounting
of present feeling and mood to a sharpened awareness of their contours
and their possibilities for instant alteration. Broadly, it is to invest present experience with a new cognitive status and importance: a lust to
extract from the living moment its full sensory and emotional potential.
For if the present is no longer to be held hostage to the future, what
other course than to ravish it at the very instant of its apprehension?

There is much about the hippie subculture that already betokens this
alteration of time-perspective and concomitant reconstitution of the experienced self. Hippie argot—some of it new, much of it borrowed with
slight connotative changes from the Negro, jazz, homosexual, and addict
subcultures—is markedly skewed toward words and phrases in the
active present tense: "happening," "where it's at," "turn on," "freak out,"
"grooving," "mind-blowing," "be-in," "cop out," "split," "drop acid" (take
LSD, "put on," "uptight" (anxious and tense), "trip out" (experience
the far-out effects of a hallucinogenic drug). The very concept of a hap-

pening signifies immediacy: Events are to be actively engaged in, impro-
vised upon, and dramatically exploited for their own sake, with little
thought about their origins, duration, or consequences. Thus, almost anything—from a massive be-in in Golden Gate Park to ingesting LSD to a
casual street conversation to sitting solitarily under a tree—is approached with a heightened awareness of its happening potential. Similarly, the vogue among Hashbury hippies for astrology, tarot cards, I
Ching, and other forms of thaumaturgic prophecy (a hippie conversation
is as likely to begin with "What's your birthday?" as "What's your
name?") seems to be an attempt to denude the future of its temporal
integrity—its unknowability and slow unfoldingness—by fusing it indis-
criminately with present dispositions and sensations. The hippie's
structureless round-of-day ("hanging loose"), his disdain for appointments, schedules, and straight society's compulsive parceling out of
minutes and hours, are all implicated in his intense reverence for the
possibilities of the present and uninterest in the future. Few wear
watches, and as a colleague who has made a close participant-observer
study of one group of hippies remarked, "None of them ever seems to
know what time it is."

It is, perhaps, from this vantage point that the widespread use of
drugs by hippies acquires its cultural significance, above and beyond the
fact that drugs are easily available in the subculture or that their use
(especially LSD) has come to symbolize a distinctive badge of membership in that culture. Denied by our Protestant-Judaic heritage the
psychological means for experiencing the moment intensively, for parlay-
ing sensation and exoticizing mundane consciousness, the hippie uses
drugs where untutored imagination fails. Drugs impart to the present—
or so it is alleged by the hippie psychedelic religionists—an aura of
aliveness, a sense of union with fellow man and nature, which—we have
been taught—can be apprehended, if not in the afterlife that few modern men still believe in, then only after the deepest reflection and self-
knowledge induced by protracted experience.

A topic of lively debate among hippie intellectuals is whether drugs
represent but a transitory phase of the hippie subculture to be discarded
once other, more self-generating, means are discovered by its members
for extracting consummatory meaning from present time, or whether
drugs are the *sine qua non* of the subculture. Whatever the case, the hippies' experiment with ways to recast our notions of time and experience
is deserving of close attention.

The Hippies' Future

As of this writing, it is by no means certain that Haight-Ashbury's
"new community," as hippie spokesmen like to call it, can survive much

beyond early 1968. Although the "great summer invasion" of émigré hippies fell far short of the 100,000 to 500,000 forecast, the influx of youth from California's and the nation's metropolitan suburbs was, despite considerable turnover, large enough to place a severe strain on the new community's meager resources. "Crash pads" for the night were simply not available in sufficient quantity; the one daily meal of soup or stew served free by the Diggers could hardly appease youthful appetites; and even the lure of free love, which to young minds might be construed as a substitute for food, tarnished for many—boys outnumbered girls by at least three to one, if not more. Besides, summer is San Francisco's most inclement season, the city being shrouded in a chilling, wind-blown fog much of the time. The result was hundreds of youths leading a hand-to-mouth existence, wandering aimlessly on the streets, panhandling, munching stale doughnuts, sleeping in parks and autos and contracting virulent upper-respiratory infections. In this milieu cases of drug abuse, notably involving Methedrine and other "body-wrecking" amphetamines, have showed an alarming increase, beginning about mid-summer and continuing up to the present. And, while the city fathers were not at first nearly so repressive as many had feared, they barely lifted a finger to ameliorate the situation in the Haight-Ashbury. Recently, however, with the upcoming city elections for Mayor and members of the Board of Supervisors, they have given evidence of taking a "firmer" attitude toward the hippies: Drug arrests are on the increase, many more minors in the area are being stopped for questioning and referral to juvenile authorities, and a leading Haight Street hippie cultural establishment, the Straight Theatre, has been denied a dance permit.

It has not, therefore, been solely the impact of sheer numbers that has subjected the new community to a difficult struggle for survival. A variety of forces, internal and external, appear to have conjoined to crush it. To begin with, there is the hippies' notorious, near-anarchic aversion to sustained and organized effort toward reaching some goal. Every man "does his own thing for as long as he likes" until another thing comes along to distract or delight him, whereupon the hippie ethos enjoins him to drop the first thing. (Shades of the early, utopian Karl Marx: ". . . in the communist society it [will be] possible for me to do this today and that tomorrow, to hunt in the morning, to fish in the afternoon, to raise cattle in the evening, to be a critic after dinner, just as I feel at the moment; without ever being a hunter, fisherman, herdsman, or critic." From *The German Ideology*.) Even with such groups as the Diggers, projects are abandoned almost as soon as they are begun. One of the more prominent examples: An ongoing pastoral idyll of summer cultural happenings, proclaimed with great fanfare in May by a group calling itself the Council for the Summer of Love, was abandoned in June when the Council's leader decided one morning to leave town. Add to this the stalling and ordinance-juggling of a city bureaucracy reluctant to grant hippies permits and licenses for their pet enterprises, and very little manages to get off the ground. With only a few notable exceptions, therefore, like the Haight-Ashbury Free Medical Clinic, which—though closed temporarily—managed through its volunteer staff to look after the medical needs of thousands of hippies during the summer, the new community badly failed to provide for the hordes of youth drawn by its paeans of freedom, love, and the new life. Perhaps there is some ultimate wisdom to "doing one's own thing"; it was, however, hardly a practical way to receive a flock of kinsmen.

Exacerbating the "uptightness" of the hippies is a swelling stream of encounters with the police and courts, ranging from panhandling misdemeanors to harboring runaway minors ("contributing to the delinquency of a minor") to, what is most unnerving for hip inhabitants, a growing pattern of sudden mass arrests for marihuana use and possession in which as many as 25 youths may be hauled off in a single raid on a flat. (Some hippies console themselves with the thought that if enough middle-class youths get "busted for grass," such a hue and cry will be generated in respectable quarters that the marihuana laws will soon be repealed or greatly liberalized.) And, as if the internal problems of the new community were not enough, apocalyptic rumors sprung up, in the wake of the Newark and Detroit riots, that "the Haight is going to be burned to the ground" along with the adjoining Fillmore Negro ghetto. There followed a series of ugly street incidents between blacks and whites—assaults, sexual attacks, window smashing—which palpably heightened racial tensions and fed the credibility of the rumors.

Finally, the area's traffic-choked main thoroughfare, Haight Street, acquired in the space of a few months so carnival and Dantesque an atmosphere as to defy description. Hippies, tourists, drug peddlers, Hell's Angels, drunks, speed freaks (people high on Methedrine), panhandlers, pamphleteers, street musicians, crackpot evangelists, photographers, TV camera crews, reporters (domestic and foreign), researchers, ambulatory schizophrenics, and hawkers of the underground press (at least four such papers are produced in the Haight-Ashbury alone) jostled, put-on, and taunted one another through a din worthy of the Tower of Babel. The street-milling was incessant, and all heads remained cocked for "something to happen" to crystallize the disarray. By early summer, so repugnant had this atmosphere become for the "old" hippies (those residing there before—the origins of Hashbury's new community barely go back two years) that many departed; those who remained did so in the rapidly fading hope that the area might revert to its normal state of abnormality following the expected post-Labor Day exodus of college and high-school hippies. And, while the exodus of summer hippies has indeed been considerable, the consensus among knowledgeable observers of the area is that it has not regained its former, less frenetic, and less disorganized ambiance. The transformations wrought by the summer influx—the growing shift to Methedrine as *the* drug of choice, the more general drift toward a wholly drug-oriented subculture, the appearance of hoodlum and thrill-seeking elements, the sleazy tourist shops, the racial tensions—persist, only on a lesser scale.

But though Haight-Ashbury's hippie community may be destined to soon pass from the scene, the roots upon which it feeds run deep in our culture. These are not only of the long-term socio-historic kind I have touched on here, but of a distinctly contemporary character as well, the pain and moral duplicity of our Vietnam involvement being a prominent wellspring of hippie alienation. As the pressures mount on middle-class youth for ever greater scholastic achievement (soon a graduate degree may be mandatory for middle-class status, as a high-school diploma was in the 1940s), as the years of adolescent dependence are further prolonged, and as the accelerated pace of technological change aggravates the normal social tendency to intergenerational conflict, an increasing number of young people can be expected to drop out, or opt out, and drift into the hippie subculture. It is difficult to foresee how long they will remain there and what the consequences for later stages of their careers will be, inasmuch as insufficient time has passed for even a single age cohort of hippies to make the transition from early to middle adulthood. However, even among those youths who "remain in" conventional society in some formal sense, a very large number can be expected to hover so close to the margins of hippie subculture as to have their attitudes and outlooks substantially modified. Indeed, it is probably through some such muted, gradual, and indirect process of social conversion that the hippie subculture will make a lasting impact on American society, if it is to have any at all.

At the same time, the hippie rebellion gives partial, as yet ambiguous, evidence of a massiveness, a universality, and a density of existential texture, all of which promise to transcend the narrowly-segregated confines of age, occupation, and residence that characterized most bohemias of the past (Greenwich Village, Bloomsbury, the Left Bank). Some hippie visionaries already compare the movement to Christianity sweeping the Roman Empire. We cannot predict how far the movement can go toward enveloping the larger society, and whether as it develops it will—as have nearly all successful social movements—significantly compromise the visions that animate it with the practices of the reigning institutional system. Much depends on the state of future social discontent, particularly within the middle classes, and on the viable political options governments have for assuaging this discontent. Judging, however, from the social upheavals and mass violence of recent decades, such options are, perhaps inevitably, scarce indeed. Just possibly, then, by opting out and making their own kind of cultural waves, the hippies are telling us more than we can now imagine about our future selves.

joseph lyford

We have looked at Main Street and Levittown and "Hashbury," three very different types of American communities. Now we turn to the "Airtight Cage," a neighborhood in the heart of Manhattan that, unlike the others, is not marked by homogeneity of values or lifestyles. Here thousands upon thousands live in a tiny area, brushing past one another but rarely really touching. Here is a community with little sense of community, despite attempts to organize it and to weld its disparate residents together.

Joseph Lyford describes the area in which he lived in the early 1960s and introduces the people and their problems. His commentary offers ample evidence of the difficulties of satisfying the needs of all and of the inevitability of conflicts—such as the New York school crisis which occurred several years after *The Airtight Cage* was published.

This is a portrait of anomie. Still Lyford sees ways out of the Cage and offers some suggestions. These, too, are worth pondering.

The Cage

Occasionally on a winter weekend the wind blows the smoke and sulphur dioxide over into New Jersey and presents the people of 105th Street with a gift of clear blue sky. If the weather is cold enough to drive the prostitutes and addicts under cover, we hear the birds in Central Park instead of the usual street obscenities. On a Sunday morning, with the schools closed, the street is quiet and almost deserted, and at the end of the day we may have a crimson sunset at the end of the street, somewhere out beyond the Hudson River.

On one of our rare good days one might get the impression, from seeing our block on the southern edge of Harlem, that we are one of those small communities in the city where the so-called "urban villager" is supposed to flourish. In fact we do have a number of these villagers—people with a very local, civic way of looking at things. One of them is Pastor Mullen, who has weekly suppers in his brownstone Jordan River Baptist Church. Another is my next-door neighbor, George Zukof. He has shoveled the snow off my sidewalk when I have been slow in getting to it, and every two weeks he cashes everybody's welfare checks in his drugstore on Columbus Avenue. Another village-minded man, Leonard Keepnews, spends his spare time making arrangements for local children to go to free summer camps.

It is the crowds of children most of all who contribute to the neighborhood atmosphere. According to my census there are about three dozen of them, mostly Negroes. Some belong to the Methodist Church Sunday school and sell Girl Scout cookies. All of them spend the summer racing up and down the block looking for something to do. Since they do not have any equipment for the usual games, they invent their own, which is a misfortune for the city because the major emphasis—in spite of Sunday school—is on breaking bottles, setting fire to trash, opening hydrants, and sending in false alarms. But with all their rushing about and daredeviling, the children regard the four corners of the block as the outermost limits of the universe. Whatever travels they take are imaginary ones in the hulk of an abandoned car that periodically turns up along the curb. Very few of the children leave the block even to climb the big rocks that loom up on the edge of Central Park a few hundred feet to the east.

Actually the children prove the opposite of what they seem to prove. Looked at more closely, they reveal that there is not much of a community here and that what we are living in is more of a temporary encampment. We know most of the children by name after seeing them out in front all summer, but at the beginning of the following summer many of the faces we know are gone and we are looking at a new set of children. It is hard to find out what happens to them although occasionally we hear something definite. One mother of five was taken off recently to an institution after trying for two years to raise her family in one room, and the children were scattered about in foster homes.

Whatever the reasons, there comes a time when the families, or the remnants of them, move to a similar street somewhere else where the children help to fill up another ancient tenement and another school.

This is the way childhood ordinarily proceeds for most of the Negro boys and girls who come and go on 105th Street, and it is probably the way things will develop in turn for their children. Communities and urban villages are not built on such life patterns as these.

Nevertheless, the upper West Side has several dozen "community" organizations, ranging from the St. Gregory's Mothers Guild to the Young Assassins. Most of them do not function as if they were on the same planet, let alone the same part of town. Some of these groups—the block associations, for example—have their handful of urban villagers and are more benign than others, but in general the villagers do not set the style of organizational life. In fact, officers of the more up-and-coming organizations consider the villager, with his preoccupation about sprucing up the local scene and doing apolitical good works, as a sentimental anachronism.

The officers may have a point. At the same time it can also be said that a good proportion of the local civic and political organizations are also becoming archaic, debilitated to the point where they have difficulty in getting together a proper quorum at meetings. The groups which do have a respectable amount of energy and financial support often burn themselves out in the most destructive competition with each other, as if there were not enough problems to go around for everybody. Many organizations have no active membership other than the people who elect each other as officers and send off resolutions to the *West Side News*. A large number of these press releases, coming at any one time, gives the impression that giant waves of public opinion are sweeping over the entire area.

On rare occasions when enough organizations are gathered into a bundle, and there is leadership, a Stryckers Bay Neighborhood Council results and can be a force for limited improvement, mainly because it has an energetic and talented leader as its president, Father Henry J. Browne. The individual organizations which make up the council membership are as anemic as the rest: without vitality or any real constituency. If at any time they were an active force for community, they are now largely neurotic reactions to the social disintegration which has overtaken the area, devices through which the people can complain about their environment. The best that can be said of many of them is that they offer their members an opportunity for self-expression.

The Area's service-directed institutions have made a more creditable response to the social situation, insofar as they have programs to do something. In some cases they have constructed an "interior community" floating in the general disorder. Perhaps the best examples of such interior communities are the public and parochial schools. A P.S. 84, a P.S. 165, or a St. Gregory's school is a place in which there is some agreed-upon direction to the proceedings, where a daily effort is under way, and where there are ideas, purposes, compassion, diversity—all essential to community. In spite of all the criticism that has been concentrated on them, the schools have an atmosphere of hope that flows over and softens the sharp edges of a good many unhappy particulars. Even in those many classes where children cling precariously to the outer edges and struggle unsuccessfully to speak and hear, something is being demanded of them and something is being given.

With a few exceptions a whole host of other service-directed enterprises in the area are isolated from each other, and the range of their effect is extremely limited. The settlement houses have acquired the knack of fund raising, but other free community-minded service enterprises are small, undermanned, and in a precarious financial state. They include an excellent day-care program run by the Children's Aid Society, the Police Athletic League recreation program, the Bloomingdale nursery school, several early-childhood education projects, a privately run mental health clinic, a college career guidance program for Negro and Puerto Rican youngsters, the many social-service and education activities housed in local churches, and a training course for unskilled teen-agers run by a Negro businessman. At the other end of this spectrum of microscopic communities is the rooming house where ex-mental patients have banded together to form their own society in exile.

In a true community, moving toward a common goal of social justice, such cooperative efforts would be running with the current, operating as part of a constructive program for the general health and welfare. In such noncommunities as the upper West Side, these enterprises have to fight the current; in fact, they are created to oppose it, antibodies in an unhealthy system, in perpetual jeopardy from the system. However, some people criticize these social-service groups because of their manifest inadequacy or because they are seen as the sort of local anesthetic an unjust society applies to its victims, and which makes the injustice bearable.

Unconsciously or consciously the people convey the feeling that they have no community worth talking about. The attitude survey conducted by the John Kraft public opinion research organization reported that West Siders then had only the vaguest idea of where they would turn in case of need. They almost never mentioned political organizations, government agencies, or elected officials, and no single institution was mentioned more than a handful of times. The despair among the poor also permeates a middle class that distrusts its public officials and is bored with its institutions. The only people who talk about community as if they believe in it are the people who are paid to be community organizers.

The one popular consensus is that there is no community. The group that cuts across all class lines is the army of noninterferers who remain passive while violence is committed on another human being, and who will tolerate the destruction of a neighborhood itself because they are resigned to its destruction. As a consequence of such a situation we have the Negro maid who puts a straight razor in her purse for protection, and the unanimous civilian boycott of Central Park after dark. These are the reflexes of people who understand that they live in a wilderness.

There are innumerable little airtight cages and bomb shelters which the citizen can build for himself as a defense against such an oppressive environment. If he is poor he can buy a police lock for his door. If he is a middle-class conservative with a suspicion of social cooperation he has no problem. It becomes almost a matter of principle to amputate himself from an immoral society and the undeserving poor who are at the bottom of the demoralization. The middle-class liberal has more difficulty in justifying his retreat into private life because his official philosophy requires him to believe in the democratic process. Nevertheless, he has plenty of plausible rationalizations at hand—the manifest futility of becoming involved, the corruption of politics, the demands of his domestic and professional life, the complexity of the problem, etc. The liberal belief in the welfare state can also ease any crisis of conscience. If there are social and economic needs to be satisfied, departments of health, education, and welfare have been created to take care of just such matters. If the old methods are inadequate, the answer is new legislation and more money. The liberal may also avoid a connection by making a connection, that is to say, instead of personally involving himself with a cause or a community, he can join an organization in which he makes a nominal commitment to the public interest on terms that allow him to be as inactive and remote as he likes.

If the political conservative never had a heart, the liberal has lost heart in the midst of the city's crisis. In most cases, he has come to accept, at least subconsciously, the idea that a trial of power is taking place in which the ultimate interests of his middle class are threatened by an invasion of the poor. His uneasy conviction that the poor—any poor (he lumps them all together in spite of himself)—constitute a public danger appears in many ways. One symptom is the congenital middle-class fear of public housing. Another is the apprehension over the influx of more and more poor children into the public schools, coupled with the conviction that only the middle class can save the city's public education system. Such apprehensions and beliefs are reinforced constantly by superstition, by rumor, and by an overwhelming array of social scientists and psychologists who maintain that a lower-class school will always be an inferior school. The soundness or unsoundness of these attitudes is beside the point. The fact that they exist is another contribution to the social disorder. Such attitudes are inevitable when the economy and politics of the city are busily promoting a class war over money and living space and services.

There are some liberals who punish themselves rather hard for this situation as if they bore the whole moral responsibility for what has happened. It is difficult to know what difference they could have made. On their side, the poor resist the sporadic and often patronizing attempts to draw them into a community for the very good reason that their style of life makes it impossible for them to become part of the customary social apparatus. The prerequisites for sharing in middle-class organizational life are jobs, baby sitters, and freedom from the health and housing problems that continually put the poor out of commission. A community institution requires stability and permanence for its people. For the poor who are temporary, such creations are designed for other people in other worlds.

The poor do not even have a unity of their own. Those who manage to escape the condition of poverty rarely look back, and those at the bottom of the heap live in almost total isolation from each other. This is particularly true of the single, unemployable Negro male, who is transient in every aspect of his life—economic, statistical, and sexual. He is sidestepped even by the Puerto Ricans, who understand that to be classified as one of the black poor is a sure road to destruction. In the worst extremes of poverty the only associations men have with each other are based on their addictions and illnesses, and in their time of greatest need they lose even these connections. Death itself does not give them any sort of personal identity: it is always a problem for the police to find someone who knows the name of the body and who can explain what has happened to the belongings of the deceased. The "culture of poverty" and the alleged community of the poor notwithstanding, there is less community in the lower depths than there was among the inmates of Auschwitz, who could not help assisting in their own destruction.

The Spanish poor would appear to be in a somewhat better position. They share a common and positive culture and, having been treated as citizens on the island, they have developed the reactions of first-class citizens. Thus, while he may be more shocked than the Negro upon colliding with color discrimination, the Puerto Rican often seems to be more vocal and less despairing. The Spanish also have local organizations to complain regularly for them, which the Negro does not. However, the very plenitude of Puerto Rican organizations obstructs their effectiveness. They have a tendency to drown one another out, and show no conspicuous ability to cooperate with one another. The aims of the Spanish organizations have been primarily social rather than political, and they do not reach out effectively to the less educated, the darker skinned, and the more recently arrived Puerto Ricans, who have a rather insecure status in the Spanish universe of the city. In fact, the local Puerto Rican aristocracy feels rather defensive toward the black island minority that arrives in the area, goes on welfare, and becomes a "social problem."

A few "leaders" of the "Spanish community" are audible and visible at public meetings, the proving ground where they build up their credentials as spokesmen. They follow the traditional pattern of generations of other politicians who have based their career on ethnic or "skin" politics. By and large, the more successful these spokesmen become, the more remote they become from their alleged constituents, until at the peak of success they may get a job with the city and disappear altogether. This process can be called assimilation in the good old American tradition, or it can be called betrayal, depending on who is making the judgment. Anyone who attends a session of a politically-minded Puerto Rican organization will hear all sorts of angry complaints about former members who, once they have "made it" politically, no longer bother to consult with their old associates.

The physical breakdown of the area, the nervous movements of the population, the forced competition among economic and social classes, and the decline of politics have all played a part in killing off the democratic dialogue that is a basic requirement of the free community. The disintegration of communication is so obvious that it is even noticed by noncontroversial generalists like Rabbi Edward Klein, of the Stephen Wise Free Synagogue, in his remark that, "we live side by side but we never learn to live together."

The difficulties of local Democrats, and the shortcomings of the city's past Democratic administrations, should not obscure the damage the city's political and economic conservatives have done to the dialogue. The *New York Herald Tribune* in an otherwise excellent series entitled "City in Crisis" left the impression before the 1965 mayoralty election that the collapse of the city has been mainly the fault of the mayor and Democratic politicians. It remained for an outsider, Edward Logue, the Redevelopment Commissioner of Boston, to point out that New York City's business community had provided neither leadership nor constructive criticism in the crisis. The conviction that the Republican party has had no interest in the thoughts or the condition of the poor is well fixed in the minds of a great majority of West Siders interviewed in the Kraft survey. It is significant that in his successful campaign for the mayoralty Congressman John Lindsay won a large West Side Democratic vote on the grounds that he was running as a liberal man who had not the heart of a real Republican.

Another factor that has prevented the construction of a community has been the fitful role of the city's major educational institutions in urban affairs. An example is Columbia University, whose expansion program is the core of a new urban renewal project on the upper West Side. It would seem that in such a situation, Columbia might have seized the chance to educate itself systematically about the political, social, and economic dislocations that always accompany urban renewal. Yet, despite its proximity to the West Side urban renewal program, Columbia made no sustained effort to get into this laboratory. Its graduate schools of education, medicine, law, and urban affairs could have invented and participated in all sorts of experimental programs, but did very little. Only a few Columbia students, far ahead of their university, saw the opportunities and volunteered to work in the area and associate themselves with local work projects. Now, Columbia, the opportunity lost and facing rising resistance among the poor to its own plans for expansion, has hired a public relations counsel to tell it what to do.

What are the immediate prospects for restoration of some semblance of community? Other than expansion in the budgets of private and public social agencies—such as piecemeal improvements in the city's educational facilities—the prospects are very few. The response will not be constructive or even corrective; it will be essentially reactive. The one significant new hope for reversing the distintegration of the city may lie in the antipoverty program, which is pumping federal aid into local rehabilitation and education projects. But, while money is in long supply, ideas and carefully thought-out programs are not, and the excessive "crash" psychology of the war on poverty has damaged its effectiveness. The power struggle over how the program shall be administered—and who shall be in charge—has also delayed its implementation and could very well destroy it in the end.

As the Office of Economic Opportunity has stated its goals, the antipoverty program would not only try to cope with unemployment and improve the health, housing, and education of the city's slum population, but it would also try to draw the poor into participation in the life of the city by asking them to elect representatives to serve in "neighborhood" poverty councils. There is considerable doubt whether this ideal can be achieved, even if the opposition of the city's political organizations can be overcome. For one thing, the poor have not responded very enthusiastically, so far, to the chance to play an active role. In addition, as has been said before, the poor have a habit of being betrayed by their own protectors. Many of the organizations most loudly demanding the participation of the poor in the antipoverty operations have themselves demonstrated neither the ability nor the desire to involve the poor in their own activities. Some nonpolitical organizations quick to criticize "the politicians" for using the antipoverty program as a patronage device have themselves used it merely to bolster their competitive position vis-à-vis other agencies. Other organizational spokesmen for the poor have spent disproportionate amounts of federal poverty money on administration and in pushing highly publicized but superficial programs.

If the antipoverty program survives its early difficulties, and is not undercut by the demands of a rising defense budget, it could reconstitute the basis of community life in America. Not only could it begin to break down the walls separating class and race, but, just as important, it could provide the opportunity for creative social experiences very similar in spirit to the communal efforts in our preindustrial past when rural families built each other's houses and harvested each other's crops. It is an irony that the communal act has almost totally vanished from our underdeveloped inner city slums at the very time when the Peace Corps is encouraging the people of underdeveloped nations to adopt this neglected American tradition in dealing with their own problems.*

Americans have been "liberated" from physical participation in community projects because of technology and the enormous proliferation of public and private services which can be bought as substitutes for personal endeavor. The availability of these substitutes allows us to disassociate ourselves from people who are unlike us and whose condition annoys us. It has also set us apart from every country which is fostering vigorous social cooperation as a means of building a healthy society. While the Chinese villagers combine to build a school and the people of India construct their own communities, we join organizations, give to the United Fund, and wash our cars on Sundays.

Progress, of course, is what makes this all inevitable. Since we are not a primitive civilization, technologically speaking, push-button methods are available to discharge our public responsibilities, thereby conserving labor, gaining leisure, and losing our personal identification with the public interest. We have even lost the ability to comprehend the significance of the communal act. The general public reaction to the civil rights march on Washington in 1963 was illustrative: over and over the question asked was—what good did it do, and how many votes did it change? The fact that this was not a political rally but an act of communion seems to have been missed by nearly everyone except the marchers themselves.

Our physical and emotional distance from each other, combined with a national reverence for competition, helps explain why we respond so much more energetically to controversy than we do to cooperation. It is natural for the isolated man to be "against" rather than "for" something, so we are against anything that threatens our equilibrium, but it is difficult for us to be actively for a positive ideal—and the only meetings we attend in very great numbers are those where a decisive and bitter argument is in the wind. Yet a civic competitiveness, and a general predilection for fake controversies do not seem to have altogether obliterated the natural human instinct for cooperation. At least the instinct is very much alive among young people, who insist on taking seriously all

---

* "In the United States, citizens are accustomed to working together in community organizations to make known their needs and solve their own problems. But in Brazil, as in many other developing nations, this tradition is almost totally lacking. The absence of local initiative and cooperative efforts in self-help is a great obstacle to economic and social development. Too often the people wait for the government to do something about their problems." *Brazil: Urban Community Development* leaflet. Peace Corps, Washington, D.C., 1965.

the homilies on justice and equality inflicted on them when they were children, and who refuse to be "realistic" now that they are growing up. A stubborn insistence that America act in accordance with its constitutional and religious proclamations may be why young people march in civil rights and peace demonstrations. The proof that young people will respond to a chance to act together for a constructive purpose lies in the Northern Students Movement, a Harlem Educational Project, in the community center, and in the Peace Corps.

If the war on poverty can win anything but very limited success it will have to try to move us toward the type of community which has been eloquently defined by philosopher Richard Lichtman. In his words:

> An authentic community commits itself to health as an end of social existence, as a primary value upon which the institutions of public life are based. Since such a community is serious in its concern it organizes itself affirmatively for the sake of human well-being. It is not simply content to correct the errors which are continually promoted in some non-communal sphere of social existence. In short, *a community is not a corrective but a constructive system of human existence.* Health is not to be cut and shaped to an ill-formed society . . . it is rather society that must be constituted to embody health, insofar as that is humanly possible. Everything communal men make of themselves and their world in their public life is infused with a concern for the vital functioning it promotes or hinders.
>
> Since one of the root concerns of a community is the equality of its participants, their equal right to well-being is one of its fundamental imperatives. But as the health of men is rooted in their whole being, and in the particular mode of their social existence, it is their "life styles" too which must bear the equalitarian imprint. It is not sufficient that those officially charged with the health of their fellows act to undo the consequences of unequal privilege and maldistributed wealth. Equality must inform the community from its inception. For what men are entitled to by right is not the partial amelioration of their inequalities, but the full equal realization of their capacities.*

If our frontier society, in which men could exist in relative isolation, found the communal life a necessity for survival, our specialized society needs even more to guard against the individual's disassociation from the whole. There is no security in our cities because there is no community in them. A society in which a fifth of the people live in poverty condemns every man to private oppression—an oppression which can be physical or a matter of conscience, or both.

The question in our cities is not whether the oppression can be avoided. The question is whether there will be a constructive outcome to the American ordeal or whether we will simply build higher walls and tighter cages to protect ourselves from the hard realities of our environment. Ideas and people who can cope with these realities will be

---

* *Toward Community*, by Richard Lichtman, p. 45. Center for the Study of Democratic Institutions, 1966.

immobilized until we get rid of the notion that we can escape into an illusory self-sufficiency, and until we understand that man's individual prosperity is not achieved by victories at the expense of others. It is a fundamental premise of a free society that the health of the community and the health of the family are inseparable, that community and family are woven together, and draw love from each other. We have, quite literally, a need to touch other human beings, and be touched by them.

The Squeeze

The government of the city has taken on many of the basic characteristics of the large, private aggregations of money and power, and has thereby become more and more the enemy of community. If the two circles of power, public and private, once functioned as countervailing forces against each other, they are now in important respects each other's agents. The corporation on one hand has become to a greater and greater degree a producer for government, and as part of the arrangement it professes a new sense of responsibility for the public welfare. On the other hand, the government agency has adopted the organization and technical innovations of the private sector and tailors its welfare programs and regulatory activities to conform to the accumulating pressures of a vast array of private interests. The resulting situation is exactly the opposite of the socialization which state power is supposed to be bringing about. Far from cutting away the base of the private sector, the governmental bureacracy has become a means through which private power—from banks to labor unions—has strengthened its grip on the development of the city, and has subordinated the general welfare to the private interest.

One can pick at random any one of thousands of case histories of the West Side poor to find an individual illustration of what happens to the unafflicted citizen at the hands of government agencies infiltrated with the private interest and paralyzed by the weight of their own anatomy. And examples of the private invasion of the public sphere can be found in every phase of municipal government:* Bernard Weissbourd's remark that the self-defeating nature of public housing policies is determined by the private developers who are its enemies can be paraphrased to fit almost any other area of municipal governmental policy; land use, taxation, city planning, urban renewal, assessments, health and welfare programs, housing, the courts and law enforcement. The very size of

---

* The situation in the city parallels that in the federal government, where agencies such as the Federal Communications Commission, Food and Drug Administration, and others are dominated by the industries they were created to regulate.

government, once seen as a threat to the private sector, has made it more susceptible to private pressure. In Lincoln Steffens' day the pressure was erratic and personal, today the science of applying pressure and yielding to it has been automated along with everything else, to the point where the private interest controls not merely individual people but the whole climate in which the governmental apparatus functions.

The division of executive government power into impersonal and nearly autonomous agencies and "authorities" has put them as far out of the range of public protest as a private monopoly like the New York Telephone Company. The New York Port Authority is one example of enormous governmental power which has accumulated out of nowhere and operates primarily as a promoter of private business interests. The experience of confronting a public agency and a private monopoly like Consolidated Edison is practically identical—in both cases one is dealing with organizations preoccupied with internal security and populated in the lower reaches by a professional class fearful of innovation and responsibility and unresponsive to any outside stimulus except organized pressure. When such government agencies are allowed to dominate the life of the poor to the minutest detail, they isolate them from participation in community life.

When even a middle-class citizen with financial and political resources has difficulty in defending himself against arbitrary government action, the position of the poor becomes hopeless. The commitments an agency makes to one of its impoverished wards are not written down, and they can be changed, lied about, or abrogated at will. The low-income Negro or Puerto Rican learns that the administrative agency is indefatigable in calling him to account for the smallest infractions, but when he seeks protection from that agency he finds that his rights are ephemeral and that his case disintegrates in a mass of technicalities. He learns that a code-enforcement agency takes little initiative on his behalf and has no will to protect him. Rather, on rare occasions when he insists on his rights vigorously, at some time or another agency officials may conspire against him because they consider the complainant a troublemaker, or because they have been corrupted by the person who has violated the rights of the complainant.

Like the public agency, the law and the judicial process also seem to work most effectively when it is the poor who are being prosecuted. The fact is no secret. Some state bar associations openly acknowledge this to be the case, and when he was attorney general, Robert Kennedy paid a great deal of attention to the problem. Patricia Wald's report to the 1965 National Conference on Law and Poverty catalogues dozens of ways in which the judicial system is rigged against the indigent, and although she draws her illustrations from many cities, she could have found all the examples she needed in the life of the West Side poor. Given this situation, it is no surprise that the minority groups' hatred and fear of legal authority has occasionally fanned an isolated act of rebellion into a sustained outbreak of mass violence.

Perhaps because they are temporary political appointees and therefore in a more exposed and precarious position, the top administrative officials in the New York City government have been more sensitive to criticism than the eternal civil service employees beneath them. But when a commissioner admits his agency operates inefficiently or unjustly "at times," he almost always concludes by a remark that there are a few rotten apples in every barrel. The condition of the barrel is never questioned. One also hears from commissioners that the city is too big and the budget too small: the manner in which a department has used its resources is never discussed. Underlying all the apologies is the assumption, which the public shares, that the city is doomed. In the face of such an attitude, of course, it becomes impossible to reduce waste, reorganize departments, or create an atmosphere that would encourage innovation. The defeatism partly explains why, even when a costly budget increase is approved, the money is channeled into expansion of the administrative apparatus rather than into improvement of direct public services.

One impressive characteristic of the civil service and political appointees in the lower levels of the bureaucracy is their peculiar attitude toward the citizen they are supposed to serve—especially if he is poor and raises a fuss. Regardless of the employee's racial or ethnic background, he very often reacts in a negative way to any situation which jiggles his procedure-centered world. Life in a municipal office building creates its own rigid habit patterns and psychological attitudes, and outsiders had better beware of them. The civil service worker in some ways resembles a member of one of the more ingrown trade unions. If he has a social attitude he lays it away when he goes on the job.

The huge mass of administrative regulations is a boon to certain agency officials, protecting the mind that avoids responsibility and shies away from the special case. It provides dozens of legal pretexts for inaction. Worst of all, the almost unlimited power which administrative rules confer on the official often results in a subconscious attitude that he personally owns the services his department is supposed to provide the public. To understand fully the results of this proprietary attitude, one must have undergone some of the insulting interrogations to which applicants for public housing are often subjected. The applicant is frequently treated as a suppliant who, if he happens to rub the official the wrong way, can be groundlessly accused of everything from immorality to cheating on his income-tax returns. Since such comments are always informal and made without witnesses present, the applicant has no recourse—he might as well be arguing with a policeman.

A bureaucratic system riddled with such attitudes will respond only if it is badly frightened. But systems don't frighten easily. Even though individual employees may be constitutionally apprehensive, the system in which they work has dispersed responsibility so widely that it is almost impossible to call anybody to account: therefore inefficiency is pursued without interruption almost as a matter of policy.

Some elements of new life have managed to take root in fissures of the bureaucratic rock. For instance, in two of the city's most absurdly organized and top-heavy agencies—the Department of Welfare and the Board of Education—case workers and teachers with a social direction to their thinking have bucked the system and forced policy and organizational changes. The pressure of the teachers, made possible by their new union (the United Federation of Teachers, AFL-CIO), has given them a small voice in influencing the educational program, while the case workers' strike against the Department of Welfare has emphasized the unworkability of traditional approaches to welfare problems. It is unlikely, however, that such low-level pressures can ever force the administrative organization to be more responsive to the poor. For one thing, the pressures are too isolated. Also, as reformers achieve substantial successes, they lose their revolutionary impulses and tend to become accretions to the system. This tendency is already noticeable among the teachers, whose union is becoming more preoccupied with teachers' prerogatives and less and less interested in general improvements in the educational system which might interfere with these prerogatives. The union's drive to prevent school principals from observing teachers in class once the teacher's probationary period is over is an indication of this trend.

Some Steps Forward

One way of forcing the bureaucracy to be more accountable to the people would be a new branch of city government—a public advocate analogous to the *ombudsman* who represents the claims of the citizen against the bureaucracy in the Scandinavian countries and in New Zealand. He has inquisitorial power, and is independent of the executive branch of government. An effective public advocate would be one way of restoring the faith of the poor in their government. The *ombudsman*'s criticism, his use of communications media, and his legal intervention could improve the efficiency of the agencies under inquiry, and his presence would also encourage those people within an agency who were trying to buck the system. The public advocate would be a useful means by which modern government could subsidize independent criticism of its internal administrative procedures and afford the citizen protection against an entrenched civil service which is out of the control of the top administrator. The idea of the *ombudsman* has already been broached on the West Side. A local city councilman, Paul O'Dwyer, has proposed an

Office of Civilian Redress, and as borough president of Manhattan Constance Baker Motley stated somewhat plaintively that she would like to function as an *ombudsman*.

Father Henry J. Browne, whose work as chairman of the Stryckers Bay Neighborhood Council has been mentioned, has actually operated as a type of unofficial *ombudsman* or local public advocate. He has the ideal equipment—expert technical knowledge, an understanding of the law and the administrative process, and a familiarity with the political relationships within city government. On behalf of the council, Browne frequently has represented the individual citizen in his complaints against administrative actions or administrative neglect. He uses all the techniques for seeking redress of grievances: meetings with agency heads, informal hearings, resort to the courts for restraining orders against city agencies, and consultation with agencies on modification of program. He has also used the press as a means of circulating information and criticism.

The results of the council's work have not always satisfied its chairman or the community, but, given the size of the council budget and the immense demands made on it, the organization has been surprisingly successful in affecting the course of the urban renewal program, and in changing attitudes and practices in such city departments as Relocation, the Housing Authority, and the Housing and Redevelopment Board. Recently the council has taken another step in its effort to make the government more responsive, by applying for a federal grant to encourage the poor to participate in the planning and operation of the local antipoverty program.

The *ombudsman* would in some ways reinforce the work of the type of civilian review board proposed for the New York City police force, and of the public member board set up by the United Auto Workers (AFL-CIO) to review grievances of union members against their own officers.* However, the *ombudsman* would not be a substitute for the civilian review board. For one thing, he could not give any single agency the close attention required, which means he could not be properly held responsible for it. The civilian review board could be a valuable supplement to the *ombudsman*, and at the same time it would not be exempt from investigation by the *ombudsman*.

Any discussion of how to render governmental bodies more accountable to the public should not overlook the civilian review board's potential. The long-standing debate over the desirability of civilian review boards for the police departments has obscured the fact that public review boards might be useful in other areas. Outside the government

---

* See *Democracy and Public Review*: An Analysis of the UAW Public Review Board, by Jack Stieber, Walter E. Oberer and Michael Harrington. Center for the Study of Democratic Institutions, 1960.

apparatus there are powerful, well-financed social agencies that solicit public financial support and thereby have a responsibility to give an accounting of themselves. But in most cases these agencies do not provide anything like a detailed and objective account of their activities. Their annual reports are usually staff-written advertisements designed to impress their own board members and serve as fund-raising documents, and the press usually accepts them at their face value. Now that many of these social agencies are receiving sizable government grants to finance antipoverty programs, there is a good argument for public review boards that could question agency officials and give their own evaluations of the agencies' programs. The boards might investigate as a matter of course the financial and administrative practices of all private agencies which use public money. United Fund officials require such an accounting from agencies that share in its fund-raising drives, but for political and public relations reasons such a system leaves something to be desired. Furthermore, a great many agencies, almost all of them receiving antipoverty money, are not included in the United Fund.

A third force on the side of justice and community would be the neighborhood law firm. Prototypes of such law groups have already been functioning in some areas of the city. The Riverside Democratic Club on the upper West Side has offered some free legal consultation to the indigent, and the Hotel Workers' Union—in spite of outcries from bar groups—has set up a legal counseling service for its members, and encourages them to use it. Gradual improvement and expansion of legal aid societies and public defender systems have also been of great help to the poor in their daily collisions with the courts, but most of the free legal assistance has been cursory and the types of cases handled have been severely restricted. The result is a legal first-aid system which may keep a defendant out of jail, but which rarely follows through to the point where it can resolve many of the defendant's most persistent legal difficulties. The tenant harassed by an administrative agency or a landlord has a chronic malady which is not cured by pill-sized doses of legal assistance, each time administered by a different lawyer.

While it is too early to tell what will become of the antipoverty program's plans for neighborhood legal service, the Community Progress antipoverty program in New Haven, Connecticut, has been in operation successfully for some time.* A privately organized Legal Assistance Association offers a strengthened legal and defender program, a neighborhood legal program, and a legal research and evaluation program which have become a key part of Community Progress. Another example of a legal aid system supported by foundation and federal money is in

---

* Mitchell Sviridoff, Executive Director of Community Progress, was the first person appointed by Mayor Lindsay to plan New York City's new poverty program.

operation on the lower East Side of New York under the supervision of Mobilization for Youth. The effectiveness of MFY's legal team in helping tenants is one of the reasons why the agency has been so bitterly attacked as "communistic" by local real estate and political interests.

Where the neighborhood legal aid program has begun to function successfully—as in New Haven and Oakland, California—it has tended to follow the lines that have also been suggested for a neighborhood public health program. The services should be comprehensive, near at hand, available at all times, and the client should as much as possible have the same practitioner throughout his difficulties. Ideally such a neighborhood legal aid system would require a regular team of adequately paid lawyers, but in fact it would probably have to rely on law students or part-time attorneys subsidized in part by public funds. The use of tax money to provide such services is quite as justifiable in principle as the use of public money to provide health, education, and welfare services. It is no more just that poverty should deprive a man of his legal rights than that it should deny him an equal chance for health and a decent education. In cases where society has placed an individual under the control of administrative agencies, it has a special responsibility to afford that individual some guarantee that his rights will be respected by those agencies. Legal counsel for the poor can be a positive public good if it enables society to police its own institutions. Perhaps in the future legal assistance to the poor might be partially financed by group insurance programs covering the less-costly types of litigation.

In discussing proposals for *ombudsmen*, neighborhood law firms, and civilian review boards, it has to be emphasized that, taken by themselves, new techniques—better ways of "making the system work"—will not reconstruct the city. One of the basic weaknesses of the "reform" approach has been its reliance on innovations that are not sufficient to alter conditions that have been mainly responsible for deforming the character of urban life. One such influence is the rapidly accumulating density of population. A second is the urban concentration of the jobless, the dependent, and the unwell. A third is the enormous, expanding complex of racial ghettoes in which overpopulation, sickness, and unemployment are centered. Proposals for a new society have little meaning in the shadow of these ghettoes.

The heart of the ghetto remains untouched. So far, urban renewal has too often been a process in which governmental power is invoked in the interest of private development; it has renewed racially mixed fringe areas which could be transformed into predominantly middle- and upper-income neighborhoods. Urban renewal has actually intensified the blackness and density of the ghetto and planted new ones. As the fringe slums are bulldozed, the thousands of displaced poor move to neighboring slums or to tubercular areas—the only type of area which will receive the poor—in other boroughs. As the D.P.'s arrive, and crowd into substandard housing, these "gray" areas turn black, and new fires burn away the economic substance and morale of the city. Thus the ghetto revenges itself on society by making fundamental improvements in the design of the city impossible.

Our automatic and unemotional acceptance of the ghetto as one of the permanent fixtures of the "free society" is an unmistakable indication of the futility of relying on the system to reform itself. This is hardly surprising in a society where almost all decisions, including moral ones, are the outcome of strenuous, competing pressures. The acceptance of the ghetto, which implies a general public disbelief in democracy itself, is responsible for the fact that even those inadequate urban renewal programs which have been undertaken have been deformed by the very influences that have a vested interest in perpetuation of the slum. The essential fact is that the slum is seen only as an inconvenience to be controlled.

It seems more than likely that effective action against the slum will have to be forced out of society by a series of explosions powerful enough to crack the surface of what Kenneth Galbraith calls the "conventional wisdom," explosions generated by the economic and political impasses that are inevitable when a fifth of the nation's population is living on or below the level of human subsistence, and much of it impacting in the urban areas. If the explosions are to be simply bigger, more destructive versions of the Harlem and Watts riots, violence or the threat of violence will be the commonly accepted way of getting attention from society. If the explosions are to be nonviolent, disciplined, protracted rebellions against irresponsible authority, of the type Martin Luther King has led in the South, they can be constructive. There has always been a place for peaceful civic insurrection in America at times when the public mind has become so insensitive to injustice that it will respond to nothing but a shocking experience.

One can argue interminably about whether the leadership for the rebellion will originate among the poor themselves, the middle class, or a coalition of both. The leadership will not have to be of the sophisticated type considered necessary to organize traditional political action; it will need only to be popular and durable. As Saul Alinsky's back-yards movement in Chicago has indicated, the leadership of the new rebellions may frankly assert that its purpose is to inflict painful discomfort on society at large exactly in the same fashion as labor unions and steel companies when they advance their claims for economic justice. The leadership will have the original character of labor unionism and will use its weapons. It will maintain a primary identification wtih jobs, economic independence, and housing; it will employ the strike, the boycott, the sitdown, and the street protest. The appeal will be to the law, not against it, an appeal that society enforce the law and improve the law where it insufficiently protects the citizen against private or governmental power.

It seems logical to assume that such rebellions would be directed initially against the slum, and that they would declare war against existing authority at the outset. Such movements would also function quite apart from politically controlled antipoverty programs and often in direct opposition to them. A significant by-product of an organized war against the slum could be new local political groupings that would supplant to some degree traditional party structures that are now quite irrelevant as far as the poor are concerned.

In New York a rebellion against the slum would require a citywide organization which, as it developed, would project itself into many other aspects of city life besides housing. Not only would the organization concern itself with racial discrimination, urban redevelopment, relocation and resettlement, code enforcement, the schools, and the police, but it might determine the prospects of the war on poverty at home. Again, the slum war organization would follow the patterns of the labor unions, which diversified their interests as they grew stronger—but, unlike the unions, which have become less and less interested in the unemployed and in many cases discriminate against the Negro (an exception is that wing of the labor movement dominated by Walter Reuther), the slum war organization could become a vital force in the life of the poor.

The organization might eventually become the basis for establishing "corporations of the poor," which could organize the political and economic power of people living in depression areas so that they could affect the direction of the poverty program and bring changes in the local environment. From the slum war could come the structural, educational, and financial groundwork for corporations that could establish credit unions, fight price discrimination in racially segregated housing areas, break down trade union barriers to Negro and Puerto Rican apprentices, and mobilize pressure on federal agencies so that they give greater support to expansion of businesses run by Negroes and other minority groups.

The tenant union movement has had its prototypes in New York City, most of them fitful and unsuccessful. One notable exception was the Harlem rent strike organized by a Negro, Jesse Gray, which tied up several dozen buildings over a protracted period and resulted in at least one court decision and in legislation that has broadened the basis on which a tenant may withhold rent. There is the example of a mass tenants' strike organized by the Stryckers Bay Neighborhood Council. The Metropolitan Committee on Housing has tried to educate organized tenants' groups and encourages rent strikes, but its effect has been mainly educational and propagandistic. The organization of a successful slum war would require much more—establishment of active committees on a district or neighborhood basis, for instance, with each committee including a legal staff. The committees would raise money, arrange for witnesses in court, recruit and plan demonstrations, circulate materials to the press and the public, publicly identify slumlords in their areas, and stimulate local institutions—churches, civic groups, parent associations, etc.—to support the campaign.

The main thrust of the rent strike would have to be directed at the core of the ghettoes, rather than its fringes. Strategy should focus a maximum of power against a sequence of selected targets. The breadth of its base and its persistence would determine what the slum war organization could do. In short-term engagements, the slumlord has always had certain advantages: he could remain anonymous behind the façade of a real-estate corporation, he could count on inefficient or corrupt housing inspectors, and he had the weapon of court delays and technicalities. But in a long-term battle, these advantages would begin to disintegrate, particularly if the opposition was supplied with lawyers and witnesses.

A slum war organization could also function as a citizens' planning board. As the slum war continued, the organization would have to think beyond code enforcement and extension of traditional public housing programs. What would happen, for instance, if a rent strike forced the city to take over large numbers of slum properties from owners who could not afford to correct widespread violations? What would be the character of the urban renewal, rehabilitation, and relocation programs? Special thought would have to be given to the problem of resettling slum tenants, the majority of whom under present relocation programs are simply moved out of one slum into another.

The growth of tenant unionism and the use of the rent strike would provoke sharp hostilities and tensions, but would also develop a new sense of community among the thousands of Negro, Spanish, and white citizens cooperating in the effort. Even the tensions would have a certain value, in that they would give the white populations of northern cities a taste of what southern whites have felt at the hands of the civil rights movement. It would not harm the northern white, who has coasted along on attitudes inherited from the Civil War, to be moved just as the southerner has been moved in spite of himself.

The whole hypothesis on which the city is built needs to be restated. We need to think more about the resources available for encouraging the growth of an entirely new type of city, different in physical structure and purpose. We need to think more about planning and the coordination of plans. We need to become dissatisfied with the fact that we are still an accidental civilization at a time when even the newest African nations have recognized the foolishness of relying on evolution by accident.

There are broad questions to be asked and answered. Why, for instance, must huge concentrations of unemployed and untrained human beings continue to pile up in financially unstable cities that no longer have the jobs, the housing, the educational opportunities, or any of the other prerequisites for a healthy and productive life? Why do we treat the consequences and ignore the causes of massive and purposeless migration to the city? Why are we not developing new uses for those rural areas that are rapidly becoming depopulated? Why do we still instinctively deal with urban and rural America as if they were separate, conflicting interests when in fact neither interest can be served independently of the other? Why have we not done more to unify federal, state, and city planning and policy so that sensible attacks on urban ailments will not be frustrated by fragmentation, delay, and bureaucratic confusion?

Although we substitute moralization for science in thinking about national policy, the responsibility for policy will more and more require a working coalition of all three levels of government—state, federal, and local—that will assume real authority for planning. The war on poverty will have to go far beyond the present concatenation of government services.

The airtight cage of poverty, frustration, and fear in which the people of the city are imprisoned can be broken open and new towns founded which could serve the purposes of the old urban center. New York City, which shortsightedly sold off precious tracts in Staten Island, could develop a land policy that would include acquisition of "rural reserves" on which it could build and incorporate subsidiary towns and cities, some of them at great distances from the old urban core. The traditional basis on which population centers have been established should be re-examined. Technology has been rapidly divorcing human beings from dependence on urban "centers" of production, of politics, of culture. In many ways the "center" has become an obsolete concept because our new technology makes it possible to diversify and disperse production and population. The President recognized this fact in his January, 1966, message to Congress asking for $3.6 billion to establish new "demonstration cities." But the magnitude of the task is still misunderstood: the President's proposal for all U.S. cities is only slightly more than what the Venezuelan government is mobilizing for construction of one new city, Ciudad Guyana.

Unless new communities are established, it is difficult to see how the poor, especially the Negro, can ever become truly integrated into American life. Efforts at so-called "desegregation" in the hostile environment of large cities have had great moral value, but in practical terms they are a mirage. Small numbers of Negro children are shifted from one school to another, and a trickle of adults manages to find its way into decent housing in middle-class neighborhoods, but that is all. Since the suburban ring about New York City has locked the Negro into the slum, new settlements would have to leap over this constricting belt. Townships could be located in areas with adequate natural resources, in every state of the Union. Migration to them would be open to everyone, regardless of economic status, perhaps under terms of a contract clearly stating the responsibilities of both parties. The citizens who signed such a "lease" would do so as volunteers in a flagship community, sponsored by government, which would set the pace for a racially integrated, heterogeneous new society.

The new communities would have to be planned architecturally, socially, administratively, and economically. They would include complexes of health and welfare services available on both a private and a public basis, and educational parks for the training of teachers as well as children. One function of the new community would be to provide housing for people relocated from urban renewal areas. The housing could be temporary or permanent, depending on the needs and resources of the individual family, and rental housing should be available for purchase by the tenant at his option. The new communities would have their defects and special problems, but they must be part of any sustained attack upon the city ghetto and on the dying towns in which the rural poor are concentrated. The redevelopment of land by these new communities would link rural America more closely to the cities.

There are the usual arguments against the new town idea: that it would be expensive, it would become economically and racially segregated, that communities cannot be created out of whole cloth without an economic base—i.e., an adequate demand for labor. However, expensive as the new towns would be, they would not begin to approach the costliness of the slum, and they could be the start toward a solution to the problems arising from high-density, badly housed city populations. Even if some new towns might become segregated or set in any number of various ways, segregation under such conditions would not necessarily be undesirable. The voluntary coming together of people with similar needs and a common purpose has always been the basis of new settlement. What is most important for the poor as a whole and for minority groups in particular is that they be provided with the resources to help themselves.

But the old arguments are disintegrating in the face of technological change and new economic and social perspectives. At the same time the traditional basis of the city as a center of industrially and commercially based employment is undergoing drastic alteration, new potentials for resettlement of our rural frontier are becoming apparent. For instance, if proposals to guarantee an annual income for people earning less than $3,000 are adopted—as suggested by the President's commission on technology, automation, and employment—they can revolutionize the future of urban and rural areas alike, by breaking the tie between jobs and income. A guaranteed income could give the poor a new mobility and choice of place to live that will affect the entire map of the United States, that could bring about a general expansion and upgrading of low-income housing, and it could help break down the walls that have kept the Negro penned up in the crowded core cities. Just as government policies have regulated the flow of credit, affected land development, agricultural production, and the dispersion of industry, they can influence distribution of the population and the opportunities of that population for self-expression.

It is not that the problems of the city are insoluble, or that the people lack the ingenuity or the resources to confront the causes of their discomfort. The difficulty lies in the failure to recognize the fearful consequences of what is being allowed to happen, to use sensibly all that we have, and to plan our national future as a whole community of individuals whose welfare is forever indivisible. The old superstition that planning will cost us our freedom has led Americans to entrust their lives to continual series of accidental developments conditioned only by the competing pressures of organized special interest. The result of this refusal to control history has cost us progress, economic security, and even our personal safety. The West Side of the city of New York is only one example of the manner in which human beings have been overwhelmed by the "monstrosities" which Arnold Toynbee says are the signs of a civilization in peril of its life—monstrosities that include the bureaucratization of life, the enormous waste of human potentiality, and the misuse of national wealth.

If the city is to be saved, it will be because the people adopt revolutionary means to save it. If it is to grow more diseased and die, it will not be the fault of the accidents that deal the final blows. If we come to the point when, as Harvey Wheeler predicts, we cannot move from one place to another without a permit from the regulators, it will be our own paralysis that will be responsible. As Toynbee contends, civilizations are never murdered; they die by their own hands.

The Process

The most important facts about the city are what I call tidal facts. These tidal facts illuminate the invisible, involuntary processes that are part of the character and the physical body of the city, processes analogous to breathing or the beating of the heart. When I say tidal facts give the essential truth, I am comparing them to facts about institutions like churches or the Department of Real Estate or what officials say about themselves. I gathered a lot of data about such institutions and people and the best that I can say about the information is that it provides a few helpful clues. The trouble is that one of the functions of a political or social institution—and of some people—is the manufacture of lies about itself and its environment. Although tidal facts cannot be counted or heard and have no color or particular shape, there is no mistaking one of them when you come across it. Tidal facts appear or they reveal themselves; they are not collected. The discovery of a tidal fact is inadvertent, sometimes, and at other times it appears in a very indistinct, bloblike shape after a great deal of lying awake and worrying about where the truth is. A bundle of data or a repetition of sights and experiences may point to where a tidal fact is buried. The main point is that the tidal fact is there and is incontrovertible. You find a rip or a hole in the surface of life and suddenly you are looking into things, not at them.

One of the tidal facts that impressed me most is the continual waste and loss of human life that is taking place in our city. I am not talking about the murders or assaults that have terrified most of the people that I know—poor people, middle-class people, well-to-do people. I am talking about the destruction of children. Of the enormous number of crimes that take place in the city, the largest number and the most terrible are committed against children. The ones who suffer the most are the children of the poor. Only a small portion of these crimes have to do with beating or physical abuse. From the time tens of thousands of newly-born infants are removed from the hospital they become subjected to what I call "the process." That is, they are introduced to a style of existence that eventually cripples or destroys huge numbers of them and occasionally other people with whom they have come in contact. I have not been able to discover any good reason why this should be taking place, even an economic reason. It is said over and over that the United States and the city of New York together do not have the public or private money to prevent the destruction of children and see that they are fed and cared for properly, that their illnesses are treated, and their minds and spirits nourished. It is said that the responsibility for such care lies with the parents, which is a non sequitur because there are no parents to speak of in this situation. Later on, when children born clean, ready and expectant begin to malfunction and cause trouble, hundreds of millions of dollars are appropriated to hire special teachers and policemen and youth workers and build special classrooms and prisons and mental institutions and hospitals to keep these children under control. The children who do survive this tempering process become adults, but in my neighborhood an adult is a dead child. In the end the justification for such procedures is that this is the way things have to be done in a system of free enterprise, but in view of the fact that all the money is wasted as well as the children, this seems to be hard to believe. Wasting money is not part of the capitalistic system.

I have thought a great deal about the reasons for the destruction of children. Obviously it tells us something about the people that we are and the character of our civilization, but what? Trying to answer the question leads to a second tidal fact. We are, practically speaking, unconscious of what is going on. We seem to have pushed whatever knowledge we have about "the process" into a part of our minds that is not directly connected with our emotions or our motor mechanisms. The knowledge is there but it is lodged in such a fashion that it does not affect our behavior, and when we are presented evidence of what is going on, we respond to it the way we do to an act of violence on television or the movies. We have the so-called vicarious experience, in which a crime is relayed to us stripped of all its meaning because it is presented as an image of crime, not as a crime itself.

The ability to respond this way, or rather not to respond, is said by some people to indicate immaturity or lack of education. This perhaps is related to what Bertrand Russell says of the proper aim of education—that is, education is supposed to develop minds sensitive enough to perceive, to feel the shock of tragedies taking place thousands of miles away and somehow communicate a feeling to the heart. In my city the sensitivity to pick up the tragedy does not extend to the corner, or even across the street.

I don't think the problem is just a plain lack of sensitivity or of education. The ability to live with "the process" has something to do with a self-induced psychic disorder. I know of no name for this state of mind, so I will invent a name: auto-anesthesia. The first step in auto-anesthesia is to turn one's eyes away from the object or the act of cruelty itself. It is not necessary to ignore the object or act completely, but it is necessary to consider it only in the abstract—in photographs, television, books, speeches, conversations, etc.; then the mind, which is naturally intolerant of pain, can erase a great deal of the shock and guilt. I have found the procedure works. I have found myself laughing when I was describing something that thoroughly frightened or nauseated me when it took place.

If we go beyond the abstract image and force ourselves to look at the object itself, moving and wriggling and making noises, or if we see the event itself—an automobile accident or someone in the process of being beaten severely (these are the more spectacular examples)—we will discover that the problem lies not in being undereducated. I recommend that we try over a period of time looking directly into the faces of autistic children or the types of babies that can be found lying on beds in our slums. I don't think it is necessary sometimes even to see the children themselves. It is enough to see the shell in which the process takes place. I can remember the experience of going to the children's ward of a mental hospital. The children were not there, and all I could see were the cots and the cells, five cots to a room, and this was enough. After we have looked at enough of such objects we can have unpredictable mental reactions, certain types of dreams, for instance, which are revealing. One may be looking into a kaleidoscope, where each piece of color can become a child's face or a characteristic sound from these children—red being a cry, blue another failure, yellow the long unbroken periods of

silence—these are the conversation of the children who are being subjected to "the process." I know it is possible for such dreams to take
place because I have had them.

When I thought about "the process" and the way we adjust to it, I
think I discovered what a good World War II German was all about—the
German who knew and disapproved and who had his own way of living
with "the process." As a matter of fact, I discovered I was one of those
"good Germans." I think perhaps most Americans are "good Germans,"
some of them better than others, and I understand something that always
mystified me before, which is how a "good German" felt when he was
led through Dachau for the first time and had a look at the objects, not
the victims but the objects. He learned how the process worked and he
saw the testimony. He cried and said he did not know. I think that he
was being honest and that he did not know. He had the tidal fact in the
back of his mind someplace. He knew about places like Dachau but he
had somehow disconnected this from the rest of his system. He had
looked at images and reports and had listened to rationalizations until
nothing was real, and the railroad cars were just taking the Jews off to a
work camp someplace. Then I think he perhaps talked about his worries
and this helped him control himself, which meant that he saved his life
I don't know what our excuse is.

I say I am a "good German" because when I was forced to look over
a long period of time at too many objects and acts in my city I felt the
German reaction, which was to justify myself by saying I have been put
into a system, that nobody asked me permission for the system, that I
hadn't wanted it. I will defend Hannah Arendt when she says that evil is
common and that most people who commit evil are asleep. She has got
hold of a tidal fact.

We are "good Germans" when we try to explain ourselves. We explain
by looking for the criminal who involved us in all this. In New York City
when we look for a culprit we usually point to the mayor or some other
highly visible politician. He is somehow responsible for all this and there
are people who would like to hang him for all of the things that are going
wrong in the city, including the destruction of children. Hanging the
mayor is another part of the auto-anesthesia, because if we can dispose
of him in some way, preferably spectacular, we can feel that something
has been done. This attitude means we are still seeing images of the
truth. I think that if we stop looking at the images we will find that exe-
cuting the mayor would be unsatisfactory and we might not even bother
to do anything about him. We would be looking for causes and we would
find them everywhere, just as the "good Germans" turned out to be
everywhere.

All of this leads to another tidal fact which explains all the others.
What has happened is that we are in the middle of a system which makes
"the process" inevitable; which requires more and more human beings in

various parts of our country—Appalachia, Selma, Chicago—to grow up to be dead children, or, as some people put it, welfare babies. The system I am talking about is turning more and more of our resources away from the nurture of human life and into the destruction of it. The system has just about been perfected and is now at the point where we have automated the process of conspicuous waste and destruction. I don't mean the waste of material and money alone. I mean the neglect or destruction of other people's lives, in Vietnam for instance, or in the last World War. I mean the piling up of children in the dark parts of our cities and leaving them to rot, the way we used to pile up boxes of 20mm guns and compasses and sextants in the jungle and leave them until sun and rain rotted the boxes and they broke apart. Over the past two or three years I have looked at many scores of children who do not look back at me because they cannot. If they could speak, I doubt that we could hear them, anyway. By some great bit of psychological magic we have surrounded ourselves with a transparent material that admits no sound or even a breath of air from the world in which they live.

The fact is that there is less and less room for all the children trying to get into the world we "good Germans" are fixing for ourselves. Sometimes, if you watch "the process," you may see the exact moment when a child gives up the struggle. I remember a plump, amiable Negro boy about thirteen named Larry who lived in a rooming house across the street. One morning the police went into the building and brought his mother out and put her in the police wagon. With all the neighborhood gathered around watching, a plainclothesman told Larry to get into the wagon with his mother. With the tears rolling down his cheeks the boy refused to move. "All right, son, you can ride with us," the plainclothesman said, and he opened the door to a black sedan. Then with a great, silent cracking of the heart the child was carried away like a seed on the wind.

harold j. abramson

Ethnicity may be defined as "a state of distinctive and shared people-hood coming out of a common past, with a shared sense of the present and future." There are all sorts of ethnic communities in America. Some are racial, and some religious. And according to Harold Abramson other groups have cultural characteristics that also allow them to be called ethnic. Such groups may be occupational, like miners and merchant seamen, or regional, such as Southerners. They all have a sense of who they are and where they belong.

In this sense most Americans are ethnics of one sort or other. But some are not, and among these we find Richard M. Nixon and his colleagues. Because they are not ethnics they could not relate to substantial sectors of society—liberal pluralists who acknowledge the validity of group interests, radicals and populists, even conservatives. They were never insiders but always the sort of persons who pressed their noses to the window hoping to be one of the gang—any gang. According to Abramson, they are without roots. They never had a real political base. And now they have nothing but their memories—and some of their tapes.

Reprinted from *The Columbia Forum*, Winter 1974, Vol. III, No. 1. Copyright 1974 by The Trustees of Columbia University in the City of New York. This article was originally entitled "Watergate: Death at the Roots."

What is clear now is at least the range of Watergate criminal charges, which includes, in alphabetical order: burglary, conspiracy to commit illegal acts, destruction of evidence, extortion, fraud, illegal distribution of campaign literature, illegal wiretapping, obstruction of justice, perjury, solicitation of illegal campaign contributions, subornation of perjury, and violation of campaign funding laws. All of these charges allege crimes against the traditional norms of the land as codified in law. As the New Year began, the House of Representatives had for the first time in one hundred years undertaken serious consideration of the impeachment of the President, who is charged to uphold the law.

Most explanations of this debacle, while useful, fail to come to terms with the uniqueness of Watergate. The historical explanation—that Watergate is American politics-as-usual, just a heightened version of the rough-and-tumble of American power—does not take into account the extent and seriousness of the crimes. American political history can offer nothing to rival Watergate in sheer scope of corruption. Moreover, as has been pointed out, the motives behind Watergate are new: this time, the scandal was not incurred for sex or money. Instead, corruption was engaged in solely to enhance the power of an ideology, and to serve a man who is presumed to represent that ideology. This is what is unique in American history, and in the history of American political scandal.

Another explanation argues that Watergate was inevitable because of the growth of power in the American Presidency. Something like it would have happened, sooner or later, regardless of who occupied the Presidency and regardless of political party, because imperial politics, the Presidency's self-aggrandizing policies vis-à-vis Congress, has been the trend ever since Roosevelt and the New Deal, quickening since the start of the Cold War. The trouble with this explanation is that nothing in the least comparable to Watergate occurred in the Truman, Eisenhower, Kennedy, or Johnson Administrations. Billy Sol Estes and Sherman Adams and Bobby Baker were the comparatively modest typifiers of American political corruption. There is nothing in their stories to rival Watergate in scope or motivation. Only Spiro Agnew can be compared with Baker, Estes, and Adams, but his problems are worse than theirs: he was, after all, the Vice President, no mere member of the "kitchen" cabinet, adviser, or ward heeler. Still, Agnew's crimes, like theirs, are old-fashioned ones: he simply wanted to live in an expensive house and have his grocery bills paid. If Watergate is the result of imperial politics and a royalist Presidency, why did we not get even a whiff of such undertakings for ideology and power in previous Administrations? We did not, I submit, because Richard Nixon is unique in the history of the American Presidency.

An explanation along economic lines: Watergate is an expression of corporate power, of the rise of new money and the characteristics of the nouveau riche. No doubt it is, but one must point out that the four previous Administrations did not show marked disdain for corporate power. (Eisenhower, an exception, did—in his Farewell Address but not before.) The well rewarded cosseting of industries (aerospace, oil, drugs) has been notable in the Nixon Administration, but the Johnson Administration drew support from similar sources, and so did other Administrations.

A more refined socio-economic theory makes much of regional or sectional bias. Watergate happened, it is said, not simply because the money was new and obtained by conspiracies of deceit, but because it was Southern Rim money, from the corporations of Southern California, the Southwest, the new South, and Florida. This is regional ethnocentrism, the East writing off the cultural, political, and moral styles of other locales in the way that Barry Goldwater writes off the East and Kevin Phillips much of the urban North. New money can be just as corrupt in New England as in Arizona, Texas, or California; and the new-money dealings of industries like aerospace and drugs are no more corrupt now, in the latter half of the twentieth century, than were the new-money dealings of the railroad and oil industries of the Harrimans and Rockefellers in the nineteenth century.

All of these interpretations are useful and thus interesting. But none takes into account the singular character of the 37th President of the United States, the man in whose name and for whose sake so many friends and associates did all that was done. Much has already been written about Nixon the man, but little that does not leave him, at heart, somehow mysterious. We know his history, yet he seems curiously unmoored. What are his roots? What are the roots of the people with whom he has surrounded himself?

I propose to approach these questions using the sociological concept of "ethnicity," a revived—and hotly debated—means of social identification which has taken shape from the writings of Max Weber, E. K. Francis, Edward Shils, Andrew Greeley, R. A. Schermerhorn, Milton Gordon, and others. Defined extremely loosely, ethnicity is a state of distinctive and shared peoplehood coming out of a common past, with a shared sense of the present and future. Time and duration are central to ethnicity.

Ethnic groups are not to be confused with minority groups, since dominant groups have their own ethnicity. Ethnic groups are subcultural populations which not only possess their own cultural styles but receive and perpetuate them. Other subcultural groups—homosexuals, dwarfs, the blind—may possess distinctive styles of life but not ethnicity, for they lack continuity over time and across generations.

Ethnicity is of course most obvious as race. But it may stem from other referents as well, often several working in conjunction with each other. Religion, for many, is a source of ethnicity. A white Episcopalian among white Jews feels like an Episcopalian; a white Baptist among white Catholics feels like a Baptist; a French Canadian Catholic among Italian Catholics feels like a French Canadian. Along with race and religion, national background persists as a source of ethnicity. America still has, after two and three generations, the self-identified Irish, Polish, Armenians, and Lithuanians—although we are not always sure of what it is to be Irish, Polish, Armenian, or Lithuanian. We have ethnic politics, ethnic novels, and ethnic communities to tell us that the culture of nationality persists, if not for always, then at least for now; if not under all social conditions, then at least under some.

And region persists as a source of ethnicity. A white Midwesterner knows the difference between Nebraska and New England. A white Southerner knows when he is not at home. And even Orange County, California (about which I shall say more later) is not the arid and anomic locale that some in the East like to think it is.

There are people who can substitute one kind of ethnicity for another in the process of assimilation, cultural change, or individual change. Some occupations—typically the more isolated ones such as railroading used to be, or fishing, or coal mining, or even laboring in the intellectual world—can also, over time, provide a sense of ethnicity. It appears that one can cast off, say, the coat of Italian-ness for that of Harvard-ness, though not always easily. One can also revive or retrieve an ethnic past out of seemingly nothing; witness the growing sense of ethnicity among somewhat assimilated Irish Americans as the troubles mount in Ulster or the renewed ethnic consciousness among Jewish Americans caught up with events in the Middle East.

We know very little about ethnic identity, but one thing we can surmise is that ethnic identity and ethnic attachments influence values, hence our behavior. How they do and to what extent is not always easy to describe. But we can, for example, point to the presence of conflicting values between the Irish and the Yankees in Boston and New England. Still more precisely, we can distinguish the proletarian conflicts between the Swamp Yankees and Shanty Irish, and the bourgeois cleavage between the Boston Brahmins and the Lace Curtain Irish. It goes without saying that such conflicts are plentiful between blacks and whites in many areas of contact, and between other groups as well.

It has been argued by some American social scientists that ethnicity leads to marginality and identity crises; it hinders getting ahead and rising in the class structure; it is embarrassing, primitive, downright un-American. (Otherwise intelligent laymen identify it only with the exotic, or with "local color": charming Methodist strawberry festivals in Zanesville, Ohio, and jolly Italian street festivals on Mulberry Street in New York. Many speak as if Anglo-Saxon Protestants do not possess it, while everyone else does.) At worst, ethnicity is judged to be reactionary: the embodiment of ethnocentrism, bigotry, and backwardness.

But ethnic difference in America has its positive side; it implies the presence of group rules and codes of behavior. To lack group ties, ethnic referents (whether racial, religious, national, regional, or occupational), is to lack an immediate and useful code of behavior. Rootlessness exposes one to the risks of behaving without a moral code, with no traditional underpinnings to support one's decisions. Ethnicity may or may not impede social mobility, but its lack may itself conduce to marginality, identity crises, and a kind of free-floating embarrassment. If one has no traditional group codes to regulate one's behavior, one has only the larger American legal-ethical system with which to handle the anonymity of the larger American mass. And one's immediate friends, all of one's "reference groups," are likely to be similarly rootless people, lacking traditions, continuity, and a sense of the past.

For that matter, not to have a home, a people within a people, a tie with the past may itself be "un-American." Lacking ethnicity, how can one relate to the American liberal tradition—to political pluralism, for example, which explicitly acknowledges the validity of group interests? Or to the American radical tradition—to populism, for example, which explicitly acknowledges the validity of group interests which are being forsaken or corrupted by the top of the hierarchy? Or to the American conservative tradition—to states' rights, for example, which explicitly acknowledges the validity of regional, decentralized group interests?

We do sometimes encounter, in the great American mix, individuals whose ethnic attachments, conscious and subconscious, are minimal, even nil. Their lives draw no meaning from their race; they derive no values from their religious past; they know and feel little about their national background; they have not much in the way of regional identity; and their occupation happens to be one which affords no sense of solidarity with others. Lacking ethnicity, such individuals lack identity. They do not know who they are in the American mass. Richard Nixon seems to me very much such a person, as do many of the characters in his cast of thousands. To call Nixon rootless is not altogether new, perhaps. But by examining his case more fully than has, I think, been done, we can see Watergate in a new way.

Of religion, Richard Nixon's Quaker mother may have tried to teach him gentleness, pacifism, forgiveness, charity; such values are difficult to see in him now. Gentleness, pacifism, forgiveness, and charity do not translate into Christmas bombings or unregulated war or secret tapings of private conversations. Nixon no longer attends Quaker services at all. He sometimes attends Presbyterian services. Bruce Mazlish, in *In Search of Richard Nixon*, reminds us that Billy Graham was the first preacher Nixon entertained in the White House. Billy Graham also preached at the funeral of Nixon's Quaker mother. But denominational-ism is by no means obsolete in American Protestantism; why then does the son ask a fundamentalist Baptist minister to officiate at the Quaker mother's funeral? Unless Nixon has in fact converted to the Billy Graham variant of fundamentalist Protestantism, no religious denom-ination would seem to anchor him securely in American society. Con-fusingly, we read that in Washington and Key Biscayne he occasionally attends the Presbyterian Church—a long way, surely, from Billy Graham's revival arenas.

Nixon is also unidentifiable in any kind of local terms. It is difficult, perhaps impossible, to see the stamp of a locale on him. He is "Amer-ican"—that is all. In this he is unique, a first-of-a-kind President. To consider only his recent predecessors: Harry Truman was always con-juring his roots in Missouri; Eisenhower, his boyhood in Kansas. John-son, even in his worst moments during the expansion of the war in Vietnam, could invoke the assurances of his Texas past. Kennedy was luckier than many. When he became President, Robert Frost counseled him "to be more Irish than Harvard." Whether or not he was, he called on both traditions and was all the richer.

Garry Wills, in *Nixon Agonistes*, puts it well:

> Nixon's background haunts him, yet does not show—not, at least, in helpful ways. Eisenhower, a virtual exile to exotic places most of his active life—Panama, the Philippines, Africa, England, Paris—could still make his grin hazily fulgurant with Kansas, with the dust-prismed sun of his childhood afternoons. All recent Presidents have had the stamp of place on them—patrician Roosevelt of upper New York, raffish Harry Truman from Missouri (almost, one feels, from a Mark Twain story), Boston-Irish Kennedy thinly veneered at Harvard, and Johnson out of Texas like a walking tall tale, comic yet redolent of danger. Nixon alone, though deeply shaped by Whittier [California], has no attractive color of place to him.

Wills continues in the same vein:

> Kennedy retreated from governmental business to native salt air at Hyannis Port; Johnson, feeling dwarfed by the central seat of power in the world, went home to play cowboys and cattle baron in Texas. Nixon, from the outset, slipped off for surcease to Mexico, the Bahamas, Key Biscayne. Johnson has, in effect, cased the "log cabin" of his birth in golden accretions of history, as a mother bronzes her baby's shoes. Nixon, returning in 1968 to the house in Yorba Linda where he was born, scuffed the floor in embarrassment, ducked his head dutifully into this hole and that corner as if each were a trap, and left like one released.

Wills does not pursue the notion of "stamp of place." But it is not merely a matter of attractiveness, the ethnicity of fun and games, of local color. Wills' passage conveys the idea not only that Nixon has no home, but that he has no local continuity to refer to. Even Eisenhower (recall their well known estrangement) knew this. According to Wills, Ike once remarked that "Nixon did not grow or mature in office; that he was not presidential timber; that he had no roots; that he was 'too political'."

Orange County, California, has often been called on to account for aspects of Richard Nixon. Southern California as a whole is said to have unusually high proportions of migrants entering, and may well shelter higher proportions of non-native-born than any other area of the United States. But there are also sufficient signs that enough people have been born there, and have lived there for more than one generation, to create some kind of continuity of traditions and cultural values. As James Q. Wilson, professor of government at Harvard, puts it:

> I grew up in Reagan country—not Hollywood, but the lower-middle-class suburbs of Los Angeles. It was a distinctive way of life. I think I could still recognize another person who grew up there no matter where I should meet him, just as surely as an Italian can spot a person from his village or region even though they are both now in Queens.

In defending his home state and region, Carey McWilliams argues that there is little reason to attribute the Watergate machinations or Nixon himself to California. "The fact is," he writes, "that Richard Nixon has few roots in any part of California and is not a typical product of its politics." It might be better, McWilliams implies, if the man did have roots in Orange County.

Others besides Wills and Mazlish have mentioned Nixon's comprehensive lack of place. In *The Making of a President, 1960*, Theodore White wrote: "His campaign has been based on home talk. But he has no real home except where his wife was: he was a stranger, even . . . in California, seeking home and friendship." To be sure, Nixon systematically romanticizes rural life and small-town America; he reminds us of the long-time strain in American political history which pits the strength of rural values against the evils of the city, straw-man fashion. This is downstate Illinois calling down doom on the sins of Chicago, upstate New York shunning the millions of New York City—the mood captured by Carl Sandburg when he wrote of painted women luring the farm boys under the lampposts. Mazlish recalls Nixon at the dedication of the Karl E. Mundt Library in Madison, South Dakota, in 1969: "I feel at home here because I, too, grew up in a small town." Mazlish concludes that Nixon was not only being politically clever but was telling the truth. I wonder. For Nixon does not show us why he would feel at home in a small town.

For all his four houses, he does not live in a small town, nor seem to want to. Mazlish reports that Richard Nixon always wanted to live in New York City, where he could work for a prestigious law firm. After law school at Duke, he did not at first make it to New York; he did not achieve that ambition until 1963, after he had lost the California gubernatorial election. He then took his place as a senior partner in a Wall Street firm. Whatever his present hostility to the so-called Eastern Establishment, he plunged into it then with a fervor. "He not only made good," Mazlish writes, "but he actively bowed to the pieties of Eastern success by sending his daughters to Finch and to Smith College and presenting them to society in a Debutante Ball (one result being their marrying boys from well known families), and by himself joining prestigious New York men's clubs such as the Metropolitan and the Links."

Nixon even now has no clear home. Rather, he has four houses and travels, travels, travels. His plane, remodeled and remodeled again, itself serves as a house. "By November 1969, after one year as President," Mazlish reports, "Nixon had, according to the Republican National Committee, already logged in Air Force One 'a total of 75,443 air miles since taking office—already three times more than the previous holder, Lyndon B. Johnson'." He flies between Florida, California, Washington, and the Bahamas, and may spend more time in the air than at any one of his present abodes. Even his famous dog, Checkers, according to a recent article, is buried in the Bide-A-Wee Memorial Park—not in Orange County, not near San Clemente, not in Key Biscayne, not even in Washington, but in Wantagh, Long Island. There is something almost pathetic about the President's continual movement. Consider only the enormous amount of time and money expended in planning for the hundreds of people in the Executive branch and elsewhere who must synchronize with all this motion. But more important, one wonders about the energy and psychic cost of all this house-hopping. The man cannot find himself. It is all reminiscent, somehow, of Citizen Kane.

Among white Protestant Americans, occupation can serve as a source of ethnic identification. Depending on certain conditions—such as continuity over time or relative isolation—some occupational subcultures in America can provide a code of conduct, a sense of solidarity, and a cultural ancestry. Often this referent works in conjunction with others, so that the ethnicity of white rural Protestant Appalachian coal miners would differ from the ethnicity of other white rural Protestants from Appalachia who are not coal miners. Similarly, we can speak of the group traditions of white Protestants who are railroaders, isolated from the ethnicity of the nearest rural and urban white Protestants who are not railroaders.

Politics, and more specifically Republicanism, might serve as a source of ethnicity for Richard Nixon; but once again the testimony and evidence stand against such a tie. This is in part due to the nature of

California politics: Republicanism in California is not at all the same as Republicanism in Iowa or in Vermont. Gary Wills once again:

> California is to America what America used to be to the world—a nation of immigrants. And the influx of outsiders is matched by a restless internal circulation of inhabitants. The state is, like its freeways, a clotting of men and machines in constant (partial) motion. Its politics, too, is fluid. There is no stable party system. Cross-filing, a huge swing vote, a changing electorate, make it possible to tumble instantly down trap doors (Goodwin Knight, Bill Knowland, and in 1962, Dick Nixon) or pop up out of nowhere (Ronald Reagan, George Murphy). There is no latticework of party structure to catch men's fall or slow their climb. It is a state with a million more registered Democrats than Republicans, which swept Reagan into office by a million votes.

Nixon's Republicanism is not at all comparable to, say, Hubert Humphrey's ties with the Democrats of Minnesota, and the immemorial traditions of local Minnesota party politics. It is also possible to show how the traditions of party politics sustained, in some sense, the identities of such disparate men as Richard Daley, George McGovern, Everett Dirksen, Sam Ervin, Robert Taft, Abraham Ribicoff, George Aiken, John Stennis, and the Kennedys. In the case of political families, where one is born to politics and has the weight of family behind one's efforts (as with the Kennedys, the Roosevelts, and the Tafts), ethnic strength and constraint stand out even clearer.

Now obviously there are many American politicians who are newcomers (Lowell Weicker), mavericks (Wayne Morse), independents (Mark Hatfield), or converts (John Lindsay), who, for these or other reasons, do not derive a sense of solidarity from party politics. I am not suggesting that identification with other politicians is essential to political success, or that all politicians derive ethnic strength from their occupation. I am only saying that this *can* be a locus of ethnicity, of a shared history and present and future. There is ample reason to believe that in the case of Richard Nixon even this boat has been missed.

One has only to look at the kinds of advisers and aides he has selected for himself. He has picked men whose loyalties to him are paramount; there is nothing unusual in this *except* for the fact that their loyalty to the boss transcends any kind of group boundaries. This is not like the loyalty found in Richard Daley's Cook County organization, or even in traditional Democratic politics in Texas, or the first and last hurrahs of Boston, or in Republican politics in rural New England or small-town Indiana. It is not even the sort of loyalty found in the Mafia. The loyalty which motivated Watergate is without ethnic—that is, cultural, regional, or party—constraint. The men around Nixon have no other attachments but to him, no competing codes of behavior, no other identity.

The best argument here is the Committee to Re-elect the President. Republicans toiling in their vineyards around the country can hardly be expected to mourn the demise of this body or the enormous legal and ethical morass in which it foundered. The election of 1972 produced a Republican victory in the Presidency, but that is about all the G.O.P. got out of it. As Senator Weicker reminded us, the Committee to Re-Elect the President was not and is not part of American Republicanism. A candidate for the Presidency ignored the national machinery of his party and set up an elaborate parallel organization to concern itself only with him. Traditional Republicans, like traditional Democrats, would hardly have undertaken such a subversion. Not only is the Committee reasonable evidence of the loyalty Richard Nixon feels to American Republicanism; it is also indicative of the strong ties that he and his palace guard felt to the essentially non-political occupations of advertising and public relations. Nixon's entourage of aides was largely recruited from business and business-related service organizations. The Committee was an invention of nonpoliticians and was designed to *compete* with traditional Republicanism, which at its best can offer a code of values, a blueprint for behavior formed by tradition.

It is to be expected that people in power will choose to surround themselves with those of similar dispositions. It is not often otherwise. Nixon and the cast of Watergate look very much like rootless people, without ethnic identity and without the constraint of tradition. This is expressed even in the language they have used in the public record and in official memos, speaking about *themselves*. John Ehrlichman says of Pat Gray: "Let him twist slowly, slowly in the wind." John Mitchell says that if he could, he would line up the Watergate defendants on the White House lawn "and would have them all shot." Charles Colson declares a loyalty above and beyond all else when he says that he "would walk over my grandmother if necessary" for Richard Nixon. (But then Nixon himself finds it expedient to wiretap his brother Donald.) Alexander Butterfield, Haldeman's former aide and the owner-up to the secret taps placed in the Oval Office, says of Ernest Fitzgerald, who told Congress about huge cost overruns on the C-5A: "We should let him bleed for a while." Or read John Dean on "how we can use the available federal machinery to screw our political enemies." All of this may or may not be shop-talk-as-usual in the nation's capital, but its lack of constraint is pretty overwhelming.

I do not at all want to suggest that an absence of ethnicity by itself explains Watergate and Richard Nixon's characteristic behavior. For instance, no part of Watergate would have been possible without vast amounts of available dollars. The characters in what the *Congressional Quarterly* has called a "medieval morality play," in their zealotry, were not greenhorn volunteers. They were all paid and paid well. The loyalty of the men around Nixon goes just so far, for they have had limited nurture in loyalty. Their unprecedented intrigue, conspiracy, subterfuge, perjury, deception, burglary, and hubris were all paid for, cash on the barrelhead. In this, Watergate resembles the industrial espionage of conglomerates and multinational corporations.

Nor would I claim that a lack of ethnicity is always translated into amorality. There are many in America for whom a grounding in race, religion, national background, region, or even occupation neither helps nor hinders a sturdy identity and moral code. For them, being "fellow Americans" seems to be enough. What is clear is that, in his circumstances, for Richard Nixon nothing was enough.

ON CLASS AND STATUS

erving goffman

More complicated than most other articles included in this collection, Erving Goffman's offers a framework for defining and understanding the ways people are ranked in society and the cues or signs they learn to recognize as symbols of class status. Status symbols, as Goffman shows, carry categorical as well as expressive significance. For example, who can acquire a second car—and who does? What does it mean to say one stayed in a fancy hotel rather than a simple but clean and perfectly adequate one? Why do some people get upset over long hair and sandals, while others find such trappings essential for social acceptance?

Who is to decide what is "in" and what is acceptable? Why do others care, which, of course, they do?

I

The terms *status*, *position*, and *role* have been used interchangeably to refer to the set of rights and obligations which governs the behavior of persons acting in a given social capacity.

In general, the rights and obligations of a status are fixed through time by means of external sanctions enforced by law, public opinion, and threat of socio-economic loss, and by inter-

From Erving Goffman, "Symbols of Class Status," from *The British Journal of Sociology*, vol. II (1951), 294–304, by permission of Routledge & Kegan Paul Ltd.

nalized sanctions of the kind that are built into a conception of self and give rise to guilt, remorse, and shame.

A status may be *ranked* on a scale of *prestige*, according to the amount of social value that is placed upon it relative to other statuses in the same sector of social life. An individual may be *rated* on a scale of *esteem*, depending on how closely his performance approaches the ideal established for that particular status.[2]

Co-operative activity based on a differentiation and integration of statuses is a universal characteristic of social life. This kind of harmony requires that the occupant of each status act toward others in a manner which conveys the impression that his conception of himself and of them is the same as their conception of themselves and him. A working consensus of this sort therefore requires adequate communication about conceptions of status.

The rights and obligations of a status are frequently ill-adapted to the requirements of ordinary communication. Specialized means of displaying one's position frequently develop. Such sign-vehicles have been called *status symbols*.[3] They are the cues which select for a person the status that is to be imputed to him and the way in which others are to treat him.

Status symbols visibly divide the social world into categories of persons, thereby helping to maintain solidarity within a category and hostility between different categories.[4] Status symbols must be distinguished from *collective symbols* which serve to deny the difference between categories in order that members of all categories may be drawn together in affirmation of a single moral community.[5]

Status symbols designate the position which an occupant has, not the way in which he fulfills it. They must therefore be distinguished from *esteem symbols* which designate the degree to which a person performs the duties of his position in accordance with ideal standards, regardless of the particular rank of his position. For example, the Victoria Cross is awarded in the British Army for heroic performance of a task, regardless of what particular task it is and regardless of the rank of the person who performs it. This is an esteem symbol. It rates above a similar one called the George Cross. On the other hand, there is an insignia which designates Lieutenant-Colonel. It is a status symbol. It tells us about the rank of the person who wears it but tells us nothing about the standard he has achieved in performing the duties of his rank. It *ranks* him above a man who wears the insignia of a Captain, although, in fact, the Captain may be *rated* higher than the Lieutenant-Colonel in terms of the esteem that is accorded to good soldiers.

Persons in the same social position tend to possess a similar pattern of behaviour. Any item of a person's behaviour is, therefore, a sign of his social position. A sign of position can be a status symbol only if it is used with some regularity as a means of "placing" socially the person who makes it. Any sign which provides reliable evidence of its maker's position—whether or not laymen or sociologists use it for evidence about position—may be called a *test of status*. This paper is concerned with the pressures that play upon behaviour as a result of the fact that a symbol of status is not always a very good test of status.

By definition, then, a status symbol carries *categorical* significance, that is, it serves to identify the social status of the person who makes it. But it may also carry *expressive* significance, that is, it may express the point of view, the style of life, and the cultural values of the person who makes it, or may satisfy needs created by the imbalance of activity in his particular social position. For example, in Europe the practice of fighting a duel of honour was for three centuries a symbol of gentlemanly status. The categorical significance of the practice was so well known that the right of taking or giving the kind of offence which led to a duel was rarely extended to the lower classes. The duel also carried an important expressive significance, however; it vividly portrayed the conception that a true man was an object of danger, a being with limited patience who did not allow a love of life to check his devotion to his principles and to his self-respect. On the whole, we must assume that any item of behaviour is significant to some degree in both a categorical and an expressive capacity.

Status symbols are used because they are better suited to the requirements of communication than are the rights and duties which they signify. This very fact, however, makes it necessary for status symbols to be distinct and separate from that which they signify. It is always possible, therefore, that symbols may come to be employed in a "fraudulent" way, i.e. to signify a status which the claimant does not in fact possess. We may say, then, that continuing use of status symbols in social situations requires mechanisms for restricting the opportunities that arise for misrepresentation. We may approach the study of status symbols by classifying the restrictive mechanisms embodied in them.

With this approach in mind, we may distinguish between two important kinds of status symbols: *occupation symbols* and *class symbols*. This paper is chiefly concerned with class symbols.

There appear to be two main types of occupation symbols. One type takes the form of credentials which testify with presumed authority to a person's training and work history. During the initiation of a work relationship reliance must frequently be placed upon symbols of this kind. They are protected from forgery by legal sanctions and, more importantly, by the understanding that corroborative information will almost certainly become available. The other type of occupation symbol comes into play after the work relation has been established and serves to mark off levels of prestige and power within a formal organization.[6]

On the whole, occupation symbols are firmly tied to an approved referent by specific and acknowledged sanctions, much in the manner in which symbols of social caste are rigidly bound. In the case of social class, however, symbols play a role that is less clearly controlled by authority and in some ways more significant.

No matter how we define social class we must refer to discrete or discontinuous levels of prestige and privilege, where admission to any one of these levels is, typically, determined by a complex of social qualifications, no one or two of which are necessarily essential. Symbols of class status do not typically refer to a specific source of status but rather to something based upon a configuration of sources. So it is that when we meet an individual who manipulates symbols in what appears to be a fraudulent way—displaying the signs yet possessing only a doubtful claim to what they signify—we often cannot justify our attitude by reference to his specific shortcomings. Furthermore, in any estimate we make of a person's class status, the multiple determinants of class position make it necessary for us to balance and weigh the person's favourable social qualifications against his less favourable ones. As we may expect, in situations where complex social judgments are required, the exact social position of a person is obscured and, in a sense, replaced by a margin of dissensus and doubt. Self-representations which fall within this margin may not meet with our approval, but we cannot prove they are misrepresentations.

No matter how we define social class we must refer to rights which are exercised and conceded but are not specifically laid down in law or contract and are not invariably recognized in practice. Legal sanctions cannot be applied against those who represent themselves as possessing a class status which an informed majority would not accord them. Offenders of this kind commit a presumption, not a crime. Furthermore, class gains typically refer to attitudes of superiority which are not officially or too openly discussed, and to preferential treatment as regards jobs, services, and economic exchanges which is not openly or officially approved. We may agree that an individual has misrepresented himself but, in our own class interests, we cannot make too clear to ourselves, to him, or to others just how he has done so. Also, we tend to justify our class gains in terms of "Cultural" values which everyone in a given society presumably respects—in our society, for example, education, skill, and talent. As a result, those who offer public proof that they possess the pet values of their society cannot be openly refused the status which their symbols permit them to demand.

On the whole, then, class symbols serve not so much to represent or misrepresent one's position, but rather to influence in a desired direction other persons' judgment of it. We shall continue to use the terms "misrepresentation" and "fraudulence," but as regards matters of social class these terms must be understood in the weakened sense in which the above discussion leaves them.

II

Every class symbol embodies one or more devices for restricting mis-representative use of it. The following restrictive devices are among the most typical.

1 / Moral Restrictions   Just as a system of economic contract is made effective by people's willingness to acknowledge the legitimacy of the rights which underlie the system, so the use of certain symbols is made effective by inner moral constraints which inhibit people from misrepresenting themselves. This compunction is typically phrased in different but functionally equivalent ways. For example, in Western society, some of the persons who can for the first time afford to emulate the conspicuous consumption of the upper classes refrain from doing so on the grounds of religious scruple, cultural disdain, ethnic and racial loyalty, economic and civic propriety, or even undisguised "sense of one's place."[7] Of course these self-applied constraints, however phrased, are reinforced by the pressure of the opinion both of one's original group and of the class whose symbols one may misemploy. But the efficacy of these external sanctions is due in part to the readiness with which they are reinforced by internalized moral constraints.

2 / Intrinsic Restrictions   One solution to the problem of misrepresentation is based on the kind of symbol which perceptibly involves an appreciable use of the very rights or characteristics which it symbolizes. We symbolize our wealth by displaying it, our power by using it, and our skill by exercising it. In the case of wealth, for example, racing stables, large homes, and jewellery obviously imply that the owner has at least as much money as the symbols can bring on the open market.

The use of certain objects as intrinsic symbols of wealth presents a special problem, for we must consider why it is that a very high market value can be placed upon them. Economists sometimes say that we have here a case of "effective scarcity," that is, a small supply in conjunction with a large demand. Scarcity alone, however, does not qualify an object for use as a status symbol, since there is an unlimited number of different kinds of scarce objects. The paintings of an unskilled amateur may be extremely rare, yet at the same time almost worthless. Why, then, do we place great value on examples of one kind of scarce object and not upon examples of another kind of similar and equally scarce object?

Sometimes an attempt is made to account for great differences in the market value of objects that are of similar kind and are equally scarce by pointing to the "expressive" difference between them. (The same

rationalization is sometimes employed to explain the difference in market value between "originals" and "reproductions.") In many cases an identifiable difference of this kind not only exists but can also be used to rank the objects on a scale in accordance with some recognized aesthetic or sensuous standard of judgment. This difference in experiential value between relatively similar objects does not, however, seem to be important enough in itself to justify the widely different market value placed upon them. We must account for the high price placed upon certain scarce objects by referring to the social gains that their owners obtain by showing these possessions to other persons. The expressive superiority of an object merely accounts for the fact that it, rather than some other equally scarce obect, was selected for use as a status symbol.

3 / Natural Restrictions The limited supply of some kinds of objects can be increased with relative ease but is not increased because persons do not have a motive for doing so or because there is a strong social sanction against doing so. On the other hand, the limited supply of certain kinds of objects cannot be increased by any means remotely available at the time, even though there may be a motive for doing so. These objects have been called "natural scarcities."

The natural scarcity of certain objects provides one kind of guarantee that the number of persons who acquire these objects will not be so large as to render the objects useless as symbols for the expression of invidious distinction. Natural scarcity, therefore, is one factor which may operate in certain symbols of status. Again we may note that not all scarce kinds of objects are valued highly. We must also note that not all highly valued scarce objects are status symbols, as may be seen, for example, in the case of certain radioactive minerals. Bases of scarcity in the case of certain status symbols nevertheless present a distinct analytical problem. If we think of it in this way we can appreciate the fact that while scarcity plays its most obvious role as an element in intrinsic symbols of wealth, there are symbols of status which are protected by the factor of natural scarcity and which cannot be directly bought and sold.

On the whole, the bases of natural scarcity may be sought in certain features of the physical production or physical structure of the symbol. More than one basis, of course, may be found combined in the same symbol.

The most obvious basis of scarcity, perhaps, can be found in objects which are made from material that is very infrequently found in the natural world and which cannot be manufactured synthetically from materials that are less scarce. This is the basis of scarcity, for example, in the case of very large flawless diamonds.

A basis of scarcity is found in what might be called "historical closure." A high value may be placed on products which derive in a verifiable way from agencies that are no longer productive, on the assumption that it is no longer physically possible to increase the supply. In New England, for example, family connection with the shipping trade is a safe thing to use as a symbol of status because this trade, in its relevant sense, no longer exists. Similarly, furniture made "solidly" from certain hardwoods, regardless of style or workmanship, is used as a symbol of status. The trees which supply the material take so long a time to grow that, in terms of the current market, existing forests can be considered as a closed and decreasing supply.

Another basis of natural scarcity is found in objects whose production requires an appreciable fraction of the total available means of production. This provides assurance on purely physical grounds that a large number of duplications will not appear. In non-industrial societies, for example, large buildings embody a significant portion of the total labour and building material available in a given region at a given time. This condition also applies in the case of some artists and craftsmen whose total life-output takes the form of a small number of distinctive objects which are characteristic of their producer.

We may consider, finally, the fact that the person who acquires the symbol may himself possess characteristics which connect him with the production of the symbol in a relatively exclusive way. This, for example, is the relation of its creator to a work of art that has become a symbol of status.

Similarly, children may share, in part, the status of their parents not only because the connection is demonstrable but also because the number of children a woman can bear is strictly limited. The family name may then be used as a symbol of status on the assumption that it can be acquired legally only by birth or by the marriage of a woman to a son of the house.

A similar basis of scarcity is found in the characteristics of social interaction. Generally speaking, personal association with individuals of high status is used as a symbol of status. The fact that there is a physical limit to the number of persons with whom any specific individual can be intimately related is one reason why this is possible. The limitation is based on the fact that personal relations imply mutual integration over a wide band of activities, and on the grounds of time and probability an individual cannot be related in this way to a large number of persons.

Finally, a play produced by a given cast must "play to" an audience of limited size. This is related to the limitations of human vision and hearing. The cast may repeat their performance for a different audience, but the performance cannot be reproduced in the sense that is possible with a cinematic performance. It is only in the cinema that the same performance may be "given" at different places simultaneously. Play-going can thus be used as a symbol of status whereas a visit to the cinema, on the whole, cannot.

4 / Socialization Restrictions An important symbol of membership in a given class is displayed during informal interaction. It consists of the kind of acts which impress others with the suitability and likeableness of one's general manner. In the minds of those present, such a person is thought to be "one of our kind." Impressions of this sort seem to be built upon a response to many particles of behaviour. These behaviours involve matters of etiquette, dress, deportment, gesture, intonation, dialect, vocabulary, small bodily movements and automatically expressed evaluations concerning both the substance and the details of life. In a manner of speaking, these behaviours constitute a social style.

Status symbols based on social style embody restrictive mechanisms which often operate in conjunction with each other. We tend to be impressed by the over-all character of a person's manner so that, in fact, we can rarely specify and itemize the particular acts which have impressed us. We find, therefore, that we are not able to analyse a desired style of behaviour into parts which are small and definite enough to make systematic learning possible.

We also find that symbolic value is given to the perceptible difference between an act performed unthinkingly under the invisible guide of familiarity and habit, and the same act, or an imitation of it, performed with conscious attention to detail and self-conscious attention to effect.

Furthermore the manner prescribed for the members of a class tends to be an expression in miniature of their style of life, of their self-conception, and of the psychological needs generated by their daily activity. In other words, social style carries deep expressive significance. The style and manners of a class are, therefore, psychologically ill-suited to those whose life experiences took place in another class.

Finally, we must note that members of a class frequently exercise exclusiveness in just those situations where the categorical significance of a particular act is taught. This accounts in part for the common social fact that one class may use as a symbol an act which another class does not know is being used in this way.[8] One-sided symbolism of this kind can occur even in cases where the persons who do the act are the ones who do not know of its significance.

5 / Cultivation Restrictions In many societies, avocational pursuits involving the cultivation of arts, "tastes," sports, and handicrafts have been used as symbols of class status. Prestige is accorded the experts, and expertness is based upon, and requires, concentrated attention over a long period of time. A command of foreign languages, for example, has provided an effective source of this sort of symbol.

It is a truism to say that anything which proves that a long span of past time has been spent in non-remunerative pursuits is likely to be used as a class symbol. Time-cost is not, however, the only mechanism of restriction which stands in the way of cultivation. Cultivation also requires discipline and perseverance, that is, it requires of a person that he exclude from the line of his attention all the distractions, deflections, and competing interests which come to plague an intention carried over an extended period of time. This restriction on the improper acquisition of symbols is especially effective where the period from preparation to exhibition is a long one.

An interesting example of cultivation is found in the quality of "restraint" upon which classes in many different societies have placed high value. Here social use is made of the discipline required to set aside and hold in check the insistent stimuli of daily life so that attention may be free to tarry upon distinctions and discriminations which would otherwise be overlooked. In a sense, restraint is a form of negative cultivation, for it involves a studied withdrawal of attention from many areas of experience. An example is seen in Japanese tea ceremonies during the Zen period of Buddhism. In Western society the negative and positive aspects of cultivation are typically combined in what is called sophistication concerning food, drink, clothes, and furnishings.

6 / Organic Restrictions Restrictions related to manner and cultivation provide evidence by means of relevant symbols as to how and where an individual has spent a great deal of his past time. Evidence concerning previous activity is crucial because class status is based not only on social qualifications but also on the length of time a person has possessed them. Owing to the nature of biological growth and development, acquired patterns of behaviour typically provide a much less reliable view of a person's past than is provided by acquired changes in his physical structure.[9] In Britain, for example, condition of hands and height in men, and secondary sexual characteristics in women, are symbols of status based ultimately on the long-range physical effects of diet, work, and environment.

III

Persons in the same social positions behave in many ways that are common to all the occupants of the position as well as particular to them. From the wide range of this activity certain items are selected and used for the special purpose of signifying status. These items are selected instead of other possible ones partly because they carry a strong expressive component and embody mechanisms for limiting misrepresentative use of them. The kind of class-consciousness which develops in a society can be understood in terms of the division between items of characteristic conduct that are employed as status symbols and those items which could be employed in this way but are not.

Six general devices for restricting misuse of class symbols have been outlined. It must be said, however, that there is no single mode of restriction which can withstand too many contingencies, nor is there any restriction which is not regularly and systematically circumvented in some fashion. An example of this is the Public School System in Britain, which may be seen as a machine for systematically re-creating middle-class people in the image of the aristocracy—a task in which twenty-six Charm Schools in Chicago are similarly engaged, but with a somewhat different clientele and a somewhat different ideal image.

The presence of routine methods of circumvention may partly explain why stable classes tend to designate their position by means of symbols which rely on many different types of restrictive devices. It would appear that the efficacy of one type of restriction acts as a check upon the failure of another. In this way the group avoids the danger, as it were, of putting all their symbols in one basket. Conversely, social situations for which analysis of status symbols is important can be classified according to the type of mechanism upon which members of a class may be over-dependent or which they may neglect.

From the point of view taken in this paper, problems in the study of class symbols have two aspects, one for the class from which the symbol originates and the other for the class which appropriates it. As a conclusion to this paper, reference will be made to three of these two-sided problem areas.

1 / Class Movement Social classes as well as individual members are constantly rising and falling in terms of relative wealth, power, and prestige. This movement lays a heavy burden upon class symbols, increasing the tendency for signs that symbolize position to take on the role of conferring it.[16] This tendency, in connection with the restrictions that are placed upon the acquisition of status symbols, retards the rise to social eminence of those who have lately acquired importance in power and wealth and retards the fall of those who have lately lost it. In this way the continuity of a tradition can be assured even though there is a change in the kind of persons who maintain the tradition.

As already suggested, we find that sources of high status which were once unchallenged become exhausted or find themselves in competition with new and different sources of status. It is therefore common for a whole class of persons to find themselves with symbols and expectations which their economic and political position can no longer support. A symbol of status cannot retain for ever its acquired role of conferring status. A time is reached when social decline accelerates with a spiral effect: members of a declining class are forced to rely more and more upon symbols which do not involve a current outlay, while at the same time their association with these symbols lowers the value of these signs in the eyes of others.

The other aspect of this problem turns upon the fact that new sources of high status typically permit the acquisition of costly symbols before symbols based on cultivation and socialization can be acquired. This tends to induce in the rising group expectations which for a time are not warranted and tends to undermine the regard in which costly symbols are held by members of other classes.[11]

2 / Curator Groups   Wherever the symbolizing equipment of a class becomes elaborate a curator personnel may develop whose task it is to build and service this machinery of status. Personnel of this kind in our society include members of such occupational categories as domestic servants, fashion experts and models, interior decorators, architects, teachers in the field of higher learning, actors, and artists of all kinds. Those who fill these jobs are typically recruited from classes which have much less prestige than the class to which such services are sold. Thus there are people whose daily work requires them to become proficient in manipulating symbols which signify a position higher than the one they themselves possess. Here, then, we have an institutionalized source of misrepresentation, false expectation, and dissensus.

An interesting complication arises when the specialist provides symbol service for a large number of persons and when the symbol to which he owes his employment at the same time carries a strongly marked expressive component. This is the case, for example, with the fashion model and interior decorator. Under these circumstances the curator comes to play much the same sacred role as those entrusted with the collective symbols of a society. It then becomes possible for the improper expectations of the curator to be realized and for the status and security of the patron class itself to be correspondingly diminished.

3 / Circulation of Symbols   The systematic circumvention of modes of restriction leads to downward and upward circulation of symbols.[12] In these cases, apparently, the objective structure of the sign-vehicle always becomes altered. A classification of these alterations or modes of vulgarization would be interesting to pursue but is beyond the scope of this paper.

From the point of view of this paper, circulation of symbols has two major consequences. First, those with whom a symbol originates must turn from that which is familiar to them and seek out, again and again, something which is not yet contaminated. This is especially true of groups which are smaller and more specialized than social classes—groups whose members feel inclined to separate themselves from their original social class, not by moving up or down but by moving out. This may be seen, for example, in the attempt of jazz musicians to create a monthly quota of new fashion to replace items of their action and speech which laymen have appropriated.[13]

The second consequence is perhaps the more significant of the two. Status symbols provide the cue that is used in order to discover the status of others and, from this, the way in which others are to be treated. The thoughts and attention of persons engaged in social activity therefore tend to be occupied with these signs of position. It is also a fact that status symbols frequently express the whole mode of life of those from whom the symbolic act originates. In this way the individual finds that the structure of his experience in one sphere of life is repeated throughout his experiences in other spheres of life. Affirmation of this kind induces solidarity in the group and richness and depth in the psychic life of its members.

As a result of the circulation of symbols, however, a sign which is expressive for the class in which it originates comes to be employed by a different class—a class for which the symbol can signify status but ill express it. In this way conscious life may become thin and meagre, focused as it is upon symbols which are not particularly congenial to it.

We may close with a plea for empirical studies which trace out the social career of particular status symbols—studies similar to the one that Dr. Mueller has given us concerning the transfer of a given kind of musical taste from one social grouping to another.[14] Studies of this kind are useful in a period when widespread cultural communication has increased the circulation of symbols, the power of curator groups, and the ranges of behaviour that are accepted as vehicles for symbols of status.

NOTES

1. A modified version of this paper was presented at the annual meeting of the University of Chicago Society for Social Research in 1949. The writer is grateful to W. Lloyd Warner for direction and to Robert Armstrong, Tom Burns, and Angelica Choate for criticism.
2. The distinction between prestige and esteem is taken from Kingsley Davis, "A Conceptual Analysis of Stratification," *Am. Soc. Rev.*, VII, June 1942, pp. 309–21.
3. The most general approach to the study of status symbols known to the writer is to be found in H. Spencer, *The Principles of Sociology*, vol. II, part IV, "Ceremonial Institutions."
4. See G. Simmel, "Fashion," *International Quarterly*, vol. X, pp. 130–55.
5. See E. Durkheim, *The Elementary Forms of the Religious Life*, trans. S. W. Swain (New York, 1926), especially pp. 230–4.
6. Examples would be private offices, segregated eating-rooms, etc. For a treatment of status symbols in formal organizations, see C. Barnard, "Functions and Pathology of Status Systems in Formal Organizations," chap. 4, pp. 46–83, in *Industry and Society*, ed. W. F. Whyte (New York, 1946).
7. Moral restrictions apply to many types of status symbols other than class. For example, in Western society, women feel that it is seemly to refrain

from using symbols of sexual attractiveness before reaching a given age and to abstain progressively from using them after attaining a given age.

8. Perhaps the structural model for this kind of symbol is found in the "password" and fraternal sign.

9. The use of inherited characteristics as symbols of status is typically found, of course, in a society of castes not classes.

10. The extreme case is found in so-called ritual transmission of charisma. See Max Weber, *Theory of Social and Economic Organization*, trans. T. Parsons (London, 1947), p. 366.

11. This has been referred to as the problem of the *nouveau riche*, of which the community of Hollywood provides an example. See Leo Rosten, *Hollywood* (New York, 1941), especially pp. 163–80. See also Talcott Parsons, "The Motivation of Economic Activity," *Essays in Sociological Theory* (Glencoe, 1948), p. 215. An extreme case in the U.S.A. is the decrease in social value of the type of expensive car favoured by the rich criminal classes.

12. It is not rare for practices which originate in one class to be adopted by the members of a higher one. Cases in point would be the argot of criminal, ethnic, and theatrical groups and such fugitive social crazes as the Lambeth Walk. In most cases these adopted practices serve only an expressive function and are not used as status symbols. Sometimes practices of low repute are adopted as status symbols in order to comment on those who cannot afford to be associated with them.

13. From conversations with Howard Becker.

14. J. H. Mueller, "Methods of Measurement of Aesthetic Folkways," *Am. J. Soc.*, vol. LI, pp. 276–82.

oscar lewis

All societies are stratified in one way or another. All have their own symbols of class status. As Erving Goffman suggests, not only do these symbols help to categorize, but they also serve to express various norms and values that have been internalized.

The late Oscar Lewis was also concerned with such cultural variations. Best known for his books on Indian, Mexican, and Puerto Rican life, he was also the first to use the phrase "the culture of poverty," a blanket expression for what he saw as a set of attitudes and behavior patterns shared by people occupying the lowest rung on the socio-economic ladder of certain societies. He made an important distinction between poverty per se and "the culture of poverty"—the former pertaining to a relative economic condition, the latter to a complex set of values related to family, friends, and the future.

In 1966, Lewis summarized his thoughts on the culture of poverty in *Scientific American*. That report is reprinted below.

Poverty and the so-called war against it provide a principal theme for the domestic program of the present Administration. In the midst of a population that enjoys unexampled material well-being—with the average annual family income exceeding $7,000—it is officially acknowledged that some 18 million families, numbering more than 50 million individuals, live below the $3,000 "poverty line." Toward the improvement of the lot of these people some $1,600 million of Federal funds are directly allocated through the Office of Economic Opportunity, and many hundreds of millions of additional dollars flow indirectly through expanded Federal expenditures in the fields of health, education, welfare and urban affairs.

Along with the increase in activity on behalf of the poor indicated by these figures there has come a parallel expansion of publication in the social sciences on the subject of poverty. The new writings advance the same two opposed evaluations of the poor that are to be found in literature, in proverbs and in popular sayings throughout recorded history. Just as the poor have been pronounced blessed, virtuous, upright, serene, independent, honest, kind and happy, so contemporary students stress their great and neglected capacity for self-help, leadership and community organization. Conversely, as the poor have been characterized as shiftless, mean, sordid, violent, evil and criminal, so other students point to the irreversibly destructive effects of poverty on individual character and emphasize the corresponding need to keep guidance and control of poverty projects in the hands of duly constituted authorities. This clash of viewpoints reflects in part the infighting for political control of the program between Federal and local officials. The confusion results also from the tendency to focus study and attention on the personality of the individual victim of poverty rather than on the slum community and family and from the consequent failure to distinguish between poverty and what I have called the culture of poverty.

The phrase is a catchy one and is used and misused with some frequency in the current literature. In my writings it is the label for a specific conceptual model that describes in positive terms a subculture of Western society with its own structure and rationale, a way of life handed on from generation to generation along family lines. The culture of poverty is not just a matter of deprivation or disorganization, a term signifying the absence of something. It is a culture in the traditional anthropological sense in that it provides human beings with a design for living, with a ready-made set of solutions for human problems, and so serves a significant adaptive function. This style of life transcends national boundaries and regional and rural-urban differences within nations. Wherever it occurs, its practitioners exhibit remarkable similarity in the structure of their families, in interpersonal relations, in spending habits, in their value systems and in their orientation in time.

Not nearly enough is known about this important complex of human behavior. My own concept of it has evolved as my work has progressed and remains subject to amendment by my own further work and that of others. The scarcity of literature on the culture of poverty is a measure of the gap in communication that exists between the very poor and the middle-class personnel—social scientists, social workers, teachers, physicians, priests and others—who bear the major responsibility for carrying out the antipoverty programs. Much of the behavior accepted in the culture of poverty goes counter to cherished ideals of the larger society. In writing about "multiproblem" families social scientists thus often stress their instability, their lack of order, direction and organization. Yet, as I have observed them, their behavior seems clearly patterned and reasonably predictable. I am more often struck by the inexorable repetitiousness and the iron entrenchment of their lifeways.

The concept of the culture of poverty may help to correct misapprehensions that have ascribed some behavior patterns of ethnic, national or regional groups as distinctive characteristics. For example, a high incidence of commonlaw marriage and of households headed by women has been thought to be distinctive of Negro family life in this country and has been attributed to the Negro's historical experience of slavery. In actuality it turns out that such households express essential traits of the culture of poverty and are found among diverse peoples in many parts of the world and among peoples that have had no history of slavery. Although it is now possible to assert such generalizations, there is still much to be learned about this difficult and affecting subject. The absence of intensive anthropological studies of poor families in a wide variety of national contexts—particularly the lack of such studies in socialist countries—remains a serious handicap to the formulation of dependable cross-cultural constants of the culture of poverty.

My studies of poverty and family life have centered largely in Mexico. On occasion some of my Mexican friends have suggested delicately that I turn to a study of poverty in my own country. As a first step in this direction I am currently engaged in a study of Puerto Rican families. Over the past three years my staff and I have been assembling data on 100 representative families in four slums of Greater San Juan and some 50 families of their relatives in New York City.

Our methods combine the traditional techniques of sociology, anthropology and psychology. This includes a battery of 19 questionnaires, the administration of which requires 12 hours per informant. They cover the residence and employment history of each adult; family relations; income and expenditure; complete inventory of household and personal possessions; friendship patterns, particularly the compadrazgo, or godparent, relationship that serves as a kind of informal social security for the children of these families and establishes special obligations among the adults; recreational patterns; health and medical history; politics; religion; world view and "cosmopolitanism." Open-end interviews and psychological tests (such as the thematic apperception test, the Rorschach test and the sentence-completion test) are administered to a sampling of this population.

All this work serves to establish the context for close-range study of a selected few families. Because the family is a small social system, it lends itself to the holistic approach of anthropology. Whole-family studies bridge the gap between the conceptual extremes of the culture at one pole and of the individual at the other, making possible observation of both culture and personality as they are interrelated in real life. In a large metropolis such as San Juan or New York the family is the natural unit of study.

Ideally our objective is the naturalistic observation of the life of "our" families, with a minimum of intervention. Such intensive study, however, necessarily involves the establishment of deep personal ties. My assistants include two Mexicans whose families I had studied; their "Mexican's-eye view" of the Puerto Rican slum has helped to point up the similarities and differences between the Mexican and Puerto Rican subcultures. We have spent many hours attending family parties, wakes and baptisms, responding to emergency calls, taking people to the hospital, getting them out of jail, filling out applications for them, hunting apartments with them, helping them to get jobs or to get on relief. With each member of these families we conduct tape-recorded interviews, taking down their life stories and their answers to questions on a wide variety of topics. For the ordering of our material we undertake to reconstruct, by close interrogation, the history of a week or more of consecutive days in the lives of each family, and we observe and record complete days as they unfold. The first volume to issue from this study is entitled *La Vida, a Puerto Rican Family in the Culture of Poverty— San Juan and New York* (Random House).

There are many poor people in the world. Indeed, the poverty of the two-thirds of the world's population who live in the underdeveloped countries has been rightly called "the problem of problems." But not all of them by any means live in the culture of poverty. For this way of life to come into being and flourish it seems clear that certain preconditions must be met.

The setting is a cash economy, with wage labor and production for profit and with a persistently high rate of unemployment and under-employment, at low wages, for unskilled labor. The society fails to provide social, political and economic organization, on either a voluntary basis or by government imposition, for the low-income population. There is a bilateral kinship system centered on the nuclear progenitive family, as distinguished from the unilateral extended kinship system of lineage and clan. The dominant class asserts a set of values that prizes thrift and the accumulation of wealth and property, stresses the possibility of upward mobility and explains low economic status as the result of individual personal inadequacy and inferiority.

Where these conditions prevail the way of life that develops among some of the poor is the culture of poverty. That is why I have described it as a subculture of the Western social order. It is both an adaptation and a reaction of the poor to their marginal position in a class-stratified, highly individuated, capitalistic society. It represents an effort to cope with feelings of hopelessness and despair that arise from the realization by the members of the marginal communities in these societies of the improbability of their achieving success in terms of the prevailing values and goals. Many of the traits of the culture of poverty can be viewed as local, spontaneous attempts to meet needs not served in the case of the poor by the institutions and agencies of the larger society because the poor are not eligible for such service, cannot afford it or are ignorant and suspicious.

Once the culture of poverty has come into existence it tends to perpetuate itself. By the time slum children are six or seven they have usually absorbed the basic attitudes and values of their subculture. Thereafter they are psychologically unready to take full advantage of changing conditions or improving opportunities that may develop in their lifetime.

My studies have identified some 70 traits that characterize the culture of poverty. The principal ones may be described in four dimensions of the system: the relationship between the subculture and the larger society; the nature of the slum community; the nature of the family, and the attitudes, values and character structure of the individual.

The disengagement, the nonintegration, of the poor with respect to the major institutions of society is a crucial element in the culture of poverty. It reflects the combined effect of a variety of factors including poverty, to begin with, but also segregation and discrimination, fear, suspicion and apathy and the development of alternative institutions and procedures in the slum community. The people do not belong to labor unions or political parties and make little use of banks, hospitals, department stores or museums. Such involvement as there is in the institutions of the large society—in the jails, the army and the public welfare system —does little to suppress the traits of the culture of poverty. A relief system that barely keeps people alive perpetuates rather than eliminates poverty and the pervading sense of hopelessness.

People in a culture of poverty produce little wealth and receive little in return. Chronic unemployment and underemployment, low wages, lack of property, lack of savings, absence of food reserves in the home and chronic shortage of cash imprison the family and the individual in a vicious circle. Thus for lack of cash the slum householder makes frequent purchases of small quantities of food at higher prices. The slum economy turns inward; it shows a high incidence of pawning of personal goods, borrowing at usurious rates of interest, informal credit arrangements among neighbors, use of secondhand clothing and furniture.

There is awareness of middle-class values. People talk about them and even claim some of them as their own. On the whole, however, they do not live by them. They will declare that marriage by law, by the church or by both is the ideal form of marriage, but few will marry. For men who have no steady jobs, no property and no prospect of wealth to pass on to their children, who live in the present without expectations of the future, who want to avoid the expense and legal difficulties involved in marriage and divorce, a free union or consensual marriage makes good sense. The women, for their part, will turn down offers of marriage from men who are likely to be immature, punishing and generally unreliable. They feel that a consensual union gives them some of the freedom and flexibility men have. By not giving the fathers of their children legal status as husbands, the women have a stronger claim on the children. They also maintain exclusive rights to their own property.

Along with disengagement from the larger society, there is a hostility to the basic institutions of what are regarded as the dominant classes. There is hatred of the police, mistrust of government and of those in high positions and a cynicism that extends to the church. The culture of poverty thus holds a certain potential for protest and for entrainment in political movements aimed against the existing order.

With its poor housing and overcrowding, the community of the culture of poverty is high in gregariousness, but it has a minimum of organization beyond the nuclear and extended family. Occasionally slum dwellers come together in temporary informal groupings; neighborhood gangs that cut across slum settlements represent a considerable advance beyond the zero point of the continuum I have in mind. It is the low level of organization that gives the culture of poverty its marginal and anomalous quality in our highly organized society. Most primitive peoples have achieved a higher degree of sociocultural organization than contemporary urban slum dwellers. This is not to say that there may not be a sense of community and *esprit de corps* in a slum neighborhood. In fact, where slums are isolated from their surroundings by enclosing walls or other physical barriers, where rents are low and residence is stable and where the population constitutes a distinct ethnic, racial or language group, the sense of community may approach that of a village. In Mexico City and San Juan such territoriality is engendered by the scarcity of low-cost housing outside of established slum areas. In South Africa it is actively enforced by the *apartheid* that confines rural migrants to prescribed locations.

The family in the culture of poverty does not cherish childhood as a specially prolonged and protected stage in the life cycle. Initiation into sex comes early. With the instability of consensual marriage the family tends to be mother-centered and tied more closely to the mother's extended family. The female head of the house is given to authoritarian rule. In spite of much verbal emphasis on family solidarity, sibling rivalry for the limited supply of goods and maternal affection is intense. There is little privacy.

The individual who grows up in this culture has a strong feeling of fatalism, helplessness, dependence and inferiority. These traits, so often remarked in the current literature as characteristic of the American Negro, I found equally strong in slum dwellers of Mexico City and San Juan, who are not segregated or discriminated against as a distinct ethnic or racial group. Other traits include a high incidence of weak ego structure, orality and confusion of sexual identification, all reflecting maternal deprivation; a strong present-time orientation with relatively little disposition to defer gratification and plan for the future, and a high tolerance for psychological pathology of all kinds. There is widespread belief in male superiority and among the men a strong preoccupation with *machismo,* their masculinity.

Provincial and local in outlook, with little sense of history, these people know only their own neighborhood and their own way of life. Usually they do not have the knowledge, the vision or the ideology to see the similarities between their troubles and those of their counterparts elsewhere in the world. They are not class-conscious, although they are sensitive indeed to symbols of status.

The distinction between poverty and the culture of poverty is basic to the model described here. There are numerous examples of poor people whose way of life I would not characterize as belonging to this subculture. Many primitive and preliterate peoples that have been studied by anthropologists suffer dire poverty attributable to low technology or thin resources or both. Yet even the simplest of these people have a high degree of social organization and a relatively integrated, satisfying and self-sufficient culture.

In India the destitute lower-caste peoples—such as the Chamars, the leatherworkers, and the Bhangis, the sweepers—remain integrated in the larger society and have their own panchayat institutions of self-government. Their panchayats and their extended unilateral kinship systems, or clans, cut across village lines, giving them a strong sense of identity and continuity. In my studies of these peoples I found no culture of poverty to go with their poverty.

The Jews of eastern Europe were a poor urban people, often confined to ghettos. Yet they did not have many traits of the culture of poverty. They had a tradition of literacy that placed great value on learning; they formed many voluntary associations and adhered with devotion to the central community organization around the rabbi, and they had a religion that taught them they were the chosen people.

I would cite also a fourth, somewhat speculative example of poverty dissociated from the culture of poverty. On the basis of limited direct observation in one country—Cuba—and from indirect evidence, I am inclined to believe the culture of poverty does not exist in socialist countries. In 1947 I undertook a study of a slum in Havana. Recently I had an opportunity to revisit the same slum and some of the same families. The physical aspect of the place had changed little, except for a beautiful new nursery school. The people were as poor as before, but I was impressed to find much less of the feelings of despair and apathy, so symptomatic of the culture of poverty in the urban slums of the U.S. The slum was now highly organized, with block committees, educational committees, party committees. The people had found a new sense of power and importance in a doctrine that glorified the lower class as the hope of humanity, and they were armed. I was told by one Cuban official that the Castro government had practically eliminated deliquency by giving arms to the delinquents!

Evidently the Castro regime—revising Marx and Engels—did not write off the so-called *lumpenproletariat* as an inherently reactionary and anti-revolutionary force but rather found in them a revolutionary potential and utilized it. Frantz Fanon, in his book *The Wretched of the Earth,* makes a similar evaluation of their role in the Algerian revolution: "It is within this mass of humanity, this people of the shantytowns, at the core of the *lumpenproletariat,* that the rebellion will find its urban spearhead. For the *lumpenproletariat,* that horde of starving men, uprooted from their tribe and from their clan, constitutes one of the most spontaneous and most radically revolutionary forces of a colonized people."

It is true that I have found little revolutionary spirit or radical ideology among low-income Puerto Ricans. Most of the families I studied were politically conservative, about half of them favoring the Statehood Republican Party, which provides opposition on the right to the Popular Democratic Party that dominates the politics of the commonwealth. It seems to me, therefore, that disposition for protest among people living in the culture of poverty will vary considerably according to the national context and historical circumstances. In contrast to Algeria, the independence movement in Puerto Rico has found little popular support. In Mexico, where the cause of independence carried long ago, there is no longer any such movement to stir the dwellers in the new and old slums of the capital city.

Yet it would seem that any movement—be it religious, pacifist or revolutionary—that organizes and gives hope to the poor and effectively promotes a sense of solidarity with larger groups must effectively destroy the psychological and social core of the culture of poverty. In this connection, I suspect that the civil rights movement among American Negroes has of itself done more to improve their self-image and self-respect than such economic gains as it has won although, without doubt, the two kinds of progress are mutually reinforcing. In the culture of poverty of the American Negro the additional disadvantage of racial discrimination has generated a potential for revolutionary protest and organization that is absent in the slums of San Juan and Mexico City and, for that matter, among the poor whites in the South.

If it is true, as I suspect, that the culture of poverty flourishes and is endemic to the free-enterprise, pre-welfare-state stage of capitalism, then it is also endemic in colonial societies. The most likely candidates for the culture of poverty would be the people who come from the lower strata of a rapidly changing society and who are already partially alienated from it. Accordingly the subculture is likely to be found where imperial conquest has smashed the native social and economic structure and held the natives, perhaps for generations, in servile status, or where feudalism is yielding to capitalism in the later evolution of a colonial economy. Landless rural workers who migrate to the cities, as in Latin America, can be expected to fall into this way of life more readily than migrants from stable peasant villages with a well-organized traditional culture, as in India. It remains to be seen, however, whether the culture of poverty has not already begun to develop in the slums of Bombay and Calcutta. Compared with Latin America also, the strong corporate nature of many African tribal societies may tend to inhibit or delay the formation of a full-blown culture of poverty in the new towns and cities of that continent. In South Africa the institutionalization of repression and discrimination under *apartheid* may also have begun to promote an immunizing sense of identity and group consciousness among the African Negroes.

One must therefore keep the dynamic aspects of human institutions forward in observing and assessing the evidence for the presence, the waxing or the waning of this subculture. Measured on the dimension of relationship to the larger society, some slum dwellers may have a warmer identification with their national tradition even though they suffer deeper poverty than members of a similar community in another country. In Mexico City a high percentage of our respondents, including those with little or no formal schooling, knew of Cuauhtémoc, Hidalgo, Father Morelos, Juárez, Díaz, Zapata, Carranza and Cárdenas. In San Juan the names of Rámon Power, José de Diego, Baldorioty de Castro, Rámon Betances, Nemesio Canales, Lloréns Torres rang no bell; a few could tell about the late Albizu Campos. For the lower-income Puerto Rican, however, history begins with Muñoz Rivera and ends with his son Muñoz Marín.

The national context can make a big difference in the play of the crucial traits of fatalism and hopelessness. Given the advanced technology, the high level of literacy, the all-pervasive reach of the media of mass communications and the relatively high aspirations of all sectors of the population, even the poorest and most marginal communities of the U.S. must aspire to a larger future than the slum dwellers of Ecuador and Peru, where the actual possibilities are more limited and where an authoritarian social order persists in city and country. Among the 50 million U.S. citizens now more or less officially certified as poor, I would guess that about 20 percent live in a culture of poverty. The largest numbers in this group are made up of Negroes, Puerto Ricans, Mexicans, American Indians and Southern poor whites. In these figures there is some reassurance for those concerned, because it is much more difficult to undo the culture of poverty than to cure poverty itself.

Middle-class people—this would certainly include most social scien-

tists—tend to concentrate on the negative aspects of the culture of poverty. They attach a minus sign to such traits as present-time orientation and readiness to indulge impulses. I do not intend to idealize or romanticize the culture of poverty—"it is easier to praise poverty than to live in it." Yet the positive aspects of these traits must not be overlooked. Living in the present may develop a capacity for spontaneity, for the enjoyment of the sensual, which is often blunted in the middle-class, future-oriented man. Indeed, I am often struck by the analogies that can be drawn between the mores of the very rich—of the "jet set" and "café society"—and the culture of the very poor. Yet it is, on the whole, a comparatively superficial culture. There is in it much pathos, suffering and emptiness. It does not provide much support or satisfaction; its pervading mistrust magnifies individual helplessness and isolation. Indeed, poverty of culture is one of the crucial traits of the culture of poverty.

The concept of the culture of poverty provides a generalization that may help to unify and explain a number of phenomena hitherto viewed as peculiar to certain racial, national or regional groups. Problems we think of as being distinctively our own or distinctively Negro (or as typifying any other ethnic group) prove to be endemic in countries where there are no segregated ethnic minority groups. If it follows that the elimination of physical poverty may not by itself eliminate the culture of poverty, then an understanding of the sub-culture may contribute to the design of measures specific to that purpose.

What is the future of the culture of poverty? In considering this question one must distinguish between those countries in which it represents a relatively small segment of the population and those in which it constitutes a large one. In the U.S. the major solution proposed by social workers dealing with the "hard core" poor has been slowly to raise their level of living and incorporate them in the middle class. Wherever possible psychiatric treatment is prescribed.

In underdeveloped countries where great masses of people live in the culture of poverty, such a social-work solution does not seem feasible. The local psychiatrists have all they can do to care for their own growing middle class. In those countries the people with a culture of poverty may seek a more revolutionary solution. By creating basic structural changes in society, by redistributing wealth, by organizing the poor and giving them a sense of belonging, of power and of leadership, revolutions frequently succeed in abolishing some of the basic characteristics of the culture of poverty even when they do not succeed in curing poverty itself.

ely chinoy

Sociologist Ely Chinoy intensively examined the aspirations and expectations of a small group of automobile workers in one town in the Midwestern United States. His detailed study relates the attitudes and behavior of factory workers to the structure of the industry, the nature of the community in which they lived, and the larger cultural tradition of American society, notably the ideals embodied in the "American Dream."

In the section of *Automobile Workers and the American Dream* reprinted here, the chronology of aspirations of auto workers is analyzed. Chinoy shows how ambitions and desires are tempered by actual experiences in the plant and in the community as young men accommodate themselves to the exigencies of circumstances and as they reinforce ties with those who share their social status and their identity.

Despite the cultural admonition to pursue large ambitions, automobile workers focus their aspirations on a narrow range of alternatives. They do not aspire to the top levels of business and industry; they want to become skilled workers, to gain promotion to supervision, to engage in small-scale farming, to open a retail store or a small service establishment of some kind. Since even most of these alternatives entail serious difficulties, however, comparatively few workers persist in hope, remain strong in intention, or persevere in effort. But desire frequently survives.

The varied patterns of desire, intention, plan, and effort revealed by the workers interviewed in Autotown must be seen as only in part the reactions of workers with different personal and social characteristics to similar concrete circumstances. To some extent, these varied patterns of aspirations with regard to both advancement in the plant and out-of-the-shop goals constitute a series linked in time; the same worker may change from one pattern to another as he moves through his occupational career. Indeed, the following hypotheses which have already emerged from our analysis suggest the existence of a more or less typical chronology of aspirations among these workers in a mass-production industry.

1. Many young men who come to work in the factory define their jobs as temporary; they do not expect to remain in the ranks of factory labor.
2. Workers with the most clearly defined out-of-the-shop goals are married men in their late twenties or early thirties who have not acquired substantial seniority.
3. Workers are most likely to develop or sustain hope for promotion to supervision if while still relatively young they gain some form of advancement as wage workers, that is, if they secure jobs at the top of the hierarchy of desirability or if they move from nonskilled to skilled work.
4. The longer workers remain in the plant, the less likely are they to muster the initiative to leave, even if they continually talk of doing so.
5. As their seniority increases, workers can look forward to the possibility of individual wage increases (however small they may be) and of transfer to more desirable jobs.
6. The weight of increasing or already heavy family responsibilities keeps men with long seniority from seriously considering out-of-the-shop goals.
7. Workers who do not gain promotion to supervision before the age of forty or thereabouts quickly lose hope because of management's preference for younger men.
8. After workers reach the low wage ceiling at the top of the hierarchy of desirability, they may be satisfied with what they have achieved or, alternatively, they may become bitter and frustrated because of their inability to go further.
9. Some workers, as they approach the age of retirement, may become interested in out-of-the-shop goals as sources of income for their remaining years.

Only a careful longitudinal study could test these hypotheses and expose in full detail the changing patterns of workers' aspirations. But we can, on the basis of our data, fill in the broad outlines of the chronology of aspirations suggested by these hypotheses.

From these propositions it seems clear that workers' aspirations emerge from a process in which hope and desire come to terms with the realities of working-class life. But this process is not one which sees simply the gradual dissolution of originally large expectations as obstacles to advancement become evident. Instead we find that workers must repeatedly accommodate new desires generated by fresh stimuli to the concrete circumstances they face at different stages of their occupational careers.

The changing patterns of workers' aspirations therefore bear little resemblance to the popular stereotype of single-minded striving toward ambitious goals. It may well be that the rational tradition in our culture has continually overplayed man's singleness of purpose, that, encouraged by the pioneer ethos of self-help, we have overstressed the power of individual effort against the press of circumstances. It is quite likely that finding oneself vocationally involves in most cases considerable floundering among available alternatives, that few men exhibit the terrible tenacity of Henry Ford or the elder Rockefeller. It seems altogether possible that for men on the level of wage labor, the period of floundering lasts longer, perhaps indefinitely, as they pitch such ambitions as they muster against the limited opportunities available to them.

The process of reconciling desire with reality begins early for industrial workers. In the public schools, if not at home, the working-class youth is repeatedly exposed to the value of success, the belief in the existence of opportunity for all, and the varied prescriptions for getting on in the world. "We were talking about Abe Lincoln in school and how he worked himself up," said the eighteen-year-old son of a machine-operator who had performed the same kind of work in the factory for eighteen years. "That shows that working yourself up depends on the person, not on the chances you have." But as soon as he leaves school, or even before, the working-class youth must come to terms with a world of limited opportunity where there are few chances. Lacking financial resources, he cannot look forward to the possibility of professional training, or even to four years of college which would widen his perspectives and increase his skills. He cannot step into a family business or acquire easily the funds with which to launch one of his own. As soon as his education ends, he must find some kind of job. And in Autotown even a large proportion of high-school graduates will probably become factory workers; a third of all employed persons in the city were engaged in factory labor of some kind, primarily in the four large automobile plants.

Many working-class boys therefore give up dreams of a rich and exciting occupational future—if they ever have such dreams—even before taking their first full-time job. In a questionnaire submitted to all boys about to graduate from Autotown's two high schools in June, 1947 and June, 1948, the question was asked: "If you could do what you wanted to what occupation would you choose?" Forty per cent of all working-class boys (forty-seven of 118) had no choice or chose occupations which carried comparatively little prestige and provided only limited rewards. (Occupations included in those with low prestige and low rewards were skilled work, clerical jobs, military service, and miscellaneous jobs which required no training. Those with high prestige and high rewards were the professions, technical and semiprofessional occupations, art and litera-ture, scientific farming, and business.) Only twenty-three per cent of the middle-class boys, on the other hand, were without a choice or chose low-prestige, low-reward occupations, indicating a statistically significant difference.[2] When asked about their actual intentions, forty per cent of the working-class boys said that they merely intended to "look for a job," without specifying any particular kind of job. Another twenty per cent intended to learn a skilled trade, to apply for some definite manual job which did not require previous training, or to enlist in the armed services. These figures compare with fifteen and twelve per cent respectively for boys of middle-class origin.

Some working-class boys, particularly those without academic apti-tudes or interests, may quit school as soon as they are able to secure a job since they feel that they will find themselves in the factory even-tually, even if they do graduate from high school. They can no longer do as their parents might have done in the past, leave school in order to learn a trade, since admission to formal apprentice training for any trade now usually require a high-school diploma. The jobs they find, there-fore, promise little for the future.

Many working-class boys only come to grips with vocational reality when they finally graduate from high school. Stimulated to a high level of aspiration by the mass media, encouraged by parents and, sometimes, by teachers, they entertain inflated ambitions until the time when they must choose a definite course of action. For example, a third of the boys whose parents were manual workers reported that they intended to go to college. While some boys with requisite academic abilities do muster the necessary financial resources and enter college, most of them in fact find themselves looking for a job after they graduate from high school. According to high-school officials, less than a third of all graduates from Autotown's two high schools go to college, most of them probably from middle-class families. An even smaller proportion ever complete work for a degree. It is therefore highly probable that a very large proportion of those working-class boys who said that they intended to go to college did not do so.

The quick surrender by working-class youth to the difficulties they face is not necessarily forced or unwilling. Although they are encouraged to focus their aspirations into a long future and to make present sacrifices

for the sake of eventual rewards, they are chiefly concerned with immediate gratifications. They may verbally profess to be concerned with
occupational success and advancement (as did fourteen working-class
boys who were interviewed), but they are likely to be more interested
in "having a good time" or "having fun." They want to "go out," to have
girl friends, to travel, to own a car or a motorcycle. When asked if "fun"
would be given up in order to take a job which might lead to advancement in the future, an eighteen-year-old boy about to graduate from high
school answered: "Do you want me to tell you the truth? I'd rather have
fun."

The concern with immediate gratifications unrelated to one's occupation is encouraged by prevalent values in American society. The massed
apparatus of commercial advertising incessantly stimulates the desire
for things which are immediately available—on the installment plan, if
necessary. Together with movies, television, radio, and magazines,
advertising sets up attractive—and expensive—models of leisure and
recreation. And these models have become increasingly important as
American culture has shifted from a central concern with the values of
production to the values of consumption.[3] In a long-range sense, the
pecuniary animus of the culture backfires among working-class youth,
for the desire for maximum income, when linked with an emphasis upon
immediate satisfactions in the sphere of consumption, leads to decisions
which virtually eliminate the possibility of a steadily increasng income
in the future. "Sometimes I say to myself," said a thirty-year-old machine-
operator who could have attended college but had instead gone to work
in the factory, ". . . you could have been somebody . . . if you hadn't been
so interested in the almighty dollar."

Since "fun" in this world of commercialized entertainment requires
money, the immediate objective becomes a well-paid job, a goal most
easily achieved by going to work in an automobile plant. Within a few
months the son of an automobile worker who goes to work in the factory
may be earning as much as his father, who may have been there for
twenty years. Despite the low status of factory work and the hope frequently expressed by automobile workers that their sons will not follow
in their steps, many boys head for factory personnel offices as soon as
they are old enough or as soon as they finish high school. And others
find themselves seeking factory employment after having tried other,
less remunerative jobs.

Many of these young workers are aware of the dead-end character of
most factory jobs. "You don't get advanced by going in the factory;
there's no future there," said one high-school senior whose father had
spent his entire adult life in the city's automobile factories. When they
do go into the factory, they therefore define their jobs as temporary,
particularly if they have earned a high-school diploma. They say that they
intend to stay in the factory only until a promising opportunity comes

along. In this fashion they can maintain the impression, both for themselves and for others, that they still intend to get ahead, that they are still ambitious.

Because the first job is frequently on the assembly line, these young workers do not quickly become satisfied. They soon seek ways of gaining a more desirable job in the factory. But beyond that limited goal they pay little attention to the possibilities of advancement. They are too young to expect a promotion to supervision. They are unwilling to undertake apprentice training, in part because they would have to accept lower wages temporarily, in part because they may not possess the necessary aptitudes or education, in part because they may define factory work itself as temporary.

Even if these young workers say that they intend, eventually, to "go into business," they make no definite plans. Their main interests lie in the things they do in their leisure hours. For example, a twenty-two-year-old single worker in the plant cared little for his work, although he boasted that he had managed to secure a transfer from the assembly line to a job which consisted of driving completed cars off the end of the line. He had gained this transfer by threatening to quit in a period of acute labor shortage. (Since he had no family responsibilities, he probably would have quit and gone to work in some other factory if he had not been transferred.) He had not thought of the possibility of foremanship or of learning a trade. He insisted, however, that he would some day leave the factory—"I don't intend to stay here forever," he said—but he had no concrete objectives or plans. His chief interests were baseball, girls, and his car. He had recently bought a new A.B.C. car, but he wanted to replace it with the model which was scheduled to appear at the beginning of the following year. One reason for going to work in the A.B.C. plant rather than elsewhere was the fact that A.B.C. employees with more than six months' seniority were given a large discount if they bought a new car.

Several older workers gave retrospective accounts of similar behavior which had preceded their "settling down." A forty-year-old union officer commented:

> Most young fellows are just like I was, they can't see ahead of their noses. They just want to have a good time and the devil take the rest of it. If they can make more money that's where they'll go. They don't think about anything else.

"Before I got married," said a thirty-nine-year-old oiler (whose work consisted of oiling moving parts of large machines, a nonskilled job), "I was only interested in three things, getting paid on Saturday, getting drunk on Saturday night, and having a girl." Others are undoubtedly more sober and conservative in their interests, but their attitudes toward their work and their future are much the same: as long as the pay is good and the job not too demanding or difficult, they are content to go along from day to day seeking their pleasures in leisure hours, careless about the future.

It seems a tenable hypothesis that this pattern of youthful aspirations represents a model type which applies to a substantial proportion of working-class youth, as well as those lower-middle-class boys who become nonskilled factory workers. The chief deviation from this pattern is the youth who decides early to become a skilled worker, or who decides after a short tenure in the factory to apply for apprentice training. His ambitions do not focus on rich images of success, but on the promise of a reasonable income, a respected status in the community, and a job which provides interesting work.

These latter values conflict, however, with the immediate gratifications which can be gained by going to work in the factory as a nonskilled laborer. The teen-age working-class youth is not likely to make the sacrifice of present satisfactions unless his aspirations gain support from a personally significant model or are encouraged by persons whom he respects, admires, or loves. One thirty-one-year-old skilled worker whose father had also been a skilled worker commented:

> When I was an apprentice I was torn by two desires. One was to go to work on the line like the rest of my friends and make some money. But there's no future in that. The other was to stick to the apprenticeship in hopes of getting some place. Seeing the way my dad worked through—even if he had his troubles and lost his home—I felt that it paid my father dividends anyway.

It is noteworthy that thirty-nine per cent of all apprentices registered with the Autotown Technical School in 1947[4] (fifty of 129) were sons of skilled workers; only eleven per cent were the sons of nonskilled workers. The rest came from the urban lower-middle class or from farm families.

The typical attitudes of young nonskilled workers toward jobs, advancement, and the future persist until marriage or, perhaps, parenthood. With the assumption of family responsibilities, workers tend to become actively concerned about the possibilities of advancement. "When I got married," said the oiler quoted above, "I suddenly realized that I'd better do something or I was really going to be stuck." The immediate need for more money leads workers to consider seriously the alternatives open to them and the arrival of children generates a fresh interest in the future.

By the time these workers marry and have children, however, they have already made decisions which limit the alternatives open to them. Some left high school in order to take jobs which offered little prospect of advancement; others went willingly into an automobile plant after graduating. Now they find that they lack the training which is requisite for advancement in the corporate hierarchy. They have gained no skills which can be used outside the factory. They have not added to their scanty knowledge about the prerequisites and potentialities of alternative jobs. Nor, in their concern with buying a car or having a good time, have they tried to acquire the resources which might enable them to buy a profitable farm or start a successful business.

The responsibilities of marriage and the uncertainties facing the non-skilled worker tend to keep attention focussed on the present and to counterbalance the new stimuli to planning for the future. The pressure of the weekly grocery bill, the rent or mortgage payment, installments on a refrigerator or a washing machine or vacuum cleaner, the need for a new pair of work pants or a pair of shoes for a child, the doctor's bill for a tonsillectomy, all keep life on a pay-day-to-pay-day basis. The future, for men in an industry known for irregular employment, bristles with threats. They are not usually well prepared to cope with unemployment or with sickness and accident, the normal hazards of life. And the future is still resonant with echoes of the depression of the 1930s; men were employed by the W.P.A. in Autotown until the eve of war in 1941. Workers may conclude, therefore, that "it doesn't pay to think about the future," as a thitrty-one-year-old line-tender put it.

As unmarried men without responsibility, these workers were careless about the future; now they are forced into taking a defensive stance toward the future despite the stimulus to aspiration and effort. There is no change, therefore, in the pattern of life to which they have been accustomed; life's rhythms of tension and release remain short, from week-end to week-end, from one good time to another. Life may occasionally be pointed toward a vacation a few months ahead, toward Christmas or Easter, toward a birthday or some other family celebration. But long-run desires and expectations are avoided as both past and future are minimized and life is compressed into the week's routine.

Lacking occupational skills and financial resources, most workers confine their aspirations to the limited array of alternatives we have already examined. Since they are unwilling or unable to plan for the long future, they see these goals as isolated small moves rather than as part of a long-range plan. Only one worker, a would-be businessman, talked of becoming rich. He was a twenty-nine-year-old toolmaker who was about to open his own tool-and-die shop. Only the two young workers who intended to go to college could see in their plans the beginning of a career. Unlike the professional or the salaried officeholder, the factory worker does not see his present job as part of a career pattern which channels his aspirations and sustains his hope. Unlike the businessman, he has no ever-beckoning goal of increasing sales and expanding profits to stimulate his efforts.

Hope for one or another of the alternatives on which workers do focus their aspirations may, for a while, run high. Despite the obstacles in their path, some workers are determined and purposeful. The period shortly after marriage when workers become concerned with their future, when they are at or near their physical peak, when family responsibilities may still serve as a stimulant to ambition and effort rather than as a brake, is probably the time of maximum ambition and of greatest expectation, for skilled as well as nonskilled workers.

* * *

But many workers see little reason for hope when they assay the possibilities of advancement in the factory and examine the problems and the risks inherent in business or farming. If they have not already gained some advancement on the level of wage labor, they are not likely to see any prospect of promotion to supervision. Indeed, if they have not had an opportunity to learn how to carry responsibility and exercise authority, they are not likely, even if offered promotion, to be willing to take on the problems which they know are inherent in the foreman's role. In order to start a business or buy a farm, one needs money; the family responsibilities which stimulate ambition also make it difficult to save. If they do manage to start a business or buy a farm, not only must they risk their savings, they must also surrender whatever security their seniority in the plant gives them. (One might therefore expect that workers most intent on leaving the factory would be those who, for one reason or another, have not been in the plant for very long. Five of the eight workers with definite out-of-the-shop plans had been there for less than a year.)

Workers who feel impelled to seek advancement despite the limited opportunities in the factory and the risks inherent in leaving tend to dilute their aspirations to a loose welter of hopes and a medley of alternative plans. And workers whose insistent hopes and positive efforts do not bear quick fruit give up their ambitions after a while and cast about as vaguely and uncertainly as the others. Without a "life-plan" which commits them to follow a series of more or less recognized steps,[5] workers simultaneously entertain alternative goals, or they continually shift their attention from one goal to another, usually without investing much hope or effort in any particular one.

While waiting for advancement in the factory which may not come and, in any case, is largely contingent upon forces over which they have little or no control, workers frequently consider the possibility of going into business or buying a farm, as twenty-three of the sixty-two workers interviewed were doing. Even those who are hopeful about advancement in the plant recognized the uncertainties involved and may therefore look elsewhere at the same time. Thus four of the six workers who felt that they would eventually become foremen had also thought of leaving the factory and said that they planned to "go into business" if they did not gain the desired promotion within some reasonable time. (None had been promoted and all were still in the plant in June, 1951.)

Interest in out-of-the-shop goals usually represents the desire for escape from the factory rather than a positive search for success. Such interest is, therefore, particularly susceptible to changes in workers' job status and the conditions of work. These changes bear no positive relationship to the objective possibilities of success or failure in business or farming or to the nature of workers' resources or skills. Interest and, in some cases, action may therefore be stimulated—or inhibited—at the wrong time.

Thus business and farming ambitions are frequently whipsawed by changes in general business conditions. In the upward phase of the business cycle, when production is being maintained at a high level or is increasing and workers are regularly employed, the desire to leave the factory is at a minimum even though opportunities for small business may be at their best. When production falls off and temporary layoffs and short workweeks occur, interest in out-of-the-shop goals increases even though workers' resources are being rapidly drained away and the chances of business failure are especially high.

Interest in out-of-the-shop goals, as well as hope for advancement in the factory, may also fluctuate with variations in workers' feelings that occur without reference to changes in their jobs. For example, a welder, when first interviewed, complained about the difficulties in his job and was anxious to leave the company despite his lack of savings and the importance he attached to his twelve years of seniority. He had been working on the second shift (4:00 P.M. to 12:30 A.M.) when interviewed and was obviously tired and irritable. When interviewed again several weeks later, he was on the first shift (workers in most departments changed shifts every four weeks), rested, and in much better spirits. He no longer complained about his job, and though he still talked about leaving the factory "some day," he did so without force or urgency.

In a moment of hope, stimulated by some unexpected suggestion, workers may undertake a correspondence course in salesmanship, in automobile repairing, in accounting, in foremanship. (Four workers volunteered the information that they had once taken some kind of correspondence course; two others were doing so at the time they were interviewed.) In a moment of discouragement, the course is dropped, the money invested in it lost completely. The tentative and uncertain character of such efforts was evident in the case of one worker who quickly asked the interviewer if he thought there was much value in the correspondence course in foremanship and supervision he was taking at the cost of $120. Two months later he dropped the course because he was not "getting anything out of it." At a time when things in the factory seem to be at their worst, workers may look into farm prices, search for a small business of some kind, perhaps answer advertisements for salesmen or look for other factory jobs. But as their mood changes, the search is ended, negotiations that may have been begun are broken off, workers fail to follow up the steps they have already taken.

It seems likely that interest in out-of-the-shop goals may be endlessly renewed by the constant turnover among workers, some of whom do go into business, farming, or white-collar jobs. (The weekly newspaper published by the Autotown C.I.O. Council frequently featured stories about union members who had gone into business for themselves.) But interest, when unsupported by knowledge or resources, rarely remains focussed on one particular objective for very long. Since many workers plan to do "something" "as soon as things get better," "if I can save up a few hundred dollars," or "when I get straightened out," they entertain in usually disorderly succession various out-of-the-shop goals which are critically scrutinized and rejected as impractical or are mulled over, dreamed about, vaguely examined, and eventually permitted to fade away. This pattern emerged clearly in the case of one worker who was interviewed three times. In the first interview he said that he was thinking of "buying some tourist property up north." When asked how much money he would need and how much he had, he admitted that he did not know how much he would need, had no savings, and did not expect to save any money within the near future. A month later he was talking of a turkey farm, again with little attention to the concrete problems he would face. A year later he said that he had been thinking of a "bee farm," but that he had finally given up any thought of leaving the plant.

The pattern of shifting goals and tentative plans may persist for the major part of a worker's occupational life. Occasionally plans congeal into positive action under the impact of a particularly strong stimulus or under the cumulative pressure of a series of events. Frequently these actions are abortive. Thus a thirty-one-year-old worker with twelve years of seniority who had been moved after the war from a job as a toolmaker-upgrader to an unskilled maintenance job to the paint line angrily left the factory in order to take a job in a small chemical plant in which his father worked, even though this move meant lower wages. Two years later he was back in the A.B.C. plant as a machine-operator, but now without the long seniority he had once had. A bitter disagreement with the foreman, an unresolved grievance, a job assignment to which he objects, these and many other specific occurrences can provoke a worker into quitting, even though he must start looking for another job without much likelihood of gaining any basic improvement. He may, as many have done, find himself back eventually at the same kind of work in the same plant.

The longer workers remain in the plant, the less seriously do they consider the possibility of leaving, even though they recognize that they are probably going to remain on the level of wage labor in the factory. Eventually they cease to entertain out-of-the-shop goals, accept the fact that they will remain in the factory, and confine their aspirations to a better job in the plant. This shift does not occur at any particular age; it may take place when a worker is thirty, it may not occur until he is fifty or even older. In some instances, of course, it may never occur. And a last burst of interest in business may appear as workers approach the age of retirement when, bedeviled by the economic problems of old age, they seek methods of supplementing whatever pension they are entitled to.

Workers give up their desire to leave the factory as they come to realize that they are not likely to be successful in business or farming and are not likely to gain much merely by changing jobs. At the same time they come to place a heavy stress upon the security provided by long seniority in the plant. This disappearance of ambition does not necessarily mean disappointment or frustration, however. Skilled workers, for example, may never consider any other alternative to their factory jobs, although many do in as amorphous a manner as do most nonskilled workers. They can count on a comparatively good income with a measure of security from a relatively interesting and satisfying job. The worker who manages to become skilled through some sort of upgrading program, formal or informal, may give up his out-of-the-shop goals and resign himself contentedly to what he has achieved. One worker, for example, was intent on buying a farm when he was interviewed in 1947. But in 1951, after he had been recalled to the electrician's job he had held as an upgrader during the war, he was no longer thinking of leaving the factory. Even nonskilled workers who manage to secure jobs at the top of the informal hierarchy of desirability may be reasonably satisfied, particularly if their ambitions were not set very high at the outset, if they have not felt pressure from their families to go into business or seek a better job elsewhere, or if they have not been stimulated by the example of friends or relatives who have done well economically.

Some workers, scarred by experience, resign themselves to a future in the factory without satisfaction, but without resentment. They no longer demand much of life except for some kind of job and some assurance that they can keep it. One fifty-two-year-old line-tender, for example, had not held a regular job from 1932 until 1941; he had tried subsistence farming, small businesses of various kinds, and had worked at a wide variety of manual jobs. Now he was grateful to have a job, although he did not like assembly-line work, and he was hoping to be permitted to remain in the factory without being disturbed or forced to look for work again.

But if workers come to feel that they must stay in the factory because there is no opportunity in business or farming, if they do not have desirable jobs in the plant, if they began their careers with large ambitions and high hopes, or if they have seen relatives or friends "get ahead in the world," then their acceptance of a future in the factory is accompanied by bitterness and resentment aimed at themselves, at others, or at the world in general.

NOTES

1. Our data consist primarily of retrospective accounts and of comparisons of workers of different ages, supplemented by the material from the dozen workers who were interviewed more than once. Both types of data must, of course, be used with caution, and their inadequacies for constructing a chronological pattern taken into account. Retrospective accounts are likely to contain some distortion of past events and attitudes; age comparisons suffer from the changing historical contexts in which men of different generations grow up and pursue their occupational careers.
2. A. B. Hollingshead reports similar findings in his discussion of class differences in the levels of aspiration among teen-age youth. See *Elmtown's Youth*, New York: John Wiley, 1949, pp. 282–287. Most studies of job choice among high-school students have stressed the generally inflated character of youthful aspirations and the inevitable comedown rather than noting the differences in the extent to which students from different classes respond to the American Dream. See, for example, D. S. Miller and W. H. Form, *Industrial Sociology*, New York: Harper, 1951, pp. 589–592.
3. See D. Riesman: *The Lonely Crowd*, New Haven: Yale University Press, 1950, and L. Lowenthal: "Biographies in Popular Magazines," in P. F. Lazarsfeld and F. Stanton (eds.)`, *Radio Research, 1942–1943*, New York: Duell, Sloan and Pearce, 1944, pp. 507–520.
4. This includes all apprentices in the city except those in the A.B.C. apprentice program. The A.B.C. plant provided its own classroom instruction for apprentices; all other apprentices received their classroom instruction at the Autotown Technical School.
5. See K. Mannheim: *Man and Society in an Age of Reconstruction*, New York: Harcourt, Brace, 1944, p. 56, 104n.

peter schrag

"The ambiguities and changes in American life that occupy discussions in university seminars and policy debates in Washington, and that form the backbone of contemporary popular sociology, become increasingly the conditions of trauma and frustration in the middle." So writes Peter Schrag.

As Schrag explains, few Americans are more misunderstood or more maligned than the lower-middle and working class. In story and song the "Yahoos" and the "Rednecks," the "Hardhats" and the "Hunkies" are stereotyped, often by those who hardly know them (though they are quick to characterize them, for example, ". . . and they all live in ticky tacky houses").

The article that follows provides an introduction to these "Forgotten Americans" and an explanation of their various beliefs and attitudes. It offers an interesting counterpoint to John Horton's comments on the "cool people" who live in a different social world.

There is hardly a language to describe him, or even a set of social statistics. Just names: racist-bigot-redneck-ethnic-Irish-Italian-Pole-Hunkie-Yahoo. The lower middle class. A blank. The man under whose hat lies the great American desert. Who watches the tube, plays the horses, and keeps the niggers out of

From *Out of Place in America*, by Peter Schrag. Copyright © 1970 by Peter Schrag. Reprinted by permission of Random House, Inc.

his union and his neighborhood. Who might vote for Wallace (but didn't). Who cheers when the cops beat up on demonstrators. Who is free, white, and twenty-one, has a job, a home, a family, and is up to his eyeballs in credit. In the guise of the working class—or the American yeoman or John Smith—he was once the hero of the civics book, the man that Andrew Jackson called "the bone and sinew of the country." Now he is "the forgotten man," perhaps the most alienated person in America.

Nothing quite fits, except perhaps omission and semi-invisibility. America is supposed to be divided between affluence and poverty, between slums and suburbs. John Kenneth Galbraith begins the foreword to *The Affluent Society* with the phrase, "Since I sailed for Switzerland in the early summer of 1955 to begin work on this book . . ." But *between* slums and suburbs, between Scarsdale and Harlem, between Wellesley and Roxbury, between Shaker Heights and Hough, there are some eighty million people (depending on how you count them) who didn't sail for Switzerland in the summer of 1955, or at any other time, and who never expect to. Between slums and suburbs: South Boston and South San Francisco, Bell and Parma, Astoria and Bay Ridge, Newark, Cicero, Downey, Daly City, Charlestown, Flatbush. Union halls, American Legion posts, neighborhood bars and bowling leagues, the Ukrainian Club and the Holy Name. Main Street. To try to describe all this is like trying to describe America itself. If you look for it, you find it everywhere: the rows of frame houses overlooking the belching steel mills in Bethlehem, Pennsylvania, two-family brick houses in Canarsie (where the most common slogan, even in the middle of a political campaign, is "curb your dog"); the Fords and Chevies with a decal American flag on the rear window (usually a cut-out from the *Reader's Digest*, and displayed in counter-protest against peaceniks and "those bastards who carry Vietcong flags in demonstrations"); the bunting on the porch rail with the inscription, "Welcome Home, Pete." The gold star in the window.

When he was Under Secretary of Housing and Urban Development, Robert C. Wood tried a definition. It is not good, but it's the best we have:

He is a white employed male . . . earning between $5,000 and $10,000. He works regularly, steadily, dependably, wearing a blue collar or white collar. Yet the frontiers of his career expectations have been fixed since he reached the age of thirty-five, when he found that he had too many obligations, too much family, and too few skills to match opportunities with aspirations.

This definition of the "working American" involves almost 23-million American families.

The working American lives in the gray area fringes of a central city or in a close-in or very far-out cheaper suburban subdivision of a large metropolitan area. He is likely to own a home and a car, especially as his income begins to rise. Of those earning between $6,000 and $7,500, 70 per cent own their own homes and 94 per cent drive their own cars.

94 per cent have no education beyond high school and 43 per cent have only completed the eighth grade.

He does all the right things, obeys the law, goes to church and insists —usually—that his kids get a better education than he had. But the right things don't seem to be paying off. While he is making more than he ever made—perhaps more than he'd ever dreamed—he's still struggling while a lot of others—"them" (on welfare, in demonstrations, in the ghettos) are getting most of the attention. "I'm working my ass off," a guy tells you on a stoop in South Boston. "My kid's don't have a place to swim, my parks are full of glass, and I'm supposed to bleed for a bunch of people on relief." In New York a man who drives a Post Office trailer truck at night (4:00 P.M. to midnight) and a cab during the day (7:00 A.M. to 2:00 P.M.), and who hustles radios for his Post Office buddies on the side, is ready, as he says, to "knock somebody's ass." "The colored guys work when they feel like it. Sometimes they show up and sometimes they don't. One guy tore up all the time cards. I'd like to see a white guy do that and get away with it."

What Counts

Nobody knows how many people in America moonlight (half of the eighteen million families in the $5,000 to $10,000 bracket have two or more wage earners) or how many have to hustle on the side. "I don't think anybody has a single job anymore," said Nicholas Kisburg, the research director for a Teamsters Union Council in New York. "All the cops are moonlighting, and the teachers; and there's a million guys who are hustling, guys with phony social-security numbers who are hiding part of what they make so they don't get kicked out of a housing project, or guys who work as guards at sports events and get free meals that they don't want to pay taxes on. Every one of them is cheating. They are underground people—*Untermenschen*. . . . We really have no systematic data on any of this. We have no ideas of the attitudes of the white worker. (We've been too busy studying the black worker.) And yet he's the source of most of the reaction in this country."

The reaction is directed at almost every visible target: at integration and welfare, taxes and sex education, at the rich and the poor, the foundations and students, at the "smart people in the suburbs." In New York State the legislature cuts the welfare budget; in Los Angeles, the voters reelect Yorty after a whispered racial campaign against the Negro favorite. In Minneapolis a police detective named Charles Stenvig, promising "to take the handcuffs off the police," is elected mayor by a margin stunning even to his supporters: in Massachusetts the voters mail tea bags to their representatives in protest against new taxes, and in state after state legislatures are passing bills to punish student demonstrators. ("We keep talking about permissiveness in training kids," said a Los Angeles labor official, "but we forget that these are our kids.")

And yet all these things are side manifestations of a malaise that lacks a language. Whatever law and order means, for example, to a man who feels his wife is unsafe on the street after dark or in the park at any time, or whose kids get shaken down in the school yard, it also means something like normality—the demand that everybody play it by the book, that cultural and social standards be somehow restored to their civics-book simplicity, that things shouldn't be as they are but as they were supposed to be. If there is a revolution in this country—a revolt in manners, standards of dress and obscenity, and, more importantly, in our official sense of what America is—there is also a counter-revolt. Sometimes it is inarticulate, and sometimes (perhaps most of the time) people are either too confused or apathetic—or simply too polite and too decent—to declare themselves. In Astoria, Queens, a white working-class district of New York, people who make $7,000 or $8,000 a year (sometimes in two jobs) call themselves affluent, even though the Bureau of Labor Statistics regards an income of less than $9,500 in New York inadequate to a moderate standard of living. And in a similar neighborhood in Brooklyn a truck driver who earns $151 a week tells you he's doing well, living in a two-story frame house separated by a narrow driveway from similar houses, thousands of them in block after block. This year, for the first time, he will go on a cruise—he and his wife and two other couples—two weeks in the Caribbean. He went to work after World War II ($57 a week) and he has lived in the same house for twenty years, accumulating two television sets, wall-to-wall carpeting in a small living room, and a basement that he recently remodeled into a recreation room with the help of two moonlighting firemen. "We get fairly good salaries, and this is a good neighborhood, one of the few good ones left. We have no smoked Irishmen around."

Stability is what counts, stability in job and home and neighborhood, stability in the church and in friends. At night you watch television and sometimes on a weekend you go to a nice place—maybe a downtown hotel—for dinner with another couple. (Or maybe your sister, or maybe bowling, or maybe, if you're defeated, a night at the track.) The wife has the necessary appliances, often still being paid off, and the money you save goes for your daughter's orthodontist, and later for her wedding. The smoked Irishmen—the colored (no one says black; few even say Negro)—represent change and instability, kids who cause trouble in school, who get treatment that your kids never got, that you never got. ("Those fucking kids," they tell you in South Boston, "raising hell, and not one of 'em paying his own way. Their fucking mothers are all on welfare.") The black kids mean a change in the rules, a double standard in grades and discipline, and—vaguely—a challenge to all you believed right. Law and order is the stability and predictability of established ways. Law and order is equal treatment—in school, in jobs, in the courts

—even if you're cheating a little yourself. The Forgotten Man is Jackson's man. He is the vestigial American democrat of 1840: "They all know that their success depends upon their own industry and economy and that they must not expect to become suddenly rich by the fruits of their toil." He is also Franklin Roosevelt's man—the man whose vote (or whose father's vote) sustained the New Deal.

There are other considerations, other styles, other problems. A postman in a Charlestown (Boston) housing project: eight children and a ninth on the way. Last year, by working overtime, his income went over $7,000. This year, because he reported it, the Housing Authority is raising his rent from $78 to $106 a month, a catastrophe for a family that pays $2.20 a day for milk, has never had a vacation, and for which an excursion is "going out for ice cream." "You try and save for something better; we hope to get out of here to someplace where the kids can play, where there's no broken glass, and then something always comes along that knocks you right back. It's like being at the bottom of the well waiting for a guy to throw you a rope." The description becomes almost Chaplinesque. Life is humble but not simple; terrors of insolent bureaucracies and contemptuous officials produce a demonology that loses little of its horror for being partly misunderstood. You want to get a sink fixed but don't want to offend the manager; want to get an eye operation that may (or may not) have been necessitated by a military injury five years earlier, "but the Veterans Administration says I signed away my benefits"; want to complain to someone about the teenagers who run around breaking windows and harassing women but get no response either from the management or the police. "You're afraid to complain because if they don't get you during the day they'll get you at night." Automobiles, windows, children, all become hostages to the vague terrors of everyday life; everything is vulnerable. Liabilities that began long ago cannot possibly be liquidated: "I never learned anything in that school except how to fight. I got tired of being caned by the teachers so at sixteen I quit and joined the Marines. I still don't know anything."

American culture? Wealth is visible, and so, now, is poverty. Both have become intimidating clichés. But the rest? A vast, complex, and disregarded world that was once—in belief, and in fact—the American middle: Greyhound and Trailways bus terminals in little cities at midnight, each of them with its neon lights and its cardboard hamburgers; acres of tarpaper beach bungalows in places like Revere and Rockaway; the hair curlers in the supermarket on Saturday, and the little girls in the communion dresses the next morning; pinball machines and the *Daily News*, the *Reader's Digest* and Ed Sullivan; houses with tiny front lawns (or even large ones) adorned with statues of the Virgin or of Sambo welcomin' de folks home; Clint Eastwood or Julie Andrews at the Palace; the trotting tracks and the dog tracks—Aurora Downs, Connaught Park, Roosevelt,

Yonkers, Rockingham, and forty others—where gray men come not for sport and beauty, but to read numbers, to study the dope. (If you win you have figured something, have in a small way controlled your world, have surmounted your impotence. If you lose, bad luck, shit. "I'll break his goddamned head.") Baseball is not the national pastime; racing is. For every man who goes to a major-league baseball game there are four who go to the track and probably four more who go to the candy store or the barbershop to make their bets. (Total track attendance in 1965: 62 million plus another 10 million who went to the dogs.)

There are places, and styles, and attitudes. If there are neighborhoods of aspiration, suburban enclaves for the mobile young executives and the aspiring worker, there are also places of limited expectation and dead-end districts where mobility is finished. But even there you can often find, however vestigial, a sense of place, the roots of old ethnic loyalties, and a passionate, if often futile, battle against intrusion and change. "Everybody around here," you are told, "pays his own way." In this world the problems are not the ABM or air pollution (have they heard of Biafra?) or the international population crisis; the problem is to get your street cleaned, your garbage collected, to get your husband home from Vietnam alive; to negotiate installment payments and to keep the schools orderly. Ask anyone in Scarsdale or Winnetka about the schools and they'll tell you about new programs, or about how many are getting into Harvard, or about the teachers; ask in Oakland or the North Side of Chicago, and they'll tell you that they have (or haven't) had trouble. Somewhere in his gut the man in those communities knows that mobility and choice in this society are limited. He cannot imagine any major change for the better; but he can imagine change for the worse. And yet for a decade he is the one who has been asked to carry the burden of social reform, to integrate his schools and his neighborhood, has been asked by comfortable people to pay the social debts due to the poor and the black. In Boston, in San Francisco, in Chicago (not to mention Newark or Oakland) he has been telling the reformers to go to hell. The Jewish schoolteachers of New York and the Irish parents of Dorchester have asked the same question: "What the hell did Lindsay (or the Beacon Hill Establishment) ever do for us?"

The ambiguities and changes in American life that occupy discussions in university seminars and policy debates in Washington, and that form the backbone of contemporary popular sociology, become increasingly the conditions of trauma and frustration in the middle. Although the New Frontier and Great Society contained some programs for those not already on the rolls of social pathology—federal aid for higher education, for example—the public priorities and the rhetoric contained little. The emphasis, properly, was on the poor, on the inner cities (e.g., Negroes) and the unemployed. But in Chicago a widow with three children who earns $7,000 a year can't get them college loans because she makes too much; the money is reserved for people on relief. New schools are built in the ghetto but not in the white working-class neighborhoods where they are just as dilapidated. In Newark the head of a white vigilante group (now a city councilman) runs, among other things, on a platform opposing pro-Negro discrimination. "When pools are being built in the Central Ward—don't they think white kids have got frustration? The white can't get a job; we have to hire Negroes first." The middle class, said Congressman Roman Pucinski of Illinois, who represents a lot of it, "is in revolt. Everyone has been generous in supporting anti-poverty. Now the middle-class American is disqualified from most of the programs."

The frustrated middle. The liberal wisdom about welfare, ghettos, student revolt, and Vietnam has only a marginal place, if any, for the values and life of the working man. It flies in the face of most of what he was taught to cherish and respect: hard work, order, authority, self-reliance. He fought, either alone or through labor organizations, to establish the precincts he now considers his own. Union seniority, the civil-service bureaucracy, and the petty professionalism established by the merit system in the public schools become sinecures of particular ethnic groups or of those who have learned to negotiate and master the system. A man who worked all his life to accumulate the points and grades and paraphernalia to become an assistant school principal (no matter how silly the requirements) is not likely to relinquish his position with equanimity. Nor is a dock worker whose only estate is his longshoreman's card. The job, the points, the credits become property:

> Some men leave their sons money [wrote a union member to the *New York Times*], some large investments, some business connections, and some a profession. I have only one worthwhile thing to give: my trade. I hope to follow a centuries-old tradition and sponsor my sons for an apprenticeship. For this simple father's wish it is said that I discriminate against Negroes. Don't all of us discriminate? Which of us . . . will not choose a son over all others?

Suddenly the rules are changing—all the rules. If you protect your job for your own you may be called a bigot. At the same time it's perfectly acceptable to shout black power and to endorse it. What does it take to be a good American? *Give the black man a position because he is black, not because he necessarily works harder or does the job better.* What does it take to be a good American? Dress nicely, hold a job, be clean-cut, don't judge a man by the color of his skin or the country of his origin. What about the demands of Negroes, the long hair of the students, the dirty movies, the people who burn draft cards and American flags? Do you have to go out in the street with picket signs, do you have to burn the place down to get what you want? What does it take to be a good American? *This is a sick society, a racist society, we are fighting an immoral war.* ("I'm against the Vietnam war, too," says the truck driver in Brooklyn. "I see a good kid come home with half an arm and a leg in a brace up to here, and what's it all for? I was glad to see *my kid* flunk the Army physical. Still, somebody has to say no to these demonstrators and enforce the law.") What does it take to be a good American?

The conditions of trauma and frustration in the middle. What does it take to be a good American? Suddenly there are demands for Italian power and Polish power and Ukrainian power. In Cleveland the Poles demand a seat on the school board, and get it, and in Pittsburgh John Pankuch, the seventy-three-year-old president of the National Slovak Society, demands "action, plenty of it to make up for lost time." Black power is supposed to be nothing but emulation of the ways in which other ethnic groups made it. But have they made it? In Reardon's Bar on East Eighth Street in South Boston, where the workmen come for their fish-chowder lunch and for their rye and ginger, they still identify themselves as Galway men and Kilkenny men; in the newsstand in Astoria you can buy *Il Progresso, El Tiempo,* the *Staats-Zeitung,* the *Irish World,* plus papers in Greek, Hungarian, and Polish. At the parish of Our Lady of Mount Carmel the priests hear confession in English, Italian, and Spanish and nearby, the biggest attraction is not the stickball game, but the *bocce* court. Some of the poorest people in America are white, native, and have lived all of their lives in the same place as their fathers and grandfathers. The problems that were presumably solved in some distant past, in that prehistoric era before the textbooks were written—problems of assimilation, of upward mobility—now turn out to be very much unsolved. The melting pot and all: millions made it, millions moved to the affluent suburbs; several million—no one knows how many—did not. The median income in Irish South Boston is $5,100 a year but the community-action workers have a hard time convincing the local citizens that any white man who is not stupid or irresponsible can be poor. Pride still keeps them from applying for income supplements or Medicaid, but it does not keep them from resenting those who do. In Pittsburgh, where the members of Polish-American organizations earn an estimated $5,000 to $6,000 (and some fall below the poverty line), the Poverty Programs are nonetheless directed primarily to Negroes, and almost everywhere the thing called urban backlash associates itself in some fashion with ethnic groups whose members have themselves only a precarious hold on the security of affluence. Almost everywhere in the old cities, tribal neighborhoods and their styles are under assault by masscult. The Italian grocery gives way to the supermarket, the ma-and-pa store and the walk-up are attacked by urban renewal. And almost everywhere, that assault tends to depersonalize and to alienate. It has always been this way, but with time the brave new world that replaces old patterns becomes increasingly bureaucratic, distant, and hard to control.

Yet beyond the problems of ethnic identity, beyond the problems of

Poles and Irishmen left behind, there are others more pervasive and more dangerous. For every Greek or Hungarian there are a dozen American-Americans who are past ethnic consciousness and who are as alienated, as confused, and as angry as the rest. The obvious manifestations are the same everywhere—race, taxes, welfare, students—but the threat seems invariably more cultural and psychological than economic or social. What upset the police at the Chicago convention most was not so much the politics of the demonstrators as their manners and their hair. (The barbershops in their neighborhoods don't advertise Beatle Cuts but the Flat Top and the Chicago Box.) The affront comes from middle-class people—and their children—who had been cast in the role of social exemplars (and from those cast as unfortunates worthy of public charity) who offend all the things on which working class identity is built: "hippies [said a San Francisco longshoreman] who fart around the streets and don't work"; welfare recipients who strike and march for better treatment; "all those [said a California labor official] who challenge the precepts that these people live on." If ethnic groups are beginning to organize to get theirs, so are others: police and firemen ("The cop is the new nigger"); schoolteachers; lower-middle-class housewives fighting sex education and bussing; small property owners who have no ethnic communion but a passionate interest in lower taxes, more policemen, and stiffer penalties for criminals. In San Francisco the Teamsters, who had never been known for such interests before, recently demonstrated in support of the police and law enforcement and, on another occasion, joined a group called Mothers Support Neighborhood Schools at a school-board meeting to oppose—with their presence and later, apparently, with their fists—a proposal to integrate the schools through bussing. ("These people," someone said at the meeting, "do not look like mothers.")

Which is not to say that all is frustration and anger, that anybody is ready "to burn the country down." They are not even ready to elect standard model demagogues. "A lot of labor people who thought of voting for Wallace were ashamed of themselves when they realized what they were about to do," said Morris Iushewitz, an officer of New York's Central Labor Council. Because of a massive last-minute union campaign, and perhaps for other reasons, the blue-collar vote for Wallace fell far below the figures predicted by the early polls last fall. Any number of people, moreover, who are not doing well by any set of official statistics, who are earning well below the national mean ($8,000 a year), or who hold two jobs to stay above it, think of themselves as affluent, and often use that word. It is almost as if not to be affluent is to be un-American. People who can't use the word tend to be angry; people who come too close to those who can't become frightened. The definition of affluence is generally pinned to what comes in, not to the quality of life as it's lived. The $8,000 son of a man who never earned more than $4,500 may, for that reason alone, believe that he's "doing all right." If life is not all right, if he can't get his curbs fixed, or his streets patrolled, if the highways are crowded and the beaches polluted, if the schools are ineffectual he is still able to call himself affluent, feels, perhaps, a social compulsion to do so. His anger, if he is angry, is not that of the wage earner resenting management—and certainly not that of the socialist ideologue asking for redistribution of wealth—but that of the consumer, the taxpayer, and the family man. (Inflation and taxes are wiping out most of the wage gains made in labor contracts signed during the past three years.) Thus he will vote for a Louise Day Hicks in Boston who promises to hold the color line in the schools or for a Charles Stenvig calling for law enforcement in Minneapolis but reject a George Wallace who seems to threaten his pocketbook. The danger is that he will identify with the politics of the Birchers and other middle-class reactionaries (who often pretend to speak for him) even though his income and style of life are far removed from theirs; that taxes, for example, will be identified with welfare rather than war, and that he will blame his limited means on the small slice of the poor rather than the fat slice of the rich.

If you sit and talk to people like Marjorie Lemlow, who heads Mothers Support Neighborhood Schools in San Francisco, or Joe Owens, a house painter who is president of a community-action organization in Boston, you quickly discover that the roots of reaction and the roots of reform are often identical, and that the response to particular situations is more often contingent on the politics of the politicians and leaders who appear to care than on the conditions of life or the ideology of the victims. Mrs. Lemlow wants to return the schools to some virtuous past; she worries about disintegration of the family and she speaks vaguely about something that she can't bring herself to call a conspiracy against Americanism. She has been accused of leading a bunch of Birchers, and she sometimes talks Birch language. But whatever the form, her sense of things comes from a small-town vision of national virtues, and her unhappiness from the assaults of urban sophistication. It just so happens that a lot of reactionaries now sing that tune, and that the liberals are indifferent.

Joe Owens—probably because of his experience as a Head Start parent, and because of his association with an effective community-action program—talks a different language. He knows, somehow, that no simple past can be restored. In his world the villains are not conspirators but bureaucrats and politicians, and he is beginning to discover that in a struggle with officials the black man in the ghetto and the working man (black or white) have the same problems. "Every time you ask for something from the politicians they treat you like a beggar, like you ought to be grateful for what you have. They try to make you feel ashamed."

The imponderables are youth and tradition and change. The civics book and the institution it celebrates—however passe—still hold the world together. The revolt is in their name, not against them. And there is simple decency, the language and practice of the folksy cliché, the small town, the Boy Scout virtues, the neighborhood charity, the obligation to support the church, the rhetoric of open opportunity: "They can keep Wallace and they can keep Alabama. We didn't fight a dictator for four years so we could elect one over here." What happens when all that becomes Mickey Mouse? Is there an urban ethic to replace the values of the small town? Is there a coherent public philosophy, a consistent set of beliefs to replace family, home, and hard work? What happens when the hang-ups of upper-middle-class kids are in fashion and those of blue-collar kids are not? What happens when Doing Your Own Thing becomes not the slogan of the solitary deviant but the norm? Is it possible that as the institutions and beliefs of tradition are fashionably denigrated a blue-collar generation gap will open to the Right as well as to the Left? (There is statistical evidence, for example, that Wallace's greatest support within the unions came from people who are between twenty-one and twenty-nine, those, that is, who have the most tenuous association with the liberalism of labor.) Most are politically silent; although SDS has been trying to organize blue-collar high-school students, there are no Mario Savios or Mark Rudds—either of the Right or the Left—among them. At the same time the union leaders, some of them old hands from the Thirties, aren't sure that the kids are following them either. Who speaks for the son of the longshoreman or the Detroit auto worker? What happens if he doesn't get to college? What, indeed, happens when he does?

Vaguely but unmistakably the hopes that a youth-worshiping nation historically invested in its young are becoming threats. We have never been unequivocal about the symbolic patricide of Americanization and upward mobility, but if at one time mobility meant rejection of older (or European) styles it was, at least, done in the name of America. Now the labels are blurred and the objectives indistinct. Just at the moment when a tradition-bound Italian father is persuaded that he should send his son to college—that education is the only future—the college blows up. At the moment when a parsimonious taxpayer begins to shell out for what he considers an extravagant state university system the students go on strike. Marijuana, sexual liberation, dress styles, draft resistance, even the rhetoric of change become monsters and demons in a world that appears to turn old virtues upside down. The paranoia that fastened on Communism twenty years ago (and sometimes still does) is increasingly directed to vague conspiracies undermining the schools, the family, order and discipline. "They're feeding the kids this generation-gap business," says a Chicago housewife who grinds out a campaign against sex education on a duplicating machine in her living room. "The kids are told to make their own decisions. They're all mixed up by situation ethics and open-ended questions. They're alienating children from their own parents." They? The churches, the schools, even the YMCA and the Girl Scouts, are implicated. But a major share of the villainy is now also attributed to "the social science centers," to the apostles of sensitivity training, and to what one California lady, with some embarrassment, called "nude therapy." "People with sane minds are being altered by psychological methods." The current major campaign of the John Birch Society is not directed against Communists in government or the Supreme Court, but against sex education.

(There is, of course, also sympathy with the young, especially in poorer areas where kids have no place to play. "Everybody's got to have a hobby," a South Boston adolescent told a youth worker. "Ours is throwing rocks." If people will join reactionary organizations to protect their children, they will also support others: community-action agencies which help kids get jobs; Head Start parent groups, Boys Clubs. "Getting this place cleaned up" sometimes refers to a fear of young hoods; sometimes it points to the day when there is a park or a playground or when the existing park can be used. "I want to see them grow up to have a little fun.")

Beneath it all there is a more fundamental ambivalence, not only about the young, but about institutions—the schools, the churches, the Establishment—and about the future itself. In the major cities of the East (though perhaps not in the West) there is a sense that time is against you, that one is living "in one of the few decent neighborhoods left," that "if I can get $125 a week upstate (or downstate) I'll move." The institutions that were supposed to mediate social change and which, more than ever, are becoming priesthoods of information and conglomerates of social engineers, are increasingly suspect. To attack the Ford Foundation (as Wright Patman has done) is not only to fan the embers of historic populism against concentrations of wealth and power, but also to arouse those who feel that they are trapped by an alliance of upper-class Wasps and lower-class Negroes. If the foundations have done anything for the blue-collar worker he doesn't seem to be aware of it. At the same time the distrust of professional educators that characterizes the black militants is becoming increasingly prevalent among a minority of lower-middle-class whites who are beginning to discover that the schools aren't working for them either. ("Are all those new programs just a cover-up for failure?") And if the Catholic Church is under attack from its liberal members (on birth control, for example) it is also alienating the traditionalists who liked their minor saints (even if they didn't exist) and were perfectly content with the Latin Mass. For the alienated Catholic liberal there are other places to go; for the lower-middle-class parishioner in Chicago or Boston there are none.

Perhaps, in some measure, it has always been this way. Perhaps none of this is new. And perhaps it is also true that the American lower middle has never had it so good. And yet surely there is a difference, and that is that the common man has lost his visibility and, somehow, his claim on public attention. There are old liberals and socialists—men like Michael Harrington—who believe that a new alliance can be forged for progressive social action:

> From Marx to Mills, the Left has regarded the middle class as a stratum of hypocritical, vacillating rear-guarders. There was often sound reason for this contempt. But is it not possible that a new class is coming into being? It is not the old middle class of small property owners and entrepreneurs, nor the new middle class of managers. It is composed of scientists, technicians, teachers, and professionals in the public sector of the society. By education and work experience it is predisposed toward planning. It could be an ally of the poor and the organized workers—or their sophisticated enemy. In other words, an unprecedented social and political variable seems to be taking shape in America.
>
> The American worker, even when he waits on a table or holds open a door, is not servile; he does not carry himself like an inferior. The openness, frankness, and democratic manner which Tocqueville described in the last century persists to this very day. They have been a source of rudeness, contemptuous ignorance, violence—and of a creative self-confidence among great masses of people. It was in this latter spirit that the CIO was organized and the black freedom movement marched.

There are recent indications that the white lower middle class is coming back on the roster of public priorities. Pucinski tells you that liberals in Congress are privately discussing the pressure from the middle class. There are proposals now to increase personal income-tax exemptions from $600 to $1,000 (or $1,200) for each dependent, to protect all Americans with a national insurance system covering catastrophic medical expenses, and to put a floor under all incomes. Yet these things by themselves are insufficient. Nothing is sufficient without a national sense of restoration. What Pucinski means by the middle class has, in some measure, always been represented. A physician earning $75,000 a year is also a working man but he is hardly a victim of the welfare system. Nor, by and large, are the stockholders of the Standard Oil Company or U.S. Steel. The fact that American ideals have often been corrupted in the cause of self-aggrandizement does not make them any less important for the cause of social reform and justice. "As a movement with the conviction that there is more to people than greed and fear," Harrington said, "the Left must . . . also speak in the name of the historic idealism of the United States."

The issue, finally, is not *the program* but the vision, the angle of view. A huge constituency may be coming up for grabs, and there is considerable evidence that its political mobility is more sensitive than anyone can imagine, that all the sociological determinants are not as significant as the simple facts of concern and leadership. When Robert Kennedy was killed last year [1969], thousands of working-class people who had expected to vote for him—if not hundreds of thousands—shifted their loyalties to Wallace. A man who can change from a progressive democrat into a bigot overnight deserves attention.

michael lerner

Who cries most loudly about bigotry? Who sings derisive songs about the awful people who live in ticky-tacky houses? Could it be that they are one and the same?

It could be and it is. According to Michael Lerner, one aspect of upper-class liberal rhetoric—on campus, in government, and in the media—is an openly expressed disdain for the working and lower-middle class. Particular targets are the police, the hard hats, and what Michael Novak calls the "PIGS"—Poles, Italians, Greeks, and Slavs.

The essay that follows was written at a time when the alternatives facing the American electorate were George Wallace and Richard Nixon. Mr. Lerner implies these men gained much support from the ire of middle Americans who resented the "respectable bigotry" of the educated elites.

When white Yale students denounce the racist university or racist American society, one has little doubt about what they refer to. One also has little doubt about the political leanings of the speaker. He is a good left-liberal or radical, upper-class or schooled in the assumptions of upper-class liberalism.

Liberal-to-radical students use these phrases and feel purged

Reprinted from *The American Scholar*, Volume 38, Number 4, Autumn 1969. Copyright © 1969 by the United Chapters of Phi Beta Kappa. By permission of the publisher. This article appeared originally in *The New Journal*, a student publication at Yale University.

of the bigotry and racism of people such as Chicago's Mayor Daley. No one could be further from bigotry, they seem to believe, than they.

But it isn't so. An extraordinary amount of bigotry on the part of elite, liberal students goes unexamined at Yale and elsewhere. Directed at the lower middle class, it feeds on the unexamined biases of class perspective, the personality predilections of elite radicals and academic disciplines that support their views.

There are certainly exceptions in the liberal-radical university society —people intellectually or actively aware of and opposed to the un-examined prejudice. But their anomalousness and lack of success in making an ostensibly introspective community face its own disease is striking.

In general, the bigotry of a lower-middle-class policeman toward a ghetto black or of a lower-middle-class mayor toward a rioter is not viewed in the same perspective as the bigotry of an upper-middle-class peace matron toward a lower-middle-class mayor; or of an upper-class university student toward an Italian, a Pole or a National Guardsman from Cicero, Illinois—that is, if the latter two cases are called bigotry at all. The violence of the ghetto is patronized as it is "understood" and forgiven; the violence of a Cicero racist convinced that Martin Luther King threatens his lawn and house and powerboat is detested without being understood. Yet the two bigotries are very similar. For one thing, each is directed toward the class directly below the resident bigot, the class that reflects the dark side of the bigot's life. Just as the upper class recognizes in lower-class lace-curtain morality the veiled up-tightness of upper-middle-class life, so the lower-middle-class bigot sees reflected in the lower class the violence, sexuality and poverty that threaten him. The radical may object that he dislikes the lower middle class purely because of its racism and its politics. But that is not sufficient explanation: Polish jokes are devoid of political content.

Empirical studies do not show it, but it is my hunch that shortly after Negro jokes became impossible in elite circles, the Polish jokes emerged. They enjoy a continuing success in universities even today. It also happens that while Frank Zappa and the Mothers of Invention or Janis Joplin may vie for top position in the hip radical affections, the cellar of their affections—the object of their ample, healthy, appropriate, unneurotic capacities for hatred—is securely in the hands of that happy team of Mayor Daley and the Chicago Police. Hip radicals in New Haven are often amused by the Italian Anti-Defamation League bumper sticker: "A.I.D.—Americans of Italian Descent." Poles, Italians, Mayor Daley and the police are safe objects for amusement, derision or hatred. They are all safely lower-middle-class.

Part of the vaunted moral development of college activists is their capacity for empathy—their ability to put themselves in the position of the Disadvantaged Other and to see the world from his circumstances. This theoretically leads them to empathize with ghetto blacks and therefore to distrust the authorities who oppress them. Unnoticed goes the fact that the "authorities" who get hated are the lower-middle-class police, the visible representatives of the more abstract and ambivalently regarded "power structure." Other favored targets for confrontation are the National Guard and the military, both bastions of the lower middle class. It is true that Dow Chemical representatives are attacked and that professors and university administrators are some-times held captive. It is also true that the police, the National Guard and the army are the agents of societal racism, student and ghetto repression and the war in Vietnam. But all these things should not blind us to the fact that the people toward whom bigotry, as well as political dislike, is directed by upper-class radicals are all too frequently lower-middle-class.

Radicals gloat over the faulty syntax of the lower middle class with the same predictability that they patronize the ghetto language as "authentic." They delight in Mayor Daley's malapropisms ("Chicago will move on to higher and higher platitudes of achievement") and in the lace-curtain cynicism of his denunciations: "They use language from the bordello, language that would shock any decent person." Why do they patronize one authenticity and mock another?

These upper-class attitudes are not a narrow phenomenon. *Time, Life* and *Newsweek* print ghetto phrases in reverent spidery italics—surrounded by space to emphasize the authentic simplicity—beneath soulful pictures of the cleansing but terrible, terrible poverty of ghetto blacks or rural poor. They reprint Daley verbatim as the fool.

One of the strongest supports for this upper-class, "respectable" bigotry lies in the academic field of psychology. In much of what practi-tioners choose to investigate and interpret, cognitive capacity, moral development and psychodynamic organization of lower-middle-class individuals are described as inferior to radical activities. Lower-middle-class people are more "authoritarian," more likely to have "closed" minds, more likely to rely on "law-and-order morality" rather than the more advanced "moral-principle orientation," and more likely to use "massive" ego-defenses such as repression instead of the more refined defenses like intellectualization and isolation. Lower-middle-class people are more likely to get stuck in a stage of "concrete cognitive opera-tions" associated with low capacity for intellectual differentiation instead of advancing into "formal cognitive operations" with its high capacity for abstract thinking.

When George Wallace said his opponent was the kind of man who couldn't park a bicycle straight, he undoubtedly confirmed for a host of academic observers how concrete and primitive his concept of success-ful intellectual operations was.

Students in elite universities are described by psychologists as possessing many of the virtues that lower-middle-class authoritarians lack. These scholars frequently find that, among the elite students, radical activists have even greater moral and intellectual virtues than classmates from lower-class or more traditional families. If you examine the incidence of these virtues, they appear, not surprisingly, to cluster. It seems that psychologists are measuring something that has connected cognitive, moral and ego-defensive manifestations. This something is related to class.

The academic yardsticks measure virtues that, as they are defined, appear most frequently in the children of elite psychologists and their classmates: in the children of the upper middle and upper class.

These virtues do seem to be the consequence of further (although not necessarily higher) development than the virtues of the lower middle class; that is, one must go through the developmentally prior lower-middle-class virtues to reach the elite virtues. Repression, obedience to law and prompt acceptance of authority are more "primitive" ways of dealing with reality than intellectualization, reflection on principles before obeying a law, and skepticism toward authority. One psychologist has urged that upper-class virtues are better in a Platonic sense than lower-middle-class virtues. It is revealing that he does not recall Plato would undoubtedly have restricted the practice of upper-class virtues to the upper class in his city, arguing that in the interest of harmony other virtues must be required of the lower classes.

Should we believe that the psychologists have discovered an empirical basis for distinguishing between more and less developed men? Should we believe that the developed men are superior? We can start with two broad possibilities. Either "further development" is the artifact of class blindness, and upper-class development is merely different from lower-class development; or upper-class development is subsequent to lower-class development. I think the weight of the argument suggests the latter.

If we opt for this possibility, we must then ask whether the further development is an achievement or a degeneration. Since this depends on our societal values, further choice is required: we can either compare directly the values of the further developed individual with the formal societal values or we can ask whether the survival of the formal societal values is enhanced by increasing the number of people whose personal values are similar to the formal values of the society.

This question forces us to be more specific about what we mean by the superiority of elite virtues in comparison with the virtues of the lower middle class. Recent analysts, lacking Plato's grasp of behavioral data and his rigorous empiricism, have been unrealistically idealistic in considering the consequences of changing a class distribution of virtues. That elite virtues are superior, Plato saw, does not mean that the society would be better or would even survive if all possessed them.

It may be that the lower-middle-class virtues provide operant support for a society that allows the upper class the luxury of elite virtues, much as Greek democracy was built on slave labor. I stress "operant support for American society" rather than "formal support of democracy" because the lower middle class is frequently denounced for disregarding formal democratic values such as regard for due process and for such freedoms as conscience, press, expression and movement.

Those who acclaim the elite radical virtues as superior to the virtues of the lower middle class would appear, if one admits that lower-class virtues provide operant support for American society, to have three alternatives. They can accept the distribution as necessary and good, in which case they espouse a troublesome elitism that cannot be reconciled with their radical views. Or they can argue that everyone should possess these virtues, in which case they are true radicals and should ask themselves whether they have considered in an unbiased light the implications of this position. Or they can do what I think most people do, which is largely to restrict—without admitting or even being conscious of the restriction—the practice of these superior virtues to the upper class.

The self-serving argument for upper-class hegemony then seems to be that the upper class is more intelligent, more moral and more finely tuned in its ego-defenses than the lower class and that this makes it more fit to govern and to preserve such democratic values as equal access. But in the name of the preservation of these values, elite virtues must be denied to the lower class because their use would be disruptive. To preserve the society that guarantees access to power to those who are virtuous, we must deny the possession of virtue to the lower class and thus deny the access we are theoretically preserving.

Leaving aside the hard choices that a believer in the superiority of radical virtues must make, we can ask in broader perspective what alternative stances one may take if it is true that an upper-class background leads to further moral and intellectual development. They appear to be—

1. In the existing world a "further developed" man may govern worse rather than better. A principled orientation can be disastrous in world politics, as the principled architects of the cold war have shown. An ability to empathize may lead to concessions in negotiation that will be misread by the Other Side as blanket willingness to retreat when faced with force. Capacity to see issues in all their complexity may lead to Hamlet-like paralysis when any action would be preferable to none.

2. The further development of the upper class might make it best qualified to rule, as its *de facto* supremacy proves. In a roughly democratic framework there is a chance for the few lower-class individuals who achieve upper-class virtues to rise to the top; that most leaders will be upper-class by birth is necessary and even desirable to preserve

social stability and to reduce the anxieties that result from situations of volatile status change.

3. Upper-class individuals are further developed than lower-class individuals, and it is an indictment of our resource-rich society that more people are not brought into these higher stages of development. Analyses claiming that this would destabilize society are too contingent to win credence; the destabilization, moreover, might result in a better society instead of a worse one.

4. This "further development" is development along a path that may lead to the overspecialization and extinction of the human race. It accepts the dubious values of a capitalist Calvinism and conceals assumptions about what constitutes higher development that are disastrous both for the individual and the species (and are rejected by the hippie culture). This building up of surplus repression in ever higher capacities for intellectualization destroys capacities for feeling, for activity, for love. Elephantiasis of intellect and atrophy of emotion are mirrored in American society, where our intellectual industry, technology, produces the anti-ballistic missile and the death-dealing gadgetry of Vietnam while our feelings are too atrophied to insist that the logic of our priorities is insane. There is the atrophy of individual sensation inherent in eating Wonder Bread, watching Johnny Carson, and smelling Right Guard.

These are a few of the attitude-policy alternatives that acceptance of the psychologists' findings could lead us to. The third and fourth arguments, which would appeal to liberals and radicals to varying degrees, have in common a disregard for the contributions of the lower-middle-class virtues to what is good as well as what is bad in American society. Let us now ask whether this disregard is based on close analysis of what American society would look like if we all possessed the "superior" elite values, or whether it is the result of an upper-class blindness toward what this might mean.

Operant supports of American society, conservatives and radicals agree, are very different from the formal democratic virtues that guarantee the procedures of a democratic policy. In the course of a brilliant denunciation of some mandarinic American political scientists, Noam Chomsky quotes Tocqueville: "I know of no country in which there is so little independence and freedom of mind as in America." Chomsky adds: "Free institutions certainly exist, but a tradition of passivity and conformism restricts their use—a cynic might say this is why they continue to exist."

Although radicals often condemn American society by juxtaposing the "traditional American virtues" of respect for democratic procedure with current breaches of those procedures, it seems probable that historically American justice was at least as pockmarked as it is today and that the lower-middle-class virtues are the real "traditional" supports that Tocqueville observed when he came to see how American democracy functioned.

These virtues—law-and-order morality, acceptance of authority, cognitive processes that present issues in broad terms, ego-defenses that prefer the violence of hockey to the savagery of the seminar table—undoubtedly play a part in whatever orderliness there is in daily American life. They help people accept and carry out decisions that affect them adversely. They help make football a high-salience issue and foreign affairs a low-salience issue, leaving the President, who should be in a better position to decide, a good deal of freedom from mass pressures. In a number of ways, one could argue, they account for what is good as well as bad in American life. Conversely, elite virtues may account for more of the bad aspects of American life than is usually assumed.

Some upper-class radicals, we suggested above, are able to assume that elite virtues are preferable to lower-middle-class virtues across the board because they unconsciously restrict their idea of who should practice these virtues and to what end. Radical students and ghetto blacks, within limits, are the groups from whom these people expect a moral-principle orientation rather than law-and-order morality. Blacks and students are expected to practice skepticism toward authority. If, on the other hand, the colonels, the police, teamsters, longshoremen or garbage collectors practice prolonged skepticism toward constituted authority or act in accordance with their principles rather than in accordance with law-and-order morality, then the elite semiradicals have a vague sense that something must be done.

The upper class has reached a plateau of security from which its liberal-radical wing believes that it can mock the politics of the policeman and the butcher and slight their aspirations while still living genteelly in the space between them. I recall a personal example of how these assumptions sometimes work:

A few months ago some black children from the ghetto that is separated from Yale by the old people and students on my street made one of their biannual pilgrimages to Lake Place to break off all the aerials and windshield wipers on the cars. I was much more enraged the next morning about my car than I was about the distant and understandable riots that are filtered to me through the New York *Times*. I called the police largely, I suspect, because I wanted to be comforted by a typical policeman's observations on what-you-can-expect-from-*those*-kids. In my protected Eastern existence I had never passed through an overtly racist stage. But sometimes I suspect I get satisfaction from the racism of others: they can say what I cannot even think, and since their racism is so vulgar, I get to feel superior to them in the bargain.

The policeman, a likely young Italian, arrived. After surveying the damage, he said: "Mr. Lerner, I know how you feel; but you've got to take into account the kind of environment in which those children were raised. I mean, if you or I lived in the places they have to live in or went through the same experiences, you can imagine. . . ." I listened stunned. Here the man from whom I expected law-and-order morality was dishing out the moral-principled upper-class capacity to imagine oneself in the situation of the other. Like that of the unconsciously hypocritical radicals, my world depended on that kind of behavior being reserved for cocktail parties and seminars at which one comments from a discreet distance on the understandability of the behavior of ghetto blacks.

The hatreds do not go one way: ghetto blacks hate policemen, and policemen hate upper-class radicals. One hates one class up as well as one class down, although the hatred downward is more violent and the hatred upward mixed with aspiration. The natural alliance is between people a class apart who hate people in the middle for different reasons. This suggests why elite intellectuals, for all their analyzed self-awareness, show immediate "understanding" for the ghetto black's hatred of the policeman yet find police violence directed at a partially upper-class political demonstration a sure sign of incipient fascism.

Examine, on the other hand, the quality of the class-apart empathy radical whites have for ghetto blacks. The radicals are upper-middle-class youths with life histories of intellectual overcontrol. They have reached a point in their lives where, as Erik Erikson suggests, they can experiment with a little controlled regression-in-the-service-of-the-ego.

The response of a permissive upper-class parent, as reflected in the New York *Times*, is, "Society may have a great deal to learn from the hippies." Translated into jargon this might read: "Upper-class psychological controls may be too strict for changing psychosexual-social-historical realities. The young people experimenting with controlled regression may be showing the way in politics, drugs and sex to a new synthesis."

From the point of view of the young people *doing* the experimenting, the value is diminished if anyone stresses the "controlled" or even experimental nature of their quest. The regression or the liberation from overcontrol is what matters. To them the lowest class shows—by fact or projective romanticization or both—a lifestyle characterized by open use of the violence, sexuality and drugs that the experimenters find appealing.

The authenticity that the experimenters sense in the ghetto derives from the fact that lower-class violence and sexuality are not a consequence of tentative and strained regression in the service of the ego but represent a normal and stable class pattern deriving from social conditions, tension levels and prevalent primitive ego-defense organizations.

When elite intellectuals urge that authentic black life-styles not be contaminated by bourgeois values, they are asking that blacks not lose temporarily the values whites lost temporarily in the process of becoming elite. In other words, the old path is from lower-class undercontrol to lower-middle-class overcontrol to the upper-class luxury of reducing controls again. Upper-class whites like to think blacks can move from undercontrol to the partial control pattern that *they* find most socially pleasing without the middle step. They do not realize partial control is usually a step taken from the strength of a background of increasingly sophisticated and differentiated overcontrol.

This self-centeredness is reflected in the programs organized for the education of blacks by upper-class whites and by blacks who have assumed university values. These programs usually stress a freedom and lack of controls that is appropriate to the fantasies of their organizers but scarcely appropriate to those who have only had ghetto experience. It is no wonder that programs organized by lower-class blacks without the funding and guidance of whites—such as the Black Muslim program for narcotics addicts, and Black Muslim educational programs in general—stress that ghetto people must learn the capacity for tight control that has characterized Mayor Daley and every other individual and group that has competed successfully in American society.

Since lower-middle-class police are repelled by the uncontrolledness of the lower class from which their families have escaped, they are understandably infuriated by the regression to violence, drugs and sexuality in the class that expects their deference. The radical students and hippies are rejecting the values to which the lower middle class aspires and by which it is able to repress the behavior that the students are flaunting at it. When a Yippie girl pulls up her skirt in front of a lower-middle-class policeman and tells him that his trouble is that he has not had what she is baring in front of his face, one cannot expect an academically oriented response. And since every cocktail party psychologist would expect the police to be authoritarian, low in capacity for differentiation and scarcely able to maintain through primitive repression the violence in himself, why is the reaction to the police riot in Chicago so unbelievably un-understanding? Why do we expect that hippies and radicals and ghetto blacks can experiment with non-restraint while the police must be models of restraint? Why can so few empathize with the frustrations of lower-middle-class life that have led to Chicago, to George Wallace and ultimately to the Presidency of Richard Nixon? It is because of the really astounding bigotry and narrowness of a class that prides itself on ridding itself of racism and having a broad perspective. There is little broad perspective in the words of the *Times* columnist who wrote in shocked tones, "Those were *our* children on the streets of Chicago." That *Times* columnist and the hip radicals did not understand a nation that approved of the police action in Chicago because its children were in the streets of Chicago, too. Its children were the police.

Racism and bigotry toward black people is frighteningly apparent at Yale. But at least the sore has been lanced and lies open. We can be aware of the ugly strains of societal racism still inside ourselves and our institutions, and we can struggle against them.

The hidden, liberal-radical bigotry toward the lower middle class is stinking and covered. When a right-wing Italian announced for Mayor in New York, a brilliant professor in New Haven said, "If Italians aren't actually an inferior race, they do the best imitation of one I've seen." Everyone at the dinner table laughed. He could not have said that about black people if the subject had been Rap Brown.

The consequences of this bigotry are tragic. It would be less serious if it were not the product of an intellectually self-righteous class that is trying to provide functioning, *electable* alternatives to Richard Nixon and George Wallace. Those dissimilar men had the common intelligence and capacity for empathy—or shrewdness—to appeal to a genuinely forgotten and highly abused segment of the American population. It may be that only when radical intellectuals begin to show again, as they did in the 1930s, empathy for the hardships of lower-middle-class life and begin to integrate the aspirations of that class into their antiwar, antiracism framework, will it be possible to break up the Nixon alliance. Not until the upper middle class learns to deal with its own hidden bigotry will it be in a position to help destroy lower-middle-class bigotry as well.

NOTE:
The terms "radical," "semiradical," "left-liberal" and "liberal-to-radical" are used in reference to "elite," "upper class" and "upper-middle-class" students to refer to a broad but splintered and diverse group of people.

M. L.

MI-
NORI-
TIES

peter i. rose

In recent years our country has witnessed an unprecedented series of challenges to time-worn traditions. Most blatant, and undoubtedly most important, is the challenge to the institutionalized patterns of discrimination that have kept certain large groups of citizens from full or even partial enjoyment of everyman's right to "life, liberty and the pursuit of happiness."

Most dramatic and widespread of all the new liberation movements is the Black Power Revolt, the culmination of years of struggle in which pride and protest finally have been joined into a powerful force with widespread political, social, and psychological effects. Indeed, for millions of people called "Negroes" it has become a time to be black.

The background of the struggle and the special problems faced by black Americans are outlined in the following article written by the editor of this volume.

History is often written in terms of the images people, or peoples, wish to project. American history, for example, was long recounted as if the English, Scottish, Irish, Welsh Protestants— and a few Dutchmen—were the only ones to have had an impact on the growth and development of the country.

Reprinted with permission from the *Social Science Quarterly*, 50 (September 1969), 286–297.

Red, White, Blue—and Black

Early books and classroom lectures dealt almost exclusively with the "Anglo-American Tradition" or "Our Christian Heritage." Throughout most of the eighteenth and nineteenth centuries, newcomers from Northwestern Europe (whom Fletcher Knebel has recently named the "out-WASPS") were encouraged to forget about the customs of Germany or Scandinavia and to adapt themselves to those eminently superior *American* lifeways. Other immigrants were most often considered beyond the pale of social acceptance. In story and song the Irish Catholics, the Poles, the Italians, and the Russian Jews—to say nothing about those who came from China or Japan—were referred to as "unassimilable aliens." Many politicians expressed serious doubts about whether such immigrants would ever have the makings of real Americans. Many noted social scientists went so far as to endorse the Dillingham Commission Reports and the restrictive legislation of the 1920's.

In time, most scholars changed their views, and their histories changed as well. Pluralism became *en vogue* and school children and college students were then told that "our differences make us strong," that "America is a multiplicity in a unity," or, as John Dewey once said, in this country "the hyphen connects instead of separates." It even became fashionable to teach about the "Judaeo-Christian Heritage" and to consider Catholics as Christians, too. Indeed, as if to bear public witness to such a revisionist view, the single Protestant preacher who had always intoned opening prayers at official gatherings was supplanted by a ubiquitous triumvirate: minister, priest, and rabbi, representatives of "our three great religions." (Sociologists even gave expression to this new phenomenon and America became known, at least in the parlance of the classroom, as a "triple melting pot.")

And now it is time to include yet another figure on the dais—and to add another "culture" to the heritage. Behavior rises to meet expectations and the behavior of academic historians and social scientists seems no exception. Today the bookstores are flooded with a thousand volumes on "the Negro problem." The problem isn't new. It is as old as America. But, worried about the future, we have once again begun to look at—and, to some extent—to rewrite the past.

The textbooks being prepared for the 1970's will indicate that there is much more to "Black History" than the slave blocks, the Old Plantation, Emancipation and the grateful darkies, Freedmen's Bureaus, the Hayes-Tilden Compromise, Plessy *vs.* Ferguson, Booker T. Washington, race riots during the two world wars, Marian Anderson, Jackie Robinson, Ralph Bunche, Thurgood Marshall, and the Supreme Court Decision of 1954. Rather, to judge by the advertising copy of the books already under preparation, they will dwell on the role played by black Americans who, "under the most adverse conditions, fought and died to gain their own freedom" and who (paradoxically it seems) "were enlisted in every major battle to save this Republic."

The new texts will continue to tell a story of life in the ante-bellum South, but the readers will learn that things were not so tranquil beneath the mimosa trees, that not all Negroes sought to emulate the ways of their masters and that none ever had good relations with them ("no matter what the romantics say"). They will also learn that black men didn't really move "north to freedom" but exchanged one kind of hell for another.

As more and more new histories appear, a far different picture of black Americans will emerge. And it will not be limited to the celebration of the martyrdom of Crispus Attucks (the Negro's Colin Kelly) or, say, to the achievements of George Washington Carver (the black Jonas Salk). The new books will include discussions of black soldiers who fought in the Union Army; they will tell of black politicians in the turbulent days of Reconstruction; they will praise the black cowboys who helped to open the West, the black troopers who rode with Teddy Roosevelt in our first Cuban adventure, the black workers who toiled along the railbeds and in the factories and on the farms. Some will go farther, too, extolling the virtues of blackness and the solidarity of "soul" and exposing the pallid character of "white culture" in contrast to "black."

The motivation for this latest attempt at re-examining American history and giving the Negro an honored place along with other "minorities" has come about as an off-shoot of the civil rights movement and the campaign to eliminate segregation.

Feeling that many of the hard-won victories of the 1950's and 1960's have not made that much difference, angry black spokesmen have begun to challenge a number of basic assumptions of the reform-minded civil rights advocates. First, they argue, liberal white leaders (whatever they wanted personally) could rarely offer much more than palliatives which, often as not, were viewed as programs to keep "their" cities from erupting rather than being expressly designed to help poor blacks. Second, they say that traditional Negro leaders have never been much better. They were either out of touch with the people for whom they claimed to speak (as many felt about the late Dr. King) or were too willing to play the "Establishment Game" (as was often said of Roy Wilkins). Arguing that their people have always been deluded by whites who had taken up the "burden" and Negroes who were trying to lighten it, the new militants wanted to turn them "blackwards," wanted them to have an identity which was truly their own. They began their campaign by excoriating white liberals, "Uncle Toms" and especially "Honkie Society." They are carrying it forward with appeals to black nationalism. They may end up by making (and, in some cases, making up) history itself.

Of course, since no group has a monopoly on ethnocentrism, it should not be surprising to find that many of the new views of Black History will be similar to most paeans to a cloudy past: compilations of vague memories which have become legends, of vague legends which have become memories, of isolated incidents swelled to monumental significance, and a good deal of hard evidence of what actually happened and, for any number of reasons, has been overlooked or purposely ignored. The history of Afro-Americans, like that of those from Europe, is almost by necessity going to turn out to be a potpourri of fancy and fact. What makes it different is that it has to serve a double function of helping to strengthen communal ties among blacks while, simultaneously, having other Americans learn that those who came from Africa also had a noble past and are a proud people.

To tell it like it really was is a difficult and frustrating task. It is difficult because there is so little data that is untainted by the biases and romanticisims of those who captured the oral tradition or the written record; it is frustrating because even the sketchy story that does emerge is so terribly ambiguous—ambiguous not in terms of the patterns of oppression so much as their effects upon the oppressed. But one thing is fairly clear: much of the old heritage was replaced by a new orientation. Western ways and southern values were absorbed and, for good or ill, countless thousands of black Africans became Negroes.

W. E. B. DuBois once suggested that "There is nothing so indigenous, so made in America, as me." And yet, as is too well known, few Negroes came to enjoy the freedoms that other Americans take for granted. Few ever got away from the stigma attached to the color of their skins. As DuBois and others repeatedly pointed out, every Negro child has always asked "Who am I?" "What am I?"

Self, Segregation, and Soul

Not very long ago, James Baldwin wrote an essay entitled "Nobody Knows My Name."[2] In a sense, it dealt with only half of the problem. White people didn't know what to call him and *he didn't know himself*. Baldwin's people—variously called blacks, coloreds, Negroes, and blacks again—had little to look forward to and even less to look back upon, or so it seemed.

Still, saying they had little is not to say they had nothing. There is such a thing as Afro-American culture and every black person in this country knows it. Like all cultures it is made up of many things—memories and moods and myths. What makes it different is that the memories and moods and even the myths "remembered" are unique: slavery and its aftermath; spiritual uplift and over-Jordan imagery;[3] continued subjugation by those who claimed and repeatedly tried to prove that "white" was always right.

Against (and, in some ways, in response to) these debilitating aspects there was resilience, richness and romance. The Negro world had (and has) its cuisine (now called "soul food"), its old-time religion, its rules of conduct, its lingo, its literature, its sound. Those who now study the black experience in America contend that it has left Negroes with different conceptions of time and space and property—and life. (Today, it is even fashionable in certain liberal circles to celebrate the unique characteristics of Negro people in this country. A mere five years ago such contentions, traditionally made by many segregationists, would have been called "racist" by the very same liberals—and by many Negro leaders, too.)

Resistance was another matter. Being frozen into the rigidity of a caste system and unable to become full partners in the society from which so many of their own customs, beliefs, and values were derived, black people often lacked the organizational apparatus characteristic of that possessed by other ethnic groups in America—the very groups to which black Americans have long been compared and, perhaps more significantly, to which they have often compared themselves. For years they talked about organizing and fighting their tormentors, but faced with retribution from large institutions and powerful men, they usually had no recourse but to adapt themselves to the system which kept them in servitude.

Segregation kept the Negro humble, and sometimes his own leaders in their innocence often aided and abetted the Man. Both spoke of their children, both tended their "flocks." (Of course, not all white men and not all leaders of Negroes acted in such a manner. But the point is that *these* were the most significant role models available for the vast majority of black people, especially in the Old South.)

There is an obvious parallel to be drawn to the plight of the Negroes in this country and those of mental patients. Some psychiatrists have recently reintroduced the notion of reality therapy. Crudely described, reality therapy is a technique used to shock patients into the realization that, yes, the world is cruel and if they are going to make it, they are going to have to do more than play out the sick role which "enlightened doctrine" has ascribed to them and which, quite understandably, they have internalized. For years now, few well-educated people have said that blacks are innately inferior; they know better. Rather the conventional wisdom sounds strikingly like that of the old planters and ministers of God. Saying, "only we know what's good for them," many social workers and school teachers have held to this view to the present day. Disadvantaged black people are viewed and treated as victims or patients or some sort of unfortunates in need of care and succor. And many Negroes, in turn, like the inmates of one asylum after another, have long been internalizing the roles ascribed to them and have acted accordingly.

This is not to say that most Negroes are (or ever were) simple "Sambos." But many did and continue to learn to act out the stereotypes others have held of them and many, even in putting the white man down by seeming to play along, came to believe—in spite of themselves— that they are in fact inferior. The late Malcolm X understood; he said, "the worst crime the white man has committed is teaching us to hate ourselves."[4]

Perhaps one can understand the bitterness of those who now claim to speak for the Negro, those who say there has really been no progress, only expanded "welfare colonialism." And one should be able to understand why young black radicals choke on that noblest of all words in the lexicon of human relationists: "brotherhood." Brotherhood, to too many, has meant: when you become like me, then we'll be as one. They have a point. Time and again Negroes have found there was always one more river to cross; white people would offer the boats if the black rowers didn't rock them too hard.

What a choice for a potential leader. Tell your people to remain supplicants in the hopes that someday the white man would overcome his prejudices, lower the barriers and welcome you into his big *white* house; or become a firebrand in the hopes that you might force his capitulation. And once having made the decision, where were you usually left? Dead on the inside or dead all around.

It is no wonder that the civil rights movement itself was always whitewardly oriented—no matter what is being said about it today. To solve the dilemma of supplication *vs.* rebellion, most efforts to redress the grievances of the past have been channeled into campaigns for integration (not quite supplication and not quite rebellion). Most black people, it seems, wanted to give the impression (and many actually wanted to believe) that, someday, somehow, color would really be overlooked. And those the angriest black spokesmen hold in contempt today—the white liberals[5]—helped to perpetuate this myth without, for the most part, realizing what they were doing and without having very much personal contact with those they claimed to accept as equals.

Attention has been focused on "most" Negroes, and "many" Negroes, but not all. There are those who have made it; some by the very same techniques used by other members of minority groups including the exploitation of those whose identity they share; some by becoming athletes and soul singers and jazz musicians performing for both their own and the wider community; some—undoubtedly the largest group—by sheer determination to overcome the barriers of segregation, often by entering government service as postmen and clerks, secretaries and soldiers, and, of course, as teachers, and working their way up. Together, these members of what have come to be called the "black bourgeoisie" and the "colored entertainers" and the "Negro respectables" represent to white folks (especially middle-class whites)living evidence that black people can make it if they try hard enough and are willing to thicken their skins (often fairly light skins) to whatever abuses the "system" and its agents mete out. Perhaps. It is true that many such people have prided themselves on their progress and, for all their difficulties, have seemed quite stable, even happy in American society, the essence of middle-class respectability: friendly, hardworking, religious and, often, community-minded.

Many of their children who are now in college think differently. They, and not just the poor people in Watts, know what a Ron Karenga means when he decries, "There are only three kinds of people in this country: white people, black people, and Negroes. Negroes? They are black people that act like white people."[6]

The message isn't lost. Those Negro college students, particularly at northern schools and the larger southern ones, know that part of Karenga's rhetoric is addressed to them and concerns their parents. ("Which side are *you* on?") Those who have suffered least from the stigma of color are beginning to suffer the most. Many are reacting by forming Afro-American organizations on the campus and by going "home" to Harlem or Hattiesburg to work and teach and organize. Some, to resolve their race/class schizophrenia, have begun to join the ranks of the most militant members of the black community and to provide the copy for the spokesman and the plans for the revolution. Stressing both poverty and race, the disorganized "black lumpen" have become their cause. With the poor, one can put to use some of the direct and fringe benefits of a college education. And for them one can try to offer a new and different view of the Americans who come from Africa.

The Past, the Present, and the Future

The young black militants are, as one said recently, "a new breed of cat." They see themselves as the vanguard of a movement to erase once and forever the stigma imposed by white slave masters and perpetuated by segregationists over the last hundred years. They want everyone— parents and peers, white liberals and conservatives—to know that times have changed and that they are black *men* not black *boys*. Often using the future as a guide to the past, they have called for a new view of the Black Experience, one in which "the real truth about black people will finally be known."

In response to mounting pressure, colleges and universities (and some public schools) have introduced Afro-American programs and curricular innovations geared to the special needs of black students. From amongst the welter of proposals and pronouncements requesting (or, more often, demanding) such programs, one message has come across loud and clear: "We will be *Negroes* no more."

This mood, its strategy and its rhetorical style, has signaled the end of an old era and the beginning of a new phase in black-white relations in the United States. In many ways, with the benefit of hindsight, one can say it was inevitable that such a shift in character and focus and leadership should come to pass.

The new ideology is a culmination of years of struggle and crisis during which black people were trying to come to grips with their unique problems and their constantly thwarted desires to become full-fledged Americans.

Among the various techniques of protest, two types of action were most prevalent from the time of emancipation to its centennial. One centered on Negroes themselves and was concerned with "uplift": the learning of useful skills, the instilling of pride in self and neighbor, and of such Puritan virtues as thrift and practicality. The other focused on integration and the gaining of civil rights. In the first instance, the underlying notion seemed to be that black people would show the white man that they were responsible, upright and talented citizens and that, in time, they would be ready to take their place beside anyone. In the latter, the argument was that the problem was not the Negro's but the white man's and *he* should be made to change. Thus the seeds were sown.

Booker T. Washington was the best known advocate of the uplift philosophy. At Tuskegee Institute, which he founded, he put into practice his bootstrap operation. A generation later a West Indian, Marcus Garvey, was to turn Washington's accommodationism into strident black nationalism. But with all the fervor and pageantry, Garvey, like Washington, exhorted his followers to prove to the world that black men were truly respectable. In time those who were to lead the many mosques of the Temple of Islam were to go beyond even Garvey, claiming black supremacy and rejecting Christianity. Yet, even the Black Muslims could not and did not reject the Puritan values. On the contrary, they built them into the basic credo of everyday life.

The reaction against Washington's accommodationist plans were publicly voiced by but a few Negro leaders. Two who did speak out were Monroe Trotter and W. E. B. DuBois. DuBois was one of the founders of the integrated and, for its time, militant National Association for the Advancement of Colored People. In time, other alphabetical labels were to be added to that of the NAACP: CORE, SCLC, SNCC, each one more militant, more "engaged" than the one before. Still, until 1964, most of those who followed the banner of INTEGRATION were possessed with a sense of mission that would ultimately culminate in that grand day, the Golden Jubilee, when color would not matter any longer, when the Dream of the Reverend Dr. Martin Luther King and a thousand other Negro preachers would no longer have to be deferred. "Free at last," they would cry out, "Free at last." "Lord, God Almighty, we're free at last."

Black Power

By the time of Emancipation's Centennial (and, for some, before), it was quite evident to many outside observers and to many of the field workers that neither apolitical blackwardness nor soulless militance could turn the tide of racism, so deep did it flow.[7] Since there was little likelihood that they could really go it alone and even less that they could (or would) ever "turn white," those called Negroes were going to have to learn (or to relearn) sooner or later that to make it, they had to take pride in themselves *and* become politicized. They had to harken to what Frederick Douglass had prescribed a hundred years before the Student Non-Violent Coordinating Committee was born. Said Douglass,

> Those who profess to favor freedom yet deprecate agitation are men who want crops without plowing up the ground; they want rain without thunder and lightning. They want the ocean without the awful roar of its many waters. . . . Power concedes nothing without demand. It never did and it never will. Find out just what any people will quietly submit to and you have found out the exact measure of injustice and wrong which will be imposed upon them, and these will continue till they are resisted with either words or blows, or with both. The limits of tyrants are prescribed by the endurance of those whom they oppress.[8]

And "Black Power" did, in fact, begin as a movement of words, impassioned words exhorting poor sharecroppers to get out and exercise their franchise. But this was not enough. Intimidation and threats raised the ire of the civil rights workers and turned many black pacifists into soldiers while turning away many white allies. The code of Thoreau and Gandhi was being replaced by the law of Hammurabi—much as Frederick Douglass had suggested.

For years, Negro leaders and their white allies had counseled patience and fortitude. Until quite recently their authority went unchallenged for it was widely felt that the liberal integrationists (black and white) were on the right path. The civil rights campaign in the late 1950's and the early 1960's, and the bills passed by Congress in their wake, seemed, to some at least, positive proof of the efficacy of non-violent direct action. But, as many of the victories proved pyrrhic, as tensions mounted between black field workers who saw radical pacifism as a tactic and whites for whom it was a way of life, as the Viet Nam war syphoned off funds that (it was said) would have been earmarked for ghetto reconstruction, and most of all, as the relative deprivation of black people became more apparent, the climate shifted. The movement went sour and the old coalitions began to break apart.

Unquestionably, the urban riots were an exacerbating factor, too. Many whites who had begun to feel some sense of sympathy with the embattled civil rights workers, or, at least, were talking of "giving Negroes

their due," grew increasingly fearful—and hostile—as they saw the flames of Rochester and Watts and Detroit on their television sets or, in some cases, from their upstairs windows. Charges and counter charges, cries of duplicity on the one hand and corruption on the other, shouts of "Burn, Baby, Burn" and "Get the Honkies ' mixed with "Send them back to Africa." Frontlash. Blacklash. A litany of curses filled the air—and the airwaves.

Given the disillusionment and the fear, the persistence of institutionalized segregation and, especially, given the fact that little was being done to satisfy those poorest blacks whose expectations had suddenly begun to rise, it is little wonder that the hymn, "We Shall Overcome" was replaced—literally and figuratively—with "Black Power."

The new mood began to reach out and develop the unorganized masses of Negroes, particularly in the northern ghettoes where few meaningful communal institutions existed around which people could rally and where even the oratory of the Reverend Martin Luther King could not arouse. The focus began to shift, too, away from integration and toward the more basic matter of "getting it together."

In the early 1920's, E. Franklin Frazier had said that "if the masses of Negroes can save their self respect and remain free of hate, so much the better. But . . . I believe, it would be better for the Negro's soul to be seared with hate than dwarfed by self abasement. . . ."[9] Again it was being argued that there is a psycho-social need for black people to call "the Man" to task rather than accepting the internalizing second-class status and all it means. As William H. Grier and Price Cobbs have recently shown, there has long been (and remains) an almost desperate need to find a sense of positive selfhood and of meaningful peoplehood, too.[10]

To accomplish this has meant that the leadership would have to change as well. And it did. Whites had to be eased or pushed out of positions of dominance to make room for those who could more easily identify with, and be identified with, the black masses. And the new leaders had to prove to their followers that black was the symbol of "light" at the end of their tunnel.

As Black Panthers gained a certain amount of notoriety, those in the "traditional organizations" changed too. SNCC became more militant. CORE turned away from its original stance of integration in favor of black consciousness. The Urban League and the NAACP sounded more militant even while trying to assuage the anxiety of white liberals who did not understand what was happening. The Southern Christian Leadership Conference continued fighting its battles for jobs and freedom, but also began forming uneasy coalitions with other embattled minority groups. Despite many differences in symbol (the clenched fist or the double bar of "equality"), in slogan, and in style, pride and protest were joined and, for many, it had become a time to be black.

It is becoming more and more difficult to predict what will happen on the racial front in the coming years than it was a few years ago. Then, the past was used as a fairly accurate guide to the future and the predictions made were based on a critical assessment of the data available to anyone bothering to sift through it. Among the evidence was a pretty clear picture that few white people were about to support any efforts to effect changes unless they were pressured into it. In celebrating the passage of the Civil Rights Acts of 1960, 1964, 1965, and even of 1968, it is easy to forget that these victories were the results of protest marches, boycotts, demonstrations and threats of disruption. Such activities, it seems, did more to bring about changes in the status quo than all the pious platitudes from segregated pulpits or the admonitions of the specialists in urban affairs and poverty.

The federal government dedicated to opening New Frontiers and making a Great Society, and dedicated to waging war on poverty, got itself so bogged down in Viet Nam that it could offer only monumental legislation and modest programs for carrying it out—programs offered to show good faith but construed by many as being proof of continued tokenism and contributing to the overall "minus-sum game," as Aaron Wildavsky has called it.

Minus-sum games are those, he says, in which every player leaves the contest worse off than when he entered.

> Promise a lot; deliver a little. . . . Lead people to believe they will be much better off, but let there be no dramatic improvement. . . . Have middle-class civil servants hire upper-class student radicals to use lower-class Negroes as a battering ram against the existing political systems; then complain that people are going around disrupting things and chastise local politicians for not cooperating with those out to do them in. . . . Feel guilty about what has happened to black people; tell them you are surprised they have not revolted before; express shock and dismay when they follow your advice."[11]

And so forth.

Those who warned about the dangers of such "games" were often told that the problem was being exaggerated or that they were "nervous Nellies" inadvertently disrupting the cause of civil rights by trying to keep everybody's expectations within certain realistic bounds. And now many other voices have been added to those who decry the sociologists and the behaviorally-oriented political scientists for their reluctance to take more radical stands.

The entry of large numbers of such spokesmen—mounting the stumps from Harlem to Watts and the campus stages from Boston to Berkeley, and writing in old Negro papers and the new black ones—has brought about many changes in the "Black Mood" and the "Black Movement." The crystal balls are far cloudier ("Whitey doesn't know what we're going to do next"—and he doesn't) and the emanations from the computers are consequently less reliable. Given what was known before, the "Black Power" movement was an almost inevitable next stage for those who were called "darker Brethren" and treated like hired hands by most Americans.

Now that many black Americans themselves have begun to question the way their past has been handled, and now that they have begun to claim that no white man can ever speak for *them*, it is difficult for anyone, black or white, to separate fancy from fact. But perhaps this is the way it has to be.

NOTES

1. Another version of this paper appears as the introduction to *Americans from Africa*, ed. by Peter I. Rose, New York: The Atherton Press, 1970.
2. James Baldwin, *Nobody Knows My Name: More Notes of a Native Son* (New York: Dial Press, 1961).
3. See, for example, James Baldwin, *Go Tell It on the Mountain* (New York: Alfred A. Knopf, 1952).
4. *The Autobiography of Malcolm X* (New York: Grove Press, 1964).
5. See, for example, Eldridge Cleaver, *Soul on Ice* (New York: McGraw-Hill, 1968), p. 46.
6. This sentiment was expressed by Ron Karenga at a Human Rights Conference at Brotherhood-in-Action, New York, May 5, 1967.
7. James Farmer, *Freedom, When?* (New York: Random House, 1965); and Stokely Carmichael and Charles V. Hamilton, *Black Power: The Politics of Liberation in America* (New York: Vintage, 1967).
8. The quotation is from a West Indian Emancipation Speech delivered by Douglass in 1857. It appears in Carmichael and Hamilton, *Black Power*, p. x.
9. This is also expressed most poignantly by Richard Wright. See his "Foreword," in St. Clair Drake and Horace Cayton, *Black Metropolis* (New York: Harcourt, Brace and Company, 1945).
10. William H. Grier and Price M. Cobbs, *Black Rage* (New York: Basic Books, 1968), esp. pp. 152–167.
11. Aaaron Wildavsky, "Recipe for Violence," *New York*, 1 (May, 1968), pp. 28–36.

eldridge cleaver

One of the most outspoken leaders of the Black Panther Party is Eldridge Cleaver who, at this writing, lives in exile in Algeria. He is the author of several important volumes on the racial crisis in America, including *Soul on Ice*, a collection of essays written while he was in prison on a murder charge.

Of all his essays, the one reprinted here offers the best summary of his and many other black men's views of American society. In the pig-Latin phrase, Cleaver is an "Ofay watcher." These are his observations on race relations and the future of our society.

White people cannot, in the generality, be taken as models of how to live. Rather, the white man is himself in sore need of new standards, which will release him from his confusion and place him once again in fruitful communion with the depths of his own being.

James Baldwin,
The Fire Next Time

Right from the go, let me make one thing absolutely clear: I am not now, nor have I ever been, a white man. Nor, I hasten to add, am I now a Black Muslim—although I used to be. But I *am* an Ofay Watcher, a member of that unchartered, amorphous league which has members on all continents and the islands of the seas.

Ofay Watchers Anonymous, we might be called, because we exist concealed in the shadows wherever colored people have known oppression by whites, by white enslavers, colonizers, imperialists, and neo-colonialists.

Did it irritate you, compatriot, for me to string those epithets out like that? Tolerate me. My intention was not necessarily to sprinkle salt over anyone's wounds. I did it primarily to relieve a certain pressure on my brain. Do you cop that? If not, then we're in trouble, because we Ofay Watchers have a pronounced tendency to slip into that mood. If it is bothersome to you, it is quite a task for me because not too long ago it was my way of life to preach, as ardently as I could, that the white race is a race of devils, created by their makers to do evil, and make evil appear as good; that the white race is the natural, unchangeable enemy of the black man, who is the original man, owner, maker, cream of the planet Earth; that the white race was soon to be destroyed by Allah, and that the black man would then inherit the earth, which has always, in fact, been his.

I have, so to speak, washed my hands in the blood of the martyr, Malcolm X, whose retreat from the precipice of madness created new room for others to turn about in, and I am now caught up in that tiny space, attempting a maneuver of my own. Having renounced the teachings of Elijah Muhammad, I find that a rebirth does not follow automatically, of its own accord, that a void is left in one's vision, and this void seeks constantly to obliterate itself by pulling one back to one's former outlook. I have tried a tentative compromise by adopting a select vocabulary, so that now when I see the whites of *their* eyes, instead of saying "devil" or "beast" I say "imperialist" or "colonialist," and everyone seems to be happier.

In silence, we have spent our years watching the ofays, trying to understand them, on the principle that you have a better chance coping with the known than with the unknown. Some of us have been, and some still are, interested in learning whether it is *ultimately* possible to live in the same territory with people who seem so disagreeable to live with; still others want to get as far away from ofays as possible. What we share in common is the desire to break the ofays' power over us.

At times of fundamental social change, such as the era in which we live, it is easy to be deceived by the onrush of events, beguiled by the craving for social stability into mistaking transitory phenomena for enduring reality. The strength and permanence of "white backlash" in America is just such an illusion. However much this rear-guard action might seem to grow in strength, the initiative, and the future, rest with those whites and blacks who have liberated themselves from the master/slave syndrome. And these are to be found mainly among the youth.

Over the past twelve years there has surfaced a political conflict between the generations that is deeper, even, than the struggle between the races. Its first dramatic manifestation was within the ranks of the Negro people, when college students in the South, fed up with Uncle Tom's hat-in-hand approach to revolution, threw off the yoke of the NAACP. When these students initiated the first sit-ins, their spirit spread like a raging fire across the nation, and the technique of nonviolent direct action, constantly refined and honed into a sharp cutting tool, swiftly matured. The older Negro "leaders," who are now all die-hard advocates of this tactic, scolded the students for sitting-in. The students rained down contempt upon their hoary heads. In the pre-sit-in days, these conservative leaders had always succeeded in putting down insurgent elements among the Negro people. (A measure of their power, prior to the students' rebellion, is shown by their success in isolating such great black men as the late W. E. B. DuBois and Paul Robeson, when these stalwarts, refusing to bite their tongues, lost favor with the U.S. government by their unstinting efforts to link up the Negro revolution with national liberation movements around the world.)

The "Negro leaders," and the whites who depended upon them to control their people, were outraged by the impudence of the students. Calling for a moratorium on student initiative, they were greeted instead by an encore of sit-ins, and retired to their ivory towers to contemplate the now phenomenon. Others, less prudent because held on a tighter leash by the whites, had their careers brought to an abrupt end because they thought they could lead a black/white backlash against the students, only to find themselves in a kind of Bay of Pigs. Negro college presidents, who expelled students from all-Negro colleges in an attempt to quash the demonstrations, ended up losing their jobs; the victorious students would no longer allow them to preside over the campuses. The spontaneous protests on southern campuses over the repressive measures of their college administrations were an earnest of the Free Speech upheaval which years later was to shake the UC campus at Berkeley. In countless ways, the rebellion of the black students served as catalyst for the brewing revolt of the whites.

What has suddenly happened is that the white race has lost its heroes. Worse, its heroes have been revealed as villains and its greatest heroes as the arch-villains. The new generations of whites, appalled by the sanguine and despicable record carved over the face of the globe by their race in the last five hundred years, are rejecting the panoply of white heroes, whose heroism consisted in erecting the inglorious edifice of colonialism and imperialism; heroes whose careers rested on a system of foreign and domestic exploitation, rooted in the myth of white supremacy and the manifest destiny of the white race. The emerging shape of a new world order, and the requisites for survival in such a world, are fostering in young whites a new outlook. They recoil in shame from the spectacle of cowboys and pioneers—their heroic forefathers whose exploits filled earlier generations with pride—galloping across a movie screen shooting down Indians like Coke bottles. Even Winston

Churchill, who is looked upon by older whites as perhaps the greatest hero of the twentieth century—even he, because of the system of which he was a creature and which he served, is an arch-villain in the eyes of the young white rebels.

At the close of World War Two, national liberation movements in the colonized world picked up new momentum and audacity, seeking to cash in on the democratic promises made by the Allies during the war. The Atlantic Charter, signed by President Roosevelt and Prime Minister Churchill in 1941, affirming "the right of all people to choose the form of government under which they may live," established the principle, although it took years of postwar struggle to give this piece of rhetoric even the appearance of reality. And just as world revolution has prompted the oppressed to re-evaluate their self-image in terms of the changing conditions, to slough off the servile attitudes inculcated by long years of subordination, the same dynamics of change have prompted the white people of the world to re-evaluate their self-image as well, to disabuse themselves of the Master Race psychology developed over centuries of imperial hegemony.

It is among the white youth of the world that the greatest change is taking place. It is they who are experiencing the great psychic pain of waking into consciousness to find their inherited heroes turned by events into villains. Communication and understanding between the older and younger generations of whites has entered a crisis. The elders, who, in the tradition of privileged classes or races, genuinely do not understand the youth, trapped by old ways of thinking and blind to the future, have only just begun to be vexed—because the youth have only just begun to rebel. So thoroughgoing is the revolution in the psyches of white youth that the traditional tolerance which every older generation has found it necessary to display is quickly exhausted, leaving a gulf of fear, hostility, mutual misunderstanding, and contempt.

The rebellion of the oppressed peoples of the world, along with the Negro revolution in America, have opened the way to a new evaluation of history, a re-examination of the role played by the white race since the beginning of European expansion. The positive achievements are also there in the record, and future generations will applaud them. But there can be no applause now, not while the master still holds the whip in his hand! Not even the master's own children can find it possible to applaud him—he cannot even applaud himself! The negative rings too loudly. Slave-catchers, slaveowners, murderers, butchers, invaders, oppressors —the white heroes have acquired new names. The great white statesmen whom school children are taught to revere are revealed as the architects of systems of human exploitation and slavery. Religious leaders are exposed as condoners and justifiers of all these evil deeds. Schoolteachers and college professors are seen as a clique of brainwashers and whitewashers.

The white youth of today are coming to see, intuitively, that to escape the onus of the history their fathers made they must face and admit the moral truth concerning the works of their fathers. That such venerated figures as George Washington and Thomas Jefferson owned hundreds of black slaves, that all of the Presidents up to Lincoln presided over a slave state, and that every President since Lincoln connived politically and cynically with the issues affecting the human rights and general welfare of the broad masses of the American people—these facts weigh heavily upon the hearts of these young people.

The elders do not like to give these youngsters credit for being able to understand what is going on and what has gone on. When speaking of juvenile delinquency, or the rebellious attitude to today's youth, the elders employ a glib rhetoric. They speak of the "alienation of youth," the desire of the young to be independent, the problems of "the father image" and "the mother image" and their effect upon growing children who lack sound models upon which to pattern themselves. But they consider it bad form to connect the problems of the youth with the central event of our era—the national liberation movements abroad and the Negro revolution at home. The foundations of authority have been blasted to bits in America because the whole society has been indicted, tried, and convicted of injustice. To the youth, the elders are Ugly Americans; to the elders, the youth have gone mad.

The rebellion of the white youth has gone through four broadly discernible stages. First there was an initial recoiling away, a rejection of the conformity which America expected, and had always received, sooner or later, from its youth. The disaffected youth were refusing to participate in the system, having discovered that America, far from helping the underdog, was up to its ears in the mud trying to hold the dog down. Because of the publicity and self-advertisements of the more vocal rebels, this period has come to be known as the beatnik era, although not all of the youth affected by these changes thought of themselves as beatniks. The howl of the beatniks and their scathing, outraged denunciation of the system—characterized by Ginsberg as Moloch, a bloodthirsty Semitic deity to which the ancient tribes sacrificed their firstborn children—was a serious, irrevocable declaration of war. It is revealing that the elders looked upon the beatniks as mere obscene misfits who were too lazy to take baths and too stingy to buy a haircut. The elders had eyes but couldn't see, ears but couldn't hear—not even when the message came through as clearly as in this remarkable passage from Jack Kerouac's *On the Road*:

> At lilac evening I walked with every muscle aching among the lights of 27th and Welton in the Denver colored section, wishing I were a Negro, feeling that the best the white world had offered was not enough ecstasy for me, not enough life, joy, kicks, darkness, music, not enough night. I wished I were a Denver Mexican, or even a poor overworked Jap, anything but what I so drearily was, a "white man" disillusioned. All my life I'd had white ambitions.

. . . I passed the dark porches of Mexican and Negro homes; soft voices were there, occasionally the dusky knee of some mysterious sensuous gal; the dark faces of the men behind rose arbors. Little children sat like sages in ancient rocking chairs.

The second stage arrived when these young people, having decided emphatically that the world, and particularly the U.S.A., was unacceptable to them in its present form, began an active search for roles they could play in changing the society. If many of these young people were content to lay up in their cool pads, smoking pot and listening to jazz in a perpetual orgy of esoteric bliss, there were others, less crushed by the system, who recognized the need for positive action. Moloch could not ask for anything more than to have its disaffected victims withdraw into safe, passive, apolitical little nonparticipatory islands, in an economy less and less able to provide jobs for the growing pool of unemployed. If all the unemployed had followed the lead of the beatniks, Moloch would gladly have legalized the use of euphoric drugs and marijuana, passed out free jazz albums and sleeping bags, to all those willing to sign affidavits promising to remain "beat." The non-beat disenchanted white youth were attracted magnetically to the Negro revolution, which had begun to take on a mass, insurrectionary tone. But they had difficulty understanding their relationship to the Negro, and what role "whites" could play in a "Negro revolution." For the time being they watched the Negro activists from afar.

The third stage, which is rapidly drawing to a close, emerged when white youth started joining Negro demonstrations in large numbers. The presence of whites among the demonstrators emboldened the Negro leaders and allowed them to use tactics they never would have been able to employ with all-black troops. The racist conscience of America is such that murder does not register as murder, really, unless the victim is white. And it was only when the newspapers and magazines started carrying pictures and stories of white demonstrators being beaten and maimed by police that the public began to protest. Negroes have become so used to this double standard that they, too, react differently to the death of a white. When white freedom riders were brutalized along with blacks, a sigh of relief went up from the black masses, because the blacks knew that white blood is the coin of freedom in a land where for four hundred years black blood has been shed unremarked and with impunity. America has never truly been outraged by the murder of a black man, woman, or child. White politicians may, if Negroes are aroused by a particular murder, say with their lips what they know with their minds they should feel with their hearts—but don't.

It is a measure of what the Negro feels that when the two white and one black civil rights workers were murdered in Mississippi in 1964, the event was welcomed by Negroes on a level of understanding beyond and deeper than the grief they felt for the victims and their families. This welcoming of violence and death to whites can almost be heard—indeed it can be heard—in the inevitable words, oft repeated by Negroes, that those whites, and blacks, do not die in vain. So it was with Mrs. Viola Liuzzo. And much of the anger which Negroes felt toward Martin Luther King during the Battle of Selma stemmed from the fact that he denied history a great moment, never to be recaptured, when he turned tail on the Edmund Pettus Bridge and refused to all those whites behind him what they had traveled thousands of miles to receive. If the police had turned them back by force, all those nuns, priests, rabbis, preachers, and distinguished ladies and gentlemen old and young—as they had done the Negroes a week earlier—the violence and brutality of the system would have been ruthlessly exposed. Or if, seeing King determined to lead them on to Montgomery, the troopers had stepped aside to avoid precisely the confrontation that Washington would not have tolerated, it would have signaled the capitulation of the militant white South. As it turned out, the March on Montgomery was a show of somewhat dim luster, stage-managed by the Establishment. But by this time the young whites were already active participants in the Negro revolution. In fact they had begun to transform it into something broader, with the potential of encompassing the whole of America in a radical reordering of society.

The fourth stage, now in its infancy, sees these white youth taking the initiative, using techniques learned in the Negro struggle to attack problems in the general society. The classic example of this new energy in action was the student battle on the UC campus at Berkeley, California —the Free Speech Movement. Leading the revolt were veterans of the civil rights movement, some of whom spent time on the firing line in the wilderness of Mississippi/Alabama. Flowing from the same momentum were student demonstrations against U.S. interference in the internal affairs of Vietnam, Cuba, the Dominican Republic, and the Congo and U.S. aid to apartheid in South Africa. The students even aroused the intellectual community to actions and positions unthinkable a few years ago: witness the teach-ins. But their revolt is deeper than single-issue protest. The characteristics of the white rebels which most alarm their elders—the long hair, the new dances, their love for Negro music, their use of marijuana, their mystical attitude toward sex—are all tools of their rebellion. They have turned these tools against the totalitarian fabric of American society—and they mean to change it.

From the beginning, America has been a schizophrenic nation. Its two conflicting images of itself were never reconciled, because never before has the survival of its most cherished myths made a reconciliation mandatory. Once before, during the bitter struggle between North and South climaxed by the Civil War, the two images of America came into conflict, although whites North and South scarcely understood it. The image of America held by its most alienated citizens was advanced neither by the North nor by the South; it was perhaps best expressed by Frederick Douglass, who was born into slavery in 1817, escaped to the North, and became the greatest leader-spokesman for the blacks of his era. In words that can still, years later, arouse an audience of black Americans, Frederick Douglass delivered, in 1852, a scorching indictment in his Fourth of July oration in Rochester:

> What to the American slave is your Fourth of July? I answer: a day that reveals to him, more than all other days in the year, the gross injustice and cruelty to which he is the constant victim. To him your celebration is a sham; your boasted liberty, an unholy license; your national greatness, swelling vanity; your sounds of rejoicing are empty and heartless; your denunciation of tyrants, brass-fronted impudence; your shouts of liberty and equality, hollow mockery; your prayers and hymns, your sermons and thanksgivings, with all your religious parade and solemnity, are, to him, more bombast, fraud, deception, impiety and hyprocrisy—a thin veil to cover up crimes which would disgrace a nation of savages. . . .

> You boast of your love of liberty, your superior civilization, and your pure Christianity, while the whole political power of the nation (as embodied in the two great political parties) is solemnly pledged to support and perpetuate the enslavement of three millions of your countrymen. You hurl your anathemas at the crown-headed tyrants of Russia and Austria and pride yourselves on your democratic institutions, while you yourselves consent to be the mere *tools* and *bodyguards* of the tyrants of Virginia and Carolina.

> You invite to your shores fugitives of oppression from abroad, honor them with banquets, greet them with ovations, cheer them, toast them, salute them, protect them, and pour out your money to them like water; but the fugitive from your own land you advertise, hunt, arrest, shoot, and kill. You glory in your refinement and your universal education; yet you maintain a system as barbarous and dreadful as ever stained the character of a nation—a system begun in avarice, supported in pride, and perpetuated in cruelty.

> You shed tears over fallen Hungary, and make the sad story of her wrongs the theme of your poets, statesmen and orators, till your gallant sons are ready to fly to arms to vindicate her cause against the oppressor; but, in regard to the ten thousand wrongs of the American slave, you would enforce the strictest silence, and would hail him as an enemy of the nation who dares to make these wrongs the subject of public discourse!

This most alienated view of America was preached by the Abolitionists, and by Harriet Beecher Stowe in her *Uncle Tom's Cabin*. But such a view of America was too distasteful to receive wide attention, and serious debate about America's image and her reality was engaged in only on the fringes of society. Even when confronted with overwhelming evidence to the contrary, most white Americans have found it possible, after steadying their rattled nerves, to settle comfortably back into their vaunted belief that America is dedicated to the proposition that all men are created equal and endowed by their Creator with certain inalienable rights—life, liberty and the pursuit of happiness. With the Constitution for a rudder and the Declaration of Independence as its guiding star, the ship of state is sailing always toward a brighter vision of freedom and justice for all.

Because there is no common ground between these two contradictory images of America, they had to be kept apart. But the moment the blacks were let into the white world—let out of the voiceless and faceless cages of their ghettos, singing, walking, talking, dancing, writing, and orating *their* image of America and of Americans—the white world was suddenly challenged to match its practice to its preachments. And this is why those whites who abandon the *white* image of America and adopt the *black* are greeted with such unmitigated hostility by their elders.

For all these years whites have been taught to believe in the myth they preached, while Negroes have had to face the bitter reality of what America practiced. But without the lies and distortions, white Americans would not have been able to do the things they have done. When whites are forced to look honestly upon the objective proof of their deeds, the cement of mendacity holding white society together swiftly disintegrates. On the other hand, the core of the black world's vision remains intact, and in fact begins to expand and spread into the psychological territory vacated by the nonviable white lies, i.e., into the minds of young whites. It is remarkable how the system worked for so many years, how the majority of whites remained effectively unaware of any contradiction between their view of the world and that world itself. The mechanism by which this was rendered possible requires examination at this point.

Let us recall that the white man, in order to justify slavery and, later on, to justify segregation, elaborated a complex, all-pervasive myth which at one time classified the black man as a subhuman beast of burden. The myth was progressively modified, gradually elevating the blacks on the scale of evolution, following their slowly changing status, until the plateau of separate-but-equal was reached at the close of the nineteenth century. During slavery, the black was seen as a mindless Supermasculine Menial. Forced to do the backbreaking work, he was conceived in terms of his ability to do such work—"field niggers," etc. The white man administered the plantation, doing all the thinking, exercising omnipotent power over the slaves. He had little difficulty dissociating himself from the black slaves, and he could not conceive of their positions being reversed or even reversible.

Blacks and whites being conceived as mutually exclusive types, those attributes imputed to the blacks could not also be imputed to the whites —at least not in equal degree—without blurring the line separating the races. These images were based upon the social function of the two races, the work they performed. The ideal white man was one who knew how to use his head, who knew how to manage and control things and get things done. Those whites who were not in a position to perform these functions nevertheless aspired to them. The ideal black man was one who did exactly as he was told, and did it efficiently and cheerfully. "Slaves," said Frederick Douglass, "are generally expected to sing as well as to work." As the black man's position and function became more varied, the images of white and black, having become stereotypes, lagged behind.

The separate-but-equal doctrine was promulgated by the Supreme Court in 1896. It had the same purpose domestically as the Open Door Policy toward China in the international arena: to stabilize a situation and subordinate a non-white population so that racist exploiters could manipulate those people according to their own selfish interests. These doctrines were foisted off as *the epitome of enlightened justice, the highest expression of morality*. Sanctified by religion, justified by philosophy and legalized by the Supreme Court, separate-but-equal was enforced by day by agencies of the law, and by the KKK & Co. under cover of night. Booker T. Washington, the Martin Luther King of his day, accepted separate-but-equal in the name of all Negroes. W. E. B. DuBois denounced it.

Separate-but-equal marked the last stage of the white man's flight into cultural neurosis, and the beginning of the black man's frantic striving to assert his humanity and equalize his position with the white. Blacks ventured into all fields of endeavor to which they could gain entrance. Their goal was to present in all fields a performance that would equal or surpass that of the whites. It was long axiomatic among blacks that a black had to be twice as competent as a white in any field in order to win grudging recognition from the whites. This produced a pathological motivation in the blacks to equal or surpass the whites, and a pathological motivation in the whites to maintain a distance from the blacks. This is the rack on which black and white Americans receive their delicious torture! At first there was the color bar, flatly denying the blacks entrance to certain spheres of activity. When this no longer worked, and blacks invaded sector after sector of American life and economy, the whites evolved other methods of keeping their distance. The illusion of the Negro's inferior nature had to be maintained.

One device evolved by the whites was to tab whatever the blacks did with the prefix "Negro." We had *Negro* literature, *Negro* athletes, *Negro* music, *Negro* doctors, *Negro* politicians, *Negro* workers. The malignant ingeniousness of this device is that although it accurately describes an objective biological fact—or, at least, a sociological fact in America— it concealed the paramount psychological fact: that to the white mind, prefixing anything with "Negro" automatically consigned it to an inferior category. A well-known example of the white necessity to deny due credit to blacks is in the realm of music. White musicians were famous for going to Harlem and other Negro cultural centers literally to steal the black man's music, carrying it back across the color line into the Great White World and passing off the watered-down loot as their own original creations. Blacks, meanwhile, were ridiculed as *Negro* musicians playing inferior coon music.

The Negro revolution at home and national liberation movements abroad have unceremoniously shattered the world of fantasy in which the whites have been living. It is painful that many do not yet see that their fantasy world has been rendered uninhabitable in the last half of the twentieth century. But it is away from this world that the white youth of today are turning. The "paper tiger" hero, James Bond, offering the whites a triumphant image of themselves, is saying what many whites want desperately to hear reaffirmed: *I am still the White Man, lord of the land, licensed to kill, and the world is still an empire at my feet.* James Bond feeds on that secret little anxiety, the psychological white backlash, felt in some degree by most whites alive. It is exasperating to see little brown men and little yellow men from the mysterious Orient, and the opaque black men of Africa (to say nothing of the impudent American Negroes!) who come to the UN and talk smart to us, who are scurrying all over *our globe* in their strange modes of dress—much as if they were new, unpleasant arrivals from another planet. Many whites believe in their ulcers that it is only a matter of time before the Marines get the signal to round up these truants and put them back securely in their cages. But it is away from this fantasy world that the white youth of today are turning.

In the world revolution now under way, the initiative rests with people of color. That growing numbers of white youth are repudiating their heritage of blood and taking people of color as their heroes and models is a tribute not only to their insight but to the resilience of the human spirit. For today the heroes of the initiative are people not usually thought of as white: Fidel Castro, Che Guevara, Kwame Nkrumah, Mao Tse-tung, Gamal Abdel Nasser, Robert F. Williams, Malcolm X, Ben Bella, John Lewis, Martin Luther King, Jr., Robert Parris Moses, Ho Chi Minh, Stokeley Carmichael, W. E. B. DuBois, James Forman, Chou En-lai.

The white youth of today have begun to react to the fact that the "American Way of Life" is a fossil of history. What do they care if their old baldheaded and crew-cut elders don't dig their caveman mops? They couldn't care less about the old, stiffassed honkies who don't like their new dances: Frug, Monkey, Jerk, Swim, Watusi. All they know is that it feels good to swing to way-out body-rhythms instead of dragassing across the dance floor like zombies to the dead beat of mind-smothered Mickey Mouse music. Is it any wonder that the youth have lost all respect for their elders, for law and order, when for as long as they can remember all they've witnessed is a monumental bickering over the Negro's place in American society and the right of people around the world to be left alone by outside powers? They have witnessed the law, both domestic and international, being spat upon by those who do not like its terms. Is it any wonder, then, that they feel justified, by sitting-in and freedom riding, in breaking laws made by lawless men? Old funny-styled, zipper-mouthed political night riders know nothing but to haul out an investigating committee *to look into the disturbance* to find the cause of the unrest among the youth. Look into a mirror! The cause is you, Mr. and Mrs. Yesterday, you with your forked tongues.

A young white today cannot help but recoil from the base deeds of his people. On every side, on every continent, he sees racial arrogance, savage brutality toward the conquered and subjugated people, genocide; he sees the human cargo of the slave trade; he sees the systematic extermination of American Indians; he sees the civilized nations of Europe fighting in imperial depravity over the lands of other people—and over possession of the very people themselves. There seems to be no end to the ghastly deeds of which his people are guilty. *GUILTY*. The slaughter of the Jews by the Germans, the dropping of atomic bombs on the Japanese people—these deeds weigh heavily upon the prostrate souls and tumultuous consciences of the white youth. The white heroes, their hands dripping with blood, are dead.

The young whites know that the colored people of the world, Afro-Americans included, do not seek revenge for their suffering. They seek the same things the white rebel wants: an end to war and exploitation. Black and white, the young rebels are free people, free in a way that Americans have never been before in the history of their country. And they are outraged.

There is in America today a generation of white youth that is truly worthy of a black man's respect, and this is a rare event in the foul annals of American history. From the beginning of the contact between blacks and whites, there has been very little reason for a black man to respect a white, with such exceptions as John Brown and others lesser known. But respect commands itself and it can neither be given nor withheld when it is due. If a man like Malcolm X could change and repudiate racism, if I myself and other former Muslims can change, if young whites can change, then there is hope for America. It was certainly strange to find myself, while steeped in the doctrine that all whites were devils by nature, commanded by the heart to applaud and acknowledge respect for these young whites—despite the fact that they are descendants of the masters and I the descendant of slave. The sins of the fathers are visited upon the heads of the children—but only if the children continue in the evil deeds of the fathers.

michael novak

The target of those Michael Lerner called "respectable bigots" are what Michael Novak calls "PIGS"—Poles, Italians, Greeks, and Slavs. Author of *The Rise of the Unmeltable Ethnics*, Novak is concerned about the extent of social, cultural, and even racial prejudice directed at people with backgrounds similar to his. In this essay, he describes his own experiences and those of other white, Catholic children and grandchildren of immigrants from eastern and southern Europe born outside the intellectual mainstream. They have their own idioms and idiosyncracies. But who knows them? Who cares?

Novak does and he claims to speak for many others.

A serious consideration of this article makes what Michael Lerner said about "respectable bigotry" far more meaningful. It will reveal why so many white ethnics hearing demands for programs beneficial to blacks, Chicanos, and Puerto Ricans are beginning to say, "We want ours, too."

Growing up in America has been an assault upon my sense of worthiness. It has also been a kind of liberation and delight.

There must be countless women in America who have known for years that something is peculiarly unfair, yet who have found it only recently possible, because of Women's Liberation, to give tongue to their pain. In recent months, I have experienced a similar inner thaw, a gradual relaxation, a willingness to think about feelings heretofore shepherded out of sight.

I am born of PIGS—those Poles, Italians, Greeks, and Slavs, non-English-speaking immigrants, numbered so heavily among the working-men of this nation. Not particularly liberal, nor radical, born into a history not white Anglo-Saxon and not Jewish—born outside what in America is considered the intellectual mainstream. And thus privy to neither power nor status nor intellectual voice.

Those Poles of Buffalo and Milwaukee—so notoriously taciturn, sullen, nearly speechless. Who has ever understood them? It is not that Poles do not feel emotion: what is their history if not dark passion, romanticism, betrayal, courage, blood? But where in America is there anywhere a language for voicing what a Christian Pole in this nation feels? He has no Polish culture left him, no Polish tongue. Yet Polish feelings do not go easily into the idiom of happy America, the America of the Anglo-Saxons and, yes, in the arts, the Jews. (The Jews have long been a culture of the word, accustomed to exile, skilled in scholarship and in reflection. The Christian Poles are largely of peasant origin, free men for hardly more than a hundred years.) Of what shall the man of Buffalo think, on his way to work in the mills, departing from his relatively dreary home and street? What roots does he have? What language of the heart is available to him?

The PIGS are not silent willingly. The silence burns like hidden coals in the chest.

All four of my grandparents, unknown to one another, arrived in America from the same county in Slovakia. My grandfather had a small farm in Pennsylvania; his wife died in a wagon accident. Meanwhile, a girl of fifteen arrived on Ellis Island, dizzy, a little ill from witnessing births and deaths and illnesses aboard the crowded ship, with a sign around her neck lettered "PASSAIC." There an aunt told her of the man who had lost his wife in Pennsylvania. She went. They were married. Inheriting his three children, each year for five years she had one of her own; she was among the lucky, only one died. When she was twenty-two, mother of seven, her husband died. And she resumed the work she had begun in Slovakia at the town home of a man known to us now only as "the Professor": she housecleaned and she laundered.

I heard this story only weeks ago. Strange that I had not asked insistently before. Odd that I should have such shallow knowledge of my roots. Amazing to me that I do not know what my family suffered, endured, learned, hoped these past six or seven generations. It is as if there were no project on which we all have been involved. As if history, in some way, began with my father and with me.

Let me hasten to add that the estrangement I have come to feel derives not only from a lack of family history. All my life, I have been made to feel a slight uneasiness when I must say my name. Under challenge in grammar school concerning my nationality, I had been instructed by my father to announce proudly: "American." When my family moved from the Slovak ghetto of Johnstown to the WASP suburb on the hill, my mother impressed upon us how well we must be dressed, and show good manners, and behave—people think of us as "different" and we mustn't give them any cause. "Whatever you do, marry a Slovak girl," was other advice to a similar end: "They cook. They clean. They take good care of you. For your own good."

When it was revealed to me that most movie stars and many other professionals had abandoned European names in order to feed American fantasies, I felt only a little sadness. One of my uncles, for business reasons and rather late in life, changed his name too, to a simple German variant. Not long, either, after World War II.

Nowhere in my schooling do I recall an attempt to put me in touch with my own history. The strategy was clearly to make an American of me. English literature, American literature; and even the history books, as I recall them, were peopled mainly by Anglo-Saxons from Boston (where most historians seemed to live). Not even my native Pennsylvania, let alone my Slovak forebears, counted for very many paragraphs. I don't remember feeling envy or regret: a feeling, perhaps, of unimportance, of remoteness, of not having heft enough to count.

The fact that I was born a Catholic also complicated life. What is a Catholic but what everybody else is in reaction against? Protestants reformed "the Whore of Babylon," others were "enlightened" from it, and Jews had reason to help Catholicism and the social structures it was rooted in to fall apart. My history books and the whole of education hummed in upon that point (during crucial years I attended a public, not a parochial, school): to be modern is decidedly not to be medieval; to be reasonable is not to be dogmatic; to be free is clearly not to live under ecclesiastical authority; to be scientific is not to attend ancient rituals, cherish irrational symbols, indulge in mythic practices. It is hard to grow up Catholic in America without becoming defensive, perhaps a little paranoid, feeling forced to divide the world between "us" and "them."

We had a special language all our own, our own pronunciation for words we shared in common with others (Augustine, contemplative), sights and sounds and smells in which few others participated (incense at Benediction of the Most Blessed Sacrament, Forty Hours, wakes, and altar bells at the silent consecration of the Host); and we had our own politics and slant on world affairs. Since earliest childhood, I have known about a "power elite" that runs America: the boys from the Ivy League in the State Department, as opposed to the Catholic boys from Hoover's FBI who, as Daniel Moynihan once put it, keep watch on them. And on a whole host of issues, my people have been, though largely Democratic, conservative: on censorship, on Communism, on abortion, on religious schools . . . Harvard and Yale long meant "them" to us.

The language of Spiro Agnew, the language of George Wallace, excepting its idiom, awakens childhood memories in me of men arguing in the barbershop, of my uncle drinking so much beer he threatened to lay his dick upon the porch rail and wash the whole damn street with steaming piss—while cursing the niggers in the mill, below, and the Yankees in the mill, above: millstones he felt pressing him. Other relatives were duly shocked, but everybody loved Uncle George: he said what he thought.

We did not feel this country belonged to us. We felt fierce pride in it, more loyalty than anyone could know. But we felt blocked at every turn. There were not many intellectuals among us, not even very many professional men. Laborers mostly. Small businessmen, agents for corporations perhaps. Content with a little, yes, modest in expectation. But somehow feeling cheated. For a thousand years the Slovaks survived Hungarian hegemony, and our strategy here remained the same: endurance and steady work. Slowly, one day, we would overcome.

A special word is required about a complicated symbol: sex. To this day my mother finds it hard to spell the word intact, preferring to write "s--." Not that much was made of sex in our environment. And that's the point: silence. Demonstrative affection, emotive dances, exuberance Anglo-Saxons seldom seem to share; but on the realities of sex, discretion. Reverence, perhaps; seriousness, surely. On intimacies, it is as though our tongues had been stolen. As though in peasant life for a thousand years the context had been otherwise. Passion, yes; romance, yes; family and children, certainly; but sex, rather a minor part of life.

Imagine, then, the conflict in the generation of my brothers, sister, and myself. (The book critic for the *New York Times* reviews on the same day two new novels of fantasy: one a pornographic fantasy to end all such fantasies [he writes], the other about a mad family representing in some comic way the redemption wrought by Jesus Christ. In language and verve, the books are rated even. In theme, the reviewer notes his embarrassment in reporting a religious fantasy, but no embarrassment at all about the preposterous pornography.) Suddenly, what for a thousand years was minor becomes an all-absorbing investigation. It is, perhaps, one drama when the ruling classes (I mean subscribers to *The New Yorker*, I suppose) move progressively, generation by generation since Sigmund Freud, toward consciousness-raising sessions in Clit. Lib., but wholly another when we stumble suddenly upon mores staggering any expectation our grandparents ever cherished.

Yet more significant in the ethnic experience in America is the intellectual world one meets: the definition of values, ideas, and purposes emanating from universities, books, magazines, radio, and television. One hears one's own voice echoed back neither by spokesmen of "Middle America" (so complacent, smug, nativist, and Protestant), nor by "the intellectuals." Almost unavoidably, perhaps, education in America leads the student who entrusts his soul to it in a direction that, lacking a better word, we might call liberal: respect for individual conscience, a sense of social responsibility, trust in the free exchange of ideas and procedures of dissent, a certain confidence in the ability of men to "reason together" and to adjudicate their differences, a frank recognition of the vitality of the unconscious, a willingness to protect workers and the poor against the vast economic power of industrial corporations, and the like.

On the other hand, the liberal imagination has appeared to be astonishingly universalist, and relentlessly missionary. Perhaps the metaphor "enlightenment" offers a key. One is initiated into light. Liberal education tends to separate children from their parents, from their roots, from their history, in the cause of a universal and superior religion. One is taught, regarding the unenlightened (even if they be one's Uncles George and Peter, one's parents, one's brothers perhaps), what can only be called a modern equivalent of *odium theologicum*. Richard Hofstadter described anti-intellectualism in America, more accurately in nativist America than in ethnic America, but I have yet to encounter a comparable treatment of anti-unenlightenment among our educated classes.

In particular, I have regretted and keenly felt the absence of that sympathy for PIGS that simple human feeling might have prodded intelligence to muster: that same sympathy that the educated find so easy to conjure up for black culture, Chicano culture, Indian culture, and other cultures of the poor. In such cases, one finds, the universalist pretensions of liberal culture are suspended: some groups, at least, are entitled to be both different and respected. Why do the educated classes find it so difficult to want to understand the man who drives a beer truck, or the fellow with a helmet working on a site across the street with plumbers and electricians, while their sensitivities race easily to Mississippi or even Bedford-Stuyvesant?

There are deep secrets here, no doubt, unvoiced fantasies and scarcely admitted historical resentments. Few persons, in describing "Middle Americans," "the Silent Majority," or Scammon and Wattenberg's "typical American voter," distinguish clearly enough between the nativist American and the ethnic American. The first is likely to be Protestant, the second Catholic. Both may be, in various ways, conservative, loyalist, and unenlightened. Each has his own agonies, fears, betrayed expectations. Neither is ready, quite, to become an ally of the other. Neither has the same history behind him here. Neither has the same hopes. Neither is living out the same psychic voyage. Neither shares the same symbols or has the same sense of reality. The rhetoric and metaphors differ.

There is overlap, of course. But country music is not a polka; a successful politician in a Chicago ward needs a very different "common touch" from the one used by the county clerk in Normal; the urban experience of immigration lacks that mellifluous, optimistic, biblical vision of the good America that springs naturally to the lips of politicians from the Bible Belt. The nativist tends to believe with Richard Nixon that he "knows America and the American heart is good." The ethnic tends to believe that every American who preceded him has an angle, and that he, by God, will one day find one too. (Often, ethnics complain that by working hard, obeying the law, trusting their political leaders, and relying upon the American Dream they now have only their own naïveté to blame for rising no higher than they have.)

It goes without saying that the intellectuals do not love Middle America, and that for all the good warm discovery of America that preoccupied them during the 1950s, no strong tide of respect accumulated in their hearts for the Yahoos, Babbitts, Agnews, and Nixons of the land. Willie Morris, in *North Toward Home*, writes poignantly of the chill, parochial outreach of the liberal sensibility, its failure to engage the humanity of the modest, ordinary little man west of the Hudson. The intellectual's map of the United States is succinct: "Two coasts connected by United Airlines."

Unfortunately, it seems, the ethnics erred in attempting to Americanize themselves, before clearing the project with the educated classes. They learned to wave the flag and to send their sons to war. (The Poles in World War I were 4 per cent of the population but took 12 per cent of the casualties.) They learned to support their President—an easy task, after all, for those accustomed abroad to obeying authority. And where would they have been if Franklin Roosevelt had not sided with them against established interests? They knew a little about Communism, the radicals among them in one way, and by far the larger number of conservatives in another. Not a few exchange letters to this day with cousins and uncles who did not leave for America when they might have, whose lot is demonstrably harder and less than free.

Finally, the ethnics do not like, or trust, or even understand the intellectuals. It is not easy to feel uncomplicated affection for those who call you "pig," "fascist," "racist." One had not yet grown accustomed not to hearing "Hunkie," "Polack," "Spic," "Mick," "Dago," and the rest. At no little sacrifice, one had apologized for foods that smelled too strong for Anglo-Saxon noses, moderated the wide swings of Slavic and Italian emotion, learned decorum, given oneself to education American style, tried to learn tolerance and assimilation. Each generation criticized the earlier for its authoritarian and European and old-fashioned ways. "Up-to-date" was a moral lever. And now when the process nears completion, when a generation appears that speaks without accent and goes to college, still you are considered pigs, fascists, and racists.

Racists? Our ancestors owned no slaves. Most of us ceased being serfs only in the last 200 years—the Russians in 1861. What have we got against blacks or blacks against us? Competition, yes, for jobs and homes and communities; competition, even, for political power. Italians, Lithuanians, Slovaks, Poles are not, in principle, against "community control," or even against ghettos of our own. Whereas the Anglo-Saxon model appears to be a system of atomic individuals and high mobility, our model has tended to stress communities of our own, attachment to family and relatives, stability, and roots. We tend to have a fierce sense of attachment to our homes, having been homeowners less than three generations: a home is almost fulfillment enough for one man's life. We have most ambivalent feelings about suburban assimilation and mobility. The melting pot is a kind of homogenized soup, and its mores only partly appeal to us: to some, yes, and to others, no.

It must be said that we think we are better people than the blacks. Smarter, tougher, harder working, stronger in our families. But maybe many of us are not so sure. Maybe we are uneasy. Emotions here are delicate. One can understand the immensely more difficult circumstances under which the blacks have suffered, and one is not unaware of peculiar forms of fear, envy, and suspicion across color lines. How much of all this we learned in America, by being made conscious of our olive skin, brawny backs, accents, names, and cultural quirks, is not plain to us. Racism is not our invention; we did not bring it with us; we found it here. And should we pay the price for America's guilt? Must all the gains of the blacks, long overdue, be chiefly at our expense? Have we, once again, no defenders but ourselves?

Television announcers and college professors seem so often to us to be speaking in a code. When they say "white racism," it does not seem to be their own traditions they are impugning. Perhaps it is paranoia, but it seems that the affect accompanying such words is directed at steelworkers, auto workers, truck drivers, and police—at us. When they say "humanism" or "progress," it seems to us like moral pressure to abandon our own traditions, our faith, our associations, in order to reap higher rewards in the culture of the national corporations—that culture of quantity, homogeneity, replaceability, and mobility. They want to grind off all the angles, hold us to the lathes, shape us to be objective, meritocratic, orderly, and fully American.

In recent years, of course, a new cleavage has sprung open among the intellectuals. Some seem to speak for technocracy—for that alliance of science, industry, and humanism whose heaven is "progress." Others seem to be taking the view once ascribed to ecclesiastical conservatives and traditionalists: that commitment to enlightenment is narrow, ideological, and hostile to the best interests of mankind. In the past, the great alliance for progress sprang from the conviction that "knowledge is power." Both humanists and scientists could agree on that, and labored in their separate ways to make the institutions of knowledge dominant in society: break the shackles of the Church, extend suffrage to the middle classes and finally to all, win untrammeled liberty for the marketplace of ideas. Today it is no longer plain that the power brought by knowledge is humanistic. Thus the parting of the ways.

Science has ever carried with it the stories and symbols of a major religion. It is ruthlessly universalist. If its participants are not "saved," they are nonetheless "enlightened," which isn't bad. And every single action of the practicing scientist, no matter how humble, could once be understood as a contribution to the welfare of the human race; each smallest gesture was invested with meaning, given a place in a scheme, and weighted with redemptive power. Moreover, the scientist was in possession of "the truth," indeed of the very meaning of and validating procedures for the word. His role was therefore sacred.

Imagine, then, a young strapping Slovak entering an introductory course in the Sociology of Religion at the nearby state university or community college. Is he sent back to his Slovak roots, led to recover paths of experience latent in all his instincts and reflexes, given an image of the life of his grandfather that suddenly, in recognition, brings tears to his eyes? Is he brought to a deeper appreciation of his Lutheran or Catholic heritage and its resonances with other bodies of religious experience? On the contrary, he is secretly taught disdain for what his grandfather *thought* he was doing when he acted or felt or imagined through religious forms. In the boy's psyche, a new religion is implanted: power over others, enlightenment, an atomic (rather than a communitarian) sensibility, a contempt for mystery, ritual, transcendence, soul, absurdity, and tragedy; and deep confidence in the possibilities of building a better world through scientific understanding. He is led to feel ashamed for the statistical portrait of Slovak immigrants which shows them to be conservative, authoritarian, not given to dissent, etc. His teachers instruct him with the purest of intentions, in a way that is value free.

To be sure, certain radical writers in America have begun to bewail "the laying on of culture" and to unmask the cultural religion implicit in the American way of science. Yet radicals, one learns, often have an agenda of their own. What fascinates *them* among working-class ethnics are the traces, now almost lost, of *radical* activities among the working class two or three generations ago. Scratch the resentful boredom of a classroom of working-class youths, we are told, and you will find hidden in their past some formerly imprisoned organizer for the CIO, some Sacco/Vanzetti, some bold pamphleteer for the IWW. All this is true. But supposing that a study of the ethnic past reveals that most ethnics have been, are, and wish to remain, culturally conservative? Suppose, for example, they wish to deepen their religious roots and defend their ethnic enclaves? Must a radical culture be "laid on" them?

America has never confronted squarely the problem of preserving diversity. I can remember hearing in my youth bitter arguments that parochial schools were "divisive." Now the public schools are attacked for their commitment to homogenization. Well, how *does* a nation of no one culture, no one language, no one race, no one history, no one ethnic stock continue to exist as one, while encouraging diversity? How can the rights of all, and particularly of the weak, be defended if power is decentralized and left to local interests? The weak have ever found strength in this country through local chapters of national organizations. But what happens when the national organizations themselves— the schools, the unions, the federal government—become vehicles of a new, universalistic, thoroughly rationalized, technological culture?

Still, it is not that larger question that concerns me here. I am content today to voice the difficulties in the way of saying what I wish to say, when I wish to say it. The tradition of liberalism is a tradition I have had to acquire, despite an innate skepticism about many of its structural metaphors (free marketplace, individual autonomy, reason naked and undisguised, enlightenment). Radicalism, with its bold and simple optimism about human potential and its anarchic tendencies, has been, despite its appeal to me as a vehicle for criticizing liberalism, freighted with emotions, sentiments, and convictions about men that I cannot bring myself to share.

In my guts, I do not feel that institutions are "repressive" in any meaning of the word that leaves it meaningful; the "state of nature" seems to me, emotionally, far less liberating, far more undifferentiated and confining. I have not dwelt for so long in the profession of the intellectual life that I find it easy to be critical and harsh. In almost everything I see or hear or read, I am struck first, rather undiscriminatingly, by all the things I like in it. Only with second effort can I bring myself to discern the flaws. My emotions and values seem to run in affirmative patterns.

My interest is not, in fact, in defining myself over against the American people and the American way of life. I do not expect as much of it as all that. What I should like to do is come to a better and more profound knowledge of who I am, whence my community came, and whither my son and daughter, and their children's children, might wish to head in the future: I want to have a history.

More and more, I think in family terms, less ambitiously, on a less than national scale. The differences implicit in being Slovak, and Catholic, and lower-middle class seem more and more important to me. Perhaps it is too much to try to speak to all peoples in this very various nation of ours. Yet it does not seem evident that by becoming more concrete, accepting one's finite and limited identity, one necessarily becomes parochial. Quite the opposite. It seems more likely that by each of us becoming more profoundly what we are, we shall find greater unity, in those depths in which unity irradiates diversity, than by attempting through the artifices of the American "melting pot" and the cultural religion of science to become what we are not.

There is, I take it, a form of liberalism not wedded to universal Reason, whose ambition is not to homogenize all peoples on this planet, and whose base lies rather in the imagination and in the diversity of human stories: a liberalism I should be happy to have others help me to find.

marlene dixon

Institutionalized segregation exists in many forms and affects many different minority groups. Of late we have seen growing militancy among the racial and ethnic minorities—"Black Power," "Red Power," "Chicano Power"; we have seen students challenge the established ways of regulating their lives; and most recently we have witnessed the birth, or rebirth, of the movement for equal rights for women.

Marlene Dixon has been a member of, a spokeswoman for, and a commentator on "Women's Lib." Initially an advocate of the view that "sisterhood is unity," she now has some second thoughts. Her article offers an analysis and critique of how a growing number of American women, especially white middle class women, came to confront the problems of economic discrimination, sexual exploitation, and psychological oppression and ended up, at least according to the author, in an all too bourgeois blind alley.

Like many other advocates and analysts, sociologist Dixon still agrees that there are certain parallels between racism and sexism. But, unlike many of her erstwhile sisters, she sees danger in accepting at face value the argument that to fight against discrimination is enough. The true struggle is against exploitation of the poor—black and white, female and male. Middle class women liberationists must join the real revolution against the forces of oppression which, she feels, affect us all.

Rise of Women's Liberation

The old women's movement burned itself out in the frantic decade of the 1920s. After a hundred years of struggle, women won a battle, only to lose the campaign: the vote was obtained, but the new millennium did not arrive. Women got the vote and achieved a measure of legal emancipation, but the real social and cultural barriers to full equality for women remained untouched.

For over thirty years the movement remained buried in its own ashes. Women were born and grew to maturity virtually ignorant of their own history of rebellion, aware only of a caricature of blue stockings and suffragettes. Even as increasing numbers of women were being driven into the labor force by the brutal conditions of the 1930s and by the massive drain of men into the military in the 1940s, the old ideal remained: a woman's place was in the home and behind her man. As the war ended and men returned to resume their jobs in factories and offices, women were forced back to the kitchen and nursery with a vengeance. This story has been repeated after each war and the reason is clear: women form a flexible, cheap labor pool that is essential to a capitalist system. When labor is scarce, they are forced onto the labor market. When labor is plentiful, they are forced out. Women and blacks have provided a reserve army of unemployed workers, benefiting capitalists and the stable male white working class alike. Yet the system imposes untold suffering on the victims—blacks and women—through low wages and chronic unemployment.

With the end of the war, the average age at marriage declined; the average size of families went up; and the suburban migration began in earnest. The political conservatism of the fifties was echoed in a social conservatism that stressed a Victorian ideal of the woman's life: a full womb and selfless devotion to husband and children.

As the bleak decade played itself out, however, three important social developments emerged that were to make a rebirth of the women's struggle inevitable. First, women came to make up more than a third of the labor force, the number of working women being twice the prewar figure. Yet the marked increase in female employment did nothing to better the position of women, who were more occupationally disadvantaged in the 1960s than they had been twenty-five years earlier. Rather than moving equally into all sectors of the occupational structure, they were being forced into the low-paying service, clerical and semi-skilled categories. In 1940, women had held 45 percent of all professional and technical positions; in 1967, they held only 37 percent. The proportion of women in service jobs meanwhile rose from 50 to 55 percent.

Second, the intoxicating wine of marriage and suburban life was turning sour; a generation of women woke up to find their children grown and a life (roughly thirty more productive years) of housework and bridge parties stretching out before them like a wasteland. For many younger women, the empty drudgery they saw in the suburban life was a sobering contradiction to adolescent dreams of romantic love and the fulfilling role of woman as wife and mother.

Third, a growing civil rights movement was sweeping thousands of young men and women into a moral crusade—a crusade that harsh political experience was to transmute into the New Left. The American Dream was riven and tattered in Mississippi and finally napalmed in Vietnam. Young Americans were drawn not to Levittown, but to Berkeley, Haight-Ashbury, and the East Village. Traditional political ideologies and cultural myths, sexual mores and sex roles with them, began to disintegrate in an explosion of rebellion and protest.

The three major groups that make up the new women's movement— working women, middle-class married women, and students—bring very different kinds of interests and objectives to women's liberation. Working women are most concerned with the economic issues of guaranteed employment, fair wages, job discrimination, and child care. Their most immediate oppression is rooted in industrial capitalism and felt directly through the vicissitudes of an exploitative labor market.

Middle-class women oppressed by the psychological mutilation and injustice of institutionalized segregation, discrimination, and imposed inferiority are most sensitive to the dehumanizing consequences of severely limited lives. Usually well educated and capable, these women are rebelling against being forced to trivialize their lives, to live vicariously through husbands and children.

Students, as unmarried, middle-class girls, have been most sensitized to the sexual exploitation of women. They have experienced the frustration of one-way relationships in which the girl is forced into a "wife" and companion role with none of the supposed benefits of marriage. Young women have increasingly rebelled not only against passivity and dependency in their relationships, but also against the notion that they must function as sexual objects, being defined in purely sexual rather than human terms, and being forced to package and sell themselves as commodities on the sex market.

Each group represents an independent aspect of the total institutionalized oppression of women. Yet, in varying degrees all women suffer from economic exploitation, from psychological deprivation, and from exploitive sexuality. Within women's liberation there is a growing understanding that the common oppression of women provides the basis for uniting to form a powerful and radical movement.

Racism and Male Supremacy

Clearly, for the liberation of women to become a reality, it is neces-sary to destroy the ideology of male supremacy that asserts the bio-logical and social inferiority of women in order to justify massive institu-tionalized oppression.

The ideology of male chauvinism can only be understood when it is perceived as a form of racism, based on stereotypes drawn from a deep belief in the biological inferiority of women. The very stereotypes that express the society's belief in the biological inferiority of women are images used to justify oppression. The nature of women is depicted as dependent, incapable of reasoned thought, childlike in its simplicity and warmth, martyred in the role of mother, and mystical in the role of sexual partner.

It has taken over fifty years to discredit the scientific and social "proof" that once gave legitimacy to the myths of black racial inferiority. Today most people can see that the theory of the genetic inferiority of blacks is absurd. Yet few are shocked by the fact that scientists are still busy "proving" the biological inferiority of women.

Yet one of the obstacles to organizing women remains women's belief in their own inferiority. This dilemma is not a fortuitous one, for the entire society is geared to socialize women to believe in and adopt as immutable necessity their traditional and inferior role. From earliest training to the grave, women are constrained and propagandized. Spend an evening at the movies or watching television and you will see a grotesque figure called woman presented in a hundred variations upon the themes of "children, church, kitchen" or "the chick sex-pot." Such contradictions as these show how pervasive and deep-rooted is the cultural contempt for women, how difficult it is to imagine a woman as a serious human being, or conversely, how empty and degrading is the image of woman that floods the culture.

Countless studies have shown that black acceptance of white stereo-types leads to mutilated identity, to alienation, to rage and self-hatred. Human beings cannot bear in their own hearts the contradictions of those who hold them in contempt. The ideology of male supremacy creates self-contempt and psychic mutilation in women; it creates trained incapacities that put women at a disadvantage in all social relationships.

It is customary to shame those who would draw the parallel between women and blacks by a great show of concern over the suffering of black people. Yet this response itself reveals a refined combination of white middle-class guilt and male chauvinism, for it overlooks several essential facts. For example, the most oppressed group within the feminine population is made up of black women, many of whom take a dim view of the black male intellectual's adoption of white male attitudes of sexual superiority. Neither are those who make this pious objection to the racial parallel addressing themselves very adequately to the millions of white working-class women living at the poverty level, who are not likely to be moved by this middle-class, guilt-ridden one-upmanship while having to deal with the boss, the factory, or the welfare worker day after day. They are already dangerously resentful of the gains made by blacks, and much of their "racist backlash" stems from the fact that they have been forgotten in the push for social change. Emphasis on the real mechanisms of oppression—on the commonality of the process—is essential lest groups such as these, which should work in alliance, become divided against one another.

White middle-class males already struggling with the acknowledgment of their own racism do not relish an added burden of recognition: that to white guilt must soon be added "male." It is therefore understandable that they should refuse to see the harshness of the lives of most women —to face honestly the facts of massive institutionalized discrimination against women.

We must never forget that the root of the ideology of male superiority, female inferiority, and white racism is a system of white male supremacy. White male supremacy is part of the ideology of imperialism, first European, then American. The European powers stripped India, China, Africa, and the New World of their wealth in raw materials— in gold, slaves, in cheap labor. Such brutal forms of exploitation required justification, and that justification was found in the doctrines of white racial superiority and the supremacy of European and American "civilization" over the "heathen" civilizations of Africa, Asia, and Latin America. Even more, we must never forget that the doctrine of white supremacy included the *supremacy of white women* as well as of white men.

The rise of capitalism in the West was based upon the wealth looted from other civilizations at the point of a gun: imperialism was the root and branch of racism and genocide then as it is now. It is at the root of mass prostitution in Saigon, of the torture and murder of innocent Vietnamese and Indochinese women and children, of all the sufferings of war inflicted upon the innocent at home and in Indochina. White American women must understand their oppression in its true context, and that context *is* a brutal, antihuman system of total exploitation having its corporate headquarters in New York and its political headquarters in Washington, D.C. And white women must understand that they are part of the system, benefiting from the loot secured through genocide.

This is why we must clearly understand that male chauvinism and racism *are not the same thing*. They are alike in that they oppress people and justify systems of exploitation, but in no way does a white woman suffer the exploitation and brutalization of women who are marked by both stigmata: being female *and* nonwhite. It is only the racism of privileged white women, self-serving in their petty, personal interests, who can claim that they must serve their own interests first, that they suffer *as much* as black women or Indochinese women or any women who experience the cruelty of white racism or the ruthless genocide of American militarism.

The contradiction of racism distorts and contaminates every sector of American life, creeps into every white insurgent movement. Understanding their own oppression can and must help white women to confront and to repudiate their own racism, for otherwise there will be no freedom, there will be no liberation.

Marriage: Genesis of Women's Rebellion

The institution of marriage is the chief vehicle for the perpetuation of the oppression of women: it is through the role of wife that the subjugation of women is maintained. In a very real way the role of wife has been the genesis of women's rebellion throughout history.

Looking at marriage from a detached point of view, one may well ask why anyone gets married, much less women. One answer lies in the economics of women's position, for women are so occupationally limited that drudgery in the home is considered to be infinitely superior to drudgery in the factory. Secondly, women themselves have no independent social status. Indeed, there is no clearer index of the social worth of a woman in this society than the fact that she has none in her own right. A woman is first defined by the man to whom she is attached, but more particularly by the man she marries, and secondly by the children she bears and rears—hence the anxiety over sexual attractiveness, the frantic scramble for boyfriends and husbands. Having obtained and married a man, the race is then on to have children, in order that their attractiveness and accomplishments may add more social worth. In a woman, not having children is seen as an incapacity somewhat akin to impotence in a man.

Beneath all of the pressures of the sexual marketplace and the marital status game, however, there is a far more sinister organization of economic exploitation and psychological mutilation. The housewife role, usually defined in terms of the biological duty of a woman to reproduce and her "innate" suitability for a nurturant and companionship role, is actually crucial to industrial capitalism in an advanced state of technological development. In fact, the housewife (some 44 million women of all classes, ethnic groups, and races) provides, unpaid, absolutely essential services and labor. In turn, her assumption of all household duties makes it possible for the man to spend the majority of his time at his work place.

It is important to understand the social and economic exploitation of the married woman, since the real productivity of her labor is denied by the commonly held assumption that she is dependent on her husband, exchanging her keep for emotional and nurturant services. Household labor, including child care, constitutes a huge amount of socially necessary labor. Nevertheless, in a society based on commodity production, it is not usually considered even as 'real work' since it is outside of trade and the marketplace. In a society in which money determines value, women are a group who work outside the money economy. Their work is not worth money, is therefore valueless, is therefore not even real work. And women themselves, who do this valueless work, can hardly be expected to be worth as much as men, who work for money.

Women are essential to the economy not only as free labor, but also as consumers. The American system of capitalism depends for its survival on the consumption of vast amounts of socially wasteful goods, and a prime target for the unloading of this waste is the housewife. She is the purchasing agent for the family, but beyond that she is eager to buy because her own identity depends on her accomplishments as a consumer and her ability to satisfy the wants of her husband and children. This is not, of course, to say that she has any power in the economy. Although she spends the wealth, she does not own or control it—it simply passes through her hands.

In addition to their role as housewives and consumers, increasing numbers of women are taking outside employment. These women leave the home to join an exploited labor force, only to return at night to assume the double burden of housework on top of wage work—that is, they are forced to work at two full-time jobs. No man is required or expected to take on such a burden. The result: two workers from one household in the labor force with no cutback in essential female functions—three for the price of two, quite a bargain. Regardless of her status in the larger society, within the context of the family, the woman's relationship to the man is one of proletariat to bourgeoisie. One consequence of this class division in the family is to weaken the capacity of oppressed men and women to struggle together against it.

For third-world people within the United States, the oppressive nature of marriage is reflected negatively—for example, motherhood out of wedlock is punished, either through discriminatory welfare legislation or through thinly disguised and genocidal programs of enforced sterilization. This society punishes unmarried women even more than it punishes married women. As a result, many third-world and poor white women want help with their families and need a husband in the home. The destruction of families among poor people, as a result of economic exploitation and social oppression, results in the deprivation of every facet of life for poor women and children. White middle-class women, bound up with the psychological oppression of marriage, have often been blind to the extent of suffering—and the extent of the needs—that the deliberate destruction of the families of the poor has created. Unemployment and pauperization through welfare programs creates very different problems than does the experience of boredom in the suburbs.

In all classes and groups, the institution of marriage nonetheless functions to a greater or lesser degree to oppress women; the unity of women of different classes hinges upon our understanding of that common oppression. The nineteenth-century women's movement refused to deal with marriage and sexuality and chose instead to fight for the vote and to elevate the feminine mystique to a political ideology. That decision retarded the movement for decades. But 1969 is not 1889. For one thing, there now exist alternatives to marriage. The cultural revolution—experimentation with life-style, communal living, collective child rearing—have all come from the rebellion against dehumanized sexual relationships, against the notion of women as sexual commodities, against the hardship, alienation, and loneliness of American life.

Lessons must be learned from the failures of the earlier movement. The feminine mystique must not be mistaken for politics or legislative reform for winning human rights. Women are now at the bottom of their respective worlds and the basis exists for a common focus of struggle for women in American society. It remains for the movement to understand this, to avoid the mistakes of the past, to respond creatively to the possibilities of the present.

Economic Exploitation

Women's oppression, although rooted in the institution of marriage, does not stop at the kitchen or the bedroom door. Indeed, the economic exploitation of women in the work place is the most commonly recognized aspect of the oppression of women.

The rise of new agitation for the occupational equality of women also coincided with the reentry of the "lost generation"—the housewives of the 1950s—into the job market. Women from middle-class backgrounds, faced with an "empty nest" (children grown or in school) and a widowed or divorced rate of one-fourth to one-third of all marriages, returned to the work place in large numbers. But once there, they discovered that women, middle class or otherwise, are the last hired, the lowest paid, the least often promoted, and the first fired. Furthermore, women are more likely to suffer job discrimination on the basis of age, so the widowed and divorced suffer particularly, even though their economic need to work is often urgent. Age discrimination also means that the option of work after child rearing is limited. Even highly qualified older women find themselves forced into low-paid, unskilled, or semiskilled work—if they are lucky enough to find a job in the first place.

Most women who enter the labor force do not work for "pin money" or "self-fulfillment." Sixty-two percent of all women working in 1967 were doing so out of economic need (that is, were either alone or with husbands earning less than $5,000 a year). In 1963, 36 percent of American families had an income of less than $5,000 a year. Women from these families work because they must; they contribute 35 to 40 percent of the family's total income when working full time and 15 to 20 percent when working part time.

Despite their need, however, women have always represented the most exploited sector of the industrial labor force. Child and female labor were introduced during the early stages of industrial capitalism, at a time when most men were gainfully employed in crafts. As industrialization developed and craft jobs were elimnted, men entered the industrial labor force, driving women and children into the lowest categories of work and pay. Indeed, the position of women and children industrial workers was so pitiful and their wages were so small that the craft unions refused to organize them. Even when women organized themselves and engaged in militant strikes and labor agitation—from the shoemakers of Lynn, Massachusetts, to the International Ladies' Garment Workers and their great strike of 1909—male unionists continued to ignore their needs. As a result of this male supremacy in the unions, women remain essentially unorganized, despite the fact that they are becoming an ever larger part of the labor force.

The trend is clearly toward increasing numbers of women entering the work force: women represented 55 percent of the growth of the total labor force in 1962, and the number of working women rose from 16.9 million in 1957 to 24 million in 1962. There is every indication that the number of women in the labor force will continue to grow as rapidly in the future.

Job discrimination against women exists in all sectors of work, even in occupations that are predominantly made up of women. This discrimination is reinforced in the field of education, where women are being short-changed at a time when the job market demands higher educational levels. In 1962, for example, while women constituted 53 percent of the graduating high school class, only 42 percent of the entering college class were women. Only one in three people who received a B.A. or M.A. in that year was a woman, and only one in ten who received a Ph.D. was a woman. These figures represent a decline in educational achievement for women since the 1930s, when women received two out of five of the B.A. and M.A. degrees given, and one out of seven of the Ph.Ds. While there has been a dramatic increase in the number of people, including women, who go to college, women have not kept pace with men in terms of educational achievement. Furthermore, women have lost ground in professional employment. In 1960 only 22 percent of the faculty and other professional staff at colleges and universities were women—down from 28 percent in 1949, 27 percent in 1930, 26 percent in 1920. 1960 does beat the 20 percent of 1919: "you've come a long way, baby"—right back to where you started! In other professional categories, 10 percent of all scientists are women, 7 percent of all physicians, 3 percent of all lawyers, and 1 percent of all engineers.

Even when women do obtain an education, in many cases it does them little good. Women, whatever their educational levels, are concentrated in the lower-paying occupations. The figures tell a story that most women know and few men will admit: most women are forced to work at clerical jobs, for which they are paid, on the average, $1,600 less per year than men doing the same work. Working-class women in the service and operative (semiskilled) categories, making up 30 percent of working women, are paid $1,900 less per year on the average than are men. Of all working women, only 13 percent are professionals (including low-pay and low-status work such as teaching, nursing, and social work), and they earn $2,600 less per year than do professional men. Household workers, the lowest category of all, are predominantly women (over 2 million) and predominantly black and third world, earning for their labor barely over $1,000 per year.

Not only are women forced onto the lowest rungs of the occupational ladder, they are in the lowest income levels as well. The most constant and bitter injustice experienced by all women is the income differential. While women might passively accept low-status jobs, limited opportunities for advancement, and discrimination in the factory, office, and university, they choke finally on the daily fact that the male worker next to them earns more and usually does less. In 1965, the median wage or salary income of year-round, full-time women workers was only 60 percent that of men, a 4 percent loss since 1955. Twenty-nine percent of working women earned less than $3,000 a year as compared with 11 percent of the men; 43 percent of the women earned from $3,000 to $5,000 a year as compared with 19 percent of the men; and 9 percent of the women earned $7,000 or more as compared with 43 percent of the men.

What most people do not know is that in certain respects all women suffer more than do nonwhite men and that black and third-world women suffer most of all.

Women, regardless of race, are more disadvantaged than are men, including nonwhite men. White women earn $2,600 less than white men and $1,500 less than nonwhite men. The brunt of the inequality is carried by 2.5 million nonwhite women, 94 percent of whom are black. They earn $3,800 less than white men, $1,900 less than nonwhite men, and $1,200 less than white women.

There is no more bitter paradox in the racism of this country than that the white man, articulating the male supremacy of the white male middle class, should provide the rationale for the oppression of black women by black men. Black women constitute the largest minority in the United States, and they are the most disadvantaged group in the labor force. The further oppression of black women will not liberate black men, for black women were never the oppressors of their men—that is a myth of the liberal white man. The oppression of black men comes from institutionalized racism and economic exploitation, from the world of the white man.

Consider the following facts and figures. The percentage of black working women has always been proportionately greater than that of white women. In 1900, 41 percent of black women were employed, as compared to 17 percent for white women. In 1963, the proportion of black women employed was still a fourth greater than that of whites. In 1960, 44 percent of black married women with children under six years were in the labor force, in contrast to 29 percent for white women. While job competition requires ever higher levels of education, the bulk of illiterate women are black. On the whole, black women—who often have the greatest need for employment—are the most discriminated against in terms of opportunity. Forced by an oppressive and racist society to carry unbelievably heavy economic and social burdens, black women stand at the bottom of that society, doubly marked by the caste signs of color and sex.

Faced with discrimination on the job—after being forced into the lower levels of the occupational structure—millions of women are inescapably presented with the fundamental contradictions in their unequal treatment and their massive exploitation. The rapid growth of women's liberation as a movement is related in part to the exploitation of working women in all occupational categories.

Conclusion

Male supremacy, marriage, and the structure of wage labor—each of these aspects of women's oppression and exploitation has been crucial to the resurgence of the women's struggle. It must be abundantly clear that revolutionary social change must occur before there can be significant improvement in the social position of *all* women.

The heart of the movement, as in all freedom movements, rests in women's knowledge, whether articulated or still only an illness without a name, that they are not inferior—not chicks or bunnies or quail or crows or bitches or ass or meat. Women hear the litany of their own dehumanization each day. Yet all the same, women know that they are not animals or sexual objects or commodities. They know their lives are mutilated, because they see within themselves a promise of creativity and personal integration. Feeling the contradiction between the essentially creative and self-actualizing human being within her and the cruel and degrading less-than-human role she is compelled to play, a woman begins to experience the internal violence that liberates the human spirit, to experience the justice of her own rebellion. This is the rage that impels women into a total commitment to women's liberation, a ferocity that stems from a denial of mutilation. It is a cry for life, a cry for the liberation of the spirit.

Yet, we must never forget that we women are not unique in our oppression, in our exploitation. Understanding ourselves should help us understand all others like us and not divide us from them. We must also remember that in one way white American women are unique, for they suffer least of all: their experience cannot approach the abysmal suffering of the third-world women or of third-world men, subject to American racism and imperialism. How does one understand rape; forced prostitution; torture; and mutilation; twisted, crippled children; deformed babies; a homeland laid waste; memories of perpetual war; perpetual oppression? It is not a question of guilt; it is a question of revolutionary struggle.

Epilogue 1969–1971

1969 was a year of explosive growth and measureless optimism for women's liberation. It was the year of sisterhood: "sisterhood is powerful!" "sisterhood is beautiful!" "sisterhood is unity!" The turning point for the women's struggle was 1969, the year in which the movement came up from underground by gaining recognition and legitimacy— recognition from the male-dominated white left and legitimacy as a protest "issue" in the larger society. The slogans of sisterhood reflected a joyful optimism, an overwhelming intuitive belief that *all* women could identify with each other, all women could struggle together— even lead—a vast movement or social transformation.

By 1971, the joyful optimism was increasingly being replaced by a sense of dismay and conflict in many women: "women's liberation is a nonstruggle movement"; "women's liberation is a racist movement"; "women's liberation is an apolitical movement"; "women's liberation is a class chauvinist movement"; "women's liberation is a liberal, middle-class movement." What did all of this mean? What had happened to the women's movement?

The United States of America had "happened" to women's liberation: all of the contradictions of a society torn by class and racial conflict, all of the contradictions of a society that is in fact based upon militarized state capitalism and institutionalized racism and class exploitation began to tear the women's movement apart. The apolitical simplicity of "sisterhood is unity" and "understand your own psychological oppression" was powerless to contend with or understand the internal, disruptive forces of the most exploitative, brutal, and complex oppressor nation in the history of Western imperialism—the United States of America.

The women's movement is no longer a struggling, tender shoot; it has become a mass movement; and women remain, often despite the movement, potentially a powerful, radical force. In the beginning, women were attacked from every quarter, most destructively from the left, for left politics became identified with male chauvinism. Originally, the attack from the left was corrupt, a ploy by radical men to keep women down. Now, however, the criticism does not come from the men, but from women within women's liberation. A movement that cannot learn from its past, that is too insecure and fearful to engage in self-criticism, that is too self-interested to be able to change its direction, too blind to see that all women are *not* sisters—that class exploitation and racism are fundamental to American society and exist *within* the women's movement—becomes a trap, not a means to liberation. In the brief critique that follows, I am correcting some of my own mistakes, for I too believed in sisterhood, I too believed that "common oppression provides the basis for uniting across class and race lines." In that belief I was wrong; this is what I have learned from the past year of the movement. There are many women and many groups within the women's struggle to which the following criticism does not apply, but there are still more who were, and still are, wrong.

Class Conflict

The mysticism of *sisterhood* disguised the reality that most women in women's liberation were white, young, and middle class, so that under all the radical rhetoric the movement's goals were reformist and its ideology was almost exclusively of middle-class female psychological oppression. The women's movement did not talk about *exploitation,* but about *oppression*—always in subjective terms. The women's movement did not talk about class struggle, nationalization of medicine, abolition of welfare, or the ultimate destruction of American imperialism. The needs of poor women, of working women, of black women were nowhere central to the demands or the rhetoric of women's liberation. The middle-class, reformist nature of the movement was not clearly and objectively revealed until the struggle over the equal rights amendment —an amendment that would have made *discrimination* unconstitutional but would not have included a single reference to exploitation, an amendment that would have benefited professional women at the expense of working-class women.

Fighting against *discrimination* is a middle-class, reformist goal—it says: let us *in* so that the privileges of our middle-class men can be extended to us middle-class women. Fighting against *exploitation* is revolutionary. To end exploitation, it is necessary to end "militarized state capitalism." To end class exploitation, it is necessary to abolish classes. To end racism, it is necessary to abolish white male supremacy, to abolish imperialism. White middle-class America, male and female, enjoys an affluence that is looted from half the world, that is stolen by means of poor white and black soldiers, that is turned into new cars and washing machines by workers, black and white, male and female. White middle-class America, *male and female,* enjoys incomes protected from inflation by means of the deliberate unemployment of workers, black and white, male and female, who suffer enforced pauperization so that the young girls of the middle class can go to the university and struggle for a women's center to give them a better education, the better to enjoy their class privileges, the better to explore the meaning of life and the adventures of a new, untrammeled sexuality. Genocide is committed against the people of Vietnam; war spreads to all the peoples of Indochina. So who cares? It's only a "penis war." It is of no concern to the young women of the middle class, who will never be soldiers, never be workers, never be on welfare, never suffer racism. The problem is *discrimination.* Women can only earn $10,000 a year teaching college while men earn $15,000 a year—that is the problem! "Sisterhood is unity! Don't criticize the movement! Don't make us feel guilty! Don't show us the blood on *our* hands—after all, we are oppressed too!"

Racism

The "black analogy" was originally used in women's liberation to help women through their understanding of their own oppression, to understand the oppression of others. By 1971 the "black analogy" has become a tool of white racism. The cries "we are oppressed too" and even more terrible "we are equally oppressed" permitted white middle-class women to dismiss the black struggle, to dismiss their complicity in a racist system, to dismiss criticisms of the movement from black women as motivated by the influence "the male chauvinism of black men" has upon them—ultimately to complete the cycle of white middle-class racism by reducing black and third-world people within the United States to invisibility. White middle-class women, bloated with their own pious claims to oppression, blind within their own racism, refused to see that black women were trying to teach them something when

they spoke at conferences, saying: "I am black and a woman, but am I first black or first a woman? First I am black." Or "we fear the abortion program, it may be used against us." Or "we must destroy exploitation and racism *before* black women can be liberated—for what does it mean to us, black women, if you white women end discrimination? We are still black; we are still exploited; we are still destroyed and our children with us." All the white women could answer with was "black male chauvinism!" They remained completely blind to the fact that third-world people are a colony and a minority within the heart of the monster, that their survival depends upon a resolution to the contradiction of male chauvinism and male supremacy that *does not* divide black women and black men into antagonistic factions.

Female Chauvinism

The purest expression of self-serving middle-class ideology is reflected in the blind hatred of men that makes no distinction between the system of white male supremacy and male chauvinism. Only very privileged women can in the security of their class status and class earning power create a little "manless Utopia" for themselves. They need only withdraw from the psychological discomfort of male chauvinism to create a new and different life for themselves—they are not faced, as a class, with the necessity to struggle against another class; they are not driven by exploitation and repression to understand that male chauvinism is reactionary but that it can also be defeated, so that men and women can resolve the contradiction between them, emerge stronger, and unite in mutual opposition to their real enemies—the generals, the corporate bosses, the corrupt politicians.

Liberal Guilt

Liberal guilt is worthless. Appealing to women who are completely devoted to their own self-serving class interests is equally useless. There is no mass movement in the United States that can avoid the contradictions of racism and class conflict, thus moralistic pleas are a waste of time. Nonetheless, women in the United States—and everywhere outside of the revolutionary world—are oppressed and exploited, suffer and die in silence. For the thousands and thousands of women who are poor, who are working class, who were born into the middle class but have turned away from it in disgust and revulsion, the women's movement, as a revolutionary struggle, remains their chief commitment and their only hope. Our challenge is to correct past mistakes, to learn what we must know to avoid future mistakes, to teach and to learn from each other. We *must* learn how to build, within the very heart of the monster, a revolutionary movement devoted to the liberation of all people *in practice*. Such a movement will not be self-serving, cannot be merely reformist. It must be political, must know history and economics, must understand that all revolutionary movements in the world today are interdependent. We can no longer be an island of affluence, blind to the lesson that what happens to women in Vietnam happens to us, that what happens to a black woman happens to us. The United States is not an empire that will stand for a thousand years, but is an oppressive monster that the peoples of the world will dismember and destroy before the world is all finished. We must choose which side we will be on—the path of revolution or the path of exploitation and genocide.

The women's movement is turning and twisting within its contradictions. Some women speed off into mysticism, claiming, but not explaining, how women by rejecting "male" politics and finding "female" politics effect world revolution—a world revolution in which the people's war in Vietnam plays no part, in which all previous world revolutions—Russian, Chinese, North Vietnamese, North Korean, Cuban—play no part. Still others seek escape in "sexual liberation," hoping to find, as does the youth movement, a personalized, individual salvation in a "life-style revolution" in which racism is dismissed as a problem of "black male chauvinism" and Vietnam is dismissed as a "penis war" of no concern to women. To be in the "vanguard," it is only necessary to love a woman sexually. Still others cling to the worn-out slogans of the early days, continuing with "consciousness raising" as weekly therapy and engaging in endless discussions of anti-elitism (an elite being anyone who does anything at all threatening to any woman in a small group) and "anti-elitist structure" in the organization of the women's center.

These tendencies reflect the other face of women's oppression, not anger or strength, but fearfulness, turning inward to avoid challenge, to avoid thinking, to avoid struggle, to avoid the large and frightening world of conflict and revolution, which cannot be contained within a small group or understood through the subjective oppression of a privileged woman. Women *are* mutilated, especially passive, nurturant middle-class women. They are made manipulative, dishonest, fearful, conservative, hypocritical, and self-serving. Celebrating women's weakness—elevating mutilation to a holy state of female grace—corrupts the movement into a reactionary and self-serving force.

Women are seen as absurd, and they blame the media. Women are criticized for being reactionary and racist. They howl "male defined," "male identified." Women are isolated from the liberation struggles of other people, and they scream that those movements are *male-dominated!* How many more excuses will be found until women have the strength to confront their mistakes and their failures? How many revolutions are we going to be called upon to make to assure rich and comforting interpersonal relationships and unhampered fucking for the people whose privilege is so great that they can afford to worry about their spirits instead of their bellies? How many more people are we going to help die in Indochina by howling that fighting against imperialism is "antiwoman" or a "penis war" or "dominated by men"? How long are we going to remain absurd because, in the eyes of the vast majority of peoples in the world, *we are absurd, self-seeking, blind,* and *ignorant*!

It is time, past time, to get our heads together, to listen to and learn from women who have made and are making revolutions, to study to fight, to fight to win, with strength and dignity and a proper respect for the suffering of others and a complete devotion to ending all oppression practiced against the majority of the peoples of the world, male and female, in the colonies of the monster and in the heart of the monster. Then, and only then, shall we know something of liberation.

irving louis horowitz

During the height of the student protest movement of the 1960s, a number of commentators and many sloganeers suggested that college students were just like blacks, an exploited minority of second-class citizens who were kept in their place by paternalism and oppression. Irving Louis Horowitz disagreed.

Horowitz saw students as a minority but did not accept the "Student-as-Nigger" argument. Rather, he saw them as analogous to Jews, people who have been traditionally marginal to the mainstream, oriented to "headwork" rather than "handwork," and suspicious of populist tendencies.

The case presented here is as controversial as its basic hypothesis and offers important food for thought for students black and white, as well as Jews, Christians, and others.

Recently an article began circulating in the underground radical press entitled "The Student as Nigger." Needless to say, the article was written by a Jew. Whatever else might be said about this essay, written by Jerry Farber, it was provocative in form, and raised by extension many situations in which students find themselves that are analogous to the historic condition of the Black people in America. Everything from separate eating facilities and separate bathrooms to demands for deferential titles

Reprinted from *The Antioch Review*, vol. 29, no. 4, by permission of the editors.

and differential treatment were raised in this article. Without accepting the soundness of the analogy, there is an overlap between the life style of the modern college student and the way of life of the modern Black man.

But style is not substance. Superficial mannerisms should not be confused with the behavioral consequences of situations. The Black condition stems from an American slave ancestry; the student condition derives from a European feudal ancestry. This is no small difference, since in slavery the master has all legal rights and is in fact the ultimate sovereign entity, whereas a slave has no legal rights and is not even a person, neither in terms of law or custom. Under feudalism there is a definite relationship between lord and serf involving mutual recognition of *persona* and mutual responsibilities to each other. These connections are formalized in a highly refined set of laws that, while clearly favorable to the class of noblemen and priests, nonetheless articulates fundamental human rights beyond which exploitation cannot be sanctioned or tolerated. Not that the feudal system particularly epitomizes egalitarian relationships. Rather, the origin of universities in this feudal culture can be seen in their symbolic remnants on every part of the modern educational plant, from graduation ceremonies conducted with the pomp of a French pre-Revolutionary court to deferential and often honorific titles that harken to days when sinecures were the normal payoff for men of breeding.

Even in this connection it would be a risky business to equate the student with the serf, since what would be done with the professors? Would they take the part of the aristocratic rulers or the downtrodden residue? Whether professors serve the tree of knowledge or serve men of power—or both—is no easy question to answer for either the thirteenth or twentieth centuries. The modern university is part of the modern corporate structure. It is linked directly and primarily to the industrial society at the economic level, the national polity, organizational level, and to the traditional cultivated élites who have in the past been fused with religious and quasi-secular institutions and agencies such as private foundations and wealthy individual benefactors. The student is the raw material for *inclusion in* this system of power, no less than for *exploitation by* this system of power.

I am suggesting that while the student-as-Black argument is provocative, it is not particularly penetrating. And on the gamble that where one analogue breaks down, another may be slightly better, I propose that the social position of the student might better be equated with the condition of the Jew than with any other large racial or ethnic bloc in American society. Indeed, the overlap in the populations of Jews and students is probably greater than that between any other two independent groupings, while the relative sizes of the college and university population (seven million) and the Jewish population (five to six million) are also roughly analogous. Thus, even in crude statistical terms one can say there is a tighter link between students and Jews than between students and Blacks. Further, if we refine our analysis, it is clear that the number of Jewish students who *finish* after enrolling in college is much higher than the norm.

The old canard that any argument by analogy is weak, weaker by far than any other form of presentation of evidence, is impossible to avoid in methodological terms; the degree to which any two independent variables can serve to "explain" each other is highly dubious. Yet these arguments do have an attractiveness and appeal in that they sharpen our focus and illuminate areas which otherwise remain obscure and whispered about only in private company.

Jews, Students, and Jewish Students

The historical grounds for discussing the student as Jew are that the Jew has a long legacy of faith in knowledge as curative and in education as the basic instrument of survival for the inner group and of upward mobility in the larger world he inhabits. There is no doubt that the post-World War II wave of college students had as its role-model the Jews who inhabited the large urban colleges just prior to World War II and who returned to fill many of the vacancies after the war. It became clear that the very essence of a credential society required just the kind of formal structure provided by the college degree. Further, what had once been true for Jews alone, namely, their need for special expertise in order to rise, became a general requisite of the more technological era that followed in the wake of the war. Thus it is that the student as Jew primarily means precisely this faith in the therapeutic powers of information and the economic powers of special service.

There are unattractive aspects of this historical analogue; namely, the Jewish working class was old and venerable—and is still shrouded in mythic if not actual form in rural Israeli society; the fact is that the highly urbanized Jew emphasized headwork not only as a superior way of getting things done but also as an escape from the drabness and deadening sameness that hand labor implied. If the Jew was confronted with alienation as a cultural fact, he was a member of the first large group dedicated to the removal of alienation as an economic fact. It is no wonder that in his world the doctrine of alienation shifted from a Marxian emphasis on the special condition of labor to a Freudian emphasis on the general condition of man.

This emphasis on head over hand complemented the status hierarchy that exists in American society, where high status occupations are generally connected with a low expenditure of physical effort (professors, judges, doctors), and low status is connected with high physical effort (the valuable garbage collectors and much maligned ditch diggers are special victims of this pecking order of man). But how does one determine the qualifications for headwork rather than handwork? Here the credentialist society emerges to solve the dilemma. It introduces a world of professional specialization and occupational definitions that mark off various levels of what constitutes satisfactory or unsatisfactory work. The entire role of colleges and universities, particularly the liberal arts sector, comes to be linked with professions rather than occupations. Gaining entrance into this world of headwork (a world that seriously downgrades claims concerning the value of human physical activities) becomes the goal, rather than the instrument.

The contrast of this situation with the life and the loss of the American Black people is clear; if there is one property that characterizes the historic role of the Blacks it is precisely an underestimation of the worth of headwork and an overestimation of the worth of handwork. It is probably not so much a matter of the Black's overemphasis upon the worth of handworth, as the simple assignment of menial tasks by the status hierarchy of the credentialist society to those who occupy the lowest rungs on the economic ladder. Given the fact that the Blacks had neither the influence nor the instrumentalities to transform handwork into headwork, they became uniquely separated from, rather than integrated into, American higher learning. Even now, despite enormous pressures to the contrary, Blacks are vastly under-represented in college education in proportion to their number in the society. American society, even by modest census figures, is at least ten percent Black; the university population is roughly one percent Black. This percentage does not include faculty, administrators, and professional staff. Indeed, among faculty and administrators the figure is closer to .01 percent, rather than 1.0 percent.

The simple mechanical equation of students to Blacks overlooks some powerful statistics indicating an acute separation between the social clusters. But if one were to take the Jewish population and match it against the college and university population, one would find a statistical over-representation with at least the same degree of marked significance as the under-representation of the Blacks. This indicates that we are not simply dealing with the student as symbolic Jew but, more to the point, the student as a very real Jew. Add to this the fact mentioned before—that Jewish students tend to drop out less frequently than non-Jewish students—and the actual degree of overlap between the two groups can scarcely be reduced to a spurious or humorous analogue. We are dealing with an isomorphism where the Jew is often a model, and the student is in fact often a Jew.

Like the Jew?

Let us proceed directly to the matter of analogues. Rather than once again urge precautions, I will say: if the shoe fits, then wear the analogue. If it doesn't, relax . . . barefooted.

Like the Jew, the student is needed both for his competence and for his special knowledge. Yet he is despised for being different and presumptuous. The student is sent to college to learn the inner workings of society, and when he learns them and then the parts fail to fit together or make a perfect whole, he is attacked both for being a dupe of his professors and for having an ivory-tower image of the world.

Like the Jew, the student is denounced for opposite reasons by the same people simultaneously. He is declared to be middle-class and opportunistic because he does not "work for a living" and because he sometimes sees college or university life as a way out of the selective service draft. Then at the same time he is attacked for being marginal to the class system, unconcerned about the future of the American economy or the importance of money, and moralistic. In the same connection, like the Jew, he becomes a sexually mysterious object: prudent, yet prurient; concerned with love, unconcerned with the institutions for lovemaking. In short, like the Jew, the student is in a can't-win moral situation with respect to the dominant sectors of society.

Like the Jews, students tend to be more politically leftist than American society in general, but not especially taken with economic utopias or political panaceas. The Jew is not only anti-Establishment; he is also anti-utopia, which makes him subject to severe assault by the political extremes. The extreme Right sees the student as Jew because of the political disaffection from the leading canons of American society, and the extreme Left sees the student as Jew for his cynicism with respect to the transforming qualities of apocalyptic revolution.

Like Jews, but quite unlike Blacks, slipping in and out of student roles is not only possible but constantly done. It is a lot easier to change your name and wear a cross than it is to wash away skin pigmentation or alter hair texture. Being a Jew and being a student are both achievement-oriented roles, while being a Black is largely an ascribed status. The options of being a student are always there, but what exactly are the options of being a Black man? It is the difference between volitional choice and a deterministic situation. While this point may seem quite obvious, it is nonetheless important enough to emphasize—particularly in light of the ambiguous status of the student subculture (perhaps the only subculture more ambiguous and amorphous than the definition of a Jew). Just as a Jew may be located on a continuum including someone who goes to Temple once a year (or never) all the way to the most devout or orthodox practitioner, the student too may be a hanger-on in a special no-credit course, or he may be someone taking five or six courses per semester for credit. In other words, role ambiguity no less than role shift is endemic as well as intrinsic to being both student and Jew. For the present at least, it is far simpler to cease being a student or even a Jew than a Black man—and this serves as a source of potential political strength for the Black, while creating a kind of political vacuity for students and Jews alike.

There is the whole issue of Jewish marginality and student marginality in relation to the larger culture. Just as a Jew rarely finds himself fully integrated whatever his wealth or social history, the student too rarely finds himself integrated into the university structure whatever his grades. It sometimes seems as if marginality is a by-product of intellect, a consequence of learning, a phenomenon that separates both student and Jewish culture from the larger society and even from the administrative aspects of university life. This marginality is not simply one that is held in fear and trembling but is almost a built-in definition of the situation itself, of being Jewish itself, of being a student itself. It is as if marginality and the extent of it defines moral activism and moral politicking. If the whole society seems terribly concerned with what Digby Baltzell describes as the Protestant art of making money or the Catholic craft of making politics, the Jew in conjunction with the student seems dedicated to the reverse proposition, namely, the worth, the moral worth, of noneconomic and nonpolitical definitions of the higher learning and the higher realities. Indeed, many of the utterances of the student youth generation are remarkably similar to the positions taken by Jewish radicals and liberals of past ages.

Jews share with students a mistrust of (or at least nonparticipation in) the American working class, and a concomitant distrust of the populist tradition. This is clearly a condition of the head-and-hand split spoken of earlier. Its existence can hardly be denied. The Jew as a working man has become a rarity; that is to say, a Jew as a factory-hand or as a field-hand is an unusual feature of the contemporary labor market. What the Jew is, almost abashedly, the student has raised to a level of ideology. Not only is he intrinsically suspicious of populist claims and mass appeals to working-class "racism" and "bigotry," but the student has often given up hope in the work and in the political propensities of the laboring classes. Not that all students have accepted this bias; the more politically conscious are aware that such a view is self-defeating. It simply remains a curious truism that of all groups in American society which have strong aversion to the working class and its current role, the Jew is most closely aligned with the student in holding this animus.

The deproletarianization of the Jew has reached epic proportions. And from this occupational clustering into middle-class activities has flowed a typical middle-class faith in machines over man, capital-intensive over labor-intensive orientations. At one and the same time, the modern Jew celebrates the victory of mind over matter, techniques over tedium; he also decries the "alienation" headwork brings about. The student has brought this condition one step further. He has trans-formed a shamefaced attitude into a boastful ideology. The working class, particularly its "blue collar" members, is criticized for selling out and copping out to capitalism, of being an unworthy heir to the heroic labor struggles of previous epochs. Whether in fact there is such a widespread "working-class authoritarianism," or if it does exist, whether such attitudes are any more prevalent among blue collar workers than among middle-class doctors and lawyers, is not examined. The arrogance of the powerful students translates itself into unabashed animosity for the working classes. Student alienation, while genuine enough, is often alienation from the laborer and the labor process, rather than alienation from the society in general, or from its oppres-sive elements in particular. Again, here the Black students clearly remain closer in background and in aspiration to the labor process—although, the fact that assaults by certain militant groups upon the Black proletariat have become old-fashioned and outdated may signify that the Black student at the white university now denies to himself the process of embourgeoisment he bitterly condemns in other religious and ethnic clusters.

Is It Good for the Jews?

There is an entire world of self-description and self-imagination, for what characterizes both Jews and students is consciousness (some-times to the point of collective autism). Neither is satisfied with observ-ing the performance of an act, but both demand explanation of the rationale behind the act and what it means to themselves as well as to others. Historically no group has been more concerned with its self-reflection than the Jews, and currently no group seems to have assimi-lated and inculcated a self-critical set of reflections more keenly than the student radical movement. Both groups are invariably involved in identity crisis questions: "What am I?" "Who am I?" These are types of questions and issues for which the man of action or the man of pure zeal has neither time nor inclination. In part this may be a function of the transitional status of being a student and the marginal status of being a Jew. Yet, whatever its causes, this self-reflective quality is certainly special, a quality that characterizes both groups more keenly than any others in the society.

Like the Jews, too, American students are increasingly in search of social justice. They seek answers to their alienation, and they are concerned not with social problems, but with social solutions. And quite unlike the Blacks, they are interested not in capitalism either of the "black" or "white" variety, nor in membership in the suburban yacht club, but in the positive value of new life-styles that made the suburb such an interesting place in the beginning. It is not true that the Jew "ran away" from the Blacks. It is rather, as Bennett Berger and Herbert Gans indicate, that they ran toward an alternative way of life, one that would be more feasible in the industrial society, and one that would provide tranquility and security without giving up either the occupational or recreational aspects of the so-called inner city. In this sense the Jew has a self-definition of living in an oasis, not a ghetto. The students too, in their deepest recesses, share with faculty and administration a belief that the college and university is an oasis in the midst of a political desert. This just as assuredly links Jews and students as it separates Jews from Blacks, and students from nearly every major segment of our society.

It might well be that this present malaise among Blacks, university administrations and the population as a whole, reflects the larger circumstance that the Black is seeking to recreate a mini-ghetto in this oasis as a proud link and symbolic identification with the macro-ghetto which Blacks occupy in American society. The Black student is often torn between direct access to the higher echelons of legitimation and status in the larger society, and the need to assist the "brothers" remaining in the ghettos. The conversion of the campus "integrationist" atmosphere into a center of Black power might be viewed as an appropriate response to this dilemma.

In the same connection students and Jews are involved in a constant dialectical dissonance with the rest of society. How they perceive themselves and how they are perceived by others remain at radical variance. What Jews see as a Jewish problem and what students see as a student problem are very different from what the larger world defines as their problems. This is the classic interest-group condition; but also a new experience for students in particular.

In these times of exacerbated Negro-Jewish tensions, it should be recollected how much the two minority groups have come to resemble each other in the less superficial things. Black people have traditionally respected Jewish mobility patterns constructed from education, the solidarity of Jewish home life, the general "soulfullness" of the way Jews live, and more recently, the transformation of a relatively docile, tranquilized people interested in survival at any price, into a militant people capable of national self-defense and national liberation. It is so easy to think of Black Power as a special *apercu* or aberration of Black militants, forgetting that less than a quarter of a century ago Jewish

Power meant precisely the sort of guerrilla struggles, national consciousness and ethnic pride that brought about the State of Israel and helped make the world Jewish community viable on the shoals of Hitlerism. This is so whatever one may think of the present tensions between Arabs and Jews in the Middle East, or Black identification with "colored" aspirations.

On the other side of the ledger, it is no less the case that Jews have played a special role in limiting the penetration of racial hatreds permeating America. Jews traditionally have been in the forefront of the struggle for Black equality and Black higher education; moreover, they have learned the most from Black people. The world of acid rock groups, so deep into the Black soul music, is populated by young Jewish musicians. The White hipster phenomenon Norman Mailer spoke of in the Fifties is not just white, but largely Jewish—and the model of cool behavior under pressure, the resurrection of sexual energies, the renewed concern with labor and work as positive values, all aspects of Black culture endemic to the Afro-American experience, have best been learned by the young Jewish people with whom Blacks interact most.

This discussion of the student as Jew is not set up as an antithesis of Black culture—rather as more nearly representative of how culture and education intersect and interpenetrate.

The Students and the Jewish Problem

The analogy of student and Jew should not be considered as unqualified or uniform. There are serious differences between the two groups. Increasingly, the majority of Jewish people in the United States tends to celebrate this country and to have a vision of America not only as a good place but as the best place. Jewish radicalism increasingly tends to be diluted into a kind of stuffy liberalism that is more rhetorical than actual, more an electoral-day pilgrimage than an everyday involvement. The students, for their part, as noted by all polls and all survey researchers, are becoming deeply disaffiliated and disaffected from the larger American society. Student criticism often times comes crashing in upon Jewish celebration. The increasingly abrasive relationships between students and Jewish officialdom—noted by many Jewish agencies—in the form of disaffiliation of Jewish youth from various congregational quasi-religious institutions, have become a major threat to Jewish solidarity.

Even here there is a peculiarity, because within the Jewish tradition there has always been strong emphasis on moral dissent in the larger Jewish matrix. Even now the proportion of Jews who are radicals is larger than the proportion of radicals to the general student population.

Though the tendency of Jews may be growing toward an acceptance of the formal system of legitimacy, whereas student tendencies may be in the reverse direction, they nonetheless share a common antipathy for a larger majority which is quite willing to accept the society on its own terms, and they move to assist the substantial minority which is unwilling or unable to participate.

Another crucial area in which Jews and students seem to be at odds is that of law, covenants, and normative restraints. The Jew has traditionally been not just law-giver but law-lover. He tends to have at least an unbounded fear, if not an unbounded admiration, for the law. For the Jew, historically, the law held all kinds of terrors, but it also held out a hope of manipulation of the power structure to gain his ends or at least to gain his survival. The law was universalism in practice. If the law was just, the Jew always was there to demand application of social justice to his brethren. The Jew, with his sacred covenant, carried over and sacerdotalized even profane covenants. As a tactic this has been historically brilliant. It has compelled institutions of law, order, and education to live up to their own rhetoric, since there would always be a Jew present to make sure that this rhetoric was widely promulgated and understood, even though implementation might be absent.

For the student, however, the acceptance of this legitimation has become sharply contested. The basis of law is viewed as a shield for authority and a sham behind which lurks unrestrained power. Coercion is faced by counter-coercion or by a flat refusal to admit the legitimate claims of either the courts of law, the police, or of any other agencies of law. If, for the Jew the phrase "moral law" has a veritable messianic force behind it, for the student the words "morality" and "legality" seem diametrically opposed to each other, with morality clearly being the superior concept if not always the operative term in student behavior.

This brings us to the confrontation of life and love. The Jew has historically been far more interested in the problems and processes of survival—and well he might be—than in the process and problems of love. It is not so much the figure of Jesus that separates Jew and Christian; it is rather the principles that are to guide the social behavior of men. The Jews willingly and consciously pay a high price for survival; and that price is at times not less than love itself. It is not that Jews, any more than other people, are not interested in or do not need affection. It is only that the time and energy that one can dedicate to matters of the heart presuppose a social, political, and economic tranquility rarely allowed the Jew. The Jewish culture, after all, is a culture of necessity—not of violence, nor of philanthropy, but of sheer necessity. Even in the current condition of abundance, the phylogenetic memory of Jews tends to push them in the direction of easy mobility through education rather than the fixed status endowed by inherited wealth.

Here the student meets the Jew, since both, the Jew above all, are the products of affluence and the consequence of a society that has promoted exactly the kind of open mobility that Jews have best survived in. And so it is no wonder that even from the "beat generation" and its poets to the present alienated generation the Jewish disaffiliate has been in the forefront of the student movement. Here again the Jew seems prominent in the heresy, in the break with tradition. The emphasis on Eastern religious cults, acid rock music, drug addiction, and all of the affairs of the private heart that are supposed to increase the quality of love and sexual freedom—these are surely characteristic of the love-oriented ethic. Nevertheless, the theme of self-destruction which appears in the youth culture and the self-sacrificing qualities of the young—whether they be viewed as foolish or heroic—are clearly gaps between the student culture and the Jewish culture that are not easily bridged and that sometimes go under the rubric of "generation gap." Again, it is not so much the formal words—"life" and "love"— but the contents of these terms, the radical difference between what Norman Podhoretz would call "making it" and Jerry Rubin would call "breaking it." A full circle is reached where the analogy, at least superficially, breaks down, and we are once more confronted with the unique claims of distinct groups.

The Jew has a final laugh, however, because within the Jewish tradition there has always been a place, a central place, for dialogue between reason and mysticism, radicalism and conservatism, self-examination and self-celebration. The Jew is a perennial seeker and very rarely the finder. Students too have opened up this world of sealed education once and for all, demanding dialogue and even confrontation. The renewed search for foundations is exactly the kind of "enterprise" that the Jew as an ideal-type has been promoting for six thousand years. The Jew can say to the student, "Welcome to the ranks." The students can say to the Jew, "We have arrived at the edge of marginality. We too are the new children of Zion." Whether these "children" will be doomed to diaspora and even holocaust is not in our hands to settle, yet it is a sobering thought that repression and ethnic destruction on a total scale not only can happen, but has happened. In this, the students have much to learn while the Jews have much to teach—if in fact, they themselves can remember the horror of repression and the tragedy of destruction.

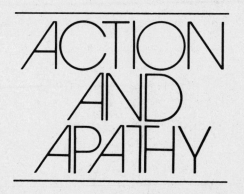

ACTION
AND
APATHY

nelson polsby, robert dentler, paul smith

Debates about power and politics in the United States focus on the question, "Who rules America?" In one camp are those who argue that there is a power elite, a small group of powerful men in business, the military, and the government. In another are those who say that power is distributed among various interest groups, each with a sort of veto power over the others.

To some political sociologists such debates are interesting but tell little about how the average citizen sees his democracy at work. Nelson Polsby, Robert Dentler, and Paul Smith concentrate their attention on the relationship between leaders, whoever and wherever they are, and nonleaders. Their research suggests that most Americans, while paying lip-service to the idea of independent judgment, tend to leave decision making to those they elect as long as they hew close to the middle of the road, whatever their party affiliation. They find or, at least, found an amazing consensus that has served to avoid extremists from gaining much of a grip on the seats of power.

One wonders how different things will be in the future as increasing numbers of young Americans use the ballot box to voice their disapproval of established policies.

From Nelson W. Polsby, Robert A. Dentler, and Paul A. Smith (eds.), *Politics and Social Life* (Boston: Houghton Mifflin, 1963), pp. 433–437, by permission of the publisher and authors.

Are American politics, broadly speaking, "democratic"? That is, are leaders in some sense controlled by nonleaders? Clearly nonleaders issue few direct instructions to leaders. Issues get all jumbled up in political campaigns. It is hard, if not impossible, to identify the mandate of any particular elected official. This is especially true in a country where Presidents and Congressmen whose policies are diametrically opposed are often elected by the same constituency. Is it true, moreover, that Americans do not *care* very much about politics? Voting turnouts run somewhat lower than in other modern societies. Few people report themselves as active participants in politics. Surprisingly few profess interest in political issues. How is it possible for a democratic political system to run under these circumstances?

One explanation may be that there is a broad substratum of agreement among most members of society, so that issues threatening in some basic way to major groups simply do not get raised and fought out in the political arena. This substratum of agreement may, indeed, be nothing more than a tacit agreement not to act. Prothro and Grigg, in their pilot study, show that Americans agree in the abstract about democratic values, but not when these values are formulated specifically.[1] Even more important, however, is the fact that so few people get up the energy to act on their anti-democratic impulses. Behaviorally, failure to overturn the results of a generally democratic system has much the same effect as "agreement" on (or lip-service to) democratic values. Issues in our system are raised in piecemeal fashion. Hence, leaders and followers alike rarely confront situations in which all-or-nothing choices must be made, where some ambiguity or room for maneuver is not present. Slogans posing alternatives such as "Red or Dead" may be useful for rallying the emotions, but they do not refer to alternatives that Americans face in the real world. Voters choose not between Red and Dead but between Kennedy and Nixon. Of the thousands of bills facing Congress in each session, none provides for one or the other. In such a system, observers may on occasion feel frustrated that issues seem rarely to be "settled" one way or another; winners seldom take all, and losers generally survive to fight another day. This fact, frustrating though it may be to the tidy-minded, has its constructive side. It builds loyalty to the preservation of the political system, on the part of winners and losers alike.

Parties and elections play key roles in maintaining this system, and in giving it democratic characteristics. One of the major necessities of a democratic society is, after all, that leaders be replaceable by the action of nonleaders. It is thus of some significance that in American national politics, turnover of leaders is legitimate. Furthermore, it is not only in theory legitimate but in fact possible for one ruling group to be replaced by another. The method by which this turnover is accomplished is peaceable, well accepted, and can be participated in by a large share of those governed. Elections are "real" as opposed to "fake" in that not only does a majority of the eligible population vote, but there exists a lively chance for one ruling group to be supplanted by another.

Secondly, election outcomes, while they have "real" consequences, do not disturb the underlying consensus. The consequences of elections are real for the contestants, but are of only minor significance for everyone else. This seems to us to be the mechanism through which turnover is legitimized: noncombatants view turnover as more or less as satisfactory as the status quo. Contestants who win are of course content. The team that loses one office always has a chance at winning others, and the fact that changes in the system are brought about only slowly and incrementally, because of the constitutional necessity of gaining the consent of so many actors within the system, means that losers of elections can often gain their policy preferences on a variety of issues. Hence, those who are mobilized and politically active have the most to gain from maintenance of the system.

Parties fit into this system by providing useful machinery for both leaders and nonleaders. For leaders, the party is the organization which supplies a method for the recruitment and advancement of contestants for public office. For nonleaders, the party is the great economizing device. Knowing what party you support makes it unnecessary to know more about individual candidates or technical issues. Information costs are cut to the point where politics is assigned its "proper" place in the scheme of things (a place of extremely low saliency for most people) and this makes noninvolvement in politics feasible while norms of civic duty are complied with.

Frank Sorauf offers the challenging hypothesis that if parties are meaningful to nonleaders only in a "sentimental" sense (i.e., if people vote for candidates because of emotional attachment, family tradition or habitual reflex favoring a particular party), then the more tangible rewards for party support, such as patronage, have much less importance in the maintenance of party organizations than was heretofore thought.[2] If anything, patronage seems to build up gratitude to *persons* rather than parties, and to local dispensers rather than central originators. If Sorauf is right, then a dominating function of political parties no longer is to dispense patronage. The usefulness of this device in generating even a modest amount of party loyalty at the polls is chimerical in today's politics. But if sentiments of loyalty are all that bind people to parties nowadays, then these can be interrupted and outweighed by other, stronger sentiments, such as adulation for a national hero. This seems to be a plausible explanation for General Eisenhower's amazing popularity among Democrats and Republicans alike, as Hyman and Sheatsley indicate.[3]

In the American political system, not only is there a peculiar disjunction between the sentiments of voters and the policies of elected leaders, but, on most substantive issues which arise in the course of governmental activity, political leaders and followers are on the whole out of touch with one another. There is no reason to suppose that the Congressman is less well informed than other leaders on the national level about what "the people" or any significant portion thereof, want. In some ways, no doubt, their communication channels to the grass roots are better than those of others in Washington. But even so-called "pressure groups" leave Congressmen pretty much alone, or contact them irregularly.

Freedom from grass roots pressure, except of the most trivial sort, does not necessarily free leaders to pursue policies whimsically since there are always the "grass tops" to contend with. In the first place, the political opposition back home is always watching. Furthermore, there are sometimes a few alert and meaningful interest groups, and indeed, often these groups are mobilized by other Congressmen in order to bring pressure to bear on their colleagues. Despite the centripetal influences enumerated by David Truman (e.g., the President's access to national publicity, the alleged growing similarity of problems from locale to locale, the growing impact of federal expenditures and standards on local outcomes) the Congressman is still sent to Washington by the people back home. And, as Truman says, "The relationships which the legislator has established and maintained within the constituency are primary and crucial; others are secondary and incidental."[4]

Many Congressmen are quite free to create their own relationships with their own peculiar clientele of interest groups and voters back home. Many, of course, are closely tied to political organizations in their home states. Nonetheless, in the American political system we have something far more complex and subtle than state organizations that get together every four years to elect a President, or Bryce's "empty-bottles-variously-labeled." Parties are becoming more cohesive under the impact of a magnified presidency and "interests and issues [such as foreign policy] which will tend to cut through rather than to unify constituencies . . . and which demand standardized national solutions." There is a definite tendency for electioneering functions of the "presidential party" to become centralized. With compelling national issues, and media capable of making them persuasive throughout the land, candidates find it increasingly difficult to cut themselves off from the head of the ticket. Their desire to reduce risks by establishing bases of support independent of the actions and fortunes of the national leadership is less and less compatible with the issues of concern to their constituents (and themselves). But both groups are still fairly immune to party discipline in the sense of overarching doctrine or centralized hierarchical demands, supervised by the President. This may change as the country grows and Congressmen come to represent more and more people who are more and more socially heterogeneous and cosmopolitan and, worst of all, from the standpoint of independence from the President, more and more estranged from him.

The costs of getting acquainted may well throw Congressional candidates into the loving grasp of the mass media, which cost big money. This in turn must come from somewhere, and perhaps the ultimate sources will be wealthy party angels who distribute their largesse through national agencies in exchange for a sympathetic hearing for their policy preferences—which could range from oil depletion allowances to civil rights action. The mass media also encourage the use of brand names for the products to be sold. But the day of party government is not upon us yet. For, among other things, it must await a much more issue-conscious electorate.

The system cannot be characterized as a simple one, where nonleaders speak with one voice. The "mandate" or "general will" does not exist in any meaningful sense. Nor do leaders respond with a set of well-articulated, logically coherent policies. In fact, fewer really pertinent demands—that is, on questions where public officials actually can do something about it—are made than is commonly supposed. Apparently even the act of making demands of government takes skill and effort far beyond what most citizens are disposed or able to marshal. At least, as Woodward and Roper show, very few citizens engage in this kind of activity.[5]

How, then, do nonleaders guide leaders in our system? Neither through directives on specific issues by their votes, nor by their lobbying activities; indeed, by adhering to partisan doctrines. Rather, nonleaders set a "zone of indifference," an underlying apathy that constrains the scope of political conflict. Secondly, they vote in contested elections. Politicians are uncertain enough of the outcomes of these to remain open to a variety of policy suggestions, particularly those advanced through skilled and dedicated lobbying activities. These characteristics result in a system which is stable, permeable, and democratic.

NOTES

1. Prothro, James W., and Charles M. Grigg, "Fundamental Principles of Democracy: Bases of Agreement and Disagreement," *The Journal of Politics*, Vol. 22 (1960), 276–294.
2. Sorauf, Frank J., "Patronage and Party," *Midwest Journal of Political Science*, Vol. 3, No. 2 (May, 1959), 115–126.
3. Hyman, Herbert H., and Paul B. Sheatsley, "The Political Appeal of President Eisenhower," *Public Opinion Quarterly*, Vol. 19 (1955–56), 26–39.
4. Truman, David B., "Federalism and the Party System" in *Politics and Social Life*, pp. 513–527.
5. Woodward, Julian L., and Elmo Roper, "Political Activity of American Citizens," *American Political Science Review*, Vol. 44 (December, 1950), 872–875.

kenneth b. clark

For several summers in the 1960s rioting became a fixed feature of urban life. In Harlem and Los Angeles, Cleveland, Detroit, and Newark, the ghetto areas burst open with explosions of pent-up frustration and bitterness. Unlike the race riots of an earlier period in which blacks and whites were pitted against each other, these were ghetto revolts: blacks against society mainly but not exclusively represented by and in its policemen.

Following two of the major riots, social psychologist Kenneth B. Clark wrote a brief essay in which he attempted to explain what was happening and why. He pointed to the appalling double standard of social morality exhibited by the public and their political representatives. The uprisings were condemned but not their causes. Indeed, says Clark, "it's a wonder there have been so few riots."

It is one measure of the depth and insidiousness of American racism that the nation ignores the rage of the rejected—until it explodes in Watts or Harlem. The wonder is that there have been so few riots, that Negroes generally are law-abiding in a world where the law itself has seemed an enemy.

To call for reason and moderation, to charge rioters with blocking the momentum of the civil-rights movement, to punish rioters by threatening withdrawal of white support for civil rights may indeed ease the fears of whites and restore confidence that a firm stern hand is enforcing order.

But the rejected Negro in the ghetto is deaf to such moral appeals. They only reinforce his despair that whites do not consider equal rights for Negroes to be their due as human beings and American citizens but as rewards to be given for good behavior, to be withheld for misbehavior. The difficulty which the average American of goodwill —white or Negro—has in seeing this as a form of racist condescension is another disturbing symptom of the complexities of racism in the United States.

It is not possible for even the most responsible Negro leaders to control the Negro masses once pent-up anger and total despair are unleashed by a thoughtless or brutal act. The prisoners of the ghetto riot without reason, without organization and without leadership, as this is generally understood. The rioting is in itself a repudiation of leadership. It is the expression of the anarchy of the profoundly alienated.

In a deeper sense such anarchy could even be a subconscious or conscious invitation to self-destruction. At the height of the Harlem riots of 1964, young Negroes could be heard to say, "If I don't get killed tonight, I'll come back tomorrow." There is evidence these outbreaks are suicidal, reflecting the ultimate in self-negation, self-rejection and hopelessness.

It was the Negro ghetto in Los Angeles which Negroes looted and burned, not the white community. When white firemen tried to enter the ghetto, they were barred by Negro snipers. Many looters did not take the trouble to avoid injury, and many were badly cut in the looting orgy. So one cannot help but wonder whether a desire for self-destruction was not a subconscious factor. Of the 36 people killed in the Los Angeles riot, 33 were Negroes, killed in the campaign to restore law and order. The fact of their deaths—the senseless deaths of human beings—has been obscured by our respectable middle-class preoccupation with the wanton destruction of property, the vandalism and the looting.

Appeals to reason are understandable; they reflect the sense of responsibility of Governmental and civil-rights leaders. But they certainly do not take into account the fact that one cannot expect individuals who have been systematically excluded from the privileges of middle-class life to view themselves as middle-class or to behave in terms of middle-class values. Those who despair in the ghetto follow their own laws—generally the laws of unreason. And though these laws are not in themselves moral, they have moral consequences and moral causes.

The inmates of the ghetto have no realistic stake in respecting property because in a basic sense they do not possess it. They are possessed by it. Property is, rather, an instrument for perpetuation of their own exploitation. Stores in the ghetto—which they rarely own—overcharge for inferior goods. They may obtain the symbols of America's vaunted high standard of living—radios, TV's, washing machines, refrigerators— but usually only through usurious carrying costs, one more symbol of the pattern of material exploitation. They do not respect property because property is almost invariably used to degrade them.

James Bryant Conant and others have warned America it is no longer possible to confine hundreds of thousands of undereducated, underemployed, purposeless young people and adults in an affluent America without storing up social dynamite. The dark ghettoes now represent a nuclear stock pile which can annihilate the very foundations of America. And if, as a minority, desperate Negroes are not able to "win over" the majority, they can nevertheless effectively undermine what they cannot win.

A small minority of Negroes can do this. Such warnings are generally ignored during the interludes of apparent quiescence and tend to be violently rejected, particularly when they come from whites, at the time of a Negro revolt.

When Senator Robert Kennedy incisively observed, after Watts, "There is no point in telling Negroes to observe the law. . . . It has almost always been used against [them]," it was described by an· individual who took the trouble to write a letter to The New York Times as an irresponsible incitement to violence. The bedeviling fact remains, however, that as long as institutionalized forms of American racism persist, violent eruptions will continue to occur in the Negro ghettoes. As Senator Kennedy warned: "All these places—Harlem, Watts, South Side—are riots waiting to happen."

When they do happen, the oversimplified term "police brutality" will be heard, but the relationship between police and residents of the ghetto is more complicated than that. Unquestionably, police brutality occurs. In the panic probably stemming from deep and complex forms of racism, inexperienced policemen have injured or killed Negroes or Puerto Ricans or other members of a powerless minority. And it is certainly true that a common denominator of most, if not all, the riots of the past two summers has been some incident involving the police, an incident which the larger society views as trivial but which prisoners of the ghetto interpret as cruel and humiliating.

In spite of the exacerbating frequency of police racism, however, the more pertinent cause of the ghetto's contempt for police is the role they are believed to play in crime and corruption within the ghetto —accepting bribes for winking at illegal activities which thrive in the ghetto. The police, rightly or wrongly, are viewed not only as significant agents in exploiting ghetto residents but also as symbols of the pathology which encompasses the ghetto. They are seen matter-of-factly as adversaries as well as burdens. The more privileged society may decide that respect for law and order is essential for its own survival, but in the dark ghettoes, survival often depends on disrespect for the law as Negroes experience it.

Thus the problem will not be solved merely by reducing the frequency of police brutality or by increasing the number of Negro policemen. It will require major reorganization and reeducation of the police and a major reorganization of the ghetto itself. To say as Police Chief William Parker did of the Los Angeles Negroes, "We are on top and they are on the bottom," is to prove to Negroes that their deep fears and hatred of established law and order are justified.

While the riots cannot be understood by attempts to excuse them, neither can they be understood by deploring them—especially by deploring them according to a double standard of social morality. For while the lawlessness of white segregationists and rebellious Negroes are expressions of deep frustrations and chronic racism, the lawlessness of Negroes is usually considered a reflection on all Negroes and countered by the full force of police and other governmental authority, but the lawlessness of whites is seen as the primitive reactions of a small group of unstable individuals and is frequently ignored by the police—when they are not themselves accessories. Moreover, rarely do the leaders of a white community in which white violence occurs publicly condemn even the known perpetrators, while almost invariably national and local Negro leaders are required to condemn the mob violence of Negroes.

As long as these double standards of social morality prevail, they reflect the forms of accepted racism which are the embers of substantial violence on the part of both Negroes and whites. And it should be obvious also, although it does not appear to be, that the violence of the Negro is the violence of the oppressed while the violence of white segregationists seeks to maintain oppression.

It is significant that the recent eruptions in Negro communities have not occurred in areas dominated by more flagrant forms of racism, by the Klan and the other institutions of Southern bigotry. They have occurred precisely in those communities where whites have prided themselves on their liberal approach to matters of race and in those states having strong laws prescribing equal opportunity, fair employment and allegedly open housing. (Some observers see a relationship between the defeat of the open housing referendum in California and the Los Angeles outbreak, but it would seem misleading to attempt to account for the riot by any single factor.)

It is revealing to hear the stunned reaction of some top political officials in Los Angeles and California who are unable to understand that such a thing could happen in Los Angeles. Here, they said, whites and blacks got along fine together; here, as reporters constantly pointed out, ghetto streets are lined with palm trees, some with private homes surrounded by tended lawns.

Americans are accustomed to judging the state of people's minds by the most visible aspects—the presence of a TV antenna indicates affluence and a neat lawn a middle-class home. The fact is a ghetto takes on the physical appearance of the particular city—in New York, rat-infested tenements and dirty streets; in Los Angeles, small homes with palm trees—but in many a small home live numerous families and in every house live segregated, desperate people with no jobs or servile jobs, little education, broken families, delinquency, drug addiction, and a burning rage at a society that excludes them from the things it values most.

It is probably not by chance that the Federal Civil Rights Act of 1964 and the Voting Rights Act of 1965 were followed by violence in the North. This was important legislation, but it was more relevant to the predicament of the Southern Negro than to Negroes in Northern ghettoes.

It may well be that the channeling of energies of Negroes in Southern communities toward eliminating the more vicious and obvious signs of racism precludes temporarily the dissipation of energy in random violence. The Northern Negro is clearly not suffering from a lack of laws. But he is suffering—rejected, segregated, discriminated against in employment, in housing, his children subjugated in de facto segregated and inferior schools in spite of a plethora of laws that imply the contrary.

He has been told of great progress in civil rights during the past 10 years and proof of this progress is offered in terms of Supreme Court decisions and civil-rights legislation and firm Presidential commitment. But he sees no positive changes in his day-to-day life. The very verbalizations of progress contribute to his frustration and rage. He is suffering from a pervasive, insensitive and at times self-righteous form of American racism that does not understand the depth of his need.

Not the civil-rights leaders who urge him to demonstrate, but the whites who urge him not to "in the light of present progress" contribute to the anger which explodes in sudden fury. He is told by liberal whites they contribute to civil-rights causes, they marched to Washington and journeyed to Selma and Montgomery to demonstrate their commitment to racial justice and equality.

But Negroes see only the continuing decay of their homes, many of them owned by liberal whites. He sees he does not own any of the means of production, distribution and sale of goods he must purchase to live. He sees his children subjected to criminally inefficient education in public schools they are required to attend, and which are often administered and staffed by liberal whites. He sees liberal labor unions which either exclude him, accept him in token numbers or, even when they do accept him en masse, exclude him from leadership or policy-making roles.

And he sees that persistent protest in the face of racism which dominates his life and shackles him within the ghetto may be interpreted by his white friends as a sign of his insatiability, his irrationality and, above all, of his ingratitude. And because this interpretation comes from his friends and allies it is much harder to take psychologically than the clear-cut bigotry of open segregationists.

It is precisely at this point in the development of race relations that the complexities, depth and intensity of American racism reveal themselves with excruciating clarity. At this point regional differences disappear. The greatest danger is an intensification of racism leading to the polarization of America into white and black. "What do they want?" the white man asks, "Don't they know they hurt their own cause!" "Get Whitey," cries the Negro. "Burn, baby, burn." At this point concerned whites and Negroes are required to face the extent of personal damage which racism has inflicted on both.

It will require from whites more than financial contributions to civil-rights agencies, more than mere verbal and intellectual support for the cause of justice. It will require compassion, willingness to accept hostility and increased resolve to go about the common business, the transformation and strengthening of our society toward the point where race and color are no longer relevant in discussing the opportunities, rights and responsibilities of Americans.

Negroes, too, are confronted with difficult challenges in the present stage of the civil rights struggle. The bitterness and rage which formed the basis for the protests against flagrant racial injustices must somehow be channeled into constructive, nondramatic programs required to translate court decisions, legislation and growing political power into actual changes in the living conditions of the masses of Negroes. Some ways must be found whereby Negro leadership and Negro organizations can redirect the volatile emotions of Negroes away from wasteful, sporadic outbursts and toward self-help and constructive social action. The need for candid communication between middle-class Negroes and the Negro masses is as imperative as the need for painful honesty and cooperation between Negroes and whites.

These demands upon whites and Negroes will not be easy to meet since it is difficult, if not impossible, for anyone growing up in America to escape some form of racist contamination. And a most disturbing fact is the tendency of racism to perpetuate itself, to resist even the most stark imperatives for change. This is the contemporary crisis in race relations which Americans must somehow find the strength to face and solve. Otherwise we will remain the victims of capricious and destructive racial animosities and riots.

The key danger is the possibility that America has permitted the cancer of racism to spread so far that present available remedies can be only palliative. One must, however, continue to believe and act on the assumption that the disease is remediable.

It is important that all three branches of the Federal Government have committed themselves to using their power to improve the status of Negroes. These commitments must be enforced despite overt or subtle attempts to resist and evade them.

But this resistance must be seen not only in the bigotry of segregationists. It must be recognized in the moralizing of Northern whites who do not consciously feel themselves afflicted with the disease of racism, even as they assert that Negro rioting justifies ending their involvement in the civil-rights cause. It must be recognized in the insistence that Negroes pull themselves up by their own bootstraps, demonstrating to the liberal and white communities they have earned the right to be treated as equal American citizens. These are satisfying, self-righteous arguments but they cannot disguise the profound realities of an unacknowledged racism.

If it is possible to talk of any value emerging from the riots it would be this: They are signals of distress, an SOS from the ghetto. They also provide the basis for therapeutically ventilating deeply repressed feelings of whites and Negroes—their underlying fear and the primitive sense of race.

In the religiously oriented, nonviolent civil rights movement in the South, courteous, neatly dressed Negroes carrying books fitted into the middle-class white image more adequately than the vulgar whites who harassed them. The middle-class white, therefore, identified with the oppressed, not the oppressor. But empathy given as a reward for respectable behavior has little value. Understanding can only be tested when one's own interests are deeply threatened, one's sensibilities violated.

These feelings of hostility must be exposed to cold reality as the prelude to realistic programs for change. If under the warmth of apparent support for civil rights lies a deeply repressed prejudice, no realistic social change can be effective.

It would be unrealistic, of course, to expect the masses of whites and Negroes who have grown up in an essentially racist society suddenly to love one another. Fortunately, love is not a prerequisite for the social reorganization now demanded. Love has not been necessary to create workable living arrangements among other ethnic groups in our society. It is no more relevant to ask Negroes and whites to love each other than to ask Italians and Irish to do the same as a prerequisite for social peace and justice.

Nevertheless, real changes in the predicament of previously rejected Negroes—changes compatible with a stable and decent society—must be made, and soon.

The Negro must be included within the economy at all levels of employment, thereby providing the basis for a sound family life and an opportunity to have an actual stake in American business and property.

The social organization of our educational system must be transformed so Negroes can be taught in schools which do not reinforce their feeling of inferiority. The reorganization, improvement and integration of our public schools is also necessary in order to re-educate white children and prepare them to live in the present and future world of racial diversity.

The conditions under which Negroes live must be improved—bad housing, infant mortality and disease, delinquency, drug addiction must be drastically reduced.

Until these minimum goals are achieved, Americans must accept the fact that we cannot expect to maintain racial ghettoes without paying a high price. If it is possible for Americans to carry out realistic programs to change the lives of human beings now confined within their ghettoes, the ghetto will be destroyed rationally, by plan, and not by random self-destructive forces. Only then will American society not remain at the mercy of primitive, frightening, irrational attempts by prisoners in the ghetto to destroy their own prison.

william kornhauser

In the mid-1960s campus confrontation became almost as commonplace as the Junior Prom once was. It began at Berkeley and spread
across the country. The issues were many and varied widely but, at
bottom, one thing was central: a challenge to the traditional authority
of university administrations and senior faculty members.

William Kornhauser, a professor at the University of California,
Berkeley, analyzed "The Politics of Confrontation" at his institution
and at nearby San Francisco State. The selection presented here deals
with the problems of powerlessness and polarization and includes
important comments on varied responses and actions of white students and blacks.

Current protest in America is marked by massive challenges
to legally constituted authority and by selective repression of
militant action. In the cities and on the campuses, politics
takes the form of confrontation. Dissident militants claim that
normal channels are inaccessible or ineffective, leaving no
choice but direct action. Authorities deny this and justify
repressive action on the grounds that normal controls are
inadequate to cope with confrontation.

Both sides increasingly believe that only one side can win,
and that there has to be a showdown. In this respect the con-

flict resembles a classic revolutionary situation, in which *polarization* of social forces destroys the efficacy of the moderates, who seek negotiation and accommodation within a common framework. In a highly polarized situation, each side draws on whatever power resources it can command. To counter institutional power, radicals seek power through mass *mobilization.* In the process of polarization, previously uncommitted people align themselves with the initially small core of radicals. The legal appeal of authority proves ineffective against mass action. Faced with mass disruption, authorities fall back on the use of force, which further undermines their legitimacy.

This paper examines the crisis of authority in the university (Berkeley) and in the city (San Francisco).

Confrontation at Berkeley

Student activism had gathered considerable momentum prior to the first massive confrontation at Berkeley in 1964, primarily as a result of the civil rights movement. Many Berkeley students participated in two large sit-ins in San Francisco business establishments only a few months before the campus demonstrations began. Students increasingly participated in political activities, and dissension built up between student political groups and university administrators. The main issues at Berkeley concerned administration restrictions on the freedom of students on campus; the only place students were allowed to conduct political activity was in a small area adjoining the main entrance to campus. Some administration concessions had been made in the years immediately preceding the major confrontation, e.g., previously banned "partisan" political speeches on campus were allowed. But no serious attempt was made to introduce new channels of consultation or participation for student expression of grievances within the university, or to change the institution's role in the community and nation.

In the fall of 1964, the Berkeley administration prohibited further political activity in the one area where it had been allowed. Students violated the new restriction on the use of university facilities, and the administration suspended leaders of the violations.

When a police car was driven into the center of the campus to remove one of the violators, students sat down around the car and immobilized it for 32 hours. They released it only after the President of the university agreed to a reconsideration of the ban on political activity and the disciplining of student violators of the ban. Two months of unsuccessful negotiations ended in a mass sit-in in the administration building. The Governor immediately ordered police to remove them, and a student strike followed. At this point, the top administrative officials withdrew (the Chancellor entered a hospital and the President made no new initiative after his proposal to end the strike was rejected by the striking students), and the faculty voted to support student demands for freedom of political activity. A new chancellor was appointed and the confrontation ended.

The Dynamics of Confrontation

The critical process underlying confrontation is polarization: (1) the tendency for a community or institution to divide into two hostile camps, and (2) the tendency for the two camps to generalize their hostility to many matters in addition to those that originally divided them.

There is an underlying and growing *distrust of authority* in the university. *This is the single most important indicator of institutional vulnerability to polarization and confrontation.* Five sample surveys at Berkeley between 1960 and 1968 support this conclusion.[1]

1. Widespread distrust of the administration preceded confrontation: about 30 percent of the 25,000 students at Berkeley said they did not think that the administration could be trusted to give sufficient consideration to the rights and needs of students in setting university policies.
2. Those who distrusted the administrators were likely to support the demonstrators, and those who trusted the administration were very unlikely to support the demonstrations: 55 percent of the former but only 13 percent of the latter supported the Free Speech Movement at Berkeley in 1964.
3. Following confrontation and the installation of a new administration, distrust declined at first. But then it increased to a new high: 32 percent and 31 percent expressed distrust in 1965 and 1966 respectively, and 46 percent expressed distrust while only 32 percent expressed trust (23 percent undecided) at Berkeley in 1968. Thus polarization continued to be very high, and escalating confrontations took place at Berkeley in the years following the Free Speech Movement of 1964.

Polarization by itself does not produce confrontation; mobilization of the opposing camps must occur. People may be sharply divided without being willing or able to act. The Berkeley students, however, mobilized. During the fall of 1964, from a student body of 27,000, 3400 students participated in one or both major sit-ins (around the police car and in the administration building), 4800 picketed during the strike, and 5600 others supported the strike by boycotting classes.

The mobilization proceeded in two steps. First the activist core, consisting of about 1000 students, was mobilized primarily by the administration's political bans and disciplinary actions against a few radical leaders. They were ready to risk arrest for civil disobedience. The strength of the student demonstrations was based on *solidarity* rather than organization, and this solidarity spread to large numbers of students. These students felt that the administration was not only out to get a few leaders, but also that it did not take the movement as a serious expression of student sentiment; they were further angered by the administration's refusal to bargain with the protesters. Instead, the Berkeley administration negotiated with the student government, which lacked legitimacy because it was widely perceived as an arm of the administration (only 18 percent of the students expressed support for the student government).

In the second stage, massive police action against the sit-ins further mobilized some 5000 strikers. These repressive disciplinary and police actions instigated by the administration were critical factors in consolidating mass opposition in a situation that was already highly polarized.

Dynamics of Order

At least three different conceptions of order are at stake here: the administration acted as if order meant the enforcement of *authority*; the faculty tended to stress the settlement of disputes for the sake of social *peace;* and the students acted on the belief that legitimate order meant recognition of student *rights*. Though enforcement of authority, settlement of conflict, and recognition of rights are all aspects of order, they may be in contradiction with one another, as this case demonstrates. Let us look at the problem of order from each of these perspectives.

Enforcement of Authority   The administration view is that only they have the responsibility for the whole institution; therefore their authority must be enforced. Thus the initial decision to ban political activity on the Berkeley campus was made on the grounds that not doing so would make the administration appear lax in enforcing its authority. (A university rule prohibited partisan advocacy on university property.) Subsequently, the Chancellor, feeling that his authority would be undermined if he seemed to condone disobedience, rejected both negotiations with students and amnesty. He believed his authority was on the line; he could not back down without jeopardizing the whole institution. Administrative authority, then, becomes *symbolic* as well as instrumental. Though the punishment of those who violated authority was not instrumentally necessary for the maintenance of the administration at that time, it was believed necessary as a means of *visibly* demonstrating the legitimacy of authority and the illegitimacy of disobedience. Symbolic and instrumental authority can be mutually contradictory, cancelling the goal of order. The effect of the symbolic discipline was the destruction of instrumental authority with a massive sit-in in the administration building. Thus, at times the choice may be between enforcing authority and minimizing disorder.

Administrators tend to view the maintenance of order as the suppression of antisocial behavior. Violations of political rules are formally treated in the same manner as violations of rules governing sex, drinking, and cheating. More important is the tendency of administrators to blame disorderly politics on "a few troublemakers" or "outside agitators."[2]

An alternative view is to regard confrontations as disputes to be settled rather than as deviant behavior to be suppressed.[3] Where disorder is defined as a dispute, there is the motivation to seek mediation or negotiation. In the Berkeley case, this would have required higher administrative levels to recognize that the Dean of Students' office might have been mistaken in issuing the initial ban, and that the affected student groups might have had a real grievance. (Much later the President admitted the ban was a mistake, but he felt that administration authority would be undermined if he had abrogated it.)

More generally, what is deviance to be suppressed in one historical period may be viewed as a dispute to be settled at another time. During the labor strife of the thirties, for example, what had previously been regarded as violence to be suppressed increasingly came to be treated as a conflict to be resolved. Where departures from order are treated as deviance, then, order will be imposed; but where they are defined as disputes, order will be negotiated. At Berkeley, order was restored only after student protest stopped being treated as deviance to be suppressed and came to be treated as a dispute to be settled.

Thus the tendency of officials to equate the maintenance of order with the enforcement of authority is a source of institutional vulnerability to the escalation of disorder. This vulnerability is deepened by the increasing centralization of authority, which in turn renders authority more remote. The danger of remoteness is much more than "the failure of communication." It is primarily the lack of responsiveness and correlatively the impoverishment of resources (energies, commitments) at the disposal of administrators—not being responsive to their constituencies, officials also lack support from their constituencies. Thus lack of confidence in the administration was widespread at Berkeley among the faculty as well as the students.

A study of university administrators concludes that: "The growth in

size and importance of universities, together with increasing specialization, has sharpened the separateness of administrators from the rest
of university life. Their authority is consequently . . . precarious . . ."[4]
This separateness engenders great vulnerability in times of crisis.
Faced with student protest, the Berkeley administration acted more
from weakness than strength, more from anticipation of outside pressure than actual demands from the "power structure," more from
concern for protecting their precarious authority than concern for
institutional interests. As a result, the administration failed to secure
order, as well as to maintain authority.

Settlement of Conflict   A second view of order equates it with settlement of conflict for the sake of social peace. This is the predominant
view of the faculty, which is more flexible than the view of order as
enforcement of authority. The weakness of this view is the tendency to
avoid the hard issues of institutional integrity. For example, by con-
demning student disorder on the one hand, and police action on the
other, the faculty avoids the student claim that no other way is open
for pressing just grievances, as well as the administration claim that no
other way exists for restoring order.

Although the faculty comprises the core of the university, neither
its organization nor its culture prepares it for institutional responsibility
and leadership. The faculty merges with the administration through
professors who are deans and other kinds of officials, and also with the
student body through graduate students who are teaching assistants
and instructors. The faculty has a corporate character of its own, of
course, but it is blurred by specialization. Especially in leading universities like Berkeley, many professors find their major identification with
their specialty, wherever it is practiced, rather than with the institution.
The most eminent professors are least likely to have strong institutional identification. Therefore, the struggle between students and
administration developed without significant faculty participation.

Small groups of professors did play a role from the beginning, especially as *mediators.* However, mediation became increasingly difficult
and ineffective as the conflict polarized; student leaders and administrators alike rejected faculty attempts at mediation. This forced the
faculty as a body to seek its own solution to the crisis. The Berkeley
faculty was much more successful in this effort than in subsequent
confrontations elsewhere. There are many reasons for this, including
the much greater collapse of administrative authority in 1964, the
clearer issue of civil liberties at that time, and the more moderate
tactics of the students.

The faculty sought "peace and quiet" rather than "law and order" (the
administration perspective) or "freedom and power" (the student
perspective). The social process underlying the insistence on peace

and quiet is *privatization* of faculty relations and activities. The individual professor above all seeks to preserve his professional sphere from interference by colleagues, administrators, and students alike. In the extreme, he wants to escape from all *institutional* obligations into the privacy of his own work. To call this privatization is to distinguish it not from the public life of the community or nation but from the institutional life of the university. Hence teaching and even research *could be* but seldom are significant modes of participation in the institutional life of the university.

To generalize this argument: privatization is a process of alienating people from a public or institutional realm. To the extent that order rests on privatization, this means that it is held together by separateness rather than concertedness, by avoidance rather than conflict, by respect for privacy rather than desire for dialogue, by exchange rather than loyalty. Such an order is highly vulnerable to breakdowns in times of stress, as people are alien to one another and to a common enterprise. Faculty privatization may be symptomatic of the broader impact of professionalization on public order and public life. While the "knowledge explosion" and the great growth of expertise greatly enhance the technical resources for solving problems, they may have a debilitating effect on social and political competence in a society, especially in times of crisis.

Establishment of Rights   A third view of order equates it with the establishment of rights. It is above all a democratic perspective held by people who believe that they (and others) are being unfairly excluded from full membership in the social order. Those who hold such beliefs initially seek entrance into the existing order. This reformist spirit wanes insofar as official responses frustrate demands for full membership. Lack of openness to reform provokes a challenge to the very legitimacy of present social arrangements. Thus the view of order as rights is potentially radical and even revolutionary.

This view of order became predominant among students during the 1960s. The unresponsiveness of institutions, including the university, has moved activist students from reform to resistance. At Berkeley, students began with specific grievances, including compulsory ROTC, restrictions on political speakers and student government, and, in the fall of 1964, the ban on campus political activity. Opinion surveys show that by this time half the student body said they did not have any say in what the administration did, and three fifths felt that students were being denied their full rights of free speech on campus. As the struggle over these specific grievances intensified, new grievances arose over the arbitrariness (e.g., in disciplining student activists) and hypocrisy of the administration, the indifference of the faculty, and the irrelevance of the curriculum. New consciousness of rights and needs continued to develop, illustrated by the increase from 51 percent in 1965 to 71 percent in 1968 in the number of students who thought that they should have more of a say in educational policies. More fundamentally, by the time students had experienced the frustration and suppression of anti-war activities, Third World struggles, and the battle over People's Park, a full-blown counter community of students and non-students had developed on the very borders of the campus.

The decisive process underlying the conception of order as the establishment of rights is *politization*, especially a growing consciousness of rights. The persistent denial of rights radicalized newly conscious students: what was happening in Vietnam came to be linked to what was happening in the ghettos and then in their own communities; and what was happening within the university came to be seen as closely intertwined with the role the university was playing in the society. This new consciousness increasingly is embodied in a movement seeking the transformation of the entire social order.

Dynamics of Change

The main concrete result of the student demonstrations at Berkeley in 1964 was liberalized rules governing political action on campus. In addition, a faculty commission to investigate needed educational reforms was established, and its report led to a number of innovations designed to improve the curriculum. Finally, there was a considerable shakeup in administrative personnel: the Berkeley Chancellor and then the university President lost their jobs, at least in part because the Regents did not like the way they had handled the student protests.

The central issue has concerned not specific changes so much as the mode of change—whether the development of a more viable order requires the correction of abuses within the existing structure or a fundamental restructuring of the university.

The notion of change that has been stressed by administration and faculty at Berkeley is reform from above. The initial settlement of the confrontation was based on faculty resolutions. The administration promulgated rules for political activity that reasonably expressed the intent of the faculty resolutions. Students saw faculty actions as support for their demands. Subsequently, however, they became disenchanted with university reforms, including the new rules, educational reforms, and the new administration. They protested that they had been given no say in the formulation of rules, that they had not been represented on the commission for educational reform, that the commission had practically nothing to recommend in the way of increased student participation in educational change, and that the new administration was no more interested than the old one in consulting student opinion or in respecting student rights. A joint faculty-student commission report on university governance in 1968 recommended numerous ways of increasing student participation in university decisions, but the administration and faculty response was generally negative. Partly for these reasons (and paralleling the civil rights movement) the cry for Student Freedom in 1964 gave way to the call for Student Power in 1968.

These conflicting approaches to change may be analyzed with an eye to what they reveal about institutional vulnerabilities to crises of authority. One approach is the administrative path to change, the other may be called the political model of change.

Administrative Mode of Change   The underlying perspective of the administrative approach is that change is to come from above rather than from below, on the basis of expertise rather than public action. Thus if the complaint is voiced, as it has been at Berkeley, that institutional channels are closed, then the administration response is to accept student membership on committees as a way of reducing the arbitrariness of power within the system. The administration and faculty, however, strongly resist politization of university decision-making (e.g., representation of campus action groups). The fear is that campus politics threatens the stability of the system, and therefore change should be sought only through administrative channels and should be made only if it does not weaken established authority.

This model of change (and it is the one that prevails at Berkeley) fails to significantly reduce institutional vulnerability to crises of authority. For it is precisely the weakness of existing channels and of established authority that prepares the way for confrontation and breakdown. The administration at Berkeley finds little support for its authority from students because it has such weak structural connections with them.[5]

Political Mode of Change   The underlying perspective of the political approach is that change comes from the community rather than from administrative authority. The community generates change through public forums, campaigns, elections, negotiations, and other devices that take account of autonomous groups and competing views.

The political model of change aims at the development of a community upon which authority rests and to which authority is responsive. The ultimate test of a political community is whether members have acquired "the effective power to criticize, to dissent, and where need be, to compel responsiveness."[6]

The primary cost of the political model is more routine disorder than in the administration model, but perhaps less severe crises of authority. In addition, the political model renders administrative authority less remote by subjecting it to more open scrutiny and criticism. It forces the faculty to be less privatized and more involved in the institutional life of the university. These consequences are already observable, if only to a small degree, as student demands for responsiveness begin to make themselves felt.

Confrontation in San Francisco

During 1964 and 1965 black leaders sought control over the newly formed Community Action Program (CAP) in San Francisco. The struggle began in response to the ambiguous concept of maximum feasible participation contained in the Economic Opportunity Act, but it soon became a general demand for power. In classical political terms, black militants demanded self-determination against alien rule; city officials claimed public responsibility against a power grab. Established black leaders joined with black militants in a prolonged confrontation with the Mayor. Subsequently, the black coalition disintegrated, and militants were driven out of the CAP, but not before the ghettos organized to gain majority representation on policy committees, as well as to determine neighborhood programs.

In 1963, militant civil rights groups (notably CORE) launched demonstrations to force selected employers to bargain with them over hiring and training programs for blacks. The demand for direct negotiations represented an effort to win recognition of black organizations as bargaining agents, in the manner of trade unions. After peaceful demonstrations failed to win agreements with the management of hotels, automobile agencies, and a large bank, massive civil disobedience followed. Some concessions on the employment of blacks were won, but mass arrests and convictions made the costs too high for the civil rights movement to sustain the confrontation. The most important result of these confrontations was the establishment of a new civil rights goal— the acquisition of authority to participate in the decision-making process. In the case of private industry, this meant the rejection of government agencies as the instruments of negotiations with employers. Thus, the civil rights groups refused to deal with a Human Rights Commission established by the Mayor in response to the crisis.

Following the confrontation with industry in April 1964, the civil rights groups turned their energies to seeking control over a major redevelopment plan in the largest (predominantly black) slum in the city. The plan was believed to be destructive to the community, and it was made without community participation. Many community residents were mobilized in opposition to the plan and in support of an alternative plan for neighborhood nonprofit corporations to handle housing and other community problems. Although direct action to stop redevelopment was threatened, the plan was not blocked or even substantially altered.

It was precisely at this time, following almost a year of unsuccessful civil rights agitation for negotiated authority, that the antipoverty program was initiated in San Francisco. The Mayor immediately appointed a council to manage the program. Just as quickly, black groups sought to wrest control of the council from the Mayor. In this case, they had the powerful weapon of the Economic Opportunity Act itself, namely the maximum feasible participation clause.

During the preceding confrontations, the militants lost primarily because moderate black leaders refused to support them. Even the NAACP split along moderate-militant lines in the employment and redevelopment struggles, while the key black politicians, ministers, and labor officials continued to operate only within existing channels. This time, however, the moderates joined the militants against the city officials, thereby making victory possible.

The civil rights movement's prior commitment to the idea of participating as an organized unit in decision-making concerning black interests led to the militants' demand for control of the antipoverty program by elected representatives of the poor. Specifically, they demanded majority representation on the citywide policy-making bodies and the organization of the ghetto to determine all programs of the poor capable of stimulating a *bargaining relationship* with city officials and agencies on all matters relating to their needs.

Black civic leaders, on the other hand, were interested in the poverty program primarily for specific services, like job training and loans to small black businesses. They had formed their own organization with the intention of becoming the official city agency to conduct the antipoverty program. When the Mayor appointed only five members of the group to the fifty member council, the group demanded at least ten additional council seats. Although the group threatened many times to demonstrate if this demand were not met, it appears to have posed no real threat to the Mayor, and he made no attempt to meet the demand. As a result, these moderate black civic leaders threw their support to the radical black civil rights leaders' demand for majority representation. The black coalition and the Mayor became increasingly antagonistic, each charging the other with attempting a power grab.

The militants were the only ones organizing the poor neighborhoods. Hence, while representatives of the federal antipoverty agency were telling the city antipoverty agency that some representation of the poor had to be included, militant-sponsored candidates were elected, preparatory to assuming positions in the agency's policy-making bodies. The militant blacks worked for weeks to get a slate of civil rights supporters elected. Most of those elected were veterans of the earlier demonstrations and confrontations.

In the early summer of 1965, faced with a united black bloc, the Mayor agreed to majority representation in the executive committee but sought to make it subordinate to the council, which he continued to control. At this point in the struggle, the rioting in Watts took place. Immediately, a black militant told the press that blacks were prepared to engage in massive civil disobedience if majority representation in the council were not forthcoming. At a mass public meeting it became clear that the black leaders had sustained their coalition and were ready to act. Shortly thereafter, the Mayor announced that he did not wish to stand in the way of majority representation.

These confrontations showed that there were only weak links between the city government and the black community. The black community was just beginning to break through its isolation. In the absence of effective institutional arrangements to compel the administration to be responsive to the black constituency, confrontation was the only way out of isolation. The Mayor's concern for enforcing his authority as the chief official responsible for public funds clashed head-on with black insistence on self-determination. Caught between the antagonists were numerous professionals, including some of the Mayor's initial appointees to the antipoverty council. They wanted a peaceful solution that would permit the efficient provision of services. During the confrontation, they were relatively powerless to affect the outcome, and many of them in fact became sympathetic to the black demands rather than siding with the Mayor. This occurred despite their natural inclination to choose reform from above on an administrative model rather than change from below on the model of political participation.

Immediately upon winning majority representation, the militants gained approval from the reconstituted council for their plan to use the antipoverty funds to build a community organization in the ghetto. This organization was intended to become capable of governing the ghetto and of bargaining with outside agencies and officials. But the militants were primarily experienced in extra-institutional means of action, not in duly constituted public programs. Once they were in, they suffered from the renewed opposition of established black leaders, as well as from their own inexperience and lack of support in the black community. A year after their victory over the Mayor, the militants were defeated by opportunist leaders backed by established leaders in the black community.

The very insistence of the militants on maximum participation of the residents, together with their concentration on elections of representatives to the area board which necessitated staffing a large organizing effort, proved to be their undoing. For the elections and the hiring immediately brought into the organization widely diverse interests and intense personal ambitions of the more active residents of the community, thereby destroying the militants' ability to sustain their leadership and goals, as well as the unity of the organization. The militants did not begin with a firm basis of support in the community, and failed to build such a basis through selective recruitment and effective indoctrination. Those who displaced them were bent on the personal benefits afforded by the antipoverty program, notably marginal power, prestige, and income in the black community; under their leadership the program became yet another limited source of public service and personal gain.

Thus, in the poverty program, too, confrontations failed to yield significant change; civic participation of blacks had not been appreciably advanced and civic authority had not been restructured or rendered more responsive. However, the series of confrontations increasingly *politicalized* the black community and made it more conscious of its *identity*.[7]

In short, during its first three years, the antipoverty organization in San Francisco became a black community organization, and therefore an arena of conflict and a vehicle for emerging community identity. That the level of controversy is presently much less than during 1965–1967 reflects not the resolution of conflict but the shift of controversy and the search for identity to another area within the black community. Correlatively, the sharp reduction in interest and participation in the antipoverty program is not a sign of the program's health but of its declining significance for the community.

The core process for resolving conflict is *bargaining* and *negotiation* between relatively autonomous centers of power. This process extends to issues of authority as well as to more limited matters.

Confrontation may be a way of forcing bargaining and negotiation. It is, however, a costly way, especially for the integrity of the institution or community. It is likely to be a common way, however, when existing channels of participation and bargaining are not readily accessible to new claimants to power.

Confrontation has been used to seek entry into the system. Blockage of entry will tend to transform the goals of confrontation from power within the system to power against the system. The civil rights movement in San Francisco sought the power to participate in decision-making. Thus the militants did not seek to destroy the antipoverty program but to acquire control over it. Insofar as these attempts fail, increasingly militant confrontations gain support, and polarization between these forces and the forces of repression gathers momentum.

The alternative to polarization of conflict and escalating crises of authority is neither the suppression of deviance nor the settlement of disputes alone. In addition, and most important for overcoming basic vulnerabilities, new claimants for power within the system must be recognized. One form of recognition is of individual rights, e.g., the ballot. But this is also inadequate, as it fails to take account of the *real sources of power, notably organized groups.*

These groups may be of two types: they may be primarily *instrumental* for individual participation in the community, that is, new channels and sources of power for their members; or, they also may be *expressive of new statuses and identities* in the community, that is, collective affirmations of positive values. Where the group is identity-affirming, it is not merely making the claim for acceptance of new participants into the existing system. It is also demanding negotiation of the *terms* of acceptance, the rules governing both the substance and the procedure.

The cardinal case in point is the black ghetto. The organization of black ghettos is not merely a way of expediting broader civic participation. Much more important, it is generating demands for the negotiation of relations between the ghetto and existing governing institutions, with the end-in-view of something like home rule. The institutionalization of both negotiation and some home rule would change the existing structure, rather than merely incorporate new participants into it. The justification for such demands is the claim of representing a valued identity, and thereby the affirmation of the dignity of the individuals who are black. This kind of claim to legitimation is consistent with the *core values* of the existing system, but not (or not totally) consistent with *present structures*.

Powerlessness, Polarization, and Authority

The central vulnerability of the American polity is the growing sense of powerlessness of individuals and, correlatively, a growing sense of arbitrariness of officials. The burgeoning acts of revolt express this sense of personal powerlessness versus arbitrary power. Large numbers of individuals define themselves as outsiders, either because they lack affiliations or because their affiliations do not provide sufficient opportunities to evoke responsiveness from the system. The critical question is whether the system is likely to increase the number of outsiders and the intensity of their alienation—in a word, whether social forces will continue to polarize.

Political and legal agencies are increasingly relied upon to prevent polarization. There are two ways such agencies seek control over processes of polarization: repression or reform. The failure of the authorities to repress political violence generally increases polarization. But repression has its severe limitations as a method of containing conflict and reversing the processes of polarization. Only a few of these limitations may be mentioned here. One problem is the vicious circle of violence. The use of police or military action against political movements may merely increase hostilities and win considerable sympathy and support for the targets of police action among heretofore uncommitted people. Second, repression may undermine the legitimacy of existing institutions, especially in a society that prizes individual rights. Third, the police may not be reliable because they give vent to their own hostilities and act in such a repressive manner as to escalate the whole conflict beyond control.

The failure of authorities to redress grievances also encourages polarization. Many a revolutionary situation has been created when a specific and limited grievance has been ignored, only to become transformed into a generalized opposition that seeks the destruction of the system. Grievances are often met with inflexibility on the part of officials who do not want to appear to be backing down under pressure. The tendency for officials to put their authority on the line in such instances is almost certain to polarize the situation further. This will be even more likely when officials themselves recognize the legitimacy of the grievances, or when they are divided or uncertain about the grievances. The attempt *first* to assert authority and only *then* to redress grievances tends to be self-defeating, as the legitimacy of that authority is viewed by those with grievances as itself dependent on how the grievances are met.

But reform or redress, like repression, has its severe limitations as a method for containing conflict and reversing the processes of polarization. Reforms may accentuate rather than mitigate underlying contradictions between institutional purposes and institutional capacities, thereby heightening revolutionary consciousness. Then, again, reforms may alienate those groups that supported a hard line in the government. Reactionary political violence may occur to stop civil authorities from making concessions, as with Reconstruction and contemporary white vigilante groups.

A more fundamental response to crises of authority than either repression or concessions is required to stop polarization: authority must be made responsive through the restructuring of authority itself. Thus, the primary political issue in America is whether authority can be democratized in all spheres of society, or whether crises of authority will continue to build up along increasingly polarized lines. Racial and generational challenges to authority are especially acute in this regard, since they cut across all communities and institutions in society, and potentially create crises in each of them. More fundamentally, the demand for responsiveness, for participation, and for power has gained such currency in the world that no society or institution is immune from either crises of authority or the need for restructuring authority. This is no small part of the revolutionary spirit in the world today.

NOTES

1. Surveys were conducted by William Nichols in 1960 and 1961 (Surveys Research Center, Berkeley); Robert Somers in 1964 and 1968 ("The Mainsprings of the Rebellion: A Survey of Berkeley Students in November, 1964," in Seymour Martin Lipset and Sheldon Wolin (eds.), *The Berkeley Student Revolt* [Garden City, N.Y.: Anchor Books, 1965], pp. 530–558, and unpublished survey of Berkeley students, Spring 1968); Kathleen Gales, "A Campus Revolution," *British Journal of Sociology*, Vol. 17 (1966), pp. 1–19; and Shirley Starr, unpublished survey of Berkeley students, Spring 1966.

2. Thus the Berkeley administration ordered only nonstudents arrested when they called the police during the campus sit-in of 1966.

3. See Philip Selznick, "Law," in Leonard Broom and Philip Selznick, *Sociology* (New York: Harper and Row, 1968), fourth edition, pp. 379–380.

4. Terry Lunsford, "Authority and Ideology in the Administered University," *American Behavioral Scientist*, Vol. 11, No. 5 (May 1968), p. 5.

5. In classic sociological terms, authority that lacks a firm social base does not have much power. A principal way of acquiring a social base is through the delegation of authority; the creation of multiple levels and centers of authority is at the same time the diffusion of responsibility throughout the system. This is completely consistent with the administrative perspective (and may therefore become a major avenue of change in universities). It, too, has its major limitations, however, as the following analysis may suggest.

6. Jeanne Cahn and Edgar Cahn, "The War on Poverty: A Civilian Perspective," *Yale Law Journal*, June 1964, p. 1329.

7. These, then, appear to be the major results of the introduction of the Community Action Program in San Francisco:
(1) The poverty program was transformed from one controlled by the city into a *black-managed program*. This was the central result of the fight for majority representation. (In 1968, as a result of national as well as local efforts, it began to revert back to city control.)
(2) Community service for the ghetto was replaced by *community organization* of the ghetto. This was the central result of the early ascendance of militant over established black leadership. (By 1968, this result also was reversed, as opportunist leadership, supported by established leadership, defeated militant leadership in the ghetto.)
(3) The ghetto was *politicalized* by the struggle for power, first in the confrontation between the black coalition and the Mayor, and second in the struggle among black factions within the antipoverty agency. This was the central result of the numerous conflicts over recruitment of staff, election of representatives and officers, and selection of programs. (By 1968, the main political arena in the ghetto was no longer the antipoverty program but, once again, the urban redevelopment program.)

tom wolfe

Tom Wolfe is not the sort of writer sociologists usually have in mind when they claim that good analysis must include a willingness to probe, to compare, and sometimes to debunk. Yet his work is all of this and more. Author of *The Electric Kool-Aid Acid Test*, *The Pumphouse Gang*, *The Kandy-Kolored Tangerine-Flake Streamline Baby*, *Radical Chic*, and many other lengthy essays about American society, Wolfe bars nothing in showing the underbelly of our culture. He moves in where most sociologists fear to tread and writes on unpopular or unmentionable themes.

In this essay, iconoclast Wolfe describes the successful confrontation tactics used by black activists against the "Flak Catchers"—the officials who serve as buffers between the people and the Establishment. "Mau-mauing," or baiting the flak catchers, began as a daring activity and continues as one of the most effective vehicles for getting concessions from the whites.

When black people first started using the confrontation tactic, they made a secret discovery. There was an extra dividend to this tactic. There was a creamy dessert. It wasn't just that you registered your protest and showed the white man that you meant business and weakened his resolve to keep up the walls of oppression. It wasn't just that you got poverty money and influence. There was something sweet that happened right there on the spot. You made the white man quake. You brought *fear* into his face.

Black people began to realize for the first time that the white man, particularly the educated white man, the leadership, had a deep dark Tarzan mumbo jungle voodoo fear of the black man's masculinity. This was a revelation. For two hundred years, wherever black people lived, north or south, mothers had been raising their sons to be meek, to be mild, to check their manhood at the front door in all things that had to do with white people, for fear of incurring the wrath of the Man. The *Man* was the white man. He was the only *man*. And now, when you got him up close and growled, this all-powerful superior animal turned out to be terrified. You could read it in his face. He had the same fear in his face as some good-doing boy who has just moved onto the block and is hiding behind his mama and the moving man and the sofa while the bad dudes on the block size him up.

So for the black man mau-mauing was a beautiful trip. It not only stood to bring you certain practical gains like money and power. It also energized your batteries. It recharged your masculinity. You no longer had to play it cool and go in for pseudo-ignorant malingering and put your head into that Ofay Pig Latin catacomb code style of protest. Mau-mauing brought you respect in its cash forms: namely, fear and envy.

This was the difference between a confrontation and a demonstration. A demonstration, like the civil-rights march on Washington in 1963, could frighten the white leadership, but it was a general fear, an external fear, like being afraid of a hurricane. But in a confrontation, in mau-mauing, the idea was to frighten white men personally, face to face. The idea was to separate the man from all the power and props of his office. Either he had enough heart to deal with the situation or he didn't. It was like saying, "You—yes, you right there on the platform— we're not talking about the *gov*ernment, we're not talking about the *Off*ice of Economic Oppor*tun*ity—we're talking about *you*, you up there with your hands shaking in your pile of papers . . ." If this worked, it created a personal, internal fear. The internal fear was, "I'm afraid I'm not man enough to deal with these bad niggers!"

That may sound like a simple case of black people being good at terrifying whites and whites being quick to run scared. But it was more than that. The strange thing was that the confrontation ritual was built into the poverty program from the beginning. The poverty bureaucrats depended on confrontations in order to know what to do.

Whites were still in the dark about the ghettos. They had been studying the "urban Negro" in every way they could think of for fifteen years, but they found out they didn't know any more about the ghettos than when they started. Every time there was a riot, whites would call on "Negro leaders" to try to cool it, only to find out that the Negro leaders didn't have any followers. They sent Martin Luther King into Chicago and the people ignored him. They sent Dick Gregory into Watts and the people hooted at him and threw beer cans. During the riot in Hunters Point, the mayor of San Francisco, John Shelley, went into Hunters Point with the only black member of the Board of Supervisors, and the brothers threw rocks at both of them. They sent in the middle-class black members of the Human Rights Commission, and the brothers laughed at them and called them Toms. Then they figured the leadership of the riot was "the gangs," so they sent in the "ex-gang leaders" from groups like Youth for Service to make a "liaison with the key gang leaders." What they didn't know was that Hunters Point and a lot of ghettos were so disorganized, there weren't even any "key gangs," much less "key gang leaders," in there. That riot finally just burnt itself out after five days, that was all.

But the idea that the real leadership in the ghetto might be the *gangs* hung on with the poverty-youth-welfare establishment. It was considered a very sophisticated insight. The youth gangs weren't petty criminals . . . they were "social bandits," primitive revolutionaries . . . Of course, they were hidden from public view. That was why the true nature of ghetto leadership had eluded everyone for so long . . . So the poverty professionals were always on the lookout for the bad-acting dudes who were the "real leaders," the "natural leaders," the "charismatic figures" in the ghetto jungle. These were the kind of people the social-welfare professionals in the Kennedy Administration had in mind when they planned the poverty program in the first place. It was a truly adventurous and experimental approach they had. Instead of handing out alms, which never seemed to change anything, they would encourage the people in the ghettos to organize. They would help them become powerful enough to force the Establishment to give them what they needed. From the beginning the poverty program was aimed at helping ghetto people rise up against their oppressors. It was a scene in which the federal government came into the ghetto and said, "Here is some money and some field advisors. Now you organize your own pressure groups." It was no accident that Huey Newton and Bobby Seale drew up the ten-point program of the Black Panther Party one night in the offices of the North Oakland Poverty Center.

To sell the poverty program, its backers had to give it the protective coloration of "jobs" and "education," the Job Corps and Operation Head Start, things like that, things the country as a whole could accept. "Jobs" and "education" were things everybody could agree on. They were part of the free-enterprise ethic. They weren't uncomfortable subjects like racism and the class structure—and giving the poor the money and the tools to fight City Hall. But from the first that was what the lion's share of the poverty budget went into. It went into "community organizing," which was the bureaucratic term for "power to the people," the term for finding the real leaders of the ghetto and helping them organize the poor.

And how could they find out the identity of these leaders of the people? Simple. In their righteous wrath they would rise up and *confront* you. It was a beautiful piece of circular reasoning. The real leaders of the ghetto will rise up and confront you . . . Therefore, when somebody rises up in the ghetto and confronts you, then you know he's a leader of the people. So the poverty program not only encouraged mau-mauing, it practically *demanded* it. Subconsciously, for administrators in the poverty establishment, public and private, confrontations became a ritual. That was the way the system worked. By 1968 it was standard operating procedure. To get a job in the post office, you filled out forms and took the civil-service exam. To get into the poverty scene, you did some mau-mauing. If you could make the flak catchers lose control of the muscles around their mouths, if you could bring fear into their faces, your application was approved.

Ninety-nine percent of the time whites were in no physical danger whatsoever during mau-mauing. The brothers understood through and through that it was a tactic, a procedure, a game. If you actually hurt or endangered somebody at one of these sessions, you were only cutting yourself off from whatever was being handed out, the jobs, the money, the influence. The idea was to terrify but don't touch. The term *mau-mauing* itself expressed this game-like quality. It expressed the put-on side of it. In public you used the same term the whites used, namely "confrontation." The term *mau-mauing* was a source of amusement in private. The term *mau-mauing* said, "The white man has a voodoo fear of us, because deep down he still thinks we're savages. Right? So we're going to do that Savage number for him." It was like a practical joke at the expense of the white man's superstitiousness.

a. m. rosenthal

At the turn of the twentieth century Emile Durkheim, the famous French sociologist, wrote about what happens when the spirit of community breaks down, when the "collective conscience" is no longer the source of an integrated life. Numerous writers have pointed to a similar phenomenon as they have witnessed people's responses to social situations, especially in the big cities of industrial societies. Durkheim wrote of *anomie,* the failure to know what to do in a situation in which old norms no longer apply. He might have also dealt with *apathy,* the (seeming) lack of concern, one of several apparent responses to anomic conditions.

In this essay journalist A. M. Rosenthal describes the murder of Kitty Genovese who lay screaming and dying while thirty-eight New Yorkers, who later identified themselves as witnesses, did nothing. "Why not?" they were asked.

"We didn't want to get involved."

It happens from time to time in New York that the life of the city is frozen by an instant of shock. In that instant the people of the city are seized by the paralyzing realization that they are one, that each man is in some way a mirror of every other man. They stare at each other—or, really, into themselves—and a look

From A. M. Rosenthal, "A Sickness Called Apathy," *New York Times Magazine* (May 3, 1964) © 1964 by The New York Times Company. Reprinted by permission.

quite like a flush of embarrassment passes over the face of the city. Then the instant passes and the beat resumes and the people turn away and try to explain what they have seen, or try to deny it.

The last 35 minutes of the young life of Miss Catherine Genovese became such a shock in the life of the city. But at the time she died, stabbed again and again by a marauder in her quiet, dark but entirely respectable, street in Kew Gardens, New York hardly took note.

It was not until two weeks later that Catherine Genovese, known as Kitty, returned in death to cry the city awake. Even then it was not her life or her dying that froze the city, but the witnessing of her murder—the choking fact that 38 of her neighbors had seen her stabbed or heard her cries, and that not one of them, during the hideous half-hour, had lifted the telephone from the safety of his own apartment to call the police and try to save her life. When it was over and Miss Genovese was dead and the murderer gone, one man did call—not from his own apartment but from a neighbor's, and only after he had called a friend and asked her what to do.

The day that the story of the witnessing of the death of Miss Genovese appeared in this newspaper became that frozen instant. "Thirty-eight!" people said over and over. "Thirty-eight!"

It was as if the number itself had some special meaning, and in a way, of course, it did. One person or two or even three or four witnessing a murder passively would have been the unnoticed symptom of the disease in the city's body and again would have passed unnoticed. But 38—it was like a man with a running low fever suddenly beginning to cough blood; his friends could no longer ignore his illness, nor could he turn away from himself.

At first there was, briefly, the reaction of shared guilt. Even people who were sure that they certainly would have acted differently felt it somehow. "Dear God, what have we come to?" a woman said that day. "We," not "they."

For in that instant of shock, the mirror showed quite clearly what was wrong, that the face of mankind was spotted with the disease of apathy —all mankind. But this was too frightening a thought to live with and soon the beholders began to set boundaries for the illness, to search frantically for causes that were external and to look for the carrier.

There was a rash of metropolitan masochism. "What the devil do you expect in a town, a jungle, like this?" Sociologists and psychiatrists reached for the warm comfort of jargon—"alienation of the individual from the group," "megalopolitan societies," "the disaster syndrome."

People who came from small towns said it could never happen back home. New Yorkers, ashamed, agreed. Nobody seemed to stop to ask whether there were not perhaps various forms of apathy and that some that exist in villages and towns do not exist in great cities.

Guilt turned into masochism, and masochism, as it often does, became

a sadistic search for a target. Quite soon, the target became the police.

There is no doubt whatsoever that the police in New York have failed, to put it politely, to instill a feeling of total confidence in the population. There are great areas in this city—fine parks as well as slums—where no person in his right mind would wander of an evening or an early morning. There is no central emergency point to receive calls for help. And a small river of letters from citizens to this newspaper testifies to the fact that patrols are often late in answering calls and that policemen on desk duty often give the bitter edge of their tongues to citizens calling for succor.

There is no doubt of these things. But to blame the police for apathy is a bit like blaming the sea wall for springing leaks. The police of this city are more efficient, more restrained and more responsive to public demands than any others the writer has encountered in a decade of traveling the world. Their faults are either mechanical or a reflection of a city where almost every act of police self-protection is assumed to be an act of police brutality, and where a night-club comedian can, as one did the other night, stand on a stage for an hour and a half and vilify the police as brutes, thieves, homosexuals, illiterates, and "Gestapo agents" while the audience howls in laughter as it drinks Scotch from bootleg bottles hidden under the tables.

There are two tragedies in the story of Catherine Genovese. One is the fact that her life was taken from her, that she died in pain and horror at the age of 28. The other is that in dying she gave every human being— not just species New Yorker—an opportunity to examine some truths about the nature of apathy and that this has not been done.

Austin Street, where Catherine Genovese lived, is in a section of Queens known as Kew Gardens. There are two apartment buildings and the rest of the street consists of one-family homes—red-brick, stucco or wood-frame. There are Jews, Catholics and Protestants, a scattering of foreign accents, middle-class incomes.

On the night of March 13, about 3 A.M., Catherine Genovese was returning to her house. She worked late as manager of a bar in Hollis, another part of Queens. She parked her car (a red Fiat) and started to walk to her death.

Lurking near the parking lot was a man. Miss Genovese saw him in the shadows, turned and walked toward a police call box. The man pursued her, stabbed her. She screamed, "Oh my God, he stabbed me! Please help me! Please help me!"

Somebody threw open a window and a man called out: "Let that girl alone!" Other lights turned on, other windows were raised. The attacker got into a car and drove away. A bus passed.

The attacker drove back, got out, searched out Miss Genovese in the back of an apartment building where she had crawled for safety, stabbed her again, drove away again.

The first attack came at 3:15. The first call to the police came at 3:50. Police arrived within two minutes, they say. Miss Genovese was dead.

That night and the next morning the police combed the neighborhood looking for witnesses. They found them, 38.

Two weeks later, when this newspaper heard of the story, a reporter went knocking, door to door, asking why, why.

Through half-opened doors, they told him. Most of them were neither defiant nor terribly embarrassed nor particularly ashamed. The underlying attitude, or explanation, seemed to be fear of involvement—any kind of involvement.

"I didn't want my husband to get involved," a housewife said.

"We thought it was a lovers' quarrel," said another woman. "I went back to bed."

"I was tired," said a man.

"I don't know," said another man.

"I don't know," said still another.

"I don't know," said others.

On March 19, police arrested a 29-year-old business-machine operator named Winston Moseley and charged him with the murder of Catherine Genovese. He has confessed to killing two other women, for one of whose murders police say they have a confession from another man.

Not much is said or heard or thought in the city about Winston Moseley. In this drama, as far as the city is concerned, he appeared briefly, acted his piece, exited into the wings.

A week after the first story appeared, a reporter went back to Austin Street. Now the witnesses no longer wanted to talk. They were harried, annoyed; they thought they should keep their mouths shut. "I've done enough talking," one witness said. "Oh, it's you again," said a woman witness and slammed the door.

The neighbors of the witnesses are willing to talk. Their sympathy is for the silent witnesses and the embarrassment in which they now live.

Max Heilbrunn, who runs a coffee house on Austin Street, talked about all the newspaper publicity and said his neighbors felt they were being picked on. "It isn't a bad neighborhood," he said.

And this from Frank Facciola, the owner of the neighborhood barber shop: "I resent the way these newspaper and television people have hurt us. We have wonderful people here. What happened could have happened any place. There is no question in my mind that people here now would rush out to help anyone being attacked on the street."

Then he said: "The same thing [failure to call the police] happens in other sections every day. Why make such a fuss when it happens in Kew Gardens? We are trying to forget it happened here."

A Frenchwoman in the neighborhood said: "Let's forget the whole thing. It is a quiet neighborhood, good to live in. What happened, happened."

Each individual, obviously, approaches the story of Catherine Genovese, reacts to it and veers away from it against the background of his own life and experience, and his own fears and shortcomings and rationalizations.

It seems to this writer that what happened in the apartments and houses on Austin Street was a symptom of a terrible reality in the human condition—that only under certain situations and only in response to certain reflexes or certain beliefs will a man step out of his shell toward his brother.

To say this is not to excuse, but to try to understand and in so doing perhaps eventually to extend the reflexes and beliefs and situations to include more people. To ignore it is to perpetuate myths that lead nowhere. Of these the two most futile philosophically are that apathy is a response to official ineptitude ("The cops never come on time anyway"), or that apathy is a condition only of metropolitan life.

Certainly police procedures must be improved—although in the story of Miss Genovese all indications were that, once called into action, the police machine behaved perfectly.

As far as is known, not one witness has said that he remained silent because he had had any unpleasant experience with the police. It is a pointless point; there are men who will jump into a river to rescue a drowner; there are others who will tell themselves that a police launch will be cruising by or that, if it doesn't, it should.

Nobody can say why the 38 did not lift the phone while Miss Genovese was being attacked, since they cannot say themselves. It can be assumed, however, that their apathy was indeed of a big-city variety. It is almost a matter of psychological survival, if one is surrounded and pressed by millions of people, to prevent them from constantly impinging on you and the only way to do this is to ignore them as often as possible.

Indifference to one's neighbor and his troubles is a conditioned reflex of life in New York as it is in other big cities. In every major city in which I have lived—in Tokyo and Warsaw, Vienna and Bombay—I have seen, over and over again, people walk away from accident victims. I have walked away myself.

Out-of-towners, and sometimes New Yorkers themselves, like to think that there is something special about New York's metropolitan apathy. It is special in that there are more people here than any place else in the country—and therefore more people to turn away from each other.

For decades, New York turned away from the truth that is Harlem or Bedford-Stuyvesant in Brooklyn. Everybody knew that in the Negro ghettos, men, women and children lived in filth and degradation. But the city, as a city, turned away with the metropolitan brand of apathy. This, most simply, consists of drowning the person-to-person responsibility in a wave of impersonal social action.

Committees were organized, speeches made, budgets passed to "do something" about Harlem or Bedford-Stuyvesant—to do something about the communities. This dulled the reality, and still does, that the communities consist of individual people who ache and suffer in the loss of their individual prides. Housewives who contributed to the N.A.A.C.P. saw nothing wrong in going down to the daily shape-up of domestic workers in the Bronx and selecting a maid for the day after looking over the coffle to see which "girl" among the Negro matrons present looked huskiest.

Now there is an acute awareness of the problems of the Negroes in New York. But, again, it is an impersonal awareness, and more and more it is tinged with irritation at the thought that the integration movement will impinge on the daily personal life of the city.

Nor are Negroes in the city immune from apathy—toward one another or toward whites. They are apathetic toward one another's right to believe and act as they please; one man's concept of proper action is labeled with the group epithet "Uncle Tom." And, until the recent unsurge of the integration movement, there was less action taken within the Negro community to improve conditions in Harlem than there was in the all-white sections of the East Side. It has become fashionable to sneer at "white liberals"—fashionable even among Negroes who for years did nothing for brothers even of their own color.

In their own sense of being wronged, some Negroes of New York have become totally apathetic to the sensitivities of all other groups. In a night club in Harlem the other night, an aspiring Negro politician, a most decent man, talked of how the Jewish shopkeepers exploited the Negroes, how he wished Negroes could "save a dollar like the Jews," totally apathetic toward the fact that Jews at the table might be as hurt as he would be if they talked in clichés of the happy-go-lucky Stepin Fetchit Negro. When a Jew protested, the Negro was stunned—because he was convinced he hated anti-Semitism. He did, in the abstract.

Since the Genovese case, New Yorkers have sought explanations of their apathy toward individuals. Fear, some say—fear of involvement, fear of reprisal from goons, fear of becoming "mixed up" with the police. This, it seems to this writer, is simply rationalization.

The self-protective shells in which we live are determined not only by the difference between big cities and small. They are determined by economics and social class, by caste and by color, and by religion, and by politics.

If I were to see a beggar starving to death in rags on the streets of Paris or New York or London I would be moved to take some kind of action. But many times I have seen starving men lying like broken dolls in the streets of Calcutta or Madras and have done nothing.

I think I would have called the police to save Miss Genovese but I know that I did not save a beggar in Calcutta. Was my failing really so much smaller than that of the people who watched from their windows on Austin Street? And what was the apathy of the people of Austin Street compared, let's say, with the apathy of non-Nazi Germans toward Jews?

Geography is a factor of apathy. Indians reacted to Portuguese imprisoning Goans, but not to Russians killing Hungarians.

Color is a factor. Ghanaians reacted toward Frenchmen killing Algerians, not toward Congolese killing white missionaries.

Strangeness is a factor. Americans react to the extermination of Jews but not to the extermination of Watusis.

There are national as well as individual apathies, all inhibiting the ability to react. The "mind-your-own business" attitude is despised among individuals, and clucked at by sociologists, but glorified as pragmatic national policy among nations.

Only in scattered moments, and then in halting embarrassment, does the United States, the most involved nation in the world, get down to hard cases about the nature of governments with which it deals, and how they treat their subject citizens. People who believe that a free government should react to oppression of people in the mass by other governments are regarded as fanatics or romantics by the same diplomats who would react in horror to the oppression of one single individual in Washington. Between apathy, regarded as a moral disease, and national policy, the line is often hard to find.

There are, it seems to me, only two logical ways to look at the story of the murder of Catherine Genovese. One is the way of the neighbor on Austin Street—"Let's forget the whole thing."

The other is to recognize that the bell tolls even on each man's individual island to recognize that every man must fear the witness in himself who whispers to close the window.

NOW—
AND
IN THE
FUTURE

richard sennett

Does familiarity breed contempt—or accommodation?

In this article Richard Sennett makes some interesting observations about the accelerating course of polarization that is occurring in American cities. He suggests that to reverse the trend drastic changes are necessary, changes that will let air into what Lyford calls "The Airtight Cage."

Since, at bottom, people must live together to learn to live together, there is a real need for mixing—rich and poor, black and white. To achieve urban peace Sennett advocates a kind of institutionalized anarchy. He argues that order will come from the chaos of everyone trying to do their own thing in a limited social setting and finding that they must make concessions.

The idea is fascinating. But will it work? Says Sennett, "A wide network of social contact that people must use in order to survive might erase the polarization of intimacy in the home circle and the impersonal tasks in the world beyond."

Let us imagine a community free to create its own patterns of life, a neighborhood of cheap rents likely to attract young people. Here also, if the functional division in city life were erased, would be found white and black blue-collar laborers, old people, perhaps some immigrant clusters, perhaps a few small shop-

---

From *The Uses of Disorder: Personal Identity and City Life*, by Richard Sennett. Copyright © 1970 by Richard Sennett. Reprinted by permission of Alfred A. Knopf, Inc.

keepers. Because the land use had not been rigidly zoned, all kinds of activities would be found—some light manufacturing, perhaps a brothel or two, many small stores, bars and inexpensive family restaurants.

The outstanding characteristic of this area would be the high level of tension and unease. It would be a vital place, to be sure, but a part of the vitality would be conflict between dissimilar groups of people. And because metropolitan-wide controls would be lessened, the threat, or assurance, of police control would be gone, for the police would not have the responsibility of keeping peace in the community by repressing deviance, but would deal with organized crime or other similar problems.

Precisely because the people had to deal with each other in order to survive, some kind of uneasy truce between these hostile camps would have to be arranged by the people themselves. And the act of participating in some sort of truce would force people to look at each other, if only to find areas in which some tenuous, unloving bond could be forged.

Fright Such a community would probably stimulate a young person, and yet scare him—make him want to find some nice, safe untroubled place. But the very diversity of the neighborhood has a built-in obligation of responsibility; the only way to avoid self-destruction in the community would be to deal with the people who live there.

Thus, the impulse to hide from pain, which is at the heart of the adolescent desire for a purified identity, would have a concrete social matrix, one in which the impulse would become untenable if the person were to survive. It is hard to imagine an 18-year-old, who suddenly has to make peace with white laborers who don't like college kids and with Negroes who don't like whites, making a snap decision about what he will do and be in the world. He can't help having to understand differences in other people whom he may not like, and who may not like him.

But these survival communities would lead men into adult concerns as well; they would not be merely a corrective to adolescence but a field for a richer life beyond it.

Conflict Since the common pattern in the relations between men is a revision to the willfully blind selfishness of the child, the materials for conflict are innate to social life. There are few areas in which it should be expected that men would want to work actively together. But there are group relationships that can be sustaining and productive as a result of letting conflicts of interests, emotional jealousies, class hatreds and racial fears express themselves. These conflicts and fears can be socialized only if they are allowed to play themselves out. If the experience of meaningful conflict were possible in cities, the young would be led to realize the blindness of talking about nonnegotiable demands.

Burn It is one of the terrible simplicities of modern city life that we believe the expression of hostile feelings will lead to violence. Perhaps this belief is so widely held because it justifies repression of our feelings, and so lets us hide from them.

Yet if men continue to believe that hostility between groups should be muted, the cities will continue to burn. By restructuring the power of city bureaucracies so that they leave to the hostile groups themselves the *need* to create some truce, hostility can take on more open and less-violent forms.

Error In any large central city there are many differences in life-styles that could be used to fragment conflict. Ethnicity, social class and race are not simple conditions of life, but complex factors that tend to inter-penetrate and become diffused. For instance, it is a popular error to sup-pose that the violence of recent summers in American cities is a race phenomenon. Most middle-class blacks are hostile to the Negro mili-tants. However, given the structure of community life and police control in American cities, middle-class blacks and poor blacks never have to deal with each other.

Yet if the police stopped their blanket repression and gave the seg-ments of the black community the responsibility to control themselves, these hostilities could be expressed. Both groups, in order to survive, would find that they could go no further to achieve their own ends with-out finding out something about each other. Let us imagine added to this situation a refusal of the police to intervene between any black group and the whites who now feel threatened. I believe that the people in-volved would learn that there is too much complex feeling involved to be taken care of by the burning of stores. When people have to come face to face in order to survive, the death instinct does not prevail.

Density If people are to deal with an environment too complex to con-trol, a small village or a suburb, with its intimacy and isolation, will hardly suffice. There needs to be an enormous number of people packed together for a truly uncontrollable environment to exist. As the number of people concentrated together in one place grows very large, the quality of human relations changes.

A massive, dense city society encourages deviance. Sexual deviations are much more easily expressed in dense urban areas than in the careful watching of sparsely populated areas. Historically, deviant subcultures, be they bohemian, ethnic, or youth-and-student, have in the same way survived much longer in dense urban areas.

The second reason large, dense communities are freed from the con-trols inherent in small ones is that movement is much more possible within them.

Contact   Large numbers of people living densely packed together thus provide the medium of diversity and instability necessary for survival communities to operate. In the old ghetto order, multiple contact points were necessary since none of the institutions in that era had the power to be self-sustaining. By removing centralized bureaucracies of social control and by eliminating preplanning with restrictive zoning, the same effect could be reproduced today. Decentralization would have the effect of necessitating multiple social contacts for survival, without leading to community cohesion.

I.S. 201   In fact, such a process occurred in New York's much-maligned [demonstration] school district I.S. 201. During the few weeks that this project had to operate on its own, conditions *within* the affected schools were remarkably nonviolent between Jewish white teachers, black teachers, and their black, Puerto Rican, and poor white students. Paths of real accommodation were beginning to emerge. Once the strike forced a we-they confrontation with a central authority—the teachers' union— the level of violence and the easy images of "us and them" again became dominant.

Contacts such as those within this school district illustrate the binding power of face-to-face tension and conflict, as opposed to the destructive power of conflict between bureaucratic institutions. For the experience of expressing hostility, or simply an alternative to the acts or the feelings of someone else, creates a certain kind of mutual commitment. People are dealing with each other rather than storing up their grievances in private. Multiple points of contact with different elements in a city diffuse hostility to such a point that an individual will despair of defining some safe, secure attributes of his own identity and social space. This sense of failure is precisely the point at which he begins to become an adult and to feel that his identity turns on his very power to reach out and explore.

Burst   In these dense, diverse communities, the process of making multiple contacts would burst the boundaries of thinking couched in homogeneous small-group terms. Since urban space would be free for all manner of incursion, the neat categories of spatial experience in cities—such as home, school, work, shopping, parks and playgrounds— could not be maintained. Men would find community problems and community experiences, as well as community conflicts, not limited to the sphere of their own small jobs, just as the region where a man lived would not be immune to a diverse circle of influences and modes of life. If an increased density in the planning of cities were connected to a limiting of central bureaucratic authority, spheres of multiple contact in the opportunities for city-wide action would emerge, as would the necessity to act in a direct and personal way.

Slaves I disagree with community thinkers who believe that diverse communities can arise naturally and spontaneously, once the system is destroyed. I believe diverse communities have to be created and urged into being.

The suburbanization and increasing organization of city spaces into functional compartments is responsive to the human desire to hide from pain and disorder. The idea that the "people" are straining at the bit against the "system" is much too naive. More realistically, the people and the system are in conspiracy to establish a comfortable slavery to the known and the routine.

Furthermore, the social dimensions of affluence in city life show themselves easily put to the service of such voluntary slavery. For affluence weakens the need for sharing of scarce goods and services, and lends each man the power to buy or control his survival necessities.

Some positive directions toward change are necessary. The first of these directions is to increase the visible density of urban areas. This can be done in a number of ways.

Vertical High-rise buildings should be thought of, Frank Lloyd Wright once said, as vertical streets. The public places should be distributed throughout the buildings.

But a more direct and perhaps more practical way of establishing visible density in cities has already been developed historically. In the great squares of such cities as Paris and Florence, the arrangement of townhouses around a common space provided a superb mingling ground for the residents. The density of these area was very high, even in modern terms. And the square surrounded by townhouses makes human density count socially. Such density permits the expression of personal deviation or idiosyncrasy in a milieu where there are too many people thrown together to discipline everyone to the same norm.

This mixture of people requires in its turn a second direction of change: a concerted effort to effect socioeconomic integration of living, working and recreational spaces.

Mix In the rebuilding of Paris by Baron Haussmann, new apartment units contained the rich on the lower floors, the middle classes on the middle floors and the poor in the roof garrets. The system worked for a long time, and contributed, David Pinkney points out, to the sense of diversity and vitality in central-city Paris. Since Haussmann's time, only sporadic and halfhearted efforts have been made to continue this form of residential building. Real-estate interests have said over and again that in private apartment or housing developments homogeneity is imposed on the builder because people feel uncomfortable unless they know that their neighbors are mostly like themselves.

True enough, but the point is that it would be *better* in the end if they did feel uncomfortable, and began to experience a sense of dislocation. If it takes government money to assist in this socioeconomic mixing, then the money ought to be spent.

Bias   Certain U.S. planners have objected that this mixing of classes has brought only unbearable racial conflict, and is inhumane to enforce when both sides don't want it. The public-housing projects these people point to certainly have been miserable failures. But this is a very biased picture. Thus social psychologist Thomas Pettigrew has estimated that a large number of communities in the United States outside the South are integrated house by house rather than with a Negro sector, and that at least passable relations have been achieved. There are also a large number of inner-city communities that are racially integrated working-class areas. The level of violence, as measured by the incidence of high-school violence and the like, is *lower* in these communities than in either homogeneously white or black working-class neighborhoods. There is tension to be sure, but it isn't escalated to violence.

Poverty   A more serious challenge to the practicality of racial integration in cities is offered by Norman Podhoretz. Podhoretz describes the strong anti-Negro feeling of Jews and the anti-Semitic feeling of blacks in integrated poverty. It may be that, for blacks and whites in poverty, socioeconomic integration of housing and schools would be only inhuman and brutalizing. However, popular stereotypes ignore the fact that the majority of urban blacks are not destitute but are working class and lower middle class. Once one gets above the poverty line, racial integration is practicable, and has proved to be a viable community structure.

Dullness   It has been said over and over by black community organizers that integration attempts only fragment further the sense of selfhood and self-dignity of ghetto residents. But for the large segment of the urban black population that has become or is becoming middle class, I am convinced that cultural insularity will lead in the end to the same kind of dullness and routine experienced by prosperous white ethnic groups. Class and wealth *do* make a difference in people's lives. What we need are affirmative, growth-producing community forms for men freed from the boundaries of poverty, and such communities seem possible only when diverse, ineradicably different kinds of people are thrown together and forced to deal with each other for mutual survival.

It may be that in such communities ethnic and racial differences would eventually be weakened. The point is that concord would not therefore be reached; the inevitable disruptions caused by regression to childhood selfishness would still be present. But in dense, visibly diverse communities these regressions would provide a constant starting point for conflict and conciliation.

City Hall   Diversifying the community through such integration raises the most important direction of replanning cities for such adult growth: the removal of central bureaucracies from their present directive power.

The closest that community workers in the last decades came to a theory of community control was the belief that functions carried on in city hall ought to be turned over to local community groups. When this kind of decentralization has been practiced it has produced some results. Hostile white school or government administrators have been replaced by less hostile black administrators. But the problem with this view of decentralization is that no changes of power *in essence* are involved. Suburbs, after all, are decentralized, local units of power, and yet the only community-control exercises at this level that grip the inhabitants are fights about open housing, gerrymandering of school districts and the like.

Police   Really decentralized power involves a change in the regulation of conflict. For example, police control of much civil disorder ought to be sharply curbed; the responsibility for making peace in neighborhood affairs ought to fall to the people involved. Because men are now so innocent and unskilled in the expression of conflict, they can only view these disorders as spiraling into violence. Until they learn through experience that they must deal with the handling of conflict, this polarization and escalation of conflict into violence will be the only end they can frame for themselves. This is as true of the small group of militant students as it is of those who call in the police "on their side."

In a less extreme dimension the spending of money for neighborhood schools or civic improvements is meaningless when the neighborhood school or community is merely spending along lines sent down from a central authority. How and why the money is to be spent needs to be the responsibility of the people who will feel its impact.

Use   There is no reason why centralized resources, like taxes, fire and police services, health and welfare benefits, have to be destroyed in order to decentralize power. It is not the existence of centralized structures that is evil, but the machinelike uses to which these structures are so easily directed. Conceivably, through social experiment we can learn how to distribute centralized resources to create decentralized, uncontrolled social situations. By breaking the machine image, and removing from massive bureaucracies the power to regulate conflict, we may be able to invent new activities for them in which they help create diversity and disorder rather than stifle it.

These suggestions for greater density, diversity, and power relations in city communities would create in general a high level of tension. They would create a sense of the need to deal with shifting combinations of people and shifting issues over the course of time. I don't imagine any sort of joyous communion in these encounters but rather a feeling of having to be involved in a social world.

Fragments   Machine politicians today have oppressive power precisely because they have captured the centralized bureaucracies for their own ends. In a fragmentation of the power of these bureaucracies, politicians of the stripe of the present mayor of Chicago would be forced back into a more modest, less dictatorial mold. City politicians would become middlemen rather than beautiful leaders; they would be successful to the extent that they channeled the revenues and coercive power of the state down to the community level.

This may seem utopian, but it is much less dangerous than the utopia invoked every election day, when one is told to vote for the cleansing savior who will restore order and decency. Decentralization is dismissed as visionary by the very people who vote out of longing for the pure leader who will "save" them and the city, state or country.

The family would be deeply affected by cities reorganized along these lines. Dense, disorderly cities would challenge family groups' capacity to act as intensive shelters, as shields from diversity.

Web   A wide network of social contact that people must use in order to survive might erase the polarization of intimacy in the home circle and the impersonal functional tasks in the world beyond. The conflicts of this city society would provide a web of confrontations whose character and personnel, unlike the family group, would be constantly in flux. This sounds as though anarchy were being brought into the city as a positive principle. That is exactly what I intend.

liza williams

There are hippies and there are "hippiebums." The former, according to Liza Williams, are the true flower children; the latter are poison ivy. The softest touch is often infectious!

In the brief essay to follow, the author writes of her observations of the pseudo-hippies who are to be found in every part of America looking for action but rarely for meaningful social relationships.

Liza Williams' description is vivid, her indictment harsh, her tone bitter. She does not exhibit the dispassionate objectivity of many social scientists. Yet she forces us all to ponder the real problems of "telling it like it is."

OK so you are wearing beads, and your hair is long and from the back you might be anyone, and from the front your face isn't too different either, your expression, is it an expression, is non-attendance, and your style is all I ever know of you. Style, it's all style and not much content, but what is the definition of decadence? Is it the substitution of style for content? Is that why so many love children smile a lot and score off you for everything they can get, cigarettes, hey man, lay a cigarette on me, or another ploy, anybody got a match? OK, now who's got a cigarette to go with it? Or you walk into an underground paper office where there is a big sign on the wall that says "Don't make magic, Be magic" and "Love" and you ask about something and receive cold indifference, they are too busy manufacturing love to give away any samples.

Hippiebums, dirty long-haired hippiebums with nowhere to go and nothing to do and they spend a lot of time using your daylight and your floor doing their nothing so that if you have something to do it is impossible. Who's that bunch of hippies out there in our garage-way mending their shoes and dancing and inviting the man to come and bust us, while we stand at the window and worry, from inside our tenuous safety, where we just got through with a lot of cleaning up after a departed hippie community, washing, wall painting, and removing piles of animal shit from under the refrigerator?

Split, that's what it's come to, a big rift, hippies and hippiebums. Upstairs the acid freaks are screaming and shouting and beating each other up and chasing each other around in lace dresses and the child who lives there sits at our table asking for food and wondering where her mother is, only not too hopefully.

Hippiebums give you presents, like dirty feathers or one bead or the clap. Hippiebums tell you about mystical experiences while they finger your breadbox. Hippiebums start off on your floor and make it to the couch and then eye your bed. When it gets tight for them they split, but they let you keep the feather or bead or the clap as a souvenir. You're materialistic they mumble at you as they drag themselves out your door, their pockets stuffed with peanut butter sandwiches.

Hippiebums write bad poetry and draw ugly pictures and make you look at them. They sing dull songs to one chord change and tell you how it is, letting you in on the secrets of life. Hippiebums hitch rides with you and roll joints in the back seat leaving seeds on the carpet. Hippiebums are just leaving for San Francisco or have just come back. Hippiebums use your telephone to call Chicago or Great Falls and three friends in New York; they pass the time on your phone. Hippiebums are always there at mealtimes but can't wipe dishes; hippiebums bring their friends over but never tell you their names.

Hippiebums come from middle-class homes and want you to be their parents, want you to pay their rent, want to make your world their high school. Hippiebums believe in the abundance of the Great Society, and want you to supply it. Hippiebums are predatory but wear a disguise of love. Hippiebums serenade you with their bells and dance for you, stepping on your feet.

I used to smile at everyone with a button or a bell or a flower, I used to think how beautiful it was all becoming, how rich it was, how sweet and good. But it's fantasy time, that's what it is, fantasy time in the twentieth century and style is where it's at, and only a few maintain content, and content, in the end, is really what creates a good world, and love, and being together with people and doing and making peace and feeling love and sustaining energy. So don't feel bad if you can't love every long-haired flower-bell child in the road; things aren't always what they seem.

peter & brigitte berger

Many readers are familiar with Charles Reich's book, *The Greening of America*, a volume which suggests that a genuine revolution is taking place in our society. In the future, it is argued, lifestyles may become closer to those of the Hippies of the Haight than those of traditional middle-America. Perhaps. But if so, what will the social structure be like—and who will mind the store(s)?

Peter and Brigitte Berger are willing to speculate. They doubt that radical youth, however much they may alter the course of culture, will have a significant effect on the basic character of technological society save to make room for a new cadre of leadership as the children of the original organization men bow out.

Long ago the Italian sociologist Vilfredo Pareto spoke of the circulation of the elites. The Bergers see something similar here today. They call it "The Bluing of America."

A considerable number of American intellectuals have been on a kick of revolution talk for the last few years. It began in a left mood, with fantasies of political revolution colored red or black. The mood now appears to have shifted somewhat. The fantasies have shifted to cultural revolution, which, we are told, will color American green.

From Peter and Brigitte Berger, "The Eve of the Bluing of America," *New York Times Magazine* (February 15, 1971) © 1971 by The New York Times Company. Reprinted by permission.

What the two varieties of revolution talk have in common is a sublime disregard for the requirements of technological society and for the realities of power and class in America. To be sure, drastic (if you like, "revolutionary") things are happening in this society, but the currently fashionable interpretations only serve to obfuscate them.

It is conceivable that technological society will collapse in America. In that case, as grass grows over the computers, we would revert to the ways of an underdeveloped country. Conceivable, yes; probable, no. The more likely assumption is that technological society will continue. If so, who will run it? We would venture, first, a negative answer: It will *not* be the people engaged in the currently celebrated cultural revolutions.

The "greening" revolution is not taking place in a sociological vacuum, but has a specific location in a society that is organized in social classes. There are enough data now to pinpoint this location. The cadres of the revolution are, in overwhelming proportions, the college-educated children of the upper middle class. Ethnically, they tend to be Wasps and Jews. Ideologically, they are in revolt against the values of this class—which is precisely the class that has been running the technological society so far. But the essentially bucolic rhetoric of this rebellion goes far beyond a radical (in the leftist sense) rejection of American class society and its allegedly evil ways. The rhetoric intends a dropping out of technological society as such.

The matrix of this revolution has been the youth culture. What are the prospects for the children of the people of the emerging counter-culture? We don't want to speculate in detail about the probable career of the son of a dropped-out sandal maker in Bella Vista—except for the suggestion that he is unlikely to make it to the upper-middle-class status of his grandfather. In sociological parlance, he is probably headed for downward social mobility.

The black revolution, for quite different reasons, is also headed for a counter or subculture, segregated from the opportunity system of technological society and subsidized through political patronage. The prospects here are for segregated social mobility. This may have its own cultural or ideological satisfactions. But upward mobility in a black ("community controlled") educational bureaucracy is unlikely to lead to positions of power and privilege in the enveloping technological society.

If the "greening" revolution will in fact continue to lure sizable numbers of upper-middle-class individuals out of "the system," and if the black revolution will succeed in arresting outward mobility among its adherents, a simple but decisively important development will take place: There will be new "room at the top." Who is most likely to take advantage of this sociological windfall? It will be the newly college-educated children of the white lower middle and working classes (and possibly those nonwhites who will refuse to stay within the resegregated racial subcultures). In other words, precisely those classes that remain most untouched by what is considered to be the revolutionary tide in contemporary America face new prospects of upward social mobility.

A technological society, given a climate of reasonable tolerance, can afford sizable regiments of sandal makers and Swahili teachers. It must have quite different people, though, to occupy its command posts and to keep its engines running. These will have to be people retaining the essentials of the old Protestant ethic—discipline, achievement orientation and, last but not least, a measure of freedom from gnawing self-doubt.

If such people are no longer available in one population reservoir, another reservoir will have to be tapped. There is no reason to think that "the system" will be unable to make the necessary accommodations. Should Yale become hopelessly "greened," Wall Street will get used to recruits from Fordham or Wichita State. Italians or Southern Baptists will have no trouble running the Rand Corporation. It is even possible that the White House may soon have its first Polish occupant (or, in a slightly different scenario, its first Greek).

There is one proviso—namely, that the children of these classes remain relatively unbitten by the "greening" bug. If they, too, should drop out, there would literally be no one left to mind the technological store. So far, the evidence does not point in this direction.

Indeed, what evidence we have of the dynamics of class in a number of European countries would indicate that the American case is not all that unique. Both England and West Germany have undergone very similar changes in their class structures, with new reservoirs of lower-middle-class and working-class populations supplying the personnel requirements of a technological society no longer serviced by the old élites.

The aforementioned process is not new in history. It is what Vilfredo Pareto (that most neglected of classical sociologists) called the "circulation of élites." Even Marx, albeit in the most ironical manner, may be proved right in the end. It may, indeed, be the blue-collar masses that are, at last, coming into their own. "Power to the people"—nothing less than that. The class struggle may be approaching a decisive new phase, with the children of the working class victorious—under the sign of the American flag. In that perspective, alas, the peace emblem represents the decline of the bourgeois enemy class, aptly symbolizing its defeat before a more robust adversary. This would not be the first time in history that the principals in the societal drama are unaware of the consequences of their actions.

"Revolutionary" America? Perhaps. We may be on the eve of its bluing.

wayne h. davis

We may be killing the goose that lays our golden eggs.

Wayne H. Davis, a biologist, describes one of the most serious social problems facing the nation, the gobbling up of resources required by our ever-increasing affluent and demanding population. Using a unique formula in which India, considered a land with great population problems, is compared to the United States, Davis suggests that the Indians will be around far longer than we.

Davis is one of many social and natural scientists who warns not so much about absolute increases in population but about our seeming insatiable desire for more of everything—land, food, material comforts.

I define as most seriously overpopulated that nation whose people by virtue of their numbers and activities are most rapidly decreasing the ability of the land to support human life. With our large population, our affluence and our technological monstrosities the United States wins first place by a substantial margin.

Let's compare the US to India, for example. We have 203 million people, whereas she has 540 million on much less land. But look at the impact of people on the land.

The average Indian eats his daily few cups of rice (or perhaps wheat, whose production on American farms contributed to our one percent per year drain in quality of our active farmland),

Reprinted from Wayne H. Davis, "Overpopulated America," *The New Republic* (January 10, 1970), 13–15. © Wayne H. Davis by permission of the author and publisher.

draws his bucket of water from the communal well and sleeps in a mud hut. In his daily rounds to gather cow dung to burn to cook his rice and warm his feet, his footsteps, along with those of millions of his countrymen, help bring about a slow deterioration of the ability of the land to support people. His contribution to the destruction of the land is minimal.

An American, on the other hand, can be expected to destroy a piece of land on which he builds a home, garage and driveway. He will contribute his share to the 142 million tons of smoke and fumes, seven million junked cars, 20 million tons of paper, 48 billion cans, and 26 billion bottles the overburdened environment must absorb each year. To run his air conditioner we will strip-mine a Kentucky hillside, push the dirt and slate down into the stream, and burn coal in a power generator, whose smokestack contributes to a plume of smoke massive enough to cause cloud seeding and premature precipitation from Gulf winds which should be irrigating the wheat farms of Minnesota.

In his lifetime he will personally pollute three million gallons of water, and industry and agriculture will use ten times this much water in his behalf. To provide these needs the US Army Corps of Engineers will build dams and flood farmland. He will also use 21,000 gallons of leaded gasoline containing boron, drink 28,000 pounds of milk and eat 10,000 pounds of meat. The latter is produced and squandered in a life pattern unknown to Asians. A steer on a Western range eats plants containing minerals necessary for plant life. Some of these are incorporated into the body of the steer which is later shipped for slaughter. After being eaten by man these nutrients are flushed down the toilet into the ocean or buried in the cemetery, the surface of which is cluttered with boulders called tombstones and has been removed from productivity. The result is a continual drain on the productivity of range land. Add to this the erosion of overgrazed lands, and the effects of the falling water table as we mine Pleistocene deposits of groundwater to irrigate to produce food for more people, and we can see why our land is dying far more rapidly than did the great civilizations of the Middle East, which experienced the same cycle. The average Indian citizen, whose fecal material goes back to the land, has but a minute fraction of the destructive effect on the land that the affluent American does.

Thus I want to introduce a new term, which I suggest be used in future discussions of human population and ecology. We should speak of our numbers in "Indian equivalents." An Indian equivalent I define as the average number of Indian citizens required to have the same detrimental effect on the land's ability to support human life as would the average American. This value is difficult to determine, but let's take an extremely conservative working figure of 25. To see how conservative this is, imagine the addition of 1000 citizens to your town and 25,000 to an Indian village. Not only would the Americans destroy much more land for

homes, highways and a shopping center, but they would contribute far more to environmental deterioration in hundreds of other ways as well. For example, their demand for steel for new autos might increase the daily pollution equivalent of 130,000 junk autos which *Life* tells us that US Steel Corp. dumps into Lake Michigan. Their demand for textiles would help the cotton industry destroy the life in the Black Warrior River in Alabama with endrin. And they would contribute to the massive industrial pollution of our oceans (we provide one third to one half the world's share) which has caused the precipitous downward trend in our commercial fisheries landings during the past seven years.

The per capita gross national product of the United States is 38 times that of India. Most of our goods and services contribute to the decline in the ability of the environment to support life. Thus it is clear that a figure of 25 for an Indian equivalent is conservative. It has been suggested to me that a more realistic figure would be 500.

In Indian equivalents, therefore, the population of the United States is at least four billion. And the rate of growth is even more alarming. We are growing at one percent per year, a rate which would double our numbers in 70 years. India is growing at 2.5 percent. Using the Indian equivalent of 25, our population growth becomes 10 times as serious as that of India. According to the Rienows in their recent book *Moment in the Sun,* just one year's crop of American babies can be expected to use up 25 billion pounds of beef, 200 million pounds of steel and 9.1 billion gallons of gasoline during their collective lifetime. And the demands on water and land for our growing population are expected to be far greater than the supply available in the year 2000. We are destroying our land at a rate of over a million acres a year. We now have only 2.6 agricultural acres per person. By 1975 this will be cut to 2.2, the critical point for the maintenance of what we consider a decent diet, and by the year 2000 we might expect to have 1.2.

You might object that I am playing with statistics in using the Indian equivalent on the rate of growth. I am making the assumption that today's child will live 35 years (the average Indian life span) at today's level of affluence. If he lives an American 70 years, our rate of population growth would be 20 times as serious as India's.

But the assumption of continued affluence at today's level is unfounded. If our numbers continue to rise, our standard of living will fall so sharply that by the year 2000 any surviving Americans might consider today's average Asian to be well off. Our children's destructive effects on their environment will decline as they sink ever lower into poverty.

The United States is in serious economic trouble now. Nothing could be more misleading than today's affluence, which rests precariously on a crumbling foundation. Our productivity, which had been increasing steadily at about 3.2 percent a year since World War II, has been falling during 1969. Our export over import balance has been shrinking steadily from $7.1 billion in 1964 to $0.15 billion in the first half of 1969. Our balance of payments deficit for the second quarter was $3.7 billion, the largest in history. We are now importing iron ore, steel, oil, beef, textiles, cameras, radios and hundreds of other things.

Our economy is based upon the Keynesian concept of a continued growth in population and productivity. It worked in an underpopulated nation with excess resources. It could continue to work only if the earth and its resources were expanding at an annual rate of 4 to 5 percent. Yet neither the number of cars, the economy, the human population, nor anything else can expand indefinitely at an exponential rate in a finite world. We must face this fact *now*. The crisis is here. When Walter Heller says that our economy will expand by 4 percent annually through the latter 1970s he is dreaming. He is in a theoretical world totally unaware of the realities of human ecology. If the economists do not wake up and devise a new system for us now somebody else will have to do it for them.

A civilization is comparable to a living organism. Its longevity is a function of its metabolism. The higher the metabolism (affluence), the shorter the life. Keynesian economics has allowed us an affluent but shortened life span. We have now run our course.

The tragedy facing the United States is even greater and more imminent than that descending upon the hungry nations. The Paddock brothers in their book, *Famine 1975!*, say that India "cannot be saved" no matter how much food we ship her. But India will be here after the United States is gone. Many millions will die in the most colossal famines India has ever known, but the land will survive and she will come back as she always has before. The United States, on the other hand, will be a desolate tangle of concrete and ticky-tacky, of strip-mined moonscape and silt-choked reservoirs. The land and water will be so contaminated with pesticides, herbicides, mercury fungicides, lead, boron, nickel, arsenic and hundreds of other toxic substances, which have been approaching critical levels of concentration in our environment as a result of our numbers and affluence, that it may be unable to sustain human life.

Thus as the curtain gets ready to fall on man's civilization let it come as no surprise that it shall first fall on the United States. And let no one make the mistake of thinking we can save ourselves by "cleaning up the environment." Banning DDT is the equivalent of the physician's treating syphilis by putting a bandaid over the first chancre to appear. In either case you can be sure that more serious and widespread trouble will soon appear unless the disease itself is treated. We cannot survive by planning to treat the symptoms such as air pollution, water pollution, soil erosion, etc.

What can we do to slow the rate of destruction of the United States as a land capable of supporting human life? There are two approaches. First, we must reverse the population growth. We have far more people now than we can continue to support at anything near today's level of affluence. American women average slightly over three children each. According to the *Population Bulletin* if we reduced this number to 2.5 there would still be 330 million people in the nation at the end of the century. And even if we reduced this to 1.5 we would have 57 million more people in the year 2000 than we have now. With our present longevity patterns it would take more than 30 years for the population to peak even when reproducing at this rate, which would eventually give us a net decrease in numbers.

Do not make the mistake of thinking that technology will solve our population problem by producing a better contraceptive. Our problem now is that people want too many children. Surveys show the average number of children wanted by the American family is 3.3. There is little difference between the poor and wealthy, black and white, Catholic and Protestant. Production of children at this rate during the next 30 years would be so catastrophic in effect on our resources and the viability of the nation as to be beyond my ability to contemplate. To prevent this trend we must not only make contraceptives and abortion readily available to everyone, but we must establish a system to put severe economic pressure on those who produce children and reward those who do not. This can be done within our system of taxes and welfare.

The other thing we must do is to pare down our Indian equivalents. Individuals in American society vary tremendously in Indian equivalents. If we plot Indian equivalents versus their reciprocal, the percentage of land surviving a generation, we obtain a linear regression. We can then place individuals and occupation types on this graph. At one end would be the starving blacks of Mississippi; they would approach unity in Indian equivalents, and would have the least destructive effect on the land. At the other end of the graph would be the politicians slicing pork for the barrel, the highway contractors, strip-mine operators, real estate developers, and public enemy number one—the US Army Corps of Engineers.

We must halt land destruction. We must abandon the view of land and minerals as private property to be exploited in any way economically feasible for private financial gain. Land and minerals are resources upon which the very survival of the nation depends, and their use must be planned in the best interests of the people.

Rising expectations for the poor is a cruel joke foisted upon them by the Establishment. As our new economy of use-it-once-and-throw-it-away produces more and more products for the affluent, the share of our resources available for the poor declines. Blessed be the starving blacks of Mississippi with their cut-door privies, for they are ecologically sound, and they shall inherit a nation. Although I hope that we will help these unfortunate people attain a decent standard of living by diverting war efforts to fertility control and job training, our most urgent task to assure this nation's survival during the next decade is to stop the affluent destroyers.

philip slater

Sociologist Philip Slater suggests that the old culture based on technological radicalism and social conservatism is no longer satisfactory for American society and should not be tolerated. He is troubled by a plasticized America and places the blame on the advertising media and other agencies that encourage the search for gadgetry and ever cleverer inventions to make life easier. Slater sees our technocracy steadily eroding the sense of human proportions and exacerbating the sense of alienation.

The revolts of the sixties were, to Slater, serious warnings by the young that all was not well. But now the Berkeley radicals of 1964 are over thirty themselves. Have they avoided the trap they saw others fall into, or have they joined the ranks of technology worshippers and become more conservative?

We need now to consider seriously what the role of those over thirty is to be during the transition to and emergence of the new culture. Many will of course simply oppose it, with varying degrees of violence. A few will greet it with a sense of liberation, finding in it an answer they have long sought, but will experience a sense of awkwardness in trying to relate themselves to what has been so noisily appropriated by the young.

Reprinted from *The Pursuit of Loneliness* by Philip Slater, pp. 126–143, by permission of Beacon Press. Copyright © 1970 by Philip E. Slater.

Many more will be tormented with ambivalence, repelled by the new culture but disillusioned by the old.

It is to this latter group that what follows is addressed, for I do not believe that a successful transition can be made without their participation. If the issue is left to generational confrontation, with new-culture adherents attempting simply to push their elders out of the way and into the grave, the results will probably be catastrophic. The old culture will not simply fall of its own weight. It is not rotten but wildly malfunctioning, not weak and failing but strong and demented, not a sick old horse but a healthy runaway. It no longer performs its fundamental task of satisfying the needs of its adherents, but it still performs the task of feeding and perpetuating itself. Nor do the young have the knowledge and skill successfully to dismantle it. If the matter is left to the collision of generational change it seems to me inevitable that a radical-right revolution will occur as a last-ditch effort to stave off change.

Only those who have participated fully in the old culture can prevent this. Only they can dismantle the old culture without calamity. Furthermore, no revolution produces total change—much of the old machinery is retained more or less intact. Those intimate with the machinery are in the best position to facilitate the retooling and redirection.

But why should they? Why should they tear down what they have built? What place is there for them in the new culture? The new culture is contemptuous of age and rejects most of the values by which moderates have ordered their lives. Yet it must be remembered that the contempt for age and tradition, the worship of modernity, is not intrinsically a new-culture trait but a foundation-stone of a technology-dominated culture. It is the old culture that systematically invalidates learning and experience, that worships innovation and turns its back on the past, on familial and community ties. The new culture is preoccupied with tradition, with community, with relationships—with many things that would reinstate the validity of accumulated wisdom. Social change is replete with paradox, and one of the most striking is the fact that the old culture worships novelty, while the new would resuscitate a more tradition-oriented way of life. The rhetoric of short-run goals, in which the young shout down the present and shout up the future, masks the fact that in the long run there is more room for the aged in the new culture than in the old. This is something about which new-culture adherents, however, are also confused, and old-culture participants will have much to do to stake out a rightful place for age in the new culture. If they fail the new culture will be corrupted into a reactionary parody of itself.

My main argument for rejecting the old culture is that it has been unable to keep any of the promises that have sustained it for so long, and as it struggles more and more violently to maintain itself, it is less and less able to hide its fundamental antipathy to human life and human satisfaction. It spends hundreds of billions of dollars to find ways of killing more efficiently, but almost nothing to enhance the joys of living. Against those who sought to humanize their physical environment in Berkeley the forces of "law and order" used a poison gas outlawed by the Geneva Conventions. The old culture is unable to stop killing people—deliberately in the case of those who oppose it, with bureaucratic indifference in the case of those who obey its dictates or consume its products trustingly. However familiar and comfortable it may seem, the old culture is threatening to kill us, like a trusted relative gone berserk so gradually that we are able to pretend to ourselves he has not changed.

But what can we cling to—what stability is there in our chaotic environment if we abandon the premises on which the old culture is based? To this I would answer that it is precisely these premises that have generated our chaotic environment. I recognize the desperate longing in America for stability, for some fixed reference point when all else is swirling about in endless flux. But to cling to old-culture premises is the act of a hopeless addict, who, when his increasingly expensive habit has destroyed everything else in his life, embraces his destroyer more fervently than ever. The radical change I am suggesting here is only the reinstatement of stability itself. It may appear highly unappealing, like all cold-turkey cures, but nothing else will stop the spiraling disruption to which our old-culture premises have brought us.

I am arguing, in other words, for a reversal of our old pattern of technological radicalism and social conservatism. Like most old-culture premises this is built upon a self-deception: we pretend that through it we actually achieve social stability—that technological change can be confined within its own sphere. Yet obviously this is not so. Technological instability creates social instability as well, and we lose both ways. Radical social change *has* occurred within the old culture, but unplanned and unheralded. The changes advocated by the new culture are changes that at least some people desire. The changes that have occurred under the old culture were desired by no one. They were not even foreseen. They just happened, and people tried to build a social structure around them; but it has always been a little like building sand castles in heavy surf and we have become a dangerously irritable people in the attempt. We have given technology carte blanche, much in the way Congress has always, in the past, given automatic approval to defense budgets, resulting in the most gigantic graft in history.

How long is it since anyone has said: "this is a pernicious invention, which will bring more misery than happiness to mankind?" Such comments occur only in horror and science-fiction films, and even there, in the face of the most calamitous outcomes that jaded and overtaxed brains can devise, the audience often feels a twinge of discomfort over the burning laboratory or the lost secret. Yet who would dare to defend even a small fraction of the technological innovations of the past century in terms of human satisfaction? The problem is that technology, industrialism, and capitalism have always been evaluated in their own terms. But it is absurd to evaluate capitalism in terms of the wealth it produces, or technology in terms of the inventions it generates, just as it would be absurd for a subway system to evaluate its service in terms of the number of tokens it manufactured. We need to find ways of appraising these systems in terms of criteria that are truly independent of the systems themselves. We need to develop a human-value index—a criterion that assesses the ultimate worth of an invention or a system or a product in terms of its total impact on human life, in terms of ends rather than means. We would then evaluate the achievements of medicine not in terms of man-hours of prolonged (and often comatose) life, or the volume of drugs sold, but in terms of the overall increase (or decrease) in human beings feeling healthy. We would evaluate city planning and housing programs not in terms of the number of bodies incarcerated in a given location, or the number of millions given to contractors, but in terms of the extent to which people take joy in their surroundings. We would evaluate the worth of an industrial firm not in terms of the money made or the number of widgets manufactured or sold, or how distended the organization has become, but in terms of how much pleasure or satisfaction has been given to people. It is not without significance that we tend to appraise a nation today in terms of its gross national product—a phrase whose connotations speak for themselves.

The problem is particularly acute in the case of technology. Freud suggested forty years ago that the much-touted benefits of technology were "cheap pleasures," equivalent to the enjoyment obtained by "sticking one's bare leg outside the bedclothes on a cold winter's night and then drawing it in again." "If there were no railway to make light of distances," he pointed out, "my child would never have left home and I should not need the telephone to hear his voice."[1] Each technological "advance" is heralded as one that will solve problems created by its predecessors. None of them have done so, however, but have merely created new ones. Heroin was first introduced into this country as a heaven-sent cure for morphine addicts, and this is the model followed by technological "progress." We have been continually misled into supporting a larger and larger technological habit.

Lest I be accused of exaggeration, let me quote from a recent newspaper article: "How would you like to have your very own flying saucer? One that you could park in the garage, take off and land in your own driveway or office parking lot. . . . Within the next few years you may own and fly just such an unusual aircraft and consider it as common as driving the family automobile. . . ." The writer goes on to describe a newly invented vertical-takeoff aircraft which will cost no more to own and operate than a sports car and is just as easy to drive. After an enthusiastic description of the design of the craft he attributes its development to the inventor's "concern for the fate of the motorist," citing the inability of the highways and city streets to handle the increasing number of automobiles. The inventor claims that his saucer "will help solve some of the big city traffic problems"![2]

The inventor is so confident of the public's groveling submission to every technological command that he does not even bother to defend this outlandish statement. Indeed, it is clear that he does not believe it himself, since he brazenly predicts that every family in the future will own a car *and* a saucer. He even acknowledges rather flippantly that air traffic might become a difficulty, but suggests that "these are not his problems," since he is "only the inventor."* He goes on to note that his invention would be useful in military operations (such as machine-gunning oriental farmers and gassing students, functions now performed by the helicopter) and in spraying poisons on our crops.

How can we account for the lack of public resistance to this arrogance? Why does the consumer abjectly comply with every technological whim, to the point where the seller scarcely bothers to justify it, or does so with tongue in cheek? Is the man in the street so punch-drunk with technological propaganda that he can conceive of the saucer as a solution to *any* problem? How can he greet with anything but horror an invention that will blot out the sky, increase a noise level which is already intense to unbearable levels, pollute the air further, facilitate crime immeasurably, and cause hundreds of thousands of horrible accidents (translating our highway death toll to the saucer domain requires the addition of bystanders, walking about the city, sitting in their yards, sleeping in their beds, or strolling in the park) each year? Is the American public really so insane or obtuse as to relish the prospect of the sky being as filled with motorized vehicles as the ground is now?

One reason for this docility is that Americans are trained by advertising media to identify immediately with the person who actually uses

---

* One is reminded of Tom Lehrer's brilliant song about the rocket scientist:

> *"Once they are up who cares where they come down:*
> *That's not my department," says Werner Von Braun.*

The Nuremberg and Eichmann trials were attempts to reverse the general rule that those who kill or make wretched a single person are severely punished, while those (heads of state, inventors, weapons manufacturers) who are responsible for the death, mutilation, or general wretchedness of thousands or millions are generally rewarded with fame, riches, and prizes. The old culture's rules speak very clearly: if you are going to rob, rob big; if you are going to kill, kill big.

the new product. When he thinks of a saucer the American imagines himself inside it, flying about and having fun. He does not think of himself trying to sleep and having other Americans roaring by his window. Nor does he think of himself trying to enjoy peace and quiet in the country with other Americans flying above. Nor does he even think of other Americans accompanying him in his flight and colliding with him as they all crowd into the city. The American in fact never thinks of other Americans at all—it is his most characteristic trait that he imagines himself to be alone on the continent.

Furthermore, Americans are always hung over from some blow dealt them by their technological environment and are always looking for a fix—for some pleasurable escape from what technology has itself created. The automobile, for example, did more than anything else to destroy community life in America. It segmented the various parts of the community and scattered them about so that they became unfamiliar with one another. It isolated travelers and decoordinated the movement of people from one place to another. It isolated and shrank living units to the point where the skills involved in informal cooperation among large groups of people atrophied and were lost. As the community became a less and less satisfying and pleasurable place to be, people more and more took to their automobiles as an escape from it. This in turn crowded the roads more which generated more road-building which destroyed more communities, and so on.

The saucers will simply extend this process further. People will take to their saucers to escape the hell of a saucer-filled environment, and the more they do the more unbearable that hell will become. Each new invention is itself a refuge from the misery it creates—a new hero, a new heroin.

How far can it go? What new inventions will be offered the staggering American to help him blow up his life? Will he finally flee to outer space, leaving the nest he has so industriously fouled behind him forever? Can he really find some means to propel himself so fast that he will escape his own inventive destructiveness? Is the man in orbit —the true Nowhere Man, whirling about in his metal womb unable to encounter anyone or anything—the destiny of all Americans?

The old-culture American needs to reconsider his commitment to technological "progress." If he fails to kick the habit he may retain his culture and lose his life. One often hears old-culture adherents saying, "what will you put in its place?" ("if you don't want me to kill you, give me something else to do"). But what does a surgeon put in the place of a malignant tumor? What does a policeman put in the place of a traffic jam? What does the Food and Drug Administration put in the place of the poisoned food it confiscates? What does a society put in the place of war when peace is declared? The question assumes, first, that what exists is safe and tolerable, and second, that social systems are mere inert mechanisms with no life of their own.

Some of this resistance comes from the old culture's dependence upon the substitutes and palliatives that its own pathology necessitates. "Without all these props, wires, crutches, and pills," its adherents ask, "how can I function? Without the 'extensions of man' I am not even a person. If you take away my gas mask, how can I breathe this polluted air? How will I get to the hospital without the automobile that has made me unfit to walk?" These questions are serious, since one cannot in fact live comfortably in our society without these props until radical changes have been made—until the diseases that necessitate these palliatives have been cured. Transitions are always fraught with risk and discomfort and insecurity, but we do not enjoy the luxury of postponement. No matter how difficult it seems to engage in radical change when all is changing anyway, the risk must be taken.

Our servility toward technology, however, is no more dangerous than our exaggerated moral commitment to the "virtues" of striving and individual achievement. The mechanized disaster that surrounds us is in no small part a result of our having deluded ourselves that a motley scramble of people trying to get the better of one another is socially useful instead of something to be avoided at all costs. It has taken us a long time to realize that seeking to surpass others might be pathological, and trying to enjoy and cooperate with others healthy, rather than the other way around.

The need to triumph over each other and the tendency to prostrate ourselves before technology are in fact closely related. We turn continually to technology to save us from having to cooperate with each other. Technology, meanwhile, serves to preserve and maintain the competitive pattern and render it ever more frantic, thus making cooperation at once more urgent and more difficult.

The essentially ridiculous premises of a competitive society are masked not only by technology, but also by the complexity of our economic system and our ability to compartmentalize our thinking about it. Since we are achievement-oriented rather than satisfaction-oriented, we always think of ourselves first as producers and only second as consumers. We talk of the "beleaguered consumer" as if this referred to some specialized group of befuddled little old ladies.

To some extent this convention is a maneuver in the American war between the sexes. Since men dominate production and women consumption, the man who produces shoddy merchandise can blame his wife for being incompetent enough to purchase it for him. Men have insulated themselves to this extent from having to deal with the consequences of their behavior.

What all of our complex language about money, markets, and profits tends to mask is the fact that ultimately, when the whole circuitous process has run its course, we are producing for our own consumption. When I exploit and manipulate others, through mass media or marketing techniques, I am also exploiting and manipulating myself. The needs I generate create a treadmill that I myself will walk upon. It is true that if I manufacture shoddy goods, create artificial needs, and sell vegetables, fruit, and meat that look well but are contaminated, I will make money. But what can I do with this money? I can buy shoddy goods and poisoned food, and satisfy ersatz needs. Our refusal to recognize our common economic destiny leads to the myth that if we all overcharge each other we will be better off.

This self-delusion is even more extraordinary when we consider issues of health and safety. Why are executives living in cities indifferent to the air pollution caused by their own factories, since it is the air they and their families breathe? Or do they all live in exurbia? And what of oil company executives: have they given up ocean beaches as places of recreation? Do they all vacation at mountain lakes? Do automobile manufacturers share a secret gas mask for filtering carbon monoxide out of the air? Are the families of canning company executives immune to botulism? Those of farming tycoons immune to insecticides?

These questions are not entirely facetious. To some extent wealth does purchase immunity from the effects of the crimes perpetrated to obtain it. But in many of the examples above the effects cannot be escaped even by those who caused them. When a tanker flushes its tanks at sea or an offshore well springs a leak the oil and tar will wash up on the most exclusive beach as well as the public one. The food or drug executive cannot tell his wife not to purchase his own product, since he knows his competitors probably share the same inadequate controls. We cannot understand the irresponsibility of corporations without recognizing that it includes and *assumes* a willingness on the part of corporate leaders to endanger themselves and their families for the short-run profit of the corporation. Men have always been able to subordinate human values to the mechanisms they create. They have the capacity to invest their libido in organizations that are then viewed as having independent life and superordinate worth. Man-as-thing (producer) can then enslave man-as-person (consumer), since his narcissism is most fully bound up in his "success" as a producer. What is overlooked, of course, is that the old-culture adherent's success as a producer may bring about his death as a consumer. Furthermore, since the Nuremberg and Eichmann trials there has been a gradual but increasing reluctance to allow individuals to hide behind the fiction of corporate responsibility.

One might object at this point that the preceding discussion places so much emphasis on individual motivation that it leaves us helpless to act. We cannot expect, after all, that everyone will arise one morning resolved simultaneously to act on different premises, and thus miraculously change the society. Competitive environments are difficult to modify, since whoever takes the first step is extremely likely to go under. "The system" is certainly a reality, no matter how much it is composed of fictions.

An action program must thus consist of two parts: (1) a long-term thrust at altering motivation and (2) a short-term attempt to redirect existing institutions. As the motivational underpinnings of the society change (and they are already changing) new institutions will emerge. But so long as the old institutions maintain their present form and thrust they will tend to overpower and corrupt the new ones. During the transitional period, then, those who seek peaceful and gradual change should work toward liberal reforms that shift the incentive *structure* as motivations in fact change.

Imagine that we are all inhabitants of a large and inescapable boat, marooned in a once ample but now rapidly shrinking lake. For generations we have been preoccupied with finding ways to make the boat sail faster around the lake. But now we find we have been all too successful, for the lake gets smaller and smaller and the boat goes faster and faster. Some people are saying that since the lake is about to disappear we must develop a new way of life, that is to say, learn to live on land. They say that in any case going in circles on a little lake is an absurd way of life. Others cling to the old ways and say that living on land is immoral. There is also a middle-of-the-road group that says living on the lake is best but perhaps we had better slow down before we smash to pieces on the ever-nearer rocks around and below us.

Now if it is true that the lake is disappearing, those who want to live on land must not only prepare themselves and convert others, but must also train the captain and crew to navigate on land. And the middle-of-the-roaders must not only try to find ways to slow the boat down, but should also seek some way to attach wheels to its bottom. Putting wheels on the boat is what I mean by liberal reform of the incentive structure. It is a technique of softening the impact of the collision between old and new.

Let me give a concrete example of adjusting institutions to match motivational changes. It seems quite clear that a far smaller proportion of college graduates today are interested in careers of personal aggrandizement, compared with twenty years ago. Far more want to devote themselves to social problems of one kind and another, or to helping individuals who are disadvantaged in some way. This is surely a beneficial shift in emphasis—we perhaps do not need as many people as we once did to enrich themselves at our expense, and we have no place to put the overpriced junk we already have. But our old-culture institutions continually place obstacles in the path of this shift. Those who seek to provide services are often prevented by established members of the professions—such as doctors, teachers, and social workers—since the principle behind any professional organization is (a) to restrict membership and (b) to provide minimum service at maximum cost. Draft boards also discriminate against this kind of social altruism, and law enforcement agencies often punish it.

The most interesting form of discrimination is that of the Internal Revenue Service. The whole complex fabric of income tax regulations rests on the principle of rewarding single-minded devotion to self-aggrandizement (the deduction for contributions is a trivial exception to this rule). If one spent all his money protecting, maintaining, or trying to increase his income he would theoretically pay no tax whatever. The tax structure rewards the moneygrubber, the wheeler-dealer, and punishes the man who simply provides a service and is paid something for it. The man who devotes his life to making money is rewarded by the United States Government with tax loopholes, while the man who devotes his life to service picks up the check.

We need to reverse these incentives. We need to reward everyone *except* the money-hungry—to reward those who are helping others rather than themselves. Actually, this could be done very easily by simply eliminating the entire absurd structure of deductions, exemptions, and allowances, and thus taxing the rich and avaricious instead of the poor and altruistic. This would have other advantages as well: discouraging overpopulation and home ownership, and saving millions of man-hours of senseless and unrewarding clerical labor.

Reforms in the kinds of priorities involved in the disbursement of federal funds would also help. At present, almost 80 percent of the federal budget is devoted to life-destroying activities, only about 10 percent to life-enhancing ones. The ending of the war should be the first item on everyone's agenda, but even without the war there is much to be done in the way of priority changes. At present most government spending subsidizes the rich: defense spending subsidizes war contractors, foreign aid subsidizes exporters, the farm program subsidizes rich farmers, highway and urban redevelopment programs subsidize building contractors, medical programs subsidize doctors and drug companies, and so on. Some programs, like the poverty program, subsidize middle-class service-oriented people to some extent, and this is helpful. It is probably impossible to subsidize the poor themselves with existing techniques—such a profound reversal of pattern requires a more radical approach, like the negative income tax or guaranteed employment.

It must be made clear that we are not trying to make moneygrubbers out of those who are not, but rather to restore money to its rightful place as a medium of exchange—to reduce the role of money as an instrument of vanity. Under present conditions those with the greatest need for narcissistic self-aggrandizement can amass enormous unused surpluses, and this process the Government tends to reward and encourage. The shortages thereby created tend to make it difficult for middle-class people who are less interested in self-aggrandizement to maintain their secular attitude toward money. The poorer working class and the destitute, meanwhile, are thrown into such an acute state of deprivation that money comes to overshadow other goals. Since we know from long experience with children of the affluent that familiarity with money tends to breed contempt, whatever we can do to equalize the distribution of wealth will tend to create disinterest. This will leave only the most pathological narcissists still money-oriented—indeed, they will be worse than ever, since they will have been deprived of their surplus millions or of the opportunity of amassing them, and will have to look elsewhere for the means of gratifying their vanity. Perhaps they will seek it through the exercise of power—becoming generals or teachers or doctors; perhaps through fame, becoming writers or artists or scholars. In any case, money would tend to be sought by the ordinary person merely to obtain specific goods or services.

Such a profound transformation is not likely to occur soon. Yet it is interesting that it is precisely the reversal of the incentive structure that is most feared by critics of such plans as the negative income tax. Why would people want to work and strive, they ask, if they could get all they wanted to eat without it? Why would they be willing to sell out their friends, sacrifice family ties, cheat and swindle themselves and everyone else, and disregard social problems and needs, if in fact they could obtain goods and services without doing these things? "They would have to be sick," we hear someone say, and this is the correct answer. Only the sick would do it—those who today when they have a million dollars keep striving for more. *But the non-sick would be free from the obligation to behave as if they were sick—an obligation our society presently enjoins.* It would not be made so difficult, if these proposals were carried out, for Americans to be motivated by something other than greed. People engaged in helping others, in making communities viable, in making the environment more attractive, would be able to live more comfortably if they wished. Some people would of course do nothing at all but amuse themselves, like the idle rich, and this seems to disturb people: "subsidized idleness," they call it, as if thus to discredit it. Yet I personally would far rather pay people *not* to make nerve gas than pay them to make it; pay them *not* to pollute the environment than pay them to do it; pay them *not* to inundate us with instant junk than pay them to do it; pay them *not* to swindle us than pay them to do it; pay them *not* to kill peasants than pay them to do it; pay them *not* to be dictators than pay them to do it; pay them *not* to replace communities with highways than pay them to do it, and so on. One thing must be said for idleness: it keeps people from doing the Devil's work. The great villains of history were busy men, since great crimes and slaughters require great industry and dedication.

Those skilled in social and political action can probably devise many more profound programs for defusing the perverse incentive structure our society now enjoys, but the foregoing will at least serve to exemplify the point I wish to make. As a general rule it can be said that every institution, every program in our society should be examined to determine whether it encourages social consciousness or personal aggrandizement.

Let us now turn to the question of long-range modifications in motivation. For no matter how much we try to eliminate scarcity assumptions from the incentive structures of our institutions, they will continue to reemerge if we do not devote some attention to reforming the psychic structures that our family patterns generate in children.

Some people may feel that this is already happening. The new culture has burgeoned among the younger generation, after all, and the new culture is founded on a rejection of scarcity assumptions. The "sexual revolution" promises to eliminate altogether the libidinal foundation for scarcity psychology. Furthermore, this liberalization of sexual norms is predictably leading to a more generalized movement toward the liberation of women (predictably because historically, sexual restrictions have been imposed primarily on women). Mothers of the future should therefore be far less inclined than in the past to flood their male children with frustrated longings and resentments. Living fuller and less constricted lives themselves they should have less need to invest their children with Oedipally tinged ambition.

I am nonetheless skeptical that this will occur in the absence of other changes—changes which will not come from, but must be learned by, the young. The problem arises at the point at which new-culture adherents enter the sphere now dominated by the old culture. This sphere has three portals: graduation, marriage, and parenthood—each one a more powerful instrument of old-culture seduction than the last. Indeed, old-culture adherents count heavily on this triple threat to force youthful "idealists" to relinquish their commitment to change. There is a gloating quality to their expectancy ("wait until they have to raise a family"), which turns rather ugly when it is disappointed ("You gotta grow up *sometime*").

These expectations are often confirmed—not because there is anything inherently mature or adult about living in a suburb or cheating your neighbor, but because the new culture has made few inroads into the structure of post-college life. New-culture students are leaving an environment in which their attitudes are widely shared and moving into one in which they will be isolated, surrounded, and shunted onto a series of conveyor belts that carry one into the old culture with a certain inevitable logic that can be resisted only with deliberate and perpetual effort.

Students know this and fear it. They dread becoming like their parents but cannot see how to avoid it. It is as if they had come to the edge of a dense, overgrown forest, penetrable only by a series of smooth, easily traversed paths, all of which, however, have signs saying "To the Quicksand."

Graduation always looks like the most dangerous seduction, but in fact it is the least. With great struggles, floundering, and anxiety, students are managing increasingly to carve out lives for themselves that do not commit them fully to the old culture. Some compromise by going to graduate school, which is more dangerous, since all professions have subtle initiation rites built into their training procedures, based on the it-must-have-been-worth-it-or-I-wouldn't-have-done-it principle. But even here some new-culture adherents have been able to hold their own, and every profession has sprouted a small but indestructible new-culture wing.

Fear of marriage and of bad marital relationships is almost as strong, but seems not to be a deterrent. Students marry in droves anyway, perhaps to obtain security for their resistance to occupational seduction. Parenthood is least feared of all, although it is clearly the most dangerous, for it was parenthood that played the largest part in the corruption of their own parents. "For the children" is second only to "for God and country" as a rallying cry for public atrocities. The new parents will undoubtedly interpret the slogan in somewhat less materialistic terms, but the old culture and the new share the same child-oriented attitude. This creates many pitfalls for unwary neophyte parents, since the old culture has a built-in system of automatic, escalating choice-points to translate this attitude into old-culture practices. The minute the parents decide they want their child to have some green grass to run about in, or a school that is not taught by rigid, authoritarian teachers, they will suddenly discover that they have eaten a piece of the gingerbread house and are no longer free.

Even in this case, of course, there are solutions, just as in the occupational sphere. But less thought and attention have been given to this problem by the young. They imagine, like every fool who ever had children, that their own experiences as children will guide them and protect them against their own parents' errors. People in our society are particularly blind to the overwhelming force of role identification, and they are also peculiarly unprepared, by the insulation of their youth culture, for its sudden onset. In more traditional cultures everyone realizes that upon becoming parents they will tend automatically to mimic their own parents' behavior, but in our society this comes as a shock, and is often not even perceived.

To this must be added still another powerful factor—peculiar in its intensity, perhaps to this generation. The parents of today's youth tended to sacrifice much of their own pleasure to the manufacturing of successful children. Much comment has been made to the effect that student protest represents a continuing expectation of adult self-sacrifice. Perhaps so, but I am even more impressed by the diffuse sense of guilt and responsibility that afflicts contemporary students. I suspect strongly that the advent of parenthood will provide a highly seductive vehicle for expression of these feelings, especially since the new culture is highly pro-child anyway, and hence provides no warning signs. Many will find not only that they have boarded the old-culture's child-oriented suburban family conveyor belt, but that the timely provision of this opportunity for the release of parent-induced feelings of guilt and responsibility will drain off much of their social concern.

It is difficult, in other words, not to repeat patterns that are as deeply rooted in primary emotional experiences as these are, particularly when one is unprepared. The new parents may not be as absorbed in material possessions and occupational self-aggrandizement as their own parents were. They may channel their parental vanity into different spheres, pushing their children to be brilliant artists, thinkers, and performers. But the hard narcissistic core on which the old culture was based will not be dissolved until the parent-child relationship itself is de-intensified, and this is precisely where the younger generation is likely to be most inadequate. While the main body of the cell of the old culture is being constantly weakened, its nucleus is in danger of being transferred, not only intact, but strengthened—like a bacterial strain resistant to drugs—to the new.

It is not that being child-oriented itself produces a narcissistic personality—quite the contrary. It is when the parent turns to the child as a vicarious substitute for satisfactions the parent fails to find in his or her own life that the child becomes vain, ambitious, hungry for glory. Both the likelihood and the intensity of this pattern are increased when the family is a small, nuclear, isolated unit and the child socialized by few other adults. Our society has from the beginning, and increasingly with each generation, tended to foster "Oedipal" children. New-culture adherents want desperately to build a cooperative, communal world, but they are in some ways the least likely people in the world to be able to do it, or to produce children that could do it. They cannot break the Oedipal pattern alone because they are even more enmeshed in it than were their parents.

Breaking the pattern means establishing communities in which (a) children are not socialized exclusively by their parents, (b) parents have lives of their own and do not live vicariously through their children, hence (c) life is lived for the present, not the future, and hence (d) middle-aged and elderly people participate in the community in the same way as youth and vice versa. This constellation of traits forms a coherent unit, as does its opposite.

Although the reasons are obvious, it is ironic that young people who try to form communes almost always create the same narrow, age-graded, class homogeneous society in which they were formed. This is in part because they know few older or working-class adults who might conceivably participate. But in part it reflects the same future-oriented psychology that produced the old-culture family system they are trying to supersede. Again we are confronted with the paradox of trying to build a future that does not always look to the future. We need desperately a social change mechanism that is self-extinguishing. Revolutionary ideologies always *assume* that change and fascination with the future will cease once the golden day arrives, but they never include any means even for slowing it down.

Older adults have a vested interest in finding a place for themselves in the new society, and whatever place they find will provide a model for new-culture adherents as they age. In the old culture there is no place at all for the aged, and old-culture adherents are growing older. They have the option of sitting back and enjoying the fact that ultimately their misery will be shared by those who follow, or of working toward a reversal of the pattern—a reversal that will profit posterity somewhat more than themselves. Their presence will help to dilute the future-orientation that new-culture adherents must of necessity have. Without this—without an attempt to establish bridges and continuities and balances, to understand where the present connects with and remodels past trends (for only the combinations and arrangements change, the elements are deathless)—the society they build will have the same defects as the old one. The old culture attempts ruthlessly to cut the past away, and thereby digs itself deeper into a morass of meaninglessness and chaos. What the new culture seeks is wholeness, and obviously it cannot achieve this by exclusion. A community that does not have old people and children, white-collar and blue-collar, eccentric and conventional, and so on, is not a community at all, but the same kind of truncated and deformed monstrosity that most people inhabit today.

What I have been saying may sound excessively utopian even to those adults who feel drawn to the new culture. Can any middle-aged person, trained as he is in the role considered appropriate to his age, find anything in the new culture to which he can attach himself without feeling absurd? Can he "act his age" in the new culture? There are indeed severe contradictions between the two, but syntheses are also to be found. Adults in encounter groups usually discover that much of what is new-culture is not at all alien or uncomfortable for them. There are many roles that can and must be carved out for older people, for otherwise we will still have the same kind of ice-floe approach to the aged that we now have.

NOTES

1. S. Freud, *Civilization and Its Discontents* (London: Hogarth, 1953), pp. 46–48. One could also make this argument for art: if our emotional life were not so impoverished by the sacrifices we make to utility, we would not need art to enrich it. See *The Glory of Hera*, pp. 463–464.
2. Alvin Smith, *Boston Sunday Globe*, January 5, 1969.

alvin toffler

Much is written about "culture shock," the result of confrontation with patterns of living dramatically different from one's own. Many people experience this when they leave their country, some when they leave their neighborhoods and venture into what Michael Harrington once called "The Other America."

According to Alvin Toffler the problem of coping with culture shock is nothing compared to what we are about to face: "future shock." To Toffler and many other futurologists, we are about to enter a new epoch in which all aspects of life, including life itself, will be altered. Yet we are doing little to prepare for a world in which social science fantasies become more and more the realities of modern life.

"It's a poor sort of memory that only works backwards."

The White Queen in *Through the Looking-Glass*

As more Americans travel abroad, the term "culture shock" is beginning to creep into the popular vocabulary. Culture shock is the effect that immersion in a strange culture has on the unprepared visitor. Peace Corps volunteers suffer from it in Borneo or Brazil, Marco Polo probably suffered from it in Cathay. Culture shock is what happens when a traveler suddenly finds himself in a place where "yes" may mean no, where a "fixed price" is negotiable, where to be kept waiting in an outer office is no cause for insult, where laughter may signify anger. It is what happens when all the familiar psychological cues that help an individual to function in society are suddenly withdrawn and replaced by new ones that are strange or incomprehensible.

The culture-shock phenomenon accounts for much of the bewilderment, frustration, and disorientation that plague Americans in their dealings with other societies. It causes a breakdown in communication, a misreading of reality, an inability to cope. Yet culture shock is relatively mild in comparison with a much more serious malady that might be called "future shock." Future shock is the dizzying disorientation brought on by the premature arrival of the future. It may well be the most important disease of tomorrow.

Future shock will not be found in *Index Medicus* or in any listing of psychological abnormalities. Yet, unless intelligent steps are taken to combat it, I believe that most human beings alive today will find themselves increasingly disoriented and, therefore, progressively incompetent to deal rationally with their environment. I believe that the malaise, mass neurosis, irrationality, and free-floating violence already apparent in contemporary life are merely a foretaste of what may lie ahead unless we come to understand and treat this psychological disease.

Future shock is a time phenomenon, a product of the greatly accelerated rate of change in society. It arises from the super-imposition of a new culture on an old one. It is culture shock in one's own society. But its impact is far worse. For most Peace Corps men, in fact most travelers, have the comforting knowledge that the culture they left behind will be there to return to. The victim of future shock does not.

Take an individual out of his own culture and set him down suddenly in an environment sharply different from his own, with a different set of cues to react to, different conceptions of time, space, work, love, religion, sex, and everything else; then cut him off from any hope of retreat to a more familiar social landscape, and the dislocation he suffers is doubly severe. Moreover, if this new culture is itself in a constant turmoil of revolutionary transition, and if—worse yet—its values are incessantly changing, the sense of disorientation will be still further intensified. Given few clues as to what kind of behavior is rational under the radically new circumstances, the victim may well become a hazard to himself and others.

Now imagine not merely an individual but an entire society, an entire generation—including its weakest, least intelligent, and most irrational members—suddenly transported into this new world. The result is mass disorientation, future shock on a grand scale.

This is the prospect that man now faces as a consequence of accelerated change—the prospect of dislocation far more subtle, complex, and continuous than any we have known. Change is avalanching down upon our heads and most people are utterly unprepared to cope with it.

Is all this exaggerated? I think not. It has become a cliché to say that we are now living through a "second industrial revolution." This phrase is supposed to impress us with the speed and profundity of the change around us. But beyond being platitudinous, it is misleading. For what is occurring now is a transformation that is, in all likelihood, bigger, deeper, and more important than the industrial revolution. In fact, there is a growing body of reputable opinion that the period we are now living through represents nothing less than the second great divide in human history, comparable in magnitude only with that first great break in historic continuity, the shift from barbarism to civilization.

This idea has begun to occur with increasing frequency in the writings of scientists, social critics, economists, business analysts, and others. For example, Sir George Thomson, the British physicist and Nobel prize winner, suggests in *The Foreseeable Future* that the nearest historical parallel with today lies in the "invention of agriculture in the neolithic age." John Diebold, the automation expert, is among many who assert that we are seriously underestimating the degree of change that will occur in our society as a result of cybernetics. "It is the *rate of change* itself which I believe to be the most significant phenomenon of all," he writes. He warns that "the effects of the technological revolution will be deeper than any social change we have experienced before." Kurt W. Marek, the student and popularizer of archeology, observes that "we, in the twentieth century, are concluding an era of mankind five thousand years in length. . . . We are not, as Spengler supposed, in the situation of Rome at the beginning of the Christian West, but in that of the year 3000 B.C. We open our eyes like prehistoric man, we see a world totally new." Lewis Mumford in *The City in History* writes ominously about the coming of "Post-historic Man."

The most recent and elaborate statement of this theme has come from Kenneth Boulding, an eminent economist and an imaginative social thinker. Referring to the twentieth century as the second great transition in the history of mankind, Boulding writes:

> The first transition was that from precivilized to civilized society. . . . This is a transition that is still going on in some parts of the world, although it can be regarded as almost complete. Precivilized society can now be found only in small and rapidly diminishing pockets in remote areas. It is doubtful whether more than 5 per cent of the world's population could now be classified as living in a genuinely precivilized society.
>
> Even as the first great transition is approaching completion, however, a second great transition is treading on its heels. It may be called the transition from civilized to postcivilized society.

Most of those who make this comparison merely state it and let it go at that. Boulding, in a series of lectures and articles and in his latest book, *The Meaning of the Twentieth Century*, attempts to justify this dramatic view of the present as a truly nodal moment in human history. Among other things, he points out that "as far as many statistical series related to activities of mankind are concerned, the date that divides human history into two equal parts is well within living memory." In effect, he is saying, our century represents The Great Median Strip running down the center of human history. This is a startling assertion, but it is borne out in many ways.

Dr. Homi Bhabha, a distinguished Indian atomic scientist and the Chairman of the first International Conference on the Peaceful Uses of Atomic Energy, once analyzed the rate at which energy consumption is rising. "To illustrate," he said, "let us use the letter Q to stand for the energy derived from burning some thirty-three thousand million tons of coal. In the eighteen and a half centuries after Christ, the total energy consumed averaged less than half a Q per century. But by 1850, the rate had risen to one Q per century. Today, the rate is about ten Q per century." This means, roughly speaking, that half of all the energy consumed by man in the past two thousand years has been consumed within the last one hundred.

A comment from Boulding serves almost as a footnote to this finding: "For many statistical series of quantities of metal or other materials extracted, this date [i.e., the dividing line] is about 1910. That is, man took about as much out of mines before 1910 as he did after 1910."

The same is true of another kind of mining—the mining of knowledge. Information, itself a prime catalytic force in the process of social change, is proliferating at a mind-numbing rate. According to Charles P. Bourne of the Stanford Research Institute, the number of significant journals now being published around the world is on the order of fifteen thousand with perhaps a million significant papers in them each year. These figures do not include books and others forms of publication. Information specialists say that the sheer quantity of information is now doubling every ten years.*

Population is, too. Sir Julian Huxley has pointed out that it took Homo sapiens at least a hundred thousand years to reach a population of two-thirds of a billion. "This was in 1650," Huxley notes. "From this date, it took nearly two hundred years for world population to double itself once, but the second doubling took only one hundred years. It has more than doubled itself again in the sixty-four years of the present century and will certainly double itself still again within the next forty years."

Similarly, ours is the century in which, at least in many countries, agriculture has ceased to be the dominant economic activity. This is particularly important because of the close historical relationship between agriculture and what we fondly call civilization.

Without the development of agriculture, Boulding reminds us, there

---

* This problem of the future was contemplated in September, 1962, by John Rader Platt in an article published by *Horizon* entitled "Where Will the Books Go?"

could have been no food surplus to support "knowledge workers" in society and there would have been no coalescence of the city. But the surplus food supply made possible by agriculture in ancient societies was meager at best. "Whether it was Sumeria, Egypt, Greece, Rome, Ancient China, the Incas, or the Mayans, all these were societies based on a food surplus . . . that rarely exceeded 20 or 25 per cent of the total product. In these circumstances three quarters to four fifths of the population [had to devote themselves to] agriculture or other food production, and these people [could] barely produce enough to feed the remaining quarter or fifth of the population. . . . Almost all the cities of classical civilization were within a few weeks of starvation at any time. . . ."

In contrast, in the United States today only 10 per cent of the population is engaged in agriculture, and this small percentage is capable of producing more food than anyone knows what to do with. Moreover, it is obvious, as Boulding observes, that "if present trends continue it will not be long before we can produce all the food that we need with 5 per cent, or even less, of the population."

In the United States a further stage has been reached. In 1900 the non-farm-labor force already outnumbered the agricultural labor pool. But of this non-farm group, 57 per cent were in blue-collar occupations. By 1960, more Americans were wearing white collars than blue. This, too, represented a qualitative change in society. For the first time in human history a society, having shrugged off the economic domination of agriculture, proceeded to shrug off the domination of manual labor.

Still another "first" is within sight. According to Professor Kingsley Davis, an authority on urbanization, by the year 2000—only thirty-five years off—one quarter of all the people in the world will be living in cities of a hundred thousand or more. By 2050 the figure will be one half of the world's population. What this shift will mean in terms of values, family structure, jobs, politics, and the structure of cities themselves, is staggering.

All these changes represent giant spurts in movements that have been continuous, in one form or another, since history began. If we add to these truly historic jumps the list of developments or processes that simply did not begin until the twentieth century—air travel and space flight, television, the development of nuclear energy, the invention of the computer, the discovery of DNA with its possibilities for the control of evolution—the sharpness of the break with the past becomes even clearer. Given these, it becomes impossible to sustain the argument that what is happening now is anything like "normal" progress, even for the kind of industrial society we have known for the past century. It is not merely a "second industrial revolution." Viewed as a violent break with historic continuity, our age takes on a significance that few ages in the past have had.

Nevertheless, isn't it possible that the life of the individual will remain largely untouched? The answer is that the mood, the pace, the very "feel" of existence, as well as one's underlying notions of time, beauty, space, and social relations will all be shaken.

Take the matter of tempo. John Diebold never wearies of pointing out to businessmen that they must begin to think in terms of shorter life spans for their products. Smith Brothers' Cough Drops, Calumet Baking Soda, Ivory Soap, have become institutions by virtue of their long reign in the market place. In the days ahead, he suggests, few products will enjoy such longevity. Corporations may create new products knowing full well that they will remain on the market for only a matter of a few weeks or months. By extension, the corporations themselves—as well as unions, government agencies, and all other organizations—may either have shorter life spans or be forced to undergo incessant and radical reorganization. Rapid decay and regeneration will be the watchwords of tomorrow. The men and women who live, work, and play in a society where whole categories of merchandise seen on the shelves of the nearby store last month are no longer manufactured today and where their own place in the bureaucratic structure of society is being constantly reshuffled, will have to use entirely new yardsticks for measuring the passage of time in their own lives.

Even our conceptions of self will be transformed in a world in which the line between man and machine grows increasingly blurred. It is now almost certain that within a matter of years the implantation of artificial organs in human bodies will be a common medical procedure. The human "body" in the future will often consist of a mixture of organic and machine components. What happens to the definition of man when one's next-door neighbor or oneself may be equipped with an electronic or mechanical lung, heart, kidney, or liver, or when a computer system can be plugged into a living brain? How will it "feel" to be part protoplasm, part transistor? What new possibilities will it open? What limitations will it place on work, play, sex, intellectual or aesthetic responses? How will it feel to have information transferred electronically between computer and brain? What happens to mind when body is changed? Such fusions of man and machine—called "Cyborgs"—are closer than most people suspect. As *Fortune* magazine, not ordinarily given to overstatement, has reported, "these are not just fantasies; they are extensions of work already being done in laboratories."

Allied to this are the implications of research being done today on the operations of the brain. For the first time, we are beginning to understand something about how the brain functions. The scientist and philosopher Percy Bridgman has observed that "thinking is done with the brain, which is a nervous system," and that "any possible thought must be subject to the limitations imposed by the system which produces it . . . all human thinking since the beginning of thought has been ignoring inexorable limitations. When we find what the limitations are I believe that our philosophy, religion, and politics will be revolutionized."

Similarly, as Professor Boulding points out, our very conception of life itself will be smashed and replaced. "The implications of the biological revolution alone are immense," he says. "We have the code of life. We can't write it yet, but that cannot be too far off. Artificial virus is close. This is the synthesis of life. Before long we may well crack the secret of aging. What happens when we do? Even if life were increased by twenty or forty years, it would shatter every relationship and institution we now know—the family, sex, marriage, the relationship between age groups, education. The work now being done raises the question: Is immortality possible?"

"Even if what is involved is only a finite extension of the life span, it creates all kinds of new ethical problems. Who gets immortality or added years? On what basis? The medical profession today already faces unusual ethical problems in connection with deciding which of many patients who need it will be lucky enough to be plugged into the new artificial kidneys. There will be other moral issues—completely new to us. All this sounds utterly farfetched, but I would not be at all surprised to see some of these things come to pass by the end of the century. Sound close? Remember that it was less than thirty-five years from Los Alamos and Hiroshima back to Rutherford's basic discoveries about the nucleus of the atom. And things are moving much faster today."

Work, too, is being transformed. There was a time when for men "the job" was a central organizing principle of life. One's living arrangements, one's hours, income, everything, was determined, or at least heavily influenced, by the nature of one's job. In the cybernetic society that lies around the corner the entire present occupational structure of society will be overthrown. A great many professions simply will not exist, and new ones as yet unpredicted will spring up. This must radically affect the texture of everyday life for millions.

In the past it was possible to know in advance what occupations would exist when a boy became a man. Today the life span of occupations has also been compressed. Individuals now train for a profession and look forward to remaining in that profession for the entire period of their working life. Yet within a generation the notion of serving in a single occupation for one's entire life may seem quaintly antique. Individuals may need to be trained to serve successively in three, four, or half a dozen different professions in the course of a career. The job will no longer serve as man's anchor and organizing principle.

The shrinking role of the job will be further diminished by the extension of leisure. Within half a century the productive machinery of society may need so few tenders that a great many individuals—and not just women—will be born who will simply never work a day in their lives at a paid job. Those who do work will, without question, work shorter hours than we do today. The work week has been cut by 50 per cent since the turn of the century. It is not out of the way to predict that it will be slashed in half again by 2000. This is not so far off that we can shrug the implications aside. How will we spend the long hours away from work? How will the role of the father be transformed with the loss of his historic role as family provider? What new forms of leisure will emerge? In a society in which work has become less central than it has been, how will we determine the esteem in which we hold a man?

Whether any or all of these developments occur precisely in the way suggested is not important. The commanding point is that we can anticipate volcanic dislocations, twists and reversals, not merely in our social structure, but also in our hierarchy of values and in the way individuals perceive and conceive reality. Such massive changes, coming with increasing velocity, will disorient, bewilder, and crush many people.

We think of ourselves as sophisticated and well educated, but how well prepared are we, as a society, to cope with the sudden new sensations, pains, intellectual turnabouts, eruptions, and shifts in perception that are likely to confront us as we speed forward into a culture in which computers can learn, and can improve upon their own performance, in which man is no longer the only manifestation of high-level intelligence on the face of the earth, and in which, in fact, he may come crash up against the realization that his globe is not the only inhabited parcel of real estate in the universe?

"We all need," says psychiatrist John R. Rees, Honorary President of the World Federation of Mental Health, "a sense of our own identity, that we have a certain place in the structure of our society, and that we fit into that. We have constantly to change our identity when we move into a different sort of world, and we often get considerable confusion of identity, something that is disturbing to many people. They cannot take it. . . ."

If the degree of change and the speed of that change is even remotely close to what I have suggested, it must be obvious that the shift to Professor Boulding's "postcivilization" may place unendurable stress on a great many people. For the current upbringing of most people, and the subtly inculcated sense of time that comes with it, are both inimical to adaptability.

A psychologist named Lawrence LeShan some years ago conducted an experiment in time orientation among groups of subjects from different socio-economic classes. Those from what he designated as the lower class tended to look at time in terms of immediate action and immediate gratification. The future was nebulous and unpredictable. There was a tendency for them to believe, as many Arabs do, that any attempt to predict the future is not only futile but evidence of mild lunacy.

In the sample highest up the economic ladder, LeShan found a pronounced identification with the past. Johnny is told, if he flunks his civics course, that his grandfather would have been ashamed of him. Family meals are set at fixed, traditional hours, rather than when hunger strikes or at convenient times. To a degree, lives are lived to carry out sequences started by previous generations.

Among the middle-class group, LeShan found a totally different time orientation. These subjects tended to think in terms of longer time sequences than the lower-class group. Children were taught to orient themselves toward goals fixed in the fairly distant future. Johnny is told to study not because his grandfather would be ashamed of him for flunking but because flunking might make it impossible for him to achieve the goal of becoming a lawyer or doctor or whatever.

But while these time orientations differ, they will assume either an unpredictable or an unchanging future. The assumption of the middle- and upper-class samples is that the contours of society will stay the same in the future. When a middle-class mother talks about Johnny becoming a lawyer, she is deceiving herself and her son because she has no conception of what being a lawyer will mean two decades hence. She has no notion of the potential, for example, of "jurimetrics." Jurimetric research, a product of the computer revolution, involves electronic data processing, information storage and retrieval (collecting, collating, and making immediately available all relevant legal precedents), the analysis of legal decisions, and the use of symbolic logic. It may have immense consequences for the making and administration of law, as well as the pleading of cases. Mama does not know it, but the lawyer of the future will not fit the mold she has in mind.

The fact is—and simple observation of one's own friends and associates will confirm it—that even the most educated people today operate on the assumption that society is relatively static. At best they attempt to plan by making simple straight-line projections of present-day trends. The result is unreadiness to meet the future when it arrives. In short, future shock.

What, if anything, can be done to lessen this shock and the disorientation and disability that come with it? Society has many built-in time spanners that help to link the present generation with the past. Our sense of the past is developed by contact with the older generation, by our knowledge of history, by the accumulated heritage of art, music, literature, and science passed down to us through the years. It is enhanced by immediate contact with the objects that surround us, each of which has a point of origin in the past, each of which provides us with a trace of identification with the past.

No such time spanners enhance our sense of the future. We have no objects, no friends, no relatives, no works of art, no music or literature, that originate in the future. We have, as it were, no heritage of the future.

Despite this, there are ways to send the human mind arching forward as well as backward. We need to begin by creating a stronger future-consciousness on the part of the public, and not just by means of Buck

Rogers comic strips and articles about the marvels of space travel or medical research. These make a contribution, but what is needed is a concentrated focus on the social and personal implications of the future, not merely on its technological characteristics.

If the contemporary individual is going to have to cope with the equivalent of millenniums of change within the compressed span of a single lifetime, he must carry within his skull a reasonably accurate (even if gross) image of the future.

Medieval men possessed one—an image of the afterlife, complete with vivid mental pictures of heaven and hell. We need now to propagate a dynamic, nonsupernatural image of what temporal life will be like, what it will sound and smell and taste and feel like in the fast-onrushing future.

To create such an image and thereby soften the impact of future shock, we must begin by making speculation about the future respectable. Instead of deriding the "crystal ball gazer," we need to encourage people, from childhood on, to speculate freely, even fancifully, not merely about what next week holds in store for them but about what the next generation holds in store for the entire human race. We offer our children courses in history; why not also make a course in "Future" a prerequisite for every student, a course in which the possibilities and probabilities of the future are systematically explored, exactly as we now explore the social system of the Romans or the rise of the feudal manor?

We train our Peace Corps volunteers by attempting to give them advance knowledge about the conditions and culture of the country to which they are assigned. In doing so, we minimize culture shock. Why not devise an education designed to minimize future shock?

We do not have a literature *of* the future, but we do have literature *about* the future, consisting not only of the great utopias but also of contemporary science fiction. Science fiction is held in low regard as a branch of literature, and perhaps it deserves this critical contempt. But if we view it as a kind of sociology of the future, rather than as literature, science fiction has immense value as a mind-stretching force for the creation of future-consciousness. Our children should be studying Arthur C. Clarke and Robert Heinlein and William Tenn not because these writers can tell them about rocket ships and time machines but, more important, because they can lead young minds through an imaginative exploration of the jungle of political, social, psychological, and ethical issues that will confront these children as adults. Science fiction should be required reading for Future I.

But science fiction is largely speculative, and while speculation is useful, we must go beyond it. We must kill, once and for all, the popular myth that the future is "unknowable."

At the last meeting of the American Association for the Advancement of Science a University of Colorado researcher named George A. Dulk predicted that a burst of radio signals from the planet Jupiter would be received in Colorado at midnight, December 31, 1964. On New Year's Eve, at 11:40 P.M.—just a few minutes ahead of schedule—a radio signal that sounded like the sizzle of a frying pan was picked up by the eighty-five-foot radio telescope at the National Center for Atmospheric Research. Since the signals did not come from intelligent creatures at the other end—there was never any question of that—the fulfillment of Dulk's prediction caused only a minor stir. For predictions—even startling predictions—of this kind are, of course, the bread and butter of science. They are entirely routine.

Every day brings improvement in man's ability to peer into the darkness ahead, and this is true in the social as well as the "hard" sciences. It is now possible to predict with fair accuracy a wide range of social phenomena—such as the number of babies to be born in Indiana in the first three months of 1970, the way in which the housewife will divide her income between purchases and savings next year, the percentage of the national production that will be allocated to wages in any given year, the number of people who will die of bathtub accidents, and, within a percentage point or two, the number of Americans who will vote for one Presidential candidate over another.

It would, of course, be foolish to oversell the ability of science, "hard" or "soft," to foretell the future. But the danger today is not that we will overestimate this ability, but that we will underutilize it. "Instead of thinking that either we can or cannot predict the future," wrote William F. Ogburn, one of the century's great students of social change, "we should admit into our thinking the idea of approximations, that is, that there are varying degrees of accuracy and inaccuracy of estimate." Furthermore, he pointed out, complete accuracy is not necessary in many fields. A rough idea of what lies ahead is better than none.

Thus, in addition to encouraging the speculative turn of mind, we must undertake to train individuals in the techniques of prediction and of scientific method in general. This does not mean more courses in biology or physics or chemistry. It means more attention to philosophy and logic, and perhaps special courses in "how to predict." How many of us, even among the educated public, understand the meaning of a random sample, or of probability, or of prediction by correlation? This does not mean that all of us need to be statisticians or logicians or mathematicians. But the principles of scientific prediction can and should be grasped by every youngster who graduates from high school, for these are *not* merely the tools of "scientific research," they are powerful instruments for dealing rationally with the problems of everyday existence. Ignorance of them constitutes a form of functional illiteracy in the contemporary world.

The willingness to speculate freely, combined with a knowledge of scientific method and predictive techniques, is coming to be valued in precisely the place where, in the past, the greatest emphasis has been placed on conservatism and feet-on-the-ground "realism." Corporations are beginning to hire men who are, in effect, staff prophets, men willing to look ahead ten years or more. "A few years ago," says Tom Alexander in *Fortune* magazine, "most such people were called crackpots. A lot of bitter recent experience has shown that such crackpots are too often likely to be right, and that it is usually the 'sound thinkers' who make fools of themselves when it comes to talking about the future." Shortly after reading this, I learned of a giant corporation that is looking for a science-fiction writer to come in, analyze its operations, and write a report about what the company will look like fifty years from now.

The idea of hiring "prophets," "wild birds," or "blue-skyers," as they are variously known, is one that should be adopted not only by corporations but by all the major institutions of our society. Schools, cultural organizations, and government agencies at the city, state, and federal level, should begin to emulate industry in this respect. It would be refreshing and healthy if some of these blue-skyers were to be retained by Congress and state legislatures. They should be invited into classrooms to lecture and lead discussions all over the country. This could have more than direct educational value. It would, I believe, thrill and inspire our children, many of whom now look forward to the future with foreboding and a sense of futility.

Finally, we might consider creating a great national or international institute staffed with top-caliber men and women from all the sciences and social sciences, the purpose of which would be to collect and systematically integrate the predictive reports that are generated by scholars and imaginative thinkers in all the intellectual disciplines all over the world. Of course, those working in such an institute would know that they could never create a single, static diagram of the future. Instead, the product of their effort would be a constantly changing geography of the future, a continually recreated overarching image based on the best predictive work available. The men and women engaged in this work would know that nothing is certain; they would know that they must work with inadequate data; they would appreciate the difficulties inherent in exploring the uncharted territories of tomorrow. But man already knows more about the future than he has ever tried to formulate and integrate in any systematic and scientific way. Attempts to bring this knowledge together would constitute one of the crowning intellectual efforts in history —and one of the most worthwhile.

Man's capacity for adaptation may have limits, but they have yet to be defined. If, as Margaret Mead has shown, the Manus of New Guinea could, within a twenty-five year period, pass from Stone Age primitivism into a twentieth-century way of life, and do so happily and successfully, modern man should be able to traverse the passage to postcivilization. But he can accomplish this grand historic advance only if he forms a better, clearer, stronger conception of what lies ahead. This is the only remedy for the phenomenon of future shock.

TO SEE OURSELVES AS OTHERS SEE US

henry morgan

Humor is a delightful if sometimes painful way of driving home a point. Humor about social scientists is often related to their frequent inability to practice what they preach.

Taking the example of cultural relativity as a basis for some barbed commentary, the following "interview" makes us laugh at ourselves. It also makes us blush as we realize how ethnocentric we often are when trying to assess the behavior of others.

Every couple of months some guy with a grant from the University of Somewhere goes to Australia or the Philippines and discovers a bunch of people who don't know about the rest of the world. The guy gets all excited and writes a big piece for one of those journals that print that kind of thing and forever after he is known among his colleagues as "McWhirtle . . . you know, the archeologist fella who found the Guaftis."

. . .

Penthouse: First, I want to thank you for taking the time for this interview.
Marsuppi: What that mean, "time"?
Penthouse: Well, time, like. I mean if you want to go from here to over there it takes time. A couple of minutes, anyway. We

all live by the clock, see. It's a dingus that tells us what time it isn't yet, so we don't have to be there until later. Now is, well, *now*, see. Later is when it gets dark. So that takes time, the difference between now and then, see.

Marsuppi: Why you care?

Penthouse: Well, that's how we do it, see. Suppose I want to see a fellow in some other place and I want to get there when he gets there. Okay, so we set a time. So we arrive together.

Marsuppi: How? If one man arrive first, other man arrive second. What first man do?

Penthouse: He waits.

Marsuppi: Then what good is the time? We don't have time. We wait anyway.

Penthouse: Look. A day has twenty-four hours. We split it up into twenty-four parts.

Marsuppi: Why?

Penthouse: Because. That's why. Each part is an hour, each hour has sixty minutes, and each minute has sixty seconds.

Marsuppi: You like that?

Penthouse: Sure I like it. Jeeze, you don't even know when it's Thursday.

Marsuppi: That bad?

Penthouse: Sure that's bad. How the hell can you get anything done? How do you expect to accomplish anything if you don't know when it is?

Marsuppi: I know when it is. What I don't know is what is when?

Penthouse: Well, when is when you don't know when it is, like. Jeez. I ask you to do something for me, but not right now. All right, then the question is, when?

Marsuppi: If I like you I do it anyway. What you care about when?

Penthouse: Because I have to go away sometime, see. I have to go back to where I came from. All right, I have to know when. It's a week from Wednesday as a matter of fact.

Marsuppi: Okay. Goodbye.

Penthouse: (sighing) Listen. Before I go, I'd like to tell you some things about how the other people in the world are living. It will help you. For instance, you don't seem to know what a government is.

Marsuppi: What is it?

Penthouse: Well, a group of people get together and they elect a chief, like you. He is the head of the government, see?

Marsuppi: Sure. Same like here.

Penthouse: No, there's more to it. They pay money to the government to do things for them that they can't do for themselves. Like, well, like hiring police.

Marsuppi: Police?

Penthouse: Yeah. See, we own a lot of things. Well, some people want to take things from other people, so you have the police to stop them

from doing that. And, of course, the police catch criminals and run the
traffic and keep the dope runners from taking over the whole place.
They keep order, see. Law and order. They stop fights and like that.

Marsuppi: When I have a thing, if somebody wants that thing, I give it
to him. Why you don't do that? Then you don't have to pay police. Easy.

Penthouse: But our things are worth a lot of money, not like the crap you
have around here. We want to keep our things.

Marsuppi: What you need them for?

Penthouse: To *use.* Say you have a radio or a camera or a TV. Why, these
creeps come around and steal them and sell them to fences and use
the money for dope. You know, mani-mani. Smoke 'em up.

Marsuppi: We give mani-mani. Take all you want. We got more. Why you
no give yours away?

Penthouse: Because you can't, that's why. You can't give everybody
everything he wants. You can't run a society that way. Some people
have a lot of things, some people don't have a lot. So the people who
have the stuff want to keep it, see?

Marsuppi: No. Me no understand you.

Penthouse: What the hell do you know. You haven't got anything worth
stealing.

Marsuppi: Right.

Penthouse: You're not living, you're just existing. Hell, you're almost a
vegetable. What good is life if you have to live this way?

Marsuppi: What way?

Penthouse: Oh, I've watched what you do. You hunt a little, you fish a
little, you sit in the sun and tell stories. . . . You have a couple of kids
and you don't care about tomorrow. Christ, you're not *responsible*
people. You don't accomplish anything.

Marsuppi: Accomplish. What that mean?

Penthouse: Achieve. Create. Advance. Progress. Get ahead. Do things,
invent things, improve your lot. I mean, man has come a long way from
the way you live. Why, you don't even have a newspaper or a radio.
You don't know what's going on. You're . . . primitive. Plain. In a thousand years, you just haven't gotten anywhere. You live the same way
your father lived, and his father, and his father. You're a . . . savage.

Marsuppi: If we make this, uh, progress, everything be better? Nobody
get sick, nobody die?

Penthouse: Well, of course, we get sick. But we have made big advances
in medicine. We live longer than you do.

Marsuppi: Ah. And what you do with the . . . uh . . . time? What you do
when you live long time?

Penthouse: Well, when our people get old—like you, for instance—we
put them up in little villages where they can meet other old people.
Then they have their shuffleboard, their social evenings, their arts and
crafts and other hobbies, and there's always a doctor in attendance and

a hospital not too far away. Or they can just sort of sit around in the sun if they feel like it.

Marsuppi: Oh. What young people do?

Penthouse: They go and visit the old people every so often. Maybe on a Sunday. Of course a lot of them live far away so their children never see them, but they write letters. What do you do with your old people?

Marsuppi: We keep them.

Penthouse: I know . . . but what do they do?

Marsuppi: They hunt a little, they fish a little. They play games. They sit in the sun. They very nice. They know a lot. They tell us what they know, then we know. Very nice.

Penthouse: *Ours* retire. They don't have to work all their lives. We give them a rest.

Marsuppi: In little village, hah? By themselves, hah?

Penthouse: Yessir, that's what progress is. You work all your life, then you get to rest.

Marsuppi: Then die, hah?

Penthouse: Well, of course, we all have to go sometime.

Marsuppi: Okay. Goodbye.

Penthouse: But wait, it's not next Wednesday yet!

Marsuppi: You forget. I can't tell time. For me is now next Wednesday. So long.

At this point the tape ends.

ABOUT THE AUTHOR

Peter I. Rose received his A.B. from Syracuse University and his Ph.D. from Cornell University. Currently Sophia Smith Professor of Sociology and Anthropology at Smith College and a member of the Graduate Faculty of the University of Massachusetts, he has also taught at Goucher, Wesleyan, the University of Colorado, Clark, and Yale and has been a Fulbright Lecturer in England, Australia, and Japan. His books include *They and We, The Study of Society, The Ghetto and Beyond, The Subject Is Race, Americans from Africa, Nation of Nations,* and *Through Different Eyes.* Professor Rose is consulting editor to the *Time-Life Series on Human Behavior,* sociology consultant to Random House and Alfred A. Knopf, Inc., and editor of the Random House series, *Ethnic Groups in Comparative Perspective.*